Srivatsa Vasudevan

Practical UVM

Step by Step with IEEE 1800.2

The programs and code in this book have been included for their instructional value. While care was taken during the preparation of this book, no warranty or fitness is implied. The author assumes no liability for errors, omissions, or for damages resulting from the use of the information contained herein. All references to known as trademarks or service marks have been appropriately indicated.

All code within this text was compiled and simulated with Synopsys® VCS P-2019.06 using Accellera UVM and the IEEE-1800.2 release.

International Edition. February 2020.   ISBN : 978-0-9977896-1-4

The author offers discounts when ordered in quantity. Special discounts are available on quantity purchases by corporations, associations, and others.

For more information, please contact:

Srivatsa Vasudevan
5567 Kimberly Street,
San Jose CA 95129
United States of America.

Cover Design: Fourth Dimension Inc.

This book is dedicated to:
The ONE by whose Grace,
A mute can speak eloquently,
A lame person can climb a mountain,
And for whom, nothing is impossible.
Our families and friends for supporting us
on this incredible journey.

Contents

Please Read! Important Note for the IEEE Edition

Dear Reader:

Thank you for purchasing this book, created to offer knowledge, theories, and practical examples to advance your knowledge and effective usage of SystemVerilog and UVM. This book is both current and rare; few publications support verification and other advancements related to the Universal Verification Methodology.

This book is the result of "blood, sweat and tears" from many, including the author, graphic designers, editors and many in the UVM community on the inner workings of UVM. It has been prepared with considerable effort for your benefit with an effort spanning multiple years. I would greatly appreciate any feedback, suggestions, or comments; you have about this book - please send me your contribution to me via email, which is provided on the inside of the book cover. It shall be gratefully acknowledged.

The greatest profit to receive from the purchases of this book is donating all funds available after recovering the costs of creating this book and its distribution, to those in real need: *Those who suffer economic hardship with insufficient food for themselves and their children, and often without a place to call home or an opportunity to better themselves.*

Unauthorized copies, such as photocopied, DRM hacked or scanned, do not help us cover the costs, or offer the privilege and compassion enabling others to succeed as well. In many ways, your support of this book gives you an opportunity to help others as you advance your working knowledge of UVM for your own personal achievements.

I hope you will join me in this endeavor. Together, we can all make this world a better place.

Thank You
Srivatsa Vasudevan
Spring 2020

Foreword

As a person that has been involved from day one on the UVM effort, serving as co-chair of the Accellera UVM WG, I am glad to embrace Srivatsa's book, which will serve as an additional means to expanding the UVM community. As a frequent user and support person for UVM, I am glad to see a book with many important details that can teach one UVM quickly. Coding up a UVM testbench rapidly and correctly is growing and required need in the Semiconductor industry. As designs are becoming more complex and schedule times are reducing, the pressure on the UVM testbench implementers is getting tougher and tougher. With this book, one can effectively learn practical aspects of UVM and can use it as a reference to get detailed information quickly.

A notable chapter is the configuration database; regular expressions are used to enable assignment of configurations to a desired set of components. The book provides detailed information about how the regular expressions are applied to achieve this.

Another notable chapter is about the register library; the books goes to great effort to point out the different register/field databases with details on how they are referenced and updated.

The author is deeply involved in the IEEE 1800.2 efforts (P1800.2). I am also looking forward towards the first book that will have details on P1800.2 as it plans to come out early next year.

To summarize, the book has truly recognized the complexities of UVM and what is needed to bring new users on board and what is needed to enable existing users better.

Austin TX, March 2016

Hillel Miller
Accellera UVM Committee Co-Chair.

Preface

SystemVerilog allows you to use a single language for both design and verification of ASIC designs. The Universal Verification Methodology (UVM) enables verification engineers to leverage the SystemVerilog language with a standardized methodology. UVM is now widely supported by EDA vendors and used by many design teams worldwide to verify complex ASIC devices. Many modern designs use UVM as a methodology for their projects moving forward. This book is a product of knowledge accumulated from many sources (UVM Users Guide and Class Reference, code comments, various DVCON presentations and papers, UVM/OVM books, UVM committee discussions, and my own experience to name a few). Many examples illustrate key concepts and show how UVM may be used to verify complex ASIC devices. The provided examples, combined with a practical hands-on approach with actual RTL cores, should enable the verification engineer to explore UVM at their own pace.

Before you get started

The subject of UVM is vast. There are new developments often concerning this class library. To keep the discussion in this book focused on UVM, knowledge of SystemVerilog, and object-oriented concepts are prerequisites not covered as a part of this book. There are many resources on the internet if you need to come up to speed on SystemVerilog.

How is this book structured?

The focus of this book is practical learning. There are a series of examples, each illustrating a concept with insight into UVM. The examples in Part 1 progress from simple examples to elaborate full-chip environments as the information progresses in Part 4. The examples are complete so that you can run them in a simulator. Part of this book's approach is that you execute/change the examples provided and work with them to learn UVM better.

During book development, a decision was made to use real-world examples. The book structure takes the form of a practical DIY (Do It Yourself) format. Download the examples to your computer and study UVM through this book as you execute the examples. The examples progress from simple to complex concepts while being complete in illustrating specific aspects of UVM. I have used many cores from opencores.org to help illustrate key concepts along the way. *The Verilog testbenches, which were originally part of the opencores offering, have also been included. This way, you can compare approaches, and make the transition from Verilog to UVM + SystemVerilog.* If you are new to UVM, you have a reference design with testcases that you can relate to as a platform.

There are four parts to this collection. After you download and install the examples, the provided Makefiles build and run these examples. Feel free to examine and modify them as you see fit. The figure below illustrates the flow of UVM concepts through this book.

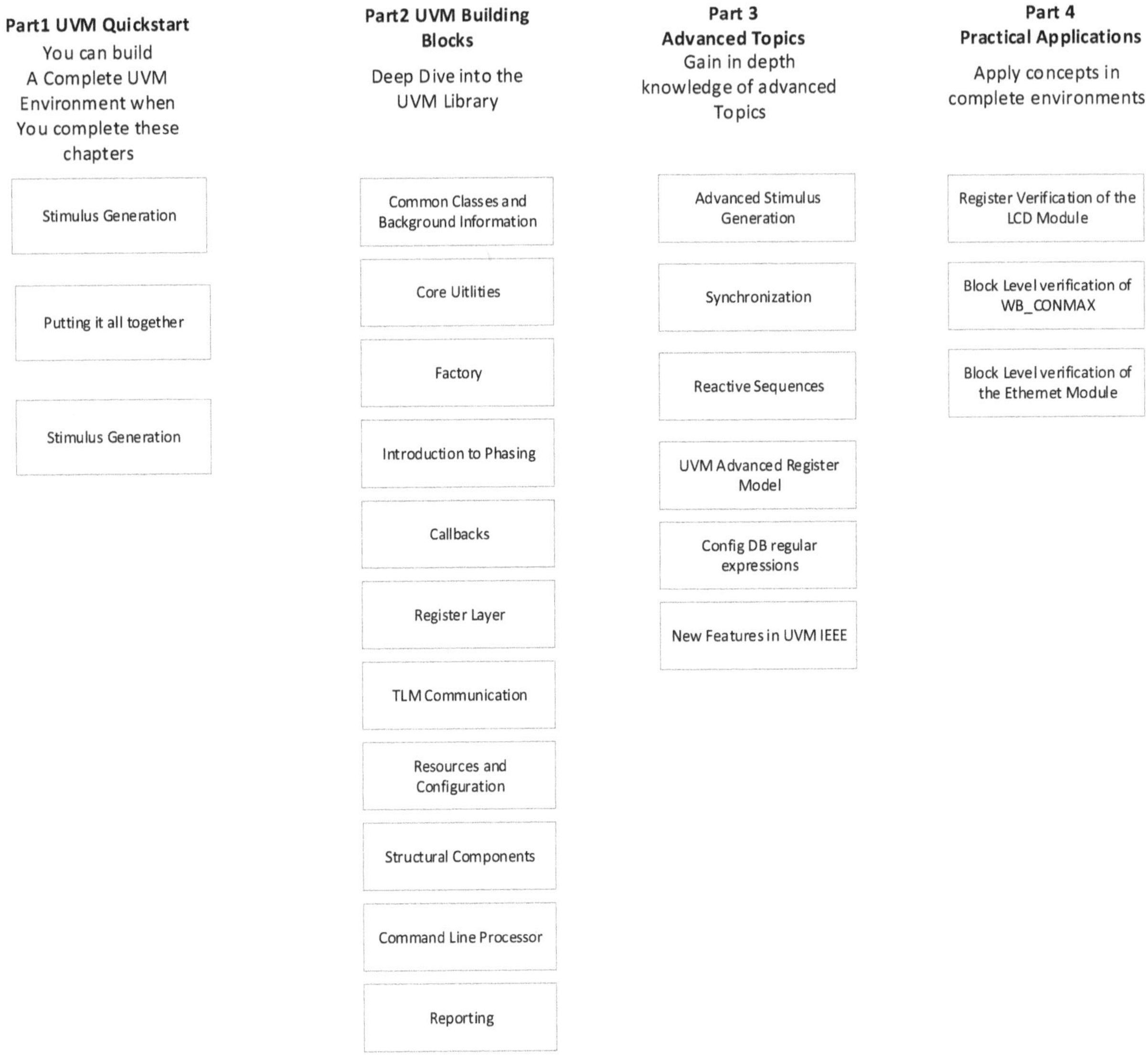

Part1 UVM Quickstart	Part2 UVM Building Blocks	Part 3 Advanced Topics	Part 4 Practical Applications
You can build A Complete UVM Environment when You complete these chapters	Deep Dive into the UVM Library	Gain in depth knowledge of advanced Topics	Apply concepts in complete environments
Stimulus Generation	Common Classes and Background Information	Advanced Stimulus Generation	Register Verification of the LCD Module
Putting it all together	Core Uitlities	Synchronization	Block Level verification of WB_CONMAX
Stimulus Generation	Factory	Reactive Sequences	Block Level verification of the Ethernet Module
	Introduction to Phasing	UVM Advanced Register Model	
	Callbacks	Config DB regular expressions	
	Register Layer	New Features in UVM IEEE	
	TLM Communication		
	Resources and Configuration		
	Structural Components		
	Command Line Processor		
	Reporting		

Fig. 0.1: Chapters in this book

Part 1: UVM Quickstart

This part is a UVM Tutorial. There are three chapters in this part. A simple DUT is used to walk you through a Verilog and a SystemVerilog in the first chapter.

The second chapter attempts to bring together concepts to put together a complete verification environment in UVM. It discusses in practical detail various aspects of a UVM environment and connects master and slave verification components through a simple pass-through DUT.

The Wishbone protocol is chosen instead of the UBUS protocol described in the UVM Users Guide. While it would have been possible to extend the UBUS protocol description to allow some other transfers and create examples using actual RTL with this protocol, such an effort would be rather significant. This book instead leverages RTL IP that has been proven elsewhere to teach UVM so that you can continue learning and exploring well-documented IP.

The third chapter goes over stimulus generation. The creation and driving of stimuli form an important activity in any verification effort. The UVM class library allows the user to write reusable code and provides some guidelines for how to structure this code. This chapter covers various concepts and considerations for stimulus generation.

Completing this Part should give you a good idea of what the UVM library contains and how it operates. If you know UVM, you can choose to skip this part, or delve deeper if you need to.

Part 2: UVM Building Blocks This part is a deep dive into the various building blocks in the UVM library. Read this part to get detailed knowledge of the library. The components and concepts developed in this chapter are reused in Part IV.

Part 3: Advanced Topics

Part3 goes into advanced topics in UVM that are not covered in earlier parts of the book. Content in this part assumes you have studied the earlier parts. Some of the primary areas covered are:

- Synchronization among processes in UVM

- Heartbeat applications to ensure your testbench is running

- Reactive sequencer applications in UVM

- Advanced Register topics

- Regular expressions in the UVM configuration database.

- Primer on Config DB regular expressions

- Advanced Core Utilities using IEEE 1800.2

Upon completion of this part of the book, you should be able to use UVM to verify your designs and tweak your environments to accomplish your specific goals.

Part 4: Block Level Verification Environments

The focus of this book is practical knowledge that you can use daily. UVM can be used to build reusable testbenches at various levels of design integration. Part IV of the book illustrates practical applications of UVM to validate several cores that are part of a SOC.

These cores mirror commonly available commercial designs. Each of the designs presented here is used to illustrate a specific aspect of the UVM library. Detailed exercises at the end of each chapter are intended to help the user to delve deeper into the design and UVM.

As some RTL cores with Verilog environments are available from www.opencores.org, it made it possible for readers who are coming into ASIC verification from a design world to relate more quickly to the concepts in UVM using these cores. Hence, all environments are built around these available cores merged into an example platform.

You may also choose to add other RTL cores to this design or delve into a variety of other topics in verification using these examples as a platform. All the cores utilize the Wishbone Protocol [18] to communicate between them. The master and slave agents developed in the previous chapters are reused in this part to verify the design.

The GitHub repository comes with all the PDF documents that describe the core. A brief description of each core is included in the relevant chapters so that you can get the context of the functionality of the core before exploring the verification environment and UVM features.

Each of the Verilog testbenches and UVM testbenches provides a Makefile. This Makefile helps compile the design with appropriate switches for the VCS simulator from Synopsys.

Note: While complete environments have been provided to you to learn and extend from, *it has never been my intention to either verify the core provided nor delve into details of each core in this book.* Such an exercise is left to you, hoping that you undertake it to explore deeper into UVM at your own pace. The provided RTL is merely a vehicle to allow you to learn.

The main areas of UVM covered in Part IV are:

- UVM Register modeling in the context of a Video Display Unit.

- The crossbar environment in UVM is used to explain many UVM concepts with multiple components in the environment.

- Data and stimulus considerations and various sequence types for random verification of the Ethernet MAC in UVM.

Example Organization

Examples are discussed using source code. Here is a sample code inset:

```
     Listing 1: A Simple Class ..//examples/part2/class2_1.sv
 2 class class_A extends uvm_object;
 3
 4     int cl_int;
 5     string cl_string;
 6     int    cl_int_arr[];
 7     int    logic_data[int];
 8
 9     `uvm_object_utils_begin(class_A)
10        `uvm_field_int(cl_int, UVM_DEFAULT)
11        `uvm_field_string(cl_string, UVM_DEFAULT)
12        `uvm_field_array_int(cl_int_arr, UVM_DEFAULT)
13        `uvm_field_aa_int_int(logic_data, UVM_DEFAULT)
14     `uvm_object_utils_end
15
16     function new(string name="");
17        int idx = 1;
18        super.new(name);
19        cl_string = name;
20        cl_int = 5;
21        cl_int_arr = new[cl_int];
22        for(int i = 0; i < cl_int; i++) begin
23           cl_int_arr[i] = i + 1;
24        end
25        repeat (16) begin
26           logic_data[idx] = idx;
27           idx = idx << 1;
28        end
29     endfunction
30 endclass
```

In this example, line numbers are relative to that file[1].

Our website for this book is http://www.uvmbook.com

Please clone the example kit repository from GitHub:

https://github.com/Practical-UVM-Step-By-Step/Practical-UVM-IEEE-Edition

We suggest you clone this repository to your work area. The directory into which you download the repository will be referred to as $DOWNLOAD in many areas of the text. We have abbreviated the listings in the book in many cases to save space

---

[1] Actual code listings are used to create the book in all cases. If you see differences between the actual line numbers in the download listing line numbers in the book, I possibly may have abstracted it to explain concepts. You should be able to find the relevant lines quickly, though.

In all the subsequent sections of this book, when we refer to a download, we are referring to a clone of this repository. If we refer to our website, we are referring to http://www.uvmbook.com.

Upon cloning this repository, you see two main sub-directories.

- IEEE_version
- uvm−1.2

The examples in these directories can be run with the VCS simulator from Synopsys. Simulation Run files and compile log files are part of the repository.

- The uvm−1.2 directory contains the **exact** same examples and directory structure as the IEEE_version but have changes to use UVM 1.2 styles and constructs and contain commands to run the VCS simulator.

- Files containing UVM API *unchanged* between IEEE 1800.2 and UVM 1.2 are identical between the IEEE_version and UVM 1.2 trees. The only changes you should see are if the IEEE UVM API was different from the UVM 1.2 API.

- Directories/examples for new features in IEEE 1800.2, which have no equivalence to UVM 1.2 are missing from the uvm−1.2 directory tree.

My intention for providing examples in this manner is to enable you to use a diff tool if you wish to compare API between UVM versions.

Each of the above two directories contains the following four subdirectories. Each of the sub-directories encapsulates a specific Part of this book and contains a directory structure under it corresponding to specific chapters.

- UVM_Quickstart - Part 1
- UVM_Building_Blocks - Part 2
- Advanced_UVM_Topics - Part 3
- Practical_Applications - Part 4

Running the examples

Please look at the file ExampleOrganization.pdf in the Github Repository for detailed instructions and ReadME for the examples. They contain additional details that have not been provided here to save space

Each example directory illustrates a particular UVM concept. This example can be compiled and run using the provided Makefile. This Makefile helps compile the design with appropriate switches for the VCS simulator from Synopsys. This can be ported to other simulators once you have identified the right switches to run UVM with other tools.

A Makefile for each example usually provides you an 'all_tests', 'comp' and 'run' target.

The most straightforward way to run an example is to execute its "all" script:

% make

This compiles, links, and runs the default example. It *does not run* all the tests in that example. You can run the other make targets manually. Please look at the README in each directory for the exact Makefile target relevant to a particular example.

The GitHub repository for the previous version of this book contains the command line switches for the other simulators that were contributed by users in the UVM community. Please use that as a baseline to get the examples running on the other simulators if you do not have access to VCS. I would appreciate a pull request contribution if you are able to get the examples running on other simulators.

Icons and Images Used in this Book and the Website

This book uses many icons to draw your attention to specific content matter in this book. We suggest you become familiar with these icons as they bring out essential features under consideration for you to be aware of as you make your journey through the UVM world.

Download the example to see the source code. The description and listings are sometimes abbreviated to save space.

This icon is calling your attention to something to be aware of.

This compass is an indicator of best practices

Limitations we found during testing which may be a GOTCHA for you
Things you really should be aware of!

This icon alerts you to a new feature in UVM 1.2 from UVM-1.1d

This book is focussed on the IEEE 1800.2 version. Many additional icons are used to indicate features related to IEEE 1800.2 version. See "IEEE-1800.2 - The New UVM Standard," describing the changes.

Book Errata

A variety of software was used to create this book. LATEX was used for typesetting this book. All code snippets are cross-references to the actual files. The GitHub Repository provides a Listings subdirectory that contains symbolic links to each of the examples listed in this book. *In a work of this magnitude, with over seven thousand source files and spanning multiple years, there are bound to be errors since it is a human effort.* If you spot any errors, please send an email to the address listed on the copyright pages or get in touch with me through the website. Your support is gratefully acknowledged.

Questions and Comments

Please tell us how you are using this book, and feel free to offer ideas and suggestions or corrections. You can email questions or comments to feedback@uvmbook.com. Again, thank you for considering and using this book, and I hope that you enjoy the content presented herein.

Srivatsa Vasudevan

Bay Area California.

Spring 2020.

UVM Coding Guidelines and UVM Linting

The coding guidelines presented in various sections of this book were synthesized combining inputs from a variety of sources, direct first-hand experience during my work with many companies, as well as expertise shared with me during my verification journey from many sources. These guidelines, while not being hard/fast reflect best practices you find in the industry. They are not exhaustive by any means. Adapt them to the needs of your project as you see fit. A good source for the guidelines is in [14] and [4], amongst others. Many of the newly added guidelines were adapted from [4], based on user feedback. Each of the guidelines is codified either as a ***Rule*** or a ***Recommendation***. These are also numbered for easy cross-reference, based on user feedback.

The following convention was used to determine where to place the rules/recommendations:

- For content where the rule fits in with the explanation and text flow, the rule/recommendation is in line with the text.

- General guidelines are often placed either at the end of a section or in a separate section. Sometimes explanations have not been provided/abbreviated because I felt that you might find these to be self-explanatory after reading the relevant sections.

The coding guidelines presented do not mention common naming conventions (class instance names, enum types, etc.) that you might come across in code at your company. I viewed these as being specific to your company and within the domain of linter tools, and in my view, easily enforceable.

Linting

The IEEE provides the LRM, and Accellera provides the implementation of the LRM. There is no documentation provided by Accellera for the methods in the IEEE LRM. Accellera documents the methods not in the LRM as extra API in their documentation.

Many companies would like to perform lint checks prior to check-in of their code. Few commercial offerings certainly exist in this area. As interest from the community increases, I am confident that this area will attract more interest. The Accellera implementation provides annotations in the code just above the class and method calls, which tell you the section number in the LRM where you can find the documentation for the relevant item. These annotations are of the form seen in the Figure below.

The line immediately preceding the declaration in the source code has these components.

- The source of the code (in this case, it's the IEEE LRM)

- The year of the standard

- The actual section number in the LRM where you will find a description of the API

- Ignore the auto/manual keywords

It is expected that linting tools designed to lint UVM code will use these annotations to identify if classes and methods comply with the UVM library and their extensions.

IEEE/Accellera Annotation   Year of Standard   Ignore this   Section Number

```
// @uvm-ieee 1800.2-2017 auto 5.3.1
virtual class uvm_object extends uvm_void;
```

Class/Method declaration

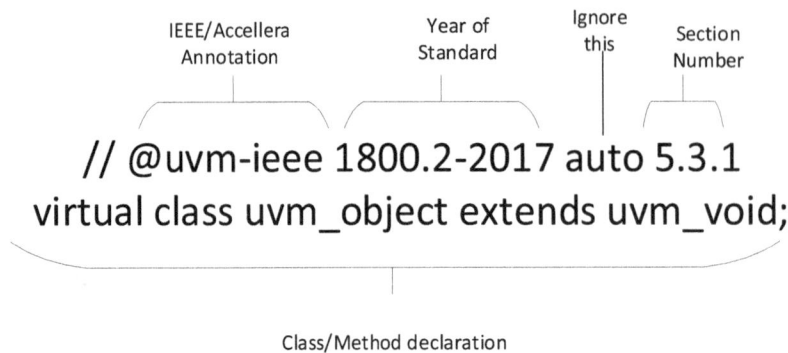

Request to Implementers of Linting Tools

Please refer to the Year and section number of the UVM LRM in your linting messages. This makes it easy for users to identify any potential issues and the appropriate remedial actions.

We have added several rules to the book, which may augment the rules you already have in your own offering. We are hoping many people will be using this book to learn and use IEEE UVM in their verification activity.

If you choose to implement any rules/recommendations from this book:

- Collecting rules and recommendations and processing all of them was a considerable effort for this author. Please acknowledge our work and obtain our permission.

- Please provide a cross-reference to the rule/recommendation number from this book. Doing so will make it easier for users transitioning into UVM and learning best practices from it.

My hope is that this provides a dual benefit to the community. Users will be able to quickly appreciate the value of the linting tool, and quickly fix any issues that are flagged. Tool vendors enjoy being able to focus on value add of their tools since explanations are provided for these rules in the appropriate context in this book.

Acknowledgements

I am grateful for the Grace of the ONE without whom none of the experiences would have ever happened to me and kept me persevering on this book. Much inspiration and strength have been derived from HIM. My parents have been a source of strength. I am especially indebted to my wife Priya who was exceedingly patient with me and made many sacrifices as this book was written. My children also helped with numerous ideas and suggestions along the way.

Putting out any book, even a second edition requires a lot of coordination, effort, and patience from many people. Rena Ayeras, a technical writer, and editor, reviewed and edited this book. She provided recommendations to fine-tune the details and flow, helping me restructure my original writing.

She patiently went through the entire book multiple times and pointed out numerous issues with the work. Shalom Bresticker helped me formulate the initial portions of the UVM Quickstart by synthesizing elements from the first edition. Fourth Dimension Inc helped create the covers for this book as well. Janick Bergeron and James Chang encouraged me to change the structure of the rules and recommendations by numbering them so that users could quickly refer to them. Janick also granted me permission to use some of the rules and recommendations he had developed earlier to benefit UVM users.

My management at Synopsys were supportive of my work in UVM and I'm grateful to them. I'd particularly like to thank Bernie Delay and Ajay Singh for their encouragement of this work which has been a long time in the making. They have patiently watched it mature into its current form.

Many gave feedback that was incorporated, some I would like to acknowledge are:

Vikram Jayaraman	Synopsys Inc	James Chang	Synopsys Inc
Nick Draghi	Microsoft	Rena Ayeras	Technical Writer
Siva Sankar Garika	Synopsys Inc	Ameesh Oza	Independent Consultant
John Stiropopulos	Synopsys Inc	Rahul Mhatre	Intel Corp
Raghavendra Kanike	Google Inc	Priyanka Sadananda	Google Inc
Alex Carlson	Google Inc	Sreeram Krishnamurthy	Synopsys Inc

First Edition:

No second edition is even possible without the first edition of this book. Many contributed to the first edition of this book in many ways.

Justin Refice and Janick Bergeron shared many concepts with me during my many interactions with them. Their insights turned out to be invaluable. For me, a lot of learning came from studying their work and asking them questions. Janick and Justin both have been very patient with me when I asked questions. Bruce Greene from Synopsys contributed the initial VGA register modeling chapter, which was modified to fit into this book's framework. Amit Sharma from Synopsys had helped me with the initial drafts of the factory chapter, which has been extended.

Srinivasan Venkataraman of CVC acted as my technical editor. I am very grateful to him for the discussions and interactions we had. He shared his insight from customers with me, and I found it invaluable.

Ajay Singh and Vikas Gautam from Synopsys provided their support. This book has been four years in the making, and they have watched its maturity through the years. Digvijay Lahe and his team at Fourth Dimension helped me with the cover design.

The following people gave me feedback and helped me with reviews. Their timely help was instrumental in making this book a reality. They took valuable time from their schedules and gave detailed feedback. I am grateful for their support.

Ashish Agarwal	Nvidia	Hillel Miller	Synopsys
Justin Refice	Nvidia	Ameesh Oza	Synopsys
John Stiropopulos	Synopsys	Adiel Khan	Synopsys
James Chang	Synopsys	Amit Sharma	Synopsys
Ole Kristoffersen	Ericsson	Cliff Cummings	Sunburst Design

I would also like to express gratitude to the many friends, colleagues and family members who offerred me feedback, provided support, and have not been mentioned here.

Srivatsa Vasudevan
San Jose CA USA

Glossary

CPU Central Processing Unit

DUT Device Under Test

SOC System On a Chip

LCD Liquid Crystal Display

VGA Video Graphics Array

PHY Physical Interface

DB DataBase

DMA Direct Memory Access

RAL Register Abstraction Layer

API Application programming interface

EDA Electronic Design Automation

FIFO First-In, First-Out

HDL Hardware description language

IP Intellectual property

TLM Transaction Level Modeling

VIP Verification Intellectual Property

LRM Language Reference Manual

IEEE 1800.2 - The New UVM Standard

The Accellera committee has donated the UVM Standard to the IEEE, and it is now available as IEEE 1800.2. The IEEE 1800.2 standard is based on the UVM 1.2 version with some additional changes described in this book. The IEEE 1800.2 standard is available via the IEEE GET program for free. Please visit www.ieee.org if you would like to obtain a copy of the standard.

The IEEE 1800.2 effort is broadly based in some key areas:

- Clarify and document all the classes and properties that are required for the UVM library to operate properly.
- Undocumented features in the library are now fully documented in the 1800.2 standard. The documentation of these classes allows anyone to develop a version of the UVM library compliant with the standard.
- Anything that was not explicitly defined in the library behavior is documented and clarified.
- Enhancing APIs that were limiting UVM from being used in some verification environments.
- Clean up the API and ensure consistency.

In the text of this book, I use IEEE 1800.2 and UVM IEEE interchangeably.

All user observable changes are highlighted using these icons and text that explains the difference between older versions of UVM and the IEEE version.

This icon alerts you to a new feature in IEEE 1800.2

This means this code was deprecated in IEEE 1800.2

This icon highlights that this feature of the library differs from the IEEE 1800.2 standard. See explanation below in the "Future Work" section.

In prior versions of UVM, the Accellera working group was responsible for providing the base class library and the LRM. With the standardization effort, ***the IEEE now provides the LRM, and Accellera now provides an implementation of the standard.*** Anybody can obtain a copy of the IEEE 1800.2 standard and develop a compliant implementation. Note that any implementation can be a superset of the provided standard by providing additional API not described in the standard.

There are some changes between UVM 1.2 and the IEEE 1800.2 standard. Users had identified many deficiencies in UVM-1.2, and where possible, new API has been added to address them. The new API allows users to accomplish tasks that were not possible earlier. As the library has been opened up, users should not need to make a copy of the library to patch it. Alternate methods provided by the library allow users to accomplish their goals.

This book discusses the Accellera implementation which contains all the API from the IEEE 1800.2 standard. In addition, the Accellera implementation also includes the following additional API:

- Debug API

- Bug Fixes

- Non-public API added to make the library work.

- New API submitted for consideration of future upcoming 1800.2 versions

- Deprecated UVM-1.2 API under a define when it does not conflict with 1800.2 API

If you use only the documented API from the IEEE standard, then your code can switch to another implementation without a problem. Note that Accellera does not provide a compliance check to determine if any extra API is used. That's the domain of any linter tools you have.

The documentation provided with the Accellera release only contains the extra end-user usable API added by Accellera and any clarifications provided by Accellera. There is no information in the Accellera provided documentation for the 1800.2 API for which you must refer the IEEE standard. There is also no information on the deprecated API for which you must consult the appropriate UVM version.

Note that any API that was in direct conflict with 1800.2 is not available in any of the Accellera 1800.2 releases. To enable a transition to 1800.2, any UVM-1.2 API not in conflict is available under the `UVM_ENABLE_DEPRECATED_API` define. Turning on this define gives you both UVM-1.2 API to a certain extent as well as the 1800.2 API.

Note that the `UVM_ENABLE_DEPRECATED_API` define is **not on** by default. The deprecation flag is "flipped" with respect to the previous UVM-1.2 version behavior. The earlier versions enabled deprecated behaviour by default.

Migrating from UVM 1.2

To begin a port to IEEE 1800.2, I suggest you move to UVM-1.2 first from any UVM-1.1x versions. You cannot make a direct jump easily from UVM-1.1x to IEEE-1800.2 easily. Note that any deprecated code in UVM-1.2 was **removed** from the code base before the IEEE 1800.2 library development began. Hence, you must first move to UVM-1.2 before contemplating a move to IEEE 1800.2. There are some scripts available to help you ease the transition from UVM-1.1x to UVM-1.2. Since you may have multiple versions of UVM in your company, You must pay some attention to the versioning mechanism in the section on UVM Versioning.

Migrating to UVM 1.2 from UVM 1.1* prior to moving to IEEE 1800.2

UVM 1.2 offers greater simulation performance compared to UVM 1.1. A script is available in the Accellera release for UVM 1.2 which can help with migrating from UVM 1.1 to UVM 1.2, which can help you get part of the way there. Some of the values of the enumerated types in UVM were renamed between UVM 1.1 and UVM 1.2 by adding a "UVM_" prefix. These are not handled by the script.

Other areas of change include the introduction of the uvm_coreservice and using it to get a handle to the factory (see Section 21.2.1), objection mechanism, phasing amongst others. These are marked in various parts of this book with the icon below.

Description of change from the UVM-1.1 version

UVM Versioning

There is a change in the versioning scheme for the UVM IEEE Version of the library. In the UVM-1.2 and UVM-1.1 versions of the library, you would find the following defines:

> `` `UVM_MAJOR_REV ``
> `` `UVM_MINOR_REV ``

The UVM version is identified by a combination of the above defines along with a Fix revision letter (like a,b,d as in the case of UVM-1.1) You could have used the define `` `UVM_POST_VERSION_1_1 `` if you were trying to detect if UVM 1.1x or UVM-1.2 versions were being used. Some of these defines are removed in the latest IEEE version which now uses the form:

> `` `UVM_VERSION 2016. ``

If your code is supporting multiple UVM versions: The `` `UVM_POST_VERSION_1_1 `` is now only available under the deprecated flag. You need to build some logic in your code to detect if the IEEE-1800.2 version is being used first, before you detect for older versions of UVM.

As newer versions of UVM are released based on the new IEEE LRM, you will see additional defines in the Accellera implementation as the IEEE standard defines them. **For example:**

The current standard was worked on in the years 2016/2017. It contains the define

> `` ` UVM_VERSION 2016 ``

If a new version of the UVM standard and implementation comes out in the year 2020 from the IEEE, the implementation would contain the defines: (notice the version changes in **bold**)

> `` `UVM_VERSION_POST_2017 ``
> `` ` `` **UVM_VERSION 2020**

to indicate that the implementation conforms to an IEEE LRM **after** the 2017 implementation version.

Assuming that a new standard comes out in the year 2024 from the IEEE after the 2020 release[2]: the implementation in 2024 ***will also contain*** the defines below to indicate that it supersedes the 2017 and 2020 IEEE standards:

> `` `UVM_VERSION_POST_2017 ``
> `` `UVM_VERSION_POST_2020 ``
> `` `UVM_VERSION 2024 ``

If you need to support multiple versions of UVM, you must build logic for version detection based on the above scheme that is dictated by the IEEE LRM.

(i)   No scripts are known to handle the change from UVM 1.2 to IEEE-1800.2 as of the writing of this book. You must therefore follow these three steps

1. Compile and Run your tests against UVM 1.2 with `` `UVM_NO_DEPRECATED `` defined. This gives you a baseline implementation that you are not relying on any deprecated UVM-1.1 API.

2. Compile against IEEE-1800.2 with `` `UVM_ENABLE_DEPRECATED_API `` defined. You may have some compile failures. These failures are the result of incompatible 1.2 APIs. You need to fix them before you continue. Use information in this book to address any issues.

---

[2] These dates are for illustrative examples, this is the not the cadence of release dates

3. Finally compile and run your tests using IEEE-1800.2 without `UVM_ENABLE_DEPRECATED_API

At the end of step 3, you should have an IEEE-1800.2 compliant UVM testbench. You may wonder whether it is worth all the effort and instead think of staying with UVM 1.2. The IEEE-1800.2 API's give you additional functionality and API that you will wish you had at some point during your verification effort. Note that the Accellera working group *no longer supports UVM-1.2 and all support and bug fixes are only going to be in IEEE-1800.2 releases.* This may possibly be true of all enhancements provided by the tool vendors as well.

Porting Hints

For the most part, the committee has kept backward compatibility unless it was impossible to do so. Some of the biggest changes you may see will be in the following areas:

- Printer Knobs removal
- Packer Metadata changes
- `uvm_do macros
- Comparer access methods and the removal of the uvm_in_order_comparer and uvm_algorithmic_comparer
- Accessor methods for all member variables in various classes.
- Messaging Changes
- Phasing and Objections

If there are very specific porting hints, They will be available with this icon in the text.

Removing Dependencies on `uvm_do Macros

The `uvm_do macros have changed in the IEEE version, and I acknowledge that many users may find this change difficult to accept. I recommend that you remove your dependencies on the `uvm_do macros which have changed. You may try the following steps which will ease the effort of porting, assuming you are familiar with PERL and its module mechanism.

I have used these steps to port the examples from the earlier version of the book into the newer version and it saved me a significant amount of time[3]

1. Download the IEEE 1800.2 implementation into a scratch directory or identify your installation directory as you will need it in the steps below.

2. Download the Verilog preprocessor from CPAN (https://metacpan.org/pod/distribution/Verilog-Perl/vppreproc). This is a good PERL module which I've used it a few times. You could probably easily install it through the CPAN shell.

   If you cannot install a module, follow the next few steps below.

3. Download a copy of PERL from http://www.perl.org.

4. Configure and compile your copy of PERL. (configure –prefix=<your install dir >; make test; make install)

5. Set your path to your newly installed copy of PERL/bin

6. Change to the CPAN module directory where you downloaded the perl module.

7. Look at the docs, and you'll probably run *perl Makefile.pl.*

8. Build using gmake and install using *make install*

9. You should get a vpppreproc binary in your PERL install *bin* directory.

---

[3] Caveat-Emptor, these worked for me. If you find another preprocessor you like, feel free to use that as well.

10. After you compile and install the module, the resulting vppreproc is the binary you will use.

11. Update your paths to point to the newly built perl binaries!

12. Run :
    vpppreproc <Your IEEE 1800.2 install Directory>/src/deprecated/macros/uvm_sequence_defines.svh <your file name>
    and redirect it to a file. You will get a file which has the macros exploded and can quickly clean up. It will dump the macro definitions at the top which you should obviously remove. You should be able to substitute other macro files as well. The resulting output file is usually more/less useful with minimal effort[4].

13. Note that most of the UVM sequences from the previous edition of this book were converted using this method.

Future Work on the IEEE Standard

The UVM standardization work continues. After the 1800.2 standardization, a project has begun under the auspices of the IEEE to address issues found in the 1800.2 standard. Some incorrect signatures were captured in the standard, and these were highlighted in the DEVIATIONS.md provided in the Accellera release. Content from this file has been distributed to the relevant chapters to provide context to users. The icon below is used to highlight issues with the standard so help users.

This icon indicates an issue with the IEEE standard and the Accellera implementation deviations from the standard. In some parts of the book, it also brings your attention to something you should be aware of. These differences will be reconciled when a new standard comes out from the IEEE.

The next release of the IEEE 1800.2 standard should have these issues addressed in addition to other clarifications. At this point, the current project in the IEEE is limited to *clarifications* only for a possible 2020 release. New enhancements are currently deferred a future release of the IEEE 1800.2 standard. The standardization work is a lengthy process, and you can contact the IEEE if you want to be a part of the process. Once the new standard has been created, Accellera will produce a compliant implementation.

---

[4] I've used this technique to explode some macros if I wanted to modify the behavior in a testcase or look at what UVM is doing under the hood.

Changes Between the First Edition and the IEEE Edition

The order of chapters varies significantly between the First and IEEE editions. This reorganization was based on feedback from UVM trainers, who indicated that most new users would prefer to come up to speed on UVM and write stimulus quickly. Hopefully, this has been addressed in the UVM Quickstart - Part 1. Readers knowing UVM and wishing to obtain a more in-depth understanding may proceed to Parts II and III to gain in-depth knowledge. Advanced topics have been moved to Part III from Part V of the previous edition. Part IV provides complete practical examples, just like the previous edition. You will find some additional examples in this part as well that address topics in UVM 1800.2.

Readers have offered feedback related to editing and typographical errors in the first edition of this book. Considerable work has been put in to eliminate as many as possible. Many paragraphs were rewritten to clarify the intent and meaning. The book has also been reviewed by a technical writer.

If you work in a company, there is a good chance that you will be working with multiple UVM versions. When you are especially dealing with an SOC, where you inherit multiple environments, each at a different UVM version; things usually get a little interesting. Hence, this book attempts to serve all three different versions of the library UVM 1.1, UVM 1.2, and IEEE 1800.2. Version specific information (where available) is marked using the following icons:

This icon is for features new to UVM 1.2 from UVM 1.1 **ONLY**. If you see an issue between migration from UVM 1.1x to UVM 1.2, watch for this icon. If this feature has changed between the UVM 1.2 and IEEE 1800.2 versions, one of the other icons will also be present in the text adjacent to this icon.

Code/behavior that has changed between UVM 1.2 and IEEE 1800.2 is marked with this icon. Note that this icon is the same one used for the Accellera to IEEE standard implementation differences.

This icon is for features of UVM deprecated between 1.2 and IEEE 1800.2 **only**. It does not cover deprecation between UVM 1.2 and UVM 1.1x. See the migration guide in the previous chapter if you are attempting to migrate to the IEEE 1800.2 version from UVM 1.2.

This icon alerts you to features **new** in IEEE 1800.2 and not present in UVM 1.2. Please do not confuse this with features between UVM 1.2 and UVM 1.1x

Part 1:

This part is specifically geared to engineers wanting to pick up UVM quickly.

- Chapter 1 presents a UVM overview and helps Verilog users understand UVM testbench architecture and philosophy and make a transition to UVM.

- Chapter 2 introduces the UVM environment.

- Chapter 3 provides you with information on creating stimulus for your DUT in UVM quickly.

Part 2:

- Chapter 4 goes over changes to uvm_object and the associated core utilities. There are a number of changes in IEEE 1800.2, and you should review this chapter as UVM 1800.2 *is not backward compatible* with earlier versions.

- Chapter 5 goes over the additions to the UVM factory class to support abstract types and aliases. Additional examples are added for abstract classes and factory replacement.

- Chapter 8 on the UVM component hierarchy adds examples explaining the changes in the build_phase in UVM 1800.2, allowing you to speed things up.

- Chapter 6 goes over the changes to reporting in IEEE 1800.2. You may see additional failures in your regressions. Please review this chapter as additional changes may be required on your part in your scripts.

- Chapter 9 goes over callbacks and their behavior. Callbacks have been enhanced in IEEE 1800.2.

- The Register Abstraction layer has additional examples to illustrate IEEE capability. Chapter 20 discusses unlocking the register model.

- Chapter 13 on Phasing discusses changes with additional examples due to capabilities added in IEEE version.

- Chapter 14 discusses Advanced Stimulus Generation. The original chapter is partitioned from the earlier book to deal solely with advanced topics. Examples now use the UVM 1800.2 style.

Advanced Topics

- Chapter 15 provides examples of how to add event callbacks to an event, a new feature introduced in IEEE version.

- Chapter 19 has descriptions of the new capabilities in the common operations. Details on how to customize your environment using the capabilities of the IEEE version are included here.

Practical Applications:

- Chapter 21 uses a different comparison function in the scoreboard.

- Content on uvm_event, uvm_barrier has been relocated from Chapter 22 to Chapter 15.

Deprecated Core Utilities

Appendix A now describes the UVM 1.2 core utilities and behavior for compare/pack/print functions which have undergone enhancements in IEEE 1800.2. Some of the API described in this appendix has been deprecated in the IEEE version.

Part I
UVM QuickStart

Chapter 1

Beginning the UVM Journey

Verification increases confidence in the design and identifies failures and bugs before a semiconductor chip is fabricated packaged and sent to a customer. In addition to creating the design and describing it in RTL or other abstractions, verification is crucial. Any errors or failure modes in the design must be corrected before the design is implemented in large volumes; this prevents expensive recalls. While not all bugs are due to coding errors, and not all mistakes result in failures, verification increases the confidence in the functionality of the design, and the future success of the product. RTL verification is typically performed by writing testbenches that send patterns to the design, and by observing the responses. Conventional approaches use the Verilog language for both design and testbench. Today, more advanced methods use the power of SystemVerilog, which is an extension of Verilog.

The first three chapters of this book provide an effective overview, a "Quickstart" to learning and using Universal Verification Methodology (UVM from now on) which is a layer on top of SystemVerilog. In this chapter, we quickly review how SystemVerilog improves upon Verilog. Chapter 2 introduces you to UVM. By the end of Chapter 3, the advantages provided by UVM should become apparent to you. All the other chapters go further into UVM, to build a more in-depth understanding, and use its many capabilities to build robust, reusable testbenches. The approaches to verification in Verilog differ significantly from SystemVerilog, as discussed in this chapter.

1.1 The DUT

Figure 1.1 shows a simple DUT design used to compare the functionalities of a Verilog testbench and a SystemVerilog testbench. Our DUT contains two ports termed a master port and a slave port. The DUT receives a transaction on its master port and operates on it before sending the transaction out on its slave port. In our example, a master writes a single 32-bit word to the master port, and the DUT merely passes it through and sends the word out on the slave port. Although this DUT is relatively trivial, it serves to highlight many key concepts in various testbenches, as well as their differences. The DUT is written in Verilog and implements the Wishbone protocol[18] for the master and slave ports.

1.2 A Verilog Testbench

The Verilog testbench shown in Figure 1.1 is implemented as a module. It contains a couple of BFMs (Bus Functional Models) and some tasks. In this case, the master port is connected to a master BFM, and the slave port is connected to a slave BFM.

The master BFM is called wb_master, and the slave BFM is called wb_slave. The BFM's contain tasks that allow you to perform operations on the DUT. Other common tasks like reset, configuration are present in the testbench and are not shown in Listing 1.1. Note that you can apply many techniques like parameters, selective inclusion of files, etc. to manage various tests during verification.

Only a small portion of the Verilog testbench is provided in Listing 1.1. It has been abbreviated for clarity. Please download for the complete listing and the Makefile if you want to study this further.

Fig. 1.1: Example DUT

Listing 1.1: Simple Verilog testbench

```verilog
module testbench;
   // Wire Declarations
   wire [31:0]  ADR_O;
   wire     CYC_O;
   ...
   dut dut(
     // Outputs
     .MDAT_I(MDAT_I[31:0]), .MRST_I(MRST_I),
     ...
     .SRTY_O(SRTY_O));
   // BFM Instances as Modules
    wb_master  wb_master(
       // Outputs
       .MDAT_I(MDAT_O[31:0]), .MRST_I(MRST_I),
       ...
       .SRTY_O(SRTY_O));
   wb_slave_behavioral wb_slave(
          // Outputs
          .TAG_O(STAG_O[3:0]), .CYC_O(SCYC_O),
       ...
          .RTY_I (SRTY_I));
    // Testcases  as tasks
    `include "tests.v"
 endmodule // testbench
```

A task included in the testbench drives the actual stimulus. Different tasks are used for different tests. Listing 1.2 provides an example of a test task. This test task would usually be called in a initial block in the testbench.

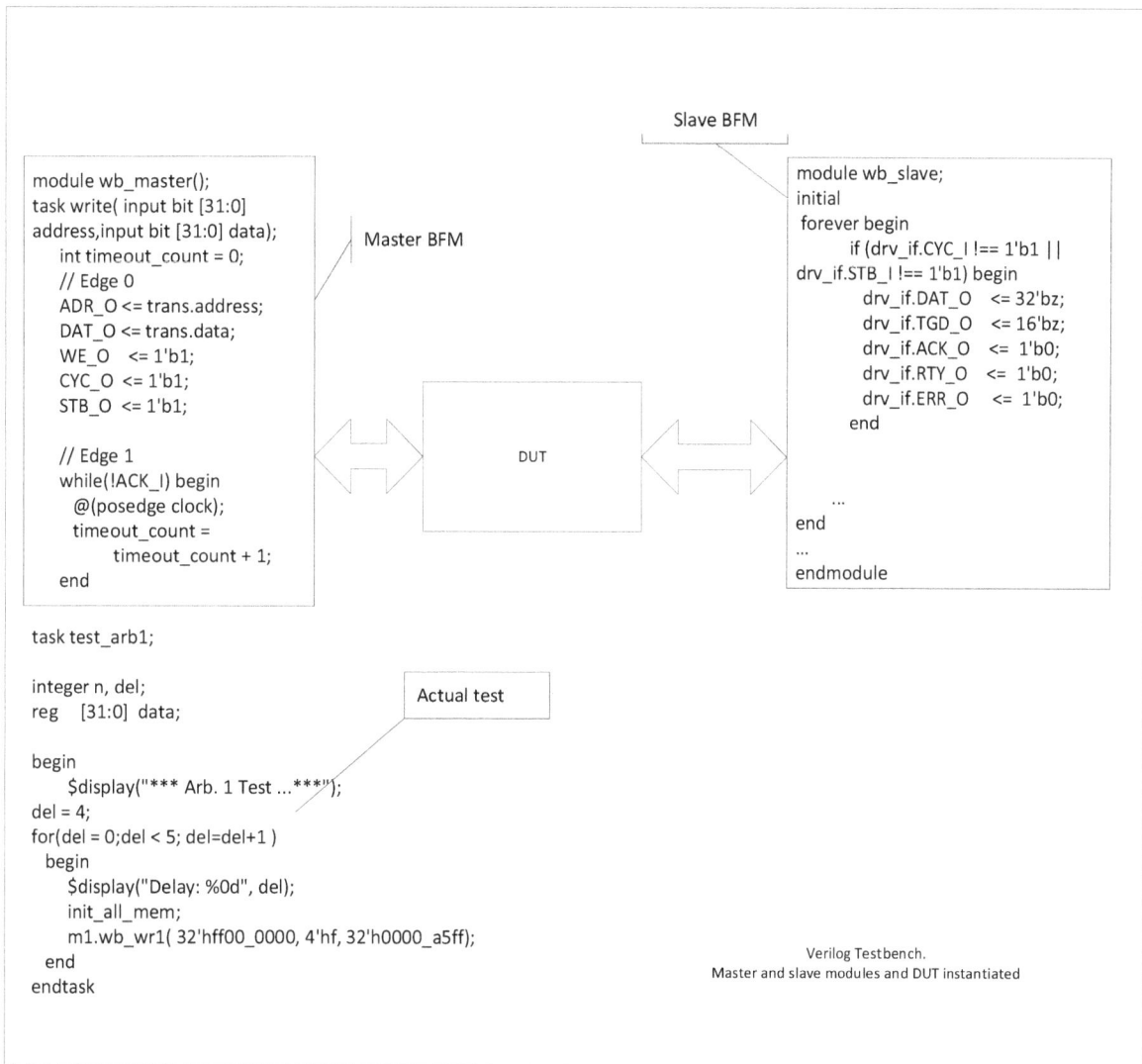

```
module wb_master();
task write( input bit [31:0]
address,input bit [31:0] data);
    int timeout_count = 0;
    // Edge 0
    ADR_O <= trans.address;
    DAT_O <= trans.data;
    WE_O   <= 1'b1;
    CYC_O <= 1'b1;
    STB_O <= 1'b1;

    // Edge 1
    while(!ACK_I) begin
      @(posedge clock);
      timeout_count =
          timeout_count + 1;
    end
```

Master BFM

```
module wb_slave;
initial
 forever begin
      if (drv_if.CYC_I !== 1'b1 ||
drv_if.STB_I !== 1'b1) begin
          drv_if.DAT_O  <= 32'bz;
          drv_if.TGD_O  <= 16'bz;
          drv_if.ACK_O  <= 1'b0;
          drv_if.RTY_O  <= 1'b0;
          drv_if.ERR_O   <= 1'b0;
        end

      ...
end
...
endmodule
```

Slave BFM

DUT

```
task test_arb1;

integer n, del;
reg   [31:0]  data;

begin
    $display("*** Arb. 1 Test ...***");
del = 4;
for(del = 0;del < 5; del=del+1 )
  begin
    $display("Delay: %0d", del);
    init_all_mem;
    m1.wb_wr1( 32'hff00_0000, 4'hf, 32'h0000_a5ff);
  end
endtask
```

Actual test

Verilog Testbench.
Master and slave modules and DUT instantiated

Fig. 1.2: Simple Verilog Testbench

Listing 1.2: Simple Verilog test

```
1 task check_main;
2   reg     [31:0] tmp;
3   reg     [31:0] tmp2;
4       tmp = 0xdeadbeef;
5       wb_master.wr(32'h0000ffff, tmp, 4'b1111);
6       wb_master.rd(32'h0000ffff, tmp2, 4'b1111);
7       if(tmp2 != 0xdeadbeef)
8         $write("error in Data");
9 endtask
```

In the Github repository[1], each of the cores I have used in the book comes with a Verilog testbench. Also, there are many examples of Verilog based tests that can be downloaded from www.opencores.org for various cores. Studying these testbenches is recommended if you are getting started in the verification world.

A basic Verilog testbench is useful in the early stages of RTL development, which is easy to write and develop. A complex testbench is usually not required in the early stages. Simple reset and read/write tasks usually help sort out basic bugs that occur at this stage. However, other approaches offer some more advantages when detailed testing is needed, especially for a complex DUT.

1.3 A SystemVerilog Testbench

The SystemVerilog language extends Verilog, and provides both design and verification constructs for creating and verifying ASIC designs. SystemVerilog improves on Verilog by introducing many additional features. The essential enhancements are:

- Data types
- Classes
- Constrained randomization
- Interfaces
- Coverage
- Packages
- Foreign language interface

This book does not cover the various aspects of SystemVerilog, as that is a vast topic. When you begin this book, it is assumed that you have a working knowledge of SystemVerilog or have taken a course on it before proceeding further.

The introduction of these constructs provides a considerable power to the language; using randomization now means that one can automate testing. Left to run long enough, a random source can eventually generate stimulus needed to cover a substantial portion of the functionality to be verified[2]. There is also a significant productivity boost when using a random approach as you see in Figure 1.3.

Translating the same testbench into SystemVerilog allows us to use the power of the various new constructs to help us during our verification. A testbench that implements the same functionality can be developed in SystemVerilog using classes, as shown in Figure 1.4.

We can model the transactions as classes and randomize them. We then drive the transactions to the DUT and collect the response from the DUT. These operations are performed using class-based objects. A generator generates the transactions and driven to the design by a driver. A monitor that is watching the interface reconstructs the transactions and puts them in a scoreboard.

In general: the changes between the Verilog and the SystemVerilog testbenches can be summarized into the following categories:

1. Testbench connections to the DUT
2. Testbench Architecture
3. Testbench components
4. Stimulus generation and monitoring

---

[1] see the preface for its location

[2] The infinite monkey theorem comes to mind, however, you can expect random generators to converge in a realistic timeframe.

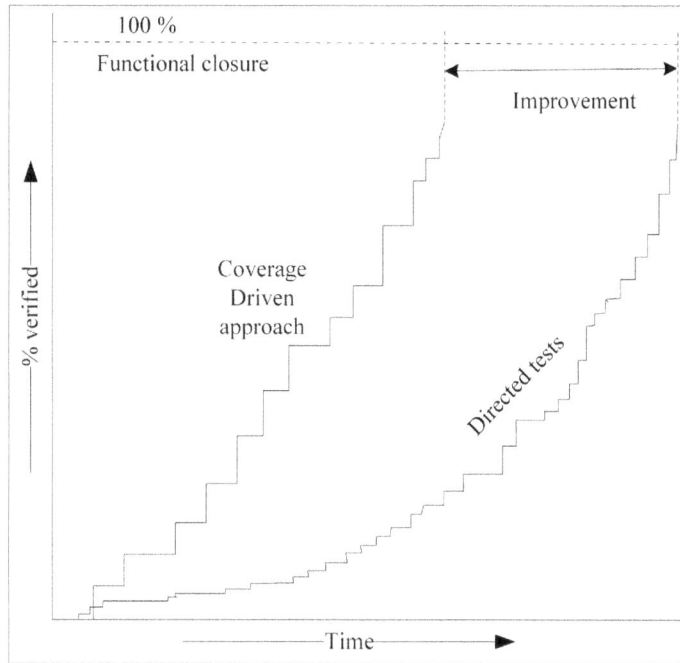

Fig. 1.3: Advantages of randomization

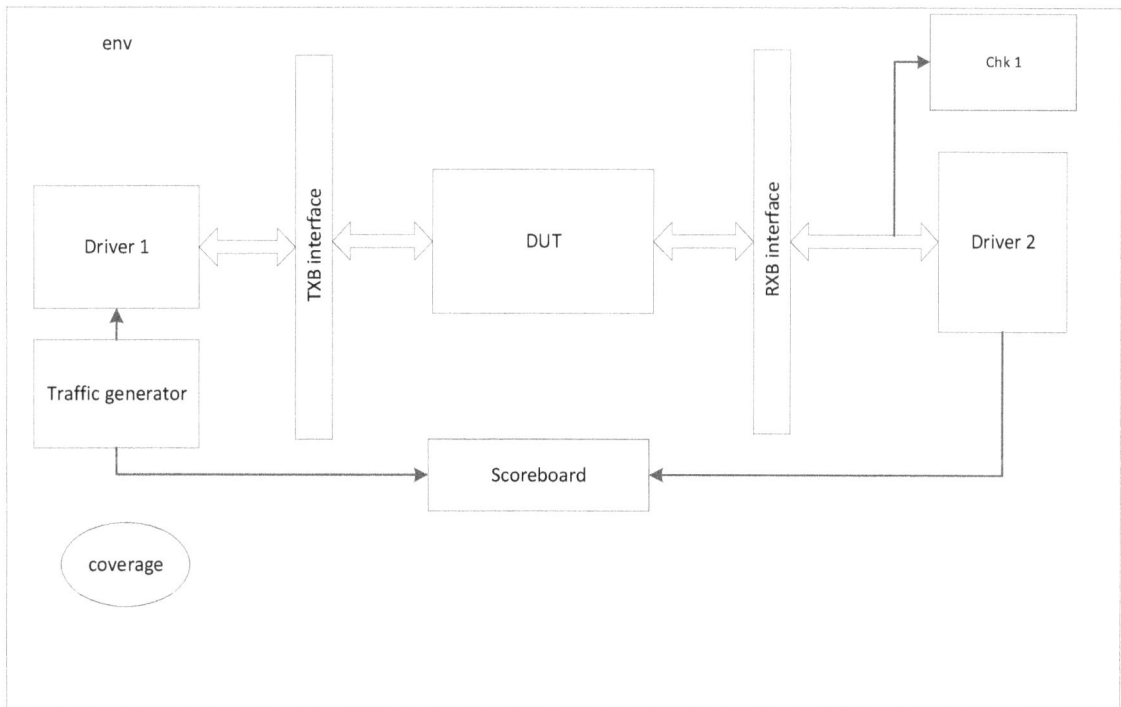

Fig. 1.4: A Simple SystemVerilog Testbench

Testbench Connections

The Verilog testbench used a collection of wires to connect the Verilog DUT and BFM models with the testbench. When using SystemVerilog, Interfaces are used to connect the models. Comparing Figure 1.2 and Figure 1.4, you can see that the connections with the DUT in the Verilog and SystemVerilog approaches are quite different.

The SystemVerilog version simplifies the connection descriptions to a single interface file. The top-level module now provides a wrapper around the DUT and connects the DUT via interfaces to the testbench. This module also provides clocks and reset. Instead of a module for the testbench, SystemVerilog uses a program block.

Listing 1.3: Top Level SystemVerilog Testbench Module

```
1    module wb_env_top_mod();
2
3      logic clk;
4      logic rst;
5
6      // Clock Generation
7      parameter sim_cycle = 10;
8
9      // Reset Delay Parameter
10     parameter rst_delay = 10;
11     initial begin
12       clk  = 0;
13       #10;
14       forever clk = #(sim_cycle/2) ~clk;
15
16     end
17
18     wb_master_if mast_if(clk,rst);
19     wb_slave_if slave_if(clk,rst);
20     wb_svtb_test test(mast_if,slave_if);
21
22     dut dut(mast_if,slave_if);
23
24     //Driver reset depending on rst_delay
25     initial
26     begin
27       clk = 0;
28       rst = 0;
29       #5 rst = 1;
30       repeat (rst_delay) @(clk);
31       rst = 1'b0;
32       @(clk);
33     end
34
35   endmodule: wb_env_top_mod
```

- Lines 18-19 are the master and slave interfaces that are connected to the testbench
- Line 20 is the instance of the Program Block.
- Line 22 is the instance of the DUT.
- Lines 25-33 are the reset & clock provided to the design.

The complete source code listing for the testbench along with a Makefile is provided in the GitHub repository. Due to page count limits, the description of the SystemVerilog testbench is abbreviated here and provided so that you can follow along. If you need more information, there is a wealth of information available on the internet.

Testbench Architecture

Compared to the Verilog testbench, the SystemVerilog testbench now uses a Program block. The testbench is now written in terms of classes and methods instead of modules and tasks. The Program block includes an environment class, which acts as a testbench container. It is passed the interfaces and parameters from the top-level test.

Listing 1.4: Top Level SVTB program Block

```
1    program test(wb_master_if m_intf wb_slave_if s_intf);
2      environment env;
3      initial begin
4        env = new(m_intf, s_intf);
5        env.gen.repeat_count = 10;
6        env.reset();
7        env.run();
8      end
```

Testbench Components

The environment class includes all the testbench components and their interconnections. The BFM models (master and slave) from the earlier approach are now written as classes and instantiated in the environment class. They are connected to the DUT via the interfaces. A generator class in the environment is used to generate traffic that used to test the DUT instead of the Verilog tasks. Mailboxes are used to connect the generator class with the driver. The generator class and the slave BFM class in this example pass abstract transaction descriptors to the scoreboard for checking. Some other approaches instantiate a set of monitor classes connected to the DUT interfaces feed the data to a scoreboard, as seen in Figure 1.4.

Listing 1.5: Top Level SVTB Environment

```
1    class environment;
2
3      // Generator and Driver and monitors & Scoreboards
4      wb_svtb_generator gen;
5
6      // mailboxes for communication
7      mailbox gen2driv;
8      // Constructor
9      function new(virtual wb_master_if mvif,wb_slave_if slvif);
10       .....
11      endfunction
12
13      // The test loop
14      task reset();
15        m_driv.reset();
16        m_mon.reset();
17        s_mon.reset();
18        scoreboard.clear();
19      endtask
20
21      task run();
22        fork
23          gen.run();
```

```
24        m_driv.run();
25        s_driv.run();
26        m_mon.run();
27        s_mon.run();
28        scoreboard.run();
29     join_any;
30   endtask
31 endclass
```

The program block creates the environment, resets the BFM's contained in the environment and configures the generator to create the specified number of transactions to be sent through the design. The test terminates after the required amount of stimulus is fed to the DUT, and the responses are accounted for by the scoreboard.

Stimulus Generation and Monitoring

In the Verilog testbench, the stimulus was generated using a task. However, in SystemVerilog, the stimulus is modeled as a transaction that contains randomizable property variables. (See Section 3 to learn how to model such a transaction) The values for the variables are determined using constraints which set the range of values that the property can take. The simulator determines the final values of the transaction properties at runtime. As a result, you can have a range of values can be accumulated when testing the DUT by running the same test with a different random seed. While SystemVerilog coverage is not shown in this example, it is typically used to capture the values that were generated and fed to the DUT during the simulation run. Coverage from multiple runs is typically merged to create a picture of the testing performed on the DUT.

Note that the SystemVerilog testbench in this section looks somewhat different from the testbench in Section 1.2. In addition to creating classes dynamically, you can have random testing with coverage measuring the extent of the stimulus applied to the DUT automatically. With this small initial investment, you gain leverage in verification with this approach. However, SystemVerilog testbenches alone are not the answer to verification. Other considerations now come into the picture when using SystemVerilog, which brings UVM into the picture.

UVM is revolutionary in the sense that it is the first verification methodology to be standardized. Note that it is also evolutionary, it's origins built on the foundations provided by the Open Verification Methodology (OVM), Universal Reuse Methodology (URM) and concepts from the e Reuse Methodology (eRM) in addition to code and concepts from Verification Methodology Manual (VMM)

Chapter 2

The UVM Testbench

There are some advantages to the simple testbenches developed in Verilog and SystemVerilog. You can write them quickly and can generate results if the design is reasonably small or doesn't need a complex protocol as part of its interface. This is the typical approach for verifying designs at the early stages. Unfortunately, it does not scale very well with design complexity. Also, it is incredibly expensive and error-prone to build and debug testbenches from scratch repeatedly. Often a simulation in one vendor's offering may need to be modified to run in another vendor's offering as the supported subsets of the SystemVerilog standard may be different.

Any change to any part of the testbench can have an impact on many other areas of the testbench. It is not feasible in the above approach to completely insulate changes to localized portions of the testbench. Consider a scenario where different groups are responsible for different interfaces on a large device. If multiple groups/people are trying to edit a single file, the entire editing and management/coordination effort becomes challenging very quickly.

While SystemVerilog provides language constructs, it does not teach you how to build reusable, layered, coverage-driven testbenches needed for verifying complex contemporary designs. With larger complex environments, merely writing much code to check a DUT does not scale well with complexity. As the designs become larger and larger, complexity increases with an exponential increase in verification effort. Moving up an abstraction layer usually helps with managing complexity. However, in addition to having the capability in the verification language, methodology is required to allow a high degree of productivity. A methodology provides features so that engineers do not have to spend much time creating an infrastructure that is common to all environments. It provides a consistent look and feel so that engineers can move quickly across various environments and still retain their productivity.

2.1 How Does UVM Help You?

In the past, many methodologies such as OVM, VMM, eRM were available from competing vendors. An Accellera committee, formed with members from both vendors and ASIC companies created a methodology and a base class library. This methodology is called Universal Verification Methodology (UVM) and combines the best features from all the contributions.

UVM is implemented as a base class library on top of SystemVerilog. It leverages object oriented techniques and concepts from the software world to provide verification engineers the ability to verify ASICs using modern programming techniques. Most vendors now ship a version of UVM with their simulators to make things easy for engineers. Many other tools leverage the UVM infrastructure making it easy to debug and lint code as well.

UVM contains many essential components which have led to its wide adoption:

1. Classes to create and organize stimulus – Chapter 3 and Chapter 14

2. Common class utilities for all class objects. – Chapter 4

3. Factory interface to create classes easily– Chapter 5

4. Common messaging platform. – Chapter 6

5. Class utilities for configuration of objects. – Chapter 7

6. Classes for verification environment hierarchy creation and management – Chapter 8

7. Classes to help manage customization of predefined components – Chapter 9

8. Classes to provide communication utilities Chapter 10.

9. Command Line interface – Chapter 11

10. Register classes to help with register programming. – Chapter 12, Chapter 17

11. Classes to provide Simulation Phasing – Chapter 13

12. Classes to help with synchronization – Chapter 15

Figure 2.1 offers a diagrammatic view. Much of the functionality is built on top of base classes. As you proceed in your study through subsequent chapters, you can appreciate the power of the UVM library since it streamlines your verification effort.

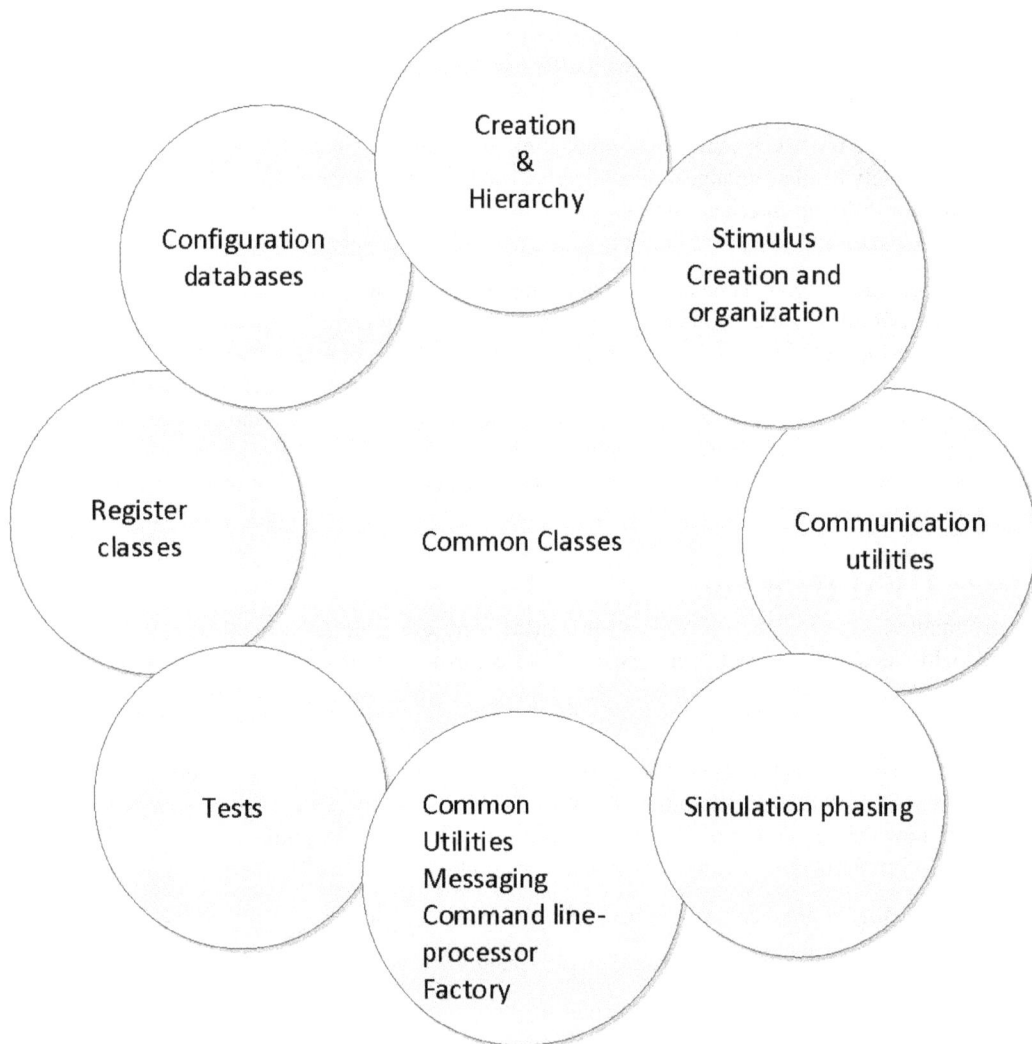

Fig. 2.1: Classes in UVM

2.2 Some UVM Terminology

As we progress through the chapters in the Quickstart and the rest of this book, you will find inter-dependency between many aspects of the UVM library. Consequently, some back and forth cross-references exist in the text. This chapter makes some forward references to content in subsequent chapters, which, ***regrettably was unavoidable*** to prevent repetitive explanations. Where possible, explanations are summarized to allow you to follow along. Concepts developed here are used with more sophisticated examples in Part IV. Those chapters are extensions of the concepts developed in this chapter. A few terms are defined here to understand the content and prevent us from getting ahead of ourselves.

Components and Dynamic Objects: The class-based structure allows the user to create class objects at runtime. The class instances can be broadly classified into two different types depending on the lifetime of objects in the simulation. Some class instances are present from the beginning of the simulation after they are created until the test is completed. For example, the class instances could be a driver, monitor scoreboard, etc. These are effectively quasi-static objects and can broadly be called **components**. Some other class instances may represent a transient packet as it transits through the simulation through the verification environment, RTL, etc. These are typically called **dynamic objects/packets** etc.

Factory: The factory is a design pattern, which allows you to create classes of different types. It allows you to substitute one class for another if is configured to do so.

Hooks: In many parts of the UVM library, the developers of the library have provided calls to some methods with a fixed signature to allow you to modify the behavior quickly without extensive changes. These 'intercept' functions are termed *hooks*.

Callbacks: Callbacks are another way for the user to add some user-defined code that is not part of the library behavior to a UVM class. These methods and signatures and 'intercept' points are called *callbacks*. The difference between hooks and callbacks is that UVM defines the position of the hooks and their signature whereas callbacks are user-defined.

Core Services: These are static classes that act as containers for some of the common uvm utilities. This approach allows you to override the core classes in the UVM library without hacking the library. The collection of these classes are the core services, and the container is called the uvm_coreservice container.

Agents. Earlier chapters discussed a driver, monitor, and a generator. While each of these components could be reused independently, every test writer would need the names, configurations, and interfaces of every entity in the system. This can be significant work, and several of the details are not usually relevant to many members in a verification team. The agent is a container class that encapsulates the components, allowing the focus on generating stimulus and reusing the work done by someone else. See Section 8.3.4 for more information.

Sequences and Sequencers. A stimulus to test a DUT is usually a recipe of traffic patterns sent to the DUT. The recipe is called a sequence, and this recipe executes on a sequencer. More information on this topic is available in Section 3 and Sections 14.1 onwards.

Command Line processor. If you have a SystemVerilog testbench, you need to write many $valueplusargs/$testplusargs code to parse the command line. A built-in command-line processor is provided that accomplishes many tasks by default.

Configuration Database. To store values, a built-in database is provided for you by default. It has a set/get API allowing you to store many types in it. In the sections that follow, we refer to this database as **config_db.** You can learn lot more about its capabilities in Chapter 7.

Objections The UVM library provides an objections infrastructure. This infrastructure is used by many classes to "have a stake" during simulation progress. You can raise and drop objections, as well as wait for objections before you perform actions.

TLM Ports. UVM operates on the basis of abstract transactions, and the methodology supports Transaction Layer Communication between component classes using a set of classes called TLM ports. TLM ports can be of different types: *ports, imports, analysis_ports and exports.* See Chapter 10 for more information.

2.3 Creating a UVM Testbench

The previous chapter described a Verilog and a SystemVerilog testbench for our DUT. The UVM testbench is similar to the SystemVerilog testbench in that it uses interfaces to allow communication between the testbench and the DUT.

However, the structure of the classes that are used to create the testbench are a little different from the approaches taken in the previous chapter. The steps described in the following sections are top down, starting with the top-level Verilog module that holds the DUT and testbench. Each of these steps has a particular significance in top-level integration with the DUT. These steps must be performed for each DUT verified using UVM in the top-level module. This top-level module is usually not reusable between environments simply because of the nature of the connections involved between the components.

The essential steps in this stage of our verification are:

1. Create a top-level module to hold the DUT instance and the testbench.

2. Create the clocks and reset to this module.

3. Instantiate the agent interfaces in the top-level environment and connect them to the DUT.

4. Create an initial block to start the UVM environment.

2.3.1 Create the Testbench Top-Level Module

The top-level module holds the DUT and several other essential components for UVM verification. The top-level testbench contains an instance of the DUT in it. It contains the clock generation, reset connections, and interface connections to connect the DUT to the testbench. Also, it contains a simple initial block that helps to get the testbench started. Listing 2.1 contains the complete listing for this testbench.

2.3.2 Clocks and Reset

Our testbench has a few initial blocks. One of the blocks acts as a clock generator. The reset is supplied by the UVM testbench.

2.3.3 Connect the Interfaces

In a typical Verilog verification environment, a collection of wires are created to connect various tasks in the testbench to the DUT. These connections are accomplished in the UVM approach using SystemVerilog interfaces. These interfaces are a named bundle of wires, making it easy to pass the collection across various UVM hierarchies. You instantiate the interfaces in the top-level testbench and pass the handle to the interface (a pointer in C parlance) to the UVM environment through an element named as a virtual interface. A virtual interface is a reference to a static interface instance, but it is treated by the SystemVerilog testbench as a variable that can be reassigned.

The complete code for the top-level testbench is listed in Section 2.3.1 after all the above steps are completed.

The top-level testbench for the wishbone class-based environment is a simple module that instantiates the DUT. It contains the SystemVerilog interfaces that allow the DUT connections to the verification environment. The clock and reset signals are created in this testbench and wired both to the DUT and the interfaces. A simple clock generator is a part of this testbench.

(i) The DUT, in this example, is deliberately kept simple to illustrate concepts. See Chapter 21 for an example of having up to 24 masters and slaves in a single system

The complete listing for the top-level testbench is in the Listing 2.1

Listing 2.1: Top-Level Testbench

```
4    module wb_env_top_mod();
5
6      logic clk;
7
8      // Clock Generation
9      parameter sim_cycle = 10;
10
11     // Reset Delay Parameter
12     parameter rst_delay = 5;
13     initial begin
14       clk  = 0;
15       forever clk = #(sim_cycle/2) ~clk;
16     end
17
18     wb_master_if mast_if(clk);
19     wb_slave_if slave_if(clk);
20
21     wb_env_tb_mod test();
22
23     dut dut(mast_if,slave_if);
24
25   endmodule: wb_env_top_mod
```

In Listing 2.1

- Lines 14-16 show the generation of the main clock to the wishbone DUT.

- Lines 18-19 show the instances of the master and slave interfaces to the DUT.

- Line 21 shows the UVM testbench module instantiated in the top-level testbench. We will learn more about this module in Section 2.5.

- Line 23 shows the instantiation of the DUT

You will notice that there is no reset in this testbench. That will be handled within the UVM environment.

2.4 Create UVM Testbench Environment for the DUT

Each interface to the DUT is connected to a container class called an agent. An agent typically encapsulates a few sub-components that generate the stimulus, drive data across the interface, and monitor values on the interface. The agent can be considered as an encapsulation of activity that occurs on a specific interface. Our previous SystemVerilog testbench had a driver that was driving either the master or the slave ports. A generator was a separate class in the environment. A monitor class was not shown in Section 1.3, but as we mentioned, it could be a part of the testbench.

In a UVM Environment, an *agent* contains a *driver* that drives the signals, a *sequencer* that acts as a generator, and a *monitor* that watches the activity on the interface and creates a transaction class out of the signals in the interface. As you go through the rest of this chapter, think of an agent as a class object that encapsulates everything to do with a specific interface.

We have two interfaces in our DUT. Similar to the SystemVerilog testbench, random stimulus needs to be applied to the DUT via the master port, an agent is needed to drive the master port. Another agent is needed to respond to the transactions on the slave port. To ensure that the transaction passed through the DUT are correctly processed, a scoreboard that connects to both the master and slave agents for checking both the input and outputs is required. Finally, to measure the stimulus that is provided by both the master and slave agents, a coverage monitor is needed.

The master and slave agents, a scoreboard and coverage monitor are all instantiated in an environment class. A test case class instantiates this environment class and also provides test specific settings and configuration to test the DUT.

This testcase instantiates the verification environment that contains the various class-based UVM components that form a part of the verification environment. The verification environment consists of the following components. Details of each of the various components are in the following sections.

- Master Agent : Section 2.4.2
- Slave Agent : Section 2.4.3
- Scoreboard : Section 2.4.4
- Environment Class : Section 2.4.1

Figure 2.2 shows the top-level testbench block diagram instantiating a testcase (see Section 2.5.1 below).

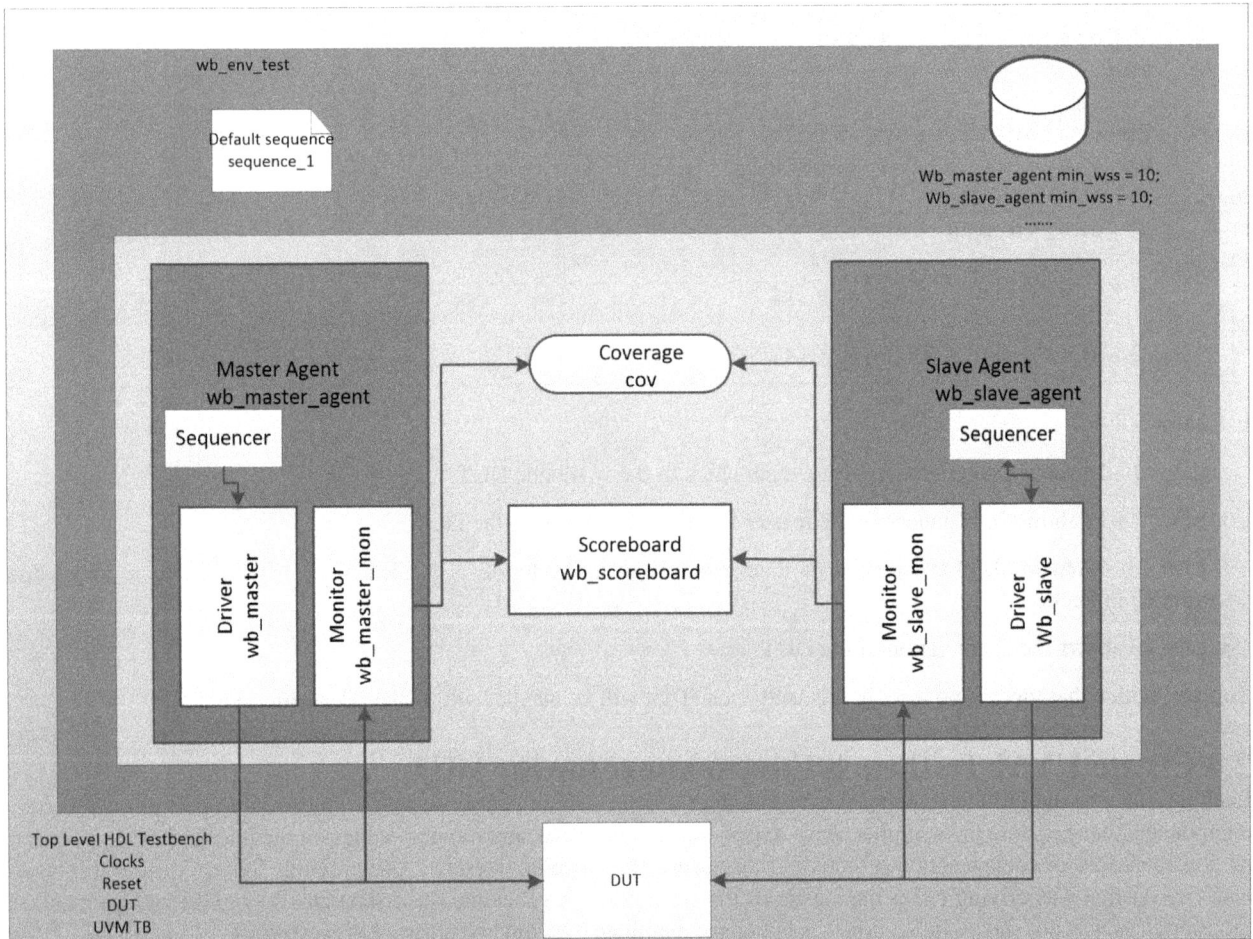

Fig. 2.2: Block Diagram Of The Class Based Environment

2.4.1 Environment Class

The environment class is a container class that contains all the subcomponents that make up the testbench. All the agents, scoreboard, and other components are instantiated in this class. The environment configures all of its subcomponents, makes connections between the various components, and sets up the testbench. Each of the subcomponents is configured by this class, which sets up the mode and parameters. An environment class cannot be reused on another design, but it may be reused in a system-level environment. One of the key things to note is that while they encapsulate all the components, environment classes *do not create any stimulus or contain any time consuming tasks*. Listing 2.2 shows the various components that are instantiated in the env class.

UVM supplies a notion of 'phasing' - an orderly sequence of tasks and functions that allow the simulation to proceed in a specific order. Classes that comprise of the environment, agents, scoreboards and tests are quasi-static in nature. They are created duing the build_phase and connections are made between them in the connect_phase. See Section 13.1.1 and sections that follow it if you want to delve into what happens in these phases. For now, all you need to know is that the build_phase creates the components and the connect_phase makes the connections between them. The methods used to invoke the phasing are shown on Lines 14 and 15 in the above listing.

Listing 2.2: The Environment Class

```
4    class wb_env extends uvm_env;
5      wb_master_agent master_agent;
6      wb_slave_agent slave_agent;
7      wb_env_cov cov;
8      wb_scoreboard sb;
9      reset_agent rst_agent;
10
11     `uvm_component_utils(wb_env)
12
13     extern function new(string name="wb_env", uvm_component parent=null);
14     extern virtual function void build_phase(uvm_phase phase);
15     extern virtual function void connect_phase(uvm_phase phase);
16
17   endclass: wb_env
```

- Line 5 is the instance of the master_agent used to drive the data to the dut

- Line 6 is the instance of the slave_agent used to drive the data to the dut

- Line 7 is the instance of the coverage component

- Line 8 is the instance of the scoreboard.

2.4.2 Master Agent

Section 2.4 described an agent as a container class. A typical agent has an interface associated with it and contains driver, monitor, and sequencer class instances along with any necessary configuration. The driver and monitor classes are connected to the interface. The sequencer class generates the transactions based on a recipe and feeds them to the driver via a TLM port. The driver class then drives the signals on the interface as per a specific protocol to the DUT.

The monitor class observes the signals on the interface and recreates an abstract transaction representation and writes out the transaction to a TLM port called an *analysis_port*.

In our case, The master agent is connected to the master interface. Note that the TLM ports for the driver and monitor are different ports.

If you want more information about Agents, See Section 8.3.1 for the driver classes, Section 8.3.3 for the sequencer and Section 8.3.2 for the monitor classes.

2.4.3 Slave Agent

The slave agent is similar to the master agent above. One major difference between the master agent and the slave agent is that the master initiates the transactions to the DUT while the slave agent *waits for the DUT to initiate transactions to it*. There are some subtle differences in the implementation of this agent because it responds to transactions instead of initiating them. See Section 16 for details of the slave agent. For now, all that is required is to identify a slave agent as one that *responds* to the stimulus given to it.

In our case, the slave agent is connected to the slave interface.

Depending on the protocol, In many UVM environments, The agents described above could be a piece of verification IP. Depending on the application, the agents could be quite complex, with many configurable parameters as in the case of PCI-E, SATA, USB, or other protocols.

2.4.4 Scoreboard

The scoreboard compares the transaction that was fed to the input of the DUT and resulting output from the DUT. It has two input ports in this example. The scoreboard compares the transaction from the master agent and the transaction provided by the slave agent. It does necessary calculations to ensure that the DUT responded to the master agent's transactions on the slave port of the DUT. By making sure that the transactions are correct, it helps verify the DUT.

The class definition of the scoreboard is shown in Listing 2.3.

For now, just recognize is that the scoreboard compares two (or possibly more) sources to determine correct behavior. The scoreboard typically connects to various components via TLM ports described later in the book.

You can reference Section 8.3.6 for more details of its operation.

Listing 2.3: The Scoreboard

```
1    class wb_scoreboard extends uvm_scoreboard;
2      `uvm_component_utils( wb_scoreboard)
3
4      uvm_tlm_analysis_fifo #(wb_transaction) expected_wb_transaction_fifo;
5      uvm_tlm_analysis_fifo #(wb_transaction) actual_wb_transaction_fifo;
6
7      // Constructor
8
9      function new( string name, uvm_component parent );
10       super.new( name, parent );
11     endfunction: new
12
13     extern virtual function void build_phase( uvm_phase phase );
14     extern virtual function void connect_phase( uvm_phase phase );
15     extern virtual task run_phase( uvm_phase phase );
16
17   endclass: wb_scoreboard
```

The master agent puts out a transaction through its driver. This is converted to an abstract transaction using the master monitor, which puts out a transaction on its analysis port. This analysis port is connected to the expected_transaction_fifo on the scoreboard in the listing above.

Similarly, the slave monitor puts out a transaction on its analysis port, which is fed into the actual_transaction_analysis_fifo.

See Section 8.3.6, to learn how the transactions are compared.

2.4.5 Coverage

Most random environments use functional coverage to assess if they have completely exhausted the range of the stimulus. Typically, a set of coverage points is identified in conjunction with the test plan. These cover points are implemented as covergroups. These covergroups can be designed to measure both the input stimulus and the output response. To use a covergroup, you create an instance of this covergroup in a component class. The monitor in the environment provides a transaction through its analysis port. This analysis port is connected to an implementation port (imp port) implemented in the component that contains the covergroup. The implementation port calls a method called write() that triggers an event which calls the sample() method of the cover group. We have only chosen to have a single covergroup here since it is a simple pass-through DUT.

Listing 2.4: The Environment Coverage Subscriber

```
5    class wb_env_cov  extends uvm_subscriber #(wb_transaction);
6      event cov_event;
7      wb_transaction tr;
8      `uvm_component_utils(wb_env_cov)
9
10     covergroup cg_trans @(cov_event);
11       coverpoint tr.kind;
12       coverpoint tr.address {
13         bins low = {[0:10]};
14         bins mid = {[10:100]};
15         bins high = {[100:$]};
16       }
17       coverpoint tr.lock ;
18       coverpoint tr.status;
19       coverpoint tr.num_wait_states {
20         bins legal[] = {[0:15]};
21         illegal_bins ib = {[16:$]};
22       }
23     endgroup: cg_trans
24
25     function new(string name, uvm_component parent);
26       super.new(name,parent);
27       cg_trans = new;
28     endfunction: new
29
30     virtual function void write(wb_transaction t);
31       this.tr = t;
32       -> cov_event;
33     endfunction: write
34
35   endclass: wb_env_cov
36
37 `endif // WB_ENV_COV__SV
```

The subscriber class contains a uvm_analysis_imp port which connects to the analysis port of the monitor. The port connections between this uvm_analysis_import class and the monitor's analysis_port class are made in the top-level environment.

- Line 5 shows the class being extended from uvm_component.
- Line 6 shows the cov_event event that is being used to trigger sampling.
- Line 8 provides the common utilities using the macros. We will discuss these in a later chapter.
- Lines 10-23 show the covergroup which cover various transaction properties.
- Lines 25-28 show the constructor.
- Lines 30-33 shows the write method for the analysis port. This write() method assigns the incoming transaction handle to the local transaction handle so that the covergroup can sample it. It triggers the event so that the sampling can occur.

2.5 Connect Testbench to DUT

In the previous sections, we studied a class based environment that would be used to verify our DUT. The class based environment used virtual interfaces inside the classes. We now need to connect the virtual interfaces to our DUT.

Listing 2.5: UVM Top-Level connections In Testbench

```
1   `include "wb_test.pkg"
2   module wb_env_tb_mod;
3
4     import uvm_pkg::*;
5     import wb_tests::*;
6
7     typedef virtual wb_master_if v_if1;
8     typedef virtual wb_slave_if v_if2;
9     initial begin
10      uvm_config_db #(v_if1)::set(null,"uvm_test_top.env.rst_agent","
            mst_if",wb_env_top_mod.mast_if);
11      uvm_config_db #(v_if1)::set(null,"uvm_test_top.env.master_agent","
            mst_if",wb_env_top_mod.mast_if);
12      uvm_config_db #(v_if2)::set(null,"uvm_test_top.env.slave_agent","
            slv_if",wb_env_top_mod.slave_if);
13      run_test();
14    end
15
16  endmodule: wb_env_tb_mod
```

The above listing shows a simple module instantiated in the top-level testbench. For reasons of clarity, we chose to keep the UVM testbench in a separate module. Note that we could have very easily have placed the contents of this module inside the top testbench; this is a matter of preference and style.

- Line 4 imports the UVM package into the module.
- Line 5 imports the testcases as a SystemVerilog Package
- Lines 7,8 declare the virtual master and slave interfaces so that they can be passed into the UVM environment.
- Lines 10,11 connect the top-level testbench to the virtual interface handles via the config_db. The config_db entries for the master and slave interfaces places handles for the DUT interface connections in the database. The UVM environment obtains the handles from the database and uses them in the class based environment.
- Line 13 starts the test. Cection 2.6.1 provides the detailed explanation of how the test proceeds.

2.5.1 The Test Class

Tests in UVM are derived from an *uvm_test* class. You usually create a base_test class that derives from uvm_test. This base_test class carries all the settings of the environment. Derived classes of base_test then define scenario-specific configurations such as specific sequences to run, coverage parameters, and so on. The test instantiates the verification environment like any other verification component.

You can create as many test classes as you want. Each test can test a specific area of the DUT. You compile all the tests into your simulator. However, you do not create an instance of the test inside the environment. You call the run_test() method with a 'testname' argument or supply this name of the test through a command-line argument. Built-in classes in the UVM library parse the command line and obtain the name of the test and create an instance of the test and its environment to begin the test. The test instantiates an instance of the environment class. The environment class contains all the agents and other components. This class instantiates and configures all the subcomponents that make up the verification environment.

The top-level test for the DUT contains all the settings required to run the test. As seen in Figure 2.3, the test class has an instance of the environment class in it. This class contains all the settings that the environment needs to configure the environment for the test. The class sets the default sequencer to be run, which provides the stimulus for the test. For now, do not worry if you are unable to understand this listing. All you need to know is that the test contains an instance of the environment, and different tests are different classes in the UVM approach.

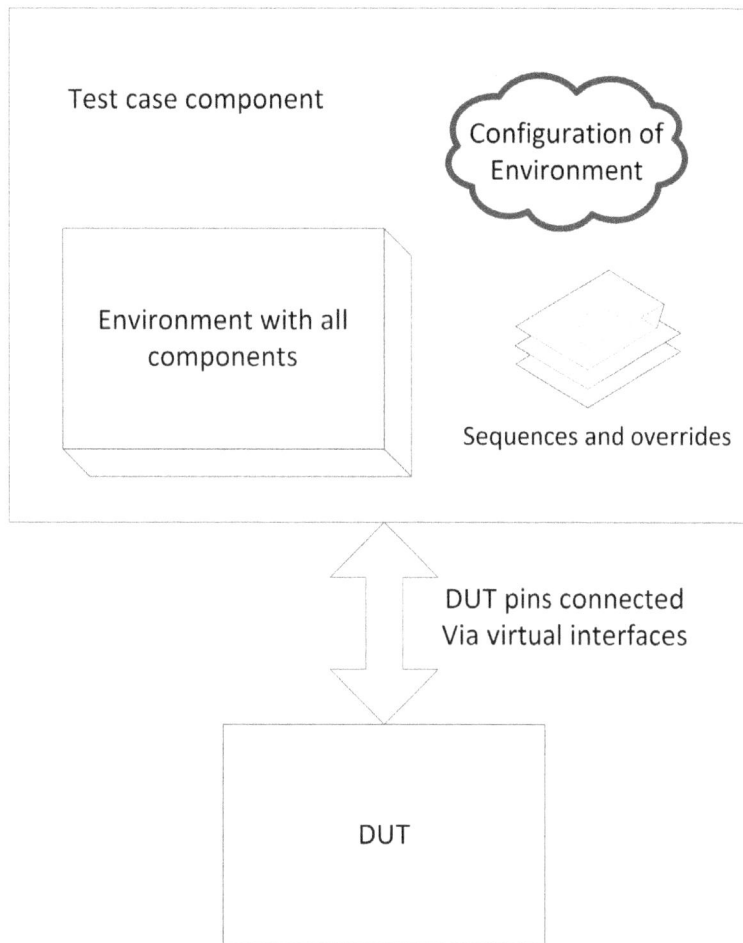

Fig. 2.3: Top-Level Test

Listing 2.6: The Test Class

```
6    class wb_env_base_test extends uvm_test;
7
8      wb_config wb_master_config;
9      wb_config wb_slave_config;
10
11     `uvm_component_utils(wb_env_base_test)
12
13     wb_env env;
14
15     function new(string name, uvm_component parent);
16       super.new(name, parent);
17     endfunction
18
19     virtual function void build_phase(uvm_phase phase);
20       super.build_phase(phase);
21       env = wb_env::type_id::create("env", this);
22       wb_master_config = new("wb_master_config");
23       wb_slave_config = new("wb_slave_config");
24
```

```
25        wb_master_config.max_n_wss = 10;
26        wb_master_config.min_addr = 0;
27        wb_master_config.max_addr = 10000000;
28
29        wb_slave_config.max_n_wss = 10;
30        wb_slave_config.min_addr = 0;
31        wb_slave_config.max_addr = 10000000;
32
33        begin: configure
34          uvm_config_db #(uvm_object_wrapper)::set(this, "env.rst_agent.
                mast_sqr.reset_phase", "default_sequence", reset_sequence::
                get_type());
35          uvm_config_db #(uvm_object_wrapper)::set(this, "env.master_agent.
                mast_sqr.main_phase", "default_sequence", sequence_1::get_type
                ());
36          uvm_config_db #(uvm_object_wrapper)::set(this, "env.slave_agent.
                slv_seqr.main_phase", "default_sequence", ram_sequence::
                get_type());
37
38          uvm_config_db #(wb_config)::set(this, "env.master_agent", "config
                ", wb_master_config);
39          uvm_config_db #(wb_config)::set(this, "env.slave_agent", "config",
                wb_slave_config);
40        end
41      endfunction
42
43    endclass : wb_env_base_test
```

- Listing 2.6 shows the top-level test, which instantiates an instance of the environment class. This environment class contains the master agent, the slave agent, and the scoreboard. It makes the connections between the scoreboard and the master and slave agents.

- The environment is created using a factory method on line 21. Note that since a factory method is used; one can substitute this environment class for another one if the test was a base class if you had additional specific customizations in another environment class.

- Line 35 sets the default sequence on the master agent sequencer.

- Lines 38-39 configure the master and slave agents with the address range via the start_addr and end_addr parameters. The configuration for the number of wait states is placed in the config_db.

2.6 Starting the Tests From the Command Line

You compile the DUT, the top-level testbench and all other related files with your simulator. You then start the test from the command line by calling the compiled testbench with +UVM_TESTNAME=*Name of the test* as an argument to the command line. The corresponding test class is then created as an instance, and the test begins execution.

2.6.1 How Does the Test Proceed?

The previous sections described the UVM environment classes, and the DUT connections between the classes. In this section, we take a look at how the test actually starts and time proceeds in the simulation.

In any simulation environment, you will observe a familiar sequence executed by almost all tests:

- Set up the test and the environment.

- Run the test

- Cleanup

You recognize that these are phases in a simulation. UVM takes this a step further and provides a phasing infrastructure to all tests. This way, all the tests have uniformity.

Since this is a class based environment, the classes need to be created and interconnected before the test can proceed. Note that this is slightly different from a Verilog simulation, since the simulator does all the work before bringing the simulation to time 0, and test can proceed from that point.

The creation of classes and interconnection between them is accomplished by specific methods at specific stages termed as "phases" in UVM. The test typically goes through the following phases. (Not all the phases are shown here: see Chapter 13 for more details.)

- Build Phase

- Connect Phase

- Run Phase

- Cleanup

Note that the build_phase and connect_phase are *functions* essentially consuming zero simulation time.

We created a separate top-level module to contain all the testbench instantiations in Listing 2.5.

Listing 2.5 shows the testbench module connecting the virtual interfaces declared on lines 12-13 to the top-level DUT connections. In the initial block of the testbench module, The path to the DUT interfaces is provided by cross-module references on lines 15-16. These interfaces are virtual in the testbench, and their handles are passed around as config_db entries. This initial block is one of the first ones to execute in the simulation.

The circles in Figure 2.4 represent the various stages, as shown below. The simulation begins with the top-level module.

1. The top-level testbench instantiates the uvm package. When the UVM package is initialized, the factory, the reporting structure, and other global objects are brought into existence. The initial module inside the testbench module (wb_env_tb_mod.sv) takes the handles of the interfaces that are connected to the DUT and places it in the config_db. The run_test() method is called.

    a. As the simulator elaborates the hierarchy, the run_test now identifies the test that is to be run using the +UVM_TESTNAME command line parameter. This test is then created. Note that the run_test() method also takes an optional string parameter which can be used, if you would like to start your tests that way. A component with the requested test (of the specific type using the factory) is created. The name of the instance is set to *uvm_test_top*. UVM Phasing now begins.

    b. The top-level testbench has an initial block. This block places the virtual interfaces inside the config_db. This is indicated by the dark circle #1 in the figure.

       See Figure 2.5 for the order of config_db calls.

    c. The top-level test now places the default sequence for the test and the configurations in the config_db. We will discuss more about this sequence in later sections and chapters. For now, all you need to know is that it contains the recipe for the actual test stimulus.

    d. The testbench now starts building the environment when it starts running the test.

2.6.1.1 Build Phase

The test now creates the environment in its build phase after setting the various configuration options to the config_db. Figure Figure 2.5 illustrates this in Step 4.

During the build _phase, the constructors are called top down and classes are created. The test is first created, and this then creates the environment. It also initializes any variables and calls super.new(). The build_phase then recursively builds all the children of each class instance.

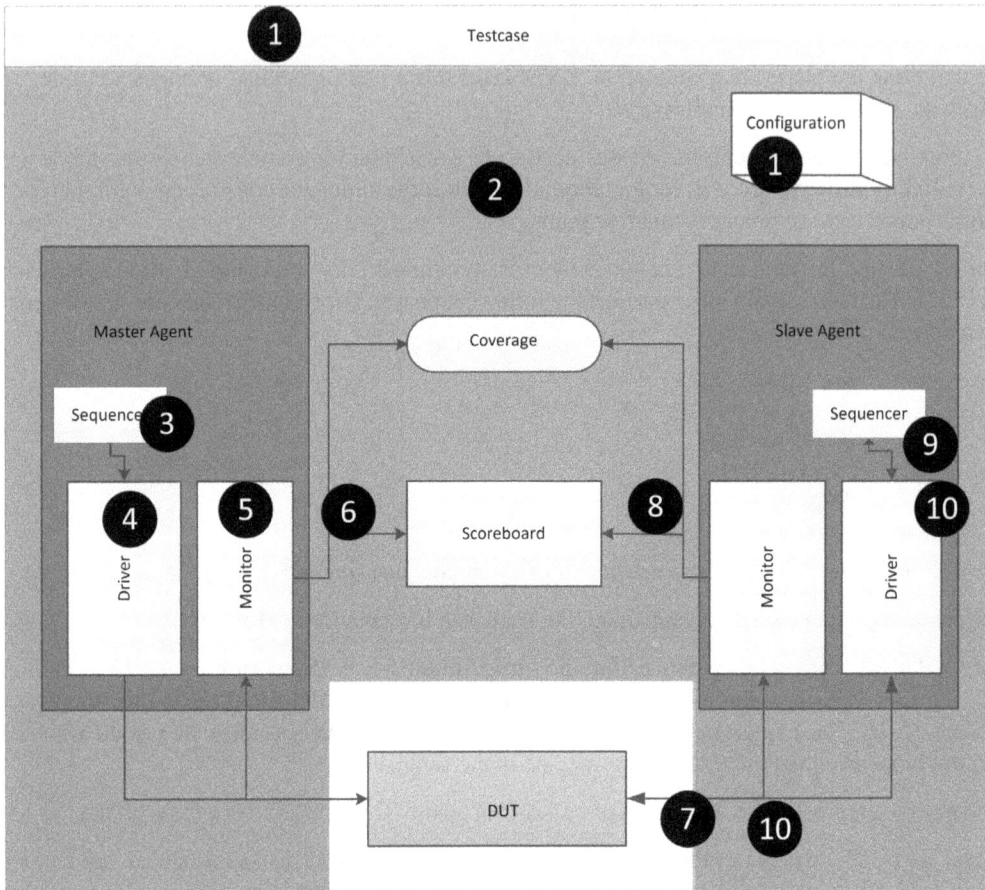

Fig. 2.4: Test Progress

All the agents, scoreboard, coverage, etc. are created in this manner. The build process is followed up by a connect_phase wherein the interconnections between the various components are established. See the listing for the test in the earlier section.

Listing 2.7: Build Phase of the Environment Class

```
23    function void wb_env::build_phase(uvm_phase phase);
24      super.build_phase(phase);
25      master_agent = wb_master_agent::type_id::create("master_agent",this)
          ;
26      slave_agent = wb_slave_agent::type_id::create("slave_agent",this);
27      cov = wb_env_cov::type_id::create("cov",this); //Instantiating the
          coverage class
28      sb = wb_scoreboard::type_id::create("sb",this);
29
30      rst_agent = reset_agent::type_id::create("rst_agent",this);
31
32    endfunction: build_phase
```

Often, the build configuration of the environment is usually controlled either through configuration database settings or via configuration class that is passed in from a specific test.

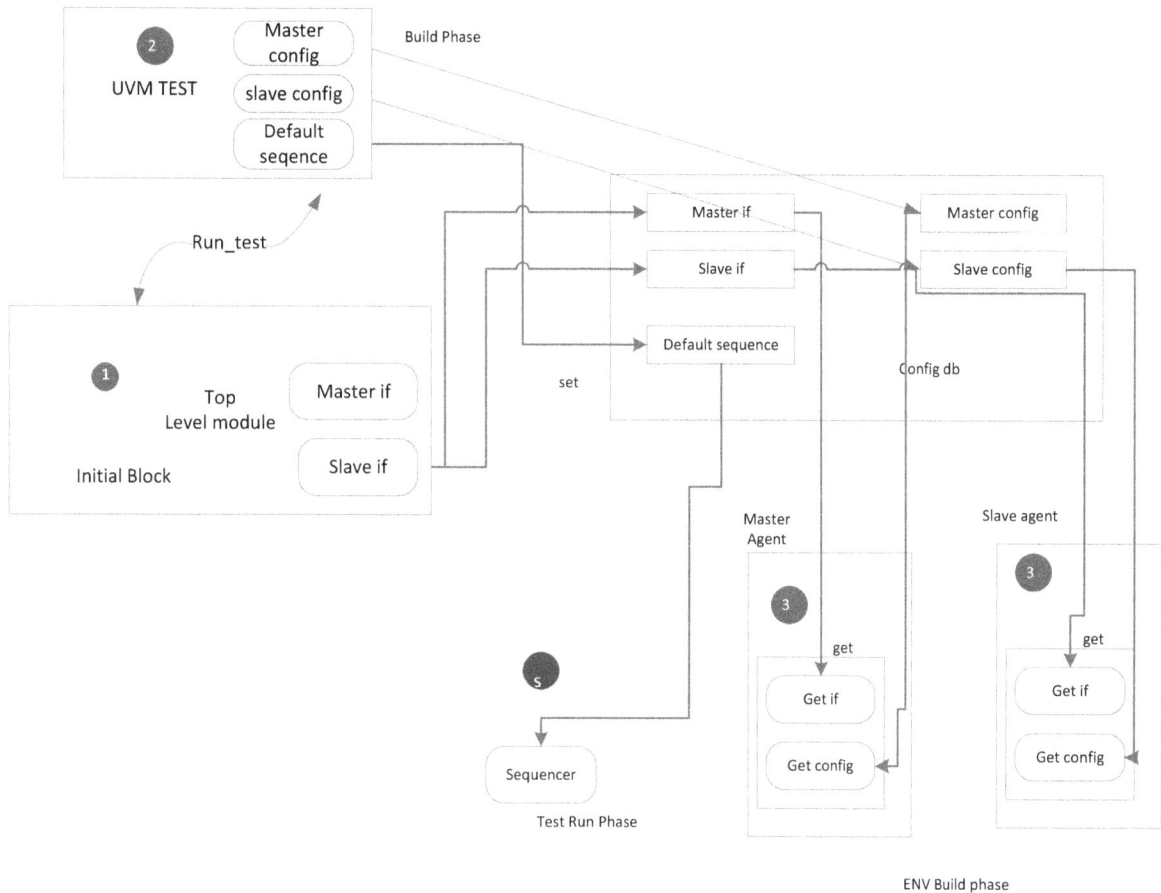

Fig. 2.5: Order of Config DB Calls

In the listing in Section 2.7

- Line 25 builds the master agent by calling the factory methods for the agent.

- Line 26 builds the slave agent by calling the factory methods for the agent.

- Line 29 builds the scoreboard.

- Lines 28 builds the coverage component and the coverage subscriber.

Here, the instance *sb* of type wb_scoreboard is created using the create() function. It is then assigned the wb_env as its parent. After the scoreboard is created, the wb_env can connect the ports on the environment slaves monitor to the after_export on the scoreboard. It connects the before_export on the master agent to the scoreboard.

(i) You can see the use of the factory pattern for the construction of the various components that make up the environment. The factory ensures that either a *type* or a *specific instance* of a component can be changed depending on the overrides provided in the test. See Section 21.2 for examples

2.6.1.2 Connect Phase
The connect phase is where all the components created in the build_phase are connected. Figure 2.6 illustrates this and Listing 2.8 shows how it is accomplished in code.

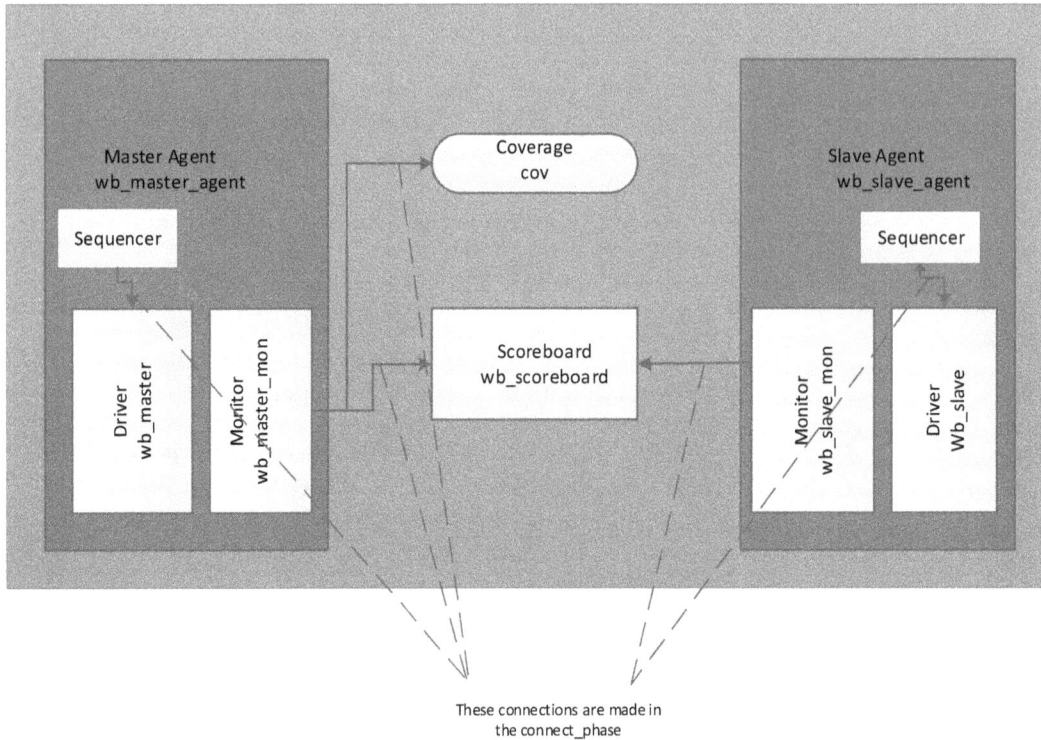

Fig. 2.6: Connect Phase

```
34    function void wb_env::connect_phase(uvm_phase phase);
35      super.connect_phase(phase);
36      master_agent.analysis_port.connect(cov.analysis_export);
37      master_agent.analysis_port.connect(sb.actual_wb_transaction_fifo.
            analysis_export);
38      slave_agent.analysis_port.connect(sb.expected_wb_transaction_fifo.
            analysis_export);
39    endfunction: connect_phase
```

- The master agent's monitor analysis port is connected to both the coverage and the scoreboard (actual_transaction_fifo tlm_analysis_fifo write_export) on line 36 and line 37

- Line 38 connects the analysis port to the expected_transaction_fifo tlm_analysis_fifo write_export inside the scoreboard. This expected_transaction comes from the slave agent's monitor analysis port.

The connect_phase is recursively called for each component in the simulation. Each of the agents makes internal connections between their sub-components in this phase.

2.6.1.3 Run Phase
1. The test selects the sequence to be run on Line 38 of Listing 2.6. The sequencer in the master agent retrieves this information from the configuration database (Step 5 in Figure 2.5) and then starts the sequence that is to be run. The sequencer then starts by creating an instance of the relevant sequence and executes the body() method in the sequence. In this particular case, the sequence is a simple sequence that creates a transaction and sends the packet to the driver.

2. The driver gets the transaction from the sequencer. This is an abstract description of the transaction. The driver examines the transaction and determines the kind of operation that needs to be generated on the bus. It then uses its knowledge of the bus protocol and drives the contents of the transaction onto the bus.

3. The monitor is connected to the pins of the DUT. Upon observing the pins, it recreates another transaction object. This transaction object is similar to the one that was obtained from the sequencer by the driver. However, one notes that the transaction object was created by the *inverse operation, IE observing the pins and creating the transaction.* The monitor then passes the transaction object to the coverage model that measures the input stimulus coverage, and to a scoreboard.

4. The DUT usually processes and sends data to the slave agent.

5. The slave agent bus monitor sees the activity on the bus and creates a transaction object that it feeds to the scoreboard.

6. The slave driver sees the transaction on its pins. It checks the address ranges and then responds back to the DUT.

The overall transaction flow for the transactions can be summarized in Figure 2.7 for the steps 3-8 above. These steps repeat until all the transactions are generated by the master agent and completed by the slave agent.

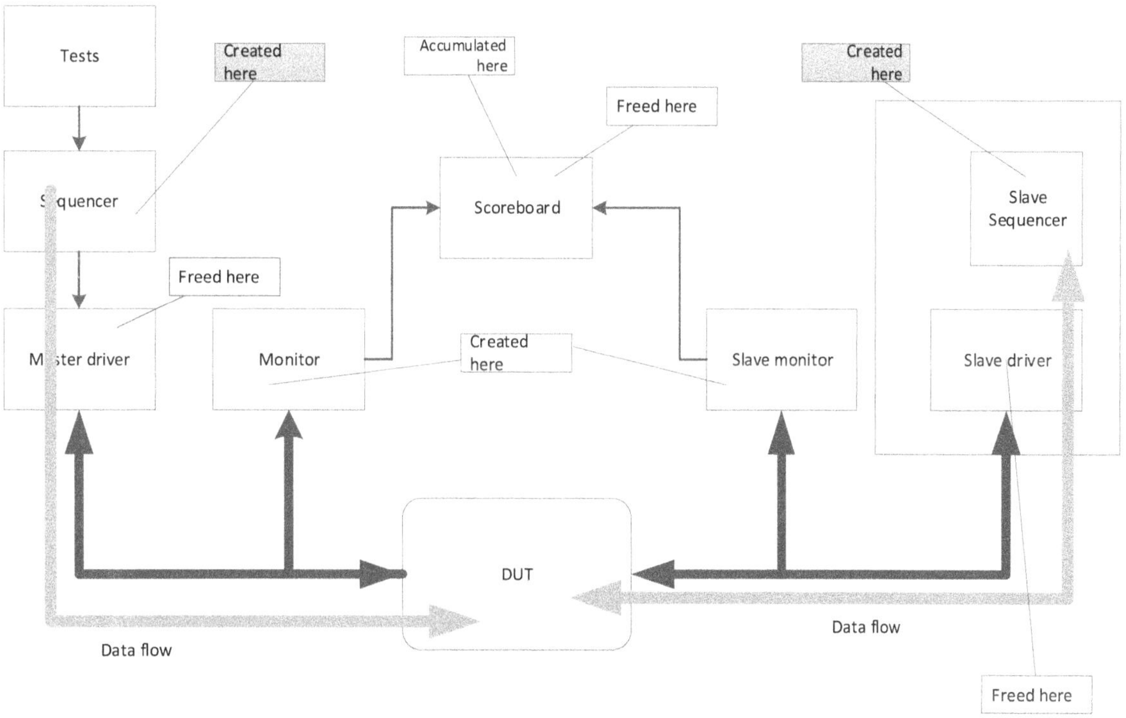

Fig. 2.7: Overall Transaction Flow

Since this DUT is a simple pass-through DUT, this transaction is seen by the master driver and the monitor. In the case of a write transaction, only the completion status is observed by the driver and monitor. In the case of a READ transaction, the slave driver provides data that is is read back and observed by the monitors on both sides of the DUT.

In some cases, the slave driver acts purely as a protocol translator and sends the transaction to its sequencer. The sequencer then generates a response depending on the sequence running on the sequencer. The sequencer sends a response back through the slave driver[1]. This completes the response. This response is monitored by the slave monitor that sends the transaction back to the scoreboard.

The scoreboard is a simple model that accepts a transaction from the master agent monitor and another from the slave agent monitor. Since the DUT has a straightforward implementation, no ordering issues are seen, the scoreboard goes on to compare the two transactions on its inputs and determine if the two are indeed equivalent. The scoreboard reports all mismatches and successful comparisons.

2.6.1.4 End of Test

UVM supplies an objection mechanism to allow hierarchical status communication among components. This objection mechanism is designed so that each component "has a say" as to when it is okay for a phase to end. When a task phase starts, the corresponding implementation method in every uvm component instance is forked. When the phase task ends, all of these forked threads are forcibly killed. The end of a task phase is indicated when there are no outstanding objections to that task phase ending. See Section 13.4 for details of the objection mechanism.

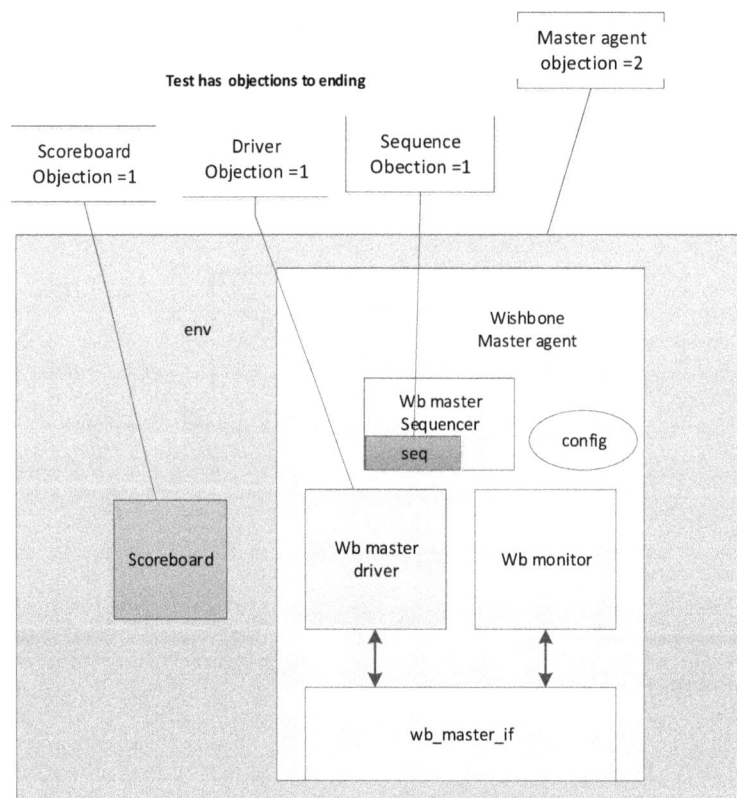

Fig. 2.8: End of test objections

When the test enters the run_phase, the sequence is started in the sequencer. This raises an objection. A transaction is generated and randomized and sent to the driver. The monitor reconstructs the transaction that it sees on the bus and forwards it to the scoreboard, which raises an objection. When the scoreboard gets a matching transaction, it drops the objection. This cycle continues until the sequence is complete, At which point, it drops its objection. The scoreboard also

---

[1] Such a driver is termed a reactive driver, and this is covered in detail in Section 16

drops its objection once it gets a transaction from the slave side, and the test advances past the run phase to the cleanup phases and the simulation eventually terminates.

2.7 Summary and Coding Guidelines

In this chapter, a complete verification environment has been created. The various agents from the later chapters were integrated into this verification environment. A collection of simple sequences to excite the DUT were developed and used to exercise the DUT and the verification environment. Various phases of the simulation were explored. The following coding guidelines will serve you well if adopted when you develop UVM environments.

Top Level Testbench Module Guidelines

Rule 2.7.0:   *The top TB module is a module with no ports. It is NOT a program block.*

The simulator simulates a program block is in the reactive region. A module on the other hand is simulated in the design region. While not having ports in the top-level module is not a hard and fast rule, this is common practice.

Rule 2.7.1:   *Generate the clocks and (optionally) reset in the module. Do not generate clocks in the testbench.*

This rule has more to do with the event regions in the testbench. SystemVerilog introduced a concept of various event regions. If you produce the clock in the reactive region, your simulation is susceptible to races between the design and the testbench. Depending on the block and a reuse methodology and the capabilities of the agents, you may implement reset in the top level module.

Recommendation 2.7.0:   *Make sure you specify the timescale in the top module.*

Some simulators provide an error if you have timescale declarations in other modules if you do not provide one. Do not assume a default timescale from the simulator.

Recommendation 2.7.1:   *Import all the tests in a package into the top module.*

After packaging, You can import the tests into the top module. Doing so, makes maintenance easier than including several files in the top module.

Interface Guidelines

Some of these guidelines are obvious for experienced verification engineers proficient in SystemVerilog. I have included these here for the benefit of engineers who are new to the verification world and SystemVerilog.

Rule 2.7.2:   *Define set-up and hold time in clocking blocks using parameters.*

Parameterizing the setup and hold time in the clocking blocks allows you to reuse the the clocking block depending on the DUT needs without modifying the interface itself. You can implement this on a per instance basis.

Rule 2.7.3:   *You should add clock generation in the top-level module. Do not clock edges at time 0.*

Clocks should be in the design region of the testbench. If you place clocks in the program block, you will be have races with your testbench. Usually, you will find races between initial blocks and always blocks that implement the clock generators. Delaying clock generation usually avoids these races.

Recommendation 2.7.2:   *Use the bit type for all clock and reset signals.*

The SystemVerilog bit type is a 2 state type. Unless you are verifying low power designs, where X-propogation is a concern, you should consider using a bit type. A corollary of this recommendation is that you must review your clock and reset signals if you choose to add low power capabilities to your design and need to verify them.

Rule 2.7.4:   *Specify the direction of asynchronous signals in the modport declaration.*

As you will see in later chapters, an agent is used with an interface to either provide stimulus or monitor the signals coming from a DUT via an interface. Depending on the functionality, the agent could either drive or monitor the signals. The interface itself is a bundle of wires, and you must specify the direction of information flow in the modport declaration.

Rule 2.7.5:   *Sample synchronous interface signals and drive using a clocking block.*

The use of a clocking block avoids races between the design and testbench.

Rule 2.7.6:   *Use one SystemVerilog interface instance per DUT interface.*

The UVM architecture defines that there is one agent per interface. The agent should be self-contained, and capable of driving the protocol on the interface.

Rule 2.7.7:   *Use virtual interfaces to access the SystemVerilog interface instances from the UVM verification environment.*

The concept of virtual interfaces has been extensively leveraged in UVM. A virtual interface is effectively a 'pointer' to an actual interface. Using a virtual interface handle allows you to modularize and package your components for reuse.

Rule 2.7.8:   *Each interface declaration must have a corresponding virtual interface.*

This rule follows the previous one in that you do not want hard cross references in your simulation.

Rule 2.7.9:   *Testcases shall access elements in the top module or design via interfaces only. Having a direct cross-module reference from the DUT signals to the UVM testbenches is not recommended.*

Cross module references cause issues not only with portability of tests, but also create issues with performance in some simulators. Hard cross references also are a challenge to debug.

I've seen a few designs where the driver is hardcoded using a `define with the actual path of the signals in the RTL. This approach defeats the purpose of the virtual interface and makes it completely non-portable. The teams had to effectively rewrite major portions of the UVM testbench when they moved from a block to a top-level simulation.

Rule 2.7.10:   *Use the config_db to send the virtual interface information to the testbench.*

The config_db introduced in later chapters provides you with a database to store the virtual interface handles. You can retrieve them from components later.

Chapter 3

Generating Stimulus to Verify The DUT

The earlier chapters provided an overview of a UVM environment with a brief discussion of both the Verilog and SystemVerilog approaches. This chapter discusses the art and science of stimulus generation and stimulus approaches commonly used in UVM testbenches. Compared to Verilog and SystemVerilog testbenches, you find that UVM creates and organizes stimulus differently with a focus on scalability of stimulus. This chapter begins with a section on deriving the *right* stimuli in UVM testbenches before delving into the art and science of stimulus generation.

The first step in the verification effort is to create a verification plan. This verification plan for the DUT can be expressed as a collection of features [21]. These features linked to tests typically have the following key attributes:

- Application level features

- Structural features (FIFO, Queue, Arbiter etc.)

- Features that are tested only at the block level

- Features that are tested only at the sub-system level

- Features that are tested only at the top-level

- Features tested at both block and subsystem and top-levels

- Features that were added to supplement the verification from a previous version of the plan

I usually attempt to obtain a comprehensive feature list by compiling information from all sources shown in the top portion of Figure 3.1. This helps me to have a complete picture of the design verification activity.

The complete list of features can be reviewed to make sure it is accurate and reflects the DUT features. Each of these features highlights some functionality in the DUT. Note that there may be some features that are interdependent on one another, and must be treated with care. The features must be broken down into actionable items like coverage, assertions, directed test cases, checker, etc. By breaking down these features into actionable items, we can divide and conquer the verification effort and prove that we verified the DUT.

Here is a technique that will help: List out all the features in your test plan and ask the following questions of each feature. I usually start out at a high level beginning with Application and Interface features and eventually drill down to Structural features like FIFO's and FSM's and Memories or glue logic [1]. This information helps the test writer create a collection of actionable verification items to test the DUT for the specific feature thoroughly.

1. What are the properties of this feature?

2. Is there any configuration associated with this feature?

3. Is there any reset behavior associated with this feature?

4. What range of values can be created for this feature?

---

[1] I usually use a PERL script since I can usually can export my test plan initially as a text file. I usually have these questions printed for each feature in a loop. I then cross out whatever is not relevant and am left with a detailed test plan.

5. What is classified as an error for this feature? Do any negative tests apply to this feature?

6. Does this test encompass multiple clock domains or interfaces?

7. What protocol associated with this feature?

8. Does the feature have interdependency on other features?

9. Do we need to break this feature down any for finer granularity?

10. Are there interactions between other features or properties for this feature?

Going through this process for all the features might appear daunting at first. However, *the opposite is true!* Usually, you will discover a high degree of commonality, which simplifies the task significantly.

Once you have gone through this process, you will have identified the drivers and other quasi-static components in the testbench environment. You will have a sense of how your stimulus should be organized. You can then create a list of actionable verification items to thoroughly test the DUT using the components you have either created or reused from elsewhere.

To test the specific feature in the DUT with your environment, you will create a sequence of data items to test the DUT in a specific way. Each data item unit is termed a *sequence item* in UVM. A collection of data items in a specific order is termed a *sequence*. The generation of stimulus in UVM is accomplished through sequences. Each verification component agent typically includes a library of basic sequences (instead of single-data items) that test writers can invoke. Sequences may call other sequences, or even be stitched together to create more complex scenarios. The library approach, therefore, enhances reuse of common stimulus patterns, thus reducing the effort in developing tests.

Various scenarios may be categorized based on a collection of sequence items, which are created and orchestrated on the DUT in UVM using sequences. The use of sequences allows a simple use model by decoupling the test writing effort from a deep understanding of the rest of the testbench components. This allows test writers to focus on coming up with interesting test scenarios rather than being bogged down by the complexity of the rest of the testbench.

You can build effective verification scenarios as a collection of sequences. A sequence can be randomized or deterministically created depending on the relevant inputs. This approach allows harnessing the power of randomization, fine-grain control of sequence creation, and supports abstraction by facilitating the creation of hierarchies of sequences. Figure 3.1 shows you the overall flow.

3.1 Creating Your Transaction Stimulus

Upon observing the features in the previous section, you should be able to either create an environment that uses preexisting agents or write your own after studying the components in Chapter 8.

Your completed environment now needs stimulus to test the DUT. In UVM, *sequence_items* are transaction objects used to represent stimulus in the verification environment. The lifetime of a sequence_item consists of the following stages:

- Creation

- Randomization

- Transfer to driver (from the sequencer)

- Execution (by the driver)

- Return to sequencer with results (if any) for further processing.

Sequences generate sequence_items, which then pass through the sequencer for transfer to a driver. The interaction between the sequence, sequencer, and the driver and DUT determines the timing of the transfer of a sequence_item. This interaction is application specific depending on the nature of the driver, and the sequencer explored in subsequent chapters of this book.

This section explores the creation of a sequence item, which acts as the transaction descriptor. The transaction descriptor can have a range of values and categories of interest to the transaction. We construct a transaction descriptor for the Wishbone protocol in this example. Note that while the protocol is simple enough, it contains many of the features found

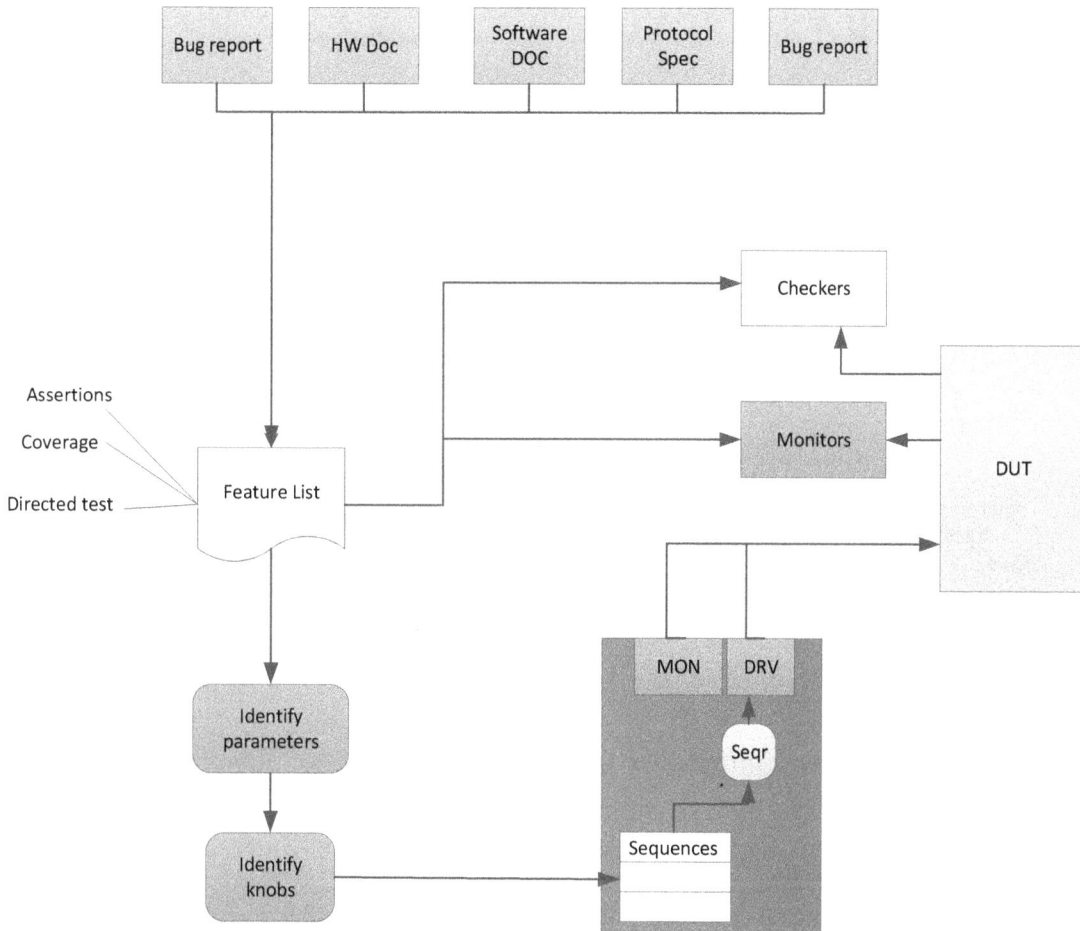

Fig. 3.1: Basic Sequence Identification Flow

in other AMBA based protocols. It serves as a foundation for the sections that follow. Refer [18] for background material. you should be able to apply the process described for the Wishbone protocol to others with a little introspection.

When observing the transaction class, asking the questions in Section 3, and introspecting, you can come up with the properties of the class shown in Figure 3.2. More complex protocols need several more knobs than the ones listed in this example; however, the process of deriving them is similar. All transactions are derived from *uvm_sequence_item* which is derived from uvm_transaction. The uvm_sequence_item is the base class for all transactions in UVM.

Listing 3.1 shows the properties of the transaction that we derived using the questions previously listed in this chapter. To constrain values, one must supply a set of constraints to be applied to the above properties, so that a reasonable set of values may be achieved and acceptable to the agent that drives the DUT.

What are the fields of the Transaction?

Address
Data
Lock
Tag

Properties of the transaction class

rand bit [31:0] address;
rand bit [31:0] data;
rand bit [3:0] sel;
rand bit [15:0] tgc;
rand bit [15:0] tga;
rand bit [15:0] tgd;
rand bit   lock;
rand bit [15:0] tag;

What are status / error for this transaction?

ACK
ERR
TIMEOUT
RTY

typedef enum {OK, ACK, RTY, ERR, TIMEOUT ,INFLIGHT ,
UNKNOWN } status_e;
rand status_e status;

What are the kinds of transactons?

Read
Write
Block Read
Block Write
RMW

typedef enum {READ, WRITE, BLK_RD, BLK_WR, RMW}
kinds_e;
rand kinds_e kind;

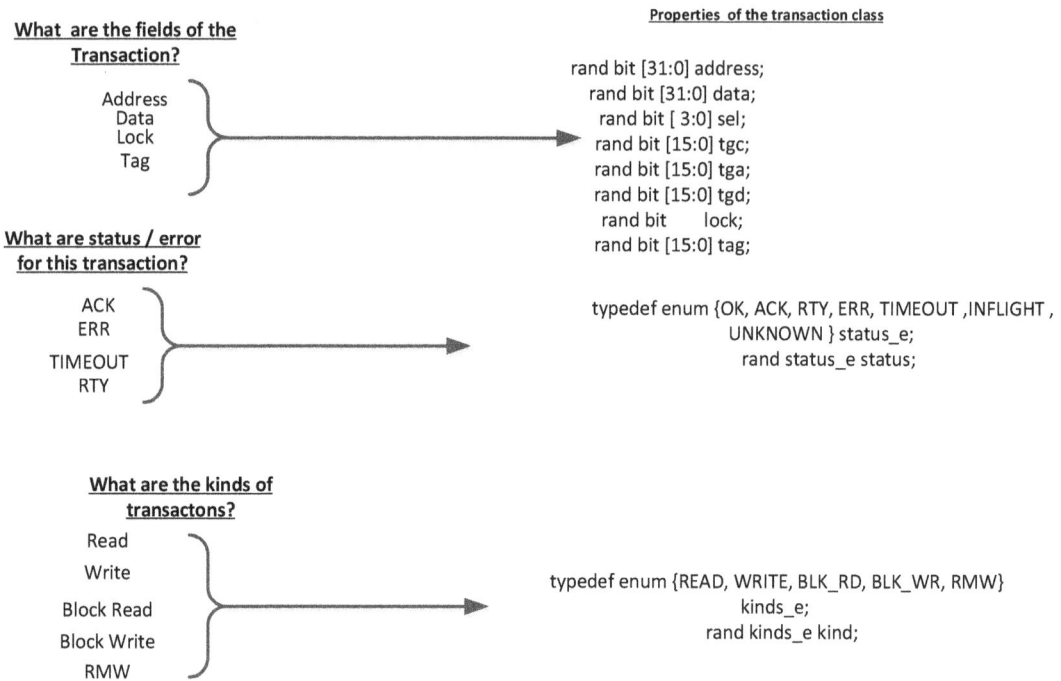

Fig. 3.2: Transaction properties by introspection

Listing 3.1: The randomizable knobs

```
27        typedef enum {READ, WRITE, BLK_RD, BLK_WR, RMW} kinds_e;
28        rand kinds_e kind;
29
30        // This is the status of the transaction
31        typedef enum {OK, ACK, RTY, ERR, TIMEOUT ,INFLIGHT , UNKNOWN }
              status_e;
32        rand status_e status;
33
34        wb_config cfg;  // Must be non-NULL to randomize
35
36        typedef enum {CLASSIC, CONSTANT,
37            LINEAR, WRAP4, WRAP8, WRAP16,
38            EOB} pipelining_e;
39        rand pipelining_e next_cycle;
40
41        rand bit [63:0] address;
42        rand bit [63:0] data[];
43        rand bit [ 7:0] sel;
44        rand bit [15:0] tgc;
45        rand bit [15:0] tga;
46        rand bit [15:0] tgd;
47        rand bit        lock;
48        rand bit [15:0] tag;
```

- Line 27 shows an enum type of various kinds of transactions.

- Lines 32 defines an enum for the status.

- Line 34 provides a handle to the configuration (see below).

- Lines 41-48 are the other properties of this transaction obtained from the above discussion.

As the transaction must have the address range and other parameters used by the agent, a reference handle to a configuration is provided in the transaction descriptor. Note that such a reference is not necessary for all environments. Agents should be able to handle such things internally. However, this example was chosen to show how the transaction properties may be affected by the protocol and the agent's capabilities.

The transaction extends from uvm_sequence_item, which extends from uvm_transaction. The uvm_transaction class extends from uvm_object. Hence, many utilities are automatically provided by macros. (These are discussed later in Section 4.5) The UVM macros help the user by providing common routines like print(), copy(), pack() and unpack() in addition to factory registration.

Listing 3.2: The UVM Macros

```
84          `uvm_object_utils_begin(wb_transaction)
85          `uvm_field_int(address,UVM_DEFAULT)
86          `uvm_field_array_int(data,UVM_DEFAULT)
87          `uvm_field_int(sel,UVM_DEFAULT)
88          `uvm_field_int(tga,UVM_DEFAULT)
89          `uvm_field_int(tgc,UVM_DEFAULT)
90          `uvm_field_int(lock,UVM_DEFAULT)
91          `uvm_field_int(num_wait_states,UVM_DEFAULT)
92          `uvm_field_enum(kinds_e,kind,UVM_DEFAULT)
93          `uvm_field_enum(status_e,status, UVM_DEFAULT)
94          `uvm_field_enum(pipelining_e,next_cycle, UVM_DEFAULT)
95          `uvm_object_utils_end
```

So, without much effort and the UVM infrastructure, you almost have a complete transaction class ready for use.

Rule 3.1.0:   *Input variables should be randomizable. I.E., make them rand when you declare them.*

If you do not declare them as *rand*, you cannot do this afterwards without modifying the class.

Rule 3.1.1:   *When you create data classes, make sure you register them with the factory.*

Listing 3.2 shows you the `uvm_object_utils macro. You will learn more about this macro in Section 5.2 and Section 4.5. Registering the classes with the factory allows you to create an class override for a specific behavior.

Recommendation 3.1.0:   *Creating sequences using the factory allows you to override them if it becomes necessary.*

This recommendation is a corollary of the previous rule. Create base sequences that have essential properties and methods and provide specific behavior in derived classes.

Rule 3.1.2:   *Initialize any sequence data members in the constructor of the sequence to have any default values.*

I have had my share of experiences during debug where I did not properly constrain the values of the property, or did not initialize them when they were non-rand variables. Keep this in mind when you write code for your classes.

3.1.1 Constraining Data Items

After creating a transaction class, you need to constrain its random values to be of interest to you. When a variable in the class is randomized, it can take any value as long as the value satisfies the constraint placed on it. It becomes essential to put bounds on the values of the properties in the wb_transaction class. This is to ensure that the values generated are within an acceptable/valid range intended by the design of the transaction class.

Note that if the range of values unacceptable for a particular scenario (for example an error scenario), you can choose to constrain the specific variable or control randomization using the constraint_mode or the rand_mode knobs in SystemVerilog.

Recommendation 3.1.1:   *While designing transaction constraints, exercise care.*

One guideline to consider if you are trading ease of writing for complexity. If you clump many variables into a small group of constraints, you will be forced to rewrite them to get an exception on a single value. If you have too many constraints, it becomes difficult to manage. Hence, some upfront care can go a long way.

Recommendation 3.1.2:   *Set up a transaction class so that it works "out of the box" for most cases.*

Following this principle implies that you can use the transaction to provide verification activity on the interface, and obtain good functional coverage. After the verification progressed far enough, you should be able to turn off some constraints either individually or in a group to create further corner cases and conditions. Given these parameters, constraints are typically defined into the following groups:

1. Valid value constraints

2. Correctness per protocol constraints

3. Reasonable constraints aka 'sane' constraints

4. Test specific/Scenario specific constraints

3.1.1.1 Valid Value Constraints

The valid constraints are used to enforce valid values on the transaction properties. Typical uses for these constraints are to enforce settings that could otherwise break the agent or its sub-components. Another use for valid value constraints is to enforce default values for class properties, which are not used in the current situation. Because the valid range constraints are retained most of the time, class extensions should prefix the name of the constraint block to ensure uniqueness. For example, the "valid_address" constraint can be seen in Listing 3.3 below. The valid values constraints are intended to be in effect all the time, as these are the primary constraints in the system. There are usually very few specific scenarios where these constraints may be turned off.

Recommendation 3.1.3:   *When you extend a class, you must name the constraint properly.*

If you do not follow this guideline, you may inadvertently override the constraint in the base class, which is undesired. I also suggest you use a naming convention.

In the case of the Wishbone protocol, there are a few constraints. However, care must be taken while designing these constraints so that they do not prevent you from generating error situations.

Listing 3.3: Valid Value Constraints on the data members

```
56        constraint supported {
57            next_cycle == CLASSIC;
58            kind == READ || kind == WRITE;
59        }
60
61        constraint valid_address {
62            if (cfg.port_size - cfg.granularity == 1) address[0:0] == 1'b0
                 ;
63            if (cfg.port_size - cfg.granularity == 2) address[1:0] == 2'
                 b00;
64            if (cfg.port_size - cfg.granularity == 3) address[2:0] == 3'
                 b000;
65        }
```

3.1.1.2 Correctness Constraints

We differentiate correctness constraints in comparison to the valid values constraints. These ensure that the transaction is correct. They further constrain the values from the valid value set. However, they are designed to be turned off if needed to generate errors and other illegal conditions.

Recommendation 3.1.4: *To achieve fine-grain control, keep only one aspect (max correct_sel in this case) in each constraint.*

If you club too many of these, you find the constraint unwieldy. The example in Listing 3.4 shows a simple correctness constraint.

Listing 3.4: Correctness Constraints on the data members

```
67          constraint valid_sel {
68              sel inside {8'h01, 8'h03, 8'h07, 8'h0F, 8'h1F, 8'h3F, 8'h7F,
                    8'hFF};
69              if (cfg.port_size - cfg.granularity == 0) sel[7:1] == 7'h00;
70              if (cfg.port_size - cfg.granularity == 1) sel[7:2] == 6'h00;
71              if (cfg.port_size - cfg.granularity == 2) sel[7:4] == 4'h0;
72          }
```

3.1.1.3 Reasonability/Sane Constraints

The objective of reasonability constraints is to help ensure that useful random values are generated. The idea for these constraints is to ensure that reasonable values are picked for the transaction. For example, in an Ethernet packet, it is desirable to ensure that the length of the transactions are reasonable and not out of bounds. The same guideline applies for the burst sizes in the wb_transaction depicted here.

These constraints are used to ensure that a transaction, when randomized, will allow the sequences and other aspects of the stimulus to work out of the box. These constraints can be shut off to get error conditions sent to your DUT.

Rule 3.1.3: *Provide a constraint block to ensure the sanity of randomized class property values.*

Note the fine line between the valid values constraints and the sane constraint, as they appear to overlap one another. Many do not distinguish one from the other. However, valid value constraints provide legal scenarios *(the entire legal space)*, while the sane constraints provide more realistic scenarios - something you would use more often. It should be a subset of the valid values constraints. I chose to separate them so that you could use the constraints in a set of testcases, on a per project basis. if you clubbed them together, you would have to shut off the whole constraint and rewrite it.

Reasonability constraints are used to:

- Prevent massive delays (e.g., most delays are int values and can result in huge delays if left unconstrained)

- Prevent extremely large arrays to avoid situations where the transaction randomization is much work for the constraint solver.

- Prevent the transaction from consuming all the memory.

- Enforce a distribution of values that may be more relevant to verification scenarios.

Rule 3.1.4: *Constrain the size of a rand array-type class property to limit its value.*

If the size of a randomized array is not constrained, it can take a very large number. Ensure that the size of the dynamic array is constrained under all circumstances. Keep this constraint separate from the others so that you can easily override it.

Listing 3.5: Reasonable Constraints on the data members

```
50          int      num_wait_states;
51
52          constraint reasonable_data_size {
53              data.size() < 64;
54          }
```

Rule 3.1.5: *Do NOT set up reasonable constraints to control multiple fields simultaneously*

You will expend effort in rewriting the constraints again and again.

Recommendation 3.1.5: *If you need a relationship between properties in a class, use the solve before constructs to enforce an ordering rule.*

Note that the configuration of the bus is sometimes required to help determine what is "reasonable" as many of the transaction features or limits are based on the configuration of the interface. If this is the case, the configuration information should be accessed via a reference to the configuration class instance with a null check before the randomization call is made. While I have divided the constraints into four groups above, it is essential to recognize that one set of constraints can easily "trump" the other set of constraints by overlapping them and reducing the verification space. As constraints are developed, they should be reviewed to ensure maximum flexibility in the environment.

Here is the final listing for the transaction class. This class has all the knobs that allow the class to be used for many test cases in sections to follow.

Listing 3.6: The WB Transaction Class

```
24    class wb_transaction extends uvm_sequence_item;
25
26        // Different types of read and Write cycles.
27        typedef enum {READ, WRITE, BLK_RD, BLK_WR, RMW} kinds_e;
28        rand kinds_e kind;
29
30        // This is the status of the transaction
31        typedef enum {OK, ACK, RTY, ERR, TIMEOUT ,INFLIGHT , UNKNOWN }
                  status_e;
32        rand status_e status;
33
34        wb_config cfg;  // Must be non-NULL to randomize
35
36        typedef enum {CLASSIC, CONSTANT,
37            LINEAR, WRAP4, WRAP8, WRAP16,
38            EOB} pipelining_e;
39        rand pipelining_e next_cycle;
40
41        rand bit [63:0] address;
42        rand bit [63:0] data[];
43        rand bit [ 7:0] sel;
44        rand bit [15:0] tgc;
45        rand bit [15:0] tga;
46        rand bit [15:0] tgd;
47        rand bit        lock;
48        rand bit [15:0] tag;
49
50        int      num_wait_states;
51
52        constraint reasonable_data_size {
```

```
53              data.size() < 64;
54          }
55
56          constraint supported {
57              next_cycle == CLASSIC;
58              kind == READ || kind == WRITE;
59          }
60
61          constraint valid_address {
62              if (cfg.port_size - cfg.granularity == 1) address[0:0] == 1'b0
                    ;
63              if (cfg.port_size - cfg.granularity == 2) address[1:0] == 2'
                    b00;
64              if (cfg.port_size - cfg.granularity == 3) address[2:0] == 3'
                    b000;
65          }
66
67          constraint valid_sel {
68              sel inside {8'h01, 8'h03, 8'h07, 8'h0F, 8'h1F, 8'h3F, 8'h7F,
                    8'hFF};
69              if (cfg.port_size - cfg.granularity == 0) sel[7:1] == 7'h00;
70              if (cfg.port_size - cfg.granularity == 1) sel[7:2] == 6'h00;
71              if (cfg.port_size - cfg.granularity == 2) sel[7:4] == 4'h0;
72          }
73
74          // ToDo: Add constraint blocks to prevent error injection
75          // ToDo: Add relevant class properties to define all transactions
76          // ToDo: Modify/add symbolic transaction identifiers to match
77
78          constraint wb_transaction_valid {
79              // Define constraint to make descriptor valid
80              status == OK;
81              if (cfg.cycles == wb_config::CLASSIC ) next_cycle == CLASSIC;
82
83          }
84          `uvm_object_utils_begin(wb_transaction)
85          `uvm_field_int(address,UVM_DEFAULT)
86          `uvm_field_array_int(data,UVM_DEFAULT)
87          `uvm_field_int(sel,UVM_DEFAULT)
88          `uvm_field_int(tga,UVM_DEFAULT)
89          `uvm_field_int(tgc,UVM_DEFAULT)
90          `uvm_field_int(lock,UVM_DEFAULT)
91          `uvm_field_int(num_wait_states,UVM_DEFAULT)
92          `uvm_field_enum(kinds_e,kind,UVM_DEFAULT)
93          `uvm_field_enum(status_e,status, UVM_DEFAULT)
94          `uvm_field_enum(pipelining_e,next_cycle, UVM_DEFAULT)
95          `uvm_object_utils_end
96
97          function new(string name="" );
98              super.new(name);
99              cfg = new(name);
100         endfunction: new
101     endclass: wb_transaction
```

With this, our wishbone transaction is now ready for use in all environments.

3.1.2 Inheritance and Constraint Layering

The transaction class from the previous section can be a base class, which can carry the essential features of the transaction. Further extended classes can add additional constraints, which can help create a transaction with the desired values. To enable extensibility, the base class for the data item (wb transaction this chapter) must use virtual methods to allow derived classes to override functionality. Organize constraint blocks so that they can override or disable constraints for a random variable without having to rewrite a large block. Otherwise, the class becomes unwieldy since derived classes must shut off constraint blocks and rewrite them, leading to a poor return on investment. If any properties are declared local or protected, access becomes restricted. This limits your ability to constrain them with an inline constraint.

Listing 3.7: An example for an completed extended class

```
4  class wb_transaction_extended extends wb_transaction;
5
6      constraint my_new_constraint {
7          address   inside {32'h01, 32'h03, 32'h07, 32'h0F, 32'h1F, 32'h3F, 32'
                h7F, 32'hFF};
8      }
9
10     `uvm_object_utils(wb_transaction_extended)
11
12     function new(string name="" );
13         super.new(name);
14     endfunction: new
15
16 endclass: wb_transaction_extended
```

- Line 4 shows the declaration of the class extending from wb_transaction.

- Lines 6 - 8 show an additional constraint placed on the address variable from the base class. The address is constrained to being inside a particular range of values.

- Line 10 uses the macros to provide the core utility functions.

- Lines 12-14 declare the constructor of the class.

In the above listing constraint, my_new_constraint shows how the base wb_transaction class is extended, adding a constraint. This class can now be used in place of the base class when using the factory overrides discussed in Chapter 5. You can replace the type wb_transaction with the type wb_transaction_extended to create specific scenarios. See Section 21.2.1 for an example on how to replace components with the factory. A simple example is shown below.

Listing 3.8: An example for using an extended class in a test

```
6   virtual function void build_phase(uvm_phase phase);
7       super.build_phase(phase);
8       wb_transaction::type_id::set_type_override(wb_transaction_extended::
            get_type());
9       uvm_config_db #(uvm_object_wrapper)::set(this, "env.master_agent.
            mast_sqr.main_phase", "default_sequence", sequence_0::get_type())
            ;
10  endfunction
```

- Line 8 sets the factory override for the wb_transaction type to be of type wb_transaction_extended. When the factory is requested for a transaction of type wb_transaction, a class instance of type wb_transaction_extended is returned instead.

There are a few other considerations that come into the picture when generating transactions. These are codified into the rules and recommendations below.

Rule 3.1.6:   *All non-local methods should be virtual.*

This recommendation comes from the fact that you cannot extend these methods in derived classes if the methods are non-virtual. (For example: If you have any methods that calculating CRC or other values based on values in the class).

Rule 3.1.7:   *Make all class properties public with a rand attribute public.*

A derived class can turn off the rand attribute for a specific case or even constrained further. This is not possible if the attribute is declared *local*.

Rule 3.1.8:   *All class properties corresponding to a protocol property or field shall have the rand attribute.*

The property can be constrained in subsequent derived classes or the rand attribute can even be turned off.

Rule 3.1.9:   *Use a rand class property to define the kind of transaction you describe.*

A class must be able to model all possible transactions for a protocol. I recommend the use of a class property that helps you identify the kind of transaction. See Line 10 of Listing 3.6 for an example.

Rule 3.1.10:   *When modeling properties that reflect scenarios, provide default constraint blocks to produce better distributions.*

Often you may want to model back-to-back/long big size transactions in your verification scenario. You can create a random property to model these in your transaction class. Create a constraint with distributions to provide you with this mix.

Rule 3.1.11:   *Solve discriminant class properties first to avoid constraint failures.*

Often, the values in some class properties depend on the values of the other properties. These other properties are called discriminant properties. These must be solved first. To prevent constraint solver errors, ensure that these properties are solved first. [2]

Rule 3.1.12:   *Derive data and transaction model classes from the uvm_sequence item class. All the field automation and other infrastructure is available to you as a result.*

Make use of the infrastructure provided by the library. Many vendors create specific optimizations to help with simulation performance. Often, these are available with vendor supplied libraries or VIP. You will miss out on potential gains if you do not choose to follow this rule.

Rule 3.1.13:   *All methods in a transaction class shall be non time-consuming functions*

When you model your transaction, you should not have the need for any time-consuming methods in this class. It should be a pure transaction descriptor. Any time consuming processing of a transaction should be relegated to components in the simulation.

3.2 Creating Sequences

Upon creation of the transaction class in the previous section, we can now create a stream of transactions is used in interesting ways to test a DUT. You do this by creating a sequence class that contains a recipe for generating an ordered list of sequence items. The recipe for the sequence is placed in a method called body().

In the UVM sequence architecture, sequences handle the stimulus generation flow, sending sequence_items to a driver via a sequencer component. The sequencer is an intermediate component, which implements communication channels and arbitration mechanisms to facilitate interactions between sequences and drivers. The benefit of sequences is that one can decouple stimulus specification from structural hierarchy with a simple API. They can be started on any matching sequencer, and have children and thereby break up large complex sequences. They are dynamic objects created in a simulation and can be customizable via the factory.

---

[2] Look at the solve-before construct in SystemVerilog

An example of a simple sequence which generates different transactions from our transaction class above is shown in Listing 3.9. This example uses a macro `uvm_do described in Section 14.2.1.2. For now, assume that the sequence macro sends the transaction to the driver and waits for it to complete before moving on to the next one.

Listing 3.9: A simple sequence

```
1 class sequence_1 extends base_sequence;
2     byte sa;
3     `uvm_object_utils(sequence_1)
4     `uvm_add_to_seq_lib(sequence_1, wb_master_seqr_sequence_library)
5     function new(string name = "seq_1");
6         super.new(name);
7     endfunction:new
8     virtual task body();
9
10        `uvm_do(req, get_sequencer(), -1, {address == 3; kind ==
               wb_transaction::WRITE; data == 63'hdeadbeef;})
11        `uvm_do(req, get_sequencer(), -1, {address == 4; kind ==
               wb_transaction::WRITE; data == 63'hbeefdead;})
12        `uvm_do(req, get_sequencer(), -1, {address == 5; kind ==
               wb_transaction::WRITE; data == 63'h0123456678;})
13
14        // Random. Should get values from Slave
15        `uvm_do(req, get_sequencer(), -1, {address inside {[10:20]}; kind
               == wb_transaction::READ ;})
16    endtask
17 endclass
```

Ⓟ Please note that this listing is for IEEE 1800.2 only. It will not compile in UVM 1.1 and UVM 1.2 because the order of macro parameters is different. It is not backward compatible!

- Line 1 declares a sequence_1 typed to the type of transaction.

- Line 3 shows the utility macros.

- Line 4 registers it with the sequence library (See Section 14.1).

- Lines 5-8 provide the constructor.

- Lines 10-15 provide the body of the sequence task. This is the main part of the sequence. You can write any code that forms the test recipe in this task.

- Lines 10-12 show the sequence items being randomized with specific addresses/data sent to the driver using additional arguments to the macro.

- Line 15 shows a completely randomized read transaction being sent to the driver. *In this listing, note that **req** is a built in data item of the type wb_transaction (the class parameter on Line 1) that is defined for you to use*

A typical sequence contains the following items depending on how it is written. UVM allows some amount of fine-grain control over the items by allowing creation, randomization, observing response before generating subsequent items, etc.

- Dynamic constraints that may be applied to each item as they are generated as seen in the listing. In addition to dynamic constraints, one can write some procedural code that may modify the sequence item using either constraint_mode() or rand_mode() to modify how the item properties are assigned values[3].

---

[3] I have not provided an example of this in this book, but the sequence body() is a task. and you should be able to write an example of this fairly easily.

- Relationships between any items generated in the sequence.
- Timing control if relevant to the sequence (by waiting for an HDL signal etc.). See Section 22.2.3.
- Reactive methods that respond to stimulus. See Chapter 16.

You can create any number of instances from a sequence type, and execute them in any desired order that is entirely dependent on the nature of verification performed. Also, sequences can be reused, and are independent of the verification environment structure. A sequence has a limited simulation lifetime and is fundamentally a transient object. From the point where it is created to the point where it is reused, it has a sense of persistence (I.E., it retains values that were in the class). Creating and executing other sequences is effectively the same as being able to call conventional subroutines, so complex functions can be built up by chaining together simple sequences.

See the examples in Chapter 22 where we have combined multiple sequences to provide enough functionality to send traffic through a DUT.

The sequence items in the body() method may be generated sequentially (See 14.4.1), in parallel (Section 14.4.3), or in response to an external event or stimulus (Section 16.1).

Unlike uvm_components, which have a lifetime of the entire simulation, sequences can be randomized to generate interesting scenarios and can be discarded once their function is complete. As sequences are registered with the factory, A user can derive it to add additional constraints and combine combinations of sequences at any time. The definition of the sequence class may contain randomizable fields that help customize the particular instance when the sequence is created using the factory.

Rule 3.2.0: *You never call body() of the sequence. Use the sequence.start() methods*

Although the actual heart of the sequence is embodied in the body() method. Recognize that you never call it. The method is called when you start the sequence in order with various callbacks that are present in the UVM library.

3.3 Using the Sequence in a Test Case

The sequence that is created in the previous sections must be run on a sequencer inside an agent. After you have created a sequence, you can start a sequence on a sequencer in many ways.

- As a default sequence on a sequencer
- Using a `uvm_do macro (see Section 14.2.1.2)
- Using methods.

An example of using starting the sequence on a sequencer is shown in the listing below.

Listing 3.10: An example a default sequence in a test

```
34          begin: configure
35              uvm_config_db #(uvm_object_wrapper)::set(this, "env.
                    master_agent.mast_sqr.run_phase", "default_sequence",
                    sequence_1::get_type());
36              uvm_config_db #(uvm_object_wrapper)::set(this, "env.
                    slave_agent.slv_seqr.run_phase", "default_sequence",
                    ram_sequence::get_type());
37
38              uvm_config_db #(wb_config)::set(this, "env.master_agent",
                    "config", wb_master_config);
39              uvm_config_db #(wb_config)::set(this, "env.slave_agent", "
                    config", wb_slave_config);
40          end
```

- Line 35 places sequence_1 type as a default_sequence in the master sequencer.

- Line 36 places ram_sequence as a default_sequence in the slave sequencer.

When the test is created and run through either run_test() or the command line using +UVM_TESTNAME=*Name of the test*, these sequences are started in the main_phase on different sequencers and started in parallel. Please see Section 14.2.1 for more examples on this topic.

3.4 Exercises for Further Exploration

A basic introduction to UVM Sequences is provided in the three chapters of this Quickstart to help you get started. Chapter 14 provides more information on Advanced Stimulus Generation along with various controls and callbacks available to sequence writers. Please also see Section 14.6 for guidelines that can help you with coding sequences effectively. The following exercises are suggested so that you can read through the output and see how the various features are implemented in this environment.

Please use the example in $DOWNLOAD_DIR/UVM_Quickstart/UVM_TestBench for these assignments. A complete environment is available for you to get started with minimal effort.

1. Create a new simple sequence and add it to the sequence library as given in Section 14.4.1.

2. Make the simple sequence above the default sequence in your test. (Hint: See Listing 3.10)

3. Add some constraints to the transaction class provided and observe the output.

Part II
UVM Building Blocks

Chapter 4

UVM Core Utilities in IEEE 1800.2

Chapter 2 provided an overview of the class library and some of the effects to consider when designing SystemVerilog environments. class based environments often create class instances and perform several operations using these instances. Upon further analysis of our simple SystemVerilog testbench in Section 1.3, you realize that creating, copying, and printing class instances for debug are common operations that occur in any class based environment. These common operations are called *core utilities*, which are described in this chapter.

UVM supplies many commonly used utilities for any object that derives from the uvm_object class. The uvm_object class is a base class for all data and hierarchical classes. The primary function of this class is defining a set of methods for common operations like copy, compare, print, pack/unpack performed during verification. These operations are available to every uvm_object and its subclasses, which extend from uvm_object.

In the sections that follow, we will explore each of these operations in some level of detail. At the end of this chapter, you should be able to perform all the common operations on classes derived from uvm_object.

There are many changes in the UVM library for the UVM Core utilities compared to the UVM-1.2 version. Many of these changes are NOT backward compatible in pure IEEE 1800.2 mode. The code and examples in this chapter refer to the IEEE 1800.2 version **only**. If you are just beginning the UVM journey, Feel free to skip over the text that discusses the difference between earlier versions and the UVM-1800.2 version.

If you are using this book to learn about UVM-1.2, See Chapter A and then continue your study with later chapters. There are subtle differences between the UVM 1.2 API and the UVM-1800.2 version. Given the importance of these UVM core utilities, I chose to separate the UVM 1.2 behavior into another chapter. When you wish to study IEEE 1800.2, you should use the contents of this chapter.

If you are migrating code and need to compare the UVM-1.2 and IEEE 1800.2 approaches, use the examples in Chapter A for an explanation of the API and behavior in the UVM 1.2 version with the content of this chapter. The examples that are illustrated in this chapter are also available when using UVM-1.2 API in the download. You should be able to use a text diff tool to identify differences between the two versions quickly.

The rest of this chapter uses examples in[1]:

$DOWNLOAD_DIR/**IEEE_version**/UVM_Building_Blocks/Uvm_Core_Utils/src

The corresponding examples for the UVM-1.2 version are in:

---

[1] See the Preface for download instructions

4.1 Simple Example Classes

To begin exploring UVM, we begin with a couple of simple SystemVerilog classes used in the examples in this chapter. The below listing presents a simple class with an integer property, string property, and an integer associative array as its members. This class extends from uvm_object class.

Listing 4.1: A Simple Class

```
2 class class_A extends uvm_object;
3
4    int cl_int;
5    string cl_string;
6    int    cl_int_arr[];
7    int unsigned logic_data[int];
8
9    `uvm_object_utils_begin(class_A)
10      `uvm_field_int(cl_int,UVM_DEFAULT)
11      `uvm_field_string(cl_string,UVM_DEFAULT)
12      `uvm_field_array_int(cl_int_arr,UVM_DEFAULT)
13      `uvm_field_aa_int_longint_unsigned(logic_data,UVM_DEFAULT)
14   `uvm_object_utils_end
15
16   function void set_value(int value);
17      cl_int  = value;
18   endfunction
19
20   function new(string name="");
21      super.new(name);
22      cl_string = name;
23      set_value(10);
24      cl_int_arr = new[cl_int];
25      for(int i = 0; i < cl_int; i++) begin
26   cl_int_arr[i] = i + 1;
27      end
28   endfunction
29
30 endclass
```

Listing 4.1 presents a simple class class_A. This class has the following properties:

- An integer: cl_int

- A dynamic array of integers: cl_int_arr

- A string: cl_string

- An associative array: logic_data

- Lines 20-28 describe the constructor new() function which initializes various properties of the class at the time of creation of an instance of the classA_cl class. Ignore all the macros on Lines 9-14. We will study them later in this chapter.

A second simple class that instances the first one shown above is provided in the next listing.

Listing 4.2: Class P

```
1 class class_P extends uvm_object;
2
3    // basic datatypes
4    rand int par_int;
5    rand byte par_address;
6    string par_string;
7
8    // Some objects to demonstrate the copy recursion policy
9
10   class_A cl1; // UVM_SHALLOW
11   class_A cl3; // UVM_DEEP
12
13   `uvm_object_utils_begin(class_P)
14      `uvm_field_int(par_int,UVM_DEFAULT)
15      `uvm_field_int(par_address,UVM_DEFAULT)
16      `uvm_field_string(par_string,UVM_DEFAULT)
17      `uvm_field_object(cl1,UVM_DEFAULT)
18      `uvm_field_object(cl3,UVM_DEFAULT)
19   `uvm_object_utils_end
20
21   function new(string name="");
22      super.new(name);
23      cl1 = new(name);
24      cl3 = new(name )  ;
25      par_string  = name;
26   endfunction
27
28 endclass
```

The above class_P has the following properties as a part of the class.

- An integer called par_int
- A byte property called par_address
- A string property called par_string
- Two child objects of the class_A class called cl1 and cl3.
- Lines 21-26 describe the constructor for the class similar to the one which is provided in Listing 4.1

The two examples for class_A and class_P classes above are not parameterized. Subtle differences between normal classes and parameterized classes exist and are discussed in Section 5.3. For now, recognize that it is possible to use parameterized classes in UVM.

Listing 4.3 shows the listing for a parameterized object class. In this file, class packet is defined as a specialization of *param_packet_base*.

Listing 4.3: Simple Parameterized Class

```
1 class param_packet_base extends uvm_object;
2    function new(string name="TypeT");
3        super.new(name);
4    endfunction
5 endclass
6
7 class packet #(type T=int) extends param_packet_base;
8   const static string type_name = $sformatf("packet#(%s)",$typename(T));
9
10    T my_var;
11    `uvm_object_param_utils(packet#(T))
12
13    function new(string name=type_name);
14        super.new(name);
15    endfunction
16
17    virtual function string get_type_name();
18        return type_name;
19    endfunction
20
21 endclass
```

- Line 11: Details about the macros are provided later in this chapter.

4.2 Object Creation

Common object creation activities with uvm_object classes are divided into the following operations:

- Create via constructor or factory
- Object cloning

UVM makes use of some well-known paradigms, such as design patterns, policies, and other concepts[9] from the software world. By leveraging these concepts, UVM offers more flexibility to the verification engineer to complete verification.

4.2.1 Create

UVM supplies the *create()* method to create a new object of a given type returning a handle to a new object. This method is implemented by every class that is derived either directly or indirectly from *uvm_object*. The factory method in Chapter 5 makes extensive use of this method to create the object. The create() method is extensively used throughout this book. The difference between using the new() method vs. the create() method is that when you call create(), the factory determines if it should substitute it with a different type. The factory calls the *new()* method after making this determination under the hood. *I recommend that you always call create().* If you call new() directly, the factory cannot substitute the object even if you want it to do so. The create() method signature is defined as:

```
virtual function uvm_object create ( string name = "" )
```

For usage examples of the create() method, see Listing 2.6 Line 21. Most of the examples in Part IV use this method.

You may notice that I did not use create() in this chapter, although I could have. I left altering examples to use create() as an exercise for you.

Recommendation 4.2.0:   *Match the object's handle name with the string name passed into the create() call; this simplifies debugging.*

UVM
1.2

UVM 1.2 requires declaring a constructor in the class. Earlier versions of UVM did not have this requirement. To use the older behavior in UVM-1.2 because you have somebody else's code that you cannot change, you must define UVM_OBJECT_DO_NOT_NEED_CONSTRUCTOR at compile time to override this behavior.

UVM
IEEE

Note that the UVM_OBJECT_DO_NOT_NEED_CONSTRUCTOR define is removed from the IEEE Version. You must migrate your code following the instructions in the IEEE 1800.2 Migration instructions at the beginning of this book.

4.2.2 Clone

UVM supplies the clone() method to help you make an exact copy of the object. The clone() method calls a constructor under the hood and creates a new object of the specific type followed by a copy().

(i) *Note that clone() returns a handle of type uvm_object and hence **you will need** to typecast it before you use it. Else your code will not compile!*

Listing 4.4: Simple Cloning operation

```
1 module top;
2     import uvm_pkg::*;
3     `include "class.sv"
4
5     // Class definition
6
7     class_A     class_A_inst1;
8     class_A     class_A_inst2;
9     initial begin
10        // free children
11        class_A_inst1 = new("child_inst1");
12
13        class_A_inst1.randomize();
14        class_A_inst1.print();
15        $cast(class_A_inst2,class_A_inst1.clone());
16        class_A_inst1.print();
17
18    end
19 endmodule
```

- Lines 7 -8 show the instantiations of the class_A class.

- Line 13-14 create a class and randomize and print it.

- Line 15 shows the use of the clone() utility. As mentioned, the $cast operation is essential.

4.3 Common Operations on Objects

UVM supplies automation for common operations like copy, compare, print, and pack/unpack using policy classes. These policy classes perform a specific task for each of these operations and are implemented separately from the uvm_object class. The intention behind this implementation is to allow the user to plug in different policies based on the desired object *without changing the uvm_object subclasses*. By simply applying a different policy, the behavior of the operation can be changed. These classes come with user-configurable parameters that have defaults, thereby making it easy for the user to use defaults wherever applicable. You can subtype the policy classes and replace the defaults in your environment using the factory mechanisms described in Chapter 5 if you need to. You can also write your own customized version of the operation by using a callback hook that is provided by UVM. There are a couple of ways to add these customizations, as shown in Figure 4.1.

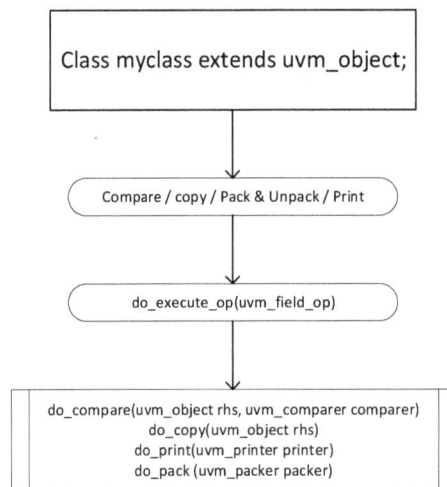

Fig. 4.1: Additional Policy Callback hooks

The do_execute_op hook infrastructure is not discussed in this chapter. Detailed examples are presented in Section 19.1.4.

4.3.1 Copy

To copy one object to another, UVM supplies built-in functions. The following two methods support the copy operation for classes derived from the uvm_object class. The copy() function copies the contents of the *rhs* to itself. To override this default mechanism, you must use the do_copy() method.

```
function void copy (uvm_object rhs, uvm_copier = null );
virtual function void do_copy (uvm_object rhs );
```

Using the classes from the earlier portions of this chapter, the listing below shows an example of how the copy function in UVM. In this listing, class class_P is instanced in a module, and illustrates the copy method.

Listing 4.5: A Simple Copy example

```
1 module top;
2     import uvm_pkg::*;
3     typedef class class_A;
4
5     `include "class.sv"
6
7     class_P  class_P_inst1;
8     class_P  class_P_inst2;
9     initial begin
10        // Create and print instances
11        class_P_inst1 = new("first_inst");
12        class_P_inst1.randomize();
13        class_P_inst1.print();
14
15        class_P_inst2 = new("second_inst");
16        class_P_inst2.randomize();
17        class_P_inst2.print();
18
19        class_P_inst2.copy(class_P_inst1);
20        class_P_inst2.print();
21
22     end
23 endmodule
```

In Listing 4.5:

- Lines 10-13 create the class_P_inst1 instance and randomize and print it.

- Lines 15-17 create the class_P_inst2 instance and randomize and print it.

- Line 19 shows the class_P_inst2 instance copying into itself the contents of class_P_inst1. Note that the contents of the children are copied as well.

Rule 4.3.0: *Note that the supplied copy() method is not virtual by design* **and should not be overloaded in derived classes**

UVM
IEEE
The UVM copier copy() method signatures have changed in the IEEE version, but the do_copy() method signature remains the same. Your existing code should not be impacted because the signature implements a default.

The underlying implementation of the copy() method from the previous example calls the do_copy() hooks in class_P. This method is used to create a customized implementation of the copy() method. The do_copy() method for class_P is shown below.

Listing 4.6: A simple do_copy() example

```
39    function void do_copy(uvm_object rhs);
40        class_P rhs_;
41        super.do_copy(rhs);
42        $cast(rhs_,rhs);
43        par_int = rhs_.par_int;
44        par_address = rhs_.par_address;
45        par_string = rhs_.par_string;
46        cl1 = new rhs_.cl1;
47        cl3 = new rhs_.cl3;
48        cl1.copy(rhs_.cl1);
49        cl3.copy(rhs_.cl3);
50    endfunction
```

In the above listing for the do_copy method for class_P:

- Lines 44-45 copy par_int, par_address, par_string over to the target.

- Lines 46 and 47 create new child objects.

- Lines 48-49 copy the children cl1 and cl3 to the target.

Rule 4.3.1:   *You must never call the do_copy() method directly. Implement the method and allow the copy() method implementation to call it under the hood.*

UVM supplies macros that provide a default copy() implementation. You can override the default implementation by calling the do_copy() method. To enable overriding the copy() method, you must set some flags in the macros to enable the do_copy() method call. We will be discussing these flags in Section 4.5.

UVM
IEEE   The IEEE version enforces the copier policy if a null copier handle is passed. Currently, in the UVM 1.2 version, no message is printed, since a copier policy did not exist, and the behavior is undefined. In the IEEE version, however, it grabs the default copier. You can get a handle to the default copier by calling the get_default_copier() method.

Rule 4.3.2:   *Perform null checks on values returned by get_default_copier()*

UVM
IEEE   The standard does not explicitly call out what happens when these default values are set to null, indicating that all of the associated get_default_copier() calls should be guarded with null checks on the return value. When get_default_copier() is called after a corresponding set_default_copier(null), the implementation returns the copier instance that would be returned if get_default had been called without any previous calls to set_default_copier().

4.3.2 Compare

Quite often, in a scoreboard or other application, you may need to compare two objects. UVM supports the comparison operation between two different uvm_objects using the following two methods. These methods use a comparer policy. A default comparer policy object is provided in UVM. To override the default, use the do_comparer() method.

```
function bit compare (uvm_object rhs, uvm_comparer comparer=null);
function bit do_compare (uvm_object rhs, uvm_comparer comparer);
```

The compare() function is used to compare all the automated fields of a class configured to be in the compare operation. You can also create an instance of the comparer policy and customize it as shown in Listing 4.7 below to control the output of the comparer. Table 4.1 shows the various policy settings available with the uvm_comparer class.

Listing 4.7: Simple Comparison

```
5 module top;
6     `include "uvm_macros.svh"
7     import uvm_pkg::*;
8     `include "class.sv"
9     // Class definition
10    class_P     class_P_inst1;
11    class_P     class_P_inst2;
12
13
14
15    initial begin
16        uvm_comparer c_comp = new();
17        c_comp.set_show_max(1);
18        c_comp.set_severity(UVM_WARNING);
19
20        class_P_inst1 = new("class_P_inst1");
21        class_P_inst1.cl1.set_value(32);
22        class_P_inst2 = new("class_P_inst2");
23        class_P_inst2.cl1.set_value(16);
24
25        class_P_inst1.randomize();
26        class_P_inst2.randomize();
27        // Make a copy into class_P_inst2.
28        class_P_inst2.copy(class_P_inst1);
29        // Change the values in class_P_inst1.
30        class_P_inst1.cl1.logic_data[16 ] = 2;
31        class_P_inst1.cl1.logic_data[32 ] = 2;
32        class_P_inst1.cl1.logic_data[64] = 2;
33        class_P_inst1.cl1.logic_data[128] = 1;
34        // We should see miscompares.
35        class_P_inst1.compare(class_P_inst2, c_comp);
36        // We can get all the miscompares into a string and print them
37        `uvm_info("COMPARES",c_comp.get_miscompares(),UVM_LOW)
38
39    end
40 endmodule
```

In this listing, class c_comp is an instance of uvm_comparer. For illustration purposes, we redefine settings that are available in class uvm_comparer and their default settings.

- Lines 17 and 18 show how the setting for these properties can be changed with the accessor methods from Table 4.1. Note that you could also do this before the policy object is passed to the compare operation line 35.

- The show_max of the compare policy object is set to 1 so that only the first compare result is printed. The rest of the miscompares are suppressed because show_max was set to 1.

- The get_miscompares() on line 37 returns a string of all the miscompares (4 in this case)

Rule 4.3.3: *Note that the supplied compare() method is not virtual by design* **and should not be overloaded in derived classes**

The do_compare() method is the override of the compare() method and is called by the class library under the hood. It allows comparing fields that need special handling or cannot be configured by the field automation macros. The listing below shows an example of this method.

Table 4.1: UVM Comparer Policy knobs

Property	Description	Method
show max	Sets the maximum number of messages to send to the messager for miscompares of an object.	set_show_max (int unsigned show_max) int get_show_max()
verbosity	Sets the verbosity for printed messages.	set_verbosity (int unsigned verbosity) int get_verbosity()
sev	Sets the severity for printed messages.	set_severity (uvm_severity severity) uvm_severity get_severity()
threshold	This string is reset to an empty string when a comparison is started.	set_threshold (int unsigned threshold) unsigned int get_threshold()
check type	This bit determines whether the type, given by uvm object::get type name, is used to verify that the types of two objects are the same.	set_check_type (bit enabled) bit get_check_type()
compare field	Compares two integral values.	compare field
compare field int	This method is the same as compare field except that the arguments are small integers, less than or equal to 64 bits.	compare field int
compare field real	This method is the same as compare field except that the arguments are real numbers.	compare field real
compare object	Compares two class objects using the policy knob to determine whether the comparison should be deep, shallow, or reference.	compare object
compare string	Compares two string variables.	compare string
print msg	Causes the error count to be incremented and the message, msg, to be appended to the miscompares string (a newline is used to separate messages).	print_msg (string msg)
policy	Determines whether comparison is UVM DEEP, UVM REFERENCE, or UVM SHALLOW	set_recursion_policy (policy)[2] uvm_recursion_policy_enum get_recursion_policy()
default comparer	get/set the default comparer	set_default (uvm_comparer comparer) uvm_comparer get_default()
result	Gets the result of the comparison	get_result()
string	Get all the miscompare strings	get_miscompares()

Listing 4.8: A simple do_compare() example

```
30    virtual function bit do_compare(uvm_object rhs, uvm_comparer comparer);
31       class_P rhs_;
32       do_compare = super.do_compare(rhs,comparer);
33       $cast(rhs_,rhs);
34       do_compare &= comparer.compare_field_int("par_int",par_int,rhs_.
            par_int,32,UVM_NORADIX);
35       do_compare &= comparer.compare_field_int("par_address",par_int,rhs_.
            par_int,32,UVM_NORADIX);
36       do_compare &= comparer.compare_string("par_string",par_string,rhs_.
            par_string);
37       do_compare &= comparer.compare_object("cl1",cl1,rhs_.cl1);
38       do_compare &= comparer.compare_object("cl3",cl3,rhs_.cl3);
39    endfunction
```

You will recognize that the operations are similar to the one for the do_copy() method.

Rule 4.3.4: *You must never call the do_compare() method directly. Instead, define the method and allow the compare() method implementation to call it under the hood.*

UVM supplies macros that provide a default compare() implementation. You can override the default implementation by calling the do_compare() method. To enable overriding the compare() method, you must set some flags in the macros to enable the do_compare() method call. We will be discussing these flags in Section 4.5.

We have found that the support for UVM_DEEP and UVM_SHALLOW are not complete as a part of the implementation under some circumstances, although they are documented in the library. Hence, we recommend that the user performs the required operations by using the do_* methods.

The IEEE version enforces the comparer policy if a null one is passed. Currently, in the UVM 1.2 version, no message is printed, and the behavior is undefined. In the IEEE version, however, it grabs the default comparer.

The standard does not explicitly call out what happens when these default values are set to null, indicating that all of the associated get_default calls should be guarded with null checks on the return value. When get_default_comparer() is called after a corresponding set_default_comparer(null), the implementation returns the instance that would be returned if get_default_comparer() had been called without any previous calls to set_default_comparer().

UVM_ABSTRACT and UVM_PHYSICAL were flags that were used only by the comparison operation. The other policies did not use them. The IEEE version removes these definitions to achieve conformity across policies.

4.3.3 Print

One of the more common operations of printing from UVM is accomplished by using the following predefined methods to support the print operation for classes derived from uvm_object:

```
function void print(uvm_printer printer=null);
function string sprint(uvm_printer printer=null);
virtual function void do_print (uvm_printer printer);
```

Rule 4.3.5: *Note that the supplied print() method is not virtual by design* **and should not be overloaded in derived classes.**

The print() function prints out all the fields configured using the macros to be a part of the print operation.

Function sprint() is similar to print() except that it returns a string instead of printing the result to the screen. The do_print() provides a callback mechanism for handling fields of the calling object that require special handling or are not configured by field automation macros to be included in the print operation. The print() and do_print() functions use a similar use model to that of the copy() policy described earlier.

The print operation makes use of print policy object uvm_printer. This policy object contains settings for controlling the print operation, as well as many methods that customize the way object data is printed. It is possible to define a new print policy object that redefines the settings of the default printer and hence achieves a modified print behavior. The following global print policy objects are automatically created by loading the UVM class library:

Listing 4.9 shows you how to use different printers that come with UVM.

uvm_printer_policy	Action
uvm_default_printer	Prints the object in a tablular formatted way
uvm_default_line_printer	Prints the object on a single line
uvm_default_tree_printer	Prints the object in a tree like format
uvm_default_table_printer	Prints the object in a tabular way (same as the default printer)

Table 4.2: Printer Policies

If no printer policy object is passed to print functions (i.e., print() and sprint()), then the global printer uvm_default_printer is used by default. Each printer policy object contains field knobs that can be used for customizing the printer output. Table 6 shows a summary of knob properties that can be configured.

When an object's print function is called without the optional printer argument specified, **then the uvm_default_printer is used**. The uvm_default_printer variable may be assigned to any printer derived from uvm_printer. Often, it is desirable to redirect the output of a printer to a file so that it may be studied later. On other occasions, a slightly different output may be desired. UVM supports these customizations quite well.

Listing 4.9: A Simple Print Example using various printers

```
1 module top;
2     import uvm_pkg::*;
3     `include "class.sv"
4
5     uvm_printer uvm_default_table_printer = uvm_table_printer::get_default
          () ;
6     uvm_printer uvm_default_tree_printer = uvm_tree_printer::get_default()
          ;
7     uvm_printer uvm_default_line_printer = uvm_line_printer::get_default()
          ;
8
9     UVM_FILE myfile;
10
11    class_A cl1 = new("Child Class");
12    initial begin
13
14        cl1.print(uvm_default_table_printer);
15        cl1.print(uvm_default_line_printer);
16
17    end
18 endmodule
```

The implementation of the print policy allows the output of print functions to either follow the global setting of the printer policy object or to be customized depending on the local requirements. Local customizations are done by instantiating a local copy of a printer policy object and then modifying its properties before passing it explicitly to the print function. The printer policy object that is passed to callback function do_print() is the same printer policy object provided as an argument to the print() functions.

The uvm_printer::set_default(), uvm_table_printer::set_default(), uvm_tree_printer::set_default(), and uvm_line_printer::set_default methods allow the user to set the associated default printer instances. The standard does not explicitly call out what happens when these default values are set to null, indicating that all of the associated get_default calls should be guarded with null checks on the return value. When get_default_printer() is called after a corresponding set_default_printer(null), the implementation returns the printer instance that would be returned if get_default had been called without any previous calls to set_default_printer().

Note that the instances of uvm_defaullt_line_printer, uvm_defaullt_tree_printer, uvm_defaullt_table_printer are not defined in the LRM. If you have code that is depending on these instances, you must instead get a handle to the required printer as shown in Listing 4.9

You could customize the output of the printer using settings in the policy class. In UVM-1.2, these settings were placed in a class called uvm_printer_knobs. The members of this class were public, and you could assign them directly.

The uvm_printer knobs have been deprecated in favor of set()/get() methods. The table below shows you the relationship between the old printer knobs settings and the new methods.

Type	UVM 1.2 Knobs	Default value	Description	Methods
int	begin elements	5	Number of elements at the head of a list that should be printed	virtual function void set_begin_elements (int elements = 5) virtual function int get_begin_elements()
string	bin radix	"b"	String prepended to integral types when UVM_BIN radix is used	virtual function void set_radix_string (uvm_radix_enum radix, string prefix) virtual function string get_radix_string (uvm_radix_enum radix)
string	dec radix	"d"	String prepended to integral types when UVM_DEC radix is used	virtual function void set_radix_string (uvm_radix_enum radix, string prefix) virtual function string get_radix_string (uvm_radix_enum radix)
enum	default	UVM_HEX	Default radix (integral values) when UVM_NORADIX is used	virtual function void set_radix_string (uvm_radix_enum radix, string prefix) virtual function string get_radix_string (uvm_radix_enum radix)
int	depth	-1	Indicates how deep to recurse when printing objects, where depth of -1 prints everything	virtual function void set_max_depth (int depth) virtual function int get_max_depth()
int	end elements	5	Number of elements at the end of a list that should be printed	virtual function void set_end_elements (int elements = 5) virtual function int get_end_elements()
string	hex radix	"h"	String prepended integral types when UVM_HEX radix is used	virtual function void set_radix_string (uvm_radix_enum radix, string prefix) virtual function string get_radix_string (uvm_radix_enum radix)
bit	identifier	1	Specifies if an identifier should be printed	virtual function void set_type_name_enabled (bit enabled) virtual function bit get_type_name_enabled()
integer	mcd	UVM_STDOUT	File descriptor	virtual function void set_line_prefix (string prefix) virtual function string get_line_prefix()
string	oct radix	"o"	String prepended to integral type when UVM_OCT radix is used	virtual function void set_radix_string (uvm_radix_enum radix, string prefix) virtual function string get_radix_string (uvm_radix_enum radix)
bit	reference	1	Specifies if a unique reference ID for an UVM object should be printed	virtual function void set_id_enabled (bit enabled) virtual function bit get_id_enabled()
bit	show radix	1	Specifies if the radix should be printed for integral types	virtual function void set_radix_enabled (bit enabled) virtual function bit get_radix_enabled()
bit	size	1	Specifies if the size of the field should be printed	virtual function void set_size_enabled (bit enabled) virtual function bit get_size_enabled()
string	unsigned radix	"d"	Default radix (integral values) when UVM_UNSIGNED specified	virtual function void set_radix_string (uvm_radix_enum radix, string prefix) virtual function string get_radix_string (uvm_radix_enum radix)

Here is an example of how to use the print policy settings to control your output:

Listing 4.10: Customizing Print

```
1  module top;
2      import uvm_pkg::*;
3      typedef class class_C;
4
5      // Class definition
6      class class_C extends uvm_object;
7
8          int cl_int;
9          string cl_string;
10         int      cl_int_arr[];
11         int      cl_int_sarr[40];
12
13         `uvm_object_utils_begin(class_C)
14         `uvm_field_int(cl_int,UVM_DEFAULT);
15         `uvm_field_string(cl_string,UVM_DEFAULT);
16         `uvm_field_array_int(cl_int_arr,UVM_DEFAULT);
17         `uvm_field_sarray_int(cl_int_sarr,UVM_DEFAULT);
18         `uvm_object_utils_end
19
20         function new(string name="");
21             super.new(name);
22             cl_string = name;
23             cl_int = 8;
24             //cl_int_arr = new[cl_int];
25             for(int i = 0; i < cl_int; i++) begin
26                 cl_int_arr[i] = i + 1;
27             end
28             for(int i = 0; i < 40; i++) begin
29                 cl_int_sarr[i] = i * 2;
30             end
31         endfunction
32
33     endclass
34
35
36     class_C class_C_inst;
37     uvm_printer my_printer;
38     initial begin
39         // free children
40         my_printer = uvm_table_printer::get_default();
41         my_printer.set_type_name_enabled(0);
42         my_printer.set_begin_elements(7);
43         my_printer.set_end_elements(3);
44         class_C_inst = new("class_C_inst");
45         class_C_inst.randomize();
46         class_C_inst.print(my_printer);
47
48     end
49  endmodule
```

- Lines 6-33 declare class_C. For now, don't worry about the macros on Lines 13-18. Their operation is described later on in this chapter.

- Line 36 creates a handle for class_C as class_C_inst.

- Line 37 creates a handle for a printer.

- Line 40 assigns the printer to the default table printer

- Line 41 sets the printer to *not display the type names*

- Line 42 -43 set the number of elements in the beginning and end of arrays to be printed

- Line 44-45 creates and randomizes the class_C_inst.

- Line 46 prints the class using the table printer.

Here is the output (partially shown) :

```
 1 17  -------------------------------------------------------------------
 2 18  Accellera:1800.2-2017:UVM:1.0.Synopsys
 3 19
 4 20  All copyright owners for this kit are listed in NOTICE.txt
 5 21  All Rights Reserved Worldwide
 6 22  -------------------------------------------------------------------
 7 23
 8 24  (Specify +UVM_NO_RELNOTES to turn off this notice)
 9 25
10 26  ------------------------------
11 27  Name Size Value
12 28  ------------------------------
13 29  class_C_inst - @113
14 30  cl_int 32 'h8
15 31  cl_string 12 class_C_inst
16 32  cl_int_arr 0 -
17 33  cl_int_sarr 40 -
18 34  [0]  32  'h0
19 35  [1]  32  'h2
20 36  [2]  32  'h4
21 37  [3]  32  'h6
22 38  [4]  32  'h8
23 39  [5]  32  'ha
24 40  [6]  32  'hc
25 41  ...  ...  ...
26 42  [37] 32  'h4a
27 43  [38] 32  'h4c
28 44  [39] 32  'h4e
29 45  ------------------------------
```

Looking at the output above, observe the settings on lines 42 and 43 of Listing 4.10 control the number of array elements in the output. Notice that the type name is also not printed in the output.

UVM supplies macros that provide a default print() implementation. You can override the default implementation by calling the do_print() method. To enable overriding the print() method, you must set some flags in the macros to enable the do_print() method call. We will be discussing these flags in Section 4.5.

The do_print() method is the override of the print() method and is called by the class library under the hood. It allows printing of fields that need special handling or cannot be configured by the field automation macros. The listing below shows an example of this method.

Listing 4.11: A simple do_print() example

```
34          function void do_print(uvm_printer printer);
35              printer.set_type_name_enabled(1);
36              printer.print_field_int("Class Integer",cl_int,32,UVM_NORADIX
                    ,".","");
37              printer.print_string("Class String",cl_string,"");
38              printer.print_array_header("cl_int_arr",3,"cl_int_sarr(int)");
39              foreach(cl_int_sarr[i])
40                  printer.print_field($sformatf("[%0d]", i), cl_int_sarr[i],
                        32);
41              printer.print_array_footer();
42          endfunction
```

Rule 4.3.6: *You must never call the do_print() method directly. Implement the method and allow the print() method implementation to call it under the hood.*

4.3.4 Packing And Unpacking

UVM supplies utility methods to pack class objects into a bitstream, as well as unpack objects from a bitstream and populate the class contents. To accomplish this goal, UVM supplies a uvm_packer class that supplies a policy object for packing and unpacking uvm_objects. This policy object determines how the packing and unpacking routines should behave. When packing an object, the object is placed into an array of bits. Such an array may then be sent across a language boundary or used inside a networking frame or other applications. The unpack operation in the application can then disassemble the bitstream array and obtain the values of the class properties. Please see Figure 10.8 for an illustration of how packing and unpacking can be used across language boundaries.

The pack operation makes use of a pack policy object called uvm_packer. This policy object has settings for controlling and customize the way the object data is packed. It is possible to define a new pack policy object that redefines the settings of the default packer and hence achieves a modified pack behavior. If you do not choose to create a new policy object and yet wish to override the default behavior, use the do_pack() callbacks.

The essential functions for packing and unpacking are:

```
function int pack ( ref bit bitstream[], input uvm_packer packer = null);
virtual function void do_pack (uvm_packer packer);
function int unpack (ref bit bitstream[],input uvm_packer packer = null);
virtual function void do_unpack (uvm_packer packer);
```

UVM supplies macros that provide a default pack() implementation. You can override the default implementation by calling the do_pack() method. To enable overriding the pack() method, you must set some flags in the macros to enable the do_pack() method call. Listing 4.12 shows you an example of a pack/unpack on a pair of classes.

Listing 4.12: A Simple Pack/Unpack Example

```
1 module top;
2     import uvm_pkg::*;
3     `include "class.sv"
4
5     bit        pack_bytes[];
6     class_P  class_P_inst1;
7     class_P  class_P_inst2;
8     initial begin
9         // Create and print children
10
11        class_P_inst1 = new("first_inst");
12        class_P_inst1.randomize();
13        class_P_inst1.print();
14        // Pack object
15        class_P_inst1.pack(pack_bytes);
16
17        class_P_inst2 = new("second_inst");
18        //       class_P_inst2.randomize();
19        class_P_inst2.print();
20
21        // Unpack object
22        class_P_inst2.unpack(pack_bytes);
23        class_P_inst2.print();
24
25    end
26 endmodule
```

In the above listing:

- The pack operation on line 15 packs class class_P_inst1 into the bitstream pack_bytes declared in Line 5.

- The unpack operation on Line 22 unpacks the bitstream into class class_P_inst2.

if you wish to use the do_pack() and do_unpack() methods, There are many helper methods available that help simplify the packing and unpacking operations.

```
virtual function void pack_field (uvm_bitstream_t value, int size);
virtual function void pack_field_int (logic[63:0] value, int size);
virtual function void pack_string (string value);
virtual function void pack_time (time value);
virtual function void pack_real (real value);
virtual function void pack_object (uvm_object value);
virtual function bit is_null ();
```

The pack_field function allows you to pack an arbitrary field of up to 4096 bits into the bitstream. The size variable can be computed for any variable by using the $bits system function. The pack_field_int, pack_string, pack_time, pack_real functions pack their corresponding variable types into the bitstream.

To unpack an object from a bitstream, you have corresponding methods as shown below: These unpacking functions take the input bitstream and unpack back the values from the bitstream into the class object.

```
virtual function logic[63:0] unpack_field_int (int size);
virtual function uvm_bitstream_t unpack_field (int size);
virtual function string unpack_string (int num_chars=-1);
virtual function time unpack_time ();
virtual function void unpack_object (uvm_object value);
virtual function int get_packed_size();
```

For queues, dynamic arrays, and associative arrays, pack 32 bits to indicate the size of the array before packing individual elements. When you unpack, the first thing you do is read the array and get the size. After obtaining the size, unpack the relevant number of array elements in the do_unpack routines.

Rule 4.3.7: *You must never call the do_pack() method directly. Implement the method and allow the pack() method implementation to call it under the hood.*

Here is an example of the do_pack() and do_unpack() methods.

Listing 4.13: A simple do_pack() example

```
54    function void do_pack (uvm_packer packer);
55       super.do_pack(packer);
56       packer.pack_field_int(par_int,32);
57       packer.pack_field_int(par_address,8);
58       packer.pack_string(par_string);
59       packer.pack_object(cl1);
60       packer.pack_object(cl3);
61    endfunction
62
63
64    function void do_unpack (uvm_packer packer);
65       super.do_unpack(packer);
66       par_int = packer.unpack_field_int(32);
67       par_address = packer.unpack_field_int(8);
68       par_string = packer.unpack_string();
69       packer.unpack_object(cl1);
70       packer.unpack_object(cl3);
71    endfunction
```

You will recognize that the operations are similar to the one for the do_copy() method.

UVM
IEEE

The IEEE version enforces the packer policy if a null one is passed. The standard does not explicitly call out what happens when these default values are set to null, indicating that all the associated get_default calls should be guarded with null checks on the return value. When get_default_packer is called after a corresponding set_default_packer(null), the implementation returns the packer instance that would be returned if get_default_packer() had been called without any previous calls to set_default_packer().

The uvm_packer::set_packed_* and uvm_packer::get_packed_* methods use signed arguments while the uvm_object::pack and uvm_object::unpack methods are unsigned. The implementation, therefore, keeps the arguments unsigned, so as to remain consistent with the other packing APIs.

The implemented signatures are:

```
virtual function void uvm_packer::get_packed_bits( ref bit unsigned stream[] );
virtual function void uvm_packer::get_packed_bytes( ref byte unsigned stream[] );
virtual function void uvm_packer::get_packed_ints( ref int unsigned stream[] );
virtual function void uvm_packer::get_packed_longints( ref longint unsigned
stream[] );
```

The uvm_packer::set_packed_* and uvm_packer::get_packed_* methods use signed arguments while the uvm_object::pack and uvm_object::unpack methods are unsigned. The implementation, therefore, keeps the arguments unsigned, so as to remain consistent with the other packing APIs.

The implemented signatures are:

```
virtual function void uvm_packer::set_packed_bits( ref bit unsigned stream[] );
virtual function void uvm_packer::set_packed_bytes( ref byte unsigned stream[] );
virtual function void uvm_packer::set_packed_ints( ref int unsigned stream[] );
virtual function void uvm_packer::set_packed_longints( ref longint unsigned
stream[] );
```

The use_metadata approach in UVM 1.2 doesn't allow streaming operations to pack and unpack objects. The use_metadata flag is therefore deprecated. Instead, one must ensure that the packer and unpacker understand each other and can understand the bitstream passed between them. If you are using UVM 1.2 see Section A.3.4

4.4 Core Operations Summary

The following table summarizes the various operations from the previous sections. In this table, you can see the various common operations and the corresponding override functions that you must call.

Table 4.3: Core operations summary and override methods

Operation	Automated	Implement your version	Options to Macros (See next section)
copy	copy	do_copy	UVM_NOCOPY
compare	compare(comparer)	do_compare	UVM_NOCOMPARE
print	print(printer)	do_print	UVM_NOPRINT
pack bytes	pack()	do_pack	UVM_NOPACK
unpack bytes	unpack(packer)	do_unpack	UVM_NOPACK

There are several advanced ways in which you can "intercept" the various do_* operations for specific scenarios without disturbing the rest of the infrastructure that you have already built. Chapter 19 discusses this in greater detail.

4.5 UVM Macros to Simplify Things

In all the above examples, note the fair amount of detail in the function calls. Creating these methods by hand is tedious and naturally, error-prone. In the footsteps of OVM and VMM, UVM also makes available macros simplify the task of creating methods for common operations using macros. If, for example, a new variable was added to a class, merely adding it to a macro ensures that the appropriate methods are automatically updated with the new variable. The alternative otherwise would be to update manually the methods, which would be a good way to create many bugs.

The `uvm macros under the hood implement some standard functions that are useful to the user. They come with utility functions and additional callback functions. The user can override or use their implementations rather than rely on what is supplied by the library. The base class implementation supplies many methods for objects in UVM. The methods provided by the macros are:

- copy
- compare
- pack/unpack
- record
- print and sprint.

There are a couple of versions of the UVM utility macros. The two versions stem from the fact that the class derived from uvm_object may or may not have any properties. Classes with no additional properties may call the following macro:

```
`uvm_object_utils(<classname>)
```

All classes with additional properties will need to invoke the field macros inside a code segment, as illustrated in Table 4.4.

```
`uvm_object_utils_begin(<classname >)
....
....
`uvm_object_utils_end
```

You can use the macros from the table below to add properties of the class to the various operations.

Table 4.4: Various Macros For UVM Objects

Field Kind	Kind of element	Automation Macro
Scalar	All integral types except enum	`uvm_field_int(FIELD,FLAG)
	enumerated types	`uvm_field_enum(TYPE,FIELD,FLAG)
	objects derived from UVM object	`uvm_field_object(FIELD,FLAG)
	string types	`uvm_field_string(FIELD,FLAG)
Array types		
STATIC Array types	All integral types except enum	`uvm_field_sarray_int(FIELD,FLAG)
	objects derived from UVM object	`uvm_field_sarray_object(FIELD,FLAG)
	string types	`uvm_field_sarray_string(FIELD,FLAG)
DYNAMIC ARRAY types	All integral types except enum	`uvm_field_array_int(FIELD,FLAG)
	objects derived from UVM object	`uvm_field_array_object(FIELD,FLAG)
	string types	`uvm_field_array_string(FIELD,FLAG)
QUEUE types	All integral types except enum	`uvm_field_queue_int(FIELD,FLAG)
	objects derived from UVM object	`uvm_field_queue_object(FIELD,FLAG)
	string types	`uvm_field_queue_string(FIELD,FLAG)
Associative Array types	objects derived from UVM object with integral key	`uvm_field_aa_object_int(FIELD,FLAG)
	string typeswith integral key	`uvm_field_aa_string_int(FIELD,FLAG)
	objects derived from UVM object with string key	`uvm_field_aa_object_string(FIELD,FLAG)
	string typeswith string key	`uvm_field_aa_string_string(FIELD,FLAG)
	string types with string key	`uvm_field_aa_string_string(FIELD,FLAG)

Depending on the type of the field, the macros have small variations in their definitions. The summary is shown in Table 4.4. Each `uvm_field_* macro is named so that it corresponds to a specific data type and usually has at least two arguments ARG and FLAG. The ARG is the instance name of the variable, which is type compatible with the macro being invoked. The argument FLAG controls the operations that are enabled by the macro.

Note that the above table lists the various macros available as per the LRM. The Accellera implementation provides many additional macros. See the uvm_object_defines.svh in the macros directory, and look for the keyword "LRM". These are newly introduced, and should make their way to the IEEE LRM after they mature.

The default value for FLAG is UVM_ALL_ON unless you do not want it as a part of a specific operation. The method to control the operations using flags, as shown below:

Table 4.5: UVM Macro Flags

Operation	Flag	Effect
Copy	UVM_NOCOPY	Do not copy this field
Compare	UVM_NOCOMPARE	Do not compare this field
Print	UVM_NOPRINT	Do not print this field
Pack	UVM_NOPACK	Do not pack this field

To illustrate flag usage, consider a small example of how you would write a field utility macro.

```
`uvm_field_int(cl_int,UVM_ALL_ON|UVM_NO_PRINT)
```

In the above example, the field cl_int from our example class will be made part of the copy() and compare() and pack() functions implemented by the macros. It is excluded from the print() function and will not print when the print functions are called unless you have created a corresponding do_print() method that prints this field. The NO_* flag attribute can be used to control whether the field is included in an operation (copy/compare, etc.) supplied by UVM or not. You can choose to turn off and exclude the field from the specific operation using the flags mentioned below. The UVM_NO_PRINT|NO_COPY|NO_COMPARE flags take precedence over including the operation signified by UVM_ALL_ON. To combine two or more flags, use the '|' operation. *Although one notices the flags are defined as integers, do not add them up.*

There is an implementation bug in the Accellera source code. If you pass any other flag other than the NO_* flags, the macros treat the flag as UVM_ALL_ON instrumenting code for every operation. This will be corrected in the next release from Accellera. Note that the change will only improve performance without changing functionality.

The UVM Library also provides other flags like UVM_COPY, UVM_PRINT, UVM_PACK, and UVM_COMPARE. *Because of the bug mentioned above,* other than passing the NO_* flags, any of UVM_COPY, UVM_COMPARE, and UVM_PRINT **is treated as UVM_ALL_ON** inside the macros. This is counter-intuitive, but that's the way it works in the 2017 release. It should be fixed in the next Accellera release.

You will notice different styles where you may see either UVM_DEFAULT or UVM_ALL_ON. There is no functional difference between UVM_ALL_ON and UVM_DEFAULT at the current time. UVM_ALL_ON turns all the operations ON, just like UVM_DEFAULT.

The reason for UVM_DEFAULT is to allow for the existence of additional flags that can be added by library implementers with a default value of OFF without impacting existing code in your codebase. Such functionality does not exist today, but maybe so in the future.

Rule 4.5.0:   *use UVM_DEFAULT instead of UVM_ALL_ON to future proof your code.*

UVM
1.2   uvm_integral_t (64b packed logic) type support in API's is added to UVM 1.2.

Expansion of the macros provides the following functions to you in addition to registering the class with the factory (discussed in the next chapter).

Name/String related functions:

1. virtual function void set_name (string name);

2. virtual function string get_name ();

3. virtual function string get_full_name ();

4. virtual function string get_type_name ();

5. virtual function string convert2string();

Transaction management

1. virtual function int get_inst_id ();

2. static function int get_inst_count();

3. static function uvm_object_wrapper get_type ();

4. virtual function uvm_object_wrapper get_object_type ();

5. virtual function uvm_object clone ();

Printing/Recording

1. virtual function void print (uvm_printer printer=null);

2. virtual function void do_print (uvm_printer printer=null);

3. function string sprint (uvm_printer printer=null);

4. function void record (uvm_recorder recorder=null);

5. function void do_record (uvm_recorder recorder=null);

Copying

1. virtual function void copy (uvm_object rhs, uvm_copier copier=null);

2. virtual function void do_copy (uvm_object rhs);

Compare:

1. virtual function bit compare (uvm_object rhs, uvm_comparer comparer=null);

2. virtual function bit do_compare (uvm_object rhs, uvm_comparer comparer=null);

Packing:

1. virtual function int pack (ref bit bitstream[], input uvm_packer packer=null);

2. virtual function int do_pack (ref bit bitstream[], input uvm_packer packer=null);

3. virtual function int pack_bytes (ref byte unsigned bytestream[], input uvm_packer packer=null);

4. virtual function int pack_ints (ref int unsigned intstream[], input uvm_packer packer=null);

5. virtual function int unpack (ref bit bitstream[], input uvm_packer packer=null);

6. virtual function int do_ unpack (ref bit bitstream[], input uvm_packer packer=null);

7. virtual function int unpack_bytes (ref byte unsigned bytestream[], input uvm_packer packer=null);

8. virtual function int unpack_ints (ref int unsigned intstream[], input uvm_packer packer=null);

4.5.1 Considerations When Using The Macros

It is essential to understand the decision of macro vs. non-macro usage is typically a "performance/creation speed /maintenance effort" decision. Making the decision is subject to the factors below:

From the UVM committee point of view, the UVM macros are effectively considered as a kind of "first-class citizens", similar to functions and tasks. *Any bug fixes, use model changes, and performance improvements inside the macros will naturally only reach the users of such macros.*

There have been studies that reveal a significant performance limitation when using the macros in UVM 1.1c. *A number of these concerns were addressed in UVM 1.2.* However, If you are concerned about performance, create your implementations using the hook methods provided.

From a performance point of view, many vendors don't like the macros, the reason being there is significant code bloat that the compiler will attempt to optimize. Performance differences between the two approaches may heavily depend upon the macro used, exact use model, UVM version, and relevant tool versions and debugging switches. Run a reasonable benchmark to study the cost of doing so before you make a switch from one approach to the other. Hard data allows you to make a subjective decision on a hand-coded implementation (non-macro) vs. less user code and more generic code. Each situation is unique in this regard.

4.6 A Complete Class in UVM

Various class methods were described for doing the most common operations used in UVM. These methods and their override callbacks were studied. The completed class, with all the macros put together, is presented here. If you wish to randomize this class, you need some additional constraints to keep the randomization within your range of values. Constraints are described in Section 3.1.1.

> Listing 4.14: A Simple Example using various core utilities with all the corresponding do hooks methods

```
3 class class_P extends uvm_object;
4
5     // basic datatypes
6     rand int par_int;
7     rand byte par_address;
8     string par_string;
9
10    // Some objects to demonstrate the copy recursion policy
11    class_A cl1; // UVM_SHALLOW
12    class_A cl3; // UVM_DEEP
13
14
```

```
15    `uvm_object_utils_begin(class_P)
16       `uvm_field_int(par_int ,UVM_DEFAULT)
17       `uvm_field_int(par_address ,UVM_DEFAULT | UVM_NOCOPY|UVM_NOPRINT|
             UVM_NOPACK)
18       `uvm_field_string(par_string ,UVM_NOCOPY|UVM_NOPRINT|UVM_NOPACK)
19       `uvm_field_object(cl1 ,UVM_DEFAULT|UVM_NOCOPY|UVM_NOPRINT|UVM_NOPACK)
20       `uvm_field_object(cl3 ,UVM_DEFAULT| UVM_NOCOPY|UVM_NOPRINT|UVM_NOPACK
             )
21    `uvm_object_utils_end
22
23    function new(string name="");
24       super.new(name);
25       cl1 = new(name);
26       cl3 = new(name )  ;
27       par_string  = name;
28    endfunction
29
30    virtual function bit do_compare(uvm_object rhs, uvm_comparer comparer);
31       class_P rhs_;
32       do_compare = super.do_compare(rhs ,comparer);
33       $cast(rhs_ ,rhs);
34       do_compare &= comparer.compare_field_int("par_int",par_int ,rhs_.
             par_int ,32,UVM_NORADIX);
35       do_compare &= comparer.compare_field_int("par_address",par_int ,rhs_.
             par_int ,32,UVM_NORADIX);
36       do_compare &= comparer.compare_string("par_string",par_string ,rhs_.
             par_string);
37       do_compare &= comparer.compare_object("cl1",cl1 ,rhs_.cl1);
38       do_compare &= comparer.compare_object("cl3",cl3 ,rhs_.cl3);
39    endfunction
40
41    function void do_copy(uvm_object rhs);
42       class_P rhs_;
43       super.do_copy(rhs);
44       $cast(rhs_ ,rhs);
45       par_int = rhs_.par_int;
46       par_address = rhs_.par_address;
47       par_string = rhs_.par_string;
48       cl1 = new rhs_.cl1;
49       cl3 = new rhs_.cl3;
50       cl1.copy(rhs_.cl1);
51       cl3.copy(rhs_.cl3);
52    endfunction
53
54    function void do_pack (uvm_packer packer);
55       super.do_pack(packer);
56       packer.pack_field_int(par_int ,32);
57       packer.pack_field_int(par_address ,8);
58       packer.pack_string(par_string);
59       packer.pack_object(cl1);
60       packer.pack_object(cl3);
61    endfunction
62
63
```

```
64    function void do_unpack (uvm_packer packer);
65        super.do_unpack(packer);
66        par_int = packer.unpack_field_int(32);
67        par_address = packer.unpack_field_int(8);
68        par_string = packer.unpack_string();
69        packer.unpack_object(cl1);
70        packer.unpack_object(cl3);
71    endfunction
72
73
74    function void do_print(uvm_printer printer);
75        printer.set_type_name_enabled(1);
76        printer.print_field_int("Integer",par_int,32,UVM_NORADIX,".","");
77        printer.print_field_int("Address",par_int,32,UVM_NORADIX,".","");
78        printer.print_string("String",par_string,"");
79        printer.print_object("cl1 Inst",cl1);
80        printer.print_object("cl3 Inst",cl3);
81    endfunction
82
83 endclass
```

In Listing 4.14:

- Lines 5-12 describe the various properties of the class.

- Lines 15-21 provide the uvm_object_utils macros to automate the creation of some of the utility methods.

- Line 16 is the par_int property using all the default implementations, excluding the default pack() implementations.

- Line 17 shows the par_address property using the default implementations except for copy() and pack(). *It is noted that although the flags are defined as integers, one is not adding up the integers but effectively OR'ing the bits.*

- Lines 23–28 is the constructor function for this class

- Lines 30-39 provide the do_compare() override method in this class. Note that this uses the comparer policy passed to the method.

- Lines 37 and 38 calls the compare() methods on the class_A classes. If a do_compare callback method is defined for class_A, it would be called as well.

- Lines 41-52 provide the do_copy() override method in this class.

- Lines 54-61 provide the do_pack() override method in this class. Note that this uses the packer policy passed to the method.

- Lines 64-71 provide the do_unpack() override method in this class. Note that this uses the packer policy passed to the method.

- Lines 74-81 provide the do_print() override method in this class. Note that this uses the printer policy passed to the method.

4.7 Coding Guidelines

This chapter discusses the core utilities provided by the UVM. The automation macros supplied by the library help the user to implement quickly commonly used functions with little effort on their part. By using various callback functions provided by the library, you can customize the behavior of the core utilities to suit a specific application requirement. User-defined hooks allow the user to alter the default behavior provided by the library. The following coding guidelines will help you significantly during your UVM journey.

Rule 4.7.0:   *There is an inherent limit of 4kbits (4096 bits) for integral variables controlled by `UVM_MAX_STREAMBITS.*

Be careful of changing this define as it has the effect of changing it to all the objects in the design and thereby affects efficiency.

Rule 4.7.1:   *Integrals are recorded as 1K bit vectors, regardless of size. Variables larger than 1K bits are* basically truncated.

Rule 4.7.2:   *Top-level function calls will call your handcrafted implementation.*

The automation provided by the uvm_field_* macros will always execute before the handcrafted implementation in the do_* methods.

Rule 4.7.3:   *The uvm_field_* macro implementations have a non-programmable execution order within the compare/copy methods.*

Your handcrafted implementations provide full control over this order via do_compare()/do_copy()/do_print() methods.

Rule 4.7.4:   *Auto-registration happens with the macros, which causes the config settings to be updated during the build_phase.*

Note that you do not have this ability when you write your functions for print() copy(), compare, and pack().

Rule 4.7.5:   *Use the provided callback hooks using the policy classes and do_execute_op to intercept the operation rather than hacking a copy of the library*

> When macros are misused, error/warning messages might not directly indicate the source of the issue, and during simulation, debugging with macros is usually more challenging.

4.8 Before Proceeding Further.

The sections in this chapter introduced the various methods available in the uvm_object class.

- Change examples provided to use create() instead of new() for examples in this chapter.

- Add a few data members to a copy of Listing 4.1 and add the corresponding macros to it from Table 4.4.

- Make changes for the added properties to the do_copy() method using Listing 4.6 as a reference and observe the output using the example similar to Listing 4.5

- Make changes for the added properties to the do_compare() method using Listing 4.8 as a reference and observe the output using the example similar to Listing 4.7

- Make changes for the added properties to the do_print() method using Listing 4.11 as a reference and observe the output using the example in Listing 4.9

- Make changes for the added properties to the do_pack() and do_unpack() methods using Listing 4.13 as a reference and observe the output using the example in Listing 4.12

- Change the macro flags using the information in Table 4.5 and observe the output.

Once you have completed the above exercises, you will have a good grasp of the UVM Core Utilities.

An important subclass of uvm_object called ***uvm_component*** is presented in Chapter 8. It uses several important capabilities that are introduced in Chapters 5 through Chapter 7.

Read Chapters 5 through 7 before studying Chapter 8 in depth. The reason for this organization is to minimize the amount of back and forth that would otherwise ensue. For now, all you need to know is that the uvm_component class is an important class in the uvm_hierarchy derived from uvm_object. You will use it to construct quasi-static objects in your simulation.

Chapter 5
UVM Factory

Earlier chapters described some of the features of the UVM methodology and various core utilities provided with UVM for classes deriving from the uvm_object class. This chapter describes the use of a software design pattern called a factory, which allows you to create objects in a UVM simulation. A discussion of the factory API along with examples of its usage is shown in this chapter.

5.1 Need for a Factory Pattern in UVM

It may be necessary to replace some of the current testbench code to test a particular aspect of the design. An example of this would be replacing a driver with another driver that injects errors. Instead of re-coding or modifying the testbench, it would be desirable to be able to create a new driver and have the existing driver replaced by the new driver at runtime for a few specific tests.

Consider the environment shown in Figure 5.1. Various classes were created using the new() function of the appropriate classes. Due to changes in the specification of the driver or to extend the functionality of the driver, a situation can arise where it would be necessary to replace the driver in the master component with a new driver. The new driver would then drive errors into the packet at runtime.

To make a change, the following classes in the environment must be changed as seen in Figure 5.1

- Driver classes

- Agent class

- Environment class

- Test class

To *change just one class*, it becomes necessary to modify many separate classes as well. Such changes are not desirable, as many issues may occur.

Having a simple uniform mechanism to handle object creation and/or override capability that minimizes confusion and maximizes reuse would be ideal. The factory is an abstract design pattern from OOP principles, which is intended to solve this problem. The factory provides a means to substitute one class object for another without making extensive changes to the testbench code. The factory is a singleton object[10] – there is only one instance of the factory in a simulation with these features:

- Global in scope and is accessible from anywhere in the hierarchy.

- Provides a mechanism to "register" objects with it.

- Provides a mechanism to create objects registered with it. During object creation, it checks to see if any objects are supposed to be replaced and returns the correct type.

- Provides a way to specify how registered objects may be replaced with other objects, namely:

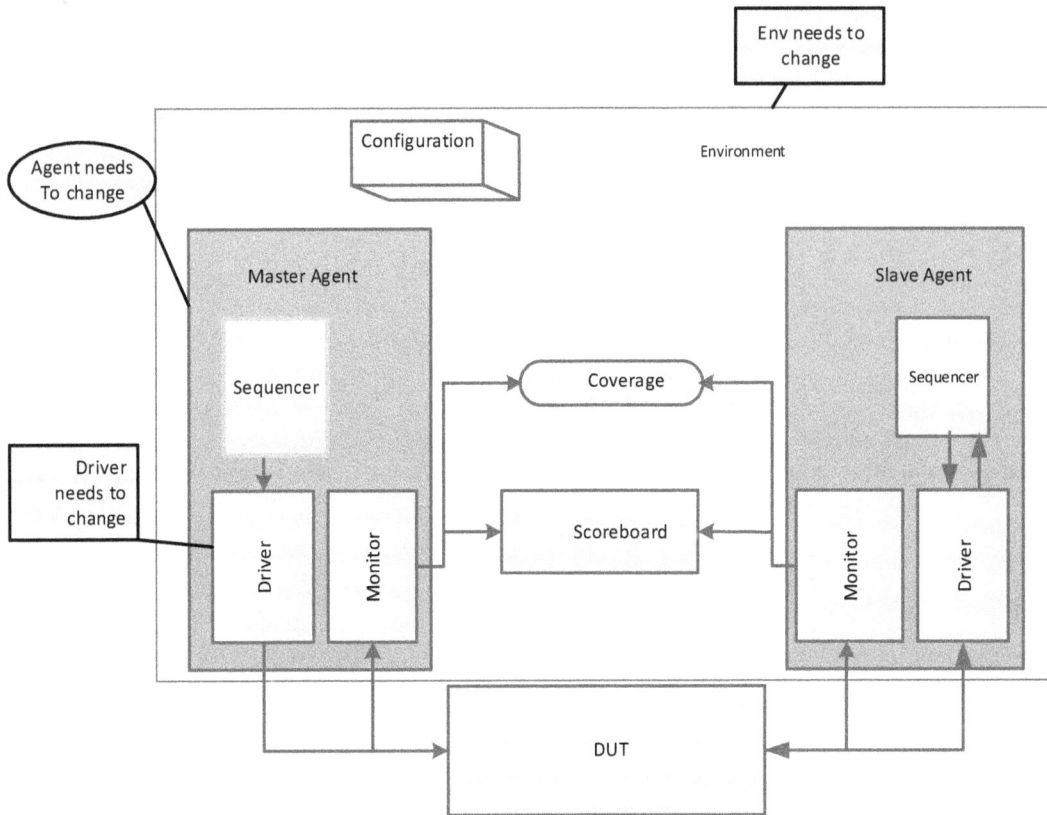

Fig. 5.1: Components that need to change if you wish to replace just the master agent driver

- Provide type overrides by replacing types: For example: return an object of type T2 when requested for an object of type T1.

- Provide instance overrides. IE. If an object of type T1 was requested for a particular instance, it can return an object of type T2, provided such an override was registered with it.

5.2 UVM Factory Operation

The UVM factory bases itself on a data structure that maps requested types to override types. There is an associative array of type handles with the key being the type handle. When you use the macros in Section 4.5, the class type registers itself with the factory. Entries are made both in the requested and override handle arrays. When registration occurs, both the original type and the override types are the same. When you override a given type, there are different entries in the two arrays for that type. When an object is requested from the factory, a lookup is performed in both the arrays. The factory then responds with the appropriate type. The factory provides a means for replacing the overrides with other types, which allows you to retrieve override types that are different from the registered type.

The inner workings of the factory may be explained as follows: Section 4.5 introduced some of the macros. Note that when a class is declared, the macros automatically register a specialized singleton class of the particular type with the appropriate registry. The macros under the hood create uvm_object_registry or uvm_component_registry classes. These classes behave as proxies that allow an object or component to be registered with the factory before any instances of the object or component are created. When the class is registered, a proxy instance is created. The proxy instance is a specialization of the registry class created automatically by the utility macros as a singleton instance of a nested class named *type_id*. This *type_id* instance contains a create() method (see Section 4.2.1).

When you request an object from the factory through its API, the factory does a lookup to determine the appropriate type of class to be created and then defers the creation of the class to the automatically generated create() function. This approach enables the factory to support specializations of parameterized classes, each type being registered separately with the factory. Calling the static create() member function of a component's or object's *type_id* nested class is the simplest way to instantiate components with the factory. It returns a handle of the correct type; no type casts are necessary.

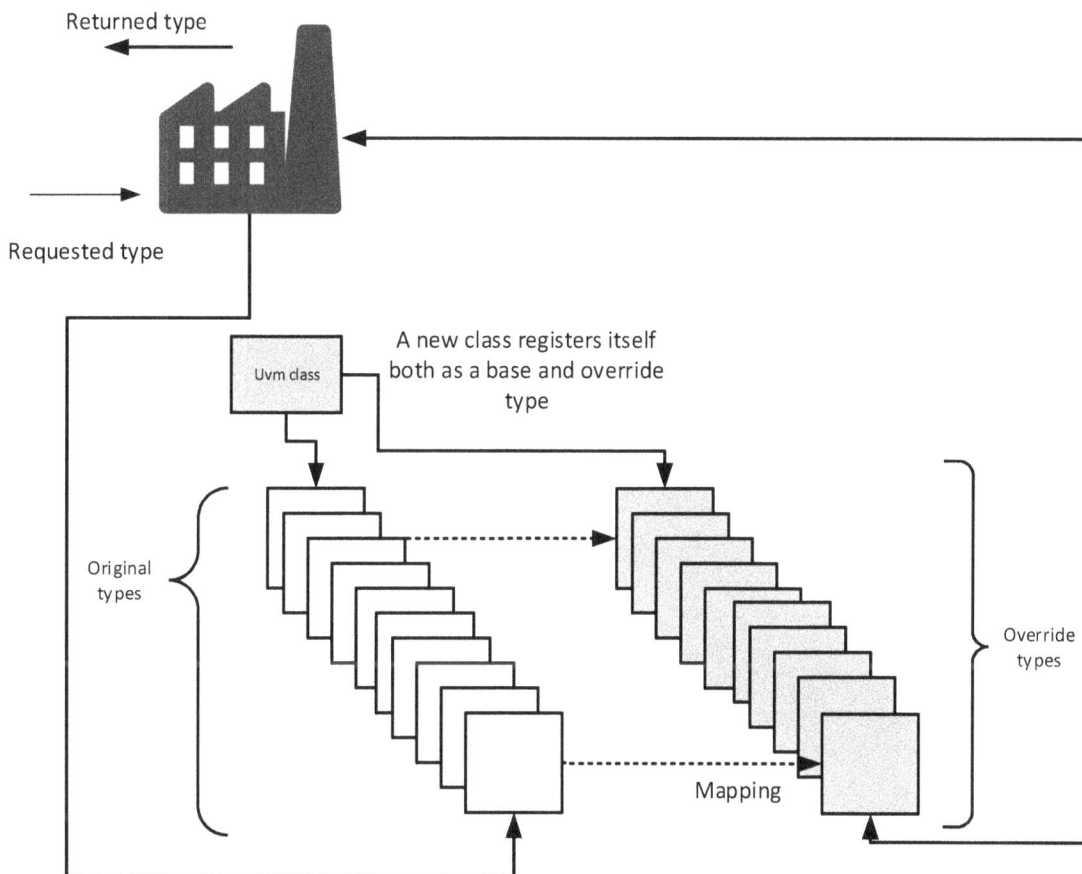

Fig. 5.2: Mapping Types Using Factory

Listing 5.1 shows the declaration of a class in UVM and the macros that help provide the factory methods.

Listing 5.1: A Simple Class

```
1 class my_class extends uvm_object;
2   `uvm_object_utils(my_class)
3   // Other class properties and methods
4
5 endclass
```

The uvm object macros add interesting functions shown in Listing 5.2.

```
Listing 5.2: Macros showing the factory methods
1 class my_class extends uvm_object;
2     static bit m_registered_converter__ = m_uvm_resource_sprint_converter#(
          my_class)::register();
3     typedef uvm_object_registry#(my_class,"my_class") type_id;
4     static function type_id get_type();
5        return type_id::get();
6     endfunction
7     virtual function uvm_object_wrapper get_object_type();
8        return type_id::get();
9     endfunction
10    function uvm_object create (string name="");
11      my_class tmp;
12      tmp = new();
13      if (name!="")
14        tmp.set_name(name);
15      return tmp;
16    endfunction
17    const static string type_name = "my_class";
18    virtual function string get_type_name ();
19       return type_name;
20    endfunction
21 endclass
```

The above source code shows the macros expanded to implement the following:

1. The get_type_name() function that returns the "my_class" as a string.
2. The create() method that allocates an object of type uvm_object by calling its constructor with no arguments.
3. The static get_type() method that returns a factory proxy object for the type.
4. The virtual get_object_type() method that works just like the static get_type() method but operates on an already allocated object.

Line 3 shows the declaration of the parameterized proxy class *type_id* which is then registered with the object_registry. The create function for this specific class is also made available from this macro. The **get_object_type(), get_type() and get_type_name()** and **type_name()** functions are also made available by this macro. The specific type *my_class* *is also* made known to the factory.

Rule 5.2.0:   *Use the `uvm_object_utils(), `uvm_object_param_utils(), `uvm_component_utils() and `uvm_component_param_utils() factory registration macros.*

Registering objects with the factory can be error-prone and difficult for the average user without the macros.

Recommendation 5.2.0:   *During the create call, the object's handle name must match the string name passed into the create() call. This simplifies debugging*[1]

Rule 5.2.1:   *Do NOT attempt to clone a component.*

Use a factory method instead to create a new component instance.

The create() and clone() methods inherited from uvm_object are disabled for components.
The factory calls the ***new()*** method under the hood (see Line 12 in the listing). Hence, it is essential to understand that the factory cannot create an abstract class since one must derive the class before using it. While the IEEE version allows you to register abstract classes, unless you derive these classes, you effectively cannot create an instance of the class.

---

[1] This is a repeat of the recommendation in Section 4.2.1. Given the importance of this guideline, it has been repeated here.

5.3 Factory Behavior for Parameterized and NonParameterized Classes

There is a difference in how the factory treats parameterized classes and the non-parameterized classes. This difference is due to the implementation of the get_type_name and other functions inferred from the nonparameterized classes. The differences are summarized in the table below.

	Non Parameterized classes	Parameterized classes
Declaration & Registration	`uvm_object_utils(packet) `uvm_component_utils(driver)	`uvm_object_param_utils(packet, (#T, WIDTH)  `uvm_component_param_utils(#T)
function get_type_name()	Automatically defined	need to implement manually (1)
static string type_name;	Automatically implemented	Needs to implement manually (2).
Print function from factory	displays correct type	displays <unknown> if (1)/(2) are not implemented.

(i) When debugging the hierarchy, sometimes you may see an <**unknown**> in your output. This is one of the things to suspect when this happens.

Listing 5.3 shows the example of a simple parameterized driver with all the functions implemented.

Listing 5.3: A simple parameterized class

```
2 class param_drv #(type T=uvm_object) extends param_driver_base #(T);
3
4   // parameterized classes must use the _param_utils macro
5   `uvm_component_param_utils(param_drv #(T))
6
7   // standard component constructor
8   function new(string name, uvm_component parent=null);
9     super.new(name,parent);
10   endfunction
11
12   // get_type_name not implemented by macro for parameterized classes
13   const static string type_name = {"param_drv #(",T::type_name,")"};
14   virtual function string get_type_name();
15     return type_name;
16   endfunction
17
18   // using the factory allows pkt overrides from outside the class
19   virtual function void build_phase(uvm_phase phase);
20     pkt= packet::type_id::create("pkt");
21   endfunction
22
23 endclass
```

- Line 2 defines param_drv as a specialized type of param_driver_base.

- Line 5 The macros help register the specialized version of the class param_drv with the factory.

- Line 13 shows the definition of the string of type_name which must be created manually in case of parameterized classes.

- Lines 18-21 show the implementation of the build_phase for this driver, which uses the factory functions to create the member called pkt.

5.4 Using the Factory

Using the factory consists of the following operations.

1. Registering objects and components types with the factory

2. Designing components to use the factory to create objects or components

3. Configuring the factory with type and instance overrides, both within and outside components

4. Creating objects using the factory's create methods.

Once an object is registered with the factory, the following methods are available for use:

Method	Description
function uvm_component create_component(string name, uvm_component parent);	Used by the factory to create instance
static function this_type get();	Returns proxy instance
function string get_type_name();	Returns type name
static function T create(string name,uvm_component parent,string)	Called by user to create instance with the factory, It returns a class instance with a name specified in the input arguments.
static function void set_type_override(uvm_object_wrapper override_type,bit replace=1);	Overrides the type used by the factory for specified type
static function void set_inst_override(uvm_object_wrapper override_type, string inst_path, uvm_component parent=null);	Overrides the type used by the factory for the specified instance (path is relative if parent specified)

5.5 Replacing Components Using a Factory.

The steps for replacing any class that registered with the factory with another class as follows:

- Define a class that derives from the appropriate UVM base class.

- Set up the override with the factory.

- Execute the override in your test class.

- Build the environment. Make sure that you call the create() methods instead of calling new() to create the various components.

  In the text below, we identify two different types of classes. There are some quasi-static classes made up of *components* and others that are dynamic. You will study more about these components in Chapter 8. The components may be built instantiating other components inside them. Therefore, the description below refers to them as hierarchical objects. The other kind of class is more dynamic in nature and exists only for a short time in the simulation. These are called non-hierarchical or dynamic objects.

  1. Regarding the requirements for replacement, there is a difference between the way the factory treats the hierarchical objects and the non-hierarchical objects. For the hierarchical objects, the instance is easily identified using the full hierarchical name of the component. For the non-hierarchical objects, the instance name and the name of its hierarchical anchor component are both needed in the function call.

  2. There are two types of overrides that are supported by the factory. These overrides make it possible for the factory to replace a particular component in the hierarchy without changing any other component in the hierarchy. The second flavor of component override replaces targeted components of the matching instance path with the new specified type.

Rule 5.5.0:   *Use the factory for creating transaction, sequence, and component objects. This allows you to use type and instance overrides.*

Remember that you often have no idea where your code will end up some time later. I'm sure you have similar experiences! Some time ago, while creating a brand new application involving both System-C and UVM, I found myself in a situation where I wanted to replace a component inside an agent with another that only provided a facade. The original component writer under the hood had used new() instead of create() from the factory, preventing an override from being used. I had to rewrite the entire agent, the component and a host of other classes rather than a small fix.

5.5.1 Type Overrides

The factory maintains an array of component types and their override types. This makes it possible to replace a component of a particular pre-defined type with one the user selected. The change can be maintained separately on a test by test basis as needed. To create a type override, you can call the function available from the factory API. This method is specified as follows:

Rule 5.5.1:   *Use the following approach to override items from the factory.*

```
set_type_override_by_type(orig_type, override_type, bit replace = 1);
or

orig_type::type_id::set_type_override(new_type)
```

The first argument is the original type of the component, which is obtained by calling the get_type() method of the original component. The second argument is the type name that is obtained by calling the get_type() method for the second component. The replace bit is used to determine whether the override type should replace the original type or an existing override. If the replace bit is set to 0, it has different behavior depending on whether it finds an override in the factory tables.

- If the override of the specified type *does not exist*, the override *is registered* with the factory.

- If an override of the specified item *does* exist, the override is *ignored*.

A practical example of the type override is shown in Section 21.2.1, in which another type replaces all the instances of a specific class type. For purposes of clarity, Figure 5.3

shows how the override operates in the case of the wb_conmax example.

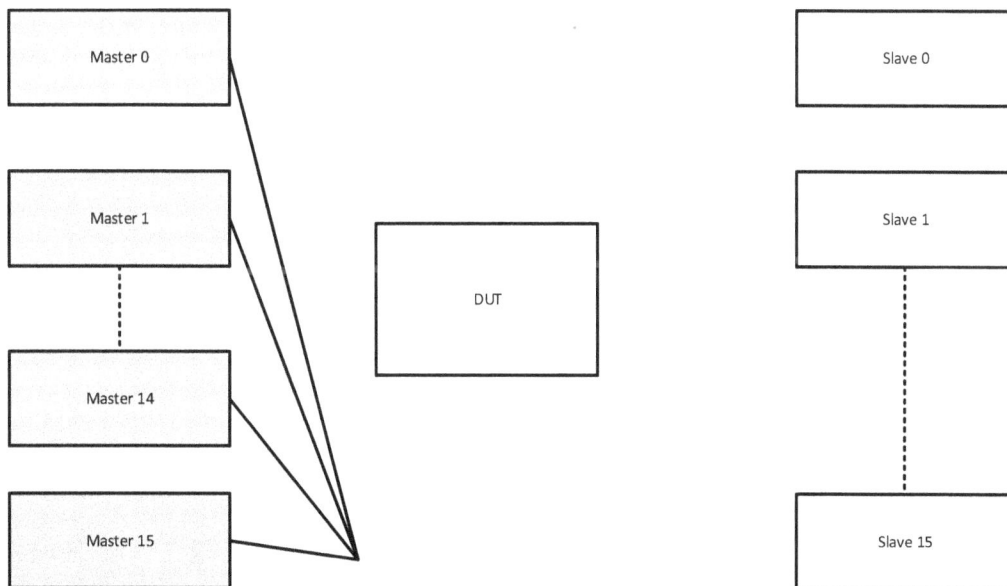

All these instances
Replaced Type Override
Figure 5.3

Type overrides are useful if you are planning a global replacement of one type of class with another. Every instance of a class that is created by the factory after the override is registered is of the override type and not the original type. In Figure 5.3, when you use a type override for the master, you will see that **all instances** of the master are replaced. For more specificity, use the instance overrides below. An example of using a type override is provided in Listing 5.4.

Listing 5.4: Type Override Example

```
30    virtual function void build_phase(uvm_phase phase);
31        // Using the uvm_coreservice_t:
32        uvm_coreservice_t cs;
33        uvm_root r;
34        uvm_factory fact;
35        super.build_phase(phase);
36        // uvm_config_db #(wb_config)::set(null,$sformatf("uvm_test_top.env.
               master_agent[%02d]",i),"mstr_agent_cfg",master_configs[i] );
37
38        cs = uvm_coreservice_t::get();
39        r = cs.get_root();
40        fact = cs.get_factory();
41        fact.set_type_override_by_type(wb_master_agent::get_type(),
               wb_master_agent_n::get_type(),1);
42        // For you to to try out. Comment above line and uncomment one of
               the below.
43        // fact.set_inst_override_by_type(wb_master_agent::get_type(),
               wb_master_agent_n::get_type(),"env.master_agent[00]");
44        // set_inst_override_by_type(wb_master_agent::get_type(),
               wb_master_agent_n::get_type(),my_full_path);
45        // wb_master_agent::type_id::set_inst_override(wb_master_agent_n::
               get_type(),my_full_path);
46        // uvm_factory::set_inst_override_by_type(wb_master_agent::get_type
               (),wb_master_agent_n::get_type(),my_full_path);
47        fact.print();
48        // Set the default sequencer in all the master agents
49        uvm_config_db #(uvm_object_wrapper)::set(this, "env.master_agent
               [00].mast_sqr.main_phase", "default_sequence", sequence_1::
               get_type());
```

- Line 38,39 gets the handle to the centralized coreservice class instance.

- Line 40 gets you a handle to the factory.

- Line 41 sets a type override.

- Line 47 prints the types and overrides registered with the factory.

This listing is also used in Section 21.2.1. For now, just recognize that it is possible to replace one type with another type by using the factory.

5.5.2 Instance Specific Overrides

In some cases, it is desirable to replace specific instances of the factory with a different type. This application is most common when there are multiple instances of the class in the environment and you would like to replace a specific class instance with a different class instance. For instance, there may be multiple driver agents in an environment just like the wb_conmax module environment, and you want to replace a single agent to change its behavior to introduce errors. The factory provides a function to override a specific instance on a particular hierarchy:

```
set_inst_override_by_name ( string original_type_name, string override_type_name, string
full_inst_path );
```

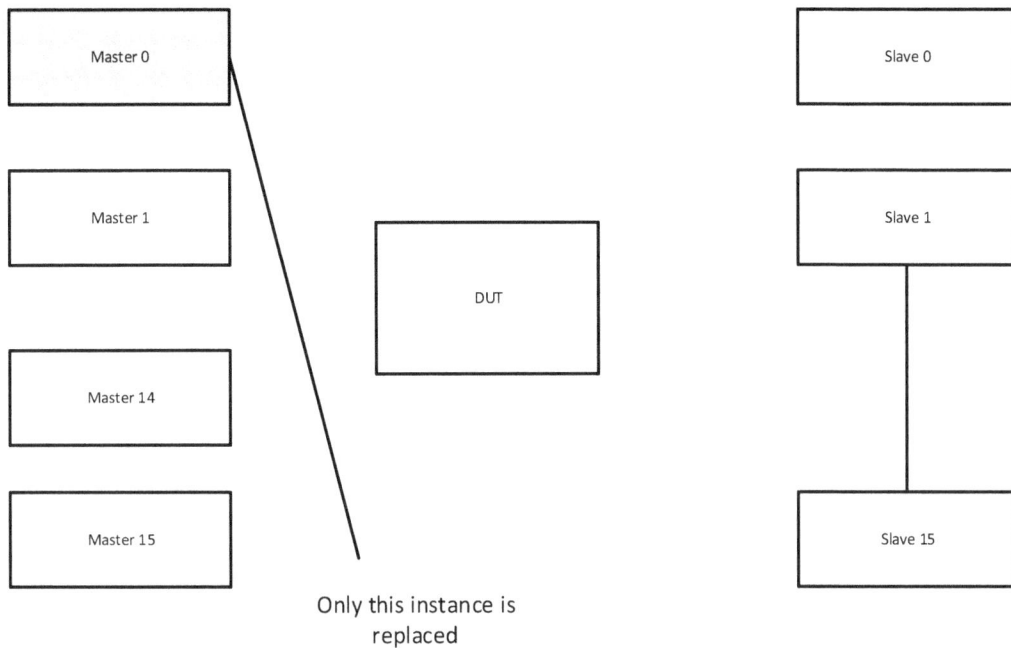

Fig. 5.4: Instance Override

The set_inst_override_by_type method configures the factory to create an object of the override type whenever the context of the object matches the complete path of the original type. In many circumstances, the original type is usually a super-class of the derived type. The full_inst_path is matched against the concatenation of {parent_inst_path, ".", name} which is provided in future create requests. The full_inst_path may include wildcards (* and ?) such that a single instance override can be applied in multiple contexts.

(i)   A full_inst_path of "*" is effectively a type override, as it shall match all paths

.

Listing 5.5 shows an example of a type override. This example has been brought forward from Section 21.2.2 and shows how a single instance of the master class may be overridden by a different type.

Listing 5.5: Instance Override Example

```
1   virtual function void build_phase(uvm_phase phase);
2       string my_full_path;
3       string orig_type_name, override_type_name;
4       uvm_coreservice_t cs;
5       uvm_root r;
6       uvm_factory fact;
7
8       cs = uvm_coreservice_t::get();
9       r = cs.get_root();
10      fact = cs.get_factory();
```

```
11        my_full_path = "env.master_agent[00]";
12        orig_type_name = "wb_master_agent";
13        override_type_name = "wb_master_agent_n";
14
15        set_inst_override(my_full_path,orig_type_name,override_type_name);
16
17        fact.print();
18        super.build_phase(phase);
19        // Set the default sequencer in one of the master agents
20        uvm_config_db #(uvm_object_wrapper)::set(this, "env.master_agent
              [00].mast_sqr.main_phase", "default_sequence", sequence_1::
              get_type());
21        r.enable_print_topology=1;
22        r.print_topology();
23
24    endfunction
```

5.5.3 Rules for Processing Overrides

Rule 5.5.2: *The factory creates objects based on name and parent.* ***Your class constructor must not have any other additional arguments.***

Using only the name and parent arguments implies that they are the only ones being used; the factory will pass along name and parent as arguments and nothing else.

When the factory processes instance overrides, the instance queue is processed in order of override registrations, and the first override match prevails. Thus, more specific overrides should be registered first, followed by more general overrides.

Many rules affect the processing of overrides[2]. You should remember the following though:

1. Wildcards can be used to specify an instance name. Just remember that wildcards affect all matching instances.

2. Wildcard characters and may be used when specifying an instance name,

   where * matches any string of characters and . matches a single character. This means that in our example for the slave agents in Section 21.1, the pattern slave[1*] matches all objects for the slave except the first nine. See examples for the regular expressions on the website for explanations of these symbols.

3. For instance, override both the type name and instance name need to match to allow the override to take effect.

4. Any new type override shall replace the previous override type for the same type.

5. Do not expect type overrides to chain. Example: class A is overridden by class type B, Class C overrides class B, and a request is made for an instance of Class A, and the factory returns class type C.

6. Instance overrides take precedence over type overrides. An instance specification provides specificity for the instances. For examples: See Listing 8.15 in Section 8.6 on line 427 in the log and Line 71 in the Listing.

7. A UVM feature can be used to make sure that a new type_override that is defined does not take effect if an existing override is already in place. To do so, use the replace bit which is set to default in the override method provided by the factory.

The "undo" capability is was introduced in UVM-1.2. To use it, replace the overridden type with the original type. In older versions of UVM (1.1d for example), if attempted to replace the overridden type by the original type resulted in an error. UVM 1.2 allows you to override types.

---

[2] Some rules above were adopted from [13] as they originated from OVM.

5.6 Debugging

UVM
1.2

Note that in UVM 1.1, the factory was a static member. In UVM 1.2, it is a part of the uvm_coreservice class newly introduced in UVM 1.2. You now have to get the instance of the coreservice first and **then** get the factory handle before using it. Listing 5.5 shows you how to do so:

Some methods are available that allow you to debug the factory as shown in Listing 5.5. You can choose to use the factory.print() or the print_topology() methods to see the components created by the factory on Line 17 of the listing.

The 2016 DVCON [8] presentation provides some detail on how to debug the factory. when you use the factory print() method, there is an optional argument *all_types* to the print() method as shown below.

- all_types = 0 – Only prints the overrides that are registered with the factory.

- all_types = 1 (default) prints *both* the registered types and the override types

- all_types = 2 prints all the types from all_types=1 and including the UVM library types. *Use this option WITH CARE. If you have a register model with many thousands of classes, this listing will be huge.*

I suggest you alter the above example, experimenting with various all_types values to the factory.print() on Line 17 in the above listing to learn the factory debug capabilities. You should see the results in the log file.

5.7 New Features in IEEE 1800.2

The factory has a few additional features added in IEEE 1800.2. Notably, it now allows you to register abstract classes that was not possible earlier. You can then create test specific overrides to exercise functionality in your DUT without disturbing the rest of your environment.

You may wonder why this capability is even needed. You cannot create an instance of an abstract class anyway! I view this as an infrastructure addition. All your common properties would be in the abstract base classes, which are mandated for use by all projects in your organization. In addition to providing effort savings by reusing code, If you don't see an override extending the base class, it becomes evident that your organization coding rules were broken. That alone makes it powerful in a verification audit.

Key features added:

- Ability to register abstract components

- Ability to register abstract objects

- Ability to set type aliases

The sections below provide you with detailed instructions on how to create and use abstract components with the factory.

5.7.1 Abstract Components

You may want to create abstract components with a set of base capabilities and use them in your environment after extending them. To register these with the factory you would use one of the following macros. Note the additional "abstract" keyword in the macros.

```
`uvm_component_abstract_utils(T)
`uvm_component_abstract_utils_begin(T)
`uvm_component_abstract_utils_end
`uvm_component_abstract_param_utils(T)
`uvm_component_abstract_param_utils_begin(T)
`uvm_component_abstract_utils_end
```

You can now declare your base components as virtual classes. The listing below shows an example.

5.7.1.1 Step 1: Create Abstract Component Class

Listing 5.6: Abstract Component Class

```
3 virtual class wb_cov_base extends uvm_component;
4    `uvm_component_abstract_utils(wb_cov_base)
5
6    uvm_analysis_imp #(wb_transaction, wb_cov_base) analysis_export;
7    wb_transaction tr;
8    event cov_event;
9    function new(string name="wb_cov_base",uvm_component parent);
10       super.new(name,parent);
11   endfunction
12
13   virtual function write(wb_transaction tr);
14       this.tr = tr;
15       -> cov_event;
16   endfunction: write
17
18 endclass
```

In this Listing:

- Class wb_cov_base extends from uvm_component. It is a virtual class.

- Line 6 is the analysis port

- Line 7 is the transaction

- Line 8 is the coverage event

- Lines 13-16 are the write() function

- Line 20 shows the derived class wb_env_cov extending from wb_cov_base. This has the actual covergroup in the class definition (not shown in above listing. See Listing 5.10).

5.7.1.2 Step 2: Instance Abstract Component in your Environment

Listing 5.7: Instance of Abstract Component in Environment

```
5 class wb_env_env extends uvm_env;
6    wb_master_agent master_agent;
7    wb_slave_agent slave_agent;
8    wb_cov_base cov;
9    wb_scoreboard sb;
10
11   `uvm_component_utils(wb_env_env)
```

- Line 8 shows the base coverage component instance. *Note that the abstract component is instantiated.*

5.7.1.3 Step 3: Create Abstract Component in build_phase()

The listing below shows the component in the build_phase. Note that this component is an abstract component that cannot be created by the factory.

Listing 5.8: Create Abstract Component in Build Phase

```
27
28     // Instantiating the coverage class. This  should  never  work  because
29     // wb_cov_base is an abstract component
30     cov = wb_cov_base::type_id::create("cov",this);
31     // Scoreboard
32     sb = wb_scoreboard::type_id::create("sb",this);
```

- Line 30 shows the base coverage component instance being created.

5.7.1.4 Step 4: Connect Abstract Component in connect_phase()

Listing 5.9: Abstract Component Connection in Environment

```
36 function void wb_env_env::connect_phase(uvm_phase phase);
37     super.connect_phase(phase);
38     master_agent.mast_mon.mon_analysis_port.connect(cov.cov_export);
39     master_agent.mast_mon.mon_analysis_port.connect(sb.
           actual_wb_transaction_fifo.analysis_export);
40     slave_agent.slv_mon.mon_analysis_port.connect(sb.
           expected_wb_transaction_fifo.analysis_export);
41 endfunction: connect_phase
```

- Line 38 shows the base coverage component instance being created. Note that there are NO covergroups in this base instance.

5.7.1.5 Step 5. Create the Override Class

.

Listing 5.10: Create Override Class

```
20 class wb_env_cov extends wb_cov_base;
21     `uvm_component_utils(wb_env_cov)
22
23     covergroup cg_trans @(cov_event);
24         coverpoint tr.kind;
25         coverpoint tr.address {
26     bins low = {[0:10]};
27     bins mid = {[10:100]};
28     bins high = {[100:$]};
29         }
30         coverpoint tr.lock ;
31         coverpoint tr.status;
32         coverpoint tr.num_wait_states {
33     bins legal[] = {[0:15]};
34     illegal_bins ib = {[16:$]};
35         }
36
37     endgroup: cg_trans
38
```

```
39
40    function new(string name, uvm_component parent);
41       super.new(name,parent);
42       cg_trans = new;
43       analysis_export = new("Coverage Analysis",this);
44    endfunction: new
45
46 endclass: wb_env_cov
```

The above listing shows the creation of the covergroup definition and its creation utilizing the capabilities provided by the base class.

5.7.1.6 Step 6: Set up Override in Top-level Testbench

Listing 5.11: Instance of Abstract Component Override in Environment

```
7 module wb_env_tb_mod;
8     import uvm_pkg::*;
9     import wb_tests::*;
10
11
12    typedef wb_transaction_ext actual_transaction_packet;
13    typedef wb_transaction base_transaction_packet;
14
15    string new_type;
16
17    // Declare interfaces
18    typedef virtual wb_master_if v_if1;
19    typedef virtual wb_slave_if v_if2;
20    initial begin
21       uvm_factory f = uvm_coreservice_t::get().get_factory() ;
22       uvm_cmdline_processor p = uvm_cmdline_processor::get_inst();
23       f.set_type_alias("BasePacket",wb_transaction::get_type());
24       f.set_type_override_by_type(wb_cov_base::get_type(),wb_env_cov::
             get_type());
25       void'(p.get_arg_value("+NEW_PACKET=",new_type));
26       if(new_type == "")
27          `uvm_fatal("MISSING_OVERRIDE","no override. test will fail")
28       else
29          f.set_type_override_by_name("BasePacket",new_type);
30       // Note that the above is equivalent to wb_transaction::type_id::
             set_type_override(wb_transaction_ext::get_type);
31       // The one difference is the use of a type alias name
32
33       uvm_config_db #(v_if1)::set(null,"uvm_test_top.env.master_agent","
             mst_if",wb_env_top_mod.mast_if);
34       uvm_config_db #(v_if2)::set(null,"uvm_test_top.env.slave_agent","
             slv_if",wb_env_top_mod.slave_if);
35       uvm_config_db #(bit) :: set(null,"env.slave_agent","is_active",1);
36       uvm_config_db #(bit) :: set(null,"env.master_agent","is_active",1);
37       run_test();
38    end
39
40 endmodule: wb_env_tb_mod
```

- Line 24 shows the base coverage component instance being overridden with the new type seen in Step 1 (Section 5.7.1.1). Note that the Listing above shows additional type aliasing features that are covered in Section 5.7.3.

There are many applications for this capability which allows for good object-oriented principles. You can design abstract components and agents with some base capabilities and create a company or project-specific library that is layered on top of UVM that you allow other component developers and verification engineers to use.

5.7.2 Abstract Classes

Abstract classes are classes with the virtual keyword in the declaration. Abstract classes are a new feature that is supported by the factory. Previously, you could not register abstract classes with the factory.

Listing 5.12: Abstract transaction Class

```
11
12 virtual class wb_transaction extends uvm_sequence_item;
13    `uvm_object_abstract_utils(wb_transaction)
```

You can extend this class to make a concrete class, as shown below.

Listing 5.13: Abstract transaction Class Concrete

```
48 class wb_transaction_ext extends wb_transaction;
49
50    constraint supported {
51       next_cycle == CLASSIC;
52       kind == READ || kind == WRITE;
53    }
```

Study the wb_transaction_ext class in the download. Since the explanations are repetitive, we have not shown the complete listing.

5.7.3 Type Aliasing

Type Aliasing is a new powerful feature of the IEEE version. Previously you could only use type name used during factory registration for overrides. the type alias capability allows you to use a different string type name in factory overrides/creates other than the original type name. Refer to Listing 5.11 for explanation below

- Line 23 sets the wb_transaction to a type alias of "BasePacket".
- Line 25 uses the command line processor to get the argument value of NEW_PACKET from the command line.
- Line 29 now sets a type override of the "BasePacket" with the new type.

Recognize that this capability is incredibly powerful. You can create typedef's of parameterized classes in your environment and give them a name. You can then use that name in the command line processor, just like the example above, and create an extremely customizable, flexible environment that you control from the command line.

Chapter 6

Reporting Infrastructure

This chapter provides an overview of the various features in the UVM reporting mechanism before delving into how you can control reporting from the simulation using practical examples. Too little information in messages forces you to continue adding messages until they clutter up the log file. Too much information makes it difficult to see what is going on. In any simulation, concise is essential for messaging.

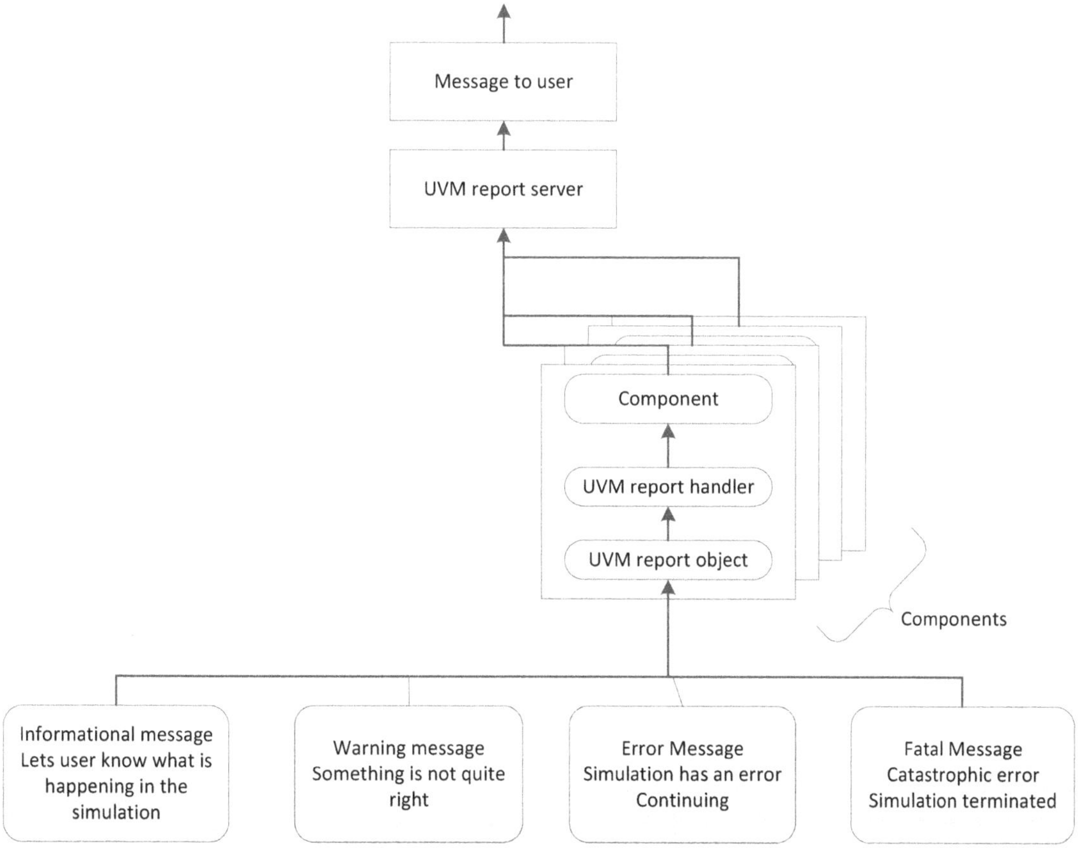

Fig. 6.1: Reporting Subsystem Overview

Figure 6.1 shows the reporting subsystem. Various uvm_report objects send their messages to the report handler. The report handler looks at the message and determines if any action is appropriate to the message that it receives. Once the relevant action is determined, the handler performs the action and forwards the message object to the global report server. The report server is a centralized class object that is instantiated by the uvm_coreservice. Earlier versions of UVM had this class as a static instance. However, in UVM 1.2 and beyond, this report server is user-replaceable.

Each UVM component contains a report handler. This report handler contains the configuration of how messages are processed and the actions that take place when the message is generated. Each component by default comes with a configuration and can be independently configured from other components in the simulation. This infrastructure is also made available to dynamically generated uvm_object based classes.

All uvm_components derive from the uvm_report_object class. By creating an interface to the UVM reporting facility through the uvm_report_object class, components provide many possible actions that are performed once messages are generated. The uvm_report_handler class does the actual heavy lifting. It interfaces with a global uvm_report_server class that processes and issues the messages as seen in the following sections.

Figure 6.1 also shows different kinds of messages obtained in a UVM environment. These messages are issued in response to different types of events happening in the UVM simulation. Some of the messages are capable of terminating the simulation by calling $finish() while others can warn you or inform of events that have occurred. Each of the messages may be called with a method or a macro as shown in Table 6.4.

Rule 6.0.0:   *You must issue all simulation messages from a UVM testbench through the reporting infrastructure.*

Doing so will allow you to leverage debug tool capabilities as well.

6.1 Elements of a UVM Report

Every report in UVM has a severity specification, a source specification, a timestamp, a verbosity specification, a component specification, an ID string, and the textual message itself. It can optionally include the filename and line number from which the message came. A report is created by the component or object and is processed by the report handler. All the reports vary depending on the application but contain the essential ingredients listed in Figure 6.2.

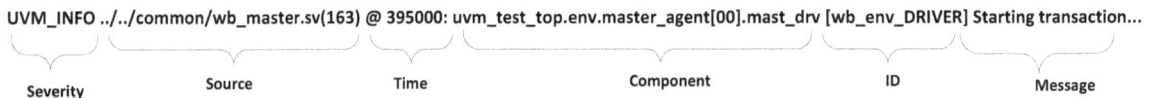

Fig. 6.2: Elements of A UVM Report

- A *Severity* specification that indicates the importance of the message to the simulation. Depending on the severity of the event, action is taken by the simulator. See Section 6.1.1.

- *Source:* The location from which the report was issued. If the predefined macros, `__FILE__ and `__LINE__ are specified, the output contains file information.

- A *Verbosity* specification that indicates WHEN the message is issued. If the message is at a higher verbosity than the simulation is configured for, then the message is not processed. This feature is useful in controlling the messaging so that one sees the minimal output in normal conditions and can change the verbosity to get more detailed output when needed. See Section 6.1.2.

- *Component:* This field tells you which component *instance* is issuing the message.

- *ID:* A unique id for the report or report group. This is user-defined and can be used to enable filtering. It is a string that you can use to tag the report any way you want.

- *Message:* This contains the actual message. If combining multiple points of information, it is essential that the message is formatted as a single string using $sformatf() or other methods.

- A *Handling* specification which dictates what should happen when the message is generated. (not shown)

- The *Time* is the simulation time at which the message was issued.

6.1.1 Severity Specification

Every message can be one of the following categories depending on what it means in the simulation:

- An **INFORMATIONAL** message that tells you what is going on. Typically, these messages are used to report the progress of events in the simulation.

- A **WARNING** message, This provides a warning to you saying something of importance is happening in the simulation. Example: A component finds that the value of a setting is outside the allowed ranges, and it has chosen to ignore it.

- An **ERROR** message. This tells you that an error occurred in the simulation. An example of this is when a component receives a bad transaction or somehow hits an internal error due to an unexpected condition.

- A **FATAL** message. This tells you that the simulation was terminated. This sort of message is usuall used when the verification environment experiences a catastrophic failure.

Rule 6.1.0:   *When failure occurs, messages use the `uvm_warning(), `uvm_error() or `uvm_fatal() macros.*

Table 6.4 shows the various methods and macros available to you in the reporting subsystem. Upon observation, one recognizes that the macros form a "convenience layer" on top of the methods provided. Users wishing for fine grain control can choose to implement the methods over the macros in their simulations.

Rule 6.1.1:   *Use `uvm_info macros instead of the uvm_report_info method() to take advantage of the check.*

Recommendation 6.1.0:   *Issue Informational messages using the `uvm_info() macro at the appropriate verbosity*

String processing is expensive in any simulator. When using uvm_info, to reduce the processing overhead associated with filtered out messages, a check is made against the report's verbosity setting and the action for the id/severity pair before any string formatting is performed.

6.1.2 Verbosity Settings

During the development of an agent or debugging, it may be quite desirable to have a high level of verbosity to debug what is going on. At other times in the component's lifecycle, a minimal output may be desired. Typically, in any simulation, you may want to simulate with minimal verbosity until a problem arises if the component is being used at higher levels. By default, UVM supplies for the following verbosity settings:

Table 6.1: UVM Verbosity Settings

Setting	Valid	Description
UVM_NONE	0	Use this for messages that should not be masked
UVM_LOW	100	Use this for higher priority messages
UVM_MEDIUM	200	Use this for messages that are normal
UVM_HIGH	300	Use this for a higher verbosity
UVM_FULL	400	Higher verbosity
UVM_DEBUG	500	Use this for debugging. All messages are shown when you choose this.

Recommendation 6.1.1:   *Use UVM_DEBUG with care. All UVM library messages are shown at this verbosity, and you may have a hard time sorting through the messages.*

Any component message configured with a verbosity setting higher than the setting configured is immediately issued. The default verbosity for any simulation can be set with a runtime switch. A good example of this is shown in Section 21.9.1

(i) *To prevent bugs from being hidden by verbosity settings, WARNINGS, ERROR and FATAL messages ignore any verbosity settings and are displayed unless a specific action called UVM_NO_ACTION is set in the report_handler or the testbench. Note that if a warning, error or fatal is demoted to an info message using the uvm_report_catcher, then, verbosity is considered*

6.1.3 Handling Specification

Once a report is generated, you must decide what to do with the generated report. Many actions are possible. For example: sending it to a file, incrementing a counter, calling a callback method, or even stopping the simulation. These actions are controlled by the UVM_ACTION specification that determines what to do with the report. When a particular message occurs of a specific severity or id type, many report handling actions are possible. UVM defines six types of actions as can be seen in the Table 6.3

These action types can be OR-ed together to enable more than one action. By default, the severity levels are configured to perform the following actions:

UVM_NO_ACTION	Do not take any action. Just leave the report as it is without causing any behavior changes to the simulation.
UVM_DISPLAY	Send report to the standard output
UVM_LOG	Assuming that a log has been set up, send the report to the specified log file (note that this is not the standard out, but an actual file on the filesystem. If a log has not been set up, the behavior is unspecified.
UVM_COUNT	increment report counter that is built into the report handler.
UVM_EXIT	Terminate the simulation by calling $finish
UVM_STOP	End the current phase and call $stop. Note that your phasing etc. is broken at this point.

Table 6.2: Various Report Actions

Any choice of which action to take is user and application-specific. One can choose to take more than one action by merely ORING the various actions as seen in Table 6.3

UVM_INFO	UVM_DISPLAY
UVM_WARNING	UVM_DISPLAY
UVM_ERROR	UVM_DISPLAY | UVM_COUNT
UVM_FATAL	UVM_DISPLAY | UVM_EXIT
UVM_INFO	UVM_DISPLAY
UVM_WARNING	UVM_DISPLAY
UVM_ERROR	UVM_DISPLAY | UVM_COUNT
UVM_FATAL	UVM_DISPLAY | UVM_EXIT

Table 6.3: Report Actions

Recommendation 6.1.2: *Do not use UVM_NO_ACTION configurations deep inside the components.*

These settings become hard to find in large environments with many agents.

Rule 6.1.2: *Keep all reporting overrides in a central location where they can be quickly referred to and audited in the base test or the top-level testbench.*

This rule is simply one of good organization. When you have a large testbench, having all the rules put in one place makes things easier. Contemplate the alternative: *Repeated compile and debug until you find all the overrides.*

The UVM_COUNT action has special behavior. If UVM_COUNT is set, a report issue counter is maintained in the report server. Once this count reaches the max_quit_count, then the die method is called.

If the UVM_EXIT action is set, then the die method is called, and the simulation ends. By default, max_quit_count is set to 0, meaning that no upper limit is set for UVM_COUNT reports.

To set an upper limit, use set_report_max_quit_count defined in the uvm_report_object class.

In UVM 1.2, all UVM Core messages are routed through the reporting subsystem compared to UVM 1.1. UVM 1.2 contains an object-based mechanism with an ability to add values/objects. You can record messages to some other storage separate from your simulation log. In addition, there has been a change in UVM 1.2 messaging to allow all C based messages from the UVM core to use the reporting subsystem.

The UVM_CALL_HOOK and associated methods have been removed both from UVM 1.2 and the IEEE standard. They are deprecated in UVM 1.2 Use the report handler (see section 6.2.4) to control messaging.

6.1.4 API Presented By UVM Components to Generate Messages

UVM supplies many macros and methods to allow you to generate messages at appropriate times and the appropriate verbosity. The Table 6.4 lists the various methods and macros. You can use either the method or the macro. **Just note that the `uvm_fatal and `uvm_error macros and their associated methods do not have a verbosity setting.** The macros enforce a verbosity setting of UVM_NONE for warnings, errors, and fatal so that they cannot be accidentally turned off.

Rule 6.1.3:   *Always use verbosity UVM_NONE for uvm_report_fatal(), uvm_report_error() and uvm_report_warning() methods. This ensures that command line verbosity does not mask issues.*

Table 6.4: Methods and Macros for UVM reports

Method	Macro
uvm report info(string id, string message, int verbosity level=100, string file-name="", int line=0);	`uvm info(string ID, string MSG,verbosity);
uvm report warning(string id, string message, int verbosity level=100, string filename="", int line=0);	`uvm warning(string ID, string MSG,verbosity);
uvm report fatal(string id, string message, string filename="", int line=0);	`uvm fatal(string ID, string MSG);
uvm report error(string id, string message, string filename="", int line=0);	`uvm error(string ID, string MSG);

A uvm_component derives from uvm_report_object, so all the reporting functions are available inside components. The uvm_component extends the reporting functions so that they can hierarchically traverse a component and all of its sub-components to set the reporting behavior. Section 8.1.4 lists the various reporting facilities that are available with the uvm_component class.

Actions can be assigned using the set_report_*_action functions (see section 8.1.4 for uvm_report_object classes). The other method uses a callback in the report server where the messages can be caught and demoted/promoted, etc. Some of these functions are used in examples in Section 21.5.

UVM_FATAL in the `uvm_fatal macro does not have a verbosity parameter. However, in the uvm_report_fatal() method, there is a verbosity parameter that you pass in. Be aware of this difference between the two.

Recommendation 6.1.3:   *Most debugging tools now support UVM. Considerable time is spent in debug of testbenches. Use the uvm_report macros or methods for logging. This will allow you to leverage debug capabilities.*

Rule 6.1.4:   *Avoid the use of $display(), $monitor, $strobe() in UVM testbenches*

You cannot use the built-in UVM mechanisms to control the output of the above constructs. In addition, you may find that these messages appear in a different spot in your log file (albeit at the same timestamp), which may make your debugging difficult.

Recommendation 6.1.4:   *Provide unique strings to quickly identify the area from which your testbenches are issuing messages*

I recommend the use of unique strings simply because you can search for these strings in your testbench and identify where the messages are coming from. If you have a small testbench, it may not appear as a problem; however, large testbenches are usually created by top-level chip integrators who may lack familiarity with your code. This practice will make debug a lot simpler.

Recommendation 6.1.5:   *Use the macros. They provide checking if the message needs to be printed before engaging in expensive string manipulations.*

This is a performance recommendation.

6.2 Reporting Subsystem - Practical Applications

Issuing messages from a simulation is easy. All you have to do is call the appropriate method/macro with the right arguments, and UVM does the rest.

Listing 6.1: Simple Reporting Example

```
1 module top;
2
3     import uvm_pkg::*;
4     `include "uvm_macros.svh"
5
6     class test extends uvm_test;
7
8         `uvm_component_utils(test)
9
10        function new(string name, uvm_component parent = null);
11            super.new(name, parent);
12        endfunction
13
14        virtual task run_phase(uvm_phase phase);
15            phase.raise_objection(this);
16
17            `uvm_info("INFO1", "first info message", UVM_LOW)
18            uvm_report_info("INFO2", "second info message", UVM_LOW);
19
20            `uvm_error("ERROR1", "first error message")
21            // Note that verbosity below ignored
22            uvm_report_error("ERROR2", "second error message",UVM_LOW);
23
24            `uvm_warning("WARNING1", "first warning message")
25            uvm_report_warning("WARNING2", "second warning message",
                    UVM_LOW);
26
27            // Only one of these two.  verbosity ignored + sim dies
28            `uvm_fatal("FATAL1", "first fatal message")
29            // uvm_report_fatal("FATAL2", "second warning message");
30
31            phase.drop_objection(this);
32        endtask
```

```
33     endclass
34
35     initial
36          run_test();
37
38 endmodule
```

In the above listing

- Line 6 begins the definition of the class test in module top
- Line 17 and 18 show the `uvm_info macro and uvm_report_info method being used to issue messages
- Lines 20 - 22 generate error messages
- Lines 24,25 show the methods and macro calls for warnings
- Only one of Line 28 or 29 should be active as they terminate the simulation

The previous sections discussed the reporting subsystem components in quite some detail. All the practical examples are available as a part of Chapter 21.

6.2.1 Controlling Reporting from the Command Line

It is possible to control the messaging from the command line of a UVM simulation. Add additional command line options to the simulation as shown below.

Listing 6.2: Altering verbosity specific Components

```
./simv -l uvm_set_inst_verbosity.dat +uvm_set_verbosity=uvm_test_top.env.
    master_agent\[00\].mast_drv,_ALL_,UVM_DEBUG,run +UVM_TESTNAME=
    wb_conmax_flat_seq_test
```

In the above example, only **one** of several components is at a higher verbosity. See the examples in Chapter 21.9, which provides details on how to quickly control the simulation from the command line.

6.2.2 Controlling Verbosity

Global controls are available to control all the components in the simulation. These controls affect every single component in the simulation.

> +UVM_VERBOSITY: allows you to specify the initial verbosity for all components.
> +UVM_MAX_QUIT_COUNT: allows users to change max quit count for the report server.

In addition to controlling the verbosity from the command line for all the components in the simulation, UVM supplies a facility to set the verbosity for a specific component. This mechanism allows you to control verbosity, action, and severity on a per-component basis. ***Note that the Wildcard for id argument not supported in UVM.***

> +uvm_set_verbosity=<comp>,<id>,<verbosity>,<phase>
> +uvm_set_verbosity=<comp>,<id>,<verbosity>,time,<time>

See Section 21.9 for usage. You can choose to set the ACTION configuration in the report handler by using the +uvm_set_action. In the example below, the UVM_ACTION is overridden so that the error is not processed.

```
+uvm_set_action=<comp>,<id>,<severity>,<action>
```
Example:
```
+uvm_set_action=uvm_test_top.env.*,_ALL_,UVM_ERROR,UVM_NO_ACTION
```

In a similar vein, one can set the severity on a particular component. The example below demotes the BAD_CRC error to a warning.

```
+uvm_set_severity=<comp>,<id>,<current severity>,<new severity>
Example:
+uvm_set_severity=uvm_test_top.*,BAD_CRC,UVM_ERROR,UVM_WARNING
```

6.2.3 Logging Messages to a File

You may sometimes choose to have messages from a certain component. In the test below from the wb_conmax chapter in Section 21.6, messages from a scoreboard are logged into a specific output file [1].

Listing 6.3: Selectively capturing messages from component

```
1   class wb_conmax_report_file_test extends wb_conmax_base_test;
2
3     UVM_FILE file_master;
4
5     `uvm_component_utils(wb_conmax_report_file_test)
6
7     function new(string name, uvm_component parent);
8       super.new(name, parent);
9       file_master = $fopen("master_output","w");
10    endfunction
11
12    virtual function void build_phase(uvm_phase phase);
13      super.build_phase(phase);
14    endfunction
15
16    virtual function void end_of_elaboration_phase(uvm_phase phase);
17      super.end_of_elaboration_phase(phase);
18      //env.set_report_default_file_hier("SCOREBOARD_MASTER",UVM_LOG);
19      env.set_report_default_file_hier(file_master);
20      env.conmax_scbd.set_report_id_file_hier("SCOREBOARD_MASTER",
             file_master);
21      env.conmax_scbd.set_report_id_action("SCOREBOARD_MASTER",
             UVM_DISPLAY|UVM_LOG);
22
23    endfunction
```

Listing 6.3 shows an example of creation of a file to log messages.

- Line 3 shows the definition of the UVM_FILE in the test. This filehandle is opened on Line 9.

- Line 20 shows the use of set_report_default_file_hier sets all the subcomponents of the test class to write to the file.

Note that some flexible options are available in the reporting subsystem to allow you to record only WARNINGS or ERRORs into a file. We do not cover them here, but you can very easily look them up in the LRM.

---

[1] By just looking at the example, It is sometimes hard for you to grasp the context and I understand that. The complete example in the correct context is shown in Section 21.6. Look at the practical applications part of this book for more ways to exercise the reporting subsystem.

6.2.4 Demoting Reports From One Level to Another

You may want to catch a report from a specific component and alter it. An example would be an uvm agent that is producing errors in a simulation, and these errors may not be relevant to the test at hand. Alternatively, you may want to promote the message from any one agent to become an error. To do this, you need a report catcher that can intercept the messages. See Section 21.5 for an example.

Note that many of the methods use string comparisons. These are inherently expensive in any simulator. If you have many messages being intercepted in a large simulation, It may be worth your time to analyze the agents and the messages issued to determine if the verification effort would benefit from re-architecting some of the messages.

Recommendation 6.2.0: *For maximum performance, use care when designing both messages and the processing that happens when using a reporting callback.*

6.2.5 Catching Reports and Changing Them

It is possible to intercept the reports when components issue them and use callbacks to make changes to the report. For example, You may want to alter the content of a particular report or make changes in a way that they are logged to a file. See Section 21.5 for a collection of complete examples on how to change reports by using the callbacks. There has been some cleanup on the messaging side for UVM 1.2:

- The reporting has been made completely object-based with the ability to add values/objects. You can record messages to some other storage.

- All UVM core messages now routed through uvm messaging,

- There are some new add-on message macros uvm_*_begin, uvm_*_end that you can use to compose your message.

6.2.6 Using Reporting Infrastructure with Assertions and Modules

The reporting infrastructure itself is extremely flexible. You can use this infrastructure inside an assertion as well. One of the advantages of doing so is that you can use the tools built for UVM for filtering. You may apply all the techniques provided in the earlier sections to catch/demote/change these messages.

After importing the uvm package, the methods/macros can be called from Verilog modules to help users ensure uniformity and other filtering capabilities provided by various tools when running a simulation. A simple example is provided below.

Listing 6.4: Using Assertions with the reporting methods

```
1
2 import uvm_pkg::*;
3 `include "uvm_macros.svh"
4
5 default clocking @ (posedge clk);
6 endclocking
7
8 property p_rd_reset;
9    (!rst_n |=> data_out == 8'd0);
10 endproperty : p_rd_reset
11
12 a_p_rd_reset : assert property (p_rd_reset)
13    else
14      `uvm_error("SVA", "data_out is not 0 after reset")
15
16 property p_wr_rd_val;
17    (wr_rd |-> wr_rd_valid);
18 endproperty : p_wr_rd_val
19
20 a_p_wr_rd_val : assert property (p_wr_rd_val)
```

```
21   else
22     `uvm_error("SVA", "Protocl violation! wr_rd is set HIGH without valid
          ")
```

In Listing 6.4:

- Lines 8-10 define a property p_rd_reset

- Line 14 shows how to issue a uvm_error from the above property

- Lines 16-18 define another property p_wr_rd_val

- Line 22 shows how to issue errors for the same property

6.3 Behavior Differences between UVM 1.2 and IEEE 1800.2

Verbosity default was UVM_LOW for uvm_report_error and UVM_NONE for `uvm_error. This means that the macro and the method were inconsistent in behavior. Depending on the source, uvm_report_server would filter errors and warnings if their verbosity was above global verbosity. This is not the behavior described in the UVM 1.2 Documentation.

To introduce consistency, the verbosity default is now UVM_NONE for all errors. This means that errors and warnings are never filtered. The verbosity only comes into the picture if you demote the errors and warnings to INFO.

UVM
IEEE

IEEE 1800.2 still shows uvm_report_warning as defaulting to UVM_MEDIUM however, the macro `uvm_warning defaults to UVM_NONE The Accellera implementation tracks the standard in this regard. **Expect changes in the next revision of the standard and implementation**.

The use of a report catcher described in Section 6.2.4 introduces some additional complexity since you can see the difference only if a catcher demotes the WARNING to INFO. Also, the following cases are something you will need to factor in when moving from UVM-1.2 to IEEE 1800.2.

- The uvm_report_error() with default verbosity in uvm 1.2 was UVM_LOW. If you had run with UVM_NONE verbosity, you would have suppressed an error that you must debug.

- If you used uvm_report_error() with default verbosity, had a catcher demote it to info, and then run with UVM_NONE verbosity, the message you were suppressing is shown in the log.

- If you used anything other than UVM_NONE with uvm_report_error(), you now see an additional error.

6.4 Exercises for Further Exploration

Please use the example in <example_home>/UVM_Quickstart/UVM_TestBench for these assignments. A complete environment is available for you to get started with minimal effort. You need to make changes to the Makefile

1. Add a report line to the report_phase to report how many transactions occurred through the DUT. You can do this by implementing a static counter that keeps track of transactions generated, and then issue a `uvm_info message with a special ID of your choosing.

Chapter 7

Configuration and Resource Databases

When you are building a testbench, you inevitably run into a situation where you may need to store values from a class object and pass it on to another. You could choose to write your own database, but that would be inefficient. The UVM Configuration Database is a database that provides you with an API to store and retrieve values easily. This database is built-in and is available as soon as UVM starts up. All you must do is use it!

As an example: typical testbenches in modern environments usually need configuration information. This information can range from simple things like the number of masters/slaves, number of transactions, a maximum number of errors, etc. Depending on the type of information and architecture of the testbench, information could be passed into the test environment using many methods. Figure 7.1 illustrates where the configuration information in a testbench is typically used. The configuration information may be present in many other locations as well.

In the case of earlier non-class based methodologies, many approaches used a configuration file or task which was placed in the testbench, which would make hierarchical references to the various elements in the testbench and DUT.

When the size of the design or testbench increases, such an approach quickly breaks down since the amount of effort to maintain it rapidly grows. In other words, a hierarchical approach is simply not scalable. Given the dynamic nature of the class-based testbenches, a component may not even exist in a certain configuration, further requiring work on the part of the testbench writer to make sure that the testbench is free from configuration errors.

One problem with dynamically created testbenches that use cross-module references or other approaches is that there is no way a test can set values for components that don't yet exist. If you consider an example of a slave agent in Chapter 2, the slave agent is not built until later in the build_phase after the test has come into existence. If the testbench is a little more sophisticated, With random configurations, it may not even be created at all. Another possibility is that the slave agent may be replaced by a factory override, which does not respect the values configured. This implies that a test cannot make a hierarchical reference to the properties of the agent. One solution is to have conditional references or use some argument parsing, but this can be quite difficult to maintain. The answer, therefore, is to build a repository not tied to the UVM component hierarchy that stores values {string, value} pairs in some form.

As the same information must be shared amongst many components built at different times, a central repository is essential. This central repository must be easily accessible and have a simple to use API, which is scalable. Another requirement is that the database should be independent of the hierarchy where it is placed.

Rule 7.0.0: *Any configuration for a sequence should come from the config_db.*[1]

7.1 Resource Database Infrastructure

Looking at the configuration problem, you realize that testbenches and test environments typically need data to configure themselves. This information usually has to be shared across many parts of a testbench. This information sharing is done by using resources. In UVM, resources are implemented using parameterized containers since the type of data can vary from application to application. Since the containers are parameterized, they can hold any data defined by SystemVerilog

---

[1] There are some examples of this in Part 4 of this book.

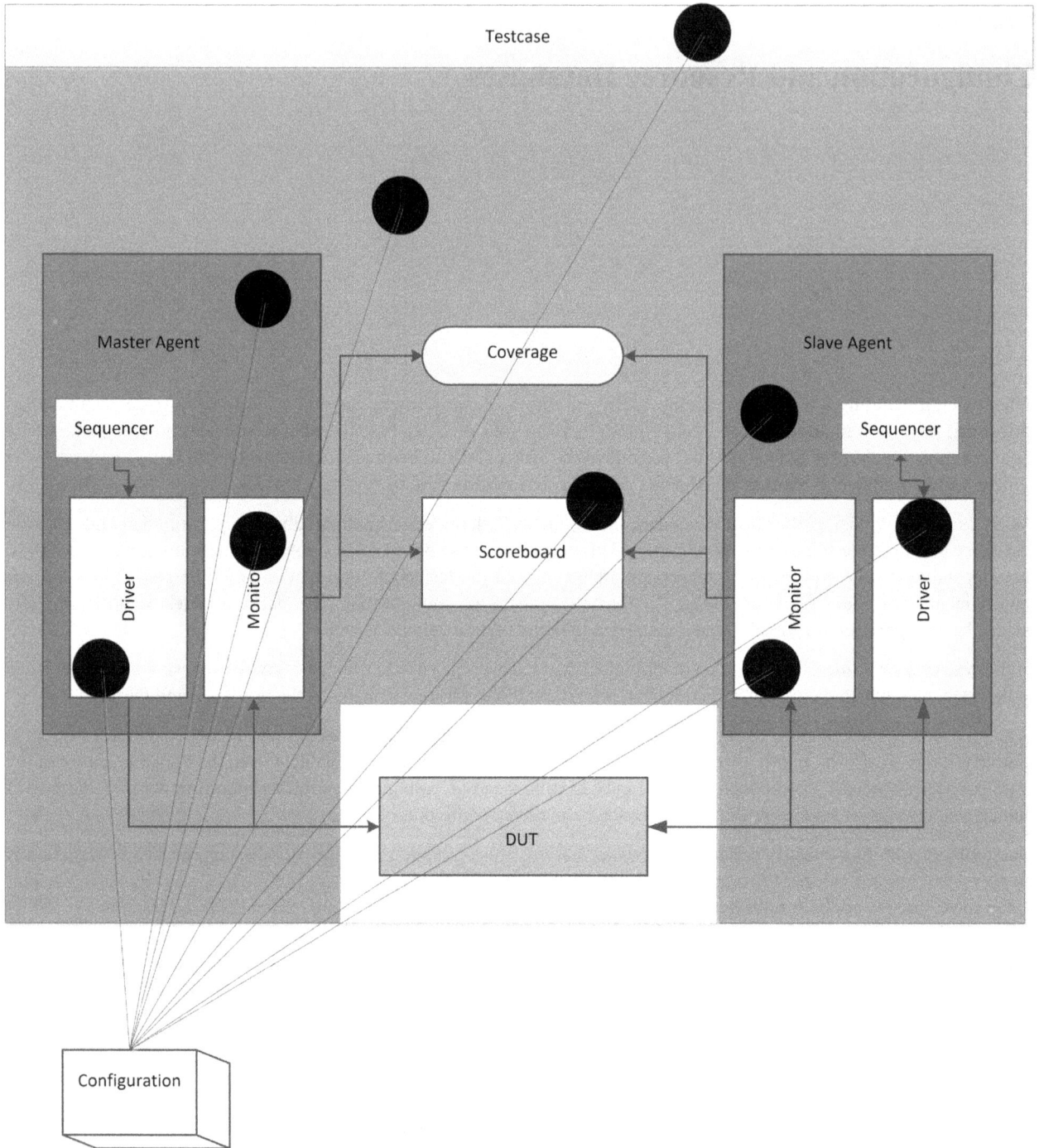

Fig. 7.1: A Testbench Needing Configuration

data types. A typical resource could contain scalar objects, and class handles, queues, lists, or virtual interfaces or any other data that the user may choose.

Each resource has a name, a value, and a set of scopes over which it is visible. A scope is a hierarchical entity or a context. The name is a string which is broken up into multiple elements separated by dots (.) which act as the separation operator. Each of the elements represents a portion of the hierarchy. Resources are stored using scoping information in a globally accessible database that implements tables for both names and types. The entries are made in both tables. As a result, one can get a resource by looking it up either by name or by type.

A regular expression can represent any set of resources. The resource is returned if the scope presented to the UVM lookup function is within the set of scopes.

The uvm_config_db and uvm_resource_db classes are convenience wrappers that access the same underlying database. Hence, it is possible to write to the database using uvm_config_db::set() and retrieve from the database using uvm_resource_db::read_by_name().

There are two different convenience wrappers because hierarchy context and information may be relevant to the setting stored in the database. When a hierarchical setting is involved, it is recommended to use uvm_config_db. If there is no hierarchical context, one may use uvm_resource_db. However, it is a bit harder to use, and engineers usually default to the config_db.

7.2 Config Database Infrastructure

(i) The configuration and resource databases are used extensively throughout this book. Look at Section 2 where the set() and get() calls are used to set various objects

The configuration database comes with many functions allowing you to set the values of a resource in the database.

```
function bit read_by_name( input string scope, input string name, inout T val, input
uvm_object accessor = null )
static function bit write_by_name( input string scope, input string name, T val, input
uvm_object accessor = null)
static function bit write_by_type( input string scope, input T val, input uvm_object
accessor = null )
static function bit read_by_type( input string scope, inout T val, input uvm_object
accessor = null )
static function void set( input string scope, input string name, T val, input
uvm_object accessor = null )
```

Y The uvm_resource_db::read_by_name and uvm_resource_db::read_by_type methods are defined as having an *output* argument *val* of type *T*. This broke backwards compatibility. As such, the Accellera implementation kept the arguments as *inout* to avoid issues. The correct functions are listed above. Expect changes in IEEE-2020 version of the LRM, not the implementation.

The read_by_name() function locates a resource by name and scope and reads its value returning it through the output argument val. The return value is a bit that indicates whether or not the read was successful. The write_by_name() function writes a resource by name and scope and value into the resource database. The return value is a bit that indicates whether or not the read was successful. A similar operation is performed by the write_by_type and read_by_type functions. The set() function create a new resource, write a value to it, and set it into the database using name and scope as the lookup parameters.

The convenience functions in the config_db API provide the following functions:

```
static function bit get(uvm_component cntxt,string inst_name,string field_name,inout T
    value)
static function void set( uvm_component cntxt, string inst_name, string field_name, T
    value)
static function bit exists(uvm_component cntxt, string inst_name, string field_name,
    bit spell_chk =0)
```

The function get() obtains the value from the config_db for field_name in inst_name using cntxt, which is the instance name as the starting search point. inst_name is an explicit instance name relative to cntxt and may be null if searching across scopes.

The set() function does the inverse, setting the value in the database, for instance, _name and field_name. The full path is added to the context when the value is set and is used to evaluate precedence.

The exists() function searches the config_db for the values pointed to by the context, the inst_name and field_name and returns 1 if it finds the value or returns 0 otherwise.

Listing 7.1: A Simple Config DB Example

```
1 module top;
2     import uvm_pkg::*;
3     import my_env_pkg::*;
4
5     my_env topenv;
6
7
8     logic unsigned [4095:0] my_int;
9     string my_string;
10
11    int     B_val;
12    int     inst1_val;
13
14    initial begin
15       //set configuration prior to creating the environment
16
17       uvm_config_db #(uvm_bitstream_t)::set(null,"topenv.inst1.u1", "v",
              30);
18       uvm_config_db #(uvm_bitstream_t)::set(null,"topenv.instB.u1", "v",
              10);
19
20       //Get configuration prior to creating the environment to make sure
              it's ok.
21
22       uvm_config_db #(uvm_bitstream_t)::get(null,"topenv.inst1.u1", "v",
              inst1_val);
23       uvm_config_db #(uvm_bitstream_t)::get(null,"topenv.instB.u1", "v",
              B_val);
24       topenv = new("topenv", null);
25
26       run_test();
27
28    end
29
30 endmodule
```

It is worthwhile to note that the set_config_int versions have been replaced by their direct methods and deprecated in UVM 1.2. However, you will see their incarnations in the uvm_commandline_processor. They are quite useful!

7.3 Priority for Setting Values in the Database

Configuration functions are set up to manage automated fields automatically. If you want to store some values in the config_db other than an automated fields, you must write code to get it from the database. Observing the functions in the earlier section, we see that the functions for the name do accept wild cards and regular expression arguments.

The base class uvm_component is defined such that all configuration settings that are part of the automated fields from the macros are applied to the component. The apply_config_settings() function is implicitly called in the build_phase() of the component. This implies that for the settings to take effect, all the configuration settings must be available before this phase.

You must be aware that there is a built-in precedence algorithm. The precedence algorithm assigns configuration settings in a higher scope more weight over the ones in a lower scope by default. This allows configuration settings at the higher layers of the hierarchy to override those specified at the lower layers. Multiple settings at the same level are pushed into a queue. Hence, within the same scope, the last configuration setting matching a field takes precedence over any previous settings for the same field. Consider Figure 7.2 of a simple agent (AGT) instantiated in an environment (Env) which is in a test (Test) This agent AGT has a driver Drv which has a value for the number of wait_cycles. The default shown in the Figure shows the driver assigning a value of 2 for this property. The agent instantiates the driver. This driver has a default value of 2 for the wait_cycles property. The agent now assigns a value of 3 to the driver's wait_cycles property. This overrides the value of 2 set by the driver. The environment class, which now instantiates the agent, sets the value of the wait_cycles to 5 as a default. This overrides the value of 3 set by the agent which has overridden the default in the driver. The driver, when fully configured by the environment without a test specific setting now has a value of 5 for the wait_cycles.

In a specific test, the test instantiates the environment, and based on the test scenario, assigns a value of 10 for to wait_cycles of the driver. As you can see, the highest level of write wins, which is the desired result.

There are many other resources on the config_db and resource_db that supplement the explanation provided in this chapter. Mark Glasser's [10] and Vanessa Coopers paper [7] are noteworthy in this area.

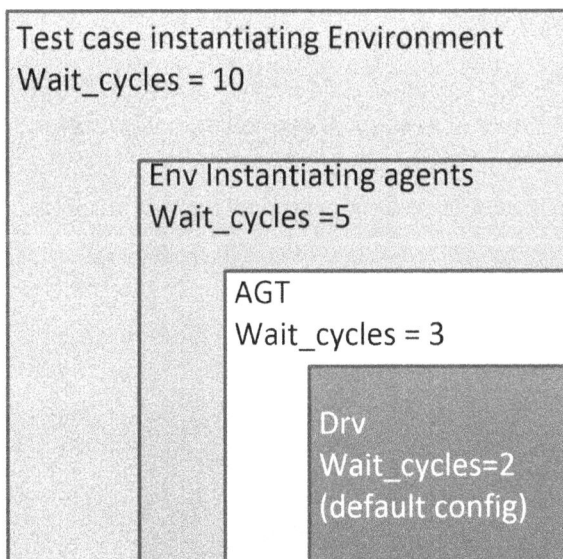

test	Env.AGT.DRV.wait_cycles	10
	AGT.DRV.wait_cycles	5
test.ENV.AGT	DRV.wait_cycles	3
Test.Env.AGT.DRV	DRV	2

Fig. 7.2: Order Of Precedence Of Config_db Settings

It is possible to alter the precedence of resources using the precedence member or by using the set_priority functions if the application demands it. A detailed walkthrough of the sequence of config_db calls and their ordering in a verification environment is presented in Section 21.3.

7.4 New Features in IEEE 1800.2

There are few changes to the config_db infrastructure between the UVM-1.2 version and the IEEE 1800.2 version with the notable deprecation of the set_config_int and set_config_string methods. Note that the command_line_processor arguments are still present. if you are migrating from UVM-1.1x to IEEE 1800.2, then you must note that the following are the changes you should make

set_config_string(...) => uvm_config_db#(string)::set
set_config_int(...) => uvm_config_db#(int)::set

Note that the Accellera implementation keeps the arguments as *inouts* to avoid backwards incompatibility problems.

```
static function bit uvm_resource_db::read_by_type(input string scope,
inout T val, input uvm_object accessor = null); static function bit
uvm_resource_db::read_by_name(input string scope, input string name, inout T val,
input uvm_object accessor = null);
```

7.5 Using Regular Expressions in UVM

The uvm_config_db and other API's in UVM can use regular expressions. This capability makes it easier for the user to perform operations on variables in the environment without having to specify everything explicitly. UVM uses the POSIX-Extended regular Expressions. Please See Chapter 18 for details on how to use regular expressions.

Regular expressions for *fields* are turned off in the 1.2 release of UVM for performance reasons. If you use it and suspect a performance problem, this is the first thing to check. Look at your simulation profile, and you should be able to narrow it down quickly.

Rule 7.5.0: *Recognize that using regular expressions can be expensive. Use them with care if you are concerned about performance.*

I recommend that you take the following approach when it comes to regular expressions in the configuration database:

1. If you are integrating a large environment and have many settings for which you don't know the path, use a regular expression to simplify your debugging.

2. Use the print() method once your simulation starts working to identify where the settings took effect. You can also use the +UVM_CONFIG_DB_TRACE command line option if your compiles are large and you do not want to spend a lot of time.

3. Replace the regular expression calls with a call that has the complete path name to the matching component/setting.

4. Ensure you save the regular expression pattern you replaced as a *commented line* in your code should you ever have to revisit it.

This approach will save you time in debug and later on in regressions also.

7.6 Debugging

The configuration database is very powerful! However, with regular expression support, some things can get difficult to spot if you have a complicated expression. The following tips can help you with your debugging.

- Code in a clear, lucid manner so that it is clear to other people who are debugging. Who knows where your code will be reused! There is a good chance that some time from now, you may have forgotten the code you wrote! It certainly happens to all of us!

- Using +UVM_CONFIG_DB_TRACE and +UVM_RESOURCE_DB_TRACE, one can usually spot the set and get calls for the component. You may need to post-process the output using a few *grep* calls to identify the relevant messages.

- Print the topology at the end of the build_phase(). That helps you determine if your regular expression is targeting the hierarchy properly once you examine the topology that is constructed.

- Use the built-in GUI debuggers available with many simulators. These debuggers are quite powerful. You can set a breakpoint at the point where the call is made, and also at the breakpoint where the settings happen and observe if the values are being set correctly,

The following common problems were observed during test development. You would do well to avoid some of these problems during your development.

- Typo in string for instance names.

- uvm_config_object::set() writes a null object during the wb_conmax examples.

- Wrong context starting points.

- Forgetting to call get() after calling set() in the tests.

- Missing super.build_phase(): as base methods did not get called.

7.7 Performance Tuning and Coding Guidelines

If you study the calls that are made to obtain a setting from the config_db, you realize that much work is done under the hood. A get or set operation performs multiple lookups before it sets/returns the value to the call. The UVM config_db is very flexible with string lookup at run-time, wildcards, priority, implicit gets, command line switches, and a 4096-bit 4-state integral value. Given the amount of code executed by the config_db, this can become a bottleneck. If this is indeed the case, simulating with a profiler can quickly point you to the source of the problem.

Recommendation 7.7.0: *Move all individual configuration variables into a class and then pass that handle to the config_db. Doing so clubs many settings into a single call. See Section 21.3 for an example.*

Rule 7.7.0: *DO NOT use a pattern for the name when doing a 'set'. The pattern becomes a regular expression.*

Rule 7.7.1: *Use unique names if possible in the set().*

Rule 7.7.2: *Use unique types so that the lookup can be minimized.*

Recommendation 7.7.1: *Remember that the implicit get mechanism, done in uvm_component::apply_config_settings() can be slow, unless you move most values into a configuration class.*

Recommendation 7.7.2: *To use UVM without any tool-specific overlay, define `UVM_NO_DPI*

Chapter 8

UVM Component Hierarchy

In RTL design or module based environments, module blocks define a fixed structure *before* the simulation runtime starts. In contrast, in a class-based environment, this restriction is removed. It now becomes possible to dynamically create objects *after* the simulation has started. This ability to create an environment and components at runtime provides a significant advantage and provides to tremendous flexibility in verification environment creation. A consistent approach is required during hierarchy creation to reuse the flexibility provided by UVM. This chapter discusses the UVM component hierarchy and the capabilities provided by the uvm component class and its derivative classes. Components developed in this chapter implement the Wishbone protocol described in [18] used in subsequent chapters. By the end of this chapter, you should be able to build all the components required for a UVM simulation.

Figure 8.1 presents the UVM component hierarchy, the primary uvm core uvm_object class is extended to form the uvm_report_object class that adds reporting infrastructure. The uvm_component class further extends the uvm_report_object class to provide hierarchy, phasing and other support as discussed below.

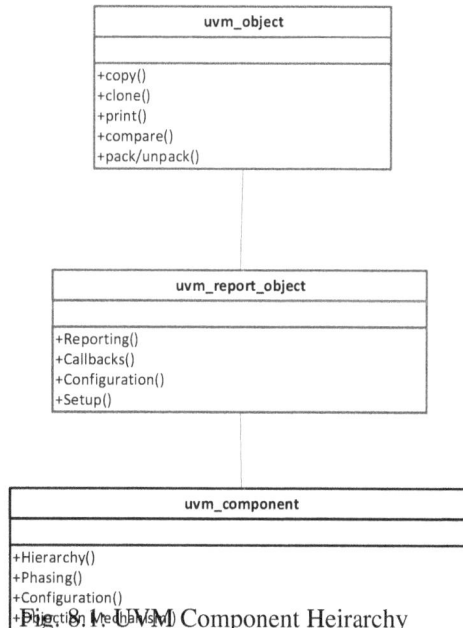

Figure 8.1 UVM Component Heirarchy

8.1 Overview of Capabilities Provided by UVM Component

The uvm_component classes provide capabilities that allow easy creation of components and other utilities that make it significantly easier to manage verification environments. Note that regularity and modularity are some of the essential features of any modern testbench. When we study Figure 8.1 above, we realize that the common class utilities derive from uvm_object. The uvm_report_object further provides messaging capabilities. The uvm_component class further derives from this class to provide the following capabilities:

- Hierarchy creation and management

- Communication Capabilities between components.

- Classes to provide Simulation Phasing

- Common messaging platform.

- Transaction Recording

- Factory interface

Sections 8.1.1 through 8.2 provide background information and the utilities available from the classes derived from uvm_component.

8.1.1 Construction and Hierarchy Management

UVM components are built for reuse and are self-contained. Self-containment indicates that each component built is independent of any values or settings not contained in its sub-hierarchy. This self-containment guideline ensures that each component is a complete unit thereby lending itself to reuse. The same self-containment guideline lends itself well to reuse with recursive construction.

Recursive construction provides a guideline as to how a testbench hierarchy is constructed. Each parent component builds only its children during the build_phase when components are created (See Chapter 13 for more information on the build_phase). The child components, in turn, create their child components that in turn create their children. In this manner, the entire hierarchy is created. To accomplish recursive construction, the build method of each component executes the following steps in their implementation:

1. Determine any local fields or fields needed by sub-components that require initialization and initialize them.

2. Create and initialize local configuration settings to determine hierarchy construction.

3. Create each subcomponent by calling the subcomponent's build method taking into account the configuration settings.

To manage the construction of objects in the environment, UVM supplies some functions to access the child components by either name or handle. The order in which the children are returned is determined by the underlying associative array that uses child component names as a key A few of these functions are listed below:

```
function new( string name, uvm_component parent);
function string get_name();
function string get_full_name();
function void set_name(string name);
function string (get_type_name();
function uvm_component (get_parent();
```

(i) Looking at the source code for uvm_component, it becomes evident that the names MUST be an exact match. Wildcards are NOT supported in these functions. If the name begins with a "." The search begins with the top-level component. Otherwise, otherwise, it looks in the current component.

The above method signatures showcase a string based hierarchy for objects. The string-based methods can be error-prone, and hence an object-based method is also available. The UVM library also provides a way to walk the hierarchy using several traversal functions:

```
function uvm_component get_child(string name);
function int get_first_child( ref string name);
function int get_next_child(ref string name);
function int get_num_children();
function int has_child(string name);
function uvm_component lookup(string name );
```

8.1.2 Component Configuration

The key to reusability is to ensure that each component follows the self-containment and recursive construction guidelines. Essentially, each component needs to be able to configure the structure and behavior of its subcomponent hierarchy. Since hierarchical creation is used to promote self-containment and reuse, any UVM component does not necessarily know the configuration values of children deep in its sub-hierarchy during its build phase. A separate mechanism is therefore provided to help provide configuration fields for values of components to support their construction. The following functions help you to get and set values to any component in the hierarchy.

```
uvm_config_db#(T)::set(uvm_component cntxt, string inst_name, string field_name, inout T
value)
uvm_config_db#(T)::get( uvm_component cntxt, string inst_name, string field_name, T
value)
```

The uvm_component class in its the build_phase() method retrieves configuration settings for a component instance. Using the build() function is mandatory for having the configuration settings for an instance to take effect. Hence, all configuration settings for a component instance must be applied by the time its function build() is called. The sub-hierarchy rooted in that instance also may obtain its configuration in this way.

- The argument *inst_name specified with each configuration function is assumed to be about the hierarchical path of the component from which it is called.*
- *Configuration settings in a higher scope take precedence over the ones in a lower scope by default. The reason for this ordering is to allow configuration parameters at the upper layers of the hierarchy to override those specified at the lower layers.*
- *Within the same scope, the last configuration setting matching a field takes precedence over previous settings for the same field. This was discussed in the previous chapter.*

See Section 7 and Section 21.3 where you will find some practical examples illustrating these concepts in greater detail.

8.1.3 Factory Interface

A set of helper functions that call the uvm_factory member functions with a simplified interface is available. These allow the user to create components quickly without having to go through much trouble to rewrite significant portions of the environment. Chapter 5 has a detailed discussion of the factory classes and the capabilities provided by the uvm_factory.

8.1.4 Reporting Interface

Components may need to emit messages during the simulation. These messages are passed through the report handler class described in Chapter 6. Components provide methods to configure the UVM report handler for a particular component and recursively for all of its children. The methods can apply to all reports of a particular severity, all reports with a matching ID or all reports whose severity and id both match. When there are overlapping conditions, reports with both ID and severity take precedence over reports where only the ID matches, and these in turn take precedence over reports where only the severity matches. Providing this reporting interface ensures that you can uniformly process component messages from various sources.

The following functions are made available to the user as a part of the reporting infrastructure. This reporting infrastructure ties into the central infrastructure for UVM described in Chapter 6.

```
set_report_id_verbosity_hier (string id, int verbosity)
set_report_severity_id_verbosity_hier (uvm_severity severity, string id, int verbosity)
set_report_severity_action_hier (uvm_severity severity, uvm_action action)
set_report_id_action_hier (string id, uvm_action action)
set_report_severity_id_action_hier (uvm_severity severity, string id, uvm_action action)
set_report_default_file_hier (uvm_FILE file)
set_report_severity_file_hier (uvm_severity severity, uvm_FILE file)
set_report_id_file_hier (string id, uvm_FILE file)
set_report_severity_id_file_hier (uvm_severity severity, string id, uvm_FILE file)
set_report_verbosity_level_hier (int verbosity)
```

The reports are written to a file previously opened (using $fopen) if the action is specified as UVM_LOG. The file descriptor used for writing can be selected according to the severity or id of the message. A number of examples of using these functions are illustrated in Section 21.6.

8.2 Macros Provided for UVM Components

Section 4.5 provided UVM macros for the uvm_object class. The utility macros greatly simplify the task of using the components in UVM. The utility macros generate factory methods and implement get_utility() macros. These macros generate factory methods and the get_type_name() function for a component. (See Utility Macros for details.)

```
`uvm_component_utils(TYPE)
or
`uvm_component_utils_begin(TYPE)
`uvm_field_*(ARG,FLAG) ...
...
`uvm_component_utils_end
```

Fields specified in field automation macros are automatically handled correctly in copy, compare, pack, unpack, record, print, and sprint. *Note that for the component_utility macros clone() and copy() are disabled.*

Parameterized components should use the parameter versions of the macros instead. Note that these do not generate a get_type_name function and register the component with the factory with the type name "<unknown>".

```
`uvm_component_param_utils(TYPE#(T))
or
uvm_component_param_utils_begin(TYPE#(T))
`uvm_field_*(ARG,FLAG)
...
...
`uvm_component_utils_end
```

The following sections in this chapter go into details of various components that are essential to a UVM simulation. These components implement the Wishbone protocol (see [18]). The concepts presented here are similar and can be transferred to other protocols as well easily. Use the examples provided herein to reinforce your concepts and build your components required to verify your DUT.

8.3 UVM Library Component Classes

Some of the component classes are wrapper classes over uvm_component while others have class instances contained in them. Nothing prevents you from creating your derivations of uvm_component instead of the provided classes, however, by using the classes developed allows the Accellera committee and the UVM working groups to add features to the derived classes of uvm_component at a future point in time. Following the methodology allows the user's code to be insulated from such changes as and when they occur.

The following sections delve into each of the common component classes in UVM. Each of these components is developed for the Wishbone protocol, but the general principles apply to any protocol of your choice.

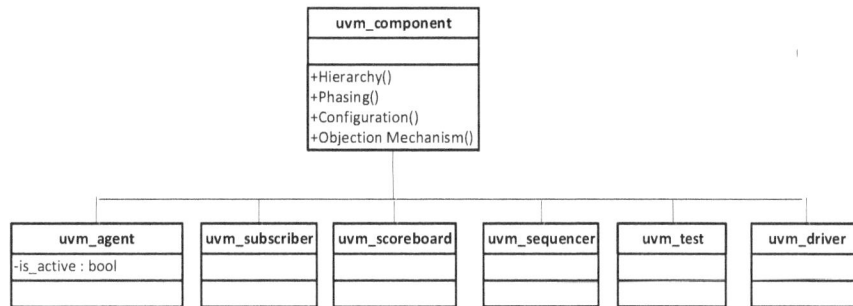

Fig. 8.2: UVM Component Classes

8.3.1 UVM Driver

The driver component is responsible for driving data items on the bus onto the physical bus. This component translates the class-based transaction it obtains from the sequencer component into pin wiggles as per the protocol it is driving.

A typical driver class extends from the uvm_component and contains a TLM like[1] port called seq_item_port that allows the driver to communicate with the sequencer and receive transactions from the sequencer. It also contains a virtual interface handle that is its interface to the external world and usually obtains a valid handle through configuration along with other parameters. It translates the abstract transaction that is provided by the sequencer onto a set of signals as per the protocol being driven on the interface and sends back the response from the bus to the sequencer.

Rule 8.3.0:   *An UVM Driver shall inherit from the uvm_driver class,*

All the timing and exchange details for the physical interface are handled by the driver[2]. Figure 8.3 shows the block diagram for the driver. The driver has a run() method that defines its operation, as well as a TLM port through which it communicates with the sequencer. The driver may also implement one or more of the parallel runtime phases (pre_reset - post_shutdown) to refine its operation further.

Listing 8.1 shows a simple wishbone driver that will be used in the sections that follow. The methods in the driver are listed with the class definition. Detailed source listings are available in the following sections along with the code.

---

[1] Note that it is not a complete implementation of a TLM port

[2] Note that in the case of a complex protocol like PCIe or USB, this driver could very well be a piece of pre-packaged verification IP

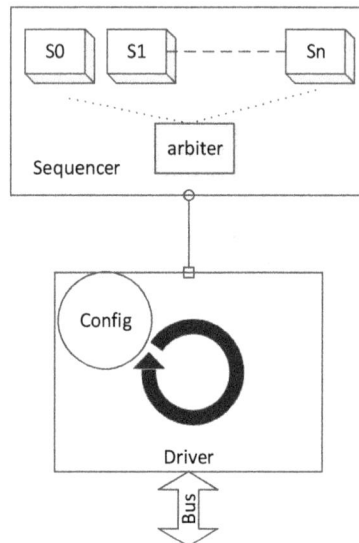

Fig. 8.3: UVM Driver

Listing 8.1: A Wishbone Driver

```
27    class wb_master extends uvm_driver # (wb_transaction);
28
29        wb_config mstr_drv_cfg;
30
31        typedef virtual wb_master_if v_if;
32        v_if drv_if;
33        `uvm_register_cb(wb_master,wb_master_callbacks);
34
35        extern function new(string name = "wb_master",
36            uvm_component parent = null);
37
38        `uvm_component_utils_begin(wb_master)
39        `uvm_component_utils_end
40
41        extern virtual function void build_phase(uvm_phase phase);
42        extern virtual function void end_of_elaboration_phase(uvm_phase
             phase);
43        extern virtual function void connect_phase(uvm_phase phase);
44        extern virtual task main_phase(uvm_phase phase);
45        extern protected virtual task main_driver();
46
47        extern protected virtual task read(wb_transaction trans);
48        extern protected virtual task write(wb_transaction trans);
49        extern protected virtual task blockRead(wb_transaction trans);
50        extern protected virtual task blockWrite( wb_transaction trans);
51        extern protected virtual task ReadModifyWrite(wb_transaction trans
             );
52
53    endclass: wb_master
```

- Line 27: shows the wb_master driver class extending from the uvm_driver class. This class is typed to the type of transaction that it uses.

- Line 29: In our example, the wb_master_driver needs to obtain configuration settings from a configuration. This is the instance of the mstr_drv_cfg class

- Line 32 shows the virtual interface that the driver uses to drive signals on the bus.

- Line 35 shows the constructor of the class

- Line 38 - the uvm_component_utils macro pair provide factory registration and other functions.

- Line 44: declares the main_driver task that is forked off in the main_phase

- Lines 47-51 are tasks that follow the Wishbone protocol and are called to drive the pins depending on which transaction is received from the sequencer.

The main_phase task does the actual work as shown in the figure below.

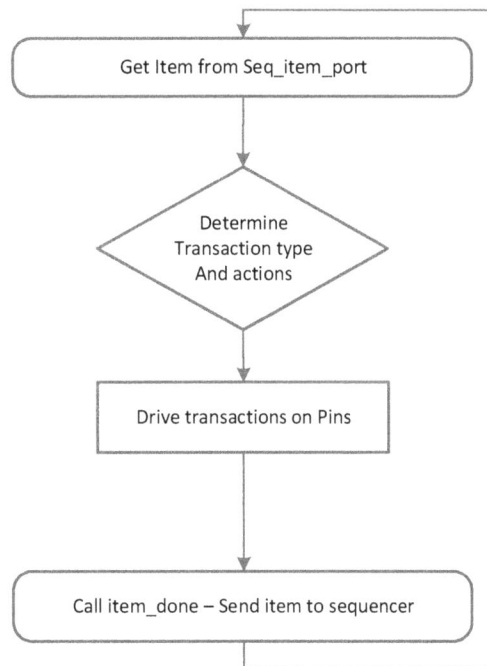

Fig. 8.4: Basic Driver Loop

The above loop is coded into the main phase task as follows:

Listing 8.2: The Main driver task

```
85    task wb_master::main_driver();
86        int count;
87        uvm_event_pool my_event_pool;  // This will become global pool
88        uvm_event      local_reset_event;  // Event to be used with global
                   pool
89
90        count = 0;
91        my_event_pool = uvm_event_pool::get_global_pool();
92        local_reset_event = my_event_pool.get("reset_event");
93        local_reset_event.wait_off();
94
95        forever begin
96            wb_transaction tr;
97            // Set output signals to their idle state
98
99            drv_if.master_cb.DAT_O <= 'bz;
100           drv_if.master_cb.TGD_O <= 'bz;
101           drv_if.master_cb.ADR_O <= 'bz;
102           drv_if.master_cb.CYC_O <= 'bz;
103           drv_if.master_cb.LOCK_O <= 'bz;
104           drv_if.master_cb.SEL_O <= 'bz;
105           drv_if.master_cb.STB_O <= 'b0;
106           drv_if.master_cb.TGA_O <= 'bz;
107           drv_if.master_cb.TGC_O <= 'bz;
108
109           seq_item_port.get_next_item(tr);
110           `uvm_info("WB_MASTER_DRV", "Starting transaction...",UVM_LOW)
111           `uvm_do_callbacks(wb_master,wb_master_callbacks, pre_tx(this,
                  tr))
112           // Since we are just beginning the transaction, we dont know
                  what kind it's yet.
113
114           tr.status = wb_transaction::UNKNOWN;
115
116           case (tr.kind)
117               wb_transaction::READ: begin
118                   read(tr);
119               end
120               wb_transaction::WRITE: begin
121                   write(tr);
122               end
123               wb_transaction::BLK_RD: begin
124                   blockRead(tr);
125               end
126               wb_transaction::BLK_WR: begin
127                   blockWrite(tr);
128               end
129               wb_transaction::RMW: begin
130                   ReadModifyWrite(tr);
131               end
```

```
132                    endcase
133
134                    seq_item_port.item_done();
135                    `uvm_info("WB_MASTER_DRV", tr.sprint(),UVM_HIGH)
136
137                    `uvm_do_callbacks(wb_master,wb_master_callbacks, post_tx(this,
                              tr))
138                    count = count + 1;
139                    `uvm_info("WB_MASTER_DRV", $sformatf("Completed %d
                              transactions...",count),UVM_LOW)
140         end
141     endtask : main_driver
```

- Line 95 onwards shows the body of a forever loop.

- Line 109 shows the get_next_item method being called on the driver's seq_item_port. This call is a blocking call that waits until the sequence is selected and an item is available.

- Line 111 shows the pre_tx callback being called. (See Section 8.3.1.1)

- Lines 116-132 show the case statement examining the transaction kind. Depending on the type of transaction, various tasks are called. Depending on the type of the transaction (Read/Write/ BurstRead/BurstWrite/ReadModifyWrite) in this example, appropriate tasks are then called. The read and write tasks are coded to provide the right pin wiggles and obtain responses from the DUT as per the Wishbone protocol.

- When the appropriate tasks complete, the post_tx callbacks are called since the data transmission is complete. Line 137 shows the post_tx callback being called. (see Section 8.3.1.1)

- Line 134 shows the item being sent back to the sequencer via the item_done() method. The driver then tells the sequencer that it is done with the item and sends the item back to the sequencer so that the sequence may process any reads.

8.3.1.1 Providing Driver Extensibility

Add some callbacks to the driver so that the user can customize driver behavior. A collection of suggested callback points is shown in Figure 8.5. You do not have to choose these exact callback points suggested in the figure. However, you must provide these hooks so that it becomes possible for users of your code to reuse all the code you have developed by merely extending the driver by using the appropriate callbacks.

An example implementation that illustrates concepts from the above figure is incorporated into the driver. Listing 8.2 shows the implementation of the callback calls on lines 111 and 137.

The following recommendations are based on Figure 8.5:

Rule 8.3.1:   *Provide a configuration mechanism to control features of your driver. You will invariably come across situations where you may want to configure specific behavior in addition to callbacks.*

Rule 8.3.2:   *If your protocol has responses, ensure that you have code in your driver to handle cases where a response is not provided within the required time interval*

The corollary of the above rule implies:
Rule 8.3.3:   *Ensure that you have a configuration property to control the response time interval in your driver.*

There are *only a few components where you would implement any of the runtime phases* (see Section 13.2 for a description of these phases). The driver implementation in the above listing drives valid values on the pins of the DUT, and hence has been implemented here.

Rule 8.3.4:   *Declare all callback methods for a driver as virtual methods in a single class derived from uvm_callbacks.*

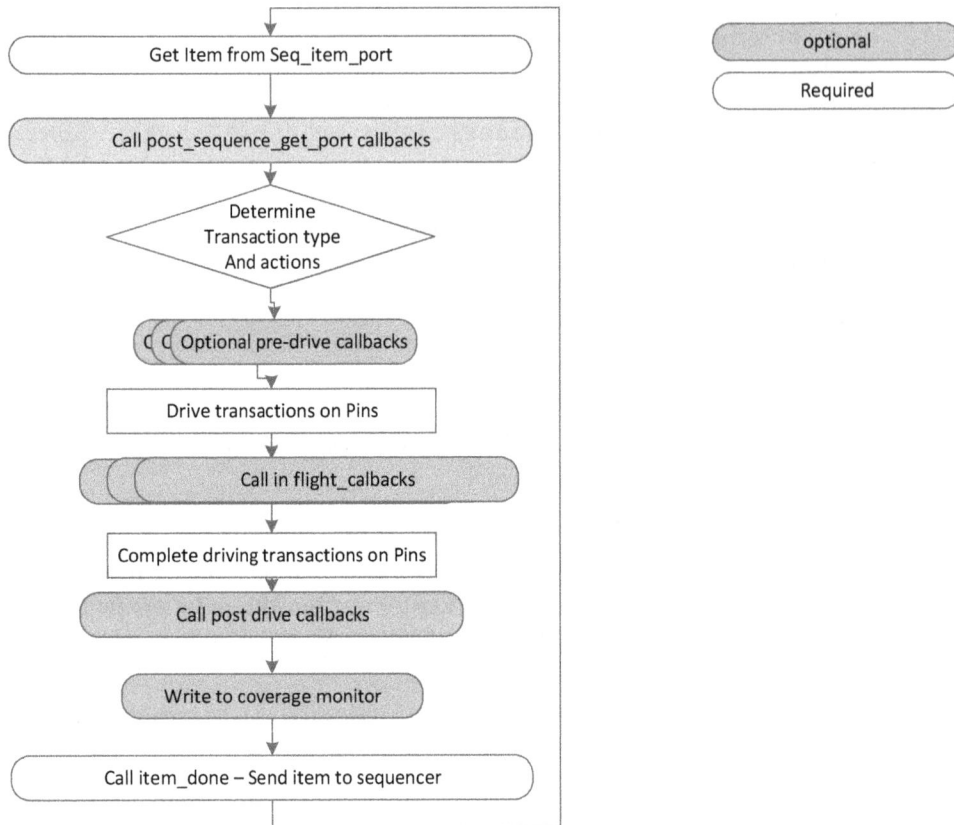

Fig. 8.5: Driver Main_phase Loop

Recommendation 8.3.0:   *Drivers shall have a rich set of callback methods.*

As a component developer, you may develop a component and move on to other parts of verification. If you provide a rich set of methods and intercept callback points in your component, chances are other users of your component will be able to make use of your work in ways you probably did not envisage.

Recommendation 8.3.1:   *Drivers should call a callback method after making a significant decision but before acting on it, letting you modify the default decision.*

Recommendation 8.3.2:   *Drivers should call a callback method before transmitting data, letting you record, modify or drop the data.*

Line 111 in the above listing shows the implementation of this rule. This is a simple protocol, so we merged the implementation for the above rules.

Recommendation 8.3.3:   *Drivers should call a callback method after receiving data, letting you record, modify or drop the data.*

Line 137 in the above listing shows the implementation of this rule.

Rule 8.3.5:   *Drivers should be able to continue with a default response if they receive receive no response after the maximum allowable time interval.*

This rule embodies a timeout to handle cases where you don't get a response from the DUT in a reasonable amount of time. You cannot create this interception from a callback, and hence, you must put in a configurable timeout and handle any errors that come from it.

8.3.1.2 Other Driver Types - Push Driver

The earlier section described a "pull" driver that is one of, the more commonly used drivers in UVM. This driver connects to a sequencer that does the arbitration between various sequences and provides serialization of the items to be driven by the driver.

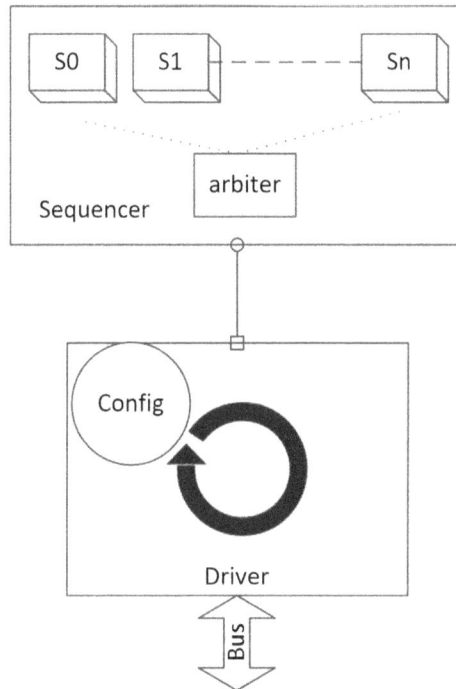

Fig. 8.6: Normal Pull Mode drivers

In another case, it is now possible for a "push mode driver" as is common with other methodologies. This driver usually derives from a uvm_push_driver component. The push driver component contains a put() task which is called by the sequencer. The sequencer now retains control of the items that are sent to the DUT from the driver.

The implementation of the push driver agent is slightly different from the commonly used pull driver. In this case, we use the sequencer extending from uvm_push_sequencer.

Listing 8.3: The Push Sequencer

```
5     class wb_master_seqr extends uvm_push_sequencer # (wb_transaction);
6
7         wb_config cfg;
8
9         `uvm_component_utils(wb_master_seqr)
10        function new (string name,
11            uvm_component parent);
12            super.new(name,parent);
13        endfunction:new
14    endclass:wb_master_seqr
```

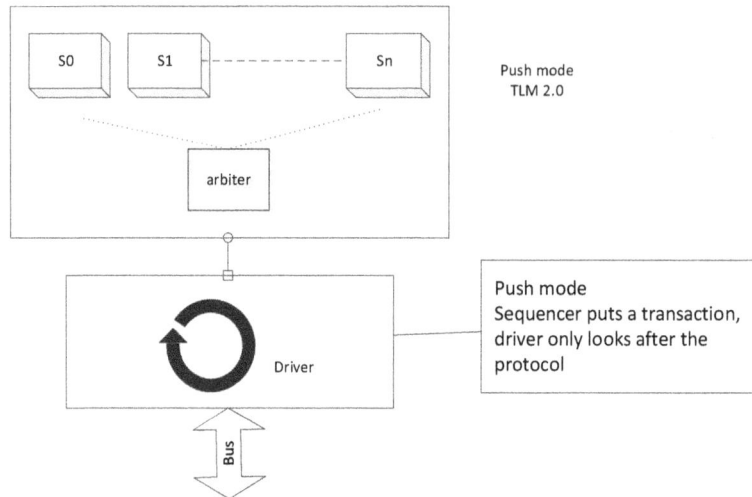

Fig. 8.7: Push Mode driver

The master driver now has a put() task which drives the transaction on the bus.

Listing 8.4: The Main driver Put() task

```
87      task wb_master::put(wb_transaction tr);
88          int count;
89          count = 0;
90          `uvm_info("wb_env_DRIVER", "Starting transaction...",UVM_LOW)
91
92          tr.status = wb_transaction::UNKNOWN;
93
94          case (tr.kind)
95              wb_transaction::READ: begin
96                  read(tr);
97              end
98              wb_transaction::WRITE: begin
99
100                 write(tr);
101             end
102             wb_transaction::BLK_RD: begin
103                 // ToDo: Implement BLK_RD transaction
104             end
105             wb_transaction::BLK_WR: begin
106                 // ToDo: Implement BLK_RD transaction
107             end
108             wb_transaction::RMW: begin
109                 // ToDo: Implement RMW transaction
110             end
111         endcase
112
113         `uvm_info("wb_env_DRIVER", "Completed transaction...",UVM_LOW)
114     endtask : put
```

Listing 8.4 shows the 'put' method implementation for a push driver. The push driver operates under control of the sequencer with the sequencer now "pushing" transactions to the driver rather than the driver "getting" them. The sequencer retains all the control. This sort of mechanism is popular in many applications, and it is a bit easier to understand than the pull mode driver which is the default UVM driver provided by UVM.

The connections in the master agent are also slightly different. In this case, the sequencer has a req_port.

Listing 8.5: The Main driver Connect Phase

```
42          virtual function void connect_phase(uvm_phase phase);
43              super.connect_phase(phase);
44              if (is_active == UVM_ACTIVE) begin
45                  mast_sqr.req_port.connect(mast_drv.req_export);
46              end
47          endfunction
```

(i) Compare the driver in Chapter 2 with this section and you can see the difference in philosophies.

8.3.1.3 Other Driver Variants

The preceding sections showed the illustration of a simple bidirectional driver where the data from the sequence is fed to the DUT, and the response from the DUT during a read is sent back to the sequence. The Wishbone protocol, like the AXI or OCP protocols, does support pipelining. This is an advanced topic, not elaborated on here. If you are attempting to write a pipelined driver [19] is a good reference on this topic.

8.3.2 Monitor

The monitor component is a subcomponent of the agent. It is similar to a driver component but performs the reverse function by translating actual signal activity to an abstract representation of that activity. One essential difference to note between a monitor and a driver is that the monitor is always present. It is also always passive and cannot drive any signals on the interface. When an agent is placed in passive mode, the monitor continues to execute. If configured, the monitor can also check for protocol correctness on a bus and with coverage collection in a CRV based environment. It can also be optionally used to print trace information about a transaction.

Rule 8.3.6:   *An UVM Monitor shall inherit from the uvm_monitor class.*

A bus monitor handles all the signals and transactions on a bus. While the code between a driver and monitor is usually common, drivers and monitors are built as separate entities so they can work independently of each other even if they reuse the same subset of signals. The monitors are built to be self-contained *It does not depend on other UVM components for any information other than configuration*. It is also highly recommended not to have monitors depend on drivers for information so that an agent can operate passively when only the monitor is present and enabled.

The monitor functionality should be limited to necessary monitoring that is always required. This can include protocol checking that should be configurable so it can be enabled or disabled and coverage collection. Additional highlevel functionality, such as scoreboards, should be implemented separately on top of the monitor.

If you choose to verify an abstract model or accelerate the pin-level functionality, you should separate the signal-level extraction, coverage, checking and the transaction-level activities. An analysis port should allow communication between the sub-monitor components.

The following example shows a simple monitor which has the following functions:

- The monitor collects bus information through a virtual interface.

- The collected data is used both coverage collection and protocol checking.

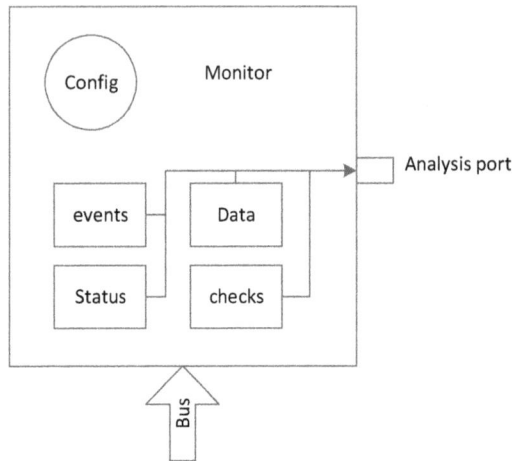

Fig. 8.8: UVM Monitor

- The collected data is exported on the built-in analysis port (item_collected_port).

The main monitor collection task is shown in the listing below.

Listing 8.6: A Wishbone Monitor

```
91     task wb_master_mon::master_monitor_task();
92
93         forever begin
94             wb_transaction tr;
95
96             do begin
97                 @(this.mon_if.CYC_O or
98                     this.mon_if.STB_O or
99                     this.mon_if.ADR_O or
100                    this.mon_if.SEL_O or
101                    this.mon_if.WE_O   or
102                    this.mon_if.TGA_O or
103                    this.mon_if.TGC_O);
104            end while (this.mon_if.CYC_O !== 1'b1 ||
105            this.mon_if.STB_O !== 1'b1);
106            tr= wb_transaction::type_id::create("tr", this);
107            tr.address = this.mon_if.ADR_O;
108            // Are we supposed to respond to this cycle?
109            if(this.mstr_mon_cfg.min_addr <= tr.address  && tr.address <=
                   this.mstr_mon_cfg.max_addr )
110            begin
111                `uvm_do_callbacks(wb_master_mon,wb_master_mon_callbacks,
112                    pre_trans(this, tr))
113
114                tr.tga = this.mon_if.TGA_O;
115                if(this.mon_if.WE_O) begin
116                    tr.kind = wb_transaction::WRITE;
```

```
117                              `uvm_info("WB master Monitor","got a write transaction
                                      from Master ",UVM_LOW)
118                          tr.data  = this.mon_if.DAT_I;
119                          tr.tgd  = this.mon_if.TGD_O;
120                          tr.status = wb_transaction::ACK;
121                      end
122                      else begin
123                          tr.kind = wb_transaction::READ ;
124                          `uvm_info("Wb_master Monitor","got a read transaction
                                  ",UVM_LOW)
125
126                          tr.status = wb_transaction::ACK;
127                      end
128
129                      `uvm_do_callbacks(wb_master_mon,wb_master_mon_callbacks,
130                          pre_ack(this, tr))
131
132                      wait(this.mon_if.master_cb.ACK_I);
133                      tr.data  = this.mon_if.DAT_O;
134                      tr.tgd  = this.mon_if.TGD_O;
135
136                      tr.sel = this.mon_if.SEL_O;
137                      tr.tgc  = this.mon_if.TGC_O;
138                      @(this.mon_if.monitor_cb);
139                  end
140                  `uvm_do_callbacks(wb_master_mon,wb_master_mon_callbacks,
141                      post_trans(this, tr))
142                  mon_analysis_port.write(tr);
143              end
144
145      endtask: master_monitor_task
```

- Line 96 begins the main portion of the monitor task. The task proceeds when there is a change in any of the signals.

- Line 106 creates a new transaction if a valid transaction has been detected. This transaction is populated and written out on the analysis port.

- Line 129 Provides a callback hook to the user to modify transaction properties.

- Lines 115-137 now populate the transaction depending on what is observed on the pins.

- Line 140 calls another callback after the transaction is detected.

- Line 142 now writes this transaction out to the analysis port.

The following recommendations will serve you well as you develop your UVM environments. Many are self explanatory.

Recommendation 8.3.4:   *During the build phase put out a message that specifies clearly what version of the protocol specification you are referring to. while this may seem initially redundant, but as specifications change, your ability to debug this will dramatically improve if your component is reusable.*

Recommendation 8.3.5:   *Specify the check. The messaging should reflect the source of the check and what is checked*

Make sure that the messages you put out have a cross-reference to the specific protocol item to allow others using your component know where to look

Rule 8.3.7:   *When performing checks using a monitor, checks must be coded as independent concurrent continuous processes.*

Rule 8.3.8:   *Provide a means to enable or disable a specific check in a monitor.* If you lump all the checks into one bucket, you may find yourself struggling with granularity

Rule 8.3.9:   *If you are checking for a protocol, make sure that you cover the protocol entirely. If you are only covering a part of the protocol, Indicate so clearly so that others can enhance your offering.*

Rule 8.3.10:   *Provide a way to accumulate statistics for the check.*

You should be able to determine from the message summary, how many checks fired, how many resulted in errors and similar execution statistics that can help users gain confidence in their design.

Rule 8.3.11:   *Monitors should issue a warning message if you receive no response after the maximum allowable time interval.*

See Section 8.3.1.1 for a suggested set of callback points. The recommendations below reflect the suggestions in that section.

Recommendation 8.3.6:   *Monitors should call a callback method after receiving data, letting you record, modify or drop the data.*

Recommendation 8.3.7:   *Monitors should call a callback method upon detection of transaction in an interface, letting you record, modify or drop the data*

Recommendation 8.3.8:   *Monitors should call a callback method after generating any new information, letting you record or modify the new information.*

8.3.3 Sequencer

The UVM sequencer is the component that runs the sequences generating stimulus for the DUT. The sequencer is a uvm_component that is built during the build phase of the environment and has fixed connections to other components in the UVM verification environment. The sequencer produces a stream of sequence items strongly typed to the type of items it creates.

Rule 8.3.12:   *Any UVM Sequencer you develop shall inherit from the uvm_sequencer class*

In addition to the methods available to the uvm_component class, The API for the sequencer component provides for many methods. These methods help provide information on the status of the sequencer as well as the ability to take control of the sequencer or affect its priority,

A typical sequencer is characterized by:

- A library of sequences running on the sequencer. These sequences can be directly run on the sequencer or used as subsequences.

- A set of running sequences

- An arbitration algorithm to select between the various sequences running on the sequencer at the current point in time.

- a TLM interface that connects to the driver component (see Section 14.2)

- A default sequence that may be defined based on the test.

The sequencer has an arbitration queue containing references to all the sequences that are trying to run on the sequencer. The default arbitration algorithm is FIFO such that the first sequence to get started gets served first and, having generated one transaction, gets sent to the back of the queue. The result is that when multiple sequences are competing to run on the same sequencer, they get scheduled in round-robin order so that the transactions are strictly interleaved. Stimulus generation is controlled via parameters that allow you to select the sequence and correspondingly the specific item sent to the driver. These parameters help the sequencer prioritize certain sequences and allow only a specific sequence to run for some time. Also, the arbitration algorithm used by each sequencer can be selected by the user from a set of built-in algorithms or can be user-defined. Section 14.3 provides some details on the sequence priority and arbitration.

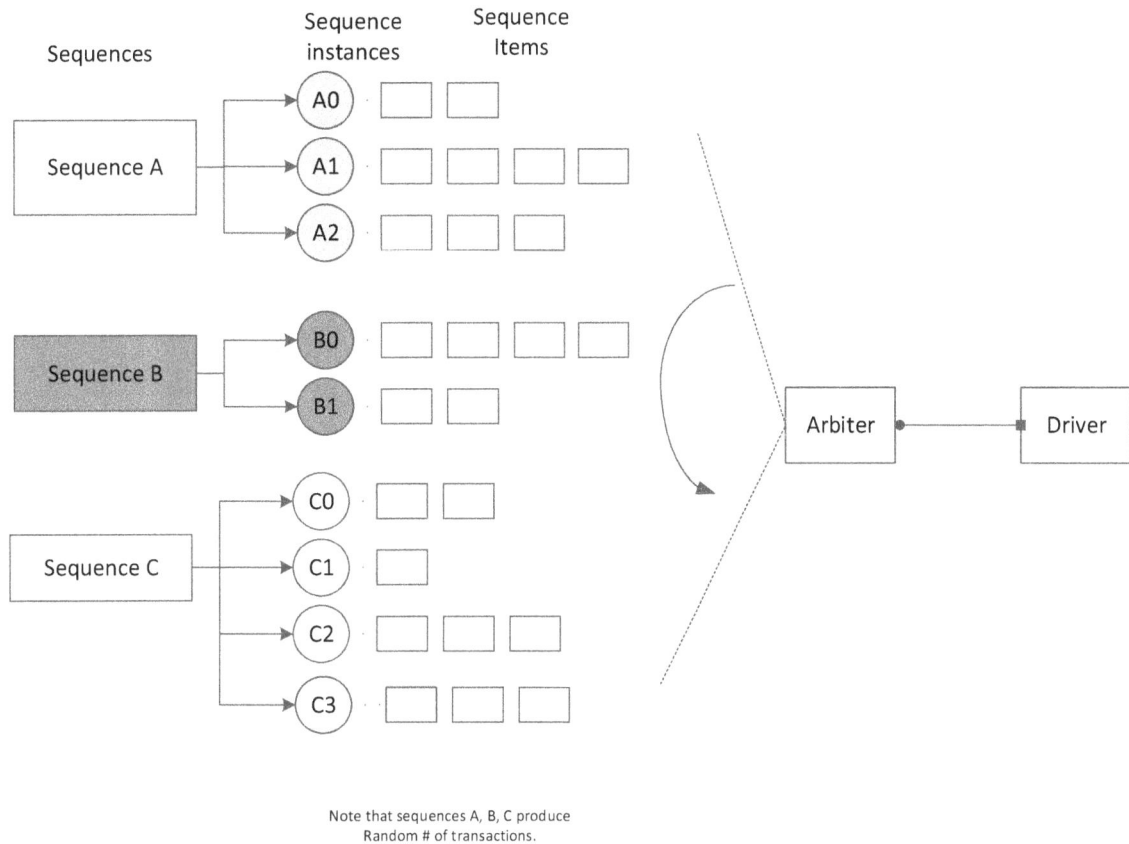

Note that sequences A, B, C produce
Random # of transactions.

Fig. 8.9: Block Diagram Of UVM Sequencer

Figure 8.9 shows the block diagram of the sequencer. The sequencer component is often parametrized to the type of transactions that are being generated by the sequences. See Section 14.2.1 onwards for a detailed description of how the sequencer interacts with the driver.

Listing 8.7: Simple Sequencer

```
1     class wb_master_seqr extends uvm_sequencer # (wb_transaction);
2         wb_config cfg;
3
4         `uvm_component_utils(wb_master_seqr)
5         function new (string name,
6             uvm_component parent);
7             super.new(name,parent);
8         endfunction:new
9     endclass:wb_master_seqr
10 `endif
```

The Listing 8.7 shows the implementation of sequencer wb_master_seqr derived from class uvm_sequencer. This class is parametrized to generate transactions of type wb_transaction. There is a sequence library also associated with this sequencer (see Section 14.1).

- Line 1 class wb_master_seqr extends from the uvm_sequencer class.

- Line 4 the macro `uvm_component_utils() is used with the sequencer class to register its type with the factory and also provide other useful utilities.

- Lines 5 - 7 describe the constructor for the sequencer.

The above example creates a minimal sequencer that produces a stream of sequence items of type wb_transaction. Once the sequencer is built during the build_phase() in a component, The sequencer's default sequence is set by using the configuration database. An example of setting the default sequence can be found in Section 14.2.2. When the test is created and started, the default sequence runs on the sequencer in the appropriate phase producing items for the device under test.

The UVM sequencer is a component. The generation of items by the sequencer involves some factors like the actual sequences running on the sequencer and also the priority of the sequences, etc. Additional information is presented in Section 14.2 where a detailed look at the sequencer operation and its relationship to the driver is explored.

8.3.4 Agent

Earlier sections of this chapter discussed the driver, the monitor, and the sequencer. Each of these components can be reused independently. However, the environment integrator needs to know the names, configuration, and interfaces of every entity in the system. This can indeed be a lot of work, and a lot of the details aren't usually relevant to many members in a verification team. UVM recommends that environment developers define a more abstract container called an agent to simplify test development. This reusable container contains three components.

- A driver the driver which does the pin wiggles

- Stimulus generating sequencer

- Monitor

- A configuration class is usually present with configuration information that provides configuration parameters.

Figure 8.10 illustrates an active agent containing a driver, a sequencer and a monitor as class instantiations along with a configuration object and some flags. There is an analysis port from the monitor that is connected to that of the agent thereby allowing the user to use it as a black box. It is noted that there can be more than just one agent in a system. For each interface, an agent usually exists, and verification components can contain more than one agent.

Rule 8.3.13:   *An agent has only one interface associated with it.*

A typical uvm_agent can be considered as a packaged verification component that is customized for a specific interface protocol and is usually interface specific. It is in effect a piece of reusable verification IP that can be reused and deployed on many projects, and care must be taken when creating the agent to ensure that it is entirely self-contained and portable. The agent's build phase handles the details of passing the connection information between its child components and also configuring them as required.

Agents can be divided into two main types

- An active agent that actively drives the pins of the interface This can be divided into two types:

  1. A master or initiator wherein it drives the signals on the interface actively. This type of agent is typically used to provide stimulus to a DUT. An example of this type of agent is the wishbone master agent is the example described below.

  2. A reactive or slave where the agent responds to pin wiggle information and provides a response. This type of agent is typically used when you are responding to signals. Example: A memory agent that incorporates a memory. See Section 16 for an example

- Passive agent who only monitors the activity on the pins of the interface

There is an error in the 1800.2 LRM where the default is set to UVM_PASSIVE. This is the opposite of UVM 1.2 behavior. Changing the implementation to be UVM_PASSIVE would have caused many environments to break. Hence, The Accellera implementation leaves it as UVM_ACTIVE, same as that of UVM 1.2. The next LRM will revert it to UVM_ACTIVE.

8.3.4.1 Agent Configuration

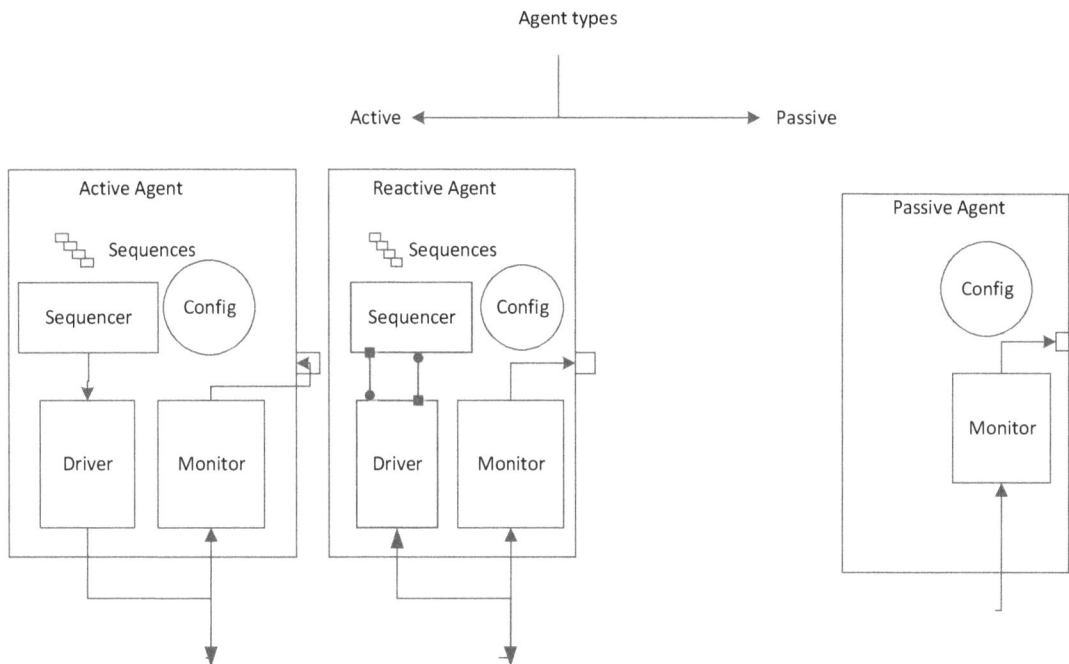

Fig. 8.10: Agent Types

By convention, UVM agents have many configuration variables. A variable of type uvm_active_passive_e that defines whether the agent is active (UVM_ACTIVE) with the sequencer and the driver constructed, or passive (UVM_PASSIVE) with neither the driver or the sequencer constructed is built into the agent. This variable is called *is_active* and by default, it is set to UVM_ACTIVE.

> If other variables are used depending on your application, make sure you use descriptive names. It simplifies debugging with all the tools.
> For Example, A property bit may control a functional coverage monitor. The property bit determines whether the functional coverage monitor gets built may be called *has_functional_coverage*.

In many agents, the agent configuration object contains a handle for the virtual interface used by the driver and the monitor. The configuration object is constructed and configured in the test which also assigns the virtual interface to it. The configuration object usually encapsulates a lot of information in case of typical modern protocol VIP classes.

> **It is critical that the passive portion does not rely on the active portion. If an agent is in passive mode and the active logic is not present, the agent cannot operate properly.** It is okay for the sequencer to accept information from the monitor but not vice versa, as we may want to perform coverage and checking on interface buses driven by some other logic. If you do not have immediate plans for using passive mode, it is often easy to add this support during agent implementation. Leave hooks in the agent for later use. Retrofitting is usually tricky when coding has finished, and all reviews are completed at the end of projects.

Please look at wb_dma_env_tb_mod.sv in
$DOWNLOAD/IEEE_version/Web_Chapters/CoverageClosure_non_UVM/bench/wb_dma_uvm/tests/ for an
example of an agent where the uvm_active_passive_enum is set to UVM_PASSIVE for some simulations.

8.3.4.2 Agent Build Phase

An agent's build function, inherited from uvm_component, can be implemented to define any agent topology. An agent
typically contains three subcomponents: a driver, sequencer, and a monitor. If the agent is active, subtypes should contain
all three subcomponents. If the agent is passive, subtypes should contain only the monitor. Determining the mode of
the agent is accomplished using the is_active property of the agent class which is built into the agent base class. During
the build_phase, the agent can decide depending on its configuration whether it needs to build the driver, sequencer and
monitor or only the monitor as illustrated by the code below.

Listing 8.8: Master agent Build Phase

```
20          virtual function void build_phase(uvm_phase phase);
21              super.build_phase(phase);
22              uvm_config_db #(wb_config)::get(this, "", "config",
                    mstr_agent_cfg);
23
24              mast_mon = wb_master_mon::type_id::create("mast_mon", this);
25              if (is_active == UVM_ACTIVE) begin
26                  mast_sqr = wb_master_seqr::type_id::create("mast_sqr",
                        this);
27                  mast_drv = wb_master::type_id::create("mast_drv", this);
28                  mast_drv.mstr_drv_cfg = mstr_agent_cfg;
29                  mast_sqr.cfg = mstr_agent_cfg;
30                  mast_mon.mstr_mon_cfg = mstr_agent_cfg;
31              end
32              if (!uvm_config_db#(vif)::get(this, "", "mst_if", mast_agt_if)
                    ) begin
33                  `uvm_fatal("AGT/NOVIF", "No virtual interface specified
                        for this agent instance Master Agent")
34              end
35              uvm_config_db# (vif)::set(this,"mast_drv","mst_if",mast_agt_if
                    );
36              uvm_config_db# (vif)::set(this,"mast_mon","mon_if",mast_agt_if
                    );
37
38              analysis_port = new("analysis_port",this);
39
40          endfunction: build_phase
```

- Line 21 calls the super() method allowing the base class build_phase to execute.

- Line 24 builds the monitor.

- Line 25 checks to see if the agent is an active agent. If the agent is an active agent, it builds both the driver and
  sequencer on Lines 27 and 28

- Line 32 gets the agent's interface from the config_db.

- Lines 35-36 set the virtual interface handle in the config_db and also assign the handles directly to the driver/monitor.

8.3.4.3 Agent Connect Phase

In the connect phase, The agent makes the connection between the sequencer and the driver that is built in the build phase. In the sub-components, the driver and monitors get the virtual interface from the config_db and connect the testbench to the interface in the design.

Listing 8.9: Connect Phase

```
42          virtual function void connect_phase(uvm_phase phase);
43              super.connect_phase(phase);
44              if (is_active == UVM_ACTIVE) begin
45                  mast_drv.seq_item_port.connect(mast_sqr.seq_item_export);
46                  mast_mon.mon_analysis_port.connect(analysis_port);
47              end
48          endfunction
```

In Listing 8.9, we note the following:

- Line 43 calls the super() method allowing the base class connections to proceed.

- Line 44 checks to see if the agent is an active agent.

- Line 45 connects the master driver item port to the sequencer item export port. With this connection, the sequencer is now connected to the driver.

- Line 46 The monitor analysis port is connected to the agent analysis port.

Rule 8.3.14:   *Identify agents to configure as Active or Passive.*

I would recommend in addition to the above rule that you provide a agent class property that allows the agent to not construct the monitor as well in the build_phase(). I recognize that this is not a standard UVM guideline. However, if you inherit a sub-environment with many agents, all of which are passive, you may be seeing a simulation slowdown with no way to shut the monitors off.

Rule 8.3.15:   *Model layers of a protocol as separate agents.*

I recommend you use layering or other concepts in case of a layered protocol. That will allow your agents to be reusable.

Rule 8.3.16:   *The agent shall be configurable if the protocol they implement has options*

If you are designing any agent with any level of complexity, ensure that you place options for configuration of the agent in a configuration class.

Rule 8.3.17:   *Configure agents using a randomizable configuration descriptor.*

Contemporary protocols have many features. You will need many class properties to model these features. Depending on protocol, you may need to set a configuration. Other sections in this book talk about using a configuration class to set agent configuration. Make the properties of the configuration class *rand* so that you can randomize the configuration for faster testing.

8.3.5 Subscriber

The UVM Subscriber class is an extension of UVM component with an analysis export port implemented as a part of the class. It finds use primarily in situations where one must process transactions emitted by an analysis port. A good example of this is a coverage collector that collects transactions emitted by a monitor. Users must implement the write() function after creating a specialized subtype of this class. This class is particularly useful when designing a coverage collector that attaches to a monitor.

Rule 8.3.18:   *UVM subscriber components shall inherit from the uvm_subscriber class,*

Figure 8.11 shows the block diagram of the uvm_subscriber class. This class acts primarily as a collector. Consider the uvm_subscriber snippet shown below. This subscriber component is used to collect information from the monitor and then used to collect coverage.

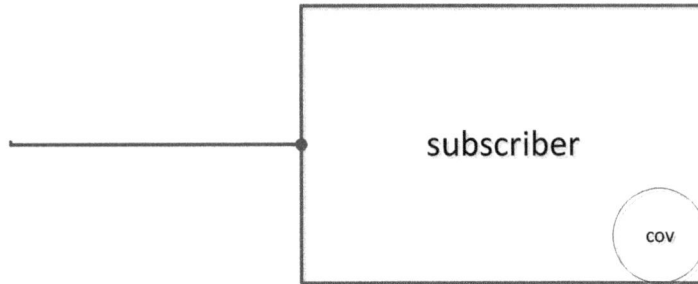

Fig. 8.11: A Simple Subscriber Component

Listing 8.10: A simple Subscriber

```
4
5      class wb_env_cov  extends uvm_subscriber #(wb_transaction);
6          event cov_event;
7          wb_transaction tr;
8          `uvm_component_utils(wb_env_cov)
9
10         covergroup cg_trans @(cov_event);
11             coverpoint tr.kind;
12             coverpoint tr.address {
13                 bins low = {[0:10]};
14                 bins mid = {[10:100]};
15                 bins high = {[100:$]};
16             }
17             coverpoint tr.lock ;
18             coverpoint tr.status;
19             coverpoint tr.num_wait_states {
20                 bins legal[] = {[0:15]};
21                 illegal_bins ib = {[16:$]};
22
23             }
24
25         endgroup: cg_trans
26
27
28         function new(string name, uvm_component parent);
29             super.new(name,parent);
30             cg_trans = new;
31         endfunction: new
32
33         virtual function void write(wb_transaction t);
34             this.tr = t;
35             -> cov_event;
36         endfunction: write
37
38     endclass: wb_env_cov
```

A complete example of this subscriber class being used as a coverage collection component to assess NON UVM testbenches is available as a web chapter in GitHub.

Complete PDF Chapter:
$DOWNLOAD/IEEE_version/Web_Chapters/CoverageClosure/CoverageClosure.pdf

Recommendation 8.3.9:   *Make coverage collection conditional to a configuration setting because it can affect simulation runtime performance.*

If you had a setting called coverage_enable that enabled coverage, you could select the coverage options on a test by test basis using the configuration mechanism. If coverage collection is enabled, the task emits the coverage sampling event (cov_transaction) which results in collecting the current values.

For example:

```
uvm_config_db#(bit)::set(this,''*.master0.monitor'', ''coverage_enable'', 0);
```

Similarly, if you need some protocol checks turned on or off, make it configurable, because it also can have an impact on runtime performance.

```
uvm_config_db#(bit)::set(this,''*.master0.monitor'', ''protocol_checks_enable'', 0);
```

8.3.6 Scoreboard

One of the most critical elements of a self-checking environment is the scoreboard. The scoreboard is a uvm_component that verifies the operation of the design at a functional level. It is usually responsible for verifying the correctness of the response to a given stimulus and also making sure that the appropriate number of responses were obtained. For the most part, in many complex environments, the scoreboard usually contains a significant amount of complexity especially if some complex data transformations are performed in the DUT. A typical scoreboard takes in input from a variety of sources and determines whether the outputs are given to the scoreboard are correct based on the logic that is coded into the scoreboard.

Rule 8.3.19:   *Any UVM scoreboard you develop shall inherit from the uvm_scoreboard class,*

Figure 8.12 shows the block diagram of the scoreboard and its operation in a typical UVM environment. This section develops the scoreboard used in Chapter 2. The monitors in the agents are driving and receiving data from the DUT both collect information from the pin level wiggles that occur on the DUT buses as seen in Figure 2.2. These are then abstracted out to transactions that are then input into the scoreboard. The scoreboard component in a sense is modular since the signal level transaction information is converted to a transaction class by the monitors that perform additional checking on the DUT interfaces that they are connected to. The uvm_scoreboard is a built-in base component in UVM library. This class extends from the uvm_component class. For all practical purposes, the uvm_scoreboard is an empty class. The bulk of the checking and work occurs within the components and tasks inside the class. In this book, two different examples of creating and instantiating a scoreboard are provided.

Creating the scoreboard involves the following steps:

1. Creating the scoreboard class

2. Intantiatating the TLM ports for connectivity

3. Creating the check/scoreboard functionality in the scoreboard class.

Figure 8.13 provides a detailed look at the scoreboard. For reasons of simplicity, this scoreboard has two FIFO ports. Connections are made between the master and slave agent monitors and the analysis ports on the FIFOs. The data is read out of the FIFO's and compared.

We can look at the implementation of the simple scoreboard class in Listing 8.11 and see the implementation of these steps and the FIFOs.

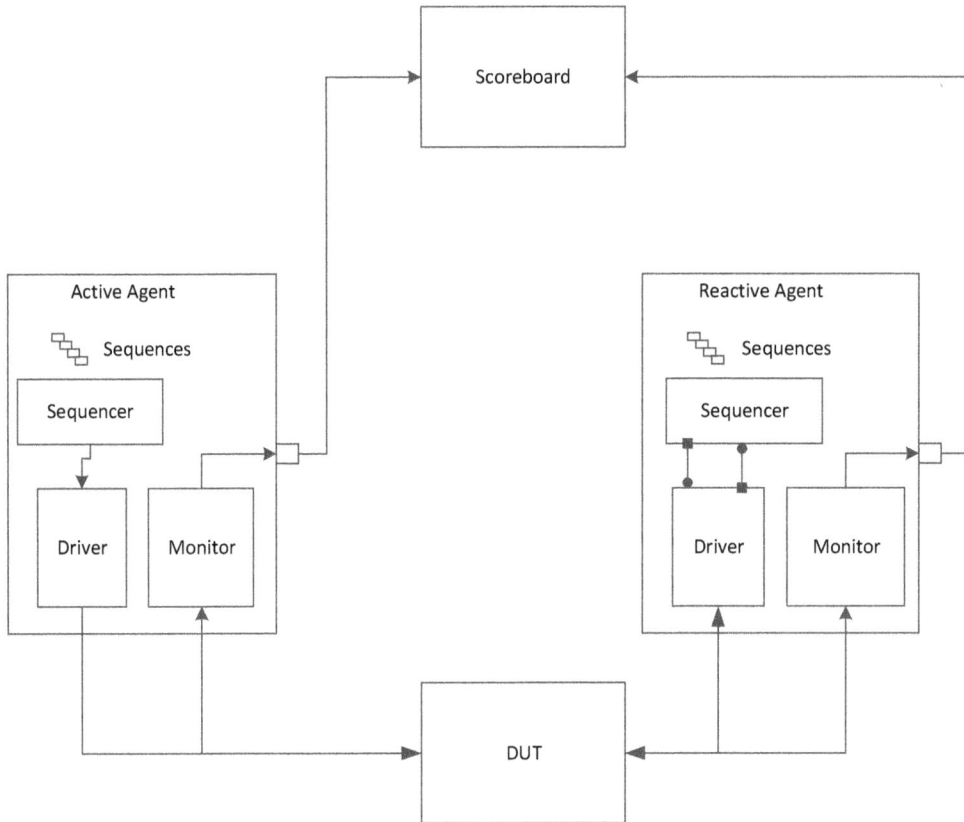

Fig. 8.12: Wishbone DUT Scoreboard

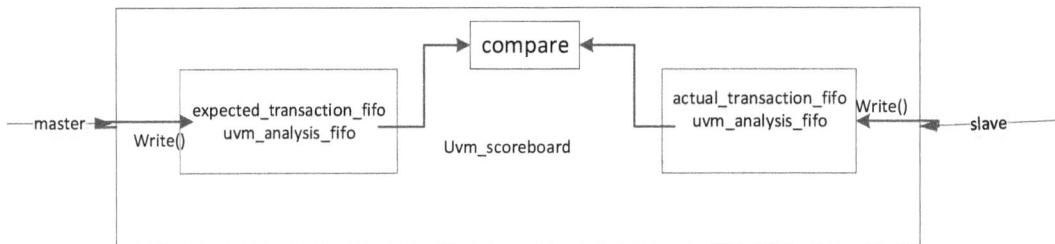

Fig. 8.13: Details of the Simple Scoreboard For The DUT

Listing 8.11: Simple Scoreboard Listing

```
4      class wb_scoreboard extends uvm_scoreboard;
5          `uvm_component_utils( wb_scoreboard)
6
7          uvm_tlm_analysis_fifo #( wb_transaction )
               expected_wb_transaction_fifo;
8          uvm_tlm_analysis_fifo #( wb_transaction )
               actual_wb_transaction_fifo;
9
10         // Constructor
11
12         function new( string name, uvm_component parent );
13             super.new( name, parent );
14         endfunction: new
15
16         extern virtual function void build_phase( uvm_phase phase );
17         extern virtual function void connect_phase( uvm_phase phase );
18         extern virtual task run_phase( uvm_phase phase );
19
20     endclass: wb_scoreboard
```

In Listing 8.11:

1. The class wb_scoreboard extends uvm_scoreboard on line 4.

2. Instantiating the tlm ports that various monitor components use to connect to the scoreboard. The TLM analysis fifos for the expected _transaction and actual_transaction TLM analysis fifos are instantiated as shown in line 7,8.

3. (Not Shown, see listing) Implemention of the checker functionality that provides the checking the mechanism for transaction classes that are input into the scoreboard is accomplished by using the comparer class which compares the transactions coming in on both the expected_transaction and actual_transaction FIFOs through the write() methods built into the ports.

8.4 The UVM Environment
8.4.1 Environment Class

The UVM Environment class encapsulates all the agents in a fashion similar to that of Section 1.3. The UVM class hierarchy is then instantiated in our top-level test. The verification environment is reused from test to test at a single integration level (Block/subsystem/System). In this example, the verification environment includes the instance of a master agent, a slave agent, a coverage component and a scoreboard. The master, slave and scoreboard component instances are created in the environment, and connections between the agents and scoreboard are done in this class.

The environment class is a container class. This class extends from uvm_component and performs the function of instantiating all the various components in the testbench. Depending on the complexity of the testbench, this environment class could contain a collection of other sub-environment classes. The environment class typically instantiates all the agents, sequencers, register models, scoreboards, etc. and any other component that is used to run the simulation.

The environment class performs the following primary functions.

1. Create and instantiate all the various components based on the configuration made available to it in its build_phase().

2. Connect all the various components in the connect_phase().

3. Apply any configuration settings relevant to each of the agents in the env in the configure_phase if needed.

4. Reporting information at the end of the test should it be desired.

The environment class extends from a uvm_env class that extends from uvm_component. The figure shows a block diagram view of an environment class that is used to verify our simple DUT.

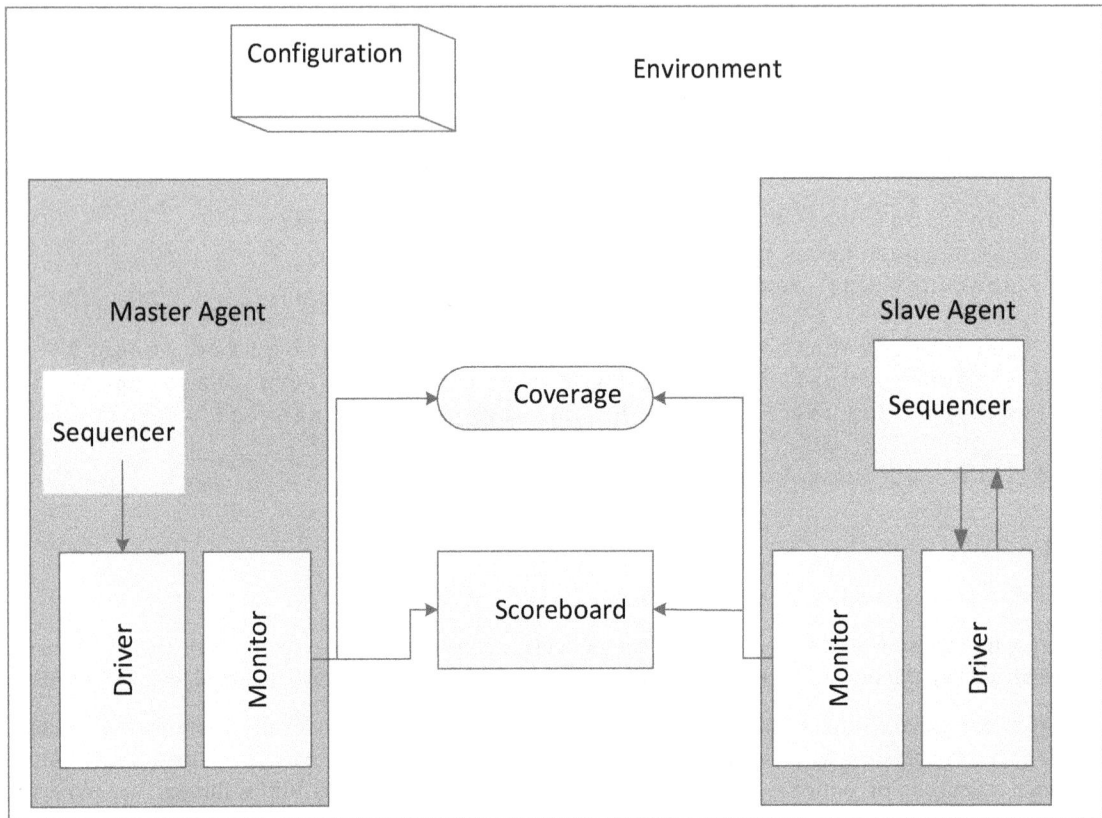

Fig. 8.14: Wishbone Environment

To understand the environment class better, consider the listing of the class below.

Listing 8.12: Testbench Environment

```
4      class wb_env extends uvm_env;
5          wb_master_agent master_agent;
6          wb_slave_agent slave_agent;
7          wb_env_cov cov;
8          wb_scoreboard sb;
9          reset_agent rst_agent;
10
11         `uvm_component_utils(wb_env)
12
13         extern function new(string name="wb_env", uvm_component parent=
                null);
14         extern virtual function void build_phase(uvm_phase phase);
15         extern virtual function void connect_phase(uvm_phase phase);
16
17     endclass: wb_env
18
19     function wb_env::new(string name= "wb_env",uvm_component parent=null);
20         super.new(name,parent);
21     endfunction:new
22
23     function void wb_env::build_phase(uvm_phase phase);
24         super.build_phase(phase);
25         master_agent = wb_master_agent::type_id::create("master_agent",
                this);
26         slave_agent = wb_slave_agent::type_id::create("slave_agent",this);
27         cov = wb_env_cov::type_id::create("cov",this); //Instantiating the
                coverage class
28         sb = wb_scoreboard::type_id::create("sb",this);
29
30         rst_agent = reset_agent::type_id::create("rst_agent",this);
31
32     endfunction: build_phase
33
34     function void wb_env::connect_phase(uvm_phase phase);
35         super.connect_phase(phase);
36         master_agent.mast_mon.mon_analysis_port.connect(cov.
                analysis_export);
37         master_agent.analysis_port.connect(sb.actual_wb_transaction_fifo.
                analysis_export);
38         slave_agent.analysis_port.connect(sb.expected_wb_transaction_fifo.
                analysis_export);
39     endfunction: connect_phase
```

In Listing 8.12:

- Line 4 declares the wb_env class

- The master agent, slave agent, coverage subscriber and scoreboard instances are defined on Lines 5-8

- The build_phase between Lines 25-30 show the use of factory methods to build the various components.

- The master and slave agents are connected to the scoreboard TLM ports in the connect phase in Lines 37-38.

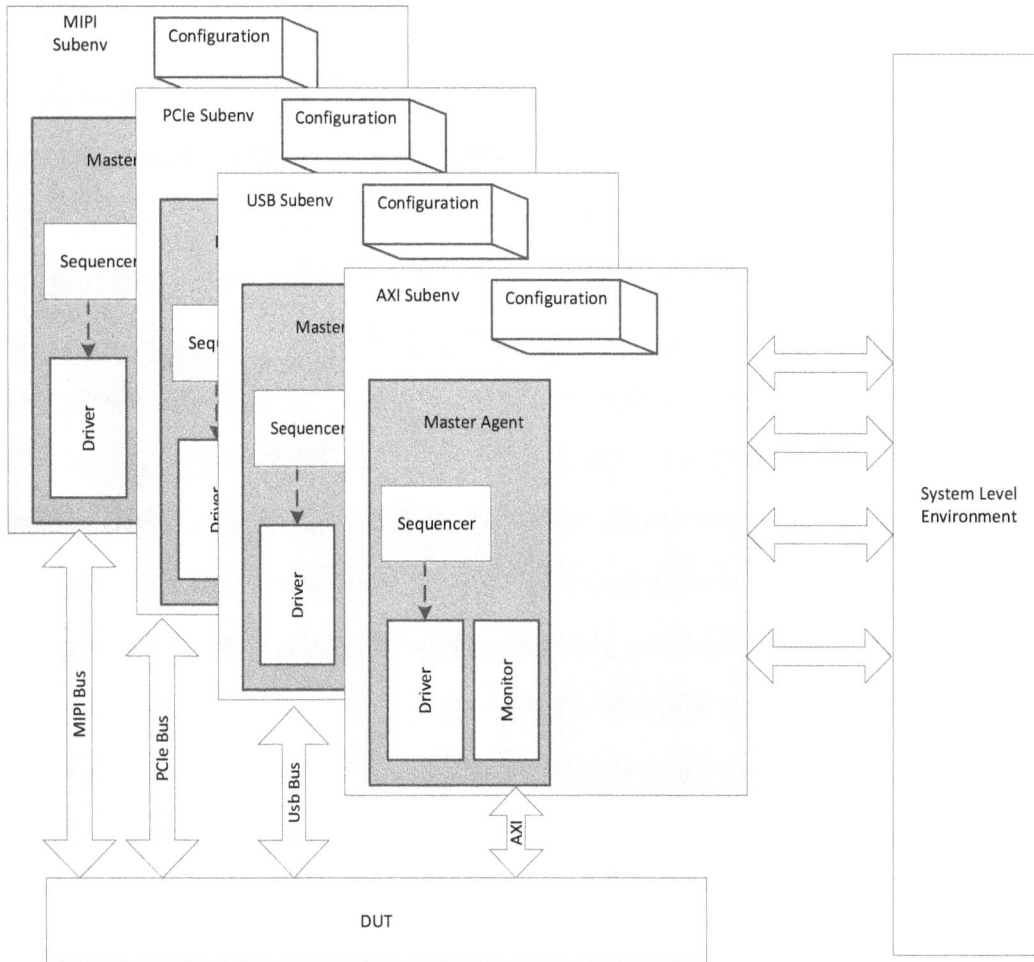

Fig. 8.15: Vertical Reuse Of The Environment Classes

A block-level environment contains all necessary block-level verification components that are used by a test to test the DUT. Once this block level testing is completed, a portion of this environment will be needed for testing the DUT at the chip level. To do so, You can extend the block level environment as necessary to communicate with system-level testbench and have the system level environment coordinate the behavior of various block-level environments

In Figure 8.15, many block level environments are all placed in a top-level subsystem/system environment. Each environment has its agents, stimuli, etc. This way, you can create a sophisticated environment by reusing some of the work done in various block level environments in your SOC.

Recommendation 8.4.0: *Create a configuration for the environment with randomizable fields*

The configuration object should instantiate the child config objects (which are also derived from uvm_object) corresponding to individual components or sub-environments.

8.4.2 Top Level Test

The uvm_test class is a class that contains information specific to a single test in the environment. It configures the environment according to specific parameters required for the test and configures the sequencers to select a specific stimulus for the test. Any information regarding the replacement of specific verification environment to facilitate the test is also contained in this test class.

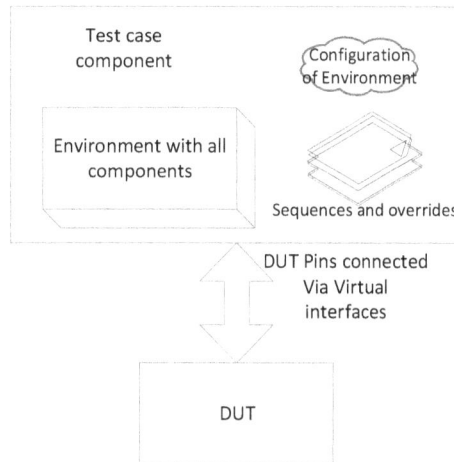

Fig. 8.16: Top Level Test

Rule 8.4.0:   *User testcases should extend uvm_test.*

The test class is derived from uvm_test and is used to represent the test case. The test creates and configures the environment required to verify particular features of the DUT. Typically, many tests are associated with any testbench, and these may be compiled together depending on the simulator, are selected from the command 'line with a single test being called with each invocation. Below is an example of a test.

Listing 8.13: The UVM test

```
5
6      class wb_env_base_test extends uvm_test;
7
8          wb_config wb_master_config;
9          wb_config wb_slave_config;
10
11         `uvm_component_utils(wb_env_base_test)
12
13         wb_env env;
14
15         function new(string name, uvm_component parent);
16             super.new(name, parent);
17         endfunction
18
19         virtual function void build_phase(uvm_phase phase);
20             super.build_phase(phase);
21             env = wb_env::type_id::create("env", this);
22             wb_master_config = new("wb_master_config");
23             wb_slave_config = new("wb_slave_config");
24
25             wb_master_config.max_n_wss = 10;
26             wb_master_config.min_addr = 0;
27             wb_master_config.max_addr = 10000000;
28
29             wb_slave_config.max_n_wss = 10;
30             wb_slave_config.min_addr = 0;
31             wb_slave_config.max_addr = 10000000;
32
33             begin: configure
34                 uvm_config_db #(uvm_object_wrapper)::set(this, "env.
                        rst_agent.mast_sqr.reset_phase", "default_sequence",
                        reset_sequence::get_type());
35                 uvm_config_db #(uvm_object_wrapper)::set(this, "env.
                        master_agent.mast_sqr.main_phase", "default_sequence",
                        sequence_1::get_type());
36                 uvm_config_db #(uvm_object_wrapper)::set(this, "env.
                        slave_agent.slv_seqr.main_phase", "default_sequence",
                        ram_sequence::get_type());
37
38                 uvm_config_db #(wb_config)::set(this, "env.master_agent",
                        "config", wb_master_config);
39                 uvm_config_db #(wb_config)::set(this, "env.slave_agent", "
                        config", wb_slave_config);
40             end
41         endfunction
42
43     endclass : wb_env_base_test
44
45 `endif //BASE_TEST__SV
```

In listing 8.13:

- Line 6 declares a test class. This class extends from the uvm_test class. Hence, one can consider it as a base class for other tests

- Line 8,9 are are the master and slave agent configurations.

- Line 11 provides factory registration and other utilities.

- Line 13 shows the environment class instance.

- Lines 15-17 are the constructor of the class.

- Lines 19-41 are the build_phase for the test class.

- Line 21 creates the environment.

- Line 34-36 sets the default sequence in the main phase for the sequencer.

8.5 Component Configuration

In the verification environment, each agent in the system needs information to configure itself properly. Building the agents with a configuration object is usually a good practice because it allows you to do many things including randomizing the config. In the case of a simple environment for the components developed in this chapter, each of the master and slave agents needs the following information:

- Start address of memory map

- End address of the memory map,

- number of wait cycles.

As you will recognize, with the growth of the number of parameters in each slave or master, there would be many config_db entries. This makes the configuration extremely hard to manage. It quickly becomes a source of bugs and debugging can also be quite challenging. One will find that with the increase in the number of configuration settings that have to be retrieved, there would be a significant performance impact on the simulation time and an adverse impact on performance.

We recommend the use of a configuration class that encapsulates these settings for many reasons. You can customize the configuration class to add additional class members that may be specific to a setting or test and also, add additional constraints allowing the class to be adequately randomized. Also, these classes can be reused in a vertical scenario, allowing for extensive reuse of the testbench components. In comparison to using many set/get calls, the use of a config class results in performance improvement when one sets up the environment correctly.

Since there are fewer lines of code in the testbench overall, you can expect fewer bugs or issues to deal with as well.

Listing 8.14: Configuration Class

```
15 class wb_config extends uvm_object;
16
17     bit enable_coverage;  // Enable coverage from monitor
18
19     typedef enum {BYTE, WORD, DWORD, QWORD} sizes_e;
20     rand sizes_e port_size;
21     rand sizes_e granularity;
22
23     typedef enum {CLASSIC, REGISTERED} cycle_types_e;
24     rand cycle_types_e cycles;
25
26     rand integer max_n_wss;
27
28     rand bit [31:0] min_addr;
29     rand bit [31:0] max_addr;
30
```

```
31      constraint wb_slave_cfg_valid {
32          max_addr >= min_addr;
33      }
34
35      constraint wb_cfg_valid {
36          granularity <= port_size;
37          max_n_wss >= 0;
38      }
39
40      constraint reasonable_max_n_wss {
41          max_n_wss < 16;
42      }
43
44      constraint supported {
45          port_size   == DWORD;
46          granularity == BYTE;
47          cycles      == CLASSIC;
48      }
49      `uvm_object_utils_begin(wb_config); // All we need is it registerd
            with factory
50      `uvm_field_enum(sizes_e,port_size,UVM_DEFAULT)
51      `uvm_field_enum(sizes_e,granularity,UVM_DEFAULT)
52      `uvm_field_enum(cycle_types_e,cycles,UVM_DEFAULT)
53      `uvm_field_int(max_n_wss,UVM_DEFAULT)
54      `uvm_field_int(min_addr,UVM_DEFAULT)
55      `uvm_field_int(max_addr,UVM_DEFAULT)
56      `uvm_object_utils_end
57
58      function new(string name ="wb_config");
59          super.new(name);
60      endfunction
61
62 endclass
```

The configuration class for the wishbone is reproduced in Listing 8.14. The class consists of a few properties.

- Line 15 shows the config class extending from uvm_object. For purposes of future expandability, the various transfer sizes that can be allowed are shown as a class property. Various allowed transfer cycles are also shown as a class property.

- Line 26 shows the number of wait states that the master/slave should expect when connected to the bus.

- Line 28 and 29 define the address range of the wishbone component.

- Line 36-42 sets a constraint to make sure that the configuration is valid. The rest of the constraints help ensure proper operation of the component.

- Lines 49- 56 are the uvm_object utils macros that do the usual functions that were described in Section 8.14

- Lines 58-60 provide the constructor for the class.

Depending on the nature of the testbench, if you are using a piece of VIP, many commercial VIP use configuration objects. In this instance, this testbench is a simple one that uses a simple configuration object. Many commercial simulator offerings now allow you to converge on coverage of these configurations. As you can recall, many RTL designs are also highly configurable, and this means that between the VIP and the other configurations in the testbench, there is a large state space that you need to verify. This consideration alone may dictate how the objects are designed.

8.6 New Features in IEEE 1800.2

In earlier versions of UVM, One of the common problems faced by environment integrators who would integrate many agents into an environment was increased time spent in the build_phase(). This behavior came from the fact that agents would query the uvm_config_db for values of properties placed in the `uvm_field_*_utils macros inside the component. Each of these queries took time, and when you had many of these, the build_phase consumed a lot of time. As indicated in Section 8.5 it Is preferable to have a wrapper container class to handle the configuration to minimize the number of lookups.

Sometimes you may have an environment where you do not want to update the properties of the class from the config_db. The IEEE version now adds additional capability to shut off configuration completely. A new virtual function has been added to IEEE 18002. you can use this function as below.

```
virtual function bit use_automatic_config();
return 1'b0;
endfunction
```

The method by default returns 1 in the UVM library to keep the default behavior. Extend the agent to set the return value of this function to 0, and the component will no longer query the config_db for values of its member properties when it is built.

Recommendation 8.6.0:   *Use this in conjunction with the set_local capability and the wrapper mechanism described in Section* 8.5

An example showing the use of this capability is shown below.

Listing 8.15: Automatic Configuration Disable

```
4   class Class_A_acs extends uvm_component;
5     int my_component_int_prop ;
6     `uvm_component_utils_begin(Class_A_acs)
7     `uvm_field_int(my_component_int_prop,UVM_ALL_ON)
8     `uvm_component_utils_end
9
10    function new(string name="Class_A_acs",uvm_component parent = null);
11      super.new(name,parent);
12    endfunction
13    virtual function bit use_automatic_config();
14      return 1;
15    endfunction
16  endclass
17
18  class Class_A_no_acs extends uvm_component;
19    int my_component_int_prop ;
20    `uvm_component_utils_begin(Class_A_no_acs)
21    `uvm_field_int(my_component_int_prop,UVM_ALL_ON)
22    `uvm_component_utils_end
23
24    function new(string name="Class_A_no_acs",uvm_component parent = null)
        ;
25      super.new(name,parent);
26    endfunction
27    virtual function bit use_automatic_config();
28      return 0;
29    endfunction
30  endclass
31
```

```
32  class Class_A_no_acs_ext extends Class_A_acs;
33      `uvm_component_utils(Class_A_no_acs_ext)
34    function new(string name="Class_A_no_acs_ext",uvm_component parent =
          null);
35      super.new(name,parent);
36    endfunction
37    virtual function bit use_automatic_config();
38      return 1;
39    endfunction
40  endclass
41
42  class Class_A_no_acs_ext_2 extends Class_A_acs;
43    `uvm_component_utils(Class_A_no_acs_ext_2)
44    function new(string name="Class_A_no_acs_ext_2",uvm_component parent =
          null);
45      super.new(name,parent);
46    endfunction
47    virtual function bit use_automatic_config();
48      return 0;
49    endfunction
50  endclass
51
52  class mytest extends uvm_test;
53    `uvm_component_utils(mytest)
54    function new(string name="mytest",uvm_component parent = null);
55      super.new(name,parent);
56    endfunction
57    Class_A_no_acs no_acs1;
58    Class_A_no_acs no_acs2;
59    Class_A_acs   acs1;
60    Class_A_acs   acs2;
61    Class_A_acs   acs_array[16];
62
63    function void build_phase(uvm_phase phase);
64      uvm_coreservice_t cs;
65      int my_comp_int = 10;
66      uvm_root r;
67      uvm_factory my_factory = uvm_factory::get();
68      cs = uvm_coreservice_t::get();
69      r = cs.get_root();
70      r.enable_print_topology = 1;
71      my_factory.set_inst_override_by_name("Class_A_acs","
          Class_A_no_acs_ext_2",{get_full_name(),".","acs_array[10]"});
72      // Type override
73      my_factory.set_type_override_by_type( Class_A_acs::get_type(),
          Class_A_no_acs_ext::get_type());
74
75      uvm_config_db #(int)::set(this,"no_acs1","my_component_int_prop",10)
          ;
76      uvm_config_db #(int)::set(this,"no_acs1","my_component_int_prop",20)
          ;
77      uvm_config_db #(int)::set(this,"acs1","my_component_int_prop",14);
78      uvm_config_db #(int)::set(this,"acs2","my_component_int_prop",15);
79      for(int i = 0; i < 16; i++) begin
```

```
80          uvm_config_db #(int)::set(this,$sformatf("acs_array[%02d]","
               my_component_int_prop",i);
81          acs_array[i]  = Class_A_acs::type_id::create($sformatf("acs_array
               [%02d]",i),this);
82       end
83       no_acs1 = Class_A_no_acs::type_id::create("no_acs1",this);
84       no_acs2 = Class_A_no_acs::type_id::create("no_acs2",this);
85       acs1 = Class_A_acs::type_id::create("acs1",this);
86       acs2 = Class_A_acs::type_id::create("acs2",this);
87       my_factory.print();
88    endfunction
89  endclass
```

There are a number of interesting observations you can make from Listing 8.15 and the below portion of the log file. Observe the config_db settings on Lines 75,76 and 80 when you look at the log file.

- Lines 4-16,18-30,32-40 and 42-50 declare various classes. Each of them returns the value of use_automatic_config() differently.

- Lines 4-16 show Class_A_acs with a integer property and the use_automatic_config() turned ON.

- Lines 18-30 show another class where the use_automatic_config() is turned OFF. Notice that it returns a 0 on line 28.

- Lines 32-40 and 42-50 show class extensions.

- Line 52 shows the test where various instances of the component are created. Some will get the configuration based on Lines 75,76,80 and some wont, based on the setting of the use_automatic_config() in the class.

- Line 71 shows an specific instance override. Note that this takes precedence over the type override on Line 73. You see this on Line 427 in the log below with the type being *Class_A_no_acs_ext_2*.

The resulting log file from this is below.

```
397
398 -----------------------------------------------------------------
399 Name                     Type                     Size   Value
400 -----------------------------------------------------------------
401 <unnamed>                uvm_root                  -      @61
402 uvm_test_top             mytest                    -      @112
403 acs1                     Class_A_no_acs_ext        -      @340
404 my_component_int_prop    integral                 32      'he
405 acs2                     Class_A_no_acs_ext        -      @349
406 my_component_int_prop    integral                 32      'hf
407 acs_array[00]            Class_A_no_acs_ext        -      @163
408 my_component_int_prop    integral                 32      'h0
409 acs_array[01]            Class_A_no_acs_ext        -      @173
410 my_component_int_prop    integral                 32      'h1
411 acs_array[02]            Class_A_no_acs_ext        -      @183
412 my_component_int_prop    integral                 32      'h2
413 acs_array[03]            Class_A_no_acs_ext        -      @193
414 my_component_int_prop    integral                 32      'h3
415 acs_array[04]            Class_A_no_acs_ext        -      @203
416 my_component_int_prop    integral                 32      'h4
417 acs_array[05]            Class_A_no_acs_ext        -      @213
418 my_component_int_prop    integral                 32      'h5
419 acs_array[06]            Class_A_no_acs_ext        -      @223
420 my_component_int_prop    integral                 32      'h6
```

```
421 acs_array[07]                Class_A_no_acs_ext      -        @233
422 my_component_int_prop        integral               32       'h7
423 acs_array[08]                Class_A_no_acs_ext      -        @243
424 my_component_int_prop        integral               32       'h8
425 acs_array[09]                Class_A_no_acs_ext      -        @253
426 my_component_int_prop        integral               32       'h9
427 acs_array[10]                Class_A_no_acs_ext_2    -        @263
428 my_component_int_prop        integral               32       'h0
429 acs_array[11]                Class_A_no_acs_ext      -        @273
430 my_component_int_prop        integral               32       'hb
431 acs_array[12]                Class_A_no_acs_ext      -        @283
432 my_component_int_prop        integral               32       'hc
433 acs_array[13]                Class_A_no_acs_ext      -        @293
434 my_component_int_prop        integral               32       'hd
435 acs_array[14]                Class_A_no_acs_ext      -        @303
436 my_component_int_prop        integral               32       'he
437 acs_array[15]                Class_A_no_acs_ext      -        @313
438 my_component_int_prop        integral               32       'hf
439 no_acs1                      Class_A_no_acs          -        @322
440 my_component_int_prop        integral               32       'h0
441 no_acs2                      Class_A_no_acs          -        @331
442 my_component_int_prop        integral               32       'h0
443 ------------------------------------------------------------------
444 UVM_INFO
```

8.7 Creating and Using UVM Components - Guidelines

There are many considerations when using UVM components in a UVM testbench. These guidelines are applicable to all classes derived from uvm_component. These considerations are designed with the view that there should be reuse enabled at all levels of the testbench without creating a significant amount of overhead and the fact that components are quasi-static objects that exist throughout the simulation.

Rule 8.7.0:   *The uvm_component class is abstract and cannot be used to create objects directly.* Components are instances of classes derived from uvm_component. You must extend the class before you can make an instance of it. This is what many of the predefined components provided by the library do

Rule 8.7.1:   *All user-defined component classes must be created by extending the appropriate subclass of class uvm_component with the intent of the component easily understandable by its users.*

Once a component hierarchy is defined, The hierarchy cannot be changed dynamically!
The clone and copy methods inherited from uvm_object are disabled for the uvm_component class.

Rule 8.7.2:   *Components may only be created, and their ports (if any) bound before the end_of_elaboration phase, the hierarchy must be fixed by the start of this phase.*

Rule 8.7.3:   *Component names must be unique at each level of the hierarchy. Else the find_by_name functions will not work.*

Rule 8.7.4:   *Do not forget to register components with the factory, using `uvm_component_utils or `uvm_component_param_utils*

Rule 8.7.5:   *new() and build() should call the base class new (super.new) and build (super.build) methods respectively.* ***You must remember to call these functions*** [3].

Recommendation 8.7.0:   *Enable build-time-control using apply_config_settings()*

Recommendation 8.7.1:   *Set the required reporting options by calling the hierarchical functions (set_report *hier) for a top-level component since these settings are applied recursively to all child components.*

Reports are only written to a file if a file descriptor has been specified and the action has been set to UVM_LOG for a particular category of report generated. See the reporting chapter.

Rule 8.7.6:   *Every component that has configuration must be configured through a configuration class. Methods for configuration are only called during the build_phase().*

Rule 8.7.7:   *If a component has sub-components, then the configuration of the components should be through the config class*

Rule 8.7.8:   *Ensure you connect all components in the connect_phase().*

Rule 8.7.9:   *Always create components using the factory.*

Instantiations should take the form:
var_name = component_type::type_id::create("var_name", this);
The string name of the component should be the same as the variable name.

Rule 8.7.10:   *Do NOT create component instances directly using new(). Use the create() method to enable factory replacement.*

Rule 8.7.11:   *Do not call randomize() within a component. Randomization is reserved for sequences and test classes.*

---

[3] You must create instantiations of components from the build_phase method ONLY. Only in the case where a user-defined component class directly extends a class from the UVM base class library and overrides the standard build_phase method, you do not call super.build_phase

Chapter 9

Callbacks

UVM allows the user to use, extend, and modify the functionality of components in a variety of ways. Often, users wish to extend the behavior of the component to test a specific mode in the DUT or handle responses in a verification environment. In many cases, extending the component entails much work on the part of the user. This chapter presents callbacks, a mechanism to allow the user to change component behavior **with less effort.**

There are many applications for callbacks. For example, you may wish to inject errors into a verification environment using an agent under specific circumstances. This implies that the error injection code is not used all the time. The requirements for error injection could also possibly change depending on circumstances. You could choose to increase the complexity of the agent by incorporating all required error injection features in your agent. However, you will have to deal with code instability that comes with such an approach. If you were using components supplied from a piece of verification IP that was encrypted, modifying it is not even an option without the involvement of the verification IP vendor. As a component developer, the best solution to these kinds of challenges is to provide a set of intercept points in the components allowing users to customize components based on their own requirements.

A callback is an ideal approach to separate customized behavior in the testbench environment. Callbacks are used for many applications and are not restricted to agents. Applications of callbacks include transaction's randomization, data generation, coverage, scoreboard operations, error injection, or any behavior that is test specific and not environment specific.

A callback is a virtual method call placed inside a uvm_component allowing you to change the behavior of the component. This mechanism allows you to change the behavior of the verification environment *without* modifying the testbench code or the component itself. This approach allows you to conduct bulk of the verification without any callbacks, incorporating changes using callbacks only where necessary. Many UVM classes provide built-in callbacks allowing you to alter the behavior of the testbench. Component developers can opt to allow the user to customize specific behaviors of their components without damaging the overall integrity of the component.

Rule 9.0.0:   *As a component developer, provide a set of virtual methods in the component at significant points to allow the user to customize the component extensively.*

(i)   Use callbacks if you need to change the default behavior (For Example: inject an error) without modifying the original component. All you need to remember is that once control is transferred to your callback during execution, the component code is effectively "stopped" until the method completes.

9.1 Creating Callbacks in Components

The sections that follow describe the various steps you should take to incorporate callbacks in components that you develop. Implementing a callback consists of four steps. As the component developer, you perform the first three steps; the user of your component performs the fourth step.

Figure 9.1 shows the steps involved in creating and using callbacks. This example uses the simple driver from Section 8.3.1. Here, we change the values driven by the driver on a write cycle without modifying the code in the driver component. The modifications are made in two distinct phases of the cycle, as shown in Figure 9.2.

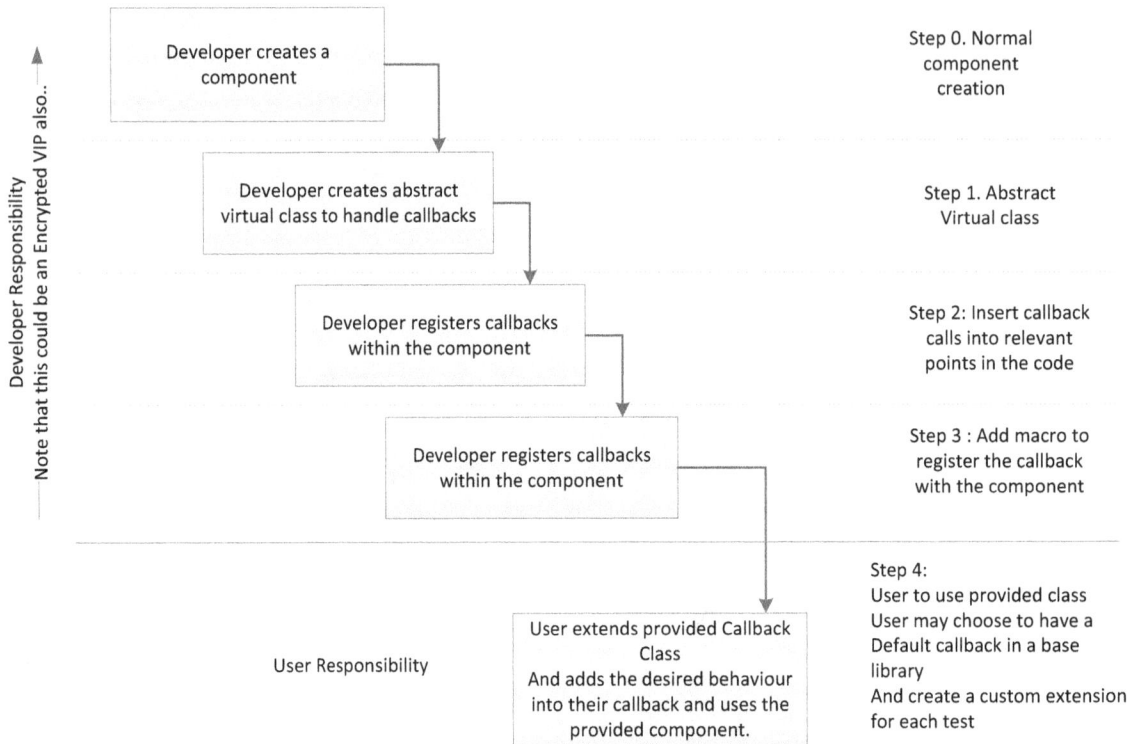

Fig. 9.1: Steps To Add Callbacks

1. Change the value of the TDA signals so that signals always have a value of 0xF *before transmission from the driver. Note that the driver probably had some other value for this field given to it as a part of a randomized packet, but this callback hard codes it to 0xF.*

2. Change the completed response to the transaction with the TDC value always set to 0x1 *after receipt, and before processing a response.*

In Figure 9.2, just before the data is driven (transmitted) on the address bus, the transaction is modified by a pre-tx() method in the callback class as indicated by marker 'a'.

After the DUT receives the transaction, the callback alters TDC. Marker 'b' indicates where the callback must change the data.

9.1.1 Step 1: Create Virtual Callback Class

The first step to adding callbacks into a component is creating an abstract (virtual) base class for the callback. This base class contains a simple skeleton definition of the callback methods to be defined. The component developer decides the names and details of the callback function and the arguments to the callback methods. These are passed into the callback when the callback method is invoked. Listing 9.1 shows the first step of the developer actions for the wishbone driver that was created in Section 8.3.1.

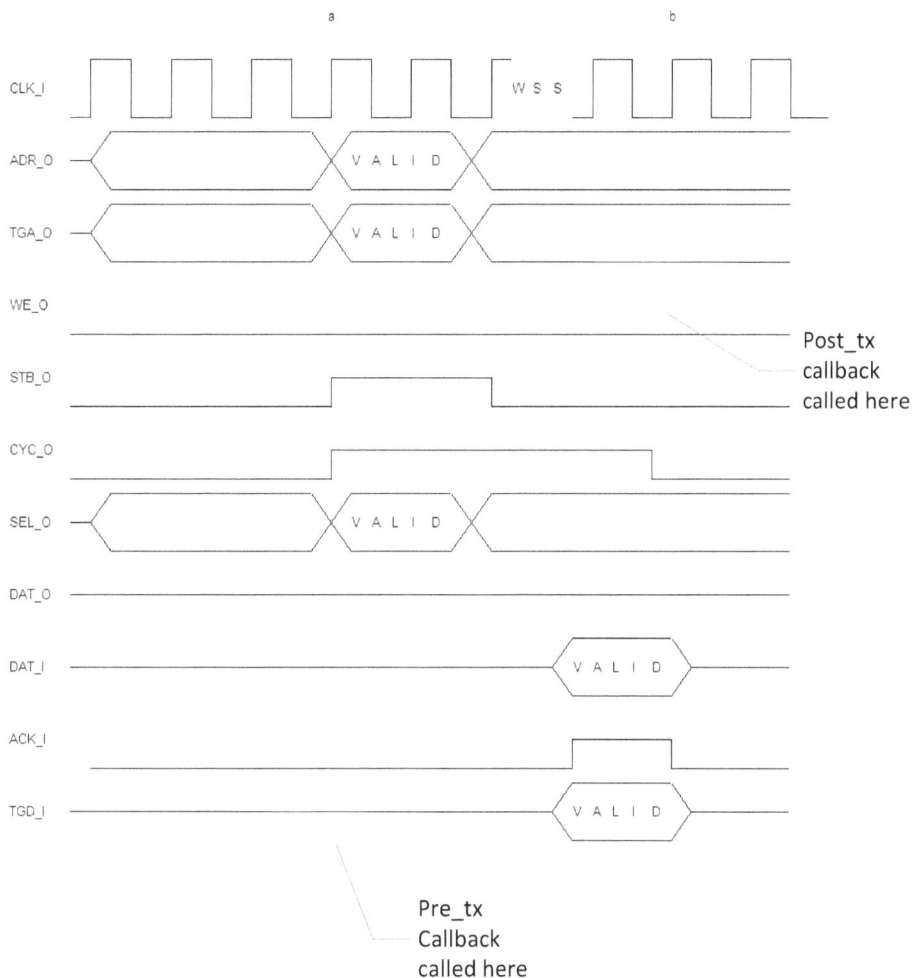

Fig. 9.2: Driver Callbacks

Listing 9.1: Driver actions in Callback

```
14   virtual class wb_master_callbacks extends uvm_callback;
15
16     // Called before a transaction is executed
17     virtual task pre_tx( wb_master xactor,
18       wb_transaction tr);
19
20     endtask: pre_tx
21
22     // Called after a transaction has been executed
23     virtual task post_tx( wb_master xactor,
24       wb_transaction tr);
25     endtask: post_tx
26
27   endclass: wb_master_callbacks
```

- Line 14 declares the callback facade class wb_master_callbacks extending from class uvm_callback.

- Line 18 shows the task pre-tx that is called at the time before the driver processes the transaction. The method prints the contents of the transaction and some simple messages. Note that this task is defined as virtual.

- Line 25 shows the driver processes the task post-tx that is called at the time after the transaction. Depending on the transaction, the contents of the transaction would vary between the pre-tx and post-tx callbacks.

Rule 9.1.0:   *You must declare all callback methods for a component as virtual tasks or void functions in a single class derived from uvm_callback.*

Rule 9.1.1:   *When developing callbacks for various components within an agent (for example driver and monitor), ensure you provide callback points in both components, which are identical in terms of protocol state.*

This is an often-ignored rule. However, it is important. If your protocol has your driver and monitor in a specific state, you must provide a callback for the *exact same* state in both the driver and monitor. If you do not do so, the issue you will run into is that your monitor may flag something, and you cannot intercept the driver in the same transaction state as the monitor in your callback.

Recommendation 9.1.0:   *Employ a delicate balance between having an excessive number of callbacks, which affect performance, to having too few callbacks.*

Too many mean that the component is going to be slow in a simulation. Too few callbacks mean that the component is very inflexible.

9.1.2 Step 2: Register the Callback Class
After creating the callback class, register the callback class with the uvm_component using `uvm_register_cb to ensure valid pairings between the class and object.

```
Listing 9.2: Callback Registration in Driver

42   class wb_master extends uvm_driver # (wb_transaction);
43
44      wb_config mstr_drv_cfg;
45
46
47      typedef virtual wb_master_if v_if;
48      v_if drv_if;
49      `uvm_register_cb(wb_master,wb_master_callbacks);
```

Listing 9.2 shows the registration of the callbacks.

- Line 49 shows the `uvm_register_cb where the type of the class and the type of the callback are registered.

As mentioned earlier, the registration function takes the type of driver and callback classes to ensure compile safety.

9.1.3 Step 3: Place the Callback Class Hook in Driver Code
The component creator defines where and when the component is expected to call the callback function.
The `uvm_do_callbacks macro calls the given METHOD_CALL of all callbacks of type TYPE_OF_CALLBACK registered with the calling object (i.e., this object), which is or is based on type COMPONENT_TYPE using the following call:

```
`uvm_do_callbacks(COMPONENT_TYPE,TYPE_OF_CALLBACK,METHOD_CALL)
```

TYPE_OF_CALLBACK is the class type of callback objects. The class type must have a function that is used in the METHOD_CALL argument. COMPONENT_TYPE is the type of the component associated with the callback. METHOD_CALL is the method call to invoke, with all required arguments as if they were invoked directly.

Rule 9.1.2:   *You must call the callback at the appropriate point using `uvm_do_callbacks*

Listing 9.3: Callback Hooks Placed in Driver

```
142   task wb_master::main_driver();
143     int count;
144     count = 0;
145     forever begin
146       wb_transaction tr;
147       bit drop = 0;
148       // Set output signals to their idle state
149       ...
150
151         seq_item_port.get_next_item(tr);
152       `uvm_info("wb_env_DRIVER", "Starting transaction...",UVM_LOW)
153       `uvm_do_callbacks(wb_master,wb_master_callbacks, pre_tx(this, tr))
154       // Since we are just beginning the transaction, we dont know what
                state it's in yet.
155       tr.status = wb_transaction::UNKNOWN;
156
157       case (tr.kind)
158         // Various kinds of transactions handled by tasks
159
160         ....
161
162       endcase
163
164       seq_item_port.item_done();
165       `uvm_do_callbacks(wb_master,wb_master_callbacks, post_tx(this, tr))
166       `uvm_info("wb_env_DRIVER", "Completed transaction...",UVM_LOW)
167       count = count + 1;
168     end
169   endtask : main_driver
```

- The main_driver task runs in an infinite loop checking the seq_item port on line 145.

- Line 153. After getting the transaction from the sequencer, the driver calls the pre_tx callback before it acts on it. The pre-tx task is defined in the wb_master_callbacks class.

- Line 165. After completing the read or write transaction, the main_driver task calls the post-tx callback

9.1.4 Step 4: Extend and Use the Callback Class

In the fourth and final step, the specific callback functions can be defined in a testcase. Once the callbacks are defined, the test case can register them with the testbench component. The component automatically invokes the callbacks at the appropriate times, using the callback macros that were included in the component in step 2. Based on Figure 9.2, The implementation of the callback class is seen in the listing:

Listing 9.4: Callback Class implementation

```
10    class wb_master_callbacks extends uvm_callback;
11
12
13      // Called before a transaction is executed
14      virtual task pre_tx( wb_master xactor,
15        wb_transaction tr);
16
17        // This callback method changes the TGA field so that it
```

```
18        // is hardcoded to  0xF as per the example
19        tr.tga = 4'hf;
20
21      endtask: pre_tx
22
23
24      // Called after a transaction has been executed
25      virtual task post_tx( wb_master xactor,
26        wb_transaction tr);
27
28        `uvm_info(this.get_fullname()," This is in the stage After the
              driver acts on a transaction phase",UVM_LOW)
29
30        tr.tgc = 4'b1;
31        // Now print the value so that one can see the value in the
              callbacks
32        tr.print();
33      endtask: post_tx
34
35    endclass: wb_master_callbacks
```

- Line 10 is the implementation of the wb_master_callbacks class.

- Line 14 shows the pre_tx method. Before driving on the bus, this method changes the value of the TGA bits on the bus to 0xF.

- Line 25 shows the implementation of the post_tx method. Line 27 shows the TGC value being fixed to 0x1 after the data is driven on the pins.

Callbacks can either be type-wide, where every instance of the component's callback for the same type is replaced, or instance-specific.

To add a callback, call:

```
`uvm_register_cb(T,CB)
or
add(T obj, uvm_callback cb, uvm_apprepend ordering=UVM_APPEND)
```

The add() method registers the given callback object, cb, with the given obj handle which is not null. The obj handle can be null, which allows registration of callbacks without an object context. If ordering is UVM_APPEND (default), the callback is executed after previously added callbacks; otherwise, the callback is executed ahead of already added callbacks. If the callback has already been added to the object instance, then a warning is issued. Note that the CB parameter is optional. The example below shows you how this call is made in the test.

Listing 9.5: Using the callback in the test

```
40      class wb_conmax_instance_callback_test extends wb_conmax_base_test;
41
42          `uvm_component_utils(wb_conmax_instance_callback_test)
43
44          wb_master_driver_new_cb new_cb1 = new("New Callback #1");
45          wb_master_driver_new_cb new_cb2 = new("New Callback #2");
46
47
48
49          function new(string name, uvm_component parent);
50              super.new(name, parent);
51          endfunction
52
53          wb_conmax_virtual_sequence virt_seq1;
54          virtual task main_phase(uvm_phase phase);
55              uvm_callbacks #(wb_master,wb_master_driver_new_cb)::add(env.
                    master_agent[00].mast_drv,new_cb1);
56              phase.raise_objection(this,"Test Main Objection");
57              virt_seq1 = wb_conmax_virtual_sequence::type_id::create("
                    wb_conmax_virtual_sequence",this);
58              virt_seq1.start(env.wb_conmax_virt_seqr,null);
59              virt_seq1.wait_for_sequence_state(UVM_FINISHED);
60              phase.drop_objection(this,"Dropping Test Main Objection");
61          endtask
62
63      endclass :  wb_conmax_instance_callback_test
```

- Line 44 shows a new instance of the callback class being created in the test
- Line 55 shows the callback added to the wb_master driver for a specific instance.

(i) Note that you can either append or prepend the callback to the queue. Experiment with this parameter during your study.

.UVM Callbacks are factory replaceable.
IEEE

9.2 User Applications of Callbacks

Callbacks can be type based (added to all instances of a specific component type) or only to a specific instance of a component. This can be controlled on a test by test basis. Users can choose, during callback instantiation, if they would like to have all the components of a specific type call the callback or only a specific component in the test without actually affecting the rest of the environment.

9.2.1 Typewide Callbacks

There are a couple of ways that callbacks can be registered in UVM. Depending on the circumstances, one may wish to add a callback to *every instance* of a specific uvm_component. Such a callback is called a type-wide callback.

Listing 9.6: Type Wide Callback Example

```
37    virtual function void build_phase(uvm_phase phase);
38        super.build_phase(phase);
39
40        uvm_callbacks #(wb_master,wb_master_driver_new_cb)::add(null,new_cb1
              );
41        // Set the default sequencer in all the master agents
42        uvm_config_db #(uvm_object_wrapper)::set(this, "env.
              wb_conmax_virt_seqr.main_phase", "default_sequence",
                                wb_conmax_virtual_sequence::get_type()); //
              uvm_report_cb::add(null,promoter);
43
44    endfunction
```

The above listing provides the code snippet for the type wide callback in the body() task of a test. All instances of the wb_master_driver class have an instance of the callback added to it. Only the listing is shown above.

See the discussion in section 21.8.2 for block diagrams and a complete example.

9.2.2 Instance Specific Callbacks

In the case of an instance-specific callback, only one specific instance of the component registers a callback as shown in the build_phase for the test below.

Listing 9.7: Instance Specific Callback Example

```
53    virtual function void end_of_elaboration_phase(uvm_phase phase);
54        super.end_of_elaboration_phase(phase);
55
56            uvm_callbacks #(wb_master,wb_master_driver_new_cb_inst)::add(env
                  .master_agent[0].mast_drv,new_cb2);
```

A complete working example of an instance-specific callback is shown in the test in Section 21.8.1. A complete description is provided in that section. In this Example, only one class instance driver[0] has a new callback. None of the other drivers of the same type have the callback registered to them.

There are many other methods available in the UVM callback class. For reasons of brevity, I have condensed the discussion to the above two callback types. You can modify the callbacks after looking at the documentation.

9.3 Order of Execution of Callbacks

Rule 9.3.0:   *Do not rely on the order of execution of the callbacks.*

The registered callbacks for any component are pushed into a queue. The callbacks can be enabled or disabled using the uvm_callback APIs. The order of execution of callbacks, therefore, depends on which callbacks are enabled in the component. Relying on it may give you unpredictable results.

9.4 New in IEEE - get_all callbacks

When you look under the macros of the `uvm_do_callbacks, you will see the following code when you expand the macro:

```
begin
uvm_callback_iter#(T,CB) iter = new(OBJ);
CB cb = iter.first();
while(cb != null) begin
... cb.METHOD;
cb = iter.next();
end
end
```

The problem is that the first() method only yields you the *enabled* callbacks and not every callback[1]. The option to process every callback was not available in the UVM-1.2 version. The IEEE 1800.2 version adds a new method that allows you to get *all* the callbacks that are registered with a component.

```
static function void get_all ( ref CB all_callbacks[$] , input T obj=null );
```

> The uvm_callbacks::get_all method the LRM describes is insufficient to retrieve all callbacks registered on a given *instance* of an object, filtering cannot be based on an object instance. The implementation, therefore, adds an argument to the method to overcome the issue of resolving the instance specific callback. This issue is corrected in the upcoming LRM. The corrected function has the signature shown above and is in UVM-IEEE-2017 implementation that you are using with this book. This will be corrected in future versions of the UVM LRM

9.5 UVM Event Callbacks

The uvm_event callback class derives from uvm_callback. Earlier versions of this class used to derive it from uvm_object. This class allows you to run a method before the event is triggered, as well as after the event is triggered.

> **UVM** **IEEE** The uvm_event callback class now extends from uvm_callback, and although the uvm_callback extends from uvm_object and is factory enabled, the uvm_event_callback class is not factory enabled. This may change in a future version of the library.

.

The methods available are:

```
virtual function bit pre_trigger (uvm_event#(T) e, T data);
virtual function void post_trigger (uvm_event#(T) e, T data);
```

The pre_trigger method is called just before triggering the associated event. In a derived class, you must override this method to implement any pre_trigger functionality. If you want to disable the event from being called, you must return 1 from the method to prevent the event from triggering. You can pass in any additional data to the callback via the data parameter.

The post_trigger callback is called after triggering the associated event. In a derived class, you must override this method to implement any post_trigger functionality. As with the previous method, you can pass additional data to the callback class.

See Section 15.2 for an example of how to use these callbacks.

9.6 Debugging Callbacks

Add +define+UVM_CB_TRACE_ON to your command line during compilation (if you are using VCS) or otherwise set this define during compile time. This setting will instrument the uvm library causing it to emit messages with message id UVMCB_TRC and UVM_NONE verbosity notifying add, delete and execution of uvm callbacks. By default, this feature is not turned on.

---

[1] Note that you could have enabled or disabled the callback using the callback_mode() on the callbacks

9.7 Exercises for Further Exploration

This chapter discussed the steps for creating callbacks in UVM_Component. A couple of different callback types with examples are illustrated above. The following exercises help you to deepen your understanding of the callback mechanism.

1. Create a type wide callback that allows the slave_driver to print out the transaction in the Example shown in Section 21.8.1. Make it instance specific.

2. For a specific slave_driver in Section 21, try to write a callback that turns the data to zero no matter what the actual data is.

3. Is it possible to have the driver shown in Section 9.3 return an error for a specific address? What kind of callback would you put and where?

Chapter 10
Transaction Layer Communication

The process of designing an electronic system involves taking an abstract idea and replacing abstractions with concrete details, which can be manufactured in silicon. This process of adding more detail to the abstract idea happens in a variety of ways, over a period of time as the design is finalized. The abstraction, therefore, can be at many levels. As the design progresses towards an implementation, details of the idea are filled in to complete the implementation.

In its simplest form, a transaction is defined as an exchange of control or data between two entities in a design. This exchange of information is from a producer to a consumer. This exchange of information manifests in the design as a quantum of activity bound spatially and temporally. Depending on the level of abstraction modeled in the design, this manifestation may be in a physical layer as a collection of pin wiggles, or it may assume a more abstract form as a function call in the implementation.

To better understand and appreciate the concept of TLM, let's take a quick look at a data transfer that is happening between a master device and a slave device. In the initial stages of the design, the master and slave components below may be abstract entities that are merely defined to have data exchanged between them. This definition is shown in Figure 10.1. At this level, all that is known and understood is that specific data exchange will occur between two entities. If there is a high-level implementation, then there are some high-level semantics that defines the transfer of information between the two entities. Moving further along with some details of the implementation, if the master and slave are coded in a system language, this transfer can now be defined as a function call between the master and slave entity. There are many ways for data exchange, and these techniques will be explored further later in this chapter. Adding detailed information on ports and pins and cycle information to the model refines the implementation further. You can now describe the information exchange as a collection of pin wiggles with timing.

In all the three cases, the information exchanged was the same. There was a change in the level of abstraction that was applied to the verification environment and the DUT. Hence, TLM can be characterized as a collection of abstraction levels ranging from cycle and timing accurate modeling to extremely abstract high levels of abstraction for transferring information from one entity to another. The terminology below refers to entities creating the transactions as producers and the ones consuming transactions as consumers.

The flow of information from a producer to a consumer can be unidirectional or bidirectional. It may also be initiated by either the producer of the data or by the consumer of the data. The exchange of information can consume time or return in zero time. All of these variables give rise to many ways that data is exchanged between two entities.

UVM provides many transaction-level interfaces as a part of the library. This feature coupled with the flexible build and configuration infrastructure supplied by the library, allows the user to swap one level of abstraction for another quickly. You can interconnect components verify one level of functionality in one configuration, and replace some components in another configuration to quickly change the level of abstraction.

There are two different modeling systems called TLM-1.0 and TLM-2.0, that codify transaction-level interfaces. Both originated from the System C Initiative (OSCI). The two systems are quite different in their capabilities. The TLM -1 is a first generation system predominantly used for message passing. There is no timing annotation with this system. TLM 2.0 is primarily designed for modeling memory-mapped bus-based systems.

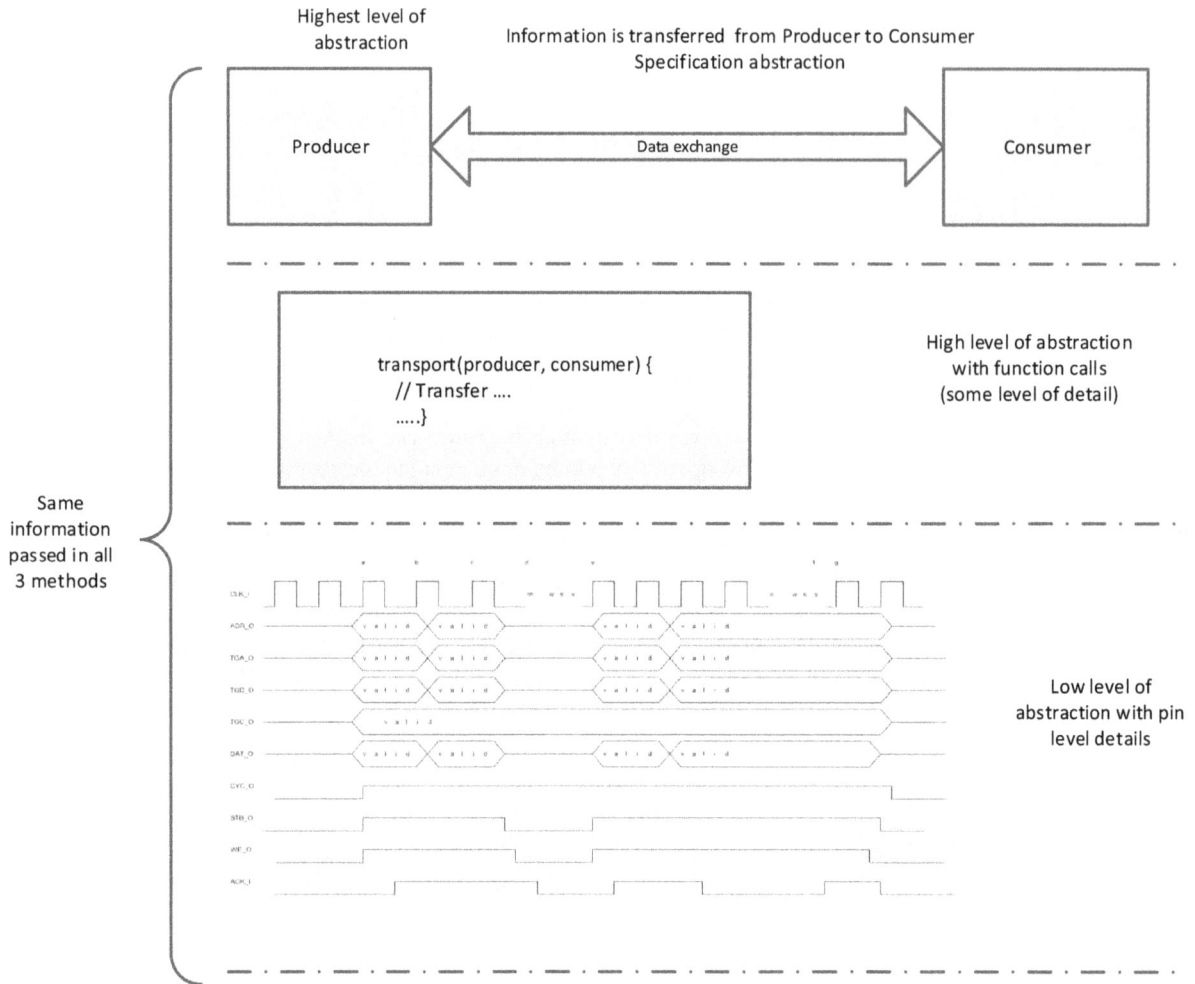

Fig. 10.1: Transaction Layer Communication

Figure 10.2 shows the origin of the various TLM standards into UVM. TLM-1.0 was introduced in AVM, made its way into OVM, and from there on to UVM. TLM 2.0 was introduced in VMM and made its way to UVM.

(i)   The standard for TLM 2.0 is quite extensive in the SystemC version of IEEE specification; only a subset of its capabilities has been translated to SystemVerilog due to language limitations and made available as a part of UVM

.

10.1 Basics of Transaction Level Communication

For information to flow from one entity to another, the process for transfer involves a ***initiator*** and a ***target*** for the transfer. Every transfer begins with an initiator and ends in a target. The initiator is the entity that starts the transaction. The target receives the transaction and consumes it. The entity that produces the data and is called a producer. The entity that consumes the transaction is the consumer. Note that the consumer may generate a response.

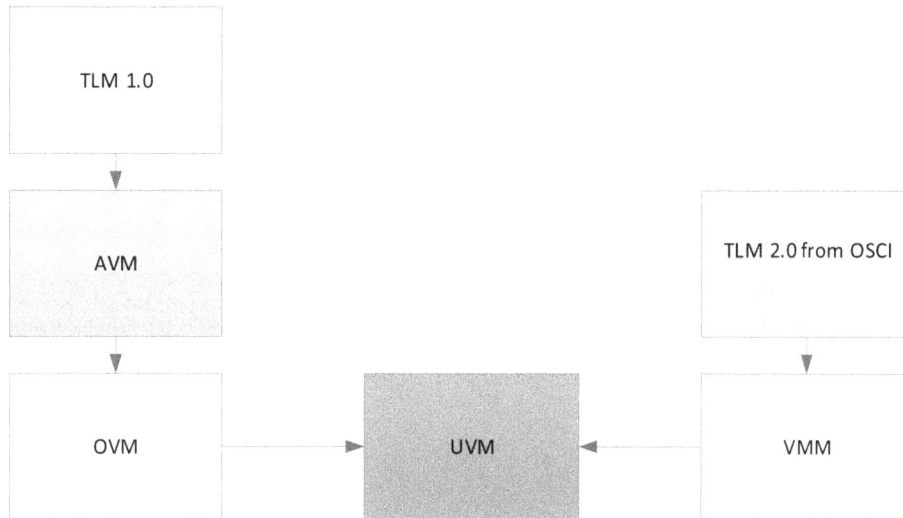

Fig. 10.2: Origins Of UVM TLM

At a high level, the producer and consumer are both concurrently running as independent processes. The consumer waits for the producer to produce data, and its process remains blocked until it receives a transfer from the producer. This blocking process in a hardware system may cause time to elapse. When the consumer completes the transaction after receiving it from the producer, the producer continues processing its thread.

Depending on who the initiator of the transaction was, we have two different variants of basic transaction-level communication. These two forms of variants are embodied in the Put() and Get() operations described in the following sections.

10.1.1 Put Port

The first is the put() operation. In this process, the producer produces some transactions and uses a port to give them to the consumer. The implementation of the put() function is supplied by the consumer, which may be replaced by any other component which provides the put() function. TLM defines the semantics of the put operation. In this case, the put() call in the producer will block until the consumer's put implementation is complete. Other than that, the operation of the producer is entirely independent of the put implementation. In fact, the consumer could be replaced by another component that also implements put() and, the producer will continue to work in the same way. The modularity provided by TLM fosters an environment encouraging easy reuse as the interfaces are well defined.

The square box on the producer indicates a port, and the circle on the consumer indicates the export. The producer generates transactions and sends them out its put_port. The example in Section 10.3 shows a producer/consumer pair. The producer on the left produces an object which is consumed by the consumer on the right.

In this figure, component A "puts" a transaction to component B. Component A contains a free-running process with its thread. Component B is a slave, operating only when invoked by component A. Component A initiates transactions that B receives and processes.

In a put operation, the transaction moves from a producer to a consumer. The producer calls put() which invokes an implementation of put() in the consumer. The data transfers from producer to consumer via the arguments to the put() method. The put operation shown here is a blocking operation. This means that when A issues the put(), A must wait until B completes the operation. B may return immediately, or it may consume time. In many cases, the producer may need to do some additional querying of the consumer before it issues a put() call. UVM offers the following methods:

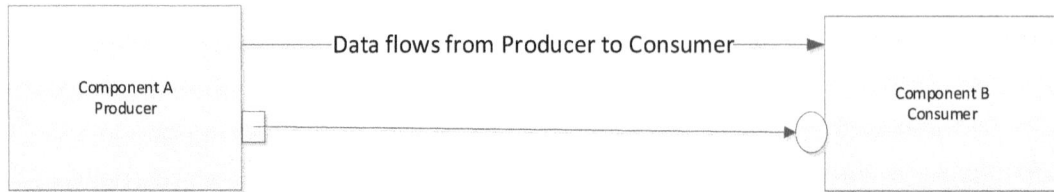

Square box on producer is the port, circle on consumer is the export
Fig. 10.3: Put Port

- **put()**: sends a transaction of type TR from the producer to the consumer. A consumer implementing the interface will block the calling thread if it cannot immediately accept delivery of the transaction. Because of the potential for waiting, only tasks may call this method.

- **try_put():** if possible, sends a transaction of type TR from the producer to the consumer. If the consumer is ready to accept the transaction argument, it does so and returns 1. Otherwise, it returns 0.

- **can_put():** returns 1 if the target is ready to accept a transaction from the producer, else it returns 0.

In the put operation, *the producer is the active component.* It determines when the transaction is sent across the interface. The consumer, in this case, is passive, and it waits for the transaction.

10.1.2 Get Ports

The converse operation of the put port is the get port. In this case, the get port is the consumer, and it obtains a transaction from the producer. The difference between this and the previous put() case is that the consumer is the initiator that gets the transaction from the producer. The transaction moves from the producer to the consumer at a timing controlled by the consumer. A get() operation moves a transaction from an initiator to a target. The initiator calls get(), which invokes an implementation of get() in the target. The data transfers via the argument to get().

The get() operation is blocking, meaning the producer may cause time to elapse in the process of producing a new value. The producer sends its value to the consumer via the return value of the get() method. As with put() above, the consumer's get() call will block until the producer's method completes.

In both the above cases, one observes that the tasks are blocking in nature. IE, the thread of execution stops until the data is available. In a multithreaded environment where multiple threads are executing at the same time, this becomes restrictive.

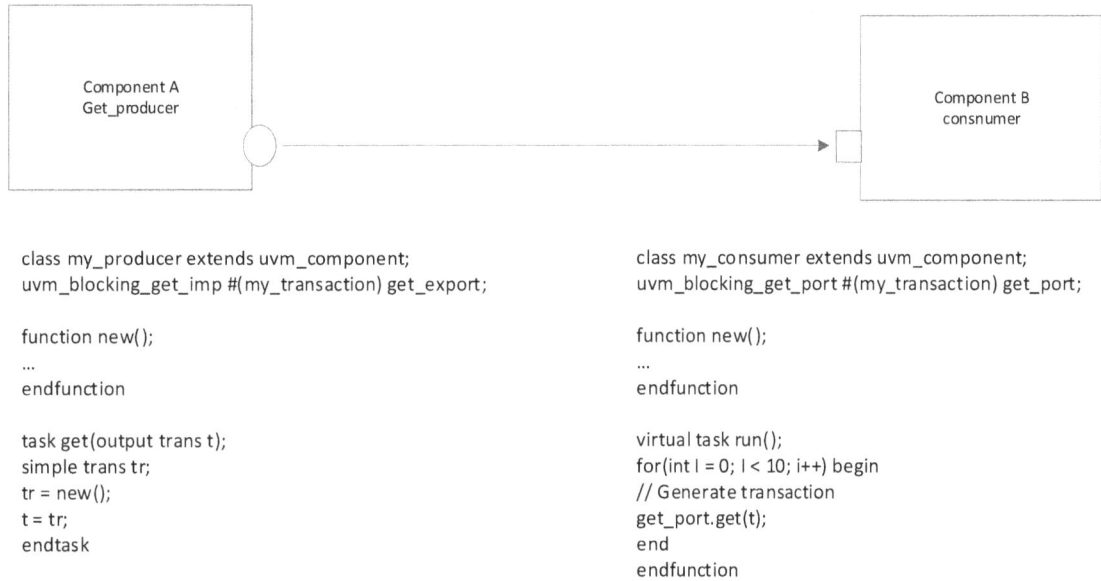

```
class my_producer extends uvm_component;          class my_consumer extends uvm_component;
uvm_blocking_get_imp #(my_transaction) get_export;  uvm_blocking_get_port #(my_transaction) get_port;

function new();                                    function new();
...                                                ...
endfunction                                        endfunction

task get(output trans t);                          virtual task run();
simple trans tr;                                   for(int I = 0; I < 10; i++) begin
tr = new();                                        // Generate transaction
t = tr;                                            get_port.get(t);
endtask                                            end
                                                   endfunction
```

Square box on consumer is the port, circle on producer is the export

Fig. 10.4: Get Port

You may want to check if transactions are indeed available before calling get(). To support such scenarios, UVM supplies a few additional methods[1]:

- **get()**: returns a new transaction of type TR from the producer to the consumer. The calling thread is blocked if the target cannot immediately provide the requested transaction. The output argument provides the new transaction. The implementation of get() must regard the transaction as consumed. Subsequent calls to get() must return a different transaction instance. Because of the potential for waiting, only tasks may call this method.

- **try_get()**: returns a new transaction of type TR from the target to the consumer. If a transaction is immediately available, it is returned in the provided output argument, and the method returns 1. Otherwise, the output argument is not modified, and it returns 0.

- **can_get()**: returns 1 if producer is ready to return a transaction immediately upon calling get() or try_get(). Otherwise, it returns 0.

10.1.3 Understanding Blocking and Non Blocking Methods.

In both the put() and get() cases, the tasks are blocking in nature. IE, the thread of execution stops until the data is available. In a multithreaded environment where multiple threads are executing at the same time, this becomes somewhat restrictive. Depending on the code that is being executed by the producer and consumer, one may desire to have considerably more flexibility in transferring transactions from the producer to the consumer. UVM adds many additional tasks and functions to help provide flexibility to the user to determine if there is data available to be processed on a port. The user can use the responses from these functions to determine if they would like to do some additional processing before accepting the put or get operations.

---

[1] These made their way to UVM from OVM. Look at [11]

Table 10.1: Blocking Vs NonBlocking Ports

Blocking	Non Blocking
Transactions can occur consuming simulation time	Transactions do not consume simulation time.
Methods are declared as tasks	Methods are declared as functions
Methods do not complete until they return their transaction	Delivery status is returned from the function
Method completion signifies transaction completion	Communication from target to initiator and from initiator to target occur along separate paths

10.1.4 Peek

Sometimes it is required to see if there is an available transaction without consuming it. The following three methods are useful:

- **peek()**: returns a new transaction from the target without consuming it. If a transaction is available, then it is written to the provided output argument. If a transaction is not available, the calling thread is blocked until one becomes available. A subsequent call to peek() or get() will return the same transaction. Because of the potential for waiting, only tasks may call this method.

- **try_peek()**: returns a new transaction without consuming it. If available, a transaction is written to the output argument, and it returns 1. A subsequent call to peek() or get() will return the same transaction. If a transaction is not available, the argument remains unmodified, and it returns 0.

- **can_peek()**: returns 1 if a new transaction is available, 0 otherwise.

10.1.5 Analysis Ports

Both get() and put() interfaces are one-to-one connections. It is not possible to have multiple components with get() ports connected to one implementation of get() in another component. The same is true of put() ports. This limitation primarily stems from the fact that with the put/get() connections, resolving the particular components implementation of get()/put() tasks results in 1-1 connections.

Considering a monitor watching a bus, the monitor could produce a single transaction that represents the activity on the bus. The verification environment containing both a scoreboard and a coverage collector may want to have a copy of the transaction. Each of these different components does different things with the transaction.

One could insert a uvm_component who's sole purpose was to forward the transaction to each of these other components, but this would be not only inelegant but also difficult to maintain if more components are added to the system. A "broadcast" system is quite useful in such cases.

The UVM analysis port is the answer to these issues. It comes in the following flavors:

```
uvm_analysis_port #(type)
uvm_ analysis_export #(type)
uvm_analysis_imp #(type, imp_parent_type)
```

This analysis port provides a single function called write with the following prototype Which is implemented by the target component.

```
function void write(transaction_type tr);
```

Consider the example in Figure 10.5. Three target_components tgt_component1, tgt_component2, and component3 are connected by means of an analysis port to the monitor.

The uvm_analysis_port (represented as a diamond on the monitor in Figure 10.5) is a specialized TLM port whose interface consists of a single function, write(). The analysis port contains a list of analysis_exports connected to it. When the component calls analysis_port.write(), the analysis_port cycles through the list and calls the write() method of each connected export. If nothing is connected, the write() call returns simply without doing anything. Hence, an analysis port may be connected to zero, one, or many analysis exports, but the operation of the component that writes to the analysis port does not depend on the number of exports connected. Because write() is specified as a void function call, the call

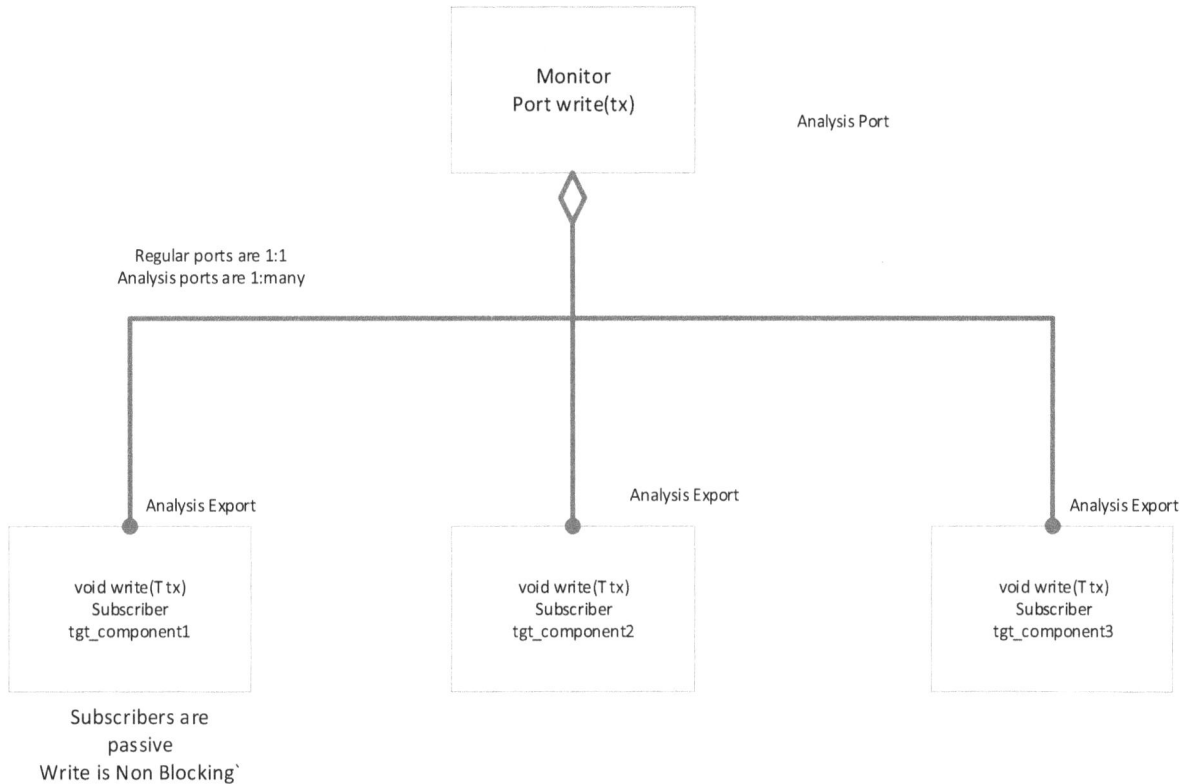

Fig. 10.5: Analysis Port Connections

is required to complete in the same simulation delta cycle. There is no count of how many components (for example, scoreboards, coverage collectors, and so on) are connected. There is no definite order though between the write calls, and you must note this.

> The effect is very similar between a callback described in Chapter 9 and an analysis port, but there are differences. Unlike UVM callbacks, the name of the method called through an analysis port is fixed as a *write()* call. A UVM callback method is permitted to modify the transaction object, ***but a transaction sent through an analysis port cannot be modified.*** Because of these differences, only UVM callbacks are appropriate for modifying the behavior of uvm_components. Analysis ports are only appropriate for sending transactions to passive components that will not attempt to modify the transaction object. On the other hand, that in itself is the feature and strength of analysis ports; they are only for analysis.

10.2 Connecting Transaction-Level Components

It is noted that the use of TLM interfaces isolates each component in a verification environment from the others. In all of the discussion presented above, the discussion was centered around put() get(), peek() and poke() methods. The discussion was presented in the context of a single producer and a single consumer class connected in a level of the hierarchy. From our study of various component classes in Section 8, we recognize that the testbench can consist of many class hierarchies and the put()/get() port in one component may need to be connected to another component in another portion of the hierarchy. Hence, there is a need to have some ports that will forward the implementation of the functions in one component to where they are needed.

The TLM standard defines three types of interfaces. The combination of these interfaces allow the user to create a method call (put/get/try_put/try_get/peek/poke) in one level of the hierarchy connect to a method in another location in the hierarchy. These are:

- **Ports** : port interfaces are instantiated in components that initiate transaction requests. Ports are used to call interface methods implemented elsewhere.

- **Exports**: export interfaces are instantiated by components that do not have an implementation of the methods themselves. They forward an implementation of the methods defined in the associated interface. The actual implementation is not found in the component where the export interface. It could be present in a child component or another component in the same hierarchy as the component itself. In the case of a child component, The child component usually provides an imp port (below). Exports effectively promote an interface (or imp) implementation from a child to its parent making it visible outside the component providing the imp port.

- **Imp port**: is instantiated by components that provide or implement an implementation of the methods defined in the associated interface. Think of this as the last link in the chain between a port and the method implementation.

The environment instantiates a component and connects its ports/exports to its neighbor(s), independent of any further knowledge of the implementation. The way the component hierarchy is set up, smaller components are grouped together and created and connected in the appropriate phases as can be seen in examples for the master agent. The access to the lower level component may be achieved by making their port/imp interfaces visible at the parent level via the appropriate exports. Each component takes care of making these connections in the build phase and connect phases, so that at any one level, it simply looks like a single component with a set of interfaces on it, regardless of its internal implementation or how many layers of the hierarchy there are.

There are a few rules[2] that can be used to characterize these connections below. Assuming the connector from_conn is connected to a port/imp/export to_conn, the following rules apply:

- A connector object can be connected only to a single next connector object. In other words, function connect() of *from_conn* cannot be called with any other connector object once it is called with argument *to_conn*. A connector object like an analysis port can, however, receive connections from multiple connector objects.

- If *from_conn* is a port connector object, then *to_conn* can be a port connector object, an export connector object, or an imp connector object.

- If *from_conn* is an export connector object, then *to_conn* can be an export connector object or an imp connector object.

- An imp connector object cannot be connected to any other connector objects since it is always the last connector on a connection path.

Table 10.2 from the UVM User's guide summarizes it for you.

Table 10.2: Port And Export Connection Rules

Connection type	connect() form
port-to-export	comp1.port.connect(comp2.export);
port-to-port	subcomponent.port.connect(port);
export-to-export	export.connect(subcomponent.export);

A number of chapters in the book provide examples of these connections. These connections may be inside an agent class or other container classes. All the environment classes in this book provide port connections between the scoreboard, coverage, and the different agents. See Section 21.1.6 for an example of an environment containing many components having port connections. To see port/export connections within an agent, see Section 8.3.4.3.

---

[2] Excerpted from [13]

10.3 UVM TLM - Ports Summary

Section 10.1.1 discussed put() operations, Section 10.1.2 discussed get() operations and peek operations were discussed in Section 10.1.4. The previous section also discussed blocking and nonblocking ports. To add to this mix, one can have a port, export or imp type of port implemented in UVM from Section 10.2, The collection of these various types leads to quite a few combinations of ports/exports. Table 10.3 below[3] summarizes the various operations and the various kinds of ports as a quick ready reference.

Table 10.3: Various Kinds Of Ports In UVM TLM 1.0

Operation	Type	Category	xxx = port—imp—export	Put methods			Get Methods			Peek		
				can_put	try_put	put	can_get	try_get	get	can_peek	try_peek	peek
put	task		uvm_put_xxx	X	X	X						
	task	blocking	uvm_blocking_put_xxx			X						
	function	non_blocking	uvm_nonblocking_put_xxx	X	X							
get	task		uvm_get_xxx				X	X	X			
	task	blocking	uvm_blocking_get_xxx						X			
	function	non_blocking	uvm_nonblocking_get_xxx				X	X				
peek	task		uvm_perk_xxx							X	X	X
	task	blocking	uvm_blocking_peek_xxx									X
	function	nonblocking	uvm_nonblocking_peek_xxx							X	X	
master	task		uvm_master_xxx	X	X	X	X	X	X	X	X	X
	task	blocking	uvm_blocking_master_xxx			X			X			X
	function	non_blocking	uvm_nonblocking_master_xxx	X	X		X	X		X	X	
slave	task		uvm_slave_xxx	X	X	X	X	X	X	X	X	X
	task	blocking	uvm_blocking_slave_xxx			X			X			X
	function	non_blocking	uvm_nonblocking_slave_xxx	X	X		X	X		X	X	

The connection rules between the various ports now remains as per the rules in Section 10.2

UVM
IEEE

The implementation of TLM in SystemVerilog is limited due to language restrictions. To differentiate between the TLM-1 and TLM-2 present in the OSCI standard, TLM-1 and TLM-2 from the earlier versions of UVM are now renamed as UVM-TLM. I have used the same convention in this book.

[3] adapted from [13]

10.4 UVM TLM 2

UVM-TLM 1.0 was the first generation standard that has been incorporated into UVM. Some of the advantages of this standard were:

- Simple, clean communication mechanism

- Many aspects in common with SystemC

- Strongly typed connections

However, this mechanism is not without its disadvantages:

- Essentially unidirectional and pass-by-value

- No standard payload type

- No explicit support for timing

- No standard way to model complex protocols

UVM-TLM2 introduces a set of features for transaction-level communication within a UVM verification environment. These features draw their inspiration from the SystemC TLM-2.0 standard. The introduction of these features was motivated in part by the need to connect a UVM testbench to a SystemC reference model.

Due to the semantics of the SystemVerilog language, only a small subset of the capabilities available in SystemC is translated to SystemVerilog. SystemVerilog does not have multiple inheritance, function pointers, function overloading capabilities. As a result, not all the features available in SystemC are available in SystemVerilog. The following table offers a summary comparison of the capabilities offered by SystemVerilog and SystemC[4].

	System C	System Verilog
Blocking transport interface	Y	Y
Nonblocking transport interface	Y	Y
Direct memory interface	Y	N
Debug transport interface	Y	N
Initiator sockets	Y	Y
Target sockets	Y	Y
Generic sockets	Y	Y
Phases	Y	Y
Convenience sockets	Y	N
Payload event queue	Y	N
Quantam keeper	Y	N
Intastance-specific extensions	Y	N
Non-ignorable and mandatory extensions	Y	Y
Temporal decoupling	Y	Y

Table 10.4: Comparison between SystemC TLM and SystemVerilog TLM2 Implementations

Section 10.1.3 presented a discussion on blocking and nonblocking methods. In UVM-TLM2, we have the concept of blocking and nonblocking *interfaces*. These interfaces are based on the uvm_tlm_if class and are parameterized to the type of the transaction object and the phase state for the transaction. Each of the interface methods take a handle to the transaction to be transported and a handle to a time value object which is independent of the timescale.

The following sections describe the various kinds of transports before exploring sockets which contain different kinds of transports built into it.

---

[4] See Janick and Mark Glasser's paper [5] and also Janick's presentation in DVCON for TLM2 [6]. The material in [6] was VMM based, and UVM TLM2 owes its origin to it. The concepts below were adapted from that presentation to explain concepts clearly

10.4.1 Blocking Transports

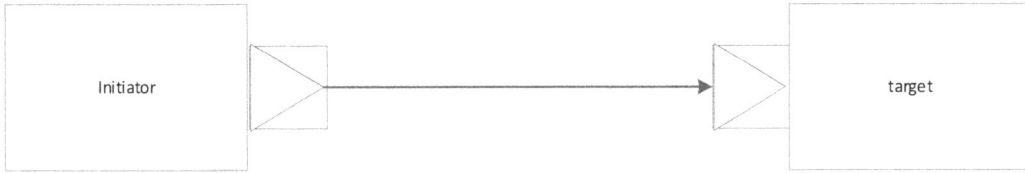

Fig. 10.6: Basic Blocking Transport

The blocking transport is implemented with following call:

    task b_transport(T t, uvm_tlm_time delay);

The b_transport task transports a transaction of type T from the initiator to the target in a blocking fashion. When the initiator makes the call to b_transport, the data is sent across to the target. Figure 10.7 presents the sequence flow when the blocking transport is used. In this figure, The initiator creates the transaction and invokes the b_transport call. The transaction is then carried over to the target. After invoking the call, the initiator cannot modify the transaction. The target that receives the transaction can then act on the transaction. For example, the transaction may ask for a read or write to be performed on a bus, which may take several cycles. After the bus operation is completed, the target updates the transaction with the results and then returns the transaction to the initiator. The initiator thread that called the b_transport call is suspended until the target returns the method. This is the reason the call to b_transport is a blocking task.

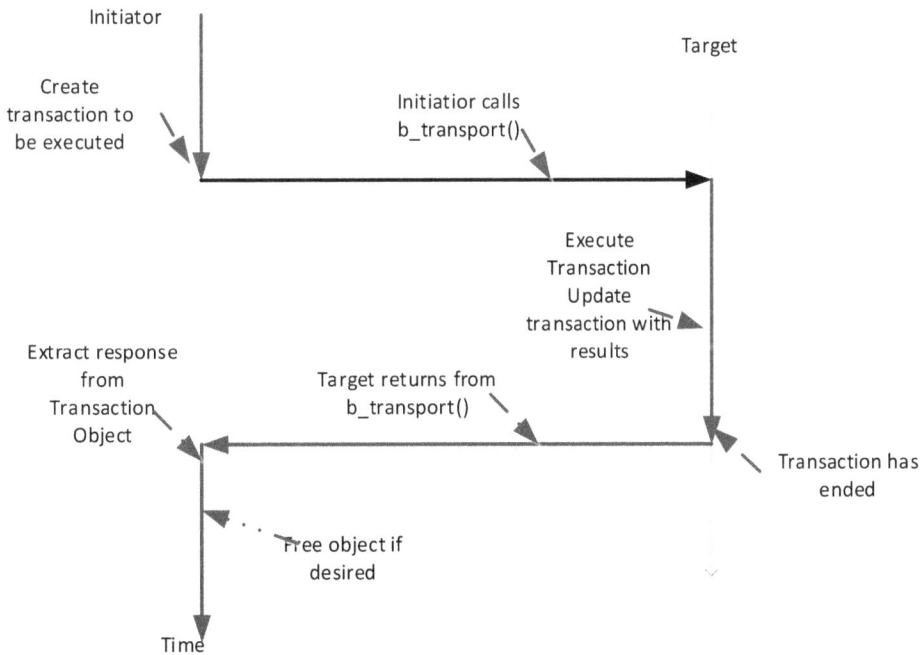

Fig. 10.7: Blocking Transport Data Flow

Across languages, however, there is an extra step. You will need to pack the SV object going into the SystemC domain, and also unpack this object when it comes back. Attention needs to be paid to memory management on the SystemC side. The steps to do this are otherwise similar. Figure 10.8 illustrates how the data flows across these boundaries.

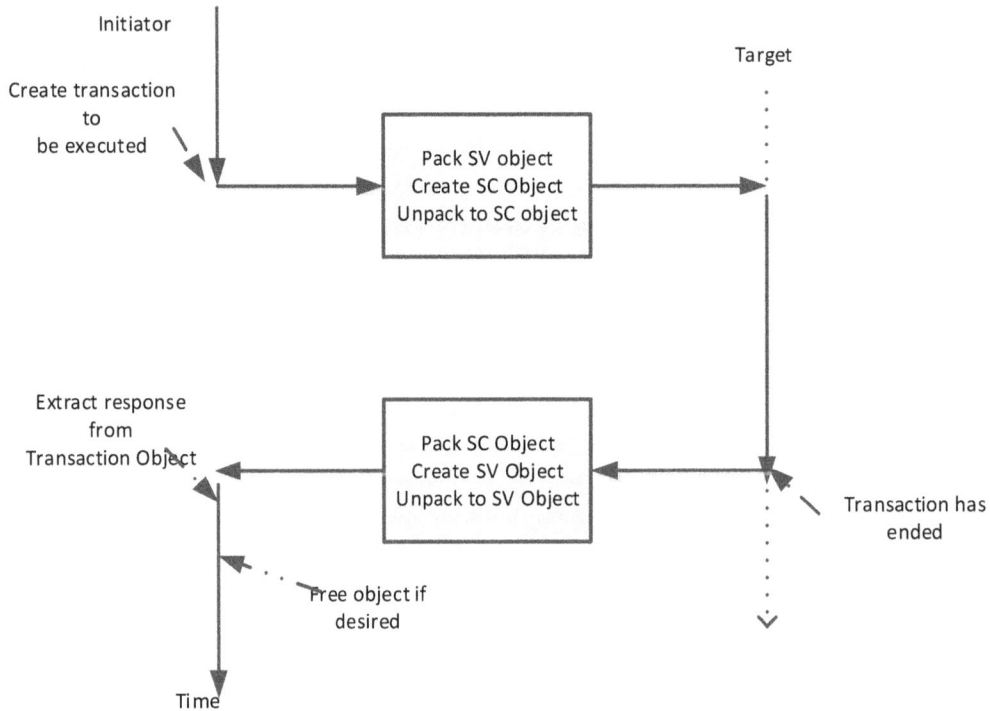

Fig. 10.8: Blocking Transport Across Language Boundaries

10.4.2 NonBlocking Transports

Compared to the blocking mechanism that was discussed in the earlier section where we had a single blocking call, nonblocking transports, on the other hand, return immediately. The nonblocking transport interface consists of a pair of methods nb_transport_fw and nb_transport_bw, called in the forward and backward directions respectively, The progress of a single transaction can be described using multiple calls to these two methods. This is shown in Figure 10.9 below. The nonblocking methods each return a value that signifies the state of the transaction, as seen in Table 10.5.

Enum value	Interpretation
UNITIALIZED_PHASE	Phase has not yet begun
BEGIN_REQ	Request has begun
END_REQ	Request has completed
BEGIN_RESP	Response has begun
END_RESP	Response has terminated

Table 10.5: Return States

The first call to nb_transport_fw by the initiator marks the first timing point in the transaction execution. Subsequent calls to nb_transport_fw and nb_transport_bw mark additional timing points in the transaction execution. The last timing point is marked by a return from nb_transport_fw or nb_transport_bw with UVM_TLM_COMPLETED.

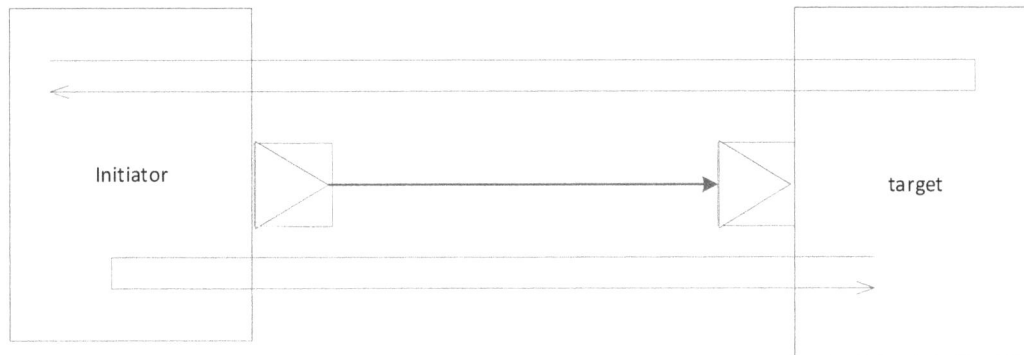

Fig. 10.9: Non Blocking Transport

The initiator is responsible for allocating the transaction object before the first call to nb_transport_fw. The same transaction object is used by all of the forward and backward calls during its execution. The transaction object is alive for
the entire duration of the transaction until the transaction is deemed completed. All timing points may be offset from the
current simulation time by the delay value specified in the delay argument. A nb_transport_fw call on the forward path
cannot call to nb_transport_bw on the backward path, and the same restriction applies in the other direction. The phase
argument represents the current state of the inbuilt protocol state machine which has several states described in Table
10.6. Any change in the value of the transaction object should be accompanied by a change in the value of phase property.
When using the base protocol provided by the library, you are not allowed to make successive calls to nb_transport_fw or
nb_transport_bw with the same phase value. When the initiator makes a call to nb_transport_fw, the transaction is taken
from the initiator to the target. Since this is a function, the call returns immediately. The method signature is shown below:

```
function uvm_tlm_sync_e nb_transport_fw(T t, ref P p, input uvm_tlm_time delay);
```

The backward (return)call from the target is given by:

```
function uvm_tlm_sync_e nb_transport_bw(T t, ref P p, input uvm_tlm_time delay);
```

nb_transport_fw transports a transaction in the forward direction, that is from the initiator to the target (the forward path).
nb_transport_bw does the reverse; it transports a transaction from the target back to the initiator (the reverse path). An
initiator and target will use the forward and backward paths to update each other on the progress of the transaction
execution. Typically, nb_transport_fw is called by the initiator whenever the protocol state change occurs in the initiator.
The nb_transport_bw is called by the target whenever the protocol state in the target changes state. The nb_* interfaces
each return an enum uvm_tlm_sync_e. The possible enum values and their meanings are shown in Table 10.6

UVM_TLM_ACCEPTED	Transaction has been accepted. Neither the transaction object, the phasenor the delay arguments have been modified.
UVM_TLM_UPDATED	Transaction has been modified. The transaction object, the phase or the delay arguments may have been modified.
UVM_TLM_COMPLETED	Transaction execution has completed. The transaction object, the phase, or the delay arguments may have been modified. There will be no further transport calls associated with this transaction.

Table 10.6: Transport states returned by the methods

The figure below shows the transactions in a nonblocking transport in greater detail.

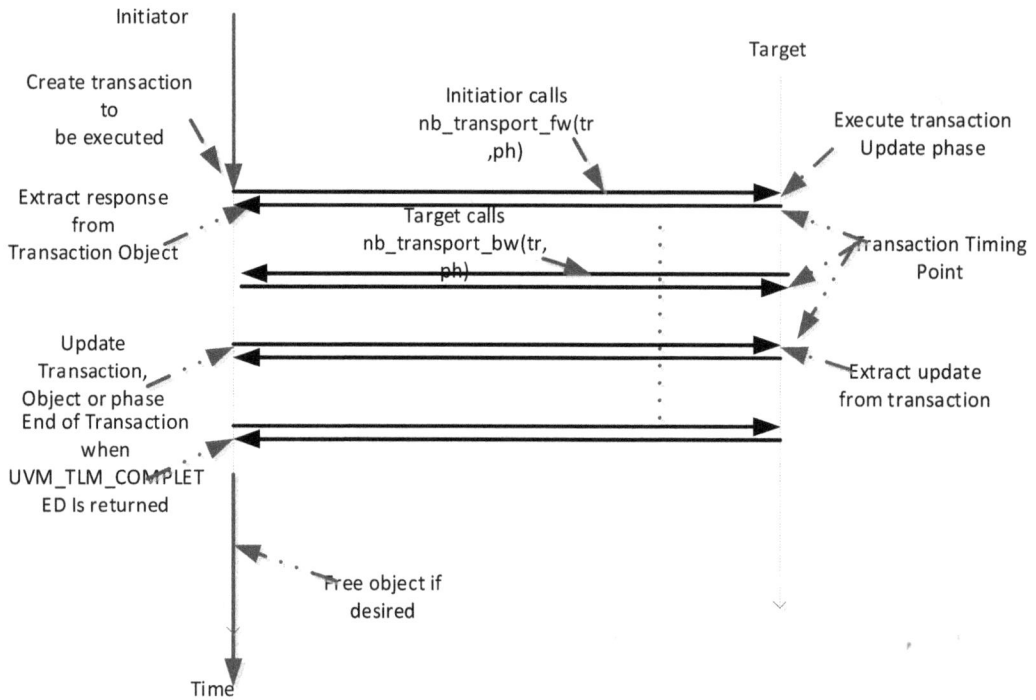

Fig. 10.10: Non Blocking Transport without Language Boundaries

In the case of language boundaries, there is an extra step that one needs to take. This step may be automated using some vendor libraries. You must pack the data so that it can be transported across the boundary. Figure 10.10 illustrates the pack/unpack operations that occur due to the language boundary crossing.

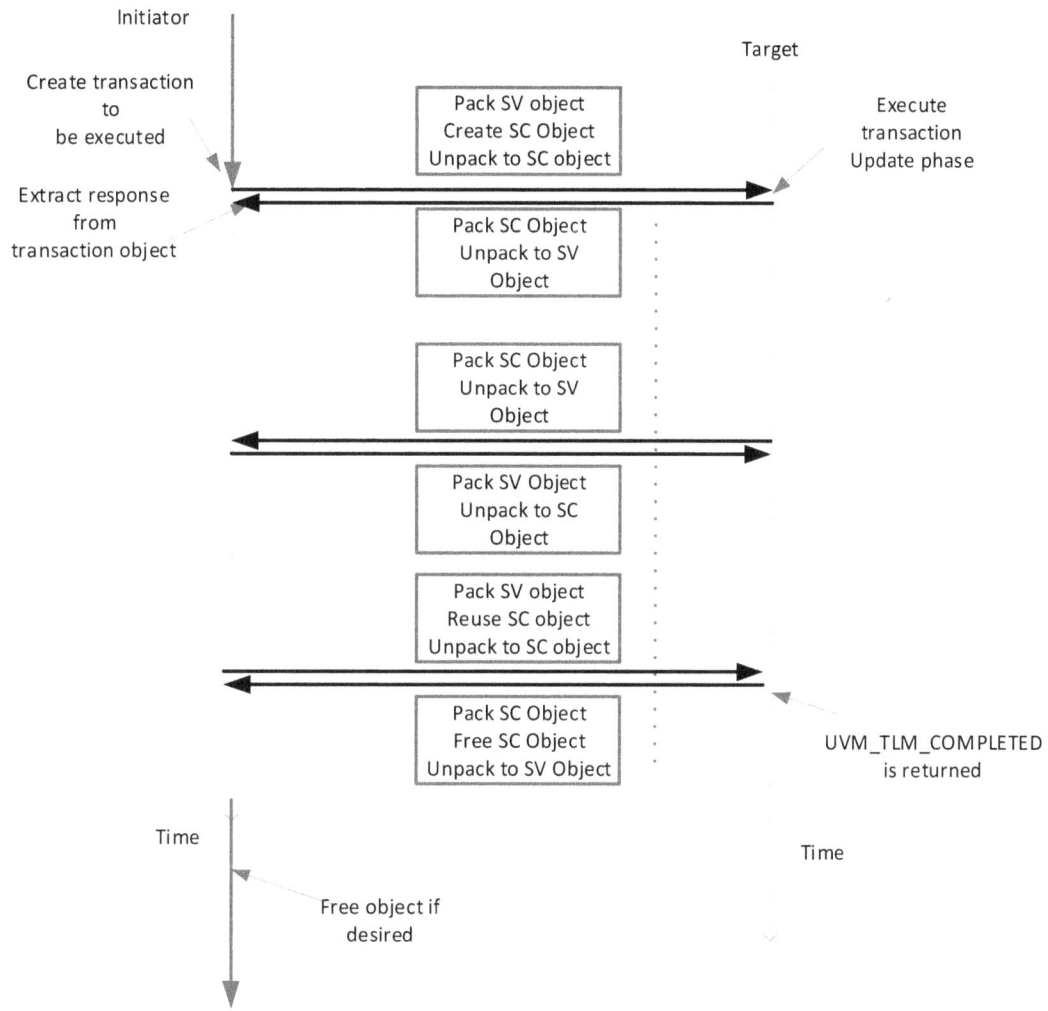

Fig. 10.11: Non Blocking Transport Across Language Boundaries

10.5 Sockets

The earlier part of this chapter showed us how to make connections between two processes using ports and exports. In the case of TLM2, this connection is made through sockets. A socket provides both a forward and backward path. Thus, you can enable asynchronous bi-directional communication by connecting sockets together.

Section 10.1 discussed how a producer and consumer interacted with one another using get() and put() ports. In the TLM2 approach, Components that initiate transactions are called initiators, and components that receive transactions sent by an initiator are called targets. An initiator contains initiator socket and targets contain target sockets. Initiator sockets can only connect to target sockets. Correspondingly target sockets can only connect to initiator sockets. Sockets are TLM2 ports. They can be of these kinds:

- Blocking or nonblocking

- Initiator or target

- Terminator or passthrough

The socket symbol is a box with an triangle with its point indicating the data and control flow direction of the forward path. The backward path is indicated by an arrow connecting the target socket back to the initiator socket.

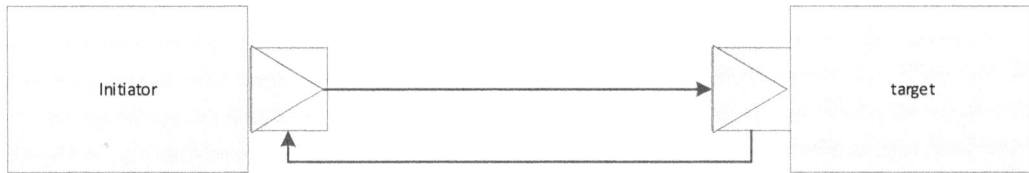

Fig. 10.12: A TLM2 Socket

If you look at the socket flavors, you will find many of them. Each socket is an initiator or a target, a passthrough, or a terminator. Furthermore, any socket implements either blocking interfaces or nonblocking interfaces. Terminator sockets are used on initiators and targets as well as interconnect components as shown in Figure 10.133. Passthrough sockets are used to enable connections to cross hierarchical boundaries.

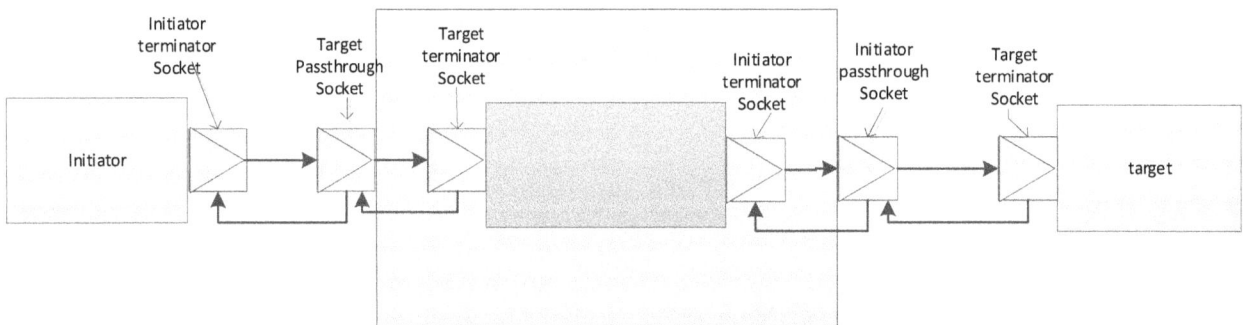

Fig. 10.13: Types of TLM2 Sockets

The various classes are listed below[5]:

```
class uvm_tlm_b_initiator_socket #(type T=uvm_tlm_generic_payload) extends
uvm_tlm_b_initiator_socket_base #(T);

class uvm_tlm_b_target_socket #(type IMP=int, type T=uvm_tlm_generic_payload) extends
uvm_tlm_b_target_socket_base #(T);

class uvm_tlm_nb_initiator_socket #(type IMP=int, type T=uvm_tlm_generic_payload, type
P=uvm_tlm_phase_e) extends uvm_tlm_nb_initiator_socket_base #(T,P);

class uvm_tlm_nb_target_socket #(type IMP=int, type T=uvm_tlm_generic_payload, type
P=uvm_tlm_phase_e) extends uvm_tlm_nb_target_socket_base #(T,P);

class uvm_tlm_b_passthrough_initiator_socket #(type T=uvm_tlm_generic_payload) extends
uvm_tlm_b_passthrough_initiator_socket_base #(T);

class uvm_tlm_b_passthrough_target_socket #(type T=uvm_tlm_generic_payload) extends
uvm_tlm_b_passthrough_target_socket_base #(T);

class uvm_tlm_nb_passthrough_initiator_socket #(type T=uvm_tlm_generic_payload, type
P=uvm_tlm_phase_e) extends uvm_tlm_nb_passthrough_initiator_socket_base #(T,P);

class uvm_tlm_nb_passthrough_target_socket #(type T=uvm_tlm_generic_payload, type
P=uvm_tlm_phase_e) extends uvm_tlm_nb_passthrough_target_socket_base #(T,P);
```

Note: Detailed examples using these sockets are not provided here.

10.6 Time

In all our simulations, time is represented as an integer. As you are well aware, an integer alone is not sufficient to represent time without ambiguity. You need to know the scale of that integer value, which is based on the timescale that was used during compilation. SystemVerilog handles time literals differently. If you use integer values, you cannot distinguish between an integer that carries an integer value and an integer that carries a time value since scaling information is not in the integer. To solve these problems, the uvm_tlm_time class contains the scaling information so that as time information is passed between processes, which may be executing under different time scales, the time can be scaled properly in each environment[6].

UVM
IEEE   IEEE renames uvm_time to uvm_tlm_time. A typedef ensures backward compatibility

10.7 Connecting TLM2 Ports and Sockets

Having studied the various aspects of UVM-TLM sockets, it now becomes necessary to interconnect components using these sockets. The UVM users guide[3] gives details on connecting these components using the connect() method. However, we think that given the origin of TLM2 in UVM, the use cases to connect a UVM-TLM2 socket to SystemC are far more interesting.

There are many approaches that allow you to connect a model in SystemVerilog with its corresponding counterpart in the SystemC world. Each of these methods either use a PLI, or DPI mechanism to connect these ports and sockets. The VCS TLI (Transaction-Level Interface) is an off-the-shelf mechanism for transaction-level communication between SystemVerilog and SystemC. The TLI provides standard transaction-level communication between a SystemVerilog testbench and a SystemC model with a considerable ease of use. You could use SystemVerilog DPI. However, DPI in itself has no native support for SystemC interface method calls or for UVM. Some other packages like UvmConnect have also been released

---

[6] See UVM Users Guide [3] for detailed explanations.

to make it easy for you to make these connections. The latest release of the TLI from Synopsys has explicit support for UVM as well as the SystemC TLM-2.0 standard, making it easy to integrate the TLM features of UVM described in this chapter.

10.8 Generic Payload

TLM-2.0 defines a base object, called the generic payload, for moving data between components. In SystemC, this is the primary transaction vehicle. In SystemVerilog, this is the default transaction type, but it is not the only type that can be used Each attribute in the SystemC version has a corresponding member in the SystemVerilog generic payload. Each of attributes also has a set/get accessor method. Table 10.7 shows the various properties of the generic payload and thier accessor methods.

Property	Type	Purpose	Accessor Methods
address	bit [31:0]	Base address of the operation	virtual function void set_address(bit [63:0] addr); virtual function bit[63:0] get_address();
command	uvm_tlm_command_e	UVM_TLM_READ_COMMAND UVM_TLM_WRITE_COMMAND UVM_TLM_IGNORE_COMMAND	virtual function void set_command(uvm_tlm_command_e command); virtual function bit is_read(); virtual function void set_read(); virtual function bit is_write(); virtual function void set_write();
data	byte unsigned []	Data to be written or read back	virtual function void get_data (output byte p []); virtual function void set_data_ptr(ref byte p []);
byte_enable	byte unsigned []	Valid bytes in data[]	virtual function void get_byte_enable(output byte p[]); virtual function void set_byte_enable(ref byte p[]); virtual function int unsigned get_byte_enable_length(); virtual function void set_byte_enable_length(int unsigned length);
response_status	uvm_tlm_response_status_e	UVM_TLM_OK_RESPONSE UVM_TLM_GENERIC_ERROR_RESPONSE UVM_TLM_ADDRESS_ERROR_RESPONSE UVM_TLM_COMMAND_ERROR_RESPONSE UVM_TLM_BURST_ERROR_RESPONSE UVM_TLM_BYTE_ENABLE_ERROR_RESPONSE UVM_TLM_IMCOMPLETE_RESPONSE	virtual function uvm_tlm_response_status_e get_response_status(); virtual function void set_response_status(uvm_tlm_response_status_e status); virtual function bit is_response_ok(); virtual function bit is_response_error(); virtual function string get_response_string();
data_length	int unsigned	Usually equal to data.size()	virtual function int unsigned get_data_length(); virtual function void set_data_length(int unsigned length);
byte_enable_length	int unsigned	Usually equal to byte_enable.size()	virtual function int unsigned get_byte_enable_length(); virtual function void set_byte_enable_length(int unsigned length);
streaming_width	int unsigned	Usually equal to 0.	virtual function int unsigned get_streaming_width(); virtual function void set_streaming_width(int unsigned width);

Table 10.7: Generic Payload members and accessor methods

10.9 Extensions

The generic payload provides a mechanism with fields to exchange data. Sometimes, you may want to have some more information to the uvm_tlm_gp object. The generic payload extension mechanism is similar to the one used in SystemC. Extensions are used to attach additional application specific/bus-specific information to the generic bus transaction described in the uvm_tlm_gp.

An extension is an instance of a user-defined container class based on the uvm_tlm_extension class. The set of extensions for any generic payload object is stored in that generic payload object instance. A generic payload object may have only one extension of a specific extension container type. However, you can have as many types as you want.

We have not provided a detailed explanation for the UVM TLM Generic payload extension mechanism in UVM. This may be covered in future editions.

Practical Examples for the UVM-TLM2 have not been provided here due to a paucity of space. The UVM to SYSTEMC connections are the most interesting ones. When discussing these examples, we would have to describe some aspects of SystemC along with details of how to cross the language boundary. This would have consumed a significant amount of space in this book and also is quite simulator specific. It is not a beginner's topic. If you desire to have some examples of the UVM-TLM2 interface, you can look at the examples provided by the UVM distribution. The only change between those examples and ones where SystemC is involved would be the details of crossing the language boundary (IE, the pack and unpack helpers)

Chapter 11

UVM Command Line Processor

Many verification environments use command line information to pass information into the simulation. The UVM command line processor is a class created at runtime, used to process command line information to take appropriate action. The UVM command line processor is architected to make it easy to pass any number of parameters to the UVM environment.

The UVM command line processor is a singleton similar to the factory. There is usually only one instance of the processor in a simulation. At the time of initialization, a global instance of the command line processor called uvm_cmdline_proc is created. It provides access to command line information. Users can get a handle to the created cmdline_processor and obtain from it a queue of all the arguments passed to it. They can then process the arguments. It typically serves the following functions:

- Configure the simulation by passing parameters
- Control simulation using overrides, verbosity or severity
- Debug the UVM environment

The following sections describe the command line processor abbreviated as CLP in the sections below.

11.1 Command Line Processor Basics
The CLP has a few built-in arguments. A convention is used to minimize ambiguity as follows:

- Any command line argument passed with *UPPERCASE* typically indicates **one instance for the entire simulation.**
- Any command line argument that is in *lowercase* **can be repeated multiple times.**

11.2 Built in Arguments
Built-in arguments are provided that are in three categories.

- Global settings that affect the entire simulation
- Configuration settings to control the simulation behavior on an instance-specific basis
- Debug Settings to help debug a UVM simulation

Examples for the CLP are merged and distributed amongst the other examples in this book. A detailed analysis of CLP capabilities is provided in following sections.

11.3 Available Global Settings
Global settings affect **all** the components in the simulation. These are typically used *once* per simulation. These settings are:

```
+UVM_TESTNAME
+UVM_VERBOSITY
+UVM_SEVERITY
+UVM_TIMEOUT
+UVM_MAX_QUIT_COUNT
+UVM_PHASE_TRACE
+UVM_OBJECTION_TRACE
+UVM_RESOURCE_DB_TRACE
+UVM_CONFIG_DB_TRACE
+UVM_DUMP_CMDLINE_ARGS
```

The UVM_TESTNAME is a mandatory option passed to the command line, and it contains the name of the test class to be executed. The simulator prints a warning if you pass more than one of these to a simulation. *It does NOT honor any other UVM_TESTNAME option other than the first instance of this option.*

The UVM_VERBOSITY setting sets the global verbosity threshold, can be any one of UVM_NONE, UVM_LOW, UVM_HIGH, UVM_FULL, UVM_DEBUG. *Note that this affects all the components in the simulation.* If you want to change the verbosity of a specific component, then use the equivalent one for a specific component. Section 21.5 shows you a good example of how to turn on the verbosity for the entire simulation.

The UVM_TIMEOUT sets the timeout for the simulation on the command line. You can use this option when you are debugging your environment. Normally tests finish as soon as all the objections are dropped; in some situations, this may not happen. To catch these situations, use this command line option to provide a way to terminate the simulation. Note that the simulation will terminate with an error condition when the timeout is hit, and this is reported in the statistics by the reporter at the end of the test.

The UVM_MAX_QUIT_COUNT=<count>,<override> sets the maximum number of COUNT actions that can be tolerated before an UVM_EXIT action is taken. This is a kill switch option that will kill the simulation. For example, you may choose to terminate a simulation after a specific number of messages from a specific ID are issued by the simulation. See Section 21.9 for information about using this command line option with any of the messages in your simulation.

The UVM_SEVERITY sets a global severity threshold, could be any one of the following: INFO, WARNING, ERROR, FATAL Note that this severity setting is **global**. *IE, it affects EVERYTHING.* So, you may want to use it sparingly if you don't want unexpected results. A component-specific setting is available in the next section.

The rest of the global command line options fall in the debug category also described further in Section 11.5.

The UVM_CONFIG_DB_TRACE and the UVM_RESOURCE_DB_TRACE options to the command line turn on the tracing so that you can see the calls that are made to set and get values from the configuration database. Use these options if you are setting some configuration variables and not seeing them take effect.

The UVM_PHASE_TRACE option is similar to the other options. Most of the useful phase traces are printed when using this option. If your simulation is stuck in reset or any other phase due to an objection, running the simulation with this option can quickly help you to find the problem. See Section 13.7 if you want to have a more enhanced implementation of this command line option.

The UVM_DUMP_CMDLINE_ARGS argument dumps all the command arguments using the reporting mechanism. You can use this to debug what is happening with the command line processor. Typically, you do not use this option unless you are trying to debug what is happening.

11.4 Controlling Simulation Behavior

The command line processor comes with a few default switches that allow one to control the behavior of the simulation. These switches can set values into a configuration database, and also help with controlling verbosity, severity, factory overrides, etc. One of the advantages of leveraging this functionality is building a simulation model a certain way, and then tweak it to the desired outcome by using a few command-line switches. This provides an alternate way of writing multiple callbacks and sequences that would otherwise be required. Note that a practical application of this would be useful when the compile times are significant as one sees in larger modern commercial designs.

11.4.1 Verbosity

This aspect of the command line processor verbosity switches affects the UVM reporting system's behavior. In a similar vein to the factory settings, one can set the verbosity of a specific component in the simulation from the command line. Such a feature might be very useful if one had earlier embedded debug level messages inside a component and now need to debug a specific component. Note that sometimes in a long simulation, one may want to restrict the verbosity for a time range. This is also possible with the same switch using the optional from_time and the to_time arguments.

```
+uvm_set_verbosity=<comp>,<id>,<verbosity>,<phase>
and the same option can also be used with an optional start and end time like below:
+uvm_set_verbosity=<comp>,<id>,<verbosity>,from_time,<to_time>
```

Here is an example of the master_agent[00] set to run at UVM_DEBUG verbosity. notice the _ALL_ which means every component.

```
./simv -l uvm_set_inst_verbosity.dat +uvm_set_verbosity=uvm_test_top.env.
   master_agent\[00\].mast_drv,_ALL_,UVM_DEBUG,run +UVM_TESTNAME=
   wb_conmax_flat_seq_test
```

See Section 21.9.7 for complete details.

> Be careful of running with UVM_DEBUG. You will get all the UVM library messages meant for UVM library debugging, which may not be what you intended. If you are debugging some issues with the library, UVM_DEBUG is appropriate. Otherwise, UVM_HIGH is more appropriate.

11.4.2 Severity

Severity options in the command line processor allow you to set the severity for the component. It also allows you to take specific actions as listed in Section 6.1.3, which specify how the simulation should behave if a certain message is received. This aspect of the command line processor affects the reporting system's behavior.

If you are debugging your environment, the two switches should be able to help you get to resolve the matter quickly. You can change from one severity (WARNING) to FATAL or ERROR etc. You can also shut off A WARNING or take no action on receipt of the message.

```
+uvm_set_action=<comp>,<id>,<severity>,<action>
+uvm_set_severity=<comp>,<id>,<current severity>,<new severity>
```

In the example below, you can see how to change the message from the "Wb Master" from a UVM_INFO message to a UVM_FATAL message. Such a promotion is possible again with the command line.

```
./simv -l uvm_set_inst_severity_no_action.dat +uvm_set_severity=
   uvm_test_top.env.master_agent[00].mast_drv,Wb master,UVM_INFO,UVM_FATAL
    +UVM_TESTNAME=wb_conmax_flat_seq_test
```

You should be able to modify the example in Section 21.9.9 to easily exercise this command line option; we leave it for you to try out after looking at the example above.

11.4.3 Configuration

UVM supplies a simple way to set configuration values for integers and strings. However, this is fairly a limited set of capabilities. As noted in section 7, when one needs to set many configuration settings, this can get very unwieldy. However, the following two built-in options are available.

```
+uvm_set_config_int=<some integer>
+uvm_set_config_string="string"
```

These settings act on a per component basis. You can repeat them as many times as needed on the command line. Several environments are presented in Part II of this book. You can attempt to use these settings in the examples presented in Section 7 and see how these settings are used. Note that you cannot set an object configuration on the command line. The workaround for this is to create a switch and use the techniques presented in Section 11.6, create the object and set it in the config_db.

Rule 11.4.0: *If you want to use the command line processor to set integer variables in the simulation, the values are only set if the target data type is uvm_bitstream_t. Otherwise, the values do not take effect. You WILL need to do a conversion from uvm_bitstream_t to type int. Otherwise use the technique in Listing 21.20*

11.4.4 Starting Sequences From a Command Line

Often one would like to use a single compiled configuration and test out many sequences from a command line since all the sequences have been analyzed and compiled into the simulator. To do so, UVM allows you to set the default sequence for the sequencers from the command line using the +uvm_set_default_sequence switch. See an example of how to use this switch in Section 21.9.3.

This is a UVM 1.2 feature

While this is a new feature in UVM, *I do NOT like it*. Just remember that if you choose to start sequences from the command line, there are now two sets of variables to maintain. The test that includes the sequence and also the *scripts* that generate the command line. While it may seem like a good idea, consider the fact that you will need to put a generic test, and then when things go wrong, you will debug the script. In the future, the environment under development could be a legacy environment, and the person who had put it in the command line may have moved on, making it a maintenance nightmare. For that reason, we have not created an example here and highlighted it.

11.4.5 Factory Command Line Interface

In the earlier section of the factory (Section 5.5), one could replace specific components in the simulation using the factory override methods. The CLP provides a similar mechanism to perform factory overrides from the command line. The principle behind this is that you can have a repertoire of components registered with the factory and use a command line argument to choose which component is connected to the interface from a command line.

In my opinion, This should have been removed from the standard! Not only is the simulation now dependent on the command line, but also your scripts that run these tests. Use these options solely to debug a simulation by replacing specific instances if you need to. Once you have a handle on the problem that you are debugging, remove these options from your command line. The only reason it is mentioned here is that it could save you a recompile.

Factory overrides are supported by the following methods:

    +uvm_set_inst_override=<req_type>,<override_type>,<full_inst_path>

    +uvm_set_type_override=<req_type>,<override_type>[,<replace>]

Command line option +uvm_set_inst_override allows you to replace a specific instance in the simulation. See Section 21.9.6 for a practical example of this option.

Command Line option +uvm_set_type_override allows you to replace a specific type for all instances in the simulation. See Section 21.9.5 for a practical example of this command line switch.

11.5 Debug Switches

(i) These debug switches are NOT in the IEEE LRM as debug switches are not deemed standard worthy. However, the Accellera implementation includes these switches.

Many command line options are available to help debug a failing UVM simulation. These options don't need to be passed to the simulation unless you would like to debug something that is going wrong and is typically used *once* per simulation.

+UVM_DUMP_CMDLINE_ARGS
+UVM_PHASE_TRACE
+UVM_OBJECTION_TRACE
+UVM_RESOURCE_DB_TRACE
+UVM_CONFIG_DB_TRACE

UVM_DUMP_CMDLINE_ARGS: option to the simulation dumps all the command line arguments using the reporting mechanism. You can see an example of this by extending the example in Section 21.9.

UVM_PHASE_TRACE: Passing this option to the simulation enables output allowing the user to debug phases. Detailed output of the phase transitions is available on the log file. Typically, if you dump the PHASE trace and the objection traces you can easily figure out the common problem of the simulation jumping through the phases and terminating too early. See Section 13.6 for the phase states it goes through.

UVM_OBJECTION_TRACE: Passing this option to the simulation enables output allowing the user to debug objections. Objection count on a per-component basis is printed in the log file as it increments and decrements the total objection count.

UVM_RESOURCE_DB_TRACE: This option allows a dump of the transactions that happen on the resource_db. If you suspect problems in your simulation are due to settings in the resource_db, pass this command line switch to the simulation. You will see a detailed report one line per set or get that happens to the resource_db.

UVM_SEVERITY: This setting puts a global severity threshold of INFO, WARNING, ERROR, FATAL.

In large environments with a lot of configuration and heavy use of the config/resource_db settings, when you use the UVM_CONFIG_DB_TRACE or the UVM_RESOURCE_DB_TRACE, especially with register settings, it can be quite challenging to see the problem since each component may be doing many config_db set/get operations.

One simple recommendation is to identify a simple search string and then use that to key off your search. Many users found such a technique quite useful.

11.6 Custom Command Line Processor Examples

To use the CLP with your own arguments that are not built-in, you must follow the following steps:

- Getting a handle to the processor
- Getting a list of arguments from the processor.
- Processing the arguments received as required.

To accomplish these tasks, the following functions listed in Table 11.1 are used in the example Listing 11.1 below. There are many examples provided in Section 21.9 that you can use to enhance your understanding of this further.

Table 11.1: Functions Available With The Command Line Processor

Method	Description
uvm_cmdline_processor get_inst()	This function helps you get the instance of the command line processor that is in the simulation
get_args (output string args[$])	Get an queue of all the arguments passed to the simulator
get_plusargs (output string args[$])	Get all the plusargs given to the simulator
get_uvm_args (output string args[$])	get a queue of all the UVM arguments passed to the simulator
get_arg_matches (string match, ref string args[$])	get a queue of all arguments that match the input string argument
get_arg_value (string match, ref string value)	get the valueof the argument that is matched with the string
get_arg_values (string match, ref string values[$])	get a queue of all values that match with the input string

Listing 11.1: Simple usage of the command line processor

```
19
20   typedef class wb_conmax_env;
21
22   class wb_conmax_simple_cmdline_proc extends wb_conmax_base_test;
23
24     wb_config master_configs[8];
25     wb_config slave_configs[16];
26
27     int slave_adr_max ;
28     int slave_adr_min;
29
30     `uvm_component_utils(wb_conmax_simple_cmdline_proc)
31
32     function new(string name, uvm_component parent);
33       super.new(name, parent);
34     endfunction
35
36     virtual function void build_phase(uvm_phase phase);
37
38       uvm_cmdline_processor clp;
39       string arg_values[$];
40       clp = uvm_cmdline_processor::get_inst();
41       void'(clp.get_arg_values("+slave_adr_max=", arg_values));
42       slave_adr_max = arg_values[0].atoi();
43       `uvm_info("CMDLINE_VALUE",$sformatf("SLAVE ADR = %h",slave_adr_max),
             UVM_LOW)
44
45       // slave_adr_max = 32'h0ffffffe;
```

In the Listing 11.1,

- A handle to the command line processor is obtained on line 40

- Line 41 shows the get_arg_values() method which gets the value of the variable slave_adr_max from the command line. The processor will parse the arguments and then populate the value of slave_adr_max with values provided on the command line for that value.

- The test now uses these values as the values instead of what is configured in the test class.

Recommendation 11.6.0: Ensure you convert the string argument from get_arg_values returns a string argument. If you want to pass an integer, such as +my_int=123456 you will get a string with value "123456" **and not an integer**. Make sure you convert it properly using the atoi() function; Otherwise *you will see unexpected results.*

11.7 Exercises for Further Exploration

Please use the example in <example_home>/UVM_Quickstart/UVM_TestBench for these assignments. A complete environment is available for you to get started with minimal effort. You need to make changes to the Makefile

1. Run the test with +UVM_CONFIG_DB_TRACE and study the output. You should be able to identify each of the config_db accesses and account for them.

2. Run the test with +UVM_OBJECTION_TRACE and study the output. You should be able to identify each of the components raising an objection and dropping it.

Chapter 12

UVM Register Abstraction Layer

This chapter provides information about the UVM register classes and helps you understand the infrastructure provided by UVM. This chapter condenses the essential material presented in [3] to help you to learn the register abstraction layer and use it effectively. The register topic is broken into three separate chapters[1]. :

- Overview of UVM register abstraction layer capabilities and API. - This chapter

- Integrating the UVM register model with a design. - Chapter 20

- Advanced capabilities of the register model. - Chapter 17

Verifying register configurations in any RTL can add significant complexity to verification. Any change to the register/memory specification has a cascade effect on both the design and testbench. Register verification usually tends to have an incredibly adverse impact on project schedules when register definitions and functionality change during a project. Unless you have an abstraction model, you find that you are dealing with a lot of high maintenance code.

The UVM register offering is designed to address this problem. It has a large number of features and supports many kinds of register access policies right out of the box. A significant amount of customization capability is built into the model so that users do not have to write a large amount of code to model and maintain registers.

This chapter provides an overview of the register model, its API, and the architecture of the model. You need this background information to understand the register model capabilities. Chapter 20 provides detailed instructions on how to integrate a register model with the design. Basics of the various kinds of accesses and various kinds of built-in tests provided as a part of the class library are covered in that chapter. Chapter 17 covers advanced register model topics, the effect of various register operations on various access policies, hooks into the register model, and various callback methods. I recommend that you read this chapter before proceeding to Chapter 20 and then proceeding to Chapter 17. Each chapter in the series builds upon the content from the earlier ones.

12.1 Typical UVM Register Use Model

The register model is typically abstracted and specified in a high-level format. The UVM user's guide [3] describes an IP-XACT specification supported by many vendors with some extensions. EDA Vendors [16] and Accellera [1] also provide offerings in this area. This abstract specification lends itself well to being maintained easily and supports various levels of integration. All essential features of the specification are captured in the abstract definition.

(i) The abstraction includes physical interfaces, Addresses, and endianness as part of the definition. It, however, does not include bus operations as a part of the abstraction.

---

[1] [17] and [2] have some good discussions on this topic.

Figure 12.1 shows the typical flow used when using the UVM register model. An abstract model is usually maintained in the user environment.

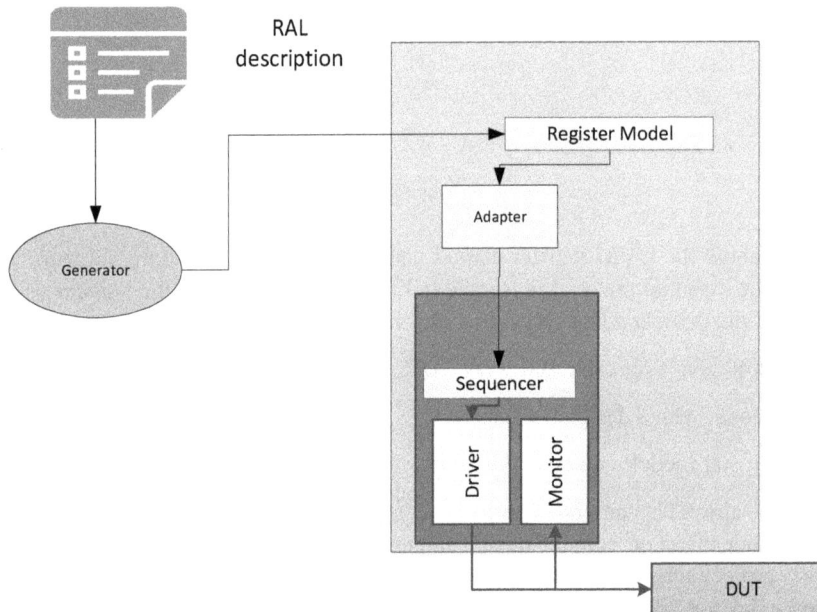

Fig. 12.1: Register Model Flow

This abstract model is then translated down to a UVM register model using a model generator. The model generator takes the abstract model as an input file and produces a SystemVerilog file comprised of classes extended from the UVM register layer. Note that contemporary generators are capable of producing register models with instrumented coverage as well. The generated register model is integrated into the verification environment. The process of integration of the model to the environment requires many steps to be performed once for each environment. These are described in Section 20.1. After integration, one can access the register model and use the power of the model.

12.2 Components of a Register Model

A typical block in a design may contain one or more registers. Each of these registers may have one or more fields, which are typically collections of bits. A group of blocks on a chip with a memory map is usually called a system.

Almost every design has registers. They are usually the first to be verified since they configure the DUT. Typically, these registers are checked for reset value and ability to program functions in the DUT. I have found that register models are usually high maintenance during the development cycle because they have a lot of updates over the cycle of the project. Figure 12.2 shows the essential elements of the register model for a typical register that you would find in a typical DUT. The register model comprises fields grouped into registers. Blocks group registers and memories. Blocks correspond to individually designed and verified components with their host processor interfaces, address decoding and memory-mapped registers and memories. If a memory is physically implemented externally to the block and accessed through the block, as part of the block's address space, the memory is considered as part of the block register model.

The smallest register model that can be used is a block. A block may contain one register and no memories or thousands of registers and gigabytes of memory in a sparse representation.

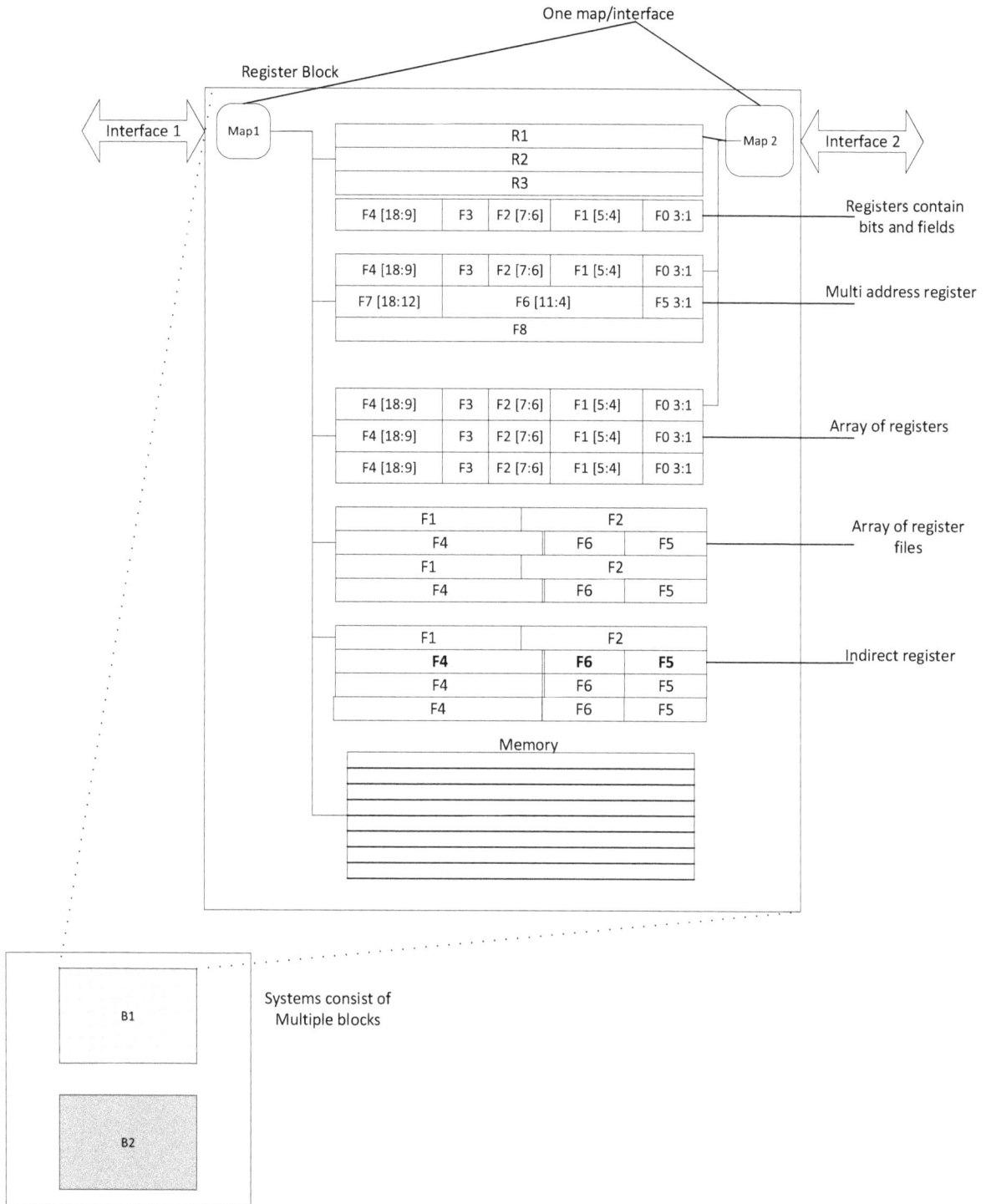

Fig. 12.2: Various components of a Register Model

A block can contain one or more registers, memories, memory maps, and register files. Each register comprises of one or more fields. Each field can represent one or more bits.

Blocks may be grouped into systems. A system may contain one or more blocks/instances of a block and optionally include other systems. The field classes are used to model the register bits in a register. Register classes model registers and block classes are used to model blocks and systems.

The UVM inheritance model for this is shown in Figure 12.6.

Given this level of complexity and a large number of details involved in correctly creating and configuring register classes, the class generation and specialization is usually accomplished by a model generator. The following main classes are present in the UVM register model. By far and large, these are found to be the most useful classes in the register model.

- Fields
- Registers
  - Normal Registers
  - Indirect Registers
  - FIFO Registers
  - Virtual Registers
  - Register Files
- Blocks
- Address Maps
- Memories

12.3 Register Maps

Some designs may have more than one physical interface, each with accessible registers or memories. Some registers or memories may even be accessible via more than one physical interface and be shared. In the register class hierarchy, Only blocks and systems can have maps. The maps contain registers and memories accessible via a specific physical interface. A register map is a class that represents a collection of registers and memories accessible via a specific physical interface and is also referred to as a *address map* in UVM documentation. Register maps can be composed into higher-level address maps.

Address maps may be composed of higher-level address maps.

The figure below shows all the various classes and how they fit together into the overall scheme[2].

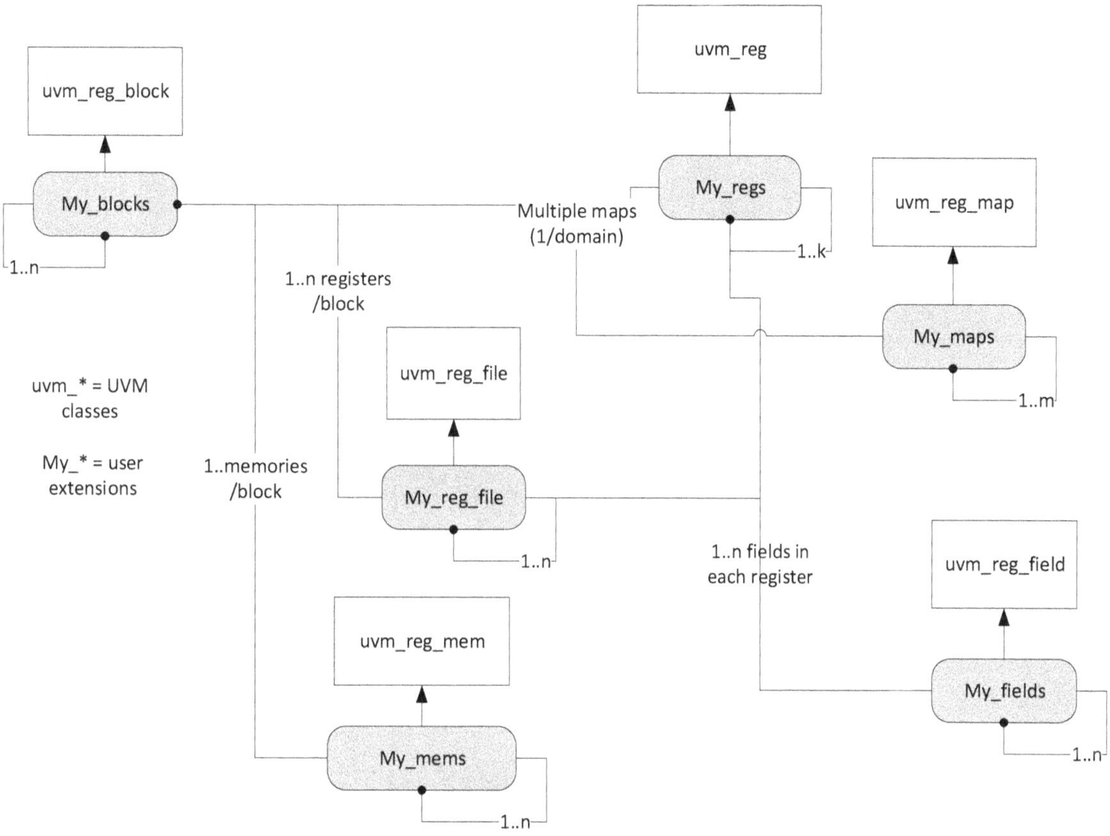

Fig. 12.3: Register Collaboration Mode

12.4 Register Model Architecture

The register model is built as a collection of classes that store many values for each of the registers.

reset value: this is implemented as an array, having multiple types of reset values associated with it, like a SOFT RESET, HARD RESET, etc.

mirror value: The register model maintains a mirror of what it believes the current value of register fields is inside the DUT. Note that the mirrored value is based upon information available to the register model through its API. It is not guaranteed to be accurate, as many drivers may modify values in the DUT, For example: forcing a value, having a value deposited on the DUT register, or having the DUT update its register values may cause it to be outdated.

Because of the above, the register model takes every opportunity to update its mirrored value. During every read operation, the mirror for the read register is updated. During every write operation, the new mirror value for the written register is predicted based on the access modes of the bits in the register (RW,RO, W1C , See Table 17.1). When you reset a register model, it sets the mirror to the reset value specified in the model. A mirror value is not a scoreboard *nor intended to be one*. While a mirror can accurately predict the content of registers that are not updated by the design, it cannot determine if an updated value is correct or not.

---

[2] Adapted from [3]

desired value: The value that the user would like the DUT to have.

value: This is the value used for functional coverage, and can be constrained when it is randomized.

Note that among these properties, only the value property is public. The other properties are local. We cannot access them directly from the outside of the class.

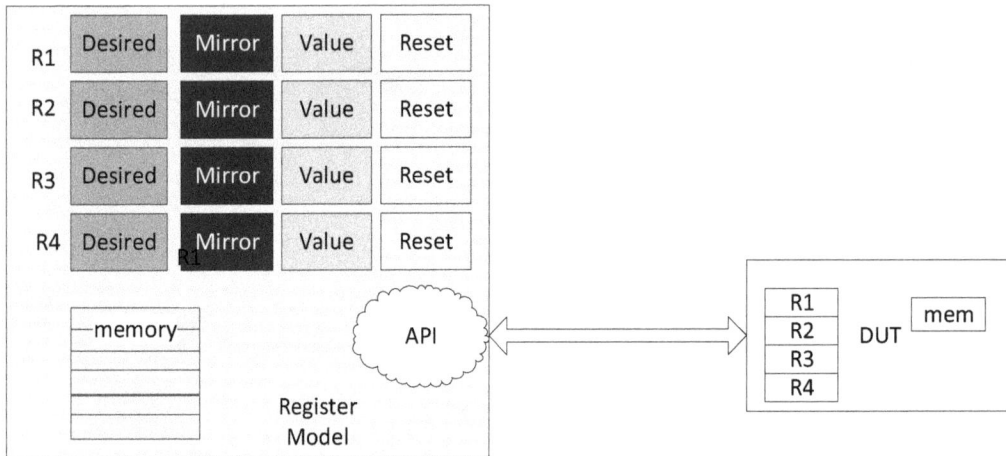

Fig. 12.4: Register Model Values and Mirror Of The DUT

12.5 Register Model API

UVM supplies base classes that you extend and configure to create a representative model of the registers in your DUT. The model you create is referred to as the register model and is composed of several classes. As you are extending from base classes, the library provides an API, categorized into three main parts, the taxonomy of which is self-evident.

- Creation API
- Heirarchy traversal API.
- Access API

12.5.1 Register Model Creation API

The creation API consists of methods to help create and configure the register model during the build_phase(). While there are many methods in this group, the most common ones are the construction and the configuration functions. A generic signature for these is shown below.

```
function void new(string name=''name'').
and
configure(......).
```

The configure methods have various parameters depending on which classes are used. Depending on the class, there are usually a few more methods that can be used to set up the class instance. Typically, you will not need to learn this category of the API, since register generators usually generate these classes for you. Read the HTML documentation of the model or [2] if you wish to know more or building a register generator.

You will notice that many of the register classes extend from uvm_object. Although the IEEE LRM mandates that all classes deriving from uvm_object shall be factory enabled, Several classes in the register layer were not factory enabled due to non-standard constructors.

12.5.2 Register Model Hierarchy Traversal API

Given the large hierarchy that can be built using the model, the class library provides for an API to allow you to traverse the hierarchy. Note that while the register model while is composed of many classes, *is not derived from uvm_component* but from uvm_object. It is usually created in the build phase, just like other agents or testbench components.

The register model provides a built-in traversal API shown in Figure 12.5.

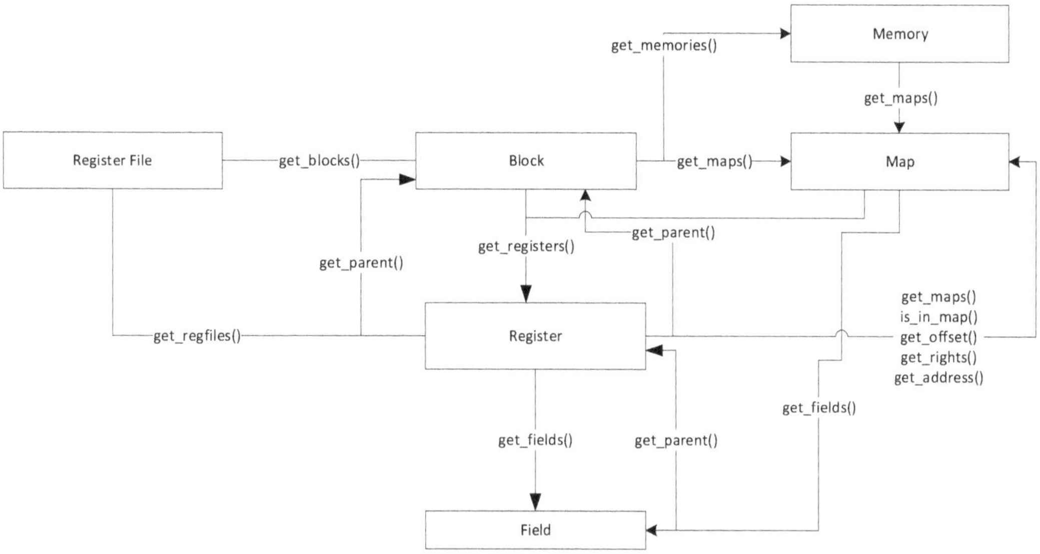

Fig. 12.5: Essential Parts of The Register Model Hierarchy API

One thing that you will observe on looking at Figure 12.5 is that from any point in the model, it is possible to go from the lowest layer in the register hierarchy to the top of the register hierarchy. All you have to do is to be aware of where you are in the hierarchy. The hierarchy API is quite extensively used in the UVM library in the pre-built tests described in Section 20.3[3].

12.5.3 Register Model Access API

Figure 12.6 shows the class diagram for the register model. This diagram also illustrates the access API. Since the model is derived from uvm_object base class, many core facilities are available to the register model classes.

---

[3] The built-in tests are in the src/reg/sequences directory of your UVM installation

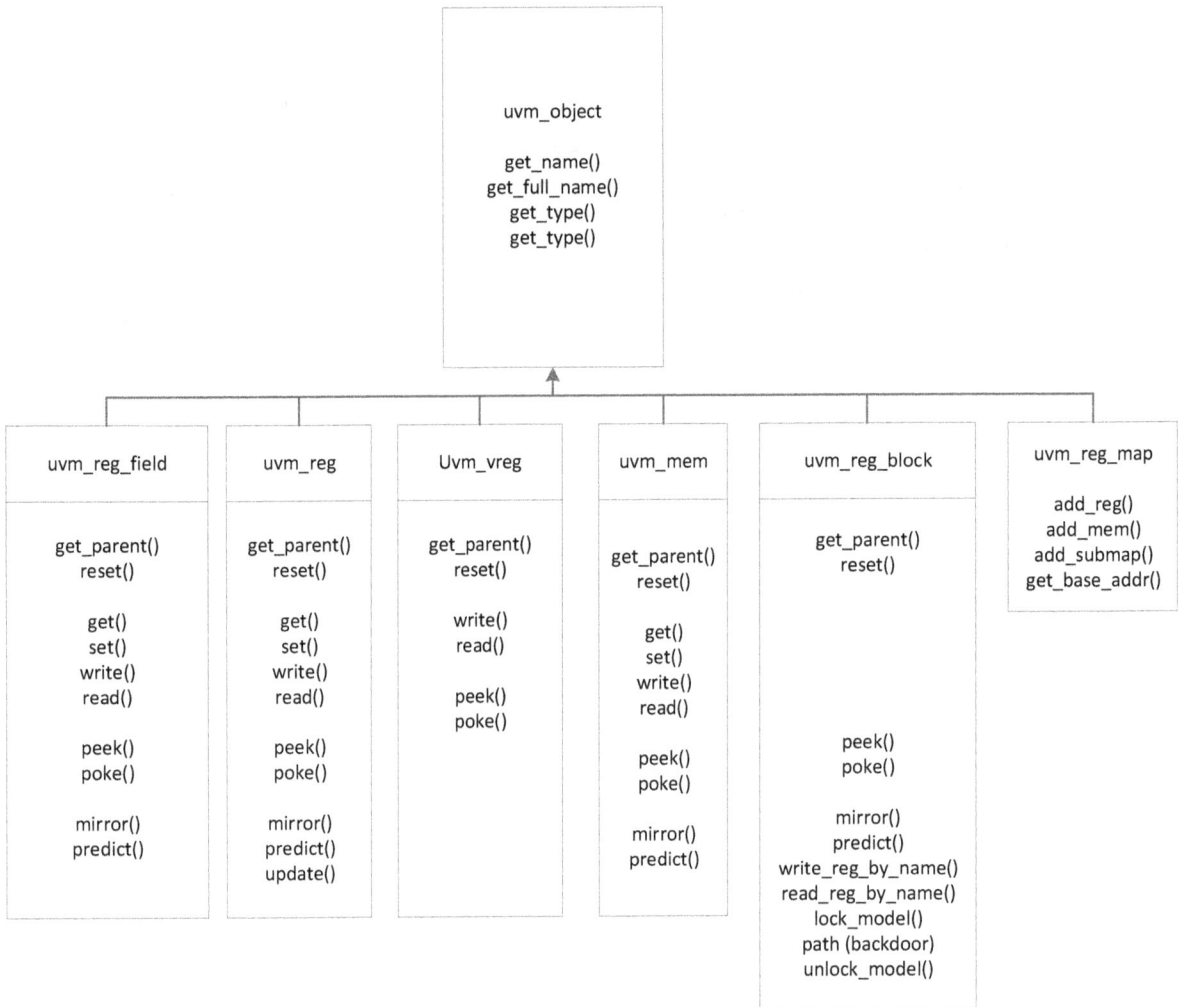

Fig. 12.6: Register Access API

12.5.3.1 Reset
Resetting a register model sets the mirror to the reset value specified in the model. An associative array inside the model allows you to specify a string that serves as a "kind" of reset such as SOFT/HARD etc. You could have any string depending on your application.

12.5.3.2 Read/Write
When you perform a read/write operation using the frontdoor mode, a transaction is issued on the bus and completed by the bus agent. The backdoor mode uses a simulator specific mechanism to update the value. The mirror value is updated with the corrected values. The mirror is checked when a read operation is performed on the DUT and updated if the values are different. During a write operation, the new mirror value for the written register is predicted based on the access modes of the bits in the register (read/write, read-only, write-1- to-clear, etc.) as the value may be different based on the policy. The listing below shows you an example of the read/write and mirror values.

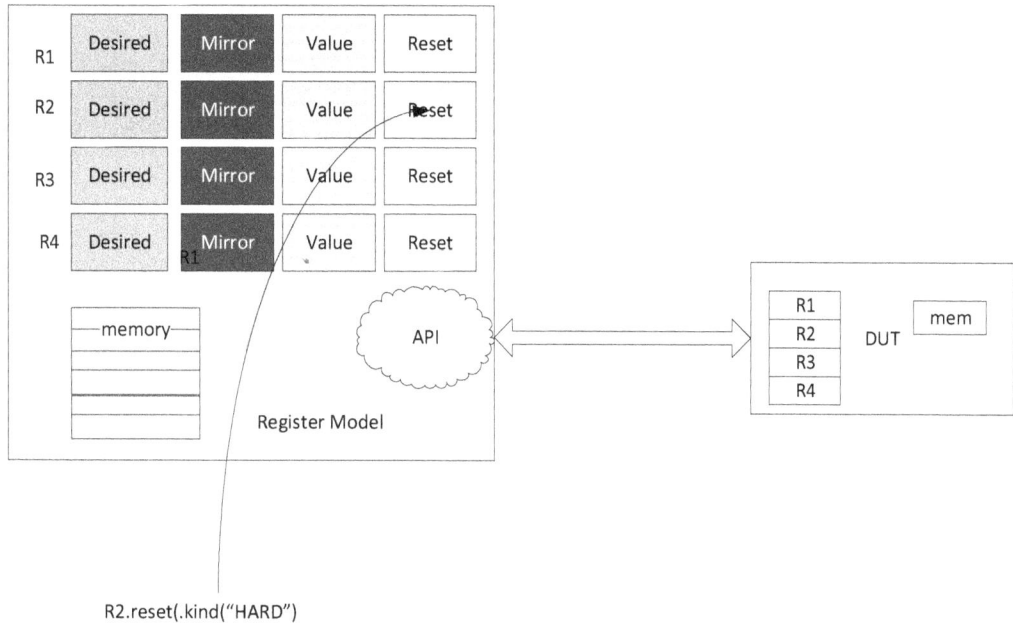

R2.reset(.kind("HARD")

Listing 12.1: Register Read/Write

```
1   task body() ;
2       string s1;
3       uvm_resource_db#(string)::read_by_name("reg_seq","regname_string",
            regname_string,this);
4       rg = regmodel.get_reg_by_name(regname_string);
5       write_val = 32'hdeadbeef;
6       set_val = 32'hbeefdead;
7       poke_val = 32'haaaabbbb;
8       if(rg == null) `uvm_fatal(get_full_name(),{regname_string ,"
            register not found"})
9
10      //Frontdoor access
11      rg.read(.status(status), .value(read_val), .path(UVM_FRONTDOOR),   .
            parent(this));
12
13      rg.write(.status(status), .value(write_val), .path(UVM_FRONTDOOR),
            .parent(this));
14
15      // backdoor access
16      rg.read(.status(status), .value(read_val), .path(UVM_BACKDOOR),   .
            parent(this));
17
18      rg.write(.status(status), .value(write_val), .path(UVM_BACKDOOR),   .
            parent(this));
19  endtask
```

12.5.3.3 Get/Set

Using the get() and set() methods access directly to the desired value respectively, without accessing the DUT. The desired value is uploaded into the DUT using the update() method.

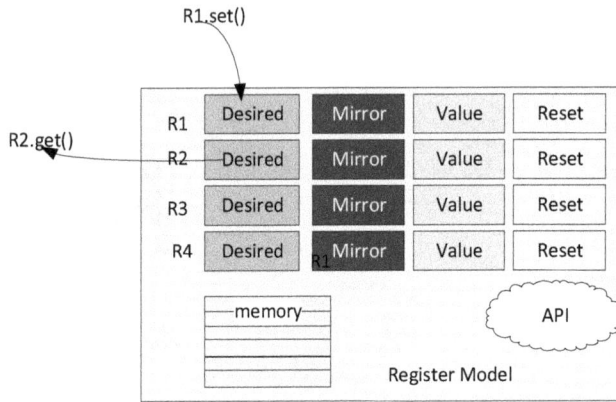

Fig. 12.7: Get And Set Operations

12.5.3.4 Peek/Poke

You must take care regarding the peek() and poke() methods with the mirror model. The peek() methods return the raw value read using the back-door *without modifying the content of the register or memory*. Depending on the register, The content can be modified by a normal read operation, such as a clear-on-read field. But a peek() or poke() will not modify it as you would expect. Therefore, reading using peek() methods may yield different results than reading through read() methods under certain circumstances. You can see this summarized in Table 17.3.

The poke() methods deposit the specified value directly in the register or memory. Should the register contain non-writable bits or bits that do not reflect the exact value written, such as read-only or write- 1-to-clear fields, they will contain a different value than if the same value had been written through normal means. The mirror will be out of sync with the design during some operations, and you must note this.

All field values, regardless of their access mode, will be forced to the poked value. Therefore, writing using poke() methods may yield different results than writing through the frontdoor. This is summarized in Table 17.3.

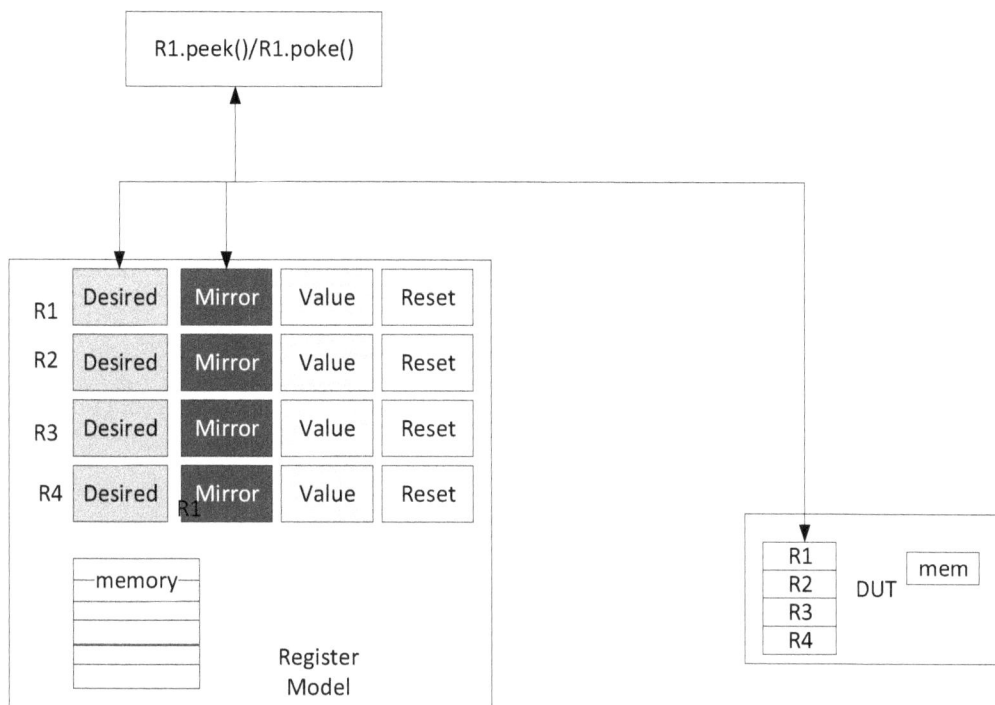

Fig. 12.8: Peek And Poke

The example below shows you how to use the peek and poke methods in your environment.

Listing 12.2: Register Peek/Poke

```
1    task body() ;
2       string s1;
3
4       uvm_resource_db#(string)::read_by_name("reg_seq","regname_string",
            regname_string,this);
5
6       rg = regmodel.get_reg_by_name(regname_string);
7       write_val = 32'hdeadbeef;
8       set_val = 32'hbeefdead;
9       poke_val = 32'haaaabbbb;
10      if(rg == null) `uvm_fatal(get_full_name(),{regname_string ,"
            register not found"})
11
12      rg.peek(.status(status), .value(peek_val), .parent(this));
13
14      rg.poke(.status(status), .value(poke_val), .parent(this));
15   endtask
```

12.5.3.5 Randomize

Using the randomize() method copies the randomized value in the uvm_reg_field::value property into the desired value of the mirror by the post_randomize() method. The desired value is uploaded into the DUT using the update() method.

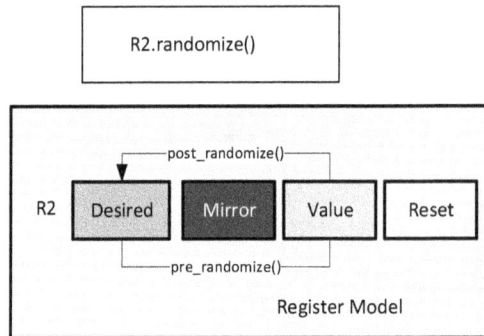

Fig. 12.9: Register Randomize Operation

12.5.3.6 Update

Using the update() method invokes the write() method if the desired value (previously modified using set() or randomize()) is different from the mirrored value. The mirrored value is then updated to reflect the expected value in the register after the executed transactions.

Once the desired value is set, you must update the DUT to match the mirror values by using the uvm_reg::update() or uvm_reg_block::update() methods. If the new mirrored value matches the old mirrored value, the register is not updated, thus saving unnecessary bus cycles and updating a block with its mirror updates all the fields and registers in the block. Updating a large block may take a lot of simulation time if physical write cycles are used; whereas, updating using backdoor access usually takes zero-time. It is recommended to use this update-from-mirror process when configuring the DUT to minimize the number of write operations performed.

A common use model for a number of environments uses update(). You typically have code that looks like below in your sequence. There are a number of other examples in the book, and only a snippet is shown here.

```
my_reg1.myfield2.set(0x11);
my_reg1.myfield3.set(1);
my_reg1.update();
```

Only when the desired value does not match the mirrored value or the register is configured as *volatile*, will an update take effect. This check is performed inside the library. Also, recall that this implies that if you have a number of registers, either configured as volatile or contains special fields (RO/RC/RS (see Table 17.1)), calling update() on a block, will always update the registers.

Recognize that other than setting the desired value and performing an operation, it is impossible to update the mirror value, which is the result of a prediction. The mirror value is *local*, and there are no accessor methods provided.

There are a few examples in the download using this API in sequences for the VGA LCD design in Chapter 20. Please refer to them in the sequences/src directory.

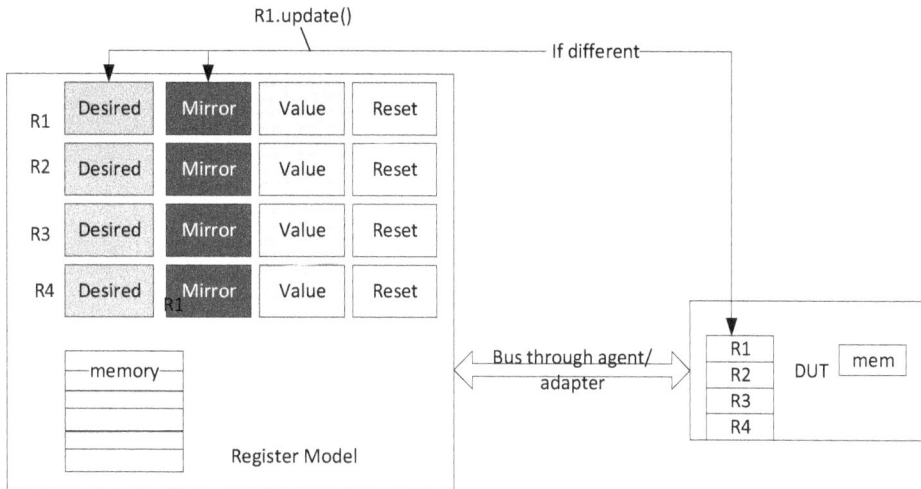

Fig. 12.10: Register Update Operation

12.5.3.7 Mirror

Using the mirror() method invokes the read() method to update the mirrored value based on the value that is read back. Mirror() can compare the read back value with the current mirrored value before updating it.

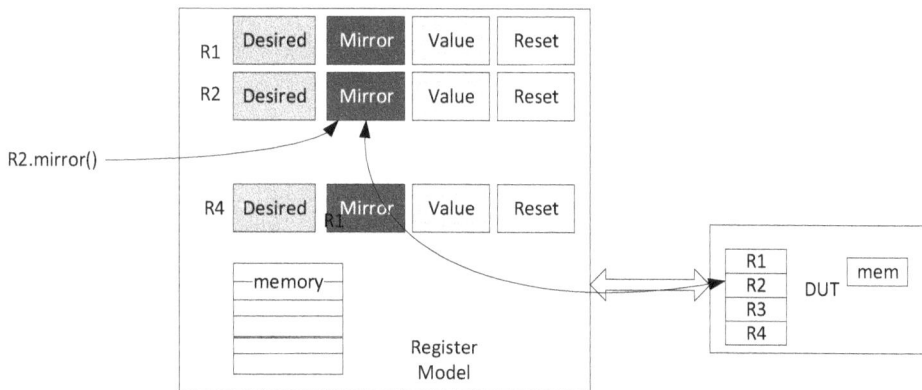

Fig. 12.11: Mirror Operation

See examples in Section 17.2.1 for this operation.

12.5.4 Front Door Access

Previous sections described the structure of the register model and the various classes that make up the register model. The frontdoor access is the access that is often used in the verification activity. When a register is written through the frontdoor, the operation looks at the map that is in effect. The operation then creates a struct where the values of the register (in case of a write) or the address (in case of a read) are transferred. The adapter is then invoked. An operation on a sequence is then initiated, which is routed through the sequencer to the driver.

Frontdoor access consumes some cycles in simulation. If you have many thousands of registers, you will find that the initialization takes an exceptionally long time. You will find many examples of front door access in Section 22.2.3.

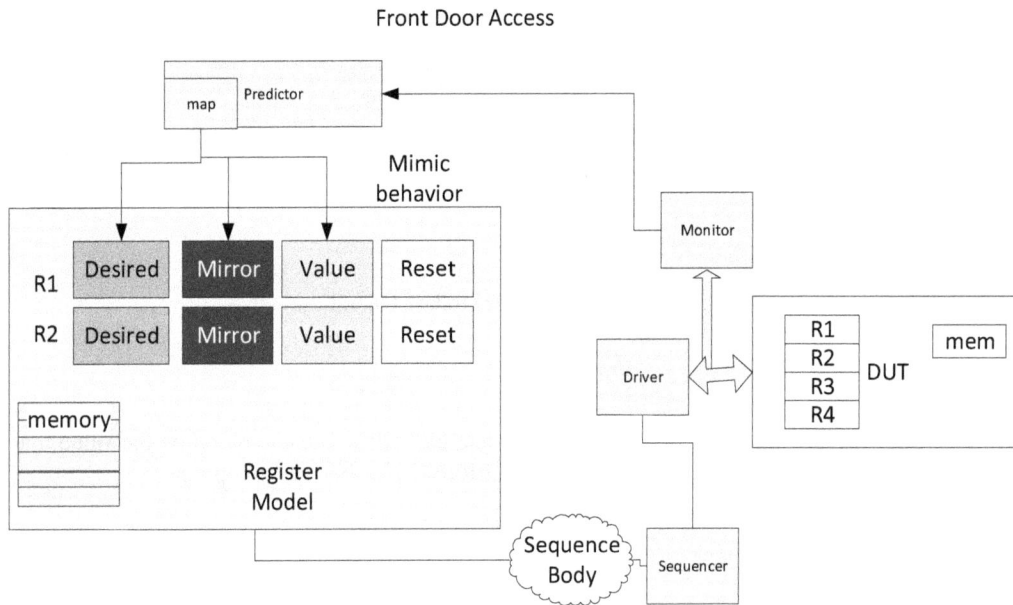

Fig. 12.12: Front Door Access

12.5.5 Back Door Access

Backdoor access can uncover bugs hidden by using the normal access path. Another advantage of backdoor access is that it's more efficient and does not consume simulation time. This access mechanism requires the user to specify the complete hierarchical reference to each of the registers.

Backdoor access can uncover hidden bugs since write and read cycles are performed using the same access path. For example, if the wrong memory is accessed or the data bits are reversed, any bug introduced on the way in (during the write cycle) will be undone on the way out (during the read cycle). You will **never** see the problem with a frontdoor access.

On the other hand, backdoor access directly accesses the simulation constructs that implement the register in the design hierarchy. One thing you should note is that the big challenge is *maintaining* the paths after identifying them. Depending on whether it is an RTL or a GATE simulation, the maintenance of the signals can either be a simple chore or something that can require a lot of maintenance.

Recommendation 12.5.0: *Plan ahead and use a proper methodology that allows the code to be reused across environments. This is essential anytime one is dealing with these backdoor paths .*

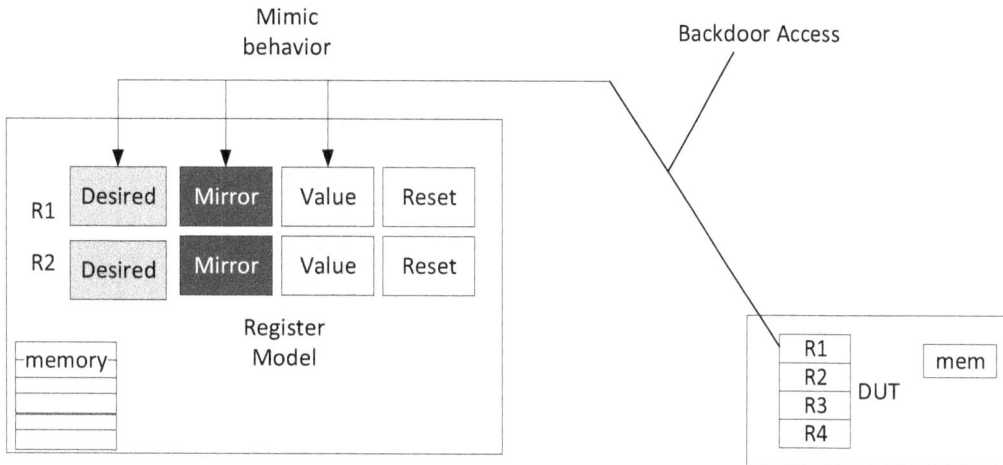

Fig. 12.13: Back Door Access

Table 12.1: Comparison Of Frontdoor And Backdoor Accesses

	Backdoor Access	Frontdoor Access
Time	Zero Simulation Time	Bus transaction may take *at least one cycle*
Changing values in DUT	Force bits to value (poke)	Write direction accesses do a normal HW write
Data Movement	read access returns values of data bits	Data returned by hardware path
Prediction	backdoor access are auto-predicted	based on prediction scheme
side effects	side effects due to other logic is possible	Side effects are modelled correctly
Potential for errors	By-passes normal HW	Simulates real timing and event sequences, catches errors due to unknown interactions

12.6 Difference Between Backdoor and Peek/Poke Operations

There are some differences between the Peek/Poke operations and the backdoor operations. These are summarized in Figure 12.14. The backdoor mechanism emulates the regular read/write processes considering the register policies that are in effect, For example, Read to Clear, etc. The Peek/Poke mechanisms, on the other hand, are effectively "hard" operators directly making/observing changes to the structure in the simulator memory.

What does this exactly mean? Take an example of a WRC register (Write to Clear). Any time you write to the register, you will clear its contents. This is true of either a frontdoor or a backdoor write. The value of the register after the operation is always *zero*. On the other hand, if you poke the register with a value, *the value will not be zero*. It will be whatever you poked it to be. This means that the mirror and DUT values are different.

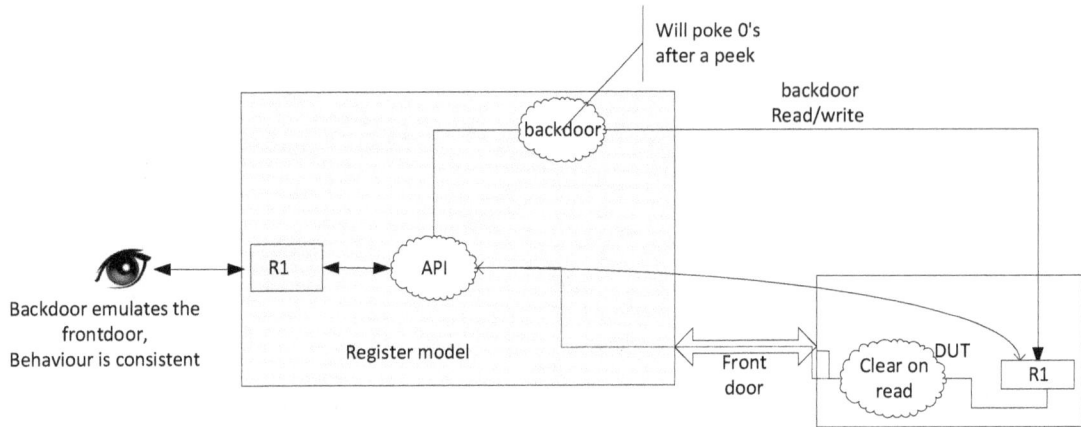

Fig. 12.14: Difference between backdoor/poke

12.7 Coverage of Register Models

The UVM register library classes do not include any coverage models since a coverage model for a register will depend on the fields it contains, as well as the layout of those fields. A coverage model for a block will depend on the registers and memories it contains and the addresses where they are located. Since the coverage model information is added to the UVM register library classes by the register model generator, the generator carries the responsibility of including a suitable coverage model. The UVM register library classes provide the necessary API for a coverage model to sample the relevant data into a coverage model. Since there are significant memory and performance impact of including a coverage model in a large register model, One must turn on the coverage explicitly to get the benefits from the model.s

If you have generated a register model with a generator and included the coverage as well, then the following controls are available to allow you to instrument the model with coverage. You would typically set these in the config_db in your test to allow the models to instrument coverage.

Identifier	Description
UVM_NO_COVERAGE	Coverage models are not created or instantiated.
UVM_CVR_REG_BITS	Coverage models for the bits read or written in registers.
UVM_CVR_ADDR_MAP	Coverage models for the addresses read or written in an address map.
UVM_CVR_FIELD_VALS	Coverage models for the values of fields
UVM_CVR_ALL	All coverage models

12.8 Customization of Register Models

This chapter provided an overview of the various register model classes supplied by UVM and the API that you use with the model. You do not instantiate the register classes directly but always extend and configure them to construct a representative model of your DUT. These extended classes use the methods supplied by UVM that were described in this chapter. Section 17.4 show you how to create these register models and how to instantiate and use them in your environment. After completing this chapter, see Chapter 17 to learn about advanced RAL features. If you would like to use the register model right away, follow the steps in Chapter 20.

Chapter 13

Phasing in UVM

If you look at any test in a verification environment, you recognize that the simulation usually passes through many stages (reset, configure DUT, stimulus checking, result summarization, etc.) Some of these stages occur in zero time, and others may consume time. When you analyze further, you will recognize that many of these steps are common, regardless of which testbench or platform you use. Pre-UVM testbenches had their own tasks that accomplished staging. This does not lend itself well to uniformity. Different engineers may call these tasks with different names with different functionality. If you just started working at a company, you would spend time coming up to speed on what the tasks and phases did, rather than helping write test cases.

UVM supplies infrastructure and standardization to help you quickly become productive. The advantage you get is that common stages are all there for you. You just need to use them. The methodology defines many stages in the methodology to help you accomplish specific tasks at each stage of the simulation. The library also has the flexibility to allow you to change the default behavior and add stages or callbacks (see Chapter 9) to intercept phase behavior if the default is not good enough for you.

This chapter reveals the working of UVM phasing[1]. The various phases and their applications are described before moving on to various considerations with phasing callbacks and other aspects.

Phasing in UVM is composed of three main parts.

1. Pre-run phases: the testbench is configured and constructed. No simulation time advances in this stage.

2. Run-time phases: time is consumed in running tests on the testbench

3. Post run phases: results of the testcase are collected and reported.

The UVM library is composed of phases, all stitched together into a schedule. You can view a schedule as a directed graph of phases[22]. The phases are grouped into groups called domains. There are essentially two domains in the current UVM implementation:

- The *common* domain intended to synchronize the construction, configuration, and eventual shutdown of the testbench.

- The *run* domain is intended to synchronize the flow and execution of a test. Typical tests go through a reset, test, sequence. However, these phases are more dynamic and can change on a test-by-test basis.

13.1 Common Domain Pre Run Stages

UVM supplies a standard way to create, configure, interconnect components in a standard way. The common pre-run stage is divided into three sections. These phases do not consume any simulation time and are usually identical in almost all the tests and testbenches. Think of these phases as something you have to do, no matter what the test does. The common domain also is used to report the test status and cleanup when the test is ending after the run domain finishes running.

---

[1] The Author is grateful to Justin Refice for granting permission to use pieces of his work [20] in this work to benefit users

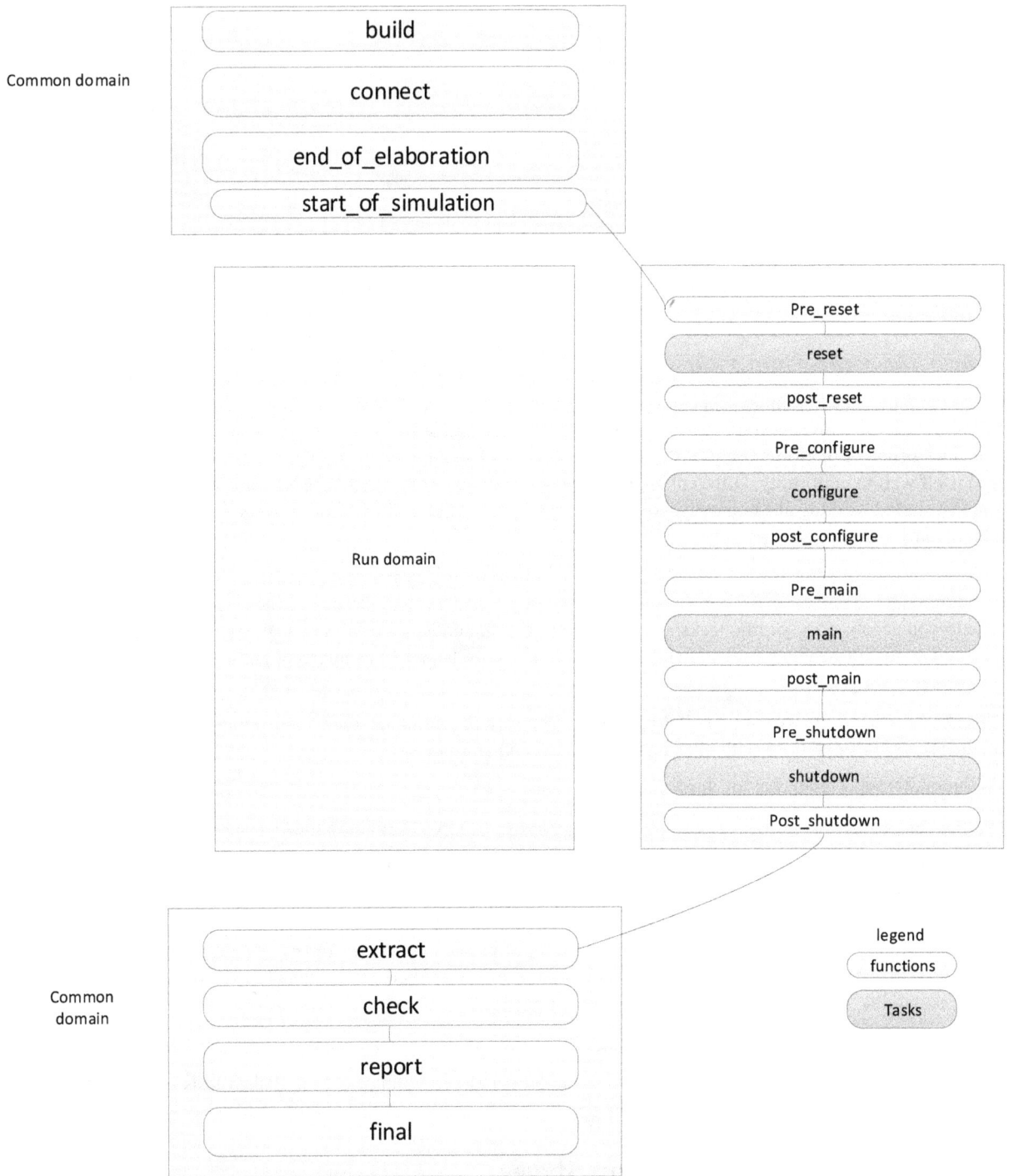

Fig. 13.1: UVM Phasing overview

13.1.1 Build_phase

Once the testbench is started from the initial block, the first phase to be executed is called the build_phase. The build_phase begins with the root node component coming into existence when the simulation starts up.

Once the UVM testbench root node component is constructed, it constructs the testbench component hierarchy in a top-down manner. Construction of each component is deferred so that each layer in the component hierarchy can be configured by the level above. During the build phase, uvm_components are constructed using the UVM factory.

Build phases are executed at the start of the UVM testbench simulation and their overall purpose is to construct, configure and connect the testbench component hierarchy. All the build phase methods are functions and, therefore, execute in zero simulation time.

13.1.2 connect_phase

The connect_phase is used to make connections between components or to assign handles to testbench resources. Since the components have to exist to be connected, this phase can only occur after the build phase has completed. This phase is executed bottom-up in the hierarchy.

13.1.3 end_of_elaboration_phase

At the end of the connect phase, all the components are built and connected. You may need to adjust the hierarchy after it has been built. The end_of_elaboration phase is provided to help with checking the constructed testbench before the simulation starts. You can also print out the simulation topology at the end of this phase.

Use this phase to check if your virtual interfaces are null.

13.1.4 start_of_simulation_phase

The start_of_simulation phase is a function that occurs before the time-consuming part of the testbench starts. Since most of the configuration and connections have been completed in the common phases earlier, this phase could be used to print out the configuration, testbench topology, and any other debug information that could help the user to get debug what is going on.

This phase can be used to make sure that proper synchronization happens in case there are other external programs like debuggers or emulators are all synchronized.

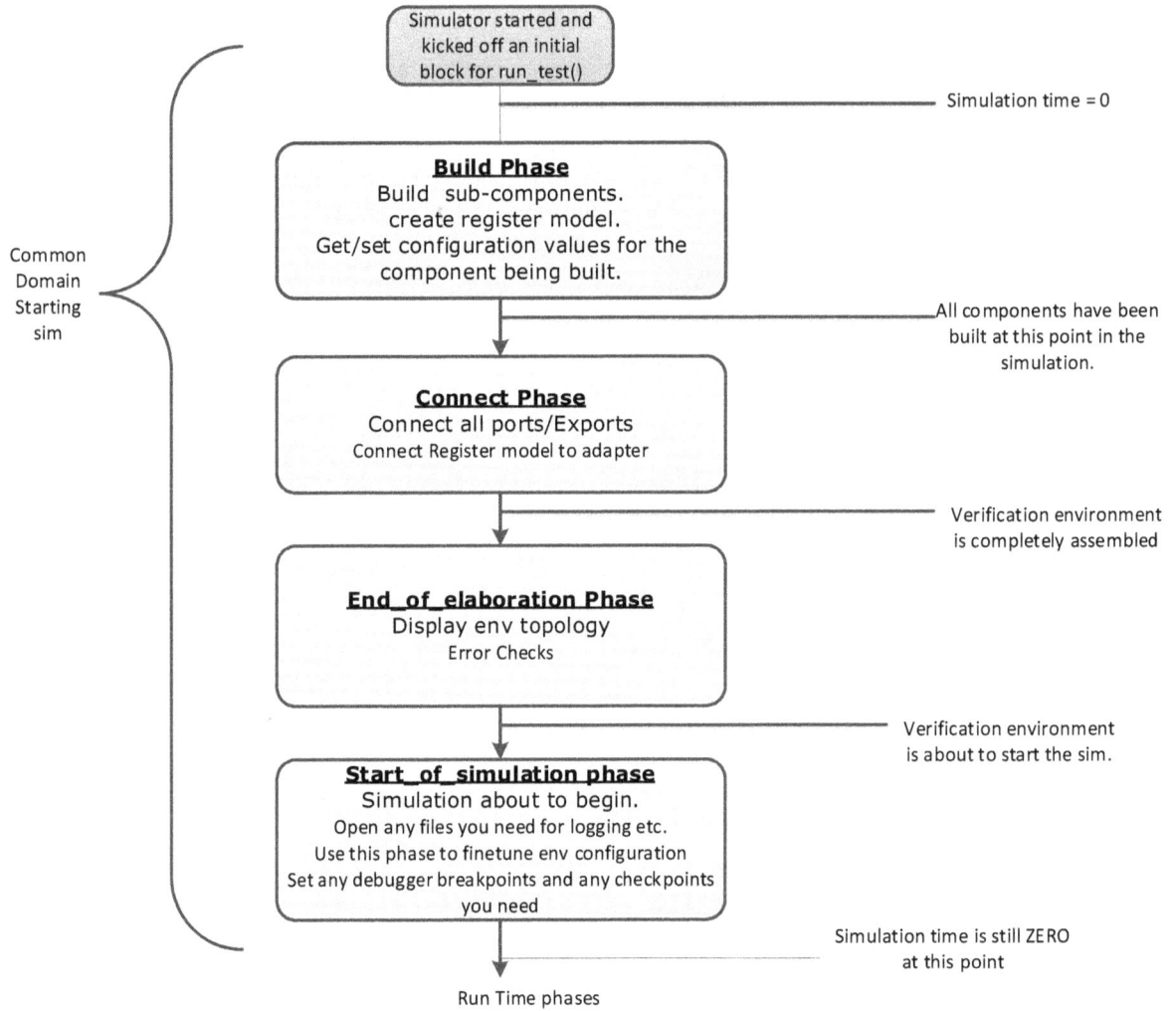

Fig. 13.2: Starting common phases

13.2 Run Time Phases

UVM defines four sequential sets of run-time phases:

- reset
- configure
- main
- shutdown

Each set is composed of three distinct phases that run in sequence: a pre-phase, the "main" part of the set, and a post-phase. This creates a total of twelve phases, from pre_reset to post_shutdown. These twelve run-time phases execute concurrently to the base "run" phase.

There is a correspondingly named task in the uvm_component class for each of these phases. When a phase starts, the corresponding task for that phase in every uvm_component instance in the testbench is forked off into a separate thread.

There is an objection mechanism (discussed in Section 13.4) that is used to determine when all components are ready to terminate the phase. Refer to the Figure 13.3. There is much detail in the diagram, which reveals the various states of the test as UVM cycles through its phases.

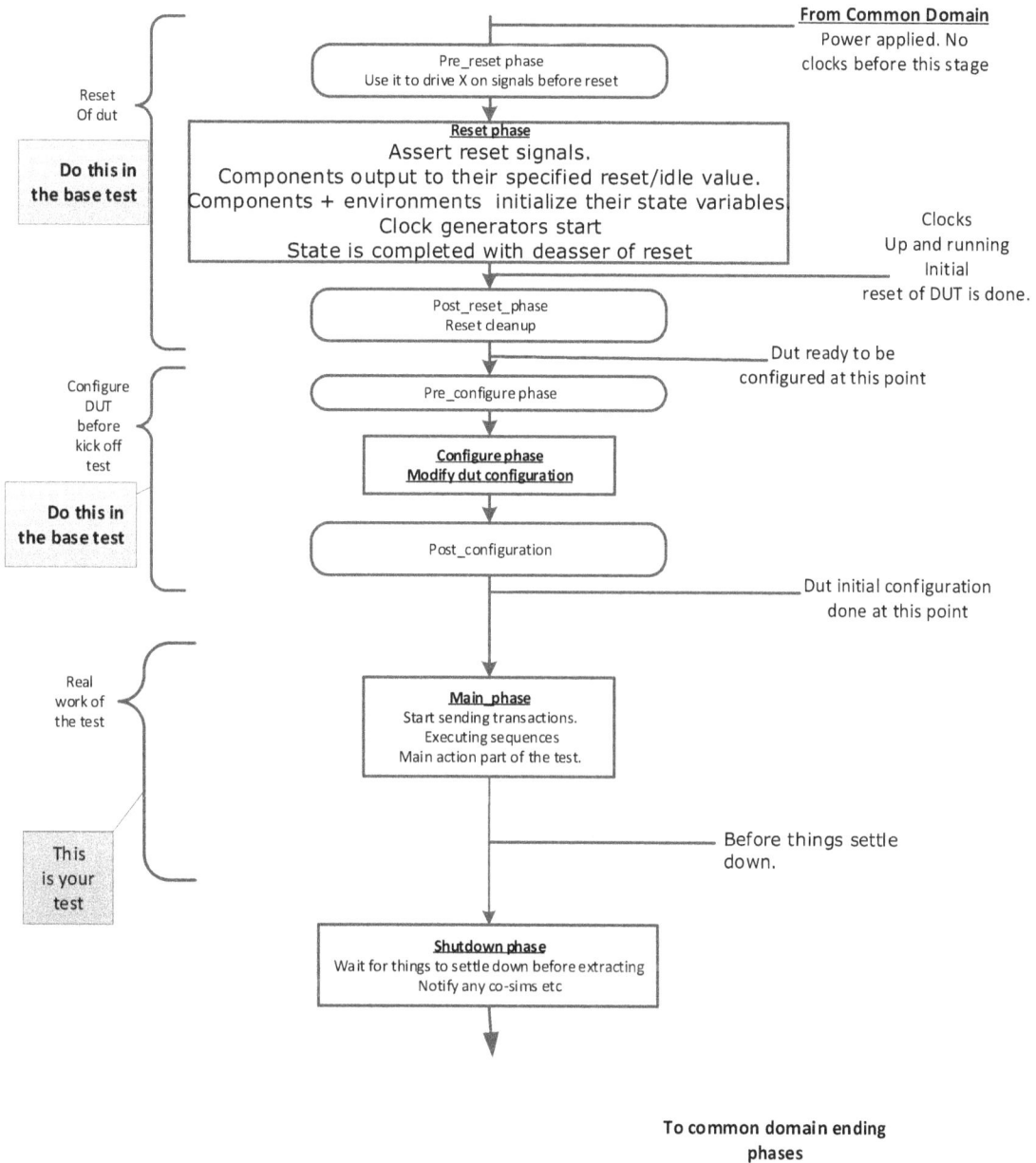

Fig. 13.3: Run Time phases

13.3 Clean Up Stages

The test has completed execution and exits the run phase allowing an orderly shutdown of the simulation. Information from the scoreboards and coverage monitors, etc. are all summarized. This is a zero time effort in simulation and is performed from the bottom to the top of the hierarchy. Cleanup activity in the phase can typically be divided into three main categories. Functional coverage/ checking/and reporting

- **extract_phase** is used to retrieve and process information from scoreboards and functional coverage monitors.

- **check_phase** is usually used by the checker components to report errors.

- **report_phase** summarizes the results from the simulation and flushes the result to a log file.

- **final phase** terminates the testbench after terminating anything that was not already terminated in the earlier phases.

Figure 13.4 provides a summary of these phases.

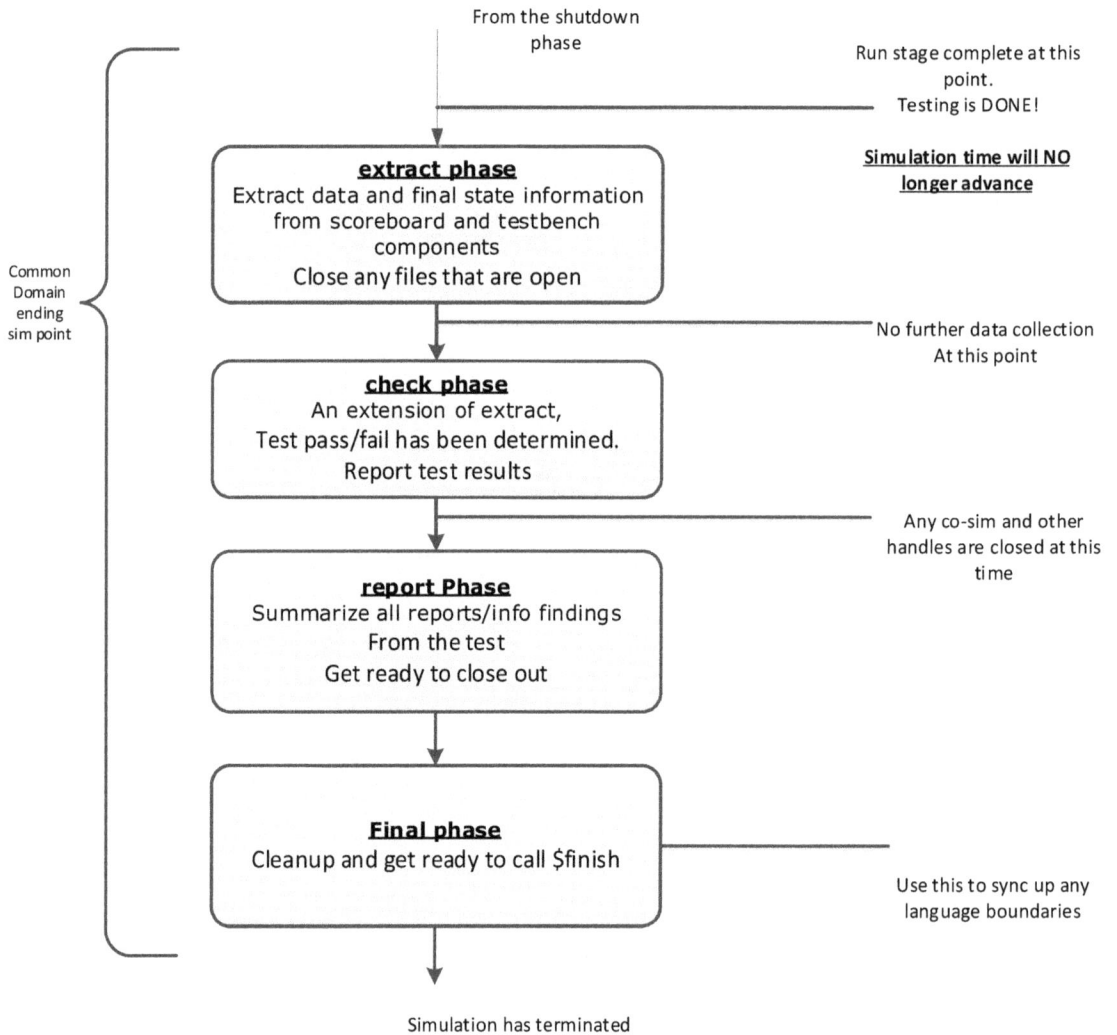

Fig. 13.4: Common Phases ending

13.4 Preventing Phases from Ending - Objections

As the simulation progresses, various uvm_components and sequences have a way to synchronize activity and indicate when it is appropriate to end the test. This mechanism is termed as an objection mechanism. The objection mechanism implements a counter under the hood. A component or sequence raises a phase objection at the beginning of any activity. It then drops the objection when the activity is completed. Once all of the raised objections are dropped, and the total objection count drops to zero, the phase then terminates. As long as there is an outstanding objection, the phase will not end.

It must be noted that each phase task implementation that is forked may object to the end of that phase. As long as any phase task objects to the end of the phase, that phase WILL continue. When no phase tasks object to the end of the phase, the objection counter is zero. The phase ends causing all processed forked during that phase to be killed. Objections are raised and dropped using the 'phase' argument to the phase task.

When a component raises an objection, Its parent effectively 'forwards' the objection. If multiple child components raise objections, all of them are forwarded as well. As a result, the global objection count increments for each objection that is forwarded by each component.

In a similar vein, when an objection is dropped, the dropped objection is now forwarded through each component to the global objection counter.

Objection mechanism comprises of three main sets of methods:

- raising objections
- dropping objections
- querying statuses

Raising objections is done by the following call:

```
raise_objection ( uvm_object obj = null, string description = "", int count = 1);
```

The effect of objecting is to increase the total objection counts. A description string is used for tracing/debug.

Recommendation 13.4.0:   *Make sure that a meaningful, unique message is placed in the description because you will be using that for debugging purposes.*

Dropping objections is done by calling the drop_objection call.

```
drop_objection ( uvm_object obj = null, string description = "", int count = 1);
```

Dropping an objection means that the source and total objection counts for the object are decreased by count. You will see an error if you inadvertently drop the objection count for object below zero. This would mean that the number of raised and dropped counts does not match up.

There is a function to set the drain time after all objections are dropped in the component and phase classes. I do not like it. The reason being that the time argument translates itself to a <delay>argument in the simulation. Depending on the timescale/time precision of the simulation, one has to adjust repeatedly the numbers depending on where the call is made, making it a high maintenance call if you think about having the sequence/component as reusable.

Recommendation 13.4.1:   *Use the all_dropped callback. This callback is triggered after all the objections are dropped. Alternately, Use a method to measure a fixed number of clock cycles on an interface using signals brought into the testbench. (see Section 22.2) for an example of bringing signals to the UVM testbench.*

Objections must be raised by a component at the beginning of the phase and dropped when the component is done processing. In Section 2.6.1.4, the simple environment raises objections to the phase ending. These objections are raised hierarchically, as shown in Figure 13.5. As you will recognize, there are many ways in which a sequence can be started. Listing 13.1 below shows one example of the objection mechanism in a sequence rather than in a component. This implies that there is more than one way in which an objection can be raised to the objection counter.

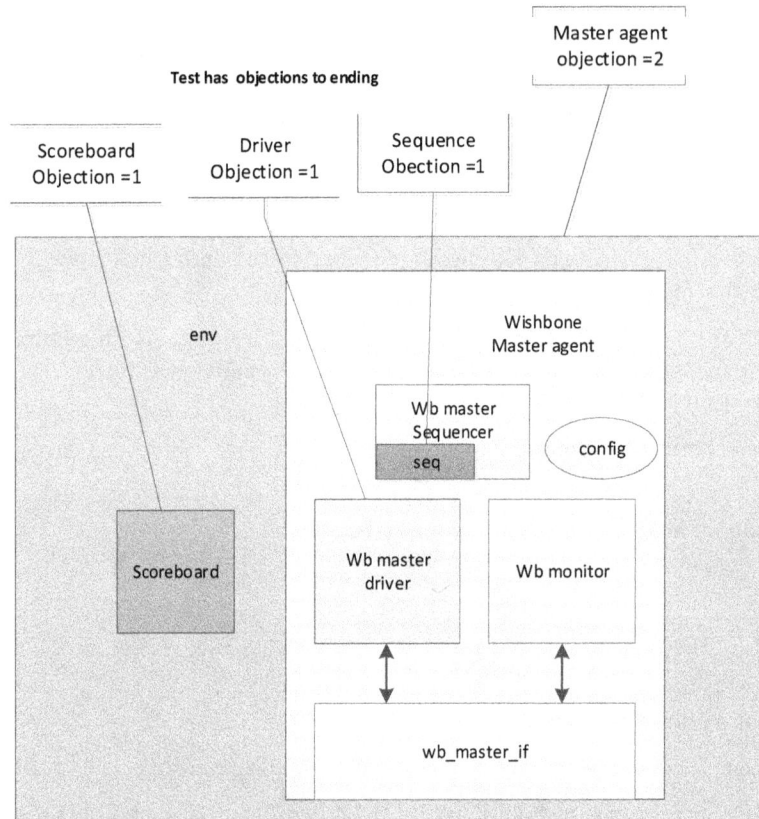

Fig. 13.5: Raising Objections

The listing below talks about tasks pre_start(), post_start() in the example. These methods are introduced in Section 14.5. For now, all you need to know is that an objection can be raised inside a component or a sequence. This is shown in the listing below.

Listing 13.1: Objections to phase ending

```
1 class base_sequence extends uvm_sequence #(wb_transaction);
2   `uvm_object_utils(base_sequence)
3
4   function new(string name = "base_seq");
5     super.new(name);
6     set_automatic_phase_objection(1);
7   endfunction:new
8
9   /*
10   virtual task pre_start();
11       uvm_phase phase_ = get_starting_phase();
12       if (phase_ != null)
13   phase_.raise_objection(this);
14    endtask:pre_start
15    virtual task post_start();
16       uvm_phase phase_ = get_starting_phase();
17       if (phase_ != null)
18   phase_.drop_objection(this);
19    endtask:post_start
20    */
21
22 endclass
```

When the sequence starts, the pre_start method raises an objection. After the sequence is completed, the post_start() method drops the objection. Since all the objections are dropped, the test proceeds to completion. Once the master agent sequencer has finished running the sequences, the end of the test is indicated by the master agent sequencer by dropping its objection from the sequence that is running on the sequencer. Since there are no more objections, the test finishes the run_phase and proceeds to extract the results and terminate the test.

> Notice that I have commented out Lines 10-19. I have set the automatic_phase_objection on Line 6. If you comment out that line, you must uncomment out the Lines 10-19.

Another option (Which I do NOT recommend, only provided as an example) is to put the objection in the sequence body, as seen in the example below. This may be needed since the pre_body()/post_body() methods is not always called (see Section 14.5).

Listing 13.2: Objections to phase ending

```
1 class objection_sequence extends base_sequence;
2   byte sa;
3   `uvm_object_utils(sequence_2)
4   `uvm_add_to_seq_lib(sequence_2, wb_master_seqr_sequence_library)
5   function new(string name = "seq_1");
6     super.new(name);
7   endfunction:new
8   virtual task body();
9     uvm_phase phase_ = get_starting_phase();
10    if (phase_ != null)
11      phase_.raise_objection(this);
12
```

```
13    `uvm_do(req, get_sequencer(), -1, {address == 6; kind ==
         wb_transaction::WRITE; data == 63'hdeadbeef;})
14    `uvm_do(req, get_sequencer(), -1, {address == 7; kind ==
         wb_transaction::WRITE; data == 63'hbeefdead;})
15    `uvm_do(req, get_sequencer(), -1, {address == 8; kind ==
         wb_transaction::WRITE; data == 63'h0123456678;})
16
17
18    `uvm_do(req, get_sequencer(), -1, {address == 6; kind ==
         wb_transaction::READ ;})
19    `uvm_do(req, get_sequencer(), -1, {address == 7; kind ==
         wb_transaction::READ;})
20    `uvm_do(req, get_sequencer(), -1, {address == 8; kind ==
         wb_transaction::READ;})
21    if (phase_ != null)
22      phase_.drop_objection(this);
23    endtask
24 endclass
```

- Lines 9-11 show the sequence getting the handle to the phase and checking it.

- Lines 13-20 show the sequence driving transactions to the DUT.

- Lines 22 show the sequence dropping the objection as the task is done.

UVM 1.2

Be careful of raising an objection and dropping an objection for every transaction. There is some overhead to propagate the objections, and you will find that your simulation runs a lot slower if you do so. The objection propagation problem has been solved in UVM 1.2 and beyond using a flag called set_propogation_mode(). Figure 13.6 shows how the objection counts are affected by this mode. When the mode is set, the propagation through each component is bypassed straight to the top. In this Figure, each of the boxes represents a component.

As we saw in the earlier sections, the implementation of the task phase in each component is forked when the phase starts. All of these threads are killed when the phase finishes. Each forked thread in the component can object to the ending of a particular phase. As long as any single phase task objects to the end of the phase, the phase will continue and not end. When no phase tasks object to the end of the phase, all process tasks forked during that phase are killed if they are still alive. The default behavior of UVM does not have any tasks objecting to any phase at all. The corresponding phase task implementation must explicitly raise and drop an objection. Objections are raised and dropped using the 'phase' argument to the phase task.

Rule 13.4.0:   *Use the objection mechanism from components to determine when to stop the test.*

In all of our examples, we had used the run_phase() method. In the example below, we show a reset_phase task in a UVM driver/monitor using the UVM phases. This task shows the raising and dropping objections once it detects a reset.

While I have used this reset_phase as an example of tasks and objections in phasing, I do not recommend you do this. If you do use this style of coding components with reset_phase() methods, remember you will not be able to use your agent in tests where you need to jump back to reset.

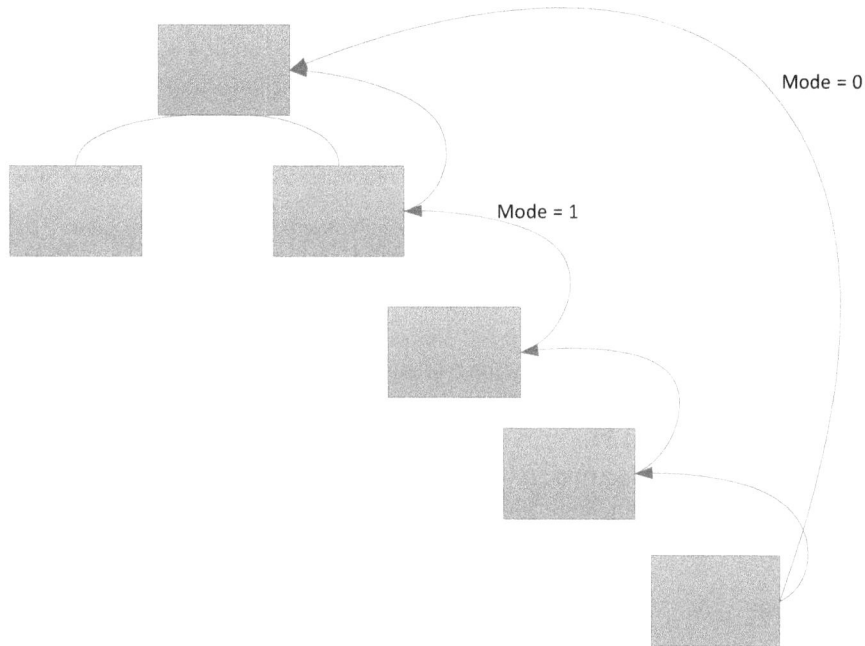

Fig. 13.6: The Way Objections Propogate With The Objection Propogation Mode

Listing 13.3: Simple Objection

```
102    task wb_master::reset_phase(uvm_phase phase);
103        super.reset_phase(phase);
104        phase.raise_objection(this,"");
105        // Driving the signals as per the spec.
106        this.drv_if.master_cb.DAT_O <= 'b0;
107        this.drv_if.master_cb.TGD_O <= 'b0;
108        this.drv_if.master_cb.ADR_O  <= 'b0;
109        this.drv_if.master_cb.WE_O   <= 'b0;
110        this.drv_if.master_cb.CYC_O <= 'b0;
111        this.drv_if.master_cb.LOCK_O <= 'b0;
112        this.drv_if.master_cb.SEL_O <= 'b0;
113        this.drv_if.master_cb.STB_O <= 'b0;
114        this.drv_if.master_cb.TGA_O <= 'b0;
115        this.drv_if.master_cb.TGC_O <= 'b0;
116        repeat (4) @(this.drv_if.master_cb);
117        wait(this.drv_if.rst);
118
119        wait(!this.drv_if.rst);
120        // Done setting signals. Now we can drop objections and move on.
121        phase.drop_objection(this);
122
123    endtask: reset_phase
```

- The reset_phase has an argument wherein the phasing mechanism passes in the phase.

- Line 103 includes the reset_phase task from the base class. Note that if the task in the base class allowed time to elapse before raising an objection, the objection mechanism could terminate the phase.

- Line 104 sets up the objection to this phase ending. There is an optional description argument. We recommend you always passing a reasonable description into the method. It will ease your debugging.

- Lines 106-115 set up some values on the interface pins.

- Line 121 shows the reset conditions are satisfied, and the objection to ending this phase is dropped.

Recommendation 13.4.2:   *Make sure that you raise the objection early on in the sequence. By design in UVM, if no phase task objects the end of the phase **before the first nonblocking assignment**, the phase will be immediately terminated, and all of the phase tasks will be killed.*

By default, phase tasks do not implicitly object to the end of the phase, nor does completion of the task execution remove any objection to the end of the phase. The objections must be explicitly raised and dropped by each phase task implementation method as required.

> The uvm_phase::get_objection method was defined as being non-virtual. The Accellera implementation made the function virtual to ensure uniformity with the other phase done objections methods.
> This is its actual signature:

```
virtual function int uvm_phase::get_objection_count( uvm_object obj=null );
```

13.5 Change in IEEE - use of get_objection before drain_time() in uvm_objection

There is a change in the way the drain_time API is used in the IEEE 1800.2 version vs the UVM 1.2 version. This change was introduced on account of the static initialization that is new in 1800.2. All internal API have been updated to call get_objection(). The creation of the phase_done objection is deferred until the first call to get_objection() and the uvm_objection phase_done variable which was *public* in the UVM 1.2 version is *local* in the IEEE 1800.2 version.

Listing 13.4: UVM 1.2 Behavior

```
phase.raise_objection(this);
...
// Your code here
....

phase.phase_done.set_drain_time(this,2000);
phase.drop_objection(this);
```

Whereas in IEEE 1800.2 you need to do this:

Listing 13.5: UVM IEEE Behavior

```
uvm_objection phase_done = phase.get_objection();
phase_done.raise_objection(this);
....
// Your code here.
...
```

```
phase_done.set_drain_time(this ,200);
phase_done.raise_objection(this);
```

Listing 17.3 contains a complete example of this API usage. See Line 33 onwards.

UVM
IEEE
Note that the above is a breaking change, and the change is in a couple of places. The first is the call to get_objection() and the second change is not referring to the phase_done property directly.

13.6 Phase States

If you look at the flow of phase states in UVM, things seem to be happening magically! It's not witchcraft by any means. UVM supplies many specific states which describe the entire lifetime of a phase. A phase usually tends to go through many states before it transitions from one phase to another. Figure 13.7 explains the various states.

When the library creates the states, they default to the "un-initialized" state. They remain in this state until they are moved into the dormant state by the phasing algorithm.

13.7 Phase Callbacks

Section 13.6 showed the various states that the phasing mechanism goes through to achieve phasing. While stepping through the phases, UVM supplies a callback mechanism through the uvm_phase_cb callback. This callback is triggered every time the phase state changes. Using the information in the callback, you can choose to raise an objection to prolong the state or do any cleanup that is required outside the normal scope of what is provided by UVM. The uvm_phase_cb class extends from the uvm_callback class. The use model for this class is identical to the ones you see in the callbacks sections. The class contains a single virtual function as below:

```
virtual function void phase_state_change(uvm_phase phase, uvm_phase_state_change
change);
```

This method is used in the listing below to illustrate how phase changes are detected. A message is printed when the phase changes state.

Listing 13.6: Simple Phasing Callbacks

```
6    class my_uvm_phase_cb extends uvm_phase_cb;
7      `uvm_object_utils(my_uvm_phase_cb)
8
9      function void phase_state_change( uvm_phase phase,
          uvm_phase_state_change change);
10       uvm_phase_state old_state = change.get_prev_state();
11       uvm_phase_state new_state = change.get_state();
12
13       `uvm_info("PHASE STATE_CHANGE ", $sformatf("phase name: %s , OLD
            STATE %s, NEW STATE : %s\n",phase.get_name(),old_state.name(),
            new_state.name()),UVM_LOW)
14
15     endfunction
16
17     function new(string name="my_phase_cb");
18       super.new(name);
19     endfunction
20
21   endclass
```

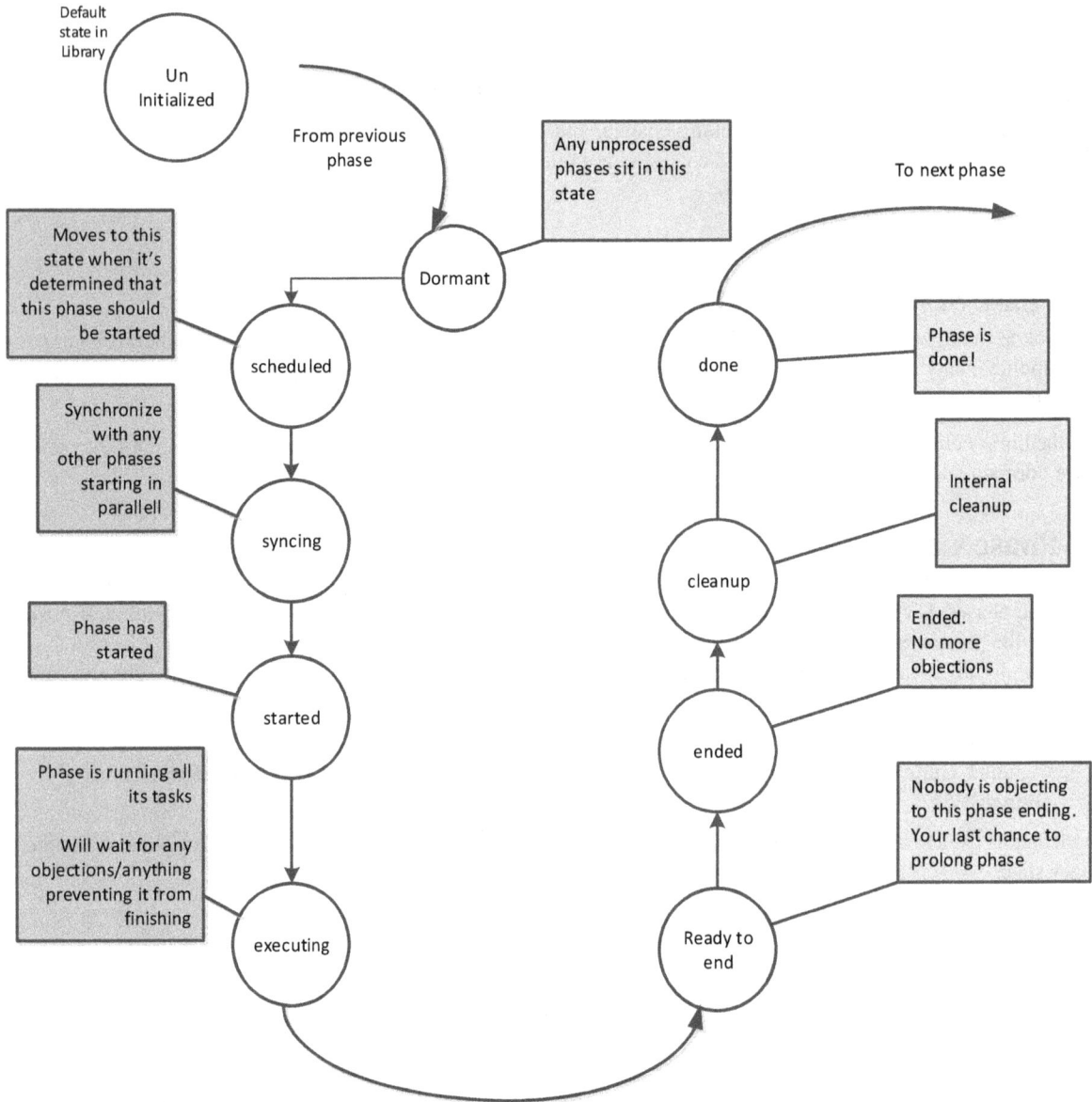

Fig. 13.7: Various states of a phase

To look at a simple example, consider Listing 13.6:

- Lines 6-21 describe a simple callback that is created extending uvm_phase_cb.
- The method phase_state_change method is shown in lines 9-15.
- Line 9 gets the previous state from which the phase changed.
- Line 11 showed the next state when the phase changed.
- All this callback does is print the state from which it is changing to the state to which it will go.

- Lines 17-19 show the constructor just like any other callback.

The top-level test that tests this callback is shown in Listing 13.7.

Listing 13.7: Simple Phasing Callbacks Test

```
23   class wb_env_phase_cb_test extends uvm_test;
24     bit test_pass = 1;
25     wb_config master_config;
26     wb_config slave_config;
27     int slave_adr_max ;
28     int slave_adr_min;
29     my_uvm_phase_cb my_phase_cb;
30
31
32     `uvm_component_utils(wb_env_phase_cb_test)
33
34     wb_env_env env;
35
36     function new(string name, uvm_component parent);
37       super.new(name, parent);
38     endfunction
39
40     virtual function void build_phase(uvm_phase phase);
41       super.build_phase(phase);
42       slave_adr_min = 32'h0;
43       slave_adr_max = 32'h0fffffe;
44       my_phase_cb = new("my simple phase callback");
45
46       uvm_phase_cb_pool::add(null,my_phase_cb);
47
48       // Create and Build the configuration
49       master_config = wb_config::type_id::create("master_configuration");
50       slave_config = wb_config::type_id::create("slave_configuration");
51       // Randomize the configuration
52       slave_config.randomize with {min_addr == slave_adr_min; max_addr ==
                 slave_adr_max; max_n_wss == 2; };
53       master_config.randomize with {min_addr == slave_adr_min; max_addr ==
                 slave_adr_max; max_n_wss == 2; };
54       // Set in Config DB
55       uvm_config_db #(wb_config)::set(null,"uvm_test_top.env.master_agent
                 ","mstr_agent_cfg",master_config);
56       uvm_config_db #(wb_config)::set(null,"uvm_test_top.env.slave_agent
                 ","slave_agent_cfg",slave_config);
57       env = wb_env_env::type_id::create("env", this);
58
59       uvm_config_db #(uvm_object_wrapper)::set(this, "env.master_agent.
                 mast_sqr.main_phase", "default_sequence", sequence_1::get_type())
                 ;
60     endfunction
61
62     function void report_phase(uvm_phase phase);
63       if(test_pass) begin
64         `uvm_info(get_type_name(), "** UVM TEST PASSED **", UVM_NONE)
65       end
```

```
66        else begin
67           `uvm_error(get_type_name(), "** UVM TEST FAIL **")
68        end
69     endfunction
70
71
72  endclass : wb_env_phase_cb_test
```

- Line 23 is a top-level test.

- Line 29 provides the callback instance.

- the build_phase has many other entries. They are not shown here.

- Line 44 creates the callback.

- Line 46 registers the callback with all the instances of the phases. You can fine tune this as per your requirements.

- The rest of the lines deal with the test configuration.

This example is simple. All it does it print the state it was in, and the state to which it is transitioning. This example shows you how to add a simple phase callback and get some basic information from it. It acts as a replacement for the +UVM_PHASE_TRACE command line option (Section 11.3). In addition to just getting notified of phase changes, one can do some introspection on where this phase is in the schedule, etc. You can then kill specific tasks or perform other cleanup or jump to some simulation task etc. in the phase_state_change method after determining exactly where you are and what needs to be done. The phasing class provides a certain amount of introspection if you look at the documentation. You can get the domain, schedule, etc. by merely making a few function calls. We have not listed these functions here to save space, as many users may not be using this functionality much. Look at the official UVM documentation if you need to accomplish something along these lines.

The UVM_PHASE_TRACE command line option does not print all of the transitions, just the important ones. If you add phases or domains etc., **you will need** an approach like the above to help you with any debug.

13.8 Spanning Multiple Phases

The previous sections explained how various phases work. When the phase task starts, each component fires off its phase task. When the phase ends, the task is terminated. Hence, there are no phase tasks that span across phases as each phase fires off its own.

In some circumstances, it may be required to have a task that spans multiple phases and remains alive through these phases. An example of something like this could be a multi-phase monitor, which is shown in the example below.

In our example, we would like the monitor task to span from the pre-reset phase to the end of the main_phase. We would like to have a task that is running all the time during the various phase transitions and report what it sees. See Figure 13.8 to see when this task is supposed to be active. This is now coded into the listing below.

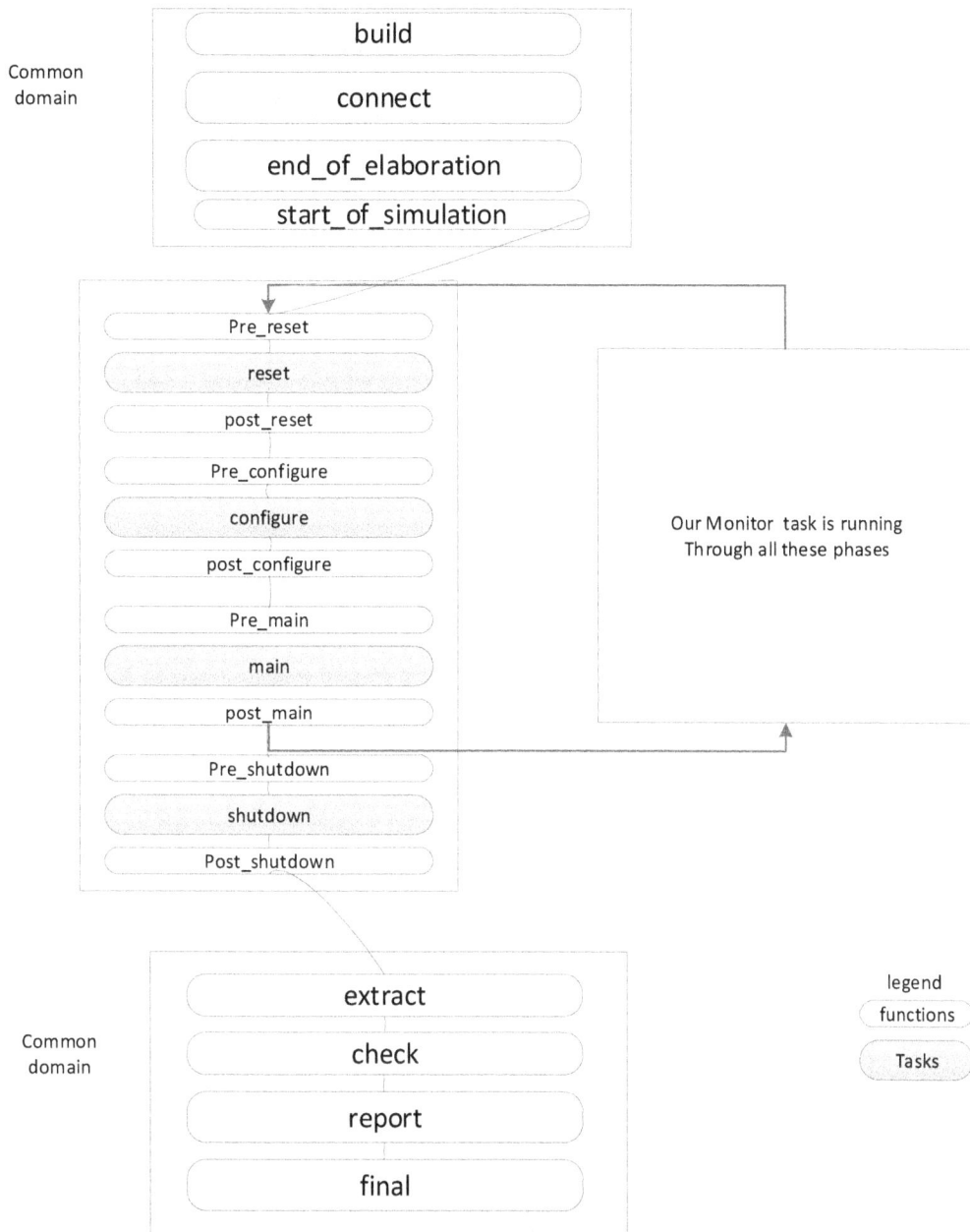

Fig. 13.8: Our Phase Spanning Task

Listing 13.8: Simple Phasing Callbacks

```
12      class wb_master_phase_mon extends uvm_monitor;
13
14          uvm_analysis_port #(wb_transaction) mon_analysis_port;   //TLM
                analysis port
15          typedef virtual wb_master_if v_if;
16          v_if mon_if;
17
18          wb_config mstr_mon_cfg;
19          process m_span_phases_process;
20
21          local uvm_phase m_pre_reset;
22          local uvm_phase m_post_run;
23          uvm_domain m_domain ;
24
25          extern function new(string name = "wb_master_phase_mon",
                uvm_component parent);
26          `uvm_component_utils_begin(wb_master_phase_mon)
27          `uvm_component_utils_end
28
29          extern virtual function void end_of_elaboration_phase(uvm_phase
                phase);
30          extern virtual function void connect_phase(uvm_phase phase);
31          extern protected virtual task multiple_phase_task();
32          extern function void phase_started(uvm_phase phase);
33          extern function void phase_ended(uvm_phase phase);
34
35
36      endclass: wb_master_phase_mon
```

The constructor of this monitor now finds the common domain and finds a couple of 'intercept' points for this monitor.

When the phase is started in the component, the generic callback for the phase_started is called.

Listing 13.9: Simple Phase Spanning Contstructor

```
38      function void wb_master_phase_mon::phase_started(uvm_phase phase);
39          if (phase == m_pre_reset) begin
40              fork
41                  begin
42                      m_span_phases_process = process::self();
43                      multiple_phase_task();
44                  end
45              join_none
46          end
47      endfunction
```

- Line 39 sees if the phase is the pre-reset phase. if so, it forks off the multiple _task_phase tasks.

- This task spans multiple phases as can be seen in Listing 13.9

When the phase is ended in the component, the generic callback for the phase_ended is called.

Listing 13.10: Simple Phase Spanning Ending

```
51    function void wb_master_phase_mon::phase_ended(uvm_phase phase);
52
53        if (phase == m_post_run) begin
54            `uvm_info("PHASE_MON_PHASE_ENDED",$sformatf("I am killing this
                   process in this %s phase", phase.get_name()),UVM_LOW)
55            m_span_phases_process.kill();
56        end
57
58    endfunction
```

- Line 55 sees if the phase is the post-run phase. If so, it kills off the multiple_task_phase tasks.

The actual task spans multiple phases. Run this simulation and you will see the reports from Lines 94,96, 139, 133 as the simulation proceeds from the listing below.

Listing 13.11: Simple Phase Spanning Task

```
83    task wb_master_phase_mon::multiple_phase_task();
84        int repeat_count ;
85        int timeout_count = 0;
86
87        integer master_transaction_timeout;
88
89        uvm_config_db#(wb_config)::get(null, "", "config",mstr_mon_cfg);
90        repeat_count = this.mstr_mon_cfg.max_n_wss + 1;
91
92        `uvm_info("WB_MASTER_MON_PHASE_TASK","This should occur before
                   reset goes high", UVM_LOW);
93        wait(this.mon_if.rst);
94        `uvm_info("WB_MASTER_MON_PHASE_TASK","Reset asserted!!!!", UVM_LOW
                   );
95        wait(!this.mon_if.rst);
96        `uvm_info("WB_MASTER_MON_PHASE_TASK","Reset deasserted!!", UVM_LOW
                   );
97
98        forever begin
99            wb_transaction tr;
100           uvm_phase phase_;
101
102           do begin
103
104               @(this.mon_if.CYC_O or
105                   this.mon_if.STB_O or
106                   this.mon_if.ADR_O or
107                   this.mon_if.SEL_O or
108                   this.mon_if.WE_O  or
109                   this.mon_if.TGA_O or
110                   this.mon_if.TGC_O);
111           end while (this.mon_if.CYC_O !== 1'b1 ||
112               this.mon_if.STB_O !== 1'b1);
113           tr= wb_transaction::type_id::create("tr", this);
```

```
114                tr.address = this.mon_if.ADR_O;
115                // Are we supposed to respond to this cycle?
116                if(this.mstr_mon_cfg.min_addr <= tr.address  && tr.address <=
                       this.mstr_mon_cfg.max_addr )
117
118            begin
119                 timeout_count = 0;
120
121
122
123                 tr.tga = this.mon_if.TGA_O;
124                 tr.tgc  =this.mon_if.TGC_O;
125                 tr.sel = this.mon_if.SEL_O;
126                 tr.lock = this.mon_if.LOCK_O;
127
128                 if(this.mon_if.WE_O) begin
129                     tr.kind = wb_transaction::WRITE;
130                     tr.data  = this.mon_if.DAT_I;
131                     tr.tgd  = this.mon_if.TGD_O;
132                     tr.status = wb_transaction::ACK;
133                     `uvm_info("WB_MASTER_MON_PHASE_TASK", $sformatf("WRITE
                             Transaction observed in this run Phase  ",),
                             UVM_LOW);
134                 end
135                 else begin
136                     tr.kind = wb_transaction::READ ;
137
138                     tr.status = wb_transaction::ACK;
139                     `uvm_info("WB_MASTER_MON_PHASE_TASK", $sformatf("READ
                             Transaction observed in  this run Phase "), UVM_LOW
                             );
140                 end
141
142
143                 // Edge 1
144                 tr.status = wb_transaction::TIMEOUT ;
145                 while(!this.mon_if.ACK_I) begin
146                     @(this.mon_if.monitor_cb);
147                     timeout_count = timeout_count + 1;
148                     // Wait states
149                     case (1'b1)
150                         this.mon_if.ERR_I: tr.status = wb_transaction::ERR
                                 ;
151                         this.mon_if.RTY_I: tr.status = wb_transaction::RTY
                                 ;
152                         this.mon_if.ACK_I: tr.status = wb_transaction::ACK
                                 ;
153                         default: continue;
154                     endcase
155                 end
156                 tr.data  = this.mon_if.DAT_O;
157                 tr.tgd  = this.mon_if.TGD_I;
158                 if ((timeout_count >  repeat_count )|| tr.status ==
                       wb_transaction::TIMEOUT ) begin
```

```
159                                  `uvm_info("wb_master_phase_monitor ", "Timeout waiting
                                          for ACK_I, RTY_I or ERR_I",UVM_LOW);
160                      end
161                 end
162           end // forever
163      endtask: multiple_phase_task
```

13.9 Adding a Domain to a Schedule

The flexibility in UVM allows you to add your specific domains and phases to the schedule. My opinion is that any time you add an additional phase to a reusable component, the corresponding environment, tests, etc. *all need to be made 'phase aware.'* If this added phase is mandatory to all environments, it could wind up being some extra work for you.

13.10 IEEE UVM New features

13.10.1 Run Test Callbacks

Looking at Section 2.6.1, you will recognize that once you call run_test(), the UVM testbench kicks off and starts executing. When the test finishes, the testbench executes a $finish call. You did not have any mechanism to create a synchronization point between the UVM testbench and possibly a C or other language model through a DPI function. You effectively wound up writing your own intercept points into the library. The run test callbacks provides a few intercept points for you to make it easier to create and use such testbenches. The new functions provided are:

```
virtual function void pre_run_test();
virtual function void post_run_test();
virtual function void pre_abort();
```

As the names suggest, The pre_run_test() callback is called before the run_test() method starts executing. Specifically, the pre_run_test callback is called **before** the uvm_component that represents the test is created.

The post_run_test() callback is called just before calling report.summarize() and $finish;

The pre_abort() callback is called from components in a bottom-up manner when the system is executing a UVM_EXIT action, which causes simulation termination. The provision of this callback allows components to provide user messages or take other actions to ensure a clean exit.

Figure 13.9 shows how it is called in the library.

This is no replacement for proper run failure detection, it's not designed to be used in that mode.

The steps below provide an example of how to add such a callback to the test. Note that these steps are similar to ones in the callback examples in Section 9.1.1.

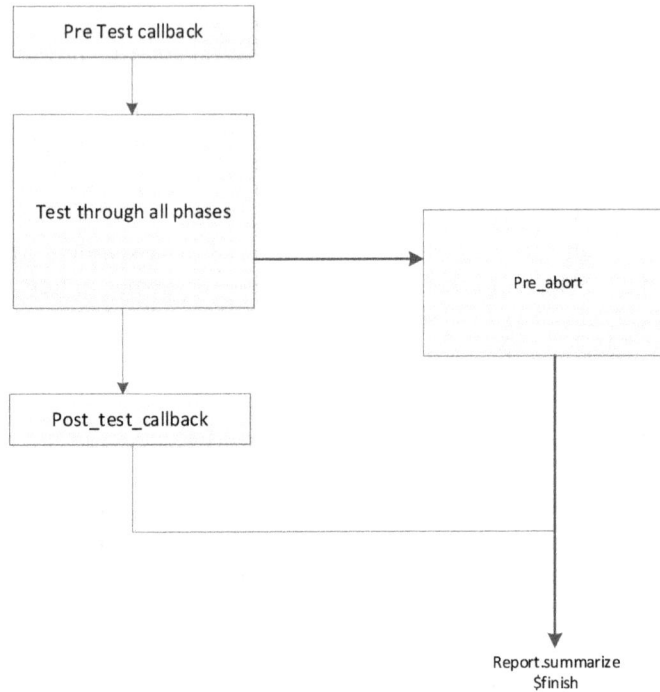

Fig. 13.9: Run Test Callbacks

13.10.1.1 Create the Run Test Callback

Consider the listing for the run_test callback class:

Listing 13.12: Declaration of Run Test Callbacks

```
6       class my_run_test_callback extends uvm_run_test_callback;
7           `uvm_object_utils(my_run_test_callback)
8
9           function new(string name="my_run_test_callback");
10              super.new(name);
11          endfunction
12          virtual function void pre_run_test();
13              super.pre_run_test();
14              `uvm_info("RUN_TEST_CALLBACK","\n\n\n\n\n\n\n This
                    pre_run_test Callback was called before run_test is called
                    \n\n\n\n\n", UVM_NONE);
15          endfunction
16          virtual function void post_run_test();
17              super.pre_run_test();
18              `uvm_info("RUN_TEST_CALLBACK"," \n\n\n\n\n\n This
                    post_run_test Callback was called is AFTER run_test was
                    done before collecting statistics \n\n\n\n\n\n", UVM_NONE);
19          endfunction
20          virtual function void pre_abort();
21              // You can call any function in here
22          endfunction
```

```
23        endclass
```

- Line 6 shows my_run_test_callback class extending from uvm_run_test_callback.

- Line 12 shows the pre_run_test callback method.

- Line 16 shows the post_run_test callback method.

Note that these are defined as *functions*. You cannot consume time in these methods.

13.10.1.2 Add Callback to Test

The previous section created the callbacks, and we now have to add them to the test. Since the test hasn't even been created, you will need to create the callback and add it to the testbench so that it can be called before run_test() is called.

Listing 13.13: Run Test Callbacks Registration

```
6        module wb_env_tb_mod;
7
8            import uvm_pkg::*;
9            typedef class my_run_test_callback;
10
11           `include "wb_env.sv"
12           `include "wb_env_base_test.sv"
13           `include "wb_env_run_test_callback_test.sv"
14
15           my_run_test_callback run_test_cb;
16           typedef virtual wb_master_if v_if1;
17           typedef virtual wb_slave_if v_if2;
18           initial begin
19               uvm_config_db #(v_if1)::set(null,"uvm_test_top.env.
                     master_agent","mst_if",wb_env_top_mod.mast_if);
20               uvm_config_db #(v_if2)::set(null,"uvm_test_top.env.slave_agent
                     ","slv_if",wb_env_top_mod.slave_if);
21               uvm_config_db #(bit) :: set(null,"env.slave_agent","is_active
                     ",1);
22               uvm_config_db #(bit) :: set(null,"env.master_agent","is_active
                     ",1);
23
24               run_test_cb = new("run_test_cb");
25               uvm_run_test_callback::add(run_test_cb);
26
27               run_test();
28           end
29       endmodule
```

- Line 15 declares an instance of the new callback class.

- Line 24 created the callback class instance.

- Line 25 registers the callback class with the testbench.

- Callback class is registered with the testbench on Line 23.

That's all there is to it. Notice that this is done differently compared to other callbacks that you are used to doing where you can put it in the test.

Note that compared to other class-based callbacks, you cannot inherit the module into another, and extend it etc. The top-level testbench is typically not portable across the block and system-level environments, and you need to be aware of this, because you are placing testbench class code in a file you would not normally look for.

13.11 Phase Jumping

One of the problems you will run into when you implement phase jumping is that all **components** will need to respect your phase jump. Phase jumping has always been considered an advanced topic since jumps must be performed safely, and all components in the simulation should be able to tolerate the jump. Sequences and other tasks are killed as the component performs the jump. If you are jumping back to the reset_phase or other phases, the components need to be *phase aware and self-initializing based on external inputs*.

Recommendation 13.11.0:   *Review your implementations before considering phase jumping. There are usually many other ways to solve the problem you face using virtual sequences or other methods.*

If a component is not written in such a manner, you will face problems. While this may not be a problem for agents and uvm_components you develop, *at some point or the other,* you will integrate with other components which may not support it, and you will have a problem. So, choose carefully.

Recommendation 13.11.1:   *Many commercial VIP are reset-aware, and you may be able to implement a virtual sequence to chain a set of test sequences together rather than implementing a phase jump.*

If you would really like to pursue this, Justin's paper [20] and Doulos Guide [15] are useful resources.

Chapter 14

Advanced Stimulus Generation

Chapter 3 presented how stimulus is generated in UVM. Many considerations when generating stimulus were presented in that chapter. This chapter builds upon the concepts that were presented earlier. The sections below delve into generating advanced scenarios for use in your testbench environments.

14.1 The Sequence Library

In UVM, it is possible to group similar sequences into a sequence library. The uvm_sequence_library is an extension of the uvm_sequence base class. The uvm_sequence_library is a sequence that contains a list of registered sequence types. This sequence library can be configured to create sequences. It can be configured to create and execute these sequences any number of times using one of the several modes of operation, including a user-defined mode. This sequence library can be started like any other sequence and treated as such. When started as a sequence, the sequence library will randomly select and execute a sequence from its sequences queue, depending on the selection_mode chosen. When it is started (like any other sequence), the sequence library selects and executes a sequence from its queue, depending on the selection mode that is chosen.

Variables that control the sequence selection from the sequence library are listed in Table 14.1.

In order to use the sequence library, there is an additional macro you must use. The macro `uvm_add_to_seq_lib simplifies the task of adding sequences to sequence libraries. An example of this macro usage is below.

Listing 14.1: A simple sequence library

```
1 class wb_master_seqr_sequence_library extends uvm_sequence_library # (
    wb_transaction);
2      `uvm_sequence_library_utils(wb_master_seqr_sequence_library)
3
4     function new(string name = "simple_seq_lib");
5          super.new(name);
6          init_sequence_library();
7     endfunction
8 endclass
9
10 class sequence_1 extends base_sequence;
11   byte sa;
12
13   `uvm_object_utils(sequence_1)
14
15   `uvm_add_to_seq_lib(sequence_1, wb_master_seqr_sequence_library)
16   function new(string name = "seq_1");
17     super.new(name);
18   endfunction:new
```

```
19
20   virtual task body();
21
22      `uvm_do(req, get_sequencer(), -1, {address == 3; kind ==
             wb_transaction::WRITE; data == 63'hdeadbeef;})
23      `uvm_do(req, get_sequencer(), -1, {address == 4; kind ==
             wb_transaction::WRITE; data == 63'hbeefdead;})
24      `uvm_do(req, get_sequencer(), -1, {address == 5; kind ==
             wb_transaction::WRITE; data == 63'h23456678;})
25
26      `uvm_do(req, get_sequencer(), -1, {address == 3; kind ==
             wb_transaction::READ ;})
27      `uvm_do(req, get_sequencer(), -1, {address == 4; kind ==
             wb_transaction::READ;})
28      `uvm_do(req, get_sequencer(), -1, {address < 5; address > 0; kind ==
             wb_transaction::READ;})
29
30   endtask
31 endclass
```

Listing 14.1 shows an example of the sequence library:

- Line 1 shows the creation of class wb_master_seqr_sequence_library as extending from the uvm_sequence_library.

- Line 2 shows the use of the macro `uvm_sequence_library_utils that defines a few maintenance functions that are needed by the library.

- Lines 4 - 7 show the definition of the constructor. Note that you **must** call the init_sequence_library() function that initializes its internal arrays.

- Line 10 shows a class sequence_1 extending from class base_sequence. The definition of the base_sequence is not shown in this listing.

- Line 15 shows the class sequence_1 added to the sequence library

(i) Many other sequences can be added to the sequence_library. For information see the file wb_master_agent_sequence_library.sv in any of the <examples>/src directories.

Table 14.1: Sequence Library Selection

selection_mode	UVM_SEQ_LIB_RAND: Randomly select from one of the sequences UVM_SEQ_LIB_RANDC : This is similar to the UVM_SEQ_LIB_RAND, but cycles through all the sequences similar to SystemVerilog randc behavior UVM_SEQ_LIB_ITEM: Execute a single item UVM_SEQ_LIB_USER: Call the select_sequence() method, which the user may override, to generate an index into the queue to select a sequence to execute
min_random_count	The minimum number of items to execute, defaults to 10
max_random_count	The maximum number of items to execute defaults to 10
sequence_count	The number of sequences to execute
select_rand	In UVM_SEQ_LIB_RAND mode, the index of the next sequence to execute. This is the INDEX number (an integer) into the registered sequences array.
select_rand	In UVM_SEQ_LIB_RANDC mode, the index of the next sequence to execute

You can create an instance of the sequence library, just like any other sequence. You can then set the selection_mode in the library.

If the sequence count is set to zero (See Table 14.1), none of the sequences will execute.

This sequence library can also be called in a test as shown in Listing 14.2.

Listing 14.2: A simple sequence library test

```
4
5    class wb_env_seq_lib_test extends wb_env_base_test;
6      `uvm_component_utils(wb_env_seq_lib_test)
7      wb_master_seqr_sequence_library seq_lib;
8
9      function new(string name, uvm_component parent);
10       super.new(name, parent);
11     endfunction
12
13     task run_phase(uvm_phase phase);
14       seq_lib = wb_master_seqr_sequence_library::type_id::create("seq_lib
             ");
15       seq_lib.set_automatic_phase_objection(1);
16       seq_lib.selection_mode = UVM_SEQ_LIB_RANDC;
17       seq_lib.randomize();
18       seq_lib.start(env.master_agent.mast_sqr);
19       seq_lib.wait_for_sequence_state(UVM_FINISHED);
20     endtask : run_phase
21
22
23   endclass : wb_env_seq_lib_test
```

In Listing 14.2:

- Line 14 shows the sequence_library instance being created. This is created just as another sequence.

- The order of sequences is defined by the selection mode described in Table 14.1.

(i) Since the sequence library is treated as a sequence, you also have the ability to choose specific sequences using a selection mode provided by an API. I have not covered it here, feel free to look at the LRM if you need this functionality

14.2 Sequencer Operation

The basic architecture of the sequencer was described in Section 8.3.3. In that section, the sequencer is shown as a component that is typed to a particular transaction type, containing a collection of sequences, and an arbiter that arbitrates between the various sequences. Section 14.3 goes into some detail on the arbitration mechanism. For now, it is sufficient to recognize that the sequencer picks a sequence item from a collection of sequences after arbitration.

The driver and sequencer components in the agent are connected via a TLM port called the seq_item_port. The driver port is connected to the sequencer's seq_item_export. The sequencer produces sequence items and provides them via the export. These are transferred to the driver via the seq_item_port.

The seq_item_port built into the uvm_driver component defines many methods to allow the driver to communicate with the sequencer and get the sequence items at an appropriate time. The seq_item_port is a bidirectional port. It includes the standard TLM methods get() and peek() for requesting an item from the sequencer and put() to provide a response. Thus, other components, which may not necessarily be derived from uvm_driver, may still connect to and communicate with the sequencer if they use the standard TLM get() and peek() calls.

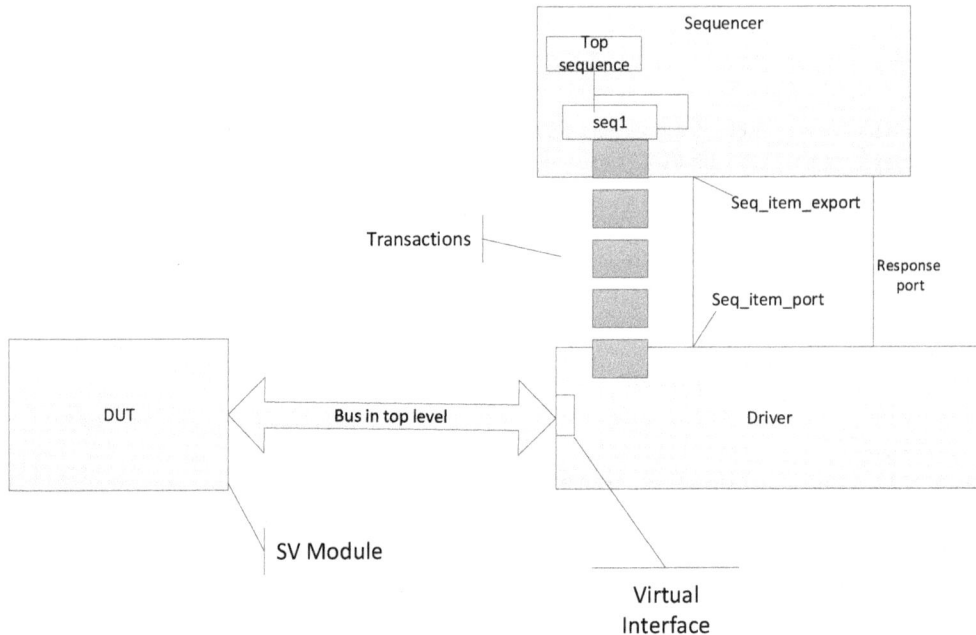

Fig. 14.1: Port Connections Between Driver And Sequencer

Note that the seq_item_port provides the following methods:

```
virtual task get_next_item(output T1 t)
virtual task try_next_item(output T1 t)
virtual function void item_done( input T2 t = null )
virtual task wait_for_sequences()
virtual function bit has_do_available()
virtual task get( output T1 t )
virtual task peek(output T1 t)
virtual task put(input T2 t)
virtual task get_response(output RSP response, input int transaction_id = -1)
virtual function void put_response(uvm_sequence_item response_item)
```

The get_next_item() and get() methods get the next available item from the sequence. It makes the sequencer arbitrate between the available relevant sequences and choose the highest priority sequence and generate an item from that sequence. Note that this is a blocking call, and will block till an item is available. The try_next_item() is similar to the get_next_item(). The one difference is that it returns immediately with a null handle if no object is available. The item_done() call indicates to the sequencer that the driver has completed processing current item. It can be removed from the sequencer's internal FIFO queues. The wait_for_sequences() and has_do_available() are handshake methods between the driver and the sequencer based on any application-specific needs. These methods, in addition to the normal TLM methods available, can be used by anyone looking to interface with the sequencer. One of the significant things to note is that the *peek() method triggers an arbitration on the sequencer if an item has already been consumed and functions just like a get().* It will otherwise return the current item from the FIFO queue if the item is available and active.

To further explore this, look at the driver component in the driver presented in Section 8.3.1. The main_phase for the driver runs in an infinite loop getting items and processing them.

14.2.1 Generating Sequences and Sequence Items on a Sequencer

The previous sections went into details of how to create a sequence item and a sequence. Various methods in the sequencer were described. If you see the sequencer, you will realize that by default, the sequencer does not do anything; it is just a component with a seq_item_port built into it and is phase aware. In each phase, the sequencer will poll for a resource called default_sequence corresponding to the specific phase it is in. This setting determines which sequence is started on entering the phase.

If such a setting is not present, one can start a sequence on the sequencer. There are many ways to start a sequence on a sequencer and make it active. You can start a sequence with either methods or macros.

The macros call many methods under the hood. In most cases, the SystemVerilog compiler expands the macros before the code is compiled. You gain additional fine-grain control when you use the methods described below.

Figure 14.2 illustrates how the macros encapsulate the various methods.

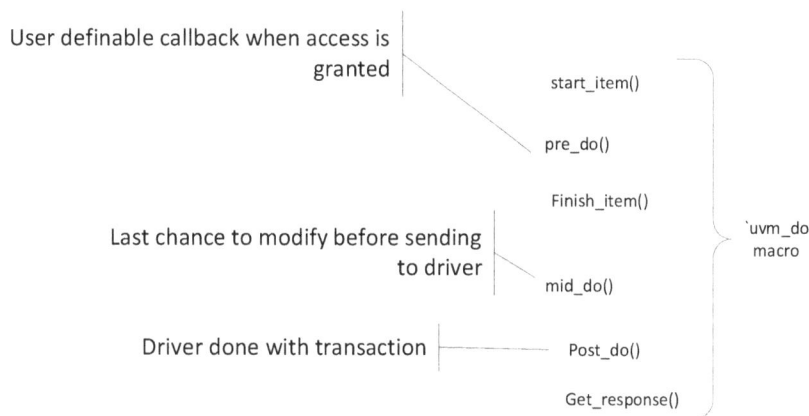

Fig. 14.2: The Encapsulation Of Sequence Methods To Macros

14.2.1.1 Using Sequence Methods

UVM supplies some methods for you to create and use sequence and sequence items. The following methods are available to you. To see how all of these fit in, see Figure 14.3.

```
function create_item( uvm_object_wrapper type_var, uvm_sequencer_base l_sequencer,
string name);
task start_item (uvm_sequence_item item, int set_priority = -1, uvm_sequencer_base
sequencer=null);
task finish_item (uvm_sequence_item item, int set_priority = -1);
task wait_for_grant(int item_priority = -1, bit lock_request = 0);
function void send_request(uvm_sequence_item request, bit rerandomize = 0);
function void send_request(uvm_sequence_item request, bit rerandomize = 0);
task wait_for_item_done(int transaction_id = -1);
task wait_for_grant(int item_priority = -1, bit lock_request = 0);
function void send_request(uvm_sequence_item request, bit rerandomize = 0);
```

The create_item() method creates, initializes a sequence item, and set it to communicate with the specific sequencer. If any override is registered with the factory, the overridden class instance is obtained by the create() method. Once an item is created, the item is "started". IE, the item is associated with a specific sequencer and randomized if needed. To ensure late generation, randomization may be applied between start_item() and finish_item(). At the end of this method, the pre_do() callback is called.

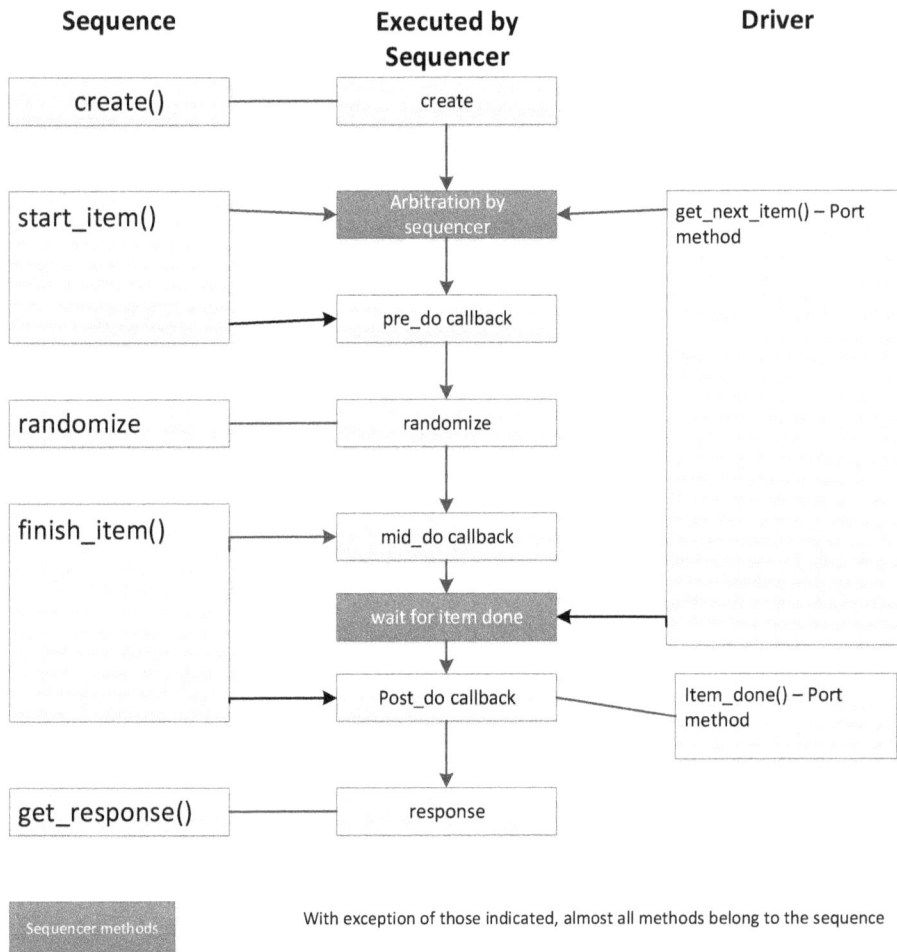

Fig. 14.3: Sequence Methods

In my view, the finish_item() method is poorly named in UVM. The finish_item() method with start_item() together initiate the operation of a sequence_item. The finish_item() method must be called after start_item() with no delays or delta-cycles. The finish_item calls the mid_do() callback and then sends the item to the sequencer.

The wait_for_item_done() is used once a sequence is sent to the driver. You may choose to wait for the driver to finish driving the item. In that case, call the wait_for_item_done() method. This task will block until the driver calls item_done or put(). If no transaction_id parameter is specified, then the call will return the next time that the driver calls item_done() or put(). If a specific transaction_id is specified, then the call will return when the driver indicates the completion of that item. The UVM documentation specifies that the call will hang, having missed the earlier notification if:

• A transaction ID that has already been specified is used

• Driver has already issued an item_done or put() for that transaction for that ID.

The figure below show how it all fits together.

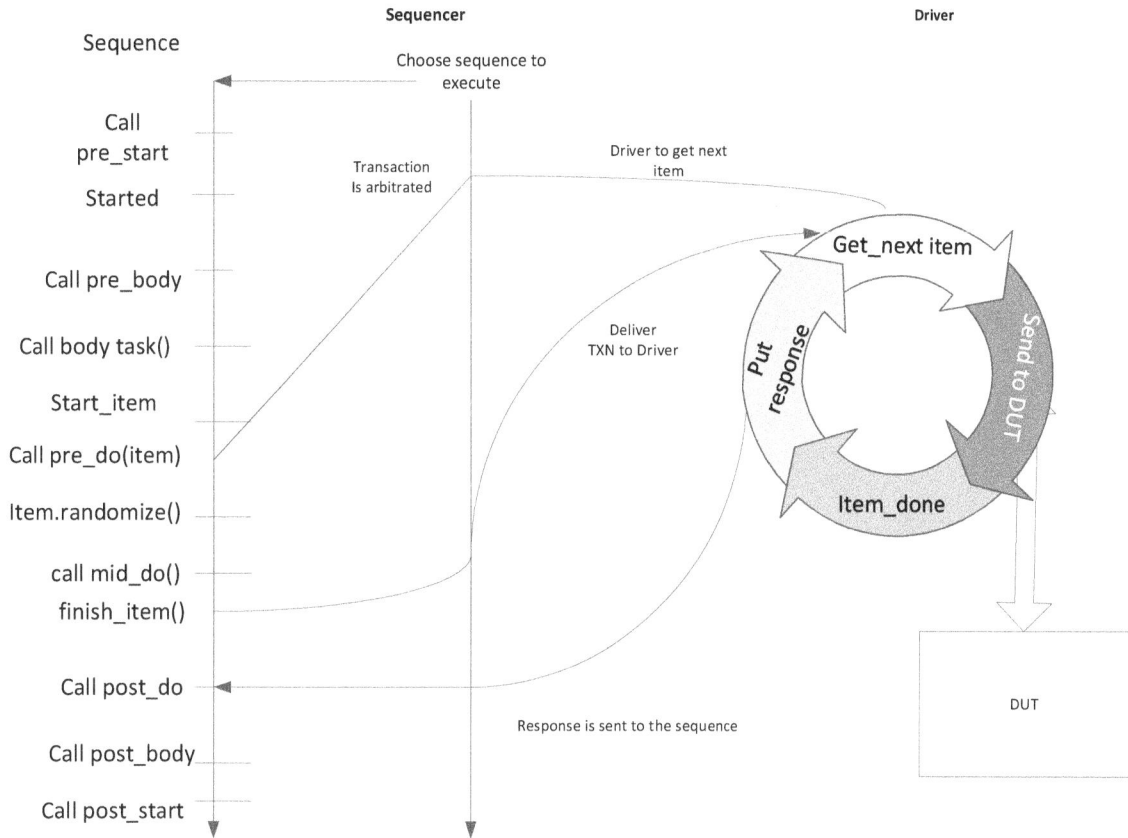

Fig. 14.4: Driver Sequencer Sequence Interaction

14.2.1.2 Using Sequence Macros

You can run the sequence on a sequencer using a macro, as shown below.

`uvm_do(SEQ_OR_ITEM, SEQR=get_sequencer(), PRIORITY=-1, CONSTRAINTS=)

This macro is a replacement for the following macros, which have been deprecated by the IEEE version. The reason being that all the macros were a variant of the single macro, and it was deemed as being easier to remember. Note that the macros are variants of a single common kind, passing along priority, constraints to the methods seen in the earlier section.

```
`uvm_create(seq_or_item)
`uvm_do(seq_or_item)
`uvm_do_pri(seq_or_item, priority)
`uvm_do_with(seq_or_item, constraints)
`uvm_do_pri_with(seq_or_item, priority, constraints)
`uvm_create_on(seq_or_item, seqr)
`uvm_do_on(seq_or_item, seqr)
`uvm_do_on_pri(seq_or_item, seqr, priority)
`uvm_do_on_with(seq_or_item, seqr, constraints)
`uvm_do_on_pri_with(seq_or_item, seqr, priority, constraints)
`uvm_send(seq_or_item)
`uvm_send_pri(seq_or_item, priority)
`uvm_rand_send(seq_or_item)
`uvm_rand_send_pri(seq_or_item, priority)
`uvm_rand_send_with(seq_or_item, constraints)
`uvm_rand_send_pri_with(seq_or_item, priority, constraints)
```

Recent developments have found some benefits to not using macros. The IEEE 1800.2 IEEE standardization deprecated the use of many of the `uvm_do macros replacing them all with a single macro. Typically, a compiler will expand these macros and attempt to do some optimization based on the signatures it observes. While this is a benefit, weigh it against maintainability. If you had used methods, you would not have encountered porting issues with code related to the macros.

14.2.2 Configuring the Sequencer's Default Sequence

Earlier, it was mentioned that a sequence could be started on a sequencer using the default_sequence resource setting. This configuration interface makes it easy to organize tests based on sequences. Listing 14.3 shows an example of setting a default sequence in the test.

Listing 14.3: Configuring the Default Sequence

```
19      virtual function void build_phase(uvm_phase phase);
20          super.build_phase(phase);
21          env = wb_env::type_id::create("env", this);
22          wb_master_config = new("wb_master_config");
23          wb_slave_config = new("wb_slave_config");
24
25          wb_master_config.max_n_wss = 10;
26          wb_master_config.min_addr = 0;
27          wb_master_config.max_addr = 10000000;
28
29          wb_slave_config.max_n_wss = 10;
30          wb_slave_config.min_addr = 0;
31          wb_slave_config.max_addr = 10000000;
32
33          begin: configure
34              uvm_config_db #(uvm_object_wrapper)::set(this, "env.
                    rst_agent.mast_sqr.reset_phase", "default_sequence",
                    reset_sequence::get_type());
35              uvm_config_db #(uvm_object_wrapper)::set(this, "env.
                    master_agent.mast_sqr.main_phase", "default_sequence",
                    sequence_1::get_type());
```

```
36                    uvm_config_db #(uvm_object_wrapper)::set(this, "env.
                         slave_agent.slv_seqr.main_phase", "default_sequence",
                         ram_sequence::get_type());
37
38                    uvm_config_db #(wb_config)::set(this, "env.master_agent",
                         "config", wb_master_config);
39                    uvm_config_db #(wb_config)::set(this, "env.slave_agent", "
                         config", wb_slave_config);
40            end
41       endfunction
```

In the above listing:

• Line 35 sets the default sequence for the master sequencer in the master agent.

14.3 Sequencer Arbitration

Sequencer arbitration controls how stimulus is received by the DUT. The UVM library provides a built-in arbiter into the sequencer. This arbiter comes with many modes that can be easily customized.

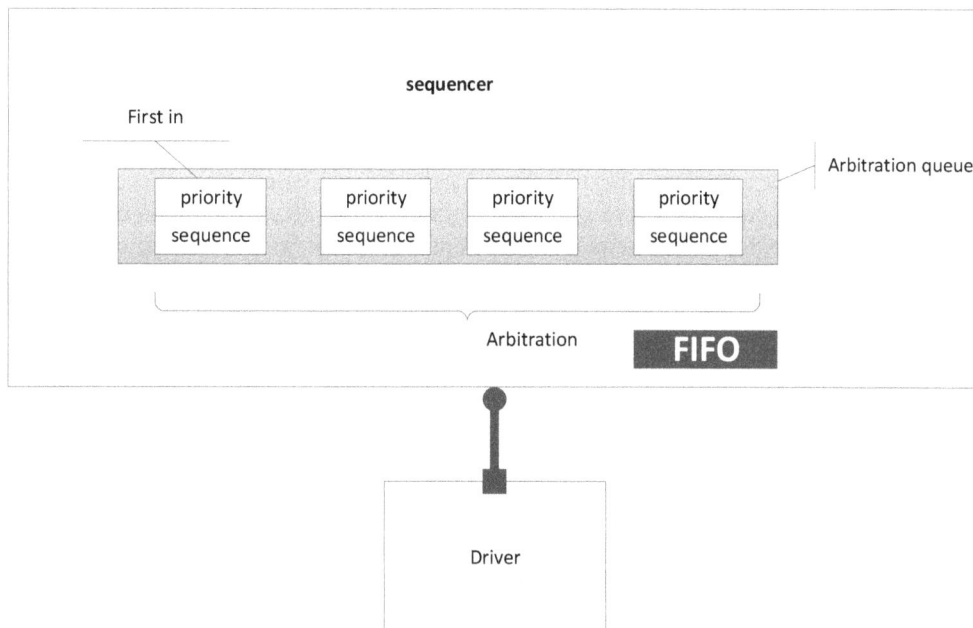

Fig. 14.5: Sequencer Arbitration

The sequencer arbitration can be set and viewed in the sequencer with the following methods:

```
function void set_arbitration( UVM_SEQ_ARB_TYPE value)
function UVM_SEQ_ARB_TYPE get_arbitration()
```

The set_arbitration method sets the current arbitration mode set for this sequencer. Value is one of the values from Table 14.2. Whereas the get_arbitration method returns the arbitration mode from the sequencer.

SEQ_ARB_FIFO	Requests are granted in FIFO order (default)
SEQ_ARB_WEIGHTED	Requests are granted randomly by weight
SEQ_ARB_RANDOM	Requests are granted randomly
SEQ_ARB_STRICT_FIFO	Requests at highest priority granted in fifo order
SEQ_ARB_STRICT_RANDOM	Requests at highest priority granted in randomly
SEQ_ARB_USER	Arbitration is delegated to the user-defined function, user_priority_arbitration. That function will specify the next sequence to grant.

Table 14.2: UVM Sequencer Arbitration Selection

Table 14.2 shows the various modes for the sequencer arbitration. Section 14.3.2 and the following sections in Section 3 contain practical examples of how to affect the sequencer arbitration.

UVM IEEE The UVM 1.2 version for the user_priority arbitration was not well documented. IEEE documents this along with accessor methods so that you can use this aspect of arbitration.

14.3.1 Getting a Handle To the Sequencer From a Sequence

Often, you may want to get a handle to the sequencer upon which the sequencer is running. Using this handle, you may want to access some other elements in the environment. Given that the sequence is dynamic in nature, and can exist for a short time, you need a standardized mechanism to do so. When a sequence is started on a sequencer, a generic sequencer handle called *m_sequencer* is initialized in the sequence. This handle is of the uvm_sequencer_base type. You can access this handle by using the m_sequencer variable in the sequence. It's primarily for internal use only, and ***I do not recommend you use m_sequencer in your sequence methods. Use the p_sequencer even if it's an extra line of code except in a few cases.***

On the other hand, you ***must*** get a type specific sequencer handle by registering the sequence to a sequencer using the `uvm_declare_p_sequencer macro. This macro performs a cast under the hood. When you use this macro, a handle p_sequencer is made available to you. The p_sequencer does not exist if the `uvm_declare_p_sequencer macros is not present in your code.

To understand the difference between m_sequencer and p_sequencer, you must recognize the fact that UVM has two different hierarchy trees in operation: the dynamically generated transaction class trees and the quasi-static component class hierarchy tree. The bridge between the two class trees is the m_sequencer variable. You may use it to access the component hierarchy or change arbitration modes etc. Since it is of type uvm_sequencer_base, *it does not have access to the derived sequencer variables or members*. Typical IP verification requires more than one sequencer/interface. A virtual sequence running on a virtual sequencer coordinates multiple sequences on multiple sequencers. This means you cannot access the subsequencers using the m_sequencer. Instead, you need the p_sequencer.

14.3.2 Sequence Priority

Often, you would like to assign a priority to the sequence. A sequence with a higher priority gets higher weight than a sequence with lower priority during arbitration. UVM supplies a mechanism for the test writer to indicate the priority of the sequence when the sequence is started. By default, the priority of a sequence is the priority of its parent sequence. If it is a root sequence (see section 14.4.2), its default priority is 100. Higher numbers indicate higher priority. You can choose to prioritize sequences by raising the priority on the sequences. Below is an example of sequences being started with different priorities.

Listing 14.4: A Simple Virtual sequence Showing Priority

```
1 class priority_sequence extends base_sequence;
2   sequence_0 sequence0;
3   sequence_1 sequence1;
4   sequence_2 sequence2;
5
6   `uvm_declare_p_sequencer(wb_master_seqr)
7   `uvm_object_utils(priority_sequence)
8   `uvm_add_to_seq_lib(priority_sequence,wb_master_seqr_sequence_library)
9
10
11  function new(string name = "seq_2");
12    super.new(name);
13  endfunction:new
14  virtual task body();
15    sequence0 = sequence_0::type_id::create("Sequence0");
16    sequence1 = sequence_1::type_id::create("Sequence1");
17    sequence2 = sequence_2::type_id::create("Sequence2");
18    p_sequencer.set_arbitration(UVM_SEQ_ARB_WEIGHTED);
19
20    `uvm_info(get_full_name(),"Running UVM SEQUENCE_3",UVM_LOW)
21
22    fork
23      begin
24        for(int i = 0; i < 10; i++) begin
25          sequence0.start(p_sequencer,this,200,0);
26        end
27      end
28
29      begin
30        for(int i = 0; i < 10; i++) begin
31          sequence2.start(p_sequencer,this,400,0);
32        end
33      end
34      begin
35        sequence1.start(p_sequencer,this,200,0);
36      end
37    join
38  endtask
39 endclass
```

- Lines 2-4 show three child subsequences in this sequence.

- Line 8 shows the handle of the sequencer being obtained to the sequencer using the `uvm_declare_p_sequencer macro. The sequencer handle is available as p_sequencer in this class from now on.

- Lines 15-18 show the three subsequences being created.

- Lines 14-38 show the body of this sequence. This sequence runs the three sequences in parallel.

- Lines 11-13 show the constructor of this class.

- The arbitration mechanism is being set in the sequencer to being weighted as per priority.

- Lines 25 and 35 show the sequence0 and sequence1 being started with a priority of 200. This means that since the two have equal priority, each of them will be chosen 2/8 times.

- Line 31 shows the sequence2 at a higher priority than the sequence0 and sequence1 subsequences. It will effectively be selected twice as often as the other two sequences by the sequencer.

14.3.3 Lock/Unlock

Quite often, there is a need to influence the arbitration in the sequencer. Depending on the nature of the stimulus, a sequence may need exclusive access to the sequencer for a duration of time. To accomplish this, one must ensure that the sequencer must not arbitrate other sequences. This is accomplished by locking down the sequence on the sequencer.

The lock functionality comes with two methods. One method is to lock the sequencer, and the other to unlock the sequencer.

```
task lock(uvm_sequence_base sequence_ptr);
task unlock(uvm_sequence_base sequence_ptr);
```

The sequencer's lock() method is called from a sequence. It forces the sequencer to get exclusive access to the driver **when it gets its *next slot* via the sequencer arbitration mechanism.**. Once the lock is granted, other sequences are locked out of arbitration until the sequence issues an unlock() call, which will then release the lock. The method is blocking and does not return until the lock() has been granted.

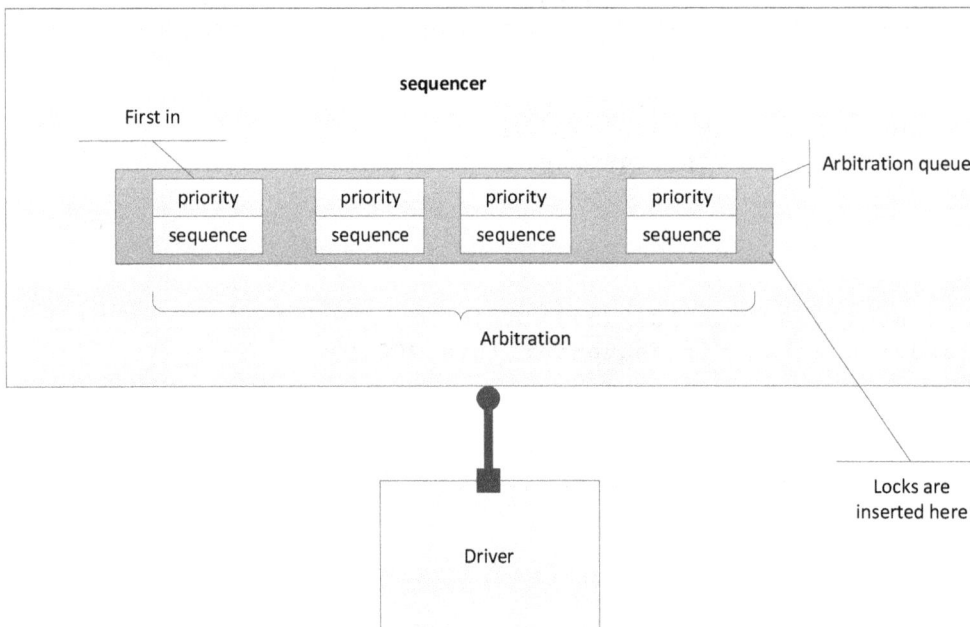

Fig. 14.6: Lock Is Inserted At The End Of The Arbitration Queue

The figure shows the action of the lock() method. The lock() method arbitrates at the end of looking at all the queues. An example of a lock() call is shown in the listing below.

Listing 14.5: A Simple Virtual sequence Showing Lock

```
1 class lock_sequence extends base_sequence;
2   `uvm_object_utils(lock_sequence)
3   `uvm_add_to_seq_lib(lock_sequence,wb_master_seqr_sequence_library)
4
5   function new(string name="my_lock_sequence");
6     super.new(name);
7   endfunction
8
9   virtual task body();
10    lock();
11    `uvm_do(req, get_sequencer(), -1, {address == 0; kind ==
        wb_transaction::READ; })
12    `uvm_do(req, get_sequencer(), -1, {address == 1; kind ==
        wb_transaction::READ; })
13    `uvm_do(req, get_sequencer(), -1, {address == 2; kind ==
        wb_transaction::READ; })
14    `uvm_do(req, get_sequencer(), -1, {address == 3; kind ==
        wb_transaction::READ; })
15    unlock();
16  endtask
17
18 endclass
```

- Line 10 shows the lock() method being used in a sequence. Note that this lock method blocks till the sequencer is available. Until then, the sequence is running on the sequencer but cannot do anything. The handle to this sequencer is called p_sequencer which was obtained by using the `uvm_declare_p_sequencer macro present in the base class.

- Lines 11-14 show the various read operations happening in the sequence after the sequence has been locked. Note that since the sequence has been locked, NO OTHER sequence can interrupt it and send anything to the driver until lock_sequence relinquishes the lock() on the sequencer.

- Line 15 shows the unlock() method being called on the sequencer. The arbiter in the sequencer is now free to arbitrate amongst all the other sequences.

14.3.4 Grab/Ungrab

The grab method is similar to the lock() method described above. ***The key difference between the grab() and the lock() methods is that the grab() takes effect on the next arbitration cycle of the sequencer without any consideration to any of the priorities in place already.*** If you can think of going straight to the ticket booth in a movie theater without paying attention to the line, you get the idea. The grab functionality comes with two methods: To grab the sequencer, and to release the grab on the sequencer.

```
function grab(uvm_sequence_base sequence_ptr);
function ungrab(uvm_sequence_base sequence_ptr);
```

The figure shows the action of the grab() method. The grab method forces the sequence to 'jump' the queues and go ahead of everybody else in the slots regardless of the priority of the sequences running on the sequencer. This call is shown in the below listing also.

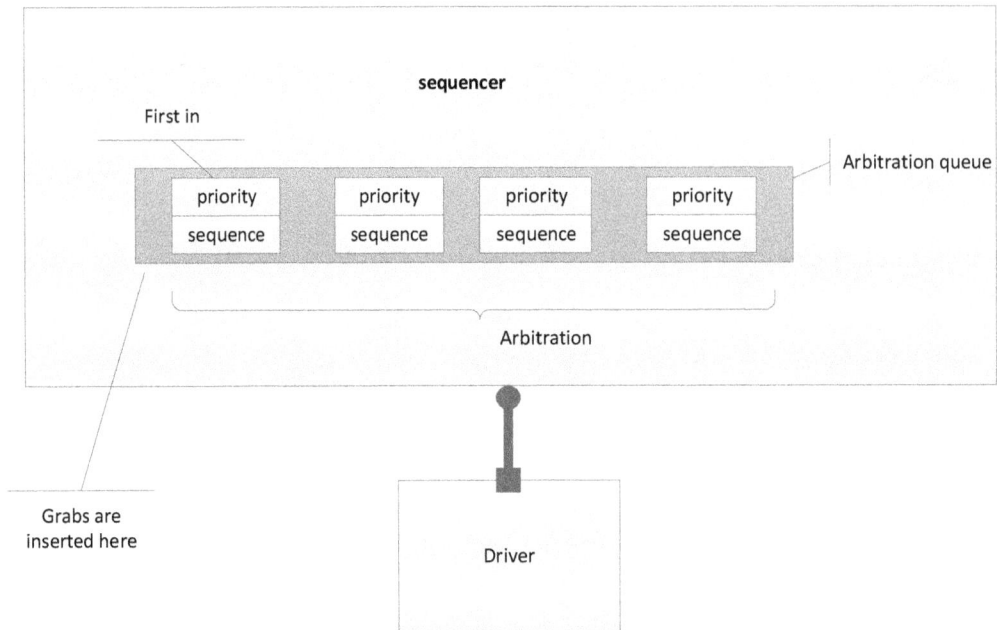

Fig. 14.7: Grab Is Inserted Before Any Of The Queue Arbitration Begins

Listing 14.6: A Simple Grab in sequence

```
1 class grabsequence extends base_sequence;
2   `uvm_object_utils(grabsequence)
3   `uvm_add_to_seq_lib(grabsequence,wb_master_seqr_sequence_library)
4
5   function new(string name="my_grabsequence");
6     super.new(name);
7   endfunction
8
9   virtual task body();
10    grab();
11    `uvm_do(req, get_sequencer(), -1, {address == 0; kind ==
         wb_transaction::READ; })
12    `uvm_do(req, get_sequencer(), -1, {address == 1; kind ==
         wb_transaction::READ; })
13    `uvm_do(req, get_sequencer(), -1, {address == 2; kind ==
         wb_transaction::READ; })
14    `uvm_do(req, get_sequencer(), -1, {address == 3; kind ==
         wb_transaction::READ; })
15    ungrab();
16  endtask
17
18 endclass
```

- Line 10 shows the grab() method being used in a sequence. Note that this grab method blocks till the sequencer is available. Until then, the sequence is running on the sequencer but cannot do anything. The handle to this sequencer is called p_sequencer which was obtained by using the `uvm_declare_p_sequencer macro present in the base class.

- Lines 11-14 show the various read operations happening in the sequence after the sequence has been grabbed. Note that since the sequence has been grabbed, NO OTHER sequence can interrupt it and send anything to the driver until this sequence relinquishes the grab() on the sequencer.

- Line 15 shows the ungrab() method being called on the sequencer. The arbiter in the sequencer is now free to arbitrate amongst all the other sequences.

Be careful with the handles to the sequencers! Other than a is_blocked method, there isn't a good way to find out if a sequencer is grabbed or locked and wait for it to become free. You can only issue either a grab() or a lock(). Both the grab() and lock() are blocking calls, and all you see is the sequencer getting blocked and no notification when it is freed up. Also, if you have a virtual sequencer and need to get the handles to multiple sequencers, you need to make sure you can get all the handles before proceeding (look at the dining philosopher's problem discussed in many texts, and you'll get the idea of what this issue entails.)

When a hierarchical sequence locks a sequencer, its child sequences will have access to the sequencer. If one of the child sequences issues a lock, then the parent sequence will not be able to start any parallel sequences or send any sequence_items until the child sequence has unlocked.

A locking or grabbing sequence must always unlock before it completes. Otherwise, the sequencer will deadlock.

Recommendation 14.3.0:   *Placing an uvm_info message at appropriate verbosity when you lock/unlock or grab/ungrab a sequencer speeds up debugging.*

The uvm_sequencer_base::ungrab and uvm_sequencer_base::unlock() methods are specified as tasks in the LRM. The Accelera implementation declares the methods as function void. Below is the correct signature. The next IEEE standard for UVM will define these methods as tasks instead of functions.

```
virtual function void unlock( uvm_sequence_base sequence_ptr )
virtual function void ungrab( uvm_sequence_base sequence_ptr )
```

14.4 Common Sequence Types

The sequence is a recipe for creating a set of transactions. Hence, depending on the application, the sequences can be timed or un-timed. Furthermore, sequences may be nested and may have interrelationships between them or dependencies on other sequences. Given the wide variety of possibilities, sequences may be broadly classified into the following areas.

- Flat sequences (series of sequence items driven by one driver)

- Parallel sequence

- Hierarchical sequences (sequence of sequences driven by one driver)

- Virtual sequences (sequence of sequences driven by multiple drivers)

- Layered sequences (sequences driving other sequences)

- Reactive sequences (ability for a sequence to react to its environment)

14.4.1 Flat Sequences

A flat sequence is defined only in terms of sequence items and has no other relationships. A flat sequence typically contains the following types of information:

- Any specific sequence item that is generated. Note that there could be more than one type of item generated in the sequence. Some of the items could be from derived classes as well. The order of items is implicit in the sequence definition.

- Any specific constraints to be applied to each sequence item generated in the previous step.

- Any specific randomization control used to modify the generated items.

- Any flow or loop flow control information that governs the number of generated items.

- The response handler for environment/DUT conditions that may affect item generation (See our section on reactive sequences in Section 16.1.3 for a different take on this topic).

- Any relationship between consecutively generated items.

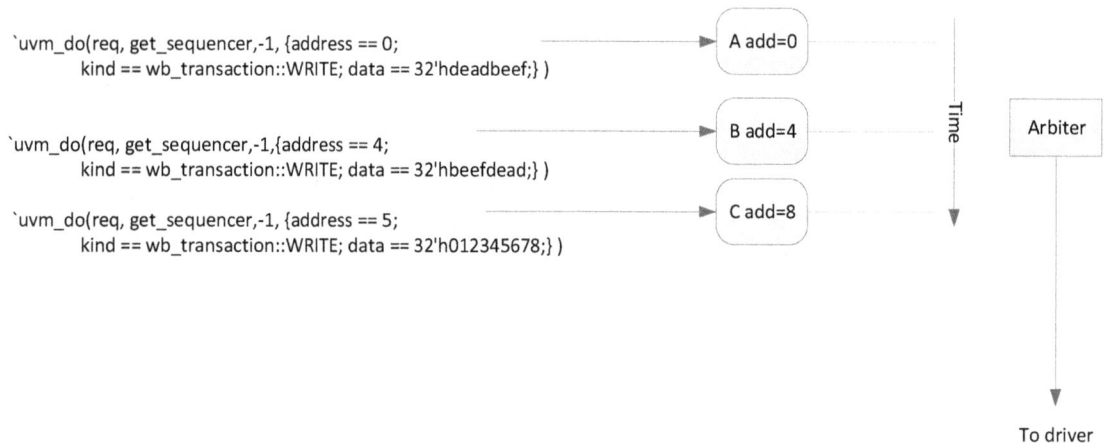

Fig. 14.8: A Simple Flat Sequence

The figure shows the composition of a simple flat sequence embodied in the listing below. The sequence sequence_0 generates three different transactions.

Listing 14.7: A Simple Flat sequence

```
1  class sequence_2 extends base_sequence;
2    byte sa;
3    `uvm_object_utils(sequence_2)
4    `uvm_add_to_seq_lib(sequence_2, wb_master_seqr_sequence_library)
5    function new(string name = "seq_1");
6      super.new(name);
7    endfunction:new
8    virtual task body();
9
10     `uvm_do(req, get_sequencer(), -1, {address == 6; kind ==
           wb_transaction::WRITE; data == 63'hdeadbeef;})
11     `uvm_do(req, get_sequencer(), -1, {address == 7; kind ==
           wb_transaction::WRITE; data == 63'hbeefdead;})
12     `uvm_do(req, get_sequencer(), -1, {address == 8; kind ==
           wb_transaction::WRITE; data == 63'h0123456678;})
13
14
15     `uvm_do(req, get_sequencer(), -1, {address == 6; kind ==
           wb_transaction::READ ;})
```

```
16      `uvm_do(req, get_sequencer(), -1, {address == 7; kind ==
            wb_transaction::READ;})
17      `uvm_do(req, get_sequencer(), -1, {address == 8; kind ==
            wb_transaction::READ;})
18   endtask
19 endclass
```

Listing 14.7 shows a simple flat sequence. This listing highlights the following guidelines that were followed when implementing a flat sequence:

- Line 1 shows a declaration for a sequence_2 class. This class is derived from a base_sequence class, which contains other properties common to all sequences in the sequence library.

- Line 5 shows the constructor for the sequence.

- Line 3 The sequence extends from uvm_object. Hence, one must use the `uvm_object_utils() macros or their begin/end variations (used when other properties need to be automated). The `uvm_add_to_seq_lib macro is used to add the sequence to a sequence library which will be running on the sequencer if you wish to use a sequence library as has been done here.

- Line 8-18 shows the sequence action block specified by defining the contents of the virtual task body(). This sequence sends three WRITE transactions to the driver followed by three READ transactions.

14.4.2 Hierarchical Sequences

A hierarchical sequence is defined in terms of both subsequences as well as sequence items. Hierarchical sequences allow previously defined sequences to be reused and provide a means of organizing a long sequence into smaller interrelated sequences. Each performs a particular operation. These inter-related sequences can be combined in many other interesting ways to form a library of sequences that may be reused to test the DUT.

You may initially begin writing simple sequences to test your DUT. Over a period of time, you would have accumulated many sequences. You can combine these sequences to a hierarchical sequence by stringing together many such sequences to form more interesting situations to test your DUT. You can then combine these sequences with other hierarchical sequences and create even more complex sequences.

Recommendation 14.4.0:   *Make sure you do an analysis of the sequences to see how much of the sequence can be reused by others. If the reuse potential is more than 50% of the time, then consider creating a base sequence so that others can leverage on it*

Some vendors use other terminologies in circulation to describe the various aspects of a hierarchical sequence. They are not described here for reasons of brevity. It is sufficient to understand that these sequences can be called from other sequences, and they, in turn, can call other sequences. The collection of these sequences in a certain order can be used to perform a specific action on the DUT.

Two types of sequences are identified during the execution of a hierarchical sequence:

- Root Sequences

- Subsequences

A root sequence is the start point of the execution of a new, completely separate tree. This means that the root sequence does not have a parent sequence attached to it. IE. its parent sequence is null. The subsequence, on the other hand, has a parent sequence. This is how you distinguish them.

The macros and methods treat root sequences and subsequences slightly differently. *Also for a subsequence, the pre_body() and post_body() methods are not called.*

Rule 14.4.0:   *The pre_body() and post_body() methods are not called in some circumstances. Use the pre_start() and post_start() instead.*

Why is this important? The parent/subsequence relationship comes into play when a sequencer that is grabbed will accept items from a subsequence if the parent is grabbing the sequencer. The same applies to the lock() mechanism. See the API for the sequences, and you will be able to see a bit & handle that signifies whether to treat the class instance as an item or as a subsequence.

The guidelines for creating a hierarchical sequence are similar to those for a flat sequence, except that a hierarchical sequence contains instances of previously defined sequences (line 134) and can optionally execute sequence items. A hierarchical sequence may include instances of both flat and other hierarchical sequences. Note that all sequence instances used in a hierarchical sequence must belong to the same sequence library and the same sequencer.

Here is an example of a simple hierarchical sequence. These simple sequences are supplied as a part of the example in chapter 22

Listing 14.8: A Simple Heirarchical sequence

```
1 class heir_sequence_w extends base_sequence;
2     `uvm_object_utils(heir_sequence_w)
3
4     write_master_single single_seq;
5
6     function new(string name = "seq_0");
7         super.new(name);
8     endfunction:new
9     virtual task body();
10        single_seq = write_master_single::type_id::create("my_sequence");
11        single_seq.write_address  = 10;
12        single_seq.write_data = 32'h12345678;
13        single_seq.start(p_sequencer);
14    endtask
15 endclass
```

Listing 14.8 shows a simple heirarchical sequence.

- Line 1 declares a hierarchical sequence.
- Line 4 shows a child sequence.
- Line 9 starts the body() method of the sequence.
- Lines 10-12 set up the sequence.
- Line 13 starts the sequence as a child sequence on the sequencer.

When the body() method of the sequence executes, the hierarchical sequence creates a child sequence, populates it, and then runs it on the sequencer. Note that the hierarchical sequence very much looks like a collection of sequences. All this sequence is doing is calling another sequence and passing some parameters to it. We have shown only one simple sequence here, but you could have any number of them.

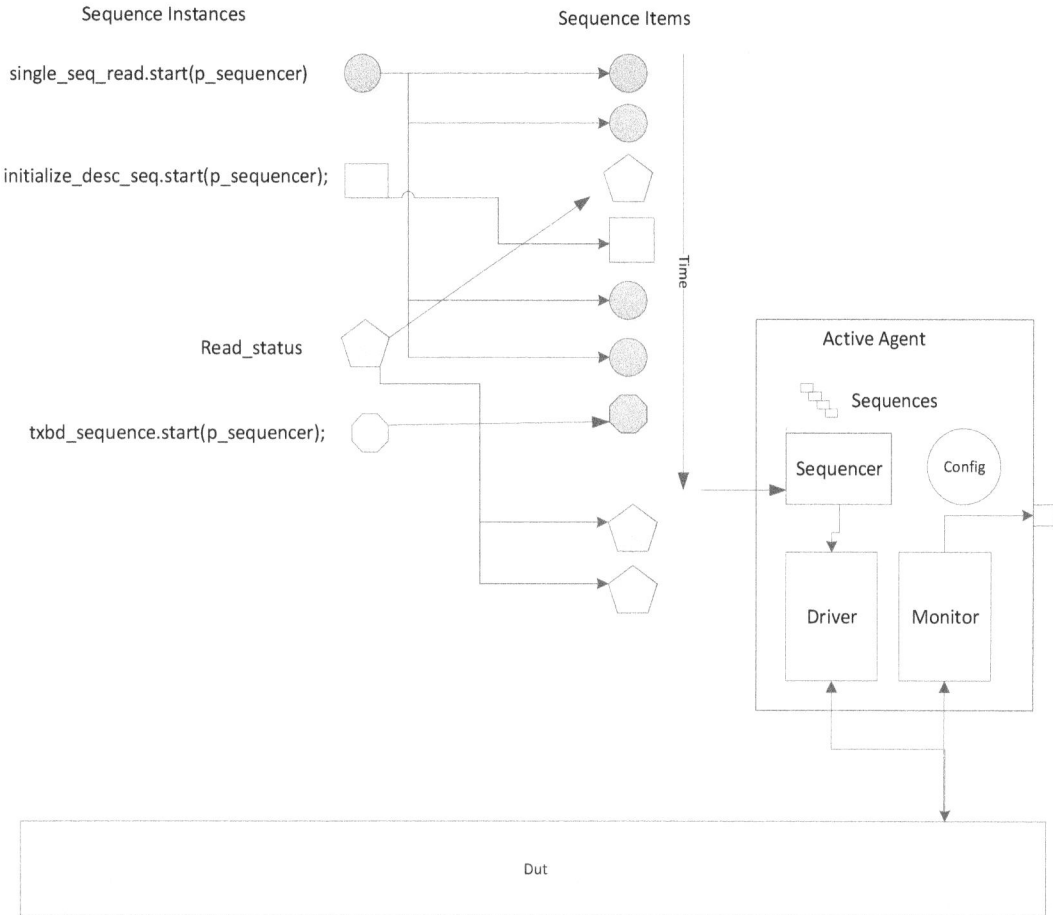

Fig. 14.9: Hierarchical Sequences

14.4.3 Parallel Sequences

Parallel sequences are just that: sequences that run in parallel on the same sequencer. These sequences are characterized by a fork-join pair. Items from each of the sequences are scheduled on the sequencer based on the sequence priority and sequencer settings. A good application of this is to generate noise traffic on a bus in addition to normal traffic. Below is an example of a parallel sequence.

Listing 14.9: A Simple Parallel sequence

```
1 class parallel_sequence extends base_sequence;
2   byte sa;
3   `uvm_object_utils(parallel_sequence)
4   `uvm_add_to_seq_lib(parallel_sequence, wb_master_seqr_sequence_library)
5   `uvm_declare_p_sequencer(wb_master_seqr)
6   function new(string name = "seq_1");
7     super.new(name);
8   endfunction:new
9   virtual task body(); uvm_phase phase_=get_starting_phase();
10
11    integer i;
12    sequence_0 seq0;
13    sequence_1 seq1;
14
15    fork
16      `uvm_do(seq0,p_sequencer,-1,{})
17      `uvm_do(seq1,p_sequencer,-1,{})
18    join
19
20  endtask
21 endclass
```

- Lines 16 -17 start sequence instances seq0 and seq1 in parallel. These will now be run on the sequencer in parallel.

14.4.4 Reactive Sequences

So far, all the sequences that were discussed drive a value to the DUT. Consider the flip side of the problem. If the DUT produces a value, and you would like to have a sequence that responds to it, *you will need first to get the DUT values in a transaction, and then look at the transaction and generate an appropriate response.* The construction of a sequence to do so is quite different from the normal sequencer/sequences as the relationship is the opposite of what you normally see. The sequencer waits for the driver in this case. Such an arrangement is an advanced topic, which is discussed in detail in Chapter 16.1.

14.4.5 Virtual Sequences and Sequencers

In all our earlier examples, a single sequencer and driver were used to drive stimulus to the DUT. Typically, one finds that interactions between multiple components are quite common. These are modeled using the multiple components in the system. While performing this kind of simulation, it often becomes necessary to co-ordinate the data between multiple channels. Frequently such scenarios can and will be reused. A virtual sequence is used to coordinate the behavior of multiple sequencers within multiple agents connected to multiple interfaces of the design-under-test.

Usually, a virtual sequence is run on a virtual sequencer. A virtual sequencer is usually a uvm_sequencer and is not typed to the type of item it creates. In early versions of OVM, virtual sequences, and virtual sequencers were distinguished from regular sequences and sequencers using separate base classes. VMM had the MultiStream Scenario Generator using this approach. Initially, virtual sequences could only run on virtual sequencers.

Listing 14.10: A Simple Virtual sequencer

```
2 class wb_virt_sequencer extends uvm_sequencer;
3
4     `uvm_component_utils(wb_virt_sequencer);
5     wb_master_seqr seqr1;
6
7
8     function new(string name = "wb_virtual_sequencer", input uvm_component
          parent=null);
9         super.new(name,parent);
10        // set_arbitration(UVM_SEQ_ARB_FIFO);
11
12    endfunction
13
14
15 endclass
```

Listing 14.10 shows the listing for a virtual sequencer. In this listing:

- Line 2 class wb_virt_sequencer is defined. Note again that this sequencer is extended from uvm_sequencer.

- Line 4 shows the `uvm macros.

- Line 5 shows the instance of another sequencer wb_master_sequencer seqr1. This sequencer is referred to in the sequence above when running child sequences.

- We have left the sequencer arbitration method in there for you. It is commented out for now, but experiment with it.

In UVM, a virtual sequence extends the same base class as a regular sequence and can run on any sequencer or a null sequencer! A virtual sequence is not obliged to be specialized with a specific transaction type when extending uvm_sequence. This is an important distinction that still causes confusion in the minds of many people.

A virtual sequence by definition will not call start_item and finish_item; There are fewer restrictions on the choice of a sequencer. A virtual sequence can run on its own dedicated sequencer. It can run on a sequencer used to run regular (non-virtual) sequences, or can even run on the null sequencer. The virtual sequence is primarily used to group together related sequences to facilitate reuse. The user can determine if the sequence needs to have access to the sequencer. If needed, it can do so either by using the p_sequencer handle or by accessing the handle depending on the sequence that is running.

Figure 14.10 shows a virtual sequence running on a virtual sequencer. Two different sequences sequence0 and sequence1 are started in parallel on this sequencer. These two sequences execute in parallel on the two different agents.

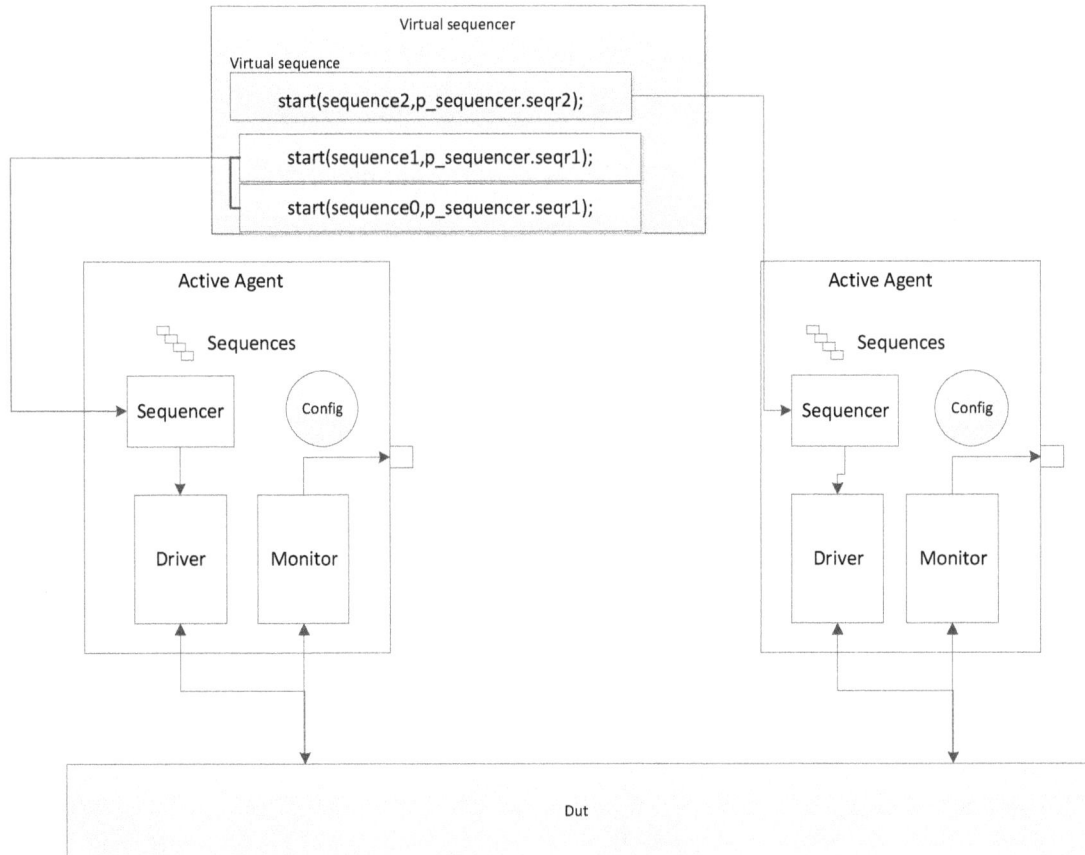

Fig. 14.10: Virtual Sequences

The listing below shows an example of a simple virtual sequence. It has three child sequences that it executes in parallel.

Listing 14.11: A Simple Virtual sequence

```
5 class wb_virtual_seq extends uvm_sequence ;
6
7    `uvm_object_utils(wb_virtual_seq);
8    `uvm_declare_p_sequencer(wb_virt_sequencer)
9    sequence_0 sequence0;
10   sequence_1 sequence1;
11   sequence_2 sequence2;
12
13   virtual task body();
14      uvm_phase phase_=get_starting_phase();
15
16      phase_.raise_objection(this);
17      `uvm_info("VIRT_SEQQ","Starting Virtual Sequence:",UVM_LOW)
18      sequence0 = sequence_0::type_id::create("Sequence0");
19      sequence1 = sequence_1::type_id::create("Sequence1");
20      sequence2 = sequence_2::type_id::create("Sequence2");
21
22      fork
23         begin
24            sequence0.start(p_sequencer.seqr1,this,20,0);
25            sequence2.start(p_sequencer.seqr1,this,50,0);
26            sequence1.start(p_sequencer.seqr1,this,1000,0);
27         end
28      join
29      phase_.drop_objection(this);
30   endtask
31
32   function new(string name="vir_sequence");
33      super.new(name);
34   endfunction
35 endclass
```

A simple virtual sequence is shown in Listing 14.11.

- Line 5 declares the wb_virtual_sequence class as an extension of uvm_sequence. Note that there is no type of transaction to which the class is parameterized.

- Line 7 provides the factory registration and other utilities for this class

- Line 8 uses the uvm_declare_p_sequencer to bring a handle of the wb_virt_sequencer into the wb_virtual_sequence class.

- Lines 9-11 show three child sequences instantiated.

- Line 13 starts the body() task for this sequence.

- Lines 18 —20 show sequence_0 , sequence_1, and sequence_2 being created as sequence0, sequence1 and sequence2, respectively.

- Lines 24-26 show the sequences all started in parallel on seqr1. Seqr1 is a handle to a sequencer present in the virtual sequencer. See Listing 14.10 for details.

- Lines 32 —32 provide the constructor to the class.

It is recommended to set the priority for a virtual sequence. When any sequence executes, the start method of the sequence calls the body() method. This body() method can start child sequences, and this process continues so on until a child sequence attempts to generate a transaction. The transaction generation is blocked by the driver at the end of the chain until the driver is ready. At that point, the priority of the sequence, passed as an argument to start, will be used as the default priority for any child sequences, and ultimately acts as the default priority of any transactions.

14.4.6 Interrupt Sequences

In addition to providing the infrastructure for detecting interrupts, there are other ways to structure these sequences. A detailed description of interrupt sequences is provided in Chapter 22.

14.4.7 Layered Sequences

Modern protocols like USB, PCIe, and others have many layers. One approach is to model them as a layer in a sequence. Look at Section 22.3 for a more detailed discussion of layering in sequences.

14.5 Sequence Callbacks

Once a sequence starts executing, there are often situations where you would like to "intercept" the sequence execution to perform some other tasks. UVM sequences have well-defined callback hooks that allow the user to perform additional actions during the sequence execution. The listing below shows one example of a sequence callback.

Listing 14.12: Sequence Callbacks Template

```
18    virtual task pre_start();
19        uvm_phase phase_ = get_starting_phase();
20        if (phase_ != null)
21            phase_.raise_objection(this);
22    endtask:pre_start
23    virtual task post_start();
24        uvm_phase phase_ = get_starting_phase();
25        if (phase_ != null)
26            phase_.drop_objection(this);
27    endtask:post_start
```

You can have callbacks before the sequence itself executes. These are the pre_start and the post_start callbacks for the sequence. The only main difference between the two mechanisms is when they are executed. The pre_start and post_start callbacks are called **on every execution of the sequence,** regardless of how that sequence was started. On the other hand, the pre_body and post_body callbacks *are only called on sequences started by calling seq.start(...)*. If a sequence is started via the `uvm_do(...) macros, then these callbacks are not executed. Figure 14.11 illustrates this clearly.

```
class sequence_1 extends base_sequence;
  byte sa;
  ...

  virtual task body();
  ....
  `uvm_do(req, get_sequencer(),-1, {address == 5; kind == wb_transaction::READ ;} )
  `uvm_do(req,get_sequencer(),-1, {address == 6; kind == wb_transaction::READ;} )
  `uvm_do(req,get_sequencer(),-1, {address == 7; kind == wb_transaction::READ;} )
  ...
  endtask
  ...
  endclass
```

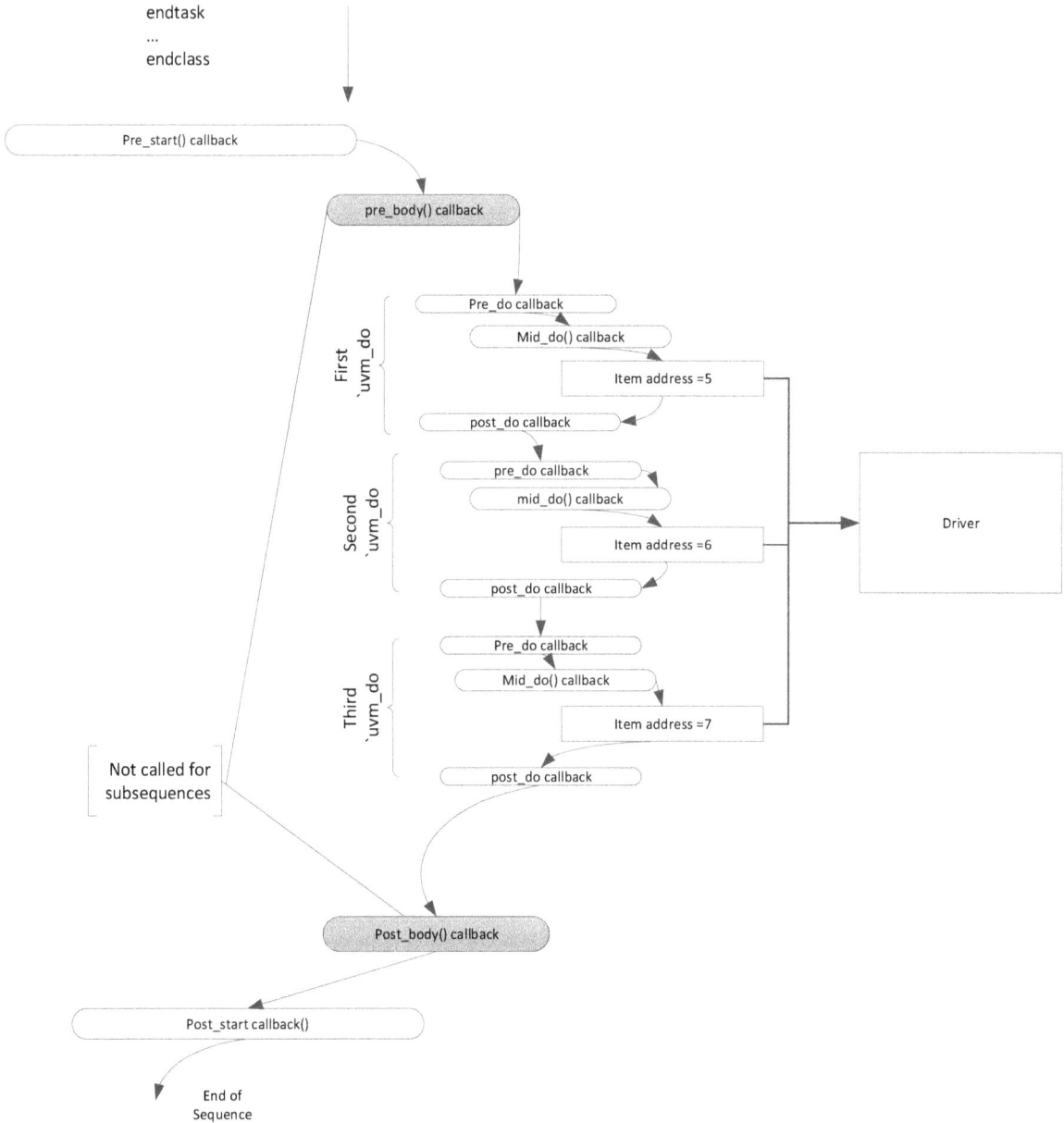

Pre_start() callback

pre_body() callback

First `uvm_do
Pre_do callback
Mid_do() callback
Item address =5
post_do callback

Second `uvm_do
pre_do callback
mid_do() callback
Item address =6
post_do callback

Third `uvm_do
Pre_do callback
Mid_do() callback
Item address =7
post_do callback

Driver

Not called for subsequences

Post_body() callback

Post_start callback()

End of Sequence

Fig. 14.11: Order of Callbacks in Sequences

14.6 Coding Guidelines

In most organizations, the uvm_sequence item class is extended from uvm_sequence item or its derived classes to provide a company-specific class. This practice allows organizations to add some customization to the base classes and have them available as a company-wide standard. You can use these classes to model transaction items of any protocol. Figure 14.12 shares one of the recommendations for how to use derivative classes with the transaction packet. Tweak these recommendations to suit your application.

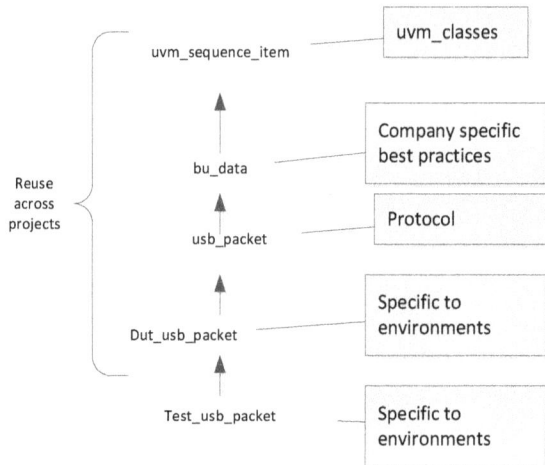

Fig. 14.12: Data Reuse

14.7 Working around Deprecated Sequence Macros

If you are moving from older versions of UVM to the IEEE 1800.2 version, you will notice that the `uvm_do macros have changed. The older version had the following arguments to the macro.

```
`uvm_do(SEQ_OR_ITEM)
```

The 1800.2 version however has the following signature:

```
`uvm_do(SEQ_OR_ITEM, SEQR=get_sequencer(), PRIORITY=-1, CONSTRAINTS={})
```

You will notice that there are default arguments in the macro. In simple cases, you normally do not have porting issues if you have simple usage in your tests. Unfortunately, this simple case is not prevalent in common usage. Many users use many of these other macros listed below. This implies you will need to pass in all the relevant parameters. You may be short of time to make this change during your verification, or it may simply not be possible to do so. *If this occurs, consider including the deprecated/macros/uvm_sequence_defines.svh from the UVM source repository. This file includes backward compatibility macros that will map to the new `uvm_do macro.*

Chapter 15

Synchronization, Watchdogs and Events

Frequently, one finds the need to synchronize across many threads that are present in the environment. An example of this is the need to wait for some configuration to take place, or some external event to occur before proceeding with a specific task while other processes are concurrently executing. UVM supplies event and barrier synchronization classes that manage concurrent processes. These classes are designed to help manage processes that may be running on various components, sequences, or other objects. The classes offer some additional functionality above the constructs provided in SystemVerilog. This chapter explores these classes with examples, along with considerations for using these classes. Concepts presented in this chapter are:

- The uvm_event class and its applications.

- The uvm_barrier class and its applications.

For this discussion, all the examples leverage complete working environments from the previous chapters.

15.1 Synchronizing Processes Across Components Using uvm_event

The uvm_event is a wrapper around the abstract uvm_event_base class that wraps around the SystemVerilog event construct. It provides additional capabilities to set callbacks and maintain the number of waiters on the event. Using uvm_event instead of SystemVerilog events allows you to attach callbacks to be executed before and after event triggering takes place.

UVM
IEEE
uvm_event class is also factory enabled, and the uvm_object* macros are in the class

Rule 15.1.0: *The uvm_event class does derive from uvm_object, and it has its own version of do_copy() and do_print() methods. Use care when using copy and other functionality on these classes.*

The main functions that are part of the uvm_event class are:

```
function new (string name="");

Trigger Functions
function void trigger (uvm_object data=null);
function uvm_object get_trigger_data ();
function time get_trigger_time ();

Status Functions
function bit is_on ();
function bit is_off ();
function void reset (bit wakeup=0);
function void cancel ();
function int get_num_waiters ();

Callback Functions
function void add_callback (uvm_event_callback cb, bit append=1);
function void delete_callback (uvm_event_callback cb);
```

The trigger functions help you to trigger the event, get the time of the triggering, and the data associated with the trigger. The status functions provide information about the triggered event while the callback functions allow you to add a set of methods to be called when the trigger executes.

Attaching a callback uses a process that is identical to that in Chapter 9. You must extend the objection class and add an instance of it to the callback queue.

The stimulus example from the Ethernet Chapter 22 is used below for synchronizing between two parallel threads using an uvm_event. The stimulus is provided by one sequence, and the interrupt sequence blocked by waiting for an interrupt signal is running in parallel. Once the transmit sequence is programmed, the event is triggered, allowing interrupts to proceed. The event is created in the top-level test and put into the config_db allowing global access. This flow is shown in the block diagram in Figure 15.1.

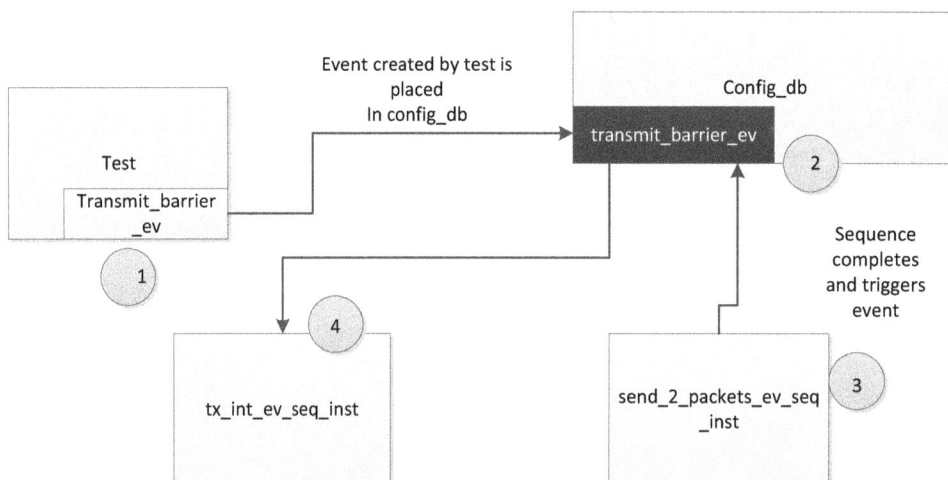

Fig. 15.1: Using an Synchronous event

The essential steps to using the uvm_events in this example are:

- Step 1: The event is created in the top-level test.

- Step 2: The event is placed in config_db.

- Step 3: The transmit_sequence picks it from config_db.

- Step 4: The interrupt sequence picks it from config_db.

This top-level test is adapted from Chapter 22. The test is set up to transmit a packet. Event synchronization occurs between sending packets and the interrupt sequence. The top-level test sets up the event, as seen in Listing 15.1. This top-level test now sets up the uvm_event and pushes it into the config_db.

Listing 15.1: Simple Transmit test with events

```
37      class eth_transmit_event_sync_test extends eth_blk_env_test;
38
39          `uvm_component_utils(eth_transmit_event_sync_test)
40
41          // Barriers and other sequences;
42          tx_interrupt_event_seq tx_int_ev_seq_inst;
43          send_2_packets_event_sync_sequence send_2_packets_ev_seq_inst;
44
45          uvm_event transmit_barrier_ev = new("transmit_complete_event") ;
46
47          function new(string name, uvm_component parent);
48              super.new(name, parent);
49          endfunction
50
51          virtual function void build_phase(uvm_phase phase);
52              super.build_phase(phase);
53              env_config = new("Ethernet configuration");
54              uvm_config_db #(eth_env_cfg)::set(this,"env","config",
                  env_config);
55              master_config = wb_config::type_id::create("WB_MASTERConf");
56              slave_config = wb_config::type_id::create("WB_SLAVEConf");
57              master_config.randomize with {min_addr == 0; max_addr == 32'
                  h0ffffffe; max_n_wss == 5;};
58              slave_config.randomize with {min_addr == 0; max_addr == 32'
                  h0ffffffe; max_n_wss == 2;};
59
60              uvm_config_db #(wb_config)::set(null,"uvm_test_top.env.
                  wb_master_agt","mstr_agent_cfg",master_config);
61              uvm_config_db #(wb_config)::set(null,"uvm_test_top.env.
                  wb_slave_agt","slv_agent_cfg",slave_config);
62
63              uvm_config_db #(int)::set(null,"*","include_coverage",0);
64
65              //      uvm_config_db #(uvm_object_wrapper)::set(this, "env.
                  wb_master_agt.mast_sqr.main_phase","default_sequence",
                  send_tx_packet2::get_type());
66              uvm_config_db #(uvm_active_passive_enum)::set(this, "env.
                  mii_tx_agt","is_active",UVM_PASSIVE);
67              uvm_config_db #(uvm_active_passive_enum)::set(this, "env.
                  mii_rx_agt","is_active",UVM_PASSIVE);
68
```

```
69              // Find the global event pool and send event to the pool
70
71              // Create the Barrier and send it to the config_db;
72              uvm_config_db #(uvm_event)::set(null,"","transmit_b",
                    transmit_barrier_ev);
73
74          endfunction
75
76          virtual task main_phase(uvm_phase phase);
77              super.main_phase(phase);
78
79              phase.raise_objection(this,"test run");
80              tx_int_ev_seq_inst = tx_interrupt_event_seq::type_id::create("
                    tx_int_bar_seq_inst",this);
81              send_2_packets_ev_seq_inst =
                    send_2_packets_event_sync_sequence::type_id::create("
                    send_2_packets_bar_ev_sync_inst");
82
83              fork
84                  begin
85                      send_2_packets_ev_seq_inst.start(env.wb_master_agt.
                            mast_sqr);
86                      send_2_packets_ev_seq_inst.wait_for_sequence_state(
                            UVM_FINISHED);
87                  end
88
89                  begin
90                      tx_int_ev_seq_inst.start(env.wb_master_agt.mast_sqr);
91                      tx_int_ev_seq_inst.wait_for_sequence_state(
                            UVM_FINISHED);
92                  end
93
94              join
95              phase.drop_objection(this,"test run");
96          endtask
97
98
99      endclass : eth_transmit_event_sync_test
```

- Line 45 illustrates the main event that is used to synchronize the processes.

- Line 51 shows the build phase where the test and environment are built.

- Line 72 enters the event into the config_db.

  The main_phase() has a couple of tasks running in parallel. The transmit sequence finishes the transmission, and the interrupt sequence waits for the event triggering.

- Upon completion of the two sequences, the test is completed.

The test is simple. The enhancements to the top-level test are listed above. Line 57 below shows the event being triggered.

```
20      virtual task body();
21          uvm_reg_data_t reg_data;
22          uvm_status_e reg_status;
23
24          uvm_config_db #(uvm_event)::get(null,"","transmit_b",
                send_2_pkt_event);
25
26          p_sequencer.regmodel.MODER.write(.status(reg_status), .value(0), .
                path(UVM_FRONTDOOR), .parent(this));
27          p_sequencer.regmodel.MAC_ADDR0.write(.status(reg_status), .value
                (32'h03040506), .path(UVM_FRONTDOOR), .parent(this));
28          p_sequencer.regmodel.MAC_ADDR1.write(.status(reg_status), .value
                (32'h00001020), .path(UVM_FRONTDOOR), .parent(this));
29          tx_seq = init_tx_seq::type_id::create("tx seq");
30          txbd_sequence = setup_txbd_sequence::type_id::create("TXBD data
                Sequence");
31          initialize_desc_seq = initialize_txbd_rxbd_sequence::type_id::
                create("initialize_desc_sequence");
32          tx_int_sequence = tx_interrupt_seq::type_id::create("
                tx_init_sequence");
33          single_seq_read = read_master_single::type_id::create("single_seq
                ");
34          single_seq = write_master_single::type_id::create("simple seq read
                ");
35          // Clean up descriptors
36          initialize_desc_seq.start(p_sequencer);
37          p_sequencer.regmodel.INT_MASK.write(.status(reg_status),.path(
                UVM_FRONTDOOR), .parent(this),.value(32'h0000007f));
38          p_sequencer.regmodel.MODER.write(.status(reg_status),.path(
                UVM_FRONTDOOR), .parent(this),.value(32'h00002403));
39
40          txbd_sequence.packet_lenght = 80;
41          txbd_sequence.buffer_num = 0;
42          txbd_sequence.mem_addr = 1000;
43          txbd_sequence.start(p_sequencer);
44          txbd_sequence.packet_lenght = 80;
45          txbd_sequence.buffer_num = 1;
46          txbd_sequence.mem_addr = 1000;
47          txbd_sequence.packet_lenght = 80;
48          txbd_sequence.buffer_num = 2;
49          txbd_sequence.mem_addr = 1000;
50          txbd_sequence.start(p_sequencer);
51
52          single_seq_read.read_address = 32'h00000400;
53          single_seq_read.read_data = 32'h007c5800;
54
55          repeat (5)   // Apparently this is a magic number that kicks off
                the machine
56              single_seq_read.start(p_sequencer);
57          send_2_pkt_event.trigger();
58      endtask
59 endclass
```

The interrupt sequence also waits for the event to trigger. This is shown in Listing 15.3 below on Line 15.

Listing 15.3: Simple Interrupt Sequence with Events

```
1 class tx_interrupt_event_seq extends base_sequence;
2      `uvm_object_utils(tx_interrupt_event_seq)
3
4      uvm_event int_event;
5
6      function new(string name = "tx_interrupt_event_seq");
7          super.new(name);
8      endfunction:new
9
10     virtual task body();
11         uvm_reg_data_t reg_data;
12         uvm_status_e reg_status;
13         uvm_config_db #(uvm_event)::get(null,"","transmit_b",int_event);
14         `uvm_info(get_full_name(),$sformatf(" Awaiting Interrupt trigger %
               d",$time),UVM_MEDIUM)
15         int_event.wait_ptrigger();
16         p_sequencer.int_if.wait_for_intr_pos();
17         `uvm_info(get_full_name(),$sformatf("Got Interrupt finally %d",
               $time),UVM_MEDIUM)
18         grab();
19         p_sequencer.regmodel.INT_MASK.read(.status(reg_status),.path(
               UVM_FRONTDOOR), .parent(this),.value(reg_data));
20         p_sequencer.regmodel.INT_MASK.write(.status(reg_status),.path(
               UVM_FRONTDOOR), .parent(this),.value(32'h0000007f));
21         p_sequencer.regmodel.INT_SOURCE.read(.status(reg_status),.path(
               UVM_FRONTDOOR), .parent(this),.value(reg_data));
22         p_sequencer.regmodel.INT_SOURCE.write(.status(reg_status),.path(
               UVM_FRONTDOOR), .parent(this),.value(reg_data));
23         ungrab();
24         `uvm_info(get_full_name(),$sformatf("Completed interrupt sequence
               %d",$time),UVM_MEDIUM)
25     endtask
26 endclass
```

Until wait_ptrigger() method is unblocked, the sequence started on the sequencer does not proceed. Once the event is triggered, the sequence waits for the interrupt signal on line 16.

(i) Compared to regular SystemVerilog events, the uvm_event class is heavy!. It can have an impact on simulation performance since additional processing occurs. Pay attention to this aspect as you design your synchronization mechanism. It does have its advantages: study the overall impact before you use it.

Recommendation 15.1.0: *You may wonder why you cannot use a callback instead of an event. Use callbacks if there is an opportunity to change the default behavior (EX: inject an error). An event is one-way. A callback can return different values or modify the state of its arguments.* **A component is "stopped" by a callback execution, but not when signaling a uvm_event.**

15.2 UVM Event Callbacks in Action

The example in the previous section illustrated the use of an uvm_event to synchronize across two different sequences. In this example, we use the features of the uvm_event from Section 15.1 to show the pre_trigger and post_trigger methods in usage. The steps to add an event callback are similar to that of any callback, as illustrated in Section 21.8.

15.2.1 Step 1: Create Event Callback Class

Listing 15.4 shows the creation of the class extending from uvm_callback.

Listing 15.4: Creating an event callback class

```
22   class int_event_callbacks extends uvm_event_callback;
23
24     function new(string name="int_event_callbacks");
25       super.new(name);
26     endfunction
27
28     virtual function bit pre_trigger(uvm_event e, uvm_object data = null);
29       `uvm_info("UVM_EVENT_CALLBACK",$sformatf("UVM EVENT Pre_trigger
             callback triggered"),UVM_LOW)
30     endfunction
31
32     virtual function void post_trigger(uvm_event e, uvm_object data = null
           );
33       `uvm_info("UVM_EVENT_CALLBACK",$sformatf("UVM EVENT post_trigger
             callback triggered"),UVM_LOW)
34     endfunction
35   endclass
```

15.2.2 Step 2: Instantiate Callback Class

Instantiation of the callback class is similar; you create the instance.

Listing 15.5: Instantiating event callback class

```
47     typedef uvm_callbacks#(uvm_event,int_event_callbacks) cbs;
48     int_event_callbacks interrupt_event_cbk = new("interrupt_event_cbk");
```

- Line 47 defines a typedef to simplify registration that we will use in Step 3.

- Line 48 creates an instance of the callback.

15.2.3 Step 3: Register Callback Class

The process of registering the callback is similar. We use the typedef from Step 2 and register the callback with the event.

Listing 15.6: Instantiating event callback class

```
74     // Create the Barrier and send it to the config_db;
75     uvm_config_db #(uvm_event)::set(null,"","transmit_b",
             transmit_barrier_ev);
76     cbs::add(transmit_barrier_ev,interrupt_event_cbk);
```

- Line 75 puts the event in the config_db.

- Line 76 registers the callback with the event.

If you check the log file for this test, you will see the messages before and after the event is triggered.

15.3 Using UVM Barrier Classes

The uvm_barrier class provides a multiprocess synchronization mechanism. The uvm_event class notifies waiting processes that they can now continue. The barrier class, on the other hand, is different. It enables a set of processes to block *until a desired number* of processes get to the synchronization point, at which time *all of them* are unblocked. Notice that unlike uvm_event, which notifies every waiting process, barriers are released once the threshold is reached.

To show the differences between barriers and events, this section uses uvm_barrier instead of uvm_ event to accomplish the same goals of the previous example. Both are similar, yet different to some extent. The stimulus is sent in from one sequence, and the parallel sequence that is forked off waits for interrupt completion. Both stimulus sequence and interrupt sequence arrive at the barrier terminating the test.

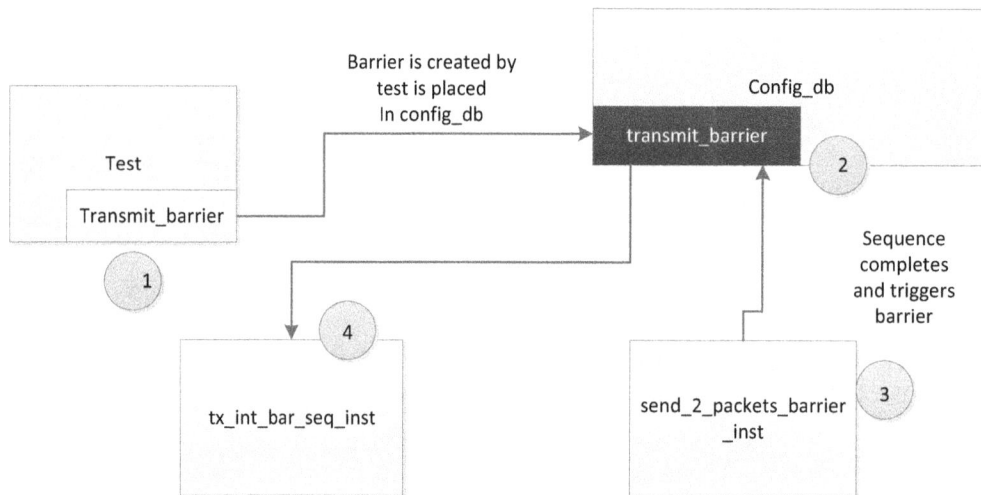

Fig. 15.2: Synchronization Using A Barrier.

Listing 15.7: Simple barrier Sequence

```
3 class send_2_packets_barrier extends base_sequence;
4
5     init_tx_seq tx_seq;
6     setup_txbd_sequence  txbd_sequence;
7     tx_interrupt_seq  tx_int_sequence;
8     initialize_txbd_rxbd_sequence  initialize_desc_seq;
9     write_master_single single_seq;
10    read_master_single single_seq_read;
11    uvm_barrier send_2_pkt_barrier;
12
13    `uvm_object_utils(send_2_packets_barrier)
14
15
16    function new(string name = "send_2_packets_barrier");
17        super.new(name);
18    endfunction:new
19
20    virtual task body();
```

```
21          uvm_reg_data_t reg_data;
22          uvm_status_e reg_status;
23
24          uvm_config_db #(uvm_barrier)::get(null,"","transmit_b",
               send_2_pkt_barrier);
25
26          p_sequencer.regmodel.MODER.write(.status(reg_status), .value(0), .
               path(UVM_FRONTDOOR), .parent(this));
27          p_sequencer.regmodel.MAC_ADDR0.write(.status(reg_status), .value
               (32'h03040506), .path(UVM_FRONTDOOR), .parent(this));
28          p_sequencer.regmodel.MAC_ADDR1.write(.status(reg_status), .value
               (32'h00001020), .path(UVM_FRONTDOOR), .parent(this));
29          tx_seq = init_tx_seq::type_id::create("tx seq");
30          txbd_sequence = setup_txbd_sequence::type_id::create("TXBD data
               Sequence");
31          initialize_desc_seq = initialize_txbd_rxbd_sequence::type_id::
               create("initialize_desc_sequence");
32          tx_int_sequence = tx_interrupt_seq::type_id::create("
               tx_init_sequence");
33          single_seq_read = read_master_single::type_id::create("single_seq
               ");
34          single_seq = write_master_single::type_id::create("simple seq read
               ");
35          // Clean up descriptors
36          initialize_desc_seq.start(p_sequencer);
37          // p_sequencer.regmodel.TX_BD_NUM.write(.status(reg_status),.path(
               UVM_FRONTDOOR), .parent(this),.value(1));
38
39          p_sequencer.regmodel.INT_MASK.write(.status(reg_status),.path(
               UVM_FRONTDOOR), .parent(this),.value(32'h0000007f));
40          p_sequencer.regmodel.MODER.write(.status(reg_status),.path(
               UVM_FRONTDOOR), .parent(this),.value(32'h00002403));
41
42          txbd_sequence.packet_lenght = 80;
43          txbd_sequence.buffer_num = 0;
44          txbd_sequence.mem_addr = 1000;
45          txbd_sequence.start(p_sequencer);
46          txbd_sequence.packet_lenght = 80;
47          txbd_sequence.buffer_num = 1;
48          txbd_sequence.mem_addr = 1000;
49          txbd_sequence.packet_lenght = 80;
50          txbd_sequence.buffer_num = 2;
51          txbd_sequence.mem_addr = 1000;
52          txbd_sequence.start(p_sequencer);
53          single_seq_read.read_address = 32'h00000400;
54          single_seq_read.read_data = 32'h007c5800;
55          single_seq_read.start(p_sequencer);
56          single_seq_read.start(p_sequencer);
57          single_seq_read.start(p_sequencer);
58          single_seq_read.start(p_sequencer);
59          // tx_int_sequence.start(p_sequencer);
60          single_seq_read.start(p_sequencer);
61          send_2_pkt_barrier.wait_for();
62      endtask
```

```
63 endclass
```

Until wait_for() method returns, the sequence does not proceed. The sequence waits on line 61 until barrier threshold is met.

Listing 15.8: Simple Transmit Sequence with barriers

```
1  class tx_interrupt_seq_barrier extends base_sequence;
2      `uvm_object_utils(tx_interrupt_seq_barrier)
3
4      uvm_barrier int_barrier;
5
6      function new(string name = "tx_interrupt_seq_barrier");
7          super.new(name);
8      endfunction:new
9
10     virtual task body();
11         uvm_reg_data_t reg_data;
12         uvm_status_e reg_status;
13         uvm_config_db #(uvm_barrier)::get(null,"","transmit_b",int_barrier
               );
14         `uvm_info(get_full_name(),$sformatf("waiting for Interrupt %d",
               $time),UVM_MEDIUM)
15         p_sequencer.int_if.wait_for_intr_pos();
16         `uvm_info(get_full_name(),$sformatf("Got Interrupt %d",$time),
               UVM_MEDIUM)
17         grab();
18         p_sequencer.regmodel.INT_MASK.read(.status(reg_status),.path(
               UVM_FRONTDOOR), .parent(this),.value(reg_data));
19         p_sequencer.regmodel.INT_MASK.write(.status(reg_status),.path(
               UVM_FRONTDOOR), .parent(this),.value(32'h0000007f));
20         p_sequencer.regmodel.INT_SOURCE.read(.status(reg_status),.path(
               UVM_FRONTDOOR), .parent(this),.value(reg_data));
21         p_sequencer.regmodel.INT_SOURCE.write(.status(reg_status),.path(
               UVM_FRONTDOOR), .parent(this),.value(reg_data));
22         ungrab();
23         `uvm_info("BARRIER",$sformatf("number of waiting %d threshold %d",
               int_barrier.get_num_waiters(),int_barrier.get_threshold()),
               UVM_LOW)
24         int_barrier.wait_for();
25
26         `uvm_info(get_full_name(),$sformatf("Completed interrupt sequence
               %d",$time),UVM_MEDIUM)
27     endtask
28 endclass
```

The interrupt sequence also waits for the barrier to unblock. This is shown in Listing 15.8 above on Line 24.

The top-level test sets up the event as seen in the listing. This top-level test now sets up the barrier and pushes it into config_db.

Listing 15.9: Simple Transmit test with events

```
22   class eth_transmit_barrier_test extends eth_blk_env_test;
23
24     `uvm_component_utils(eth_transmit_barrier_test)
25
26     // Barriers and other sequences;
27     tx_interrupt_seq_barrier  tx_int_bar_seq_inst;
28     send_2_packets_barrier       send_2_packets_bar_seq_inst;
29
30     uvm_barrier transmit_barrier = new("transmit_barrier",2);
31
32     function new(string name, uvm_component parent);
33       super.new(name, parent);
34     endfunction
35
36     virtual function void build_phase(uvm_phase phase);
37       super.build_phase(phase);
38       env_config = new("Ethernet configuration");
39       uvm_config_db #(eth_env_cfg)::set(this,"env","config",env_config);
40       master_config = wb_config::type_id::create("WB_MASTERConf");
41       slave_config = wb_config::type_id::create("WB_SLAVEConf");
42       master_config.randomize with {min_addr == 0; max_addr == 32'
           h0fffffe; max_n_wss == 5;};
43       slave_config.randomize with {min_addr == 0; max_addr == 32'h0fffffe
           ; max_n_wss == 2;};
44
45       uvm_config_db #(wb_config)::set(null,"uvm_test_top.env.wb_master_agt
           ","mstr_agent_cfg",master_config);
46       uvm_config_db #(wb_config)::set(null,"uvm_test_top.env.wb_slave_agt
           ","slv_agent_cfg",slave_config);
47
48       uvm_config_db #(int)::set(null,"*","include_coverage",0);
49
50       //       uvm_config_db #(uvm_object_wrapper)::set(this, "env.
           wb_master_agt.mast_sqr.main_phase","default_sequence",
           send_tx_packet2::get_type());
51       uvm_config_db #(uvm_active_passive_enum)::set(this, "env.mii_tx_agt
           ","is_active",UVM_PASSIVE);
52       uvm_config_db #(uvm_active_passive_enum)::set(this, "env.mii_rx_agt
           ","is_active",UVM_PASSIVE);
53
54       // Create the Barrier and send it to the config_db;
55       uvm_config_db #(uvm_barrier)::set(null,"","transmit_b",
           transmit_barrier);
56
57
58     endfunction
59
60     virtual task main_phase(uvm_phase phase);
61       super.main_phase(phase);
62       phase.raise_objection(this,"test run");
63       tx_int_bar_seq_inst = tx_interrupt_seq_barrier::type_id::create("
           tx_int_bar_seq_inst",this);
```

```
64      send_2_packets_bar_seq_inst = send_2_packets_barrier::type_id::
            create("send_2_packets_bar_seq_inst");
65
66      fork
67        begin
68          send_2_packets_bar_seq_inst.start(env.wb_master_agt.mast_sqr);
69          send_2_packets_bar_seq_inst.wait_for_sequence_state(UVM_FINISHED
                );
70          `uvm_info(get_full_name(), "looking for Interrupt", UVM_MEDIUM);
71        end
72
73        begin
74          tx_int_bar_seq_inst.start(env.wb_master_agt.mast_sqr);
75          tx_int_bar_seq_inst.wait_for_sequence_state(UVM_FINISHED);
76          `uvm_info(get_full_name(), "Done looking for Interrupt",
                UVM_MEDIUM);
77        end
78
79      join
80      `uvm_info("TEST","Test Completed",UVM_LOW)
81      phase.drop_objection(this,"test run");
82    endtask
83
84
85  endclass : eth_transmit_barrier_test
```

In this example, two sequences are running in parallel in the top-level test. When the barrier drops, the test finishes. In your application, you could do a host of other things, for example, make multiple sequences wait for one another, or even use a voting system to allow components to wait for certain occurrences in the simulation.

I have not provided a detailed explanation for this barrier class. The execution of this sequence is similar to the event sequence test presented in the earlier section. The difference between the two is the type of blocking mechanism involved. While the event mechanism is a" one size fits all", the barrier mechanism is a little more versatile. This allows unblocking various sequences based on the barrier threshold. For example, if you used an event and had a few sequences waiting for the event, all sequences are unblocked. In the barrier case, however, you can set that a few sequences had a higher barrier, and a few others could be unblocked with a lower barrier. This gives you much flexibility in creating many sequence behaviors. Use the one that is most relevant to your application.

15.4 Heartbeats From Simulations

Catastrophic events in the simulation can kill some parts of a testbench. For example, this situation may occur if the RTL DUT timed out while responding to stimulus. Depending on how agent/driver/monitors were developed, a deadlock may have also occurred. UVM supplies a heartbeat class to help ensure that the simulation is still up and running. The class uvm heartbeat checks for events occurring in a time window. Just like a beating heart, one expects that each component being tracked by a heartbeat instance must raise (or correspondingly drop) a synchronizing objection during a heartbeat window.

The synchronizing objection is of a class type must be a uvm_callbacks_objection, which provides for callback methods when the objection methods are called. To implement a heartbeat mechanism, the following class instances are needed in test/environment classes.

1. Creation of a heartbeat event that is used to trigger the heartbeat.

2. An instance of a heartbeat class.

3. An objection class instance of type uvm_callbacks_objection used to indicate to the heartbeat class instance that the component is alive

4. Optionally a report catcher class (see Section 6.2.5 and the example in Section 21.5) if you want to change the heartbeat verbosity.

Once the heartbeat architecture is determined, it becomes relatively easy to create a simple heartbeat that monitors the simulation. In the example below, we monitor the Ethernet example in Section 22.3.1, adding a heartbeat to the wb_master_agent component to make sure that the component is alive during programming of the DUT. One could add the heartbeat to other components quickly and extend it if needed.

The heartbeat class includes the following API methods:

```
new (string name, uvm_component cntxt, uvm_callbacks_objection objection=null);
uvm_heartbeat_modes set_mode (uvm_heartbeat_modes mode=UVM_NO_HB_MODE);
set_heartbeat (uvm_event e, ref uvm_component comps[$]);
add (uvm_component comp)
remove (uvm_component comp);
```

The heartbeat has a few modes, UVM_ALL_ACTIVE, UVM_ONE_ACTIVE, UVM_ANY_ACTIVE, UVM_NO_HB_MODE. The names are self-explanatory, depending on configuration, Either all, one or any component can trigger an objection. The UVM_NO_HB_MODE shuts off the heartbeat mechanism. Our suggestion is to use these settings in a command line/config_db mechanism as needed.

The UVM heartbeat class in its current avatar is not very flexible or useful. Part of the problem is that it uses a single event and a one-size-fits-all from an objection perspective. It also enforces the same time out on all the connected components. In addition, the message ID HBFAIL that it issues is a UVM_FATAL message. You need an additional report catchers to process it.

This example was described in the previous edition of this book. However, I removed it from this version because of the above limitations.

I suggest you either extend this class to add the above functionality or create your own. I would suggest you extend the heartbeat class and customize it before you use it. See the example provided by Brian Hunter [12]

Chapter 16

Agents That React To Stimulus

Earlier sections of the book provided details of how to use an agent to drive data into a DUT. The agent described in Chapter 8 allowed the user to drive data from a wishbone master into a DUT slave device. This master agent was able to read and write data from the DUT in its current implementation. In many verification situations, it becomes necessary to have a testbench component that is a *slave* for a certain interface. I.E. In this case, ***the DUT is the master,*** and ***the agent is the slave*** for that interface. A master agent on one port may configure a DUT, and it may send/receive traffic on a second port. The agent connected to the second port must observe the command presented to it by the DUT and then respond. In this case, it becomes necessary to have the agent respond to the stimulus provided to it instead of having the agent create the stimulus to drive into the DUT. The agent has to wait for the DUT to apply a stimulus to its pins, analyze it, and send back a response to the DUT. One must also be able to run sequences on the sequencer in the agent so that one can customize the response of the agent and provide maximum flexibility to the testbench writer. You need an architectural tweak compared to the classic agent modes studied you have studied so far. ***The sequence in the agent must react to the stimulus rather than create it.***

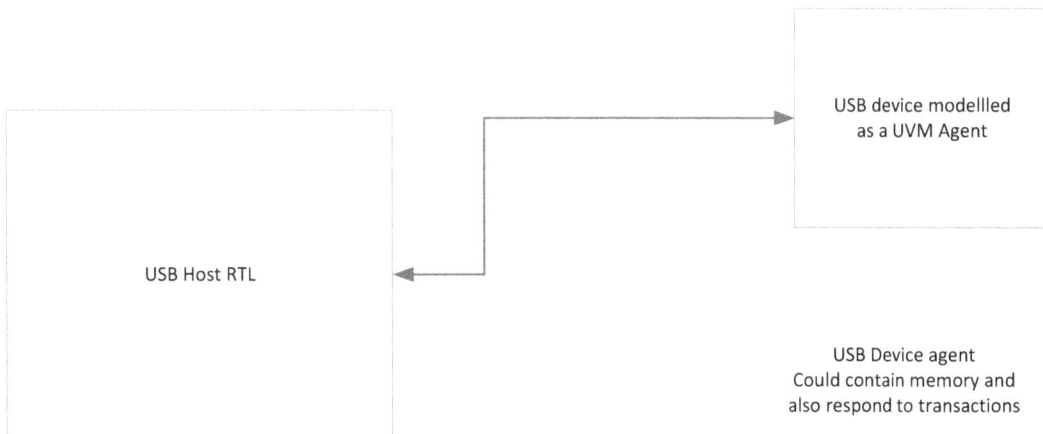

USB Host RTL

USB device modellled
as a UVM Agent

USB Device agent
Could contain memory and
also respond to transactions

Fig. 16.1: The Challenge Of A Reactive Agent

Figure 16.1 above shows the block diagram of the problem and the need for a reactive agent. The USB device must respond to transactions that are given to it by the host. The USB device does not create transactions on the bus until requested by the host.

By default, agents, sequencers, drivers and sequencers are "active". A sequence (via a sequencer and driver in an agent) can initiate a transaction at any time by calling `uvm_do() or start_item ()/finish_item() combination. Since this is a reactive agent, the start_item()/finish_item() and get_next_item() / item_done() protocol between the sequence and the driver will not work. The driver must be able to notify the sequencer that a transaction has been started as and provide all known information about the transaction so a proper response can be composed, and the sequence must wait for that indication before composing its response.

The reactive agent in this section is designed to address this problem. It creates a transaction out of the incoming activity on the pins and forwards them to the sequencer. Since reactive agents do not initiate the transaction, they cannot call_start_item() before a transaction that they must respond to has started. Furthermore, they often need information about the transaction before they can supply the response. ***The approach described here is one of many ways you can approach this problem.***

16.1 Example of a Reactive Agent

The reactive agent shown below is similar to the master agent described in earlier chapters. There are a few key differences in the communication between the children of the agent subcomponents. The agent includes a reactive sequencer and a reactive driver. The driver has an additional uvm_blocking_get_imp port in addition to the usual sequencer port through which it receives data from the sequencer. Using this port, the driver communicates the transaction it has seen on its pins. The sequencer waits for the driver to signal that a transaction is available before proceeding to generate a response which it places on the seq_item_port just like the normal sequencer driver communication described in Section 14.2.

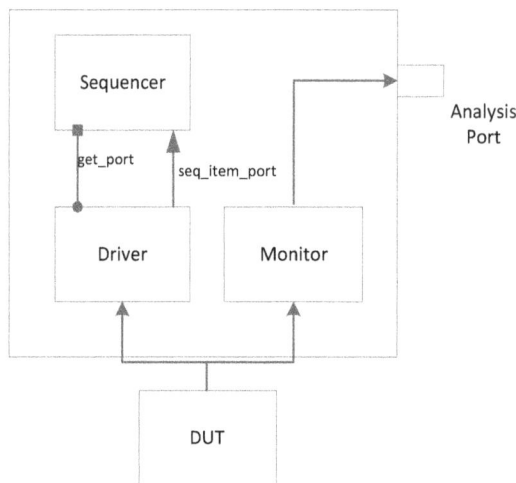

Fig. 16.2: Reactive Agent Block Diagram

The following sections explore the connections between the driver, the sequencer, and their operations. Our study begins with the reactive driver, which has a slightly different implementation from the one in Chapter 8. You can easily draw parallels between the implementation below and the one in Chapter 8.

16.1.1 Reactive Driver

The reactive driver mimics part of the monitor functionality as a reactive component. The driver must first detect a transaction, create a transaction descriptor, and populate it with available information. It must then make the transaction available to the get() task before calling the get_next_item() method. Once the get_next_item() method returns, the provided transaction has the necessary information to complete the transaction execution then call item_done(). This process repeats in a forever loop.

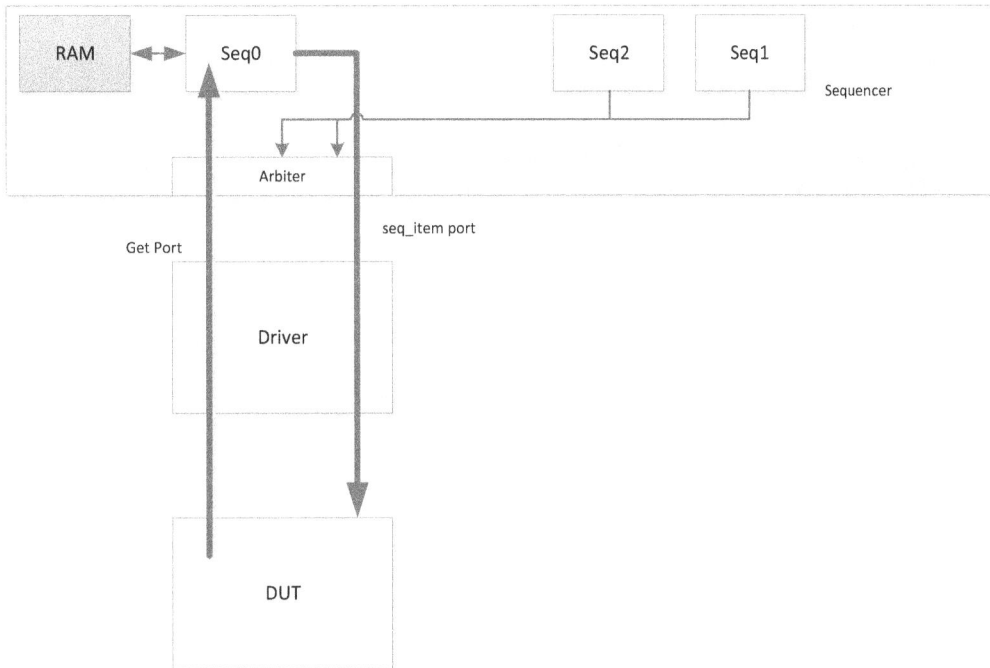

Fig. 16.3: Driver Data Flow

The data flow for the reactive driver is shown in Figure 16.3. Data is collected from the pins and sent to the sequencer, which responds with a transaction for the driver to drive through the pins. The basic driver class is shown in Listing 16.1.

Listing 16.1: Simple Reactive Driver Class

```
24    class wb_slave extends uvm_driver # (wb_transaction);
25
26        wb_transaction m_tr; // This is what is captured
27        local bit [63:0] ram [*];
28
29        uvm_blocking_get_imp #(wb_transaction,wb_slave) getp;
30
31        wb_config wb_slave_cfg;
32
33        typedef virtual  wb_slave_if v_if;
34        v_if drv_if;
35        `uvm_register_cb(wb_slave,wb_slave_callbacks);
36
37        extern function new(string name = "wb_slave",
38            uvm_component parent = null);
39
40        `uvm_component_utils(wb_slave)
41
42        extern virtual function void build_phase(uvm_phase phase);
43        extern virtual function void end_of_elaboration_phase(uvm_phase
              phase);
44        extern virtual function void connect_phase(uvm_phase phase);
45        extern virtual task reset_phase(uvm_phase phase);
46        extern virtual task configure_phase(uvm_phase phase);
47        extern virtual task run_phase(uvm_phase phase);
48        extern protected virtual task slave_driver();
49
50        task get(output wb_transaction transaction);
51            wait(m_tr != null )
52                transaction = m_tr;
53            m_tr = null;
54        endtask: get
55
56    endclass: wb_slave
```

All the necessary action happens in the slave_driver() task. The task detects the transaction occurring on the pins and creates an abstract transaction out of it. It then puts it across the get() port so that the sequencer can process it and provide a response. The response from the sequencer is put on the seq_item_port, and that response is consumed by the driver which drives a transaction back on the pins.

Listing 16.2: Simple Reactive Driver Task Class

```
109   task wb_slave::slave_driver();
110       bit [63:0] read_data;
111       wb_slave_cfg.print();
112       forever begin
113           wb_transaction tr;
114
115           do begin
116               if (this.drv_if.CYC_I !== 1'b1 || this.drv_if.STB_I !== 1'
                      b1) begin
117                   this.drv_if.DAT_O    <= 64'bz;
```

```
118                              this.drv_if.TGD_O       <= 16'bz;
119                              this.drv_if.ACK_O       <=  1'bz;
120                              this.drv_if.RTY_O       <=  1'bz;
121                              this.drv_if.ERR_O        <=  1'bz;
122                      end
123
124              @(this.drv_if.CYC_I or
125                      this.drv_if.STB_I or
126                      this.drv_if.ADR_I or
127                      this.drv_if.SEL_I or
128                      this.drv_if.WE_I  or
129                      this.drv_if.TGA_I or
130                      this.drv_if.TGC_I);
131          end while (this.drv_if.CYC_I !== 1'b1 ||
132          this.drv_if.STB_I !== 1'b1);
133          tr= wb_transaction::type_id::create("tr", this);
134          tr.address = this.drv_if.ADR_I;
135          // Are we supposed to respond to this cycle?
136          if(this.wb_slave_cfg.min_addr <= tr.address  && tr.address <=
                 this.wb_slave_cfg.max_addr )
137          begin
138              tr.sel = this.drv_if.SEL_I;
139              tr.tgc  = this.drv_if.TGC_I;
140              `uvm_do_callbacks(wb_slave,wb_slave_callbacks, pre_tx(this
                     , tr))
141              tr.tga = this.drv_if.TGA_I;
142              if(this.drv_if.WE_I) begin
143                  tr.kind = wb_transaction::WRITE;
144                  `uvm_info("Wb_slave","got a write transaction  from
                         Master ",UVM_LOW)
145                  tr.data  = this.drv_if.DAT_I;
146                  tr.tgd  = this.drv_if.TGD_I;
147              end
148              else  begin
149                  tr.kind = wb_transaction::READ ;
150                  `uvm_info("Wb_slave","got a read transaction  ",
                         UVM_LOW)
151              end
152              m_tr = tr;
153              seq_item_port.get_next_item(tr);
154              this.drv_if.DAT_O    = 64'bz;
155              if(tr.kind == wb_transaction::READ) begin
156                  this.drv_if.DAT_O = tr.data;
157              end
158
159              repeat (this.wb_slave_cfg.max_n_wss) begin
160                  @ (this.drv_if.slave_cb);
161              end
162              this.drv_if.ACK_O <= 1'b1;
163              this.drv_if.RTY_O <= 1'b0;
164              this.drv_if.ERR_O <= 1'b0;
165              @ (this.drv_if.slave_cb);
166              this.drv_if.ACK_O <= 1'b0;
167              @(this.drv_if.slave_cb);
```

```
168                        this.drv_if.DAT_O    <= 64'bz;
169                        `uvm_do_callbacks(wb_slave,wb_slave_callbacks, post_tx(
                                this, tr))
170                        `uvm_info("SLAVE_DRIVER", "Completed transaction...",
                                UVM_LOW)
171                        seq_item_port.item_done(tr);
172                end // if
173            end //forever
174        endtask : slave_driver
```

- Line 133 creates a transaction if the driver senses a transaction occurring on its pins (lines 116-122).

- Lines 138-147 populate the transaction with all the available details.

- Line 152 assigns this new transaction to m_tr. At this point, it is picked up by the get_port() and sent to the sequencer.

- If the transaction is a write, the relevant data has been sent to the sequencer.

- If the transaction is a read, a response is required from the sequencer.

- Line 153. After sequencer is done arbitrating, a response is made available on the seq_item port.

- If the transaction is a READ transaction, the data is driven on the pins.

- Line 171 signals to the sequencer that the driver is done with the item.

- Lines 162-168 handle the wait state logic and the status of the driver.

16.1.2 Reactive Sequencer

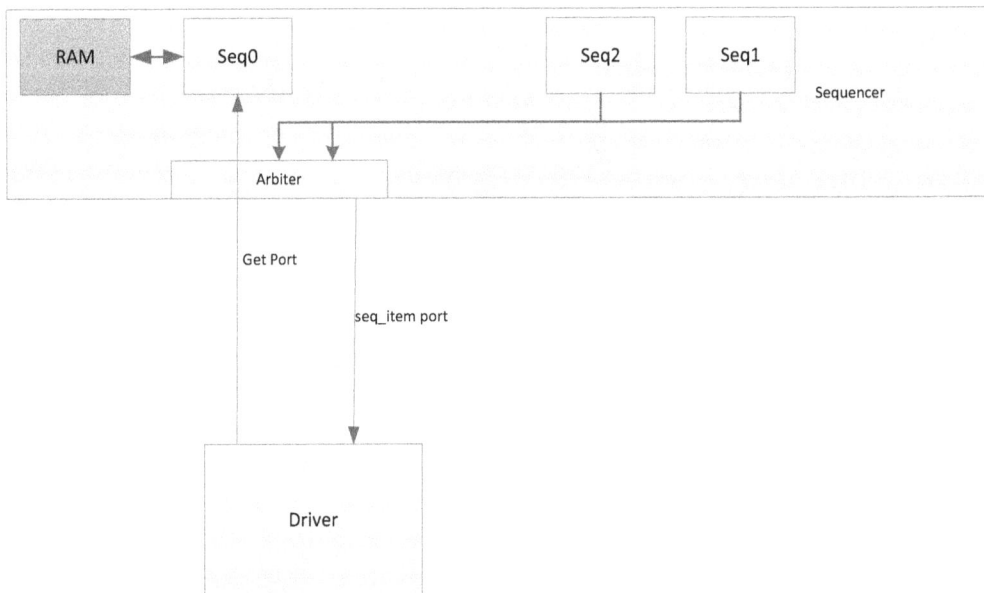

Fig. 16.4: The Reactive Slave Sequencer

The reactive sequencer uses the information from the transaction in the get port provided by the reactive driver to obtain information about an on-going transaction. To simplify the task of writing reactive sequences, the reactive sequencer provides a wait_for_req() method that will wait for a transaction to be available and blocks until a transaction is available. Once a transaction is available, it calls wait_for_grant() to arbitrate between the different reactive sequences that may be running before fetching the transaction information from the get port.

Figure 16.4 shows the sequencer with many sequences running on it. The arbiter arbitrates between the various sequences, and its seq_item_port provides the driver with a transaction as a response on the driver pins.

Listing 16.3 shows the implementation of the sequencer. In this implementation of the sequencer, a RAM has been modeled. Rather than placing the ram in a sequence, it has been kept in the sequencer so that multiple sequences can access the memory, and it acts as a shared resource. For example, you could run a sequence initially on the sequencer to fill the memory with specific content, or have the sequences respond with bad data to a range of addresses, or even corrupt the memory between some transactions.

Listing 16.3: The reactive sequencer

```
4      class wb_slave_seqr extends uvm_sequencer # (wb_transaction);
5
6          uvm_blocking_get_port #(wb_transaction) m_getp;
7
8          local bit [63:0] ram [*];
9          `uvm_component_utils(wb_slave_seqr)
10         function new (string name,
11             uvm_component parent);
12             super.new(name,parent);
13             m_getp = new("slave_get_port",this);
14             set_arbitration(UVM_SEQ_ARB_STRICT_FIFO);
15         endfunction:new
16
17         task wait_for_req(uvm_sequence_base seq, output wb_transaction req
               );
18             wait_for_grant(seq);
19             m_getp.get(req);
20         endtask
21
22         task send_rsp(uvm_sequence_base seq, wb_transaction rsp);
23             rsp.set_item_context(seq);
24             seq.finish_item(rsp);
25         endtask
26
27         function bit [63:0] read(bit [63:0] addr);
28             read = (this.ram.exists(addr)) ? this.ram[addr] : 64'bx;
29         endfunction: read
30
31         function void write(bit [63:0] addr,
32             bit [63:0] data);
33             this.ram[addr] = data;
34         endfunction: write
35
36         function void start_of_simulation_phase(uvm_phase phase);
37             integer          i;
38             super.start_of_simulation_phase(phase);
39             `uvm_info("WB_SLAVE_SEQR","Initializing memory",UVM_MEDIUM)
40             for(i = 0; i < 1000; i++) begin
41                 write(i,i * 10);
42             end
```

```
43        endfunction
44
45    endclass:wb_slave_seqr
46 `endif
```

Listing 16.3 shows the reactive sequencer with the get port in addition to the seq_item_port.

- Line 14 declares the class for the wb_slave_seqr

- Line 6 shows the additional m_getp port in the sequencer.

- Lines 10-16 show the constructor.

- Line 13 shows the get_port being created

- The arbitration mode for the sequencer is set to SEQ_ARB_STRICT_FIFO mode. This ensures that the sequencer processes transactions on a FIFO basis and not the random mode that is the default of the sequencer.

- To write a reactive sequence, a wait_for_req() method is provided on lines 17-20. The sequence will wait for a transaction to be available and return all available information so far.

- Lines 22-25 show the send_resp task that allows the transaction to be sent by the sequencer to the driver.

- Lines 27-34 show the read and write methods placed in the sequencer. Note that one could have implemented them another way using sequence persistence or other approaches. This method was chosen for simplicity.

- Lines 36-43 show the memory being initialized. Note that Memory initialization may not be needed for proper operation. However, the code between lines 36-43 places some values in the memory.

Note that start_item() is not called. The functionality of start_item() is split between the call to wait_for_grant () and set_item_context() methods.

16.1.3 The Creation of a Reactive Sequence

Rather than having the sequence generate the data items, the sequence waits for the get_port to unblock with an available transaction. The unblocking by the get port indicates that the driver has detected a transaction on the pins, and the abstract version of the transaction has been made available through the port. Listing 16.4 illustrates how this sequence is implemented.

Listing 16.4: Simple Reactive Sequence

```
38 class ram_sequence extends uvm_sequence #(wb_transaction);
39    `uvm_object_utils(ram_sequence)
40    `uvm_declare_p_sequencer(wb_slave_seqr)
41    `uvm_add_to_seq_lib(ram_sequence,wb_slave_seqr_sequence_library)
42    function new(string name = "seq_0");
43        super.new(name);
44    endfunction:new
45    virtual task body();
46        wb_transaction tr;
47        forever begin
48            p_sequencer.wait_for_req(this, tr);
49            `uvm_info(get_full_name(),$sformatf("In SLAVE SEQUENCER,
                 Transaction address = %h   kind = %s",tr.address,tr.kind.
                 name()),UVM_LOW)
50            case (tr.kind)
51                wb_transaction::WRITE: p_sequencer.write(tr.address, tr.
                     data);
```

```
52                    wb_transaction::READ: tr.data = p_sequencer.read(tr.
                         address);
53               endcase
54               tr.status = wb_transaction::ACK;
55               `uvm_info(get_full_name(),$sformatf("SLAVE SEQUENCER OUTPUT,
                    Transaction address = %h   kind = %s data = %h",tr.address,
                    tr.kind.name(), tr.data),UVM_LOW)
56               p_sequencer.send_rsp(this, tr);
57          end
58     endtask
59
60 endclass
```

- Line 45 shows the body() task at the heart of reactive sequence. this task contains a forever loop.

- Line 48 waits for a request to come on the get_port(). Until the get() unblocks, the sequence does not move forward. The unblocking of the get() method indicates a transaction is available.

- Depending on the transaction kind WRITE/READ, the sequencer's write or read tasks (from Listing 16.4, lines 50-53 in the earlier listing) are called.

- Line 54 sets the transaction status to ACK, but, depending on the sequence, it could be different.

- Line 56 sends the control back to the sequencer to send the item to the driver. The send_rsp method sets the sequence context in the item, and calls finish_item(), which enables the sequence to send the transaction to the driver and wait for it to be consumed.

Note that you could write any number of sequences depending on addresses, data, or other variables, which could customize the response of this sequencer to the stimulus.

16.1.4 The Completed Reactive Agent

The operations of the sequencer, driver, and sequence were explored in the earlier sections of this chapter. Now, the driver, sequencer must be packaged as a reusable component so that it can be used in any project. It is only required is to create an agent that instantiates the driver and the sequencer and connects them properly to create a component that is ready for use. Listing 16.5 shows the creation of the reactive agent.

Listing 16.5: Reactive Slave Agent

```
1     class wb_slave_agent extends uvm_agent;
2
3          wb_slave slv_drv;
4          wb_slave_mon slv_mon;
5          wb_slave_seqr slv_seqr;
6          typedef virtual wb_slave_if vif;
7          vif slv_agt_if;
8
9          wb_config slv_agent_cfg;
10
11         `uvm_component_utils_begin(wb_slave_agent)
12         `uvm_field_object(slv_seqr, UVM_DEFAULT)
13         `uvm_field_object(slv_drv, UVM_DEFAULT)
14         `uvm_field_object(slv_mon, UVM_DEFAULT)
15         `uvm_component_utils_end
16
17         function new(string name = "slv_agt", uvm_component parent = null)
               ;
```

```
18                      super.new(name, parent);
19              endfunction
20
21              virtual function void build_phase(uvm_phase phase);
22                      super.build_phase(phase);
23                      uvm_config_db #(wb_config)::get(this, "", "config",
                            slv_agent_cfg);
24
25                      slv_mon = wb_slave_mon::type_id::create("slv_mon", this);
26                      if (is_active == UVM_ACTIVE) begin
27                          slv_seqr = wb_slave_seqr::type_id::create("slv_seqr",this)
                                ;
28                          slv_drv = wb_slave::type_id::create("slv_drv", this);
29                          slv_drv.wb_slave_cfg  = slv_agent_cfg;
30                          slv_mon.slv_mon_cfg = slv_agent_cfg;
31                      end
32                      if (!uvm_config_db#(vif)::get(this, "", "slv_if", slv_agt_if))
                            begin
33                          `uvm_fatal("AGT/NOVIF", "No virtual interface specified
                                for this agent instance")
34                      end
35                      uvm_config_db# (vif)::set(this,"slv_drv","slv_if",slv_agt_if);
36                      uvm_config_db# (vif)::set(this,"slv_mon","mon_if",slv_agt_if);
37              endfunction: build_phase
38
39              virtual function void connect_phase(uvm_phase phase);
40                      super.connect_phase(phase);
41                      if (is_active == UVM_ACTIVE) begin
42                          slv_drv.seq_item_port.connect(slv_seqr.seq_item_export);
43                          slv_seqr.m_getp.connect(slv_drv.getp);
44                      end
45              endfunction
46
47      endclass: wb_slave_agent
```

The various components are built during the build_phase and connected during the connect_phase.

- Line 5 shows the wb_slave_agent. Lines 2-4 show various sub-components of the slave agent.

- Lines 17-19 describe the constructor.

- Lines 21-37 show the build_phase(), which is similar to the master_agent studied earlier.

- Lines 39-45 show the connections between the sequencer and the driver. Not only is the normal seq_item_port connected, but the additional get_port from the driver to the sequencer is also connected in this phase.

16.2 Other Approaches to the Reactive Agent

There are many other alternative methods for creating reactive agents. One approach uses the analysis port on the monitor to tell the sequencer about the incoming transaction on the interface. This is shown in the figure below. The sequencer runs sequences similar to the earlier approach, and one may be able to use some commercial VIP components in case the protocol is quite complex.

This may look to be an attractive proposition; it does involve a little more work and has some other tradeoffs. A comparison of the two based on our opinion is provided in Table 16.1. Make your decisions based on the tradeoffs in your specific situation.

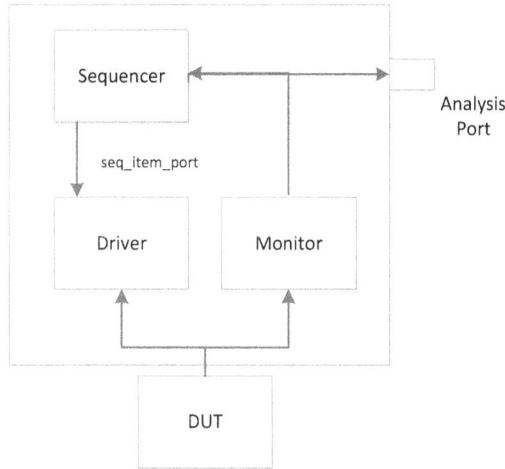

Fig. 16.5: Another Approach To A Reactive Agent

Using a Driver with a get port	Using Analysis ports on the monitor.
The driver will send a transaction to the sequencer as soon as it can detect as much as it can	You may be able to leverage some VIP components. However, you may also be constrained by the timing in which the transaction is available to the sequencer. The monitor may not put out a transaction until the transaction is complete
Coupling with the Sequencer is tight.	Loose coupling.
Driver mimics part of the monitor functionality. Complexity is limited to the driver.	monitor becomes a little more complicated. Not only does it need to report partial transactions if you use the analysis port, but also complete transactions. Since there is more than one transaction on the analysis port, every component connected to the analysis port must be aware of what happens.
The driver has two sets of ports to connect to the sequencer. The monitor has its analysis port	sequencer has two ports. One port connects to the driver, and the other is an analysis port that connects to the monitor.
Callbacks may be placed at specific points in the driver. It is all contained in one callback class attached to one component.	Remember that you have two different components in this agent. You will have to figure out where the callback is going and what it can do. When you see the messages from the agent, realize that one set of messages is coming from the driver, and another set of messages is coming from the monitor when you're debugging.

Table 16.1: Using a driver versus using a monitor

Chapter 17
Advanced Register Concepts

This chapter is the third in a series of chapters discussing the UVM register portion of the library. Chapter 12 presented an overview of the register abstraction classes. Chapter 20 presented details on how to integrate a register model into the environment and provided details of various kinds of predictors and tests built into RAL. This chapter now covers additional advanced topics in register modeling. You must explore the discussions presented in the earlier chapters *first*. You need that background material to completely understand the material presented in this chapter and explore the following areas:

- Field access policies and their effect on register model operations.

- Various register types in the register model

- The effect of various operations on the various register types

- Factory replacement of various registers in register model

- Callback facilities in the register model

17.1 Example DUT

A DUT with all the register types, and a register model and its associated environment, are essential to explore the register model features in depth. However, the challenge is that not all the register types are usually supported in a single core. Many cores have only a subset of the capabilities that are available using the register model. An example DUT has been provided to explore these additional features. It is based on a wishbone slave built with the various register policies. The DUT incorporates a wishbone slave interface and an address decoder along with a collection of registers at various offsets that incorporate the respective register/field policy.

(i) Note that the implementation of the RTL in the DUT is only ONE of many possible implementations. Conceptually, this chapter provides a platform that you can modify to learn about the UVM register library. Feel free to modify the RTL to add your features to the RTL and see how the model behaves with this example.

Refer to Table 17.1 for the exact registers implemented in the design.

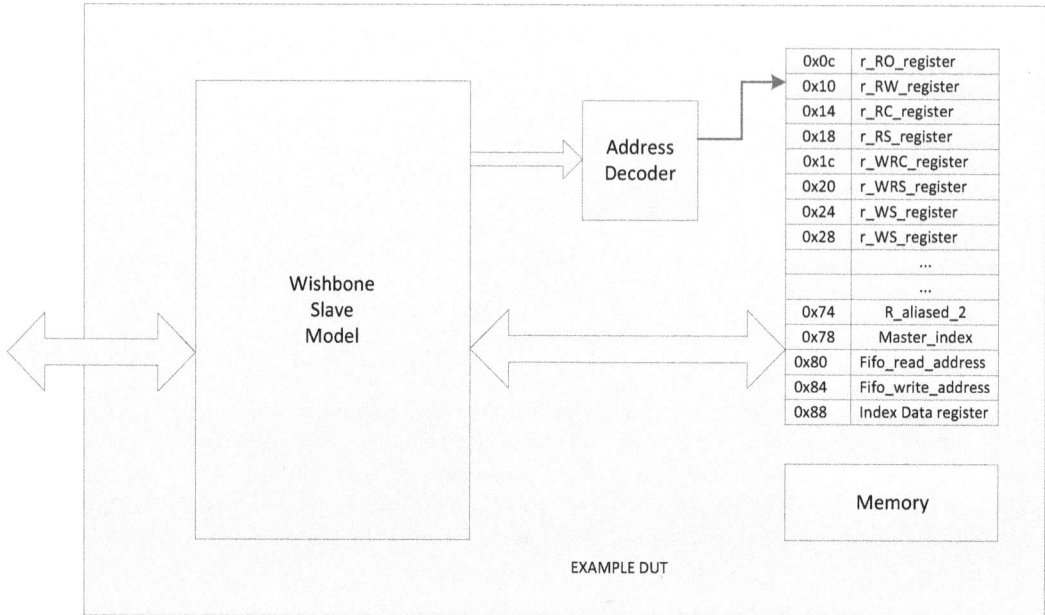

Fig. 17.1: Example DUT

17.2 Verification Environment for the DUT

Figure 17.2 shows the block diagram of the verification environment built for the DUT. It incorporates a wishbone master agent; a register model created using RALGEN©. A register adapter is created and connected to the master agent. An independent predictor has been connected to the monitor so that the predictions from the master agent monitor are fed into the register model. Refer to Section 20.1 for the various steps that have taken to integrate the register model into the environment.

Table 17.1: Various register Types in Example DUT

Address	Register Name	Policy	Description
0x0c	r_RO_register	**RO**	Read Only
0x10	r_RW_register	**RW**	Read, Write
0x14	r_RC_register	**RC**	Read Clears All
0x18	r_RS_register	**RS**	Read Sets All
0x1c	r_WRC_register	**WRC**	Write, Read Clears All
0x20	r_WRS_register	**WRS**	Write, Read Sets All
0x24	r_WC_register	**WC**	Write Clears All
0x28	r_WS_register	**WS**	Write Sets All
0x2c	r_WSRC_register	**WSRC**	Write Sets All, Read Clears All
0x30	r_WCRS_register	**WCRS**	Write Clears All, Read Sets All
0x34	r_W1C_register	**W1C**	Write 1 to Clear
0x38	r_W1S_register	**W1S**	Write 1 to Set
0x3c	r_W1T_register	**W1T**	Write 1 to Toggle
0x40	r_W0C_register	**W0C**	Write 0 to Clear
0x44	r_W0S_register	**W0S**	Write 0 to Set
0x48	r_W0T_register	**W0T**	Write 0 to Toggle
0x4c	r_W1SRC_register	**W1SRC**	Write 1 to Set, Read Clears All
0x50	r_W1CRS_register	**W1CRS**	Write 1 to Clear, Read Sets All
0x54	r_W0SRC_register	**W0SRC**	Write 0 to Set, Read Clears All
0x58	r_W0CRS_register	**W0CRS**	Write 0 to Clear, Read Sets All
0x5c	r_WO_register	**WO**	Write Only
0x60	r_WOC_register	**WOC**	Write Only Clears All
0x64	r_WOS_register	**WOS**	Write Only Sets All
0x68	r_W1_register	**W1**	Write Once
0x6c	r_WO1_register	**WO1**	Write Only, Once
0x70	r_aliased_1		register to show aliasing
0x74	r_aliased_2		register to show aliasing
0x78	master_index		Index register
0x80	Fifo_read_address		Fifo register read address
0x84	Fifo_write_address		Fifo register Write address
0x88	Index Data register		Data for read/write from Index register

17.2.1 Master Agent Sequence

To learn the effects of each operation on the registers, a simple sequence is developed. This sequence runs on the master agent's sequencer and does many reads/writes/get/peek/poke operations for each register. After each operation is complete, the sequence displays the value it obtained using the `uvm_info macro. This sequence is shown in Listing 17.1 below.

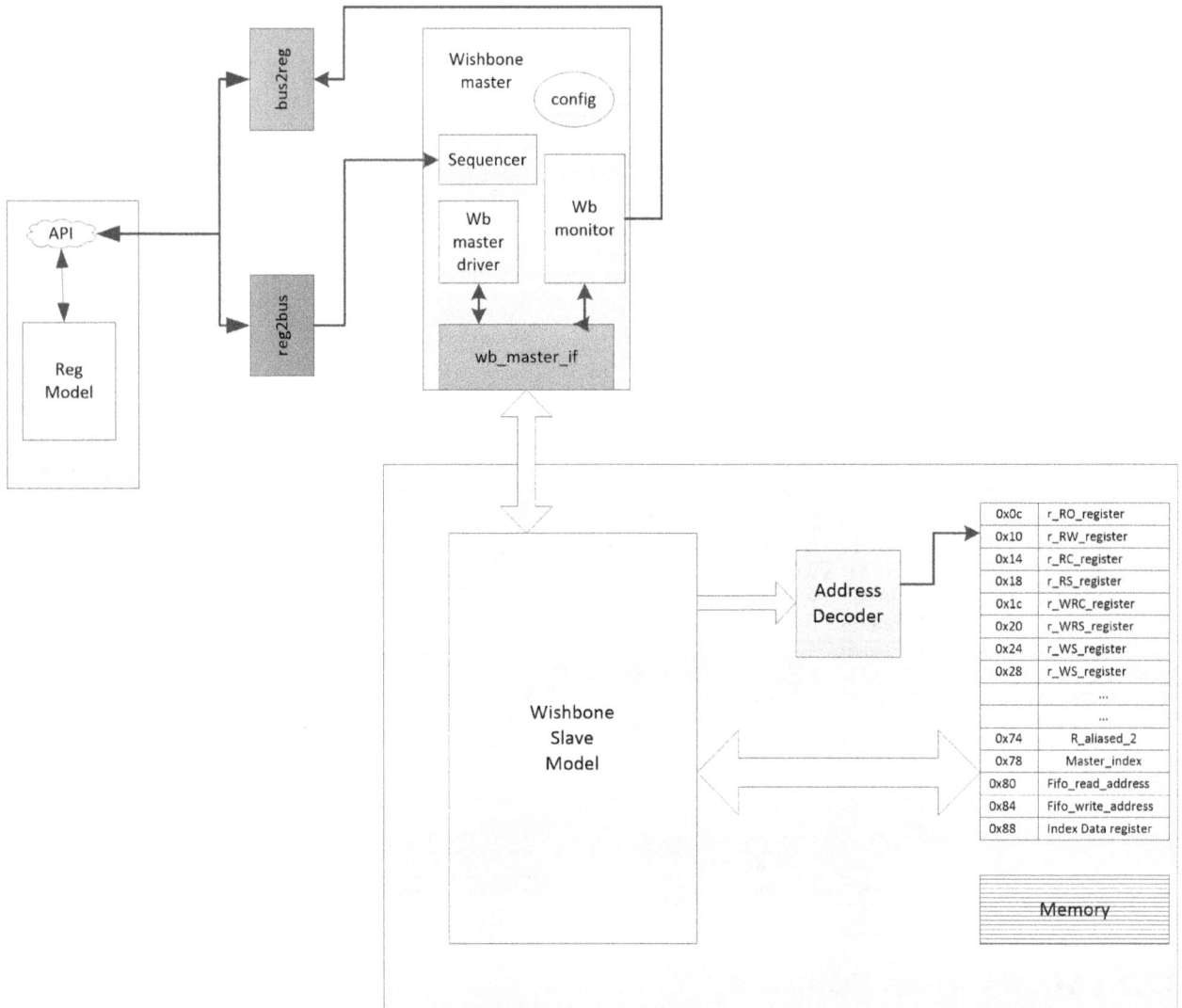

Fig. 17.2: Verification Environment for the example DUT

Listing 17.1: Simple DUT sequence for registers

```
130 class uvm_reg_single_all_access_seq_resdb extends uvm_reg_sequence #(
        uvm_sequence #(uvm_reg_item));
131
132     // Variable: rg
133     // The register to be tested
134     uvm_reg rg;
135     ral_block_simple_ral_env regmodel;
136     string regname_string;
137
138     uvm_status_e status;
139     uvm_reg_data_t  read_val, write_val, set_val, mirror_val, get_val,
            peek_val, poke_val;
140     uvm_reg_data_t  peek_bkup_1, read_bkup1;
141
142     `uvm_object_utils(uvm_reg_single_all_access_seq_resdb)
```

```
143
144    function new(string name="uvm_reg_single_access_seq");
145        super.new(name);
146    endfunction
147
148    task body() ;
149        string s1;
150
151        uvm_resource_db#(string)::read_by_name("reg_seq","regname_string",
               regname_string,this);
152
153        rg = regmodel.get_reg_by_name(regname_string);
154        write_val = 32'hdeadbeef;
155        set_val = 32'hbeefdead;
156        poke_val = 32'haaaabbbb;
157
158        if(rg == null) `uvm_fatal(get_full_name(),{regname_string ,"
               register not found"})
159
160        rg.peek(.status(status), .value(peek_val), .parent(this));
161        `uvm_info("reg_single_all_access_seq_resdb" , $sformatf("Status
               was %s when performing peek() from %s peek_value = %x",status.
               name(), rg.get_full_name(),peek_val),UVM_LOW)
162
163        rg.poke(.status(status), .value(poke_val), .parent(this));
164        `uvm_info("reg_single_all_access_seq_resdb" , $sformatf("Status
               was %s when performing poke() from %s poke_value = %x",status.
               name(), rg.get_full_name(),poke_val),UVM_LOW)
165
166        rg.peek(.status(status), .value(peek_val),  .parent(this));
167        `uvm_info("reg_single_all_access_seq_resdb" , $sformatf("Status
               was %s when performing peek() from %s peek_value = %x",status.
               name(), rg.get_full_name(),peek_val),UVM_LOW)
168
169        rg.read(.status(status), .value(read_val), .path(UVM_FRONTDOOR),
               .parent(this));
170        `uvm_info("reg_single_all_access_seq_resdb" , $sformatf("Status
               was %s when performing read() from %s read_value = %x",status.
               name(), rg.get_full_name(),read_val),UVM_LOW)
171
172        rg.peek(.status(status), .value(peek_val),   .parent(this));
173        `uvm_info("reg_single_all_access_seq_resdb" , $sformatf("Status
               was %s when performing peek() from %s peek_value = %x",status.
               name(), rg.get_full_name(),peek_val),UVM_LOW)
174
175        rg.write(.status(status), .value(write_val), .path(UVM_BACKDOOR),
               .parent(this));
176        `uvm_info("reg_single_all_access_seq_resdb" , $sformatf("Status
               was %s when performing FRONTDOOR write() from %s write_value =
               %x",status.name(), rg.get_full_name(),write_val),UVM_LOW)
177
178        rg.peek(.status(status), .value(peek_val),    .parent(this));
```

```
179        `uvm_info("reg_single_all_access_seq_resdb" , $sformatf("Status
              was %s when performing peek() from %s peek_value = %x",status.
              name(), rg.get_full_name(),peek_val),UVM_LOW)
180
181        rg.poke(.status(status), .value(poke_val), .parent(this));
182        `uvm_info("reg_single_all_access_seq_resdb" , $sformatf("Status
              was %s when performing poke() from %s poke_value = %x",status.
              name(), rg.get_full_name(),poke_val),UVM_LOW)
183        mirror_val = rg.get_mirrored_value();
184        `uvm_info(get_full_name(),$sformatf("BEFORE Read Value : %08h\
              nWrite Value %08h \nSet Value: %08h\n MirrorValue:%08h\n
              GetValue : %08h\n", read_val, write_val, set_val, mirror_val,
              get_val),UVM_LOW);
185
186        rg.read(.status(status), .value(read_val), .path(UVM_BACKDOOR), .
              parent(this));
187        `uvm_info("reg_single_all_access_seq_resdb" , $sformatf("Status
              was %s when performing BACKDOOR read() from %s read_value = %x
              ",status.name(), rg.get_full_name(),read_val),UVM_LOW)
188
189        rg.write(.status(status), .value(write_val), .path(UVM_BACKDOOR),
              .parent(this));
190        `uvm_info("reg_single_all_access_seq_resdb" , $sformatf("Status
              was %s when performing BACKDOOR WRITE() from %s write_value = %
              x",status.name(), rg.get_full_name(),write_val),UVM_LOW)
191
192        rg.read(.status(status), .value(read_val), .path(UVM_BACKDOOR), .
              parent(this));
193        `uvm_info("reg_single_all_access_seq_resdb" , $sformatf("Status
              was %s when performing BACKDOOR READ() from %s write_value = %x
              ",status.name(), rg.get_full_name(),read_val),UVM_LOW)
194
195        rg.peek(.status(status), .value(peek_val),    .parent(this));
196        `uvm_info("reg_single_all_access_seq_resdb" , $sformatf("Status
              was %s when performing peek() from %s peek_value = %x",status.
              name(), rg.get_full_name(),peek_val),UVM_LOW)
197        // mirror_val =   rg.get_mirrored_value("r_R_field");
198        `uvm_info(get_full_name(),$sformatf("AFTER Read Value : %08h\
              nWrite Value %08h \nSet Value: %08h\n MirrorValue:%08h\n
              GetValue : %08h\n", read_val, write_val, set_val, mirror_val,
              get_val),UVM_LOW);
199        //  `uvm_info("reg_single_all_access_seq_resdb_resdb" , {"
              Mirrored value was : ", $sformatf("%d",rg.get_mirrored_value())
              }, UVM_LOW)
200    endtask
201
202 endclass
```

The above listing (partially shown above) illustrates the various actions that occur for each register. A number of peek()/poke()/read()/write() operations are performed in a sequence. After each operation, the value is printed to the log file. You can alter the order of these methods and study the behavior of the different register types. The effect of these register policies are explored in the next section.

17.3 Effect of Register Operations on Various Field Access Policies

The UVM RAL library contains pre-defined field access policies. These policies are built-in by default and cover some aspects of commonly used field policies that are in use in contemporary designs with callbacks and hooks; one can build a register model that mirrors accurately the mechanism that is represented in the DUT. The use of various callback mechanisms is discussed in Section 17.5

Table 17.3 provides a summary of the various field access policies available for the UVM register types. Depending on the type of field/register, the access policy, and the corresponding operation, different values are seen in the various copies of the register model and the DUT.

Some of the values in the table in some cases may be *specific to the sequence* (peek/poke/write/read order sequence in a test). If a write/read occurs to a special register (W0/R0/W1T/W0T, etc.), our DUT will perform the special operation on the negative edge of the clock. The mirror and other values, however, *may be updated right away*. You could modify the RTL to have the behavior based on your preferences. I have tried to keep the spirit of the DUT implementation as close as possible to typical RTL implementations and match the intent of the register types. You should be able to modify to reflect this RTL fairly easily.

Table 17.2: Read Policies and their operations

Access Policy	Description	Write	read	Read-back Value	peek	poke	get	set	get_mirror	update
RO	Read Only	No effect.	No effect.	Note 1	Note 1	depends on access	Note 2	Note 7	Note 1	undefined
RW	Read, Write	Note 5	No effect.	Note 1	Note 1	Note 5	Note 2	Note 7	Note 1	sync
RC	Read Clears All	No effect.	Sets all bits to 0's.	Note 1	Note 1	Note 5	Note 2	Note 7	Note 1	Note 3
RS	Read Sets All	No effect.	Sets all bits to 1's.	Note 1	Note 1	Note 5	Note 2	Note 7	Note 1	Note 3

Note 1 Current Value
Note 2 Current Value in Model
Note 3 Depends on Back/Frontdoor access
Note 4 Undefined
Note 5 Changed to Poke Value
Note 6 Unchanged
Note 7 Set value in model

Table 17.3: Write Policies with various operations

Access Policy	Description	Write	read	Readbk	peek	poke	get	set	get_mirror	update
WRC	Write, Read Clears All	Note 5	Sets all bits to 0's.	Note 1	Note 1	Note 5	Note 2	Note 7	Note 1	Note 3
WRS	Write, Read Sets All	Note 5	Sets all bits to 1's.	Note 1	Note 1	Note 5	Note 2	Note 7	Note 1	Note 3
WC	Write Clears All	Sets all bits to 0's.	No effect.	Note 1	Note 1	Note 5	Note 2	Note 7	Note 1	Note 3
WS	Write Sets All	Sets all bits to 1's.	No effect.	Note 1	Note 1	Note 5	Note 2	Note 7	Note 1	Note 3
WSRC	Write Sets All, Read Clears All	Sets all bits to 1's.	Sets all bits to 0's.	Note 1	Note 1	Note 5	Note 2	Note 7	Note 1	Note 3
WCRS	Write Clears All, Read Sets All	Sets all bits to 0's.	Sets all bits to 1's.	Note 1	Note 1	Note 5	Note 2	Note 7	Note 1	Note 3
W1C	Write 1 to Clear	Clear any bit set to 1	No effect.	Note 1	Note 1	Note 5	Note 2	Note 7	Note 1	Note 3
W1S	Write 1 to Set	Set any bit set to 1	No effect.	Note 1	Note 1	Note 5	Note 2	Note 7	Note 1	Note 3
W1T	Write 1 to Toggle	Toggle any bit set to 1	No effect.	Note 1	Note 1	Note 5	Note 2	Note 7	Note 1	Note 3
W0C	Write 0 to Clear	Clear any bit set to 0	No effect.	Note 1	Note 1	Note 5	Note 2	Note 7	Note 1	Note 3
W0S	Write 0 to Set	Set any bit set to 0 (opposite of W1S)	No effect.	Note 1	Note 1	Note 5	Note 2	Note 7	Note 1	Note 3
W0T	Write 0 to Toggle	Clear any bit set to 0 (opposite of W1T)	No effect.	Note 1	Note 1	Note 5	Note 2	Note 7	Note 1	Note 3
W1SRC	Write 1 to Set, Read Clears All	leave alone if bit = 1	Sets all bits to 0's.	Note 1	Note 1	Note 5	Note 2	Note 7	Note 1	Note 3
W1CRS	Write 1 to Clear, Read Sets All	clear any bit set to 1	Sets all bits to 1's.	Note 1	Note 1	Note 5	Note 2	Note 7	Note 1	Note 3
W0SRC	Write 0 to Set, Read Clears All	If the bit in the written value is a 0, the corresponding bit in the field is set to 1. Otherwise, the field bit is not affected.	Sets all bits to 0's.	Note 1	Note 1	Note 5	Note 2	Note 7	Note 1	Note 3
W0CRS	Write 0 to Clear, Read Sets All	If the bit in the written value is a 0, the corresponding bit in the field is set to 0. Otherwise, the field bit is not affected.	Sets all bits to 1's.	Note 1	Note 1	Note 5	Note 2	Note 7	Note 1	Note 3
WO	Write Only	Note 5	No effect.	Undefined	Undefined	Note 5	Note 2	Note 7	Undefined	Note 3
WOC	Write Only Clears All	Sets all bits to 0's.	No effect.	Undefined	Undefined	Note 5	Note 2	Note 7	Undefined	Note 3
WOS	Write Only Sets All	Sets all bits to 1's.	No effect.	Undefined	Undefined	Note 5	Note 2	Note 7	Undefined	Note 3
W1	Write Once	Changed to written value if this is the first write operation after a hard reset. Otherwise, has no effect.	No effect.	Note 1	Note 1	Note 5	Note 2	Note 7	Note 1	Note 3
WO1	Write Only, Once	Changed to written value if this is the first write operation after a hard reset. Otherwise, has no effect.	No effect.	Undefined	Undefined	Note 5	Note 2	Note 7	Undefined	Note 3

* Please check the implementation of your DUT for the undefined values in get_mirror().

Note 1 Current Value
Note 2 Current Value in Model
Note 3 Depends on Back/Frontdoor access
Note 4 Undefined
Note 5 Changed to Poke Value
Note 6 Unchanged
Note 7 Set value in model

17.4 Customizing Register Models

The UVM RAL flow, as described in Figure 12.1 shows the code generated from an abstracted specification. Naturally, users would like to customize the register models depending on their needs. The figure below indicates the best practices when customizing the register model.

Recommendation 17.4.0:   *Modify the specification that is used to generate the register model to allow you to generate the desired output from a tool.* RAL Generator

The register specification is usually is used for multiple purposes, be it documentation or C firmware code generation. Staying at an abstract level allows you to make use of features in the generator to simplify testing. You can use any number of generators either provided by CAD vendor, or your own, depending on the need.

Sometimes it is not possible for the generator to create the appropriate model. In such instances, use the factory approach (see Section 17.5.1) if you are making global changes, or add callbacks that offer fine grain control (see Section 17.5). Doing so will allow the user to keep most of the flow intact.

Do NOT edit the code that is produced by the generator. When you make a change to the code generated by the generator, you find that whatever you did is effectively wiped out the moment a new run from the generator is required should the specification change. Maintenance becomes a problem when the output code of the generator is edited.

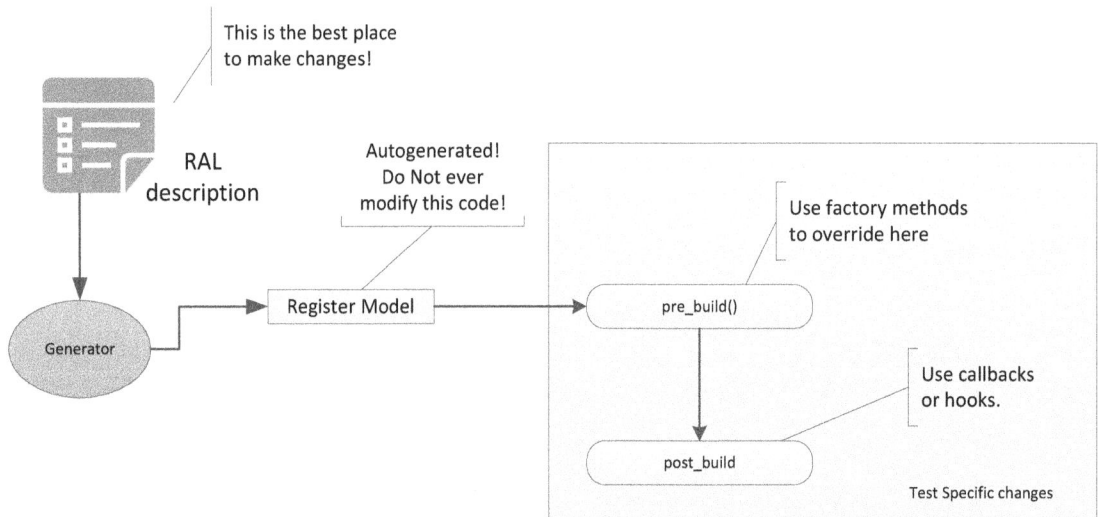

Fig. 17.3: Opportunities to customize a RAL Model

17.5 Hooks and Callback Facilities in Register Models

The UVM register model is generated from an abstract description, as shown in the previous chapters. The class library also provides a few hooks and callback mechanisms to allow customizing the behavior of the model over and above what is presented in the library classes. Often, most of the provided policies are not enough to complete the verification activity. It is often necessary to model some behavior that is not covered by the UVM built-in models.

The register and field classes provide a set of empty virtual methods. These methods are called hooks. These methods are called at specific points during register operations. These methods are:

- pre_write()

- post_write()

- pre_read

- post_read()

You can modify any of the register data or do anything (modify status, readback/write values etc) in any of these methods[1].

Listing 17.2: A Simple register Extension

```
1    // class simple_WR_extension extends uvm_reg;
2  class simple_WR_extension extends ral_reg_simple_ral_env_r_RW_register;
3    rand uvm_reg_field r_RW_field;
4
5    function new(string name = "simple_ral_env_r_RW_register");
6       super.new(name);
7    endfunction: new
8    virtual function void build();
9       this.r_RW_field = uvm_reg_field::type_id::create("r_RW_field",,
           get_full_name());
10      this.r_RW_field.configure(this, 15, 0, "RW", 0, 15'h10, 1, 0, 1);
11   endfunction: build
12
13   `uvm_object_utils(simple_WR_extension)
14
15
16   virtual task pre_write( uvm_reg_item  rw);
17      `uvm_info(get_full_name(), $sformatf("calling task pre_write with
           value %h",rw.value[0]),UVM_LOW)
18   endtask
19
20
21   virtual task post_write(uvm_reg_item   rw);
22      `uvm_info(get_full_name(), $sformatf("calling task post_write() with
           value %h",rw.value[0]),UVM_LOW)
23   endtask
24
25   virtual task pre_read( uvm_reg_item  rw);
26      `uvm_info(get_full_name(), $sformatf("calling task pre_read() with
           value %h",rw.value[0]),UVM_LOW)
27   endtask
28   virtual task post_read(uvm_reg_item   rw);
29      `uvm_info(get_full_name(), $sformatf("calling task post_read() with
           value %h",rw.value[0]),UVM_LOW)
```

---

[1] In addition to the concepts and discussions presented in this chapter, please see the paper from Mark Litterick and others [17].

```
30    endtask
31
32 endclass : simple_WR_extension
```

In the above listing, we call a `uvm_info method is called to print out on the display, This extension class can be used to observe and learn how the code can impact the different access policies in the hooks.

17.5.1 Factory Replacement for RAL Registers

In order to test our simple class extension, we use the factory's capabilities.

Listing 17.3: Factory replacement of RAL registers

```
1  class simple_reg_access_test_factory extends simple_ral_env_test;
2
3    `uvm_component_utils(simple_reg_access_test_factory)
4    uvm_reg_data_t value_w;
5    uvm_reg_data_t value_r;
6    uvm_reg rg;
7    uvm_status_e status;
8    uvm_reg_single_all_access_seq_resdb m_reg_access_seq;
9
10
11   uvm_coreservice_t cs = uvm_coreservice_t::get();
12   uvm_factory f = cs.get_factory();
13
14   function new(string name, uvm_component parent);
15     super.new(name, parent);
16   endfunction
17
18   virtual function void build_phase(uvm_phase phase);
19     super.build_phase(phase);
20     f.set_type_override_by_type(ral_reg_simple_ral_env_r_RW_register::
          get_type(),simple_WR_extension::get_type(),1);
21   endfunction
22
23   task run_phase(uvm_phase phase) ;
24     uvm_objection phase_done;
25     value_w = 32'h12345678;
26     phase.raise_objection(this);
27
28     uvm_resource_db #(string)::set("reg_seq","regname_string","
          r_RW_register",this);
29     m_reg_access_seq = new("m_reg_access_seq");
30     m_reg_access_seq.regmodel = env.regmodel;
31     m_reg_access_seq.start(null);
32     m_reg_access_seq.wait_for_sequence_state(UVM_FINISHED);
33
34     phase_done = phase.get_objection();
35     phase_done.set_drain_time(this,2000);
36     phase.drop_objection(this);
37   endtask
38 endclass : simple_reg_access_test_factory
```

- Line 20 in the above listing shows the factory replacement of the r_RW register class with the simple_WR_extension class.

- Line 23 shows the main phase of the test. This test now uses the r_RW register which was replaced in the test.

17.5.2 Register Callbacks

There are some situations where it is useful to perform some actions that are based on a register operation, or customize register mirror values based on DUT behavior. To do so, use hooks and callbacks in the register model. The nature of the actual operation may be user-defined. Some examples of when to use callbacks are:

1. Quirky registers – register cleared on 3rd read (or some count).

2. Registers whose write has side effects. An example is writing something that sets a bit in some other register.

3. Aliased register: When one register is written, another register takes a new value.

4. Changing a prediction based on your algorithm.

5. Making a write to one register add a write to some other register via backdoor/poke, etc.

In addition to this functionality, the UVM classes provide the means to use many callbacks. These callbacks are derived from uvm_reg_cbs;. The following methods are defined in the class:

```
virtual task pre_write(uvm_reg_item rw) ;
virtual task post_write(uvm_reg_item rw);
virtual task pre_read(uvm_reg_item rw);
virtual task post_read(uvm_reg_item rw);
virtual task post_predict(uvm_reg_item rw);
virtual function encode(ref uvm_reg_data_t data[]);
virtual function decode(ref uvm_reg_data_t data[]);
```

17.5.2.1 Step 1: Create the Callback with the Appropriate Tasks

You can have as many callback classes as one desires and pass in values you think are appropriate. For example, a constructor for the class can have some values that are used by the callbacks.

Listing 17.4: RAL Callback example

```
1
2 class simple_reg_field_cb extends uvm_reg_cbs;
3
4    virtual task pre_write(  uvm_reg_item  rw);
5       `uvm_info(get_full_name(), $sformatf("calling task inside callback
            pre_write with value %h",rw.value[0]),UVM_LOW)
6    endtask
7
8    virtual task post_write(uvm_reg_item   rw);
9       rw.value[0] = 32'h0000ffff;
10      `uvm_info(get_full_name(), $sformatf("calling task inside callback
            post_write() with value %h",rw.value[0]),UVM_LOW)
11   endtask
12
13   virtual task pre_read( uvm_reg_item  rw);
14      `uvm_info(get_full_name(), $sformatf("calling task inside callback
            pre_read() with value %h",rw.value[0]),UVM_LOW)
15   endtask
16   virtual task post_read(uvm_reg_item   rw);
```

```
17        `uvm_info(get_full_name(), $sformatf("calling task inside callback
              post_read() with value %h",rw.value[0]),UVM_LOW)
18     endtask
19     virtual function void post_predict( input uvm_reg_field fld, input
           uvm_reg_data_t previous,
20                   inout uvm_reg_data_t value, input uvm_predict_e kind, input
                         uvm_path_e path, input uvm_reg_map map);
21
22        `uvm_info(get_full_name(), $sformatf("calling task inside callback
              post_predict() with previous value %h , current : %h predict kind
              %s",value,previous,kind.name()),UVM_LOW)
23
24     endfunction
25     function new(string name="simple_reg_field_cb");
26        super.new();
27     endfunction
```

The listing shows a collection of callbacks for the registers. During the post_write task, the value of the register is set to 32`h0000ffff; The concept is similar to that in Chapter 9 and is not discussed in detail here.

17.5.2.2 Step 2: Add the Callback to the test
The above callback can then be created and attached to the register.

Listing 17.5: RAL Callback and Factory example

```
1  class simple_reg_access_test_callback_test extends simple_ral_env_test;
2
3     `uvm_component_utils(simple_reg_access_test_callback_test)
4     uvm_reg_data_t value_w;
5     uvm_reg_data_t value_r;
6     uvm_reg rg;
7     uvm_status_e status;
8     uvm_reg_single_all_access_seq_resdb m_reg_access_seq;
9     simple_reg_field_cb my_cb  ;
10
11    uvm_coreservice_t cs = uvm_coreservice_t::get();
12    uvm_factory f = cs.get_factory();
13
14    function new(string name, uvm_component parent);
15       super.new(name, parent);
16    endfunction
17
18    virtual function void build_phase(uvm_phase phase);
19       super.build_phase(phase);
20       my_cb = new("simple_reg_field_cb");
21    endfunction
22
23    function void start_of_simulation_phase(uvm_phase phase);
24       super.start_of_simulation_phase(phase);
25       uvm_reg_field_cb::add(env.regmodel.r_RW_register.r_RW_field,my_cb);
26    endfunction
```

The concepts are similar to those covered in Chapter 9. Lines 23 and 25 are the noteworthy items in this listing.

17.6 Summary

A number of callbacks and effect of register operations were covered in this chapter. Although the implementation of some of the field access policies in your RTL may be different, the results will be in line with to information presented in Tables 17.3 and 17.2 because the operations are abstracted. If you have additional policies that are **not** covered by the built in policies, you have a few options:

1. Use callbacks as described in this chapter if you can do so. You will only need to define a few methods and in my opinion, this is a preferred option. You still can leverage subsequent versions of the library because your customizations are independent of the library.

2. If the above option is not viable, create your own variant after copying the uvm_reg_field.svh and modifying it. You can include this file seperately in your compilation, as long as you can modify your register generator to use this file instead of the class built into UVM. This way, you leave the rest of the library intact and can easily migrate to another version of UVM if needed.

3. Copy out the library and add your behavior to uvm_reg_field.svh - This is an invasive step. Use this as a last resort if the above two options are infeasible. It appears that you may not be able to override the class because some of the methods and properties are *local* not *protected*. You also lose all ability to migrate easily because you need to keep maintaining *the entire library*. This also prevents the simulator vendor from providing you with performance optimizations and bug fixes since they have to do more work to optimize your specific code.

Chapter 18

A Primer for UVM Config DB Regular Expressions

Regular Expressions in UVM form one of the most challenging topics in UVM API to date. Multiple challenges deter widespread adoption of regular expressions. Regular expressions are not easily understood. Also, UVM implementation of the POSIX regular expression standard has many escaped characters. Using the wrong character here or there may need to undesired results. This chapter attempts to shed some light on these expressions so that you can use them in your work. A series of examples on how to use expressions by setting values in the config_db database and seeing their effects on various field values are explored.

In simple terms, a regular expression is a pattern describing a certain amount of text. Their name comes from the mathematical theory on which they are based. You will usually find it being abbreviated to "regex" or "regexp" in various literature online and in books. The regexp is a shorthand way of expressing a pattern in the text.

UVM allows for a regular expression syntax to set values in the config and resource databases. The regular expression syntax is quite powerful and can save you a lot of time if it is desired to set the values in many components at once.

UVM supports a POSIX-style extended regular expression syntax, and some characters are escaped as part of the syntax which is described below with a few examples. To understand the syntax a little better, consider a few basic component classes. These classes have some properties which are set by the component's apply_config_settings() method when the components are created.

Just be aware that using regular expressions is a simulation performance hit. The UVM source code provides documentation in the comments about how the regular expression is converted into globs and stored. See the source code if you want to understand the whole flow in the code. The DPI functions wind up creating the regular expression glob after compiling the expression and then only storing the values in the database. The following sections cover only the application of regular expressions in code as that is of more practical use to verification engineers.

The examples in this chapter use uvm_component classes for clarity. However, nothing prevents you from using them in config_db calls with sequences and other classes in your work on UVM. They should work as long as you set the context and other fields correctly.

18.1 Component Classes

A simple component class C as shown below in Listing 18.1

```
4 class C extends uvm_component;
5    int v=0;
6    int s=0;
7
8    function new(string name, uvm_component parent);
9        super.new(name, parent);
10   endfunction
11
12   function void build_phase(uvm_phase phase);
13       super.build_phase(phase);
14   endfunction
15
16   `uvm_component_utils_begin(C)
17       `uvm_field_int(v, UVM_DEFAULT)
18       `uvm_field_int(s, UVM_DEFAULT)
19   `uvm_component_utils_end
20
21 endclass
```

- Component C contains two properties for two integers called v and s.

- Lines 5 and 6 declare the two properties.

- Lines 17 and 18 show the use of the UVM macros with these properties. All automation is provided by these macros.

Component Class A now instantiates 4 copies of this component C as seen in listing below.

```
4 class A extends uvm_component;
5    bit debug = 0;
6    C u1;
7    C u2;
8    C u3;
9    C u4;
10   int s;
11   `uvm_component_utils_begin(A)
12       `uvm_field_int(debug, UVM_DEFAULT)
13       `uvm_field_int(s, UVM_DEFAULT)
14   `uvm_component_utils_end
15
16   function new(string name, uvm_component parent);
17       super.new(name, parent);
18   endfunction
19
20   function void build_phase(uvm_phase phase);
21       super.build_phase(phase);
22       uvm_config_db #(uvm_bitstream_t)::set(this,"*","v",7);
23
24       u1 = new("u1", this);
25       u2 = new("u2", this);
```

```
26          u3 = new("u3", this);
27          u4 = new("u4", this);
28      endfunction
29 endclass
```

- Lines 6-9 show that Class A has four instances of Class C.

- Line 20 shows the build_phase for this component. During the build_phase, all the child components are constructed.

- Line 22 shows the property v of the child components u1,u2,u3,u4 being set to 7 using the wildcard. Note that the uvm_config_db has "this" as the context.

- Lines 24 - 28 show the child components being built. These components now call apply_config_settings as a part of their build_phases.

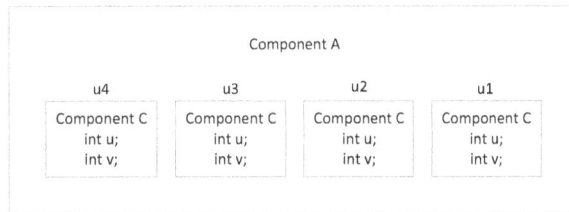

Fig. 18.1: Component Class A With Component C Instances

The top-level environment now instantiates many these components in the topenv class. To keep the listing simple, we present a graphical view of the instances in the top env class. The listing also contains a few display statements that print the values of the properties of instance u1, which is not shown in the listing. Each of the instances in Figure 18.2 is an instance of class A in the top-level environment. Each instance of class A contains four instances of class C as shown in Listing 18.1. Each instance is named separately as seen in the Figure 18.2.

The top-level module has an initial block where we will use some regular expressions.

```
instB = new("instB", this);
instD = new("instD",this);

for(int i = 0; i < 5; i++) begin
 inst_arr[i] = new($sformatf("inst%02d",i),this);
end
for(int i = 5; i < 10; i++) begin
 inst_arr[i] = new($sformatf("tom%02d",i),this);
end
for(int i = 10; i < 12; i++) begin
 inst_arr[i] = new($sformatf("tomm%02d",i),this);
end
for(int i = 12; i < 14; i++) begin
 inst_arr[i] = new($sformatf("tommm%02d",i),this);
end
for(int i = 14; i < 15; i++) begin
 inst_arr[i] = new($sformatf("tommmm%02d",i),this);
end

inst_arr[15] = new($sformatf("tomm%02d",15),this);
inst_arr[16] = new($sformatf("tommommomm%02d",16),this);
inst_arr[17] = new($sformatf("tommommommomm%02d",17),this);

for(int i = 18; i <20 ; i++) begin
 inst_arr[i] = new($sformatf("TOMMMM%02d",i),this);
end
for(int i = 20; i <25 ; i++) begin
 inst_arr[i] = new($sformatf("tom%02d",i),this);
end

inst_arr[25] = new($sformatf("a"),this);
inst_arr[26] = new($sformatf("aa"),this);
inst_arr[27] = new($sformatf("aaa"),this);
inst_arr[28] = new($sformatf("aaaaa"),this);
inst_arr[29] = new($sformatf("b"),this);
inst_arr[30] = new($sformatf("ab"),this);
inst_arr[31] = new($sformatf("aaaaab"),this);
inst_arr[32] = new($sformatf("abc"),this);
inst_arr[33] = new($sformatf("abbc"),this);
inst_arr[34] = new($sformatf("abbbc"),this);
inst_arr[35] = new($sformatf("aaaaabbbb"),this);
inst_arr[36] = new($sformatf("aaabbbccc"),this);
inst_arr[37] = new($sformatf("abd"),this);
inst_arr[38] = new($sformatf("abcdef"),this);
inst_arr[39] = new($sformatf("abcdefabc"),this);
inst_arr[40] = new($sformatf("cab"),this);
inst_arr[41] = new($sformatf("caab"),this);
inst_arr[42] = new($sformatf("cb"),this);
inst_arr[43] = new($sformatf("def"),this);
```

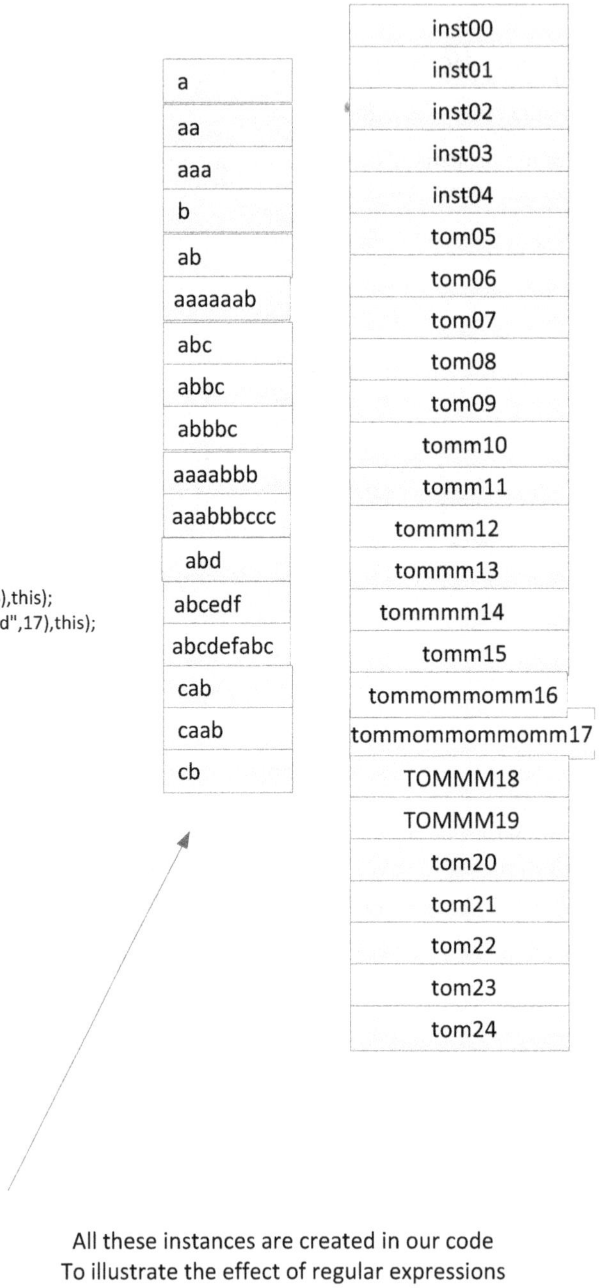

a	inst00
aa	inst01
aaa	inst02
b	inst03
ab	inst04
aaaaaab	tom05
abc	tom06
abbc	tom07
abbbc	tom08
aaaabbb	tom09
aaabbbccc	tomm10
abd	tomm11
abcedf	tommm12
abcdefabc	tommm13
cab	tommmm14
caab	tomm15
cb	tommommomm16
	tommmommommomm17
	TOMMM18
	TOMMM19
	tom20
	tom21
	tom22
	tom23
	tom24

All these instances are created in our code
To illustrate the effect of regular expressions

Fig. 18.2: Component Instances

Listing 18.3: Top class

```
1 module top;
2    import uvm_pkg::*;
3    import my_env_pkg::*;
4
5    my_env topenv;
6
7
8
9    initial begin
10       // UVM_CONFIG_DB_EXPRESSION
11
12       topenv = new("topenv", null);
13       run_test();
14    end
15
16 endmodule
```

The above listing has a simple top-level module that instantiates our env class. The initial block on Line 9 in the testbench helps us set the config_db expressions before the environment is constructed. Line 12 creates the top-level environment.

Each config_db expression shown is shown

With this basic UVM component classes, we can now go on to explore the UVM regular expression. On line 10, we will use various regular expressions to set values for the component properties.

18.2 Config DB Regular Expressions in UVM

Now that a complete example has been set up to explore UVM expressions, we can go on to write a few expressions and see the effect it has on the properties of the members. Note that the regular expressions in UVM, which are described in the following sections, are a subset of the POSIX standard.

18.2.1 Case Sensitivity And Other Things To Note

One essential item to note is that the UVM regular expression implementation is case specific. I.E. pattern /TOMM/ is not the same as /tomm/. There are a couple of instances of varying case in the above environment class, and you are encouraged to take note of this.

Another thing to note is that the expression matching mechanism appears to be "lazy" based on our observations below. It stops after the match or returns if it doesn't see the match.

Recommendation 18.2.0:   *Use regular expressions with care. Debugging why it did not work is not easy especially if the expression is complex*

18.2.2 WildCards

As per the UVM regular expression syntax, several characters are escaped. These characters do indeed have a special meaning when used in a regular expression.
. { [( ) \ * ? + ^ $

The sections below use the term "atom" for a character/marked subexpression/class of characters that need to be matched. An atom can be a single character or a group of characters that is marked by a subexpression or a class of characters (explained below).

18.2.2.1 '*' Wildcards

The single character * will match the preceding atom ZERO or MORE times. The * wildcard is used as a "match all" in most cases. It matches the preceding atom which is nothing in this case zero or more times, which implies it matches all instances.

Listing 18.4: Class A variable set to 7

```
        uvm_config_db #(uvm_bitstream_t)::set(this,"*","v",7);
```

In the above example, the value of the property v is set to 7 in all instances of all classes instantiated in Class A. For reasons of brevity; we only printed the value of the property in the u1 instance. This can be seen in the result below.

Listing 18.5: Setting Property to 7

```
value of v in inst00.u1.v is              7
value of v in inst01.u1.v is              7
value of v in inst02.u1.v is              7
value of v in inst03.u1.v is              7
value of v in inst04.u1.v is              7
value of v in tom05.u1.v is            7
value of v in tom06.u1.v is            7
value of v in tom07.u1.v is            7
value of v in tom08.u1.v is            7
value of v in tom09.u1.v is            7
value of v in tomm10.u1.v is            7
value of v in tomm11.u1.v is            7
value of v in tommm12.u1.v is             7
value of v in tommm13.u1.v is             7
value of v in tommmm14.u1.v is             7
value of v in tomm15.u1.v is            7
value of v in tommommomm16.u1.v is              7
value of v in tommommommomm17.u1.v is               7
value of v in TOMMMM18.u1.v is             7
value of v in TOMMMM19.u1.v is             7
value of v in tom20.u1.v is            7
value of v in tom21.u1.v is            7
value of v in tom22.u1.v is            7
value of v in tom23.u1.v is            7
value of v in tom24.u1.v is            7
value of v in a.u1.v is          7
value of v in aa.u1.v is           7
value of v in aaa.u1.v is            7
value of v in aaaaa.u1.v is            7
value of v in b.u1.v is          7
value of v in ab.u1.v is           7
value of v in aaaaab.u1.v is             7
value of v in abc.u1.v is           7
value of v in abbc.u1.v is            7
value of v in abbbc.u1.v is            7
value of v in aaaaabbbb.u1.v is             7
value of v in aaabbbccc.u1.v is             7
value of v in abd.u1.v is           7
value of v in abcdef.u1.v is           7
value of v in abcdefabc.u1.v is             7
```

```
value of v in cab.u1.v is                7
value of v in caab.u1.v is                 7
value of v in cb.u1.v is               7
value of v in def.u1.v is                7
```

18.2.2.2 '?' Wildcards

The single character '?' Will match the preceding atom ZERO or ONE times. See show the ? wildcard is used in the following config_db setting

Listing 18.6: Using the ? wildcard

```
            uvm_config_db #(uvm_bitstream_t)::set(null,"/ab?d/", "s", 21);
            uvm_config_db #(uvm_bitstream_t)::set(null,"/ca?b/", "v", 22);
```

This will get a match in the following instances: abd, cab and cb and it will NOT match anything else. Note that it does NOT match instance caab.

```
value of s in a.u1.s is                0
value of s in aa.u1.s is                 0
value of s in aaa.u1.s is                  0
value of s in aaaaa.u1.s is                  0
value of s in b.u1.s is                0
value of s in ab.u1.s is                 0
value of s in aaaaab.u1.s is                   0
value of s in abc.u1.s is                 0
value of s in abbc.u1.s is                  0
value of s in abbbc.u1.s is                  0
value of s in aaaaabbbb.u1.s is                  0
value of s in aaabbbccc.u1.s is                  0
value of s in abd.u1.s is               21
value of s in abcdef.u1.s is                  0
value of s in abcdefabc.u1.s is                  0
value of s in cab.u1.s is                 0
value of s in caab.u1.s is                  0
value of s in cb.u1.s is               0
value of s in def.u1.s is                 0
value of v in a.u1.v is                7
value of v in aa.u1.v is                7
value of v in aaa.u1.v is                 7
value of v in aaaaa.u1.v is                  7
value of v in b.u1.v is                7
value of v in ab.u1.v is                 7
value of v in aaaaab.u1.v is                   7
value of v in abc.u1.v is                 7
value of v in abbc.u1.v is                  7
value of v in abbbc.u1.v is                  7
value of v in aaaaabbbb.u1.v is                  7
value of v in aaabbbccc.u1.v is                  7
value of v in abd.u1.v is                7
value of v in abcdef.u1.v is                  7
value of v in abcdefabc.u1.v is                  7
value of v in cab.u1.v is               22
```

```
value of v in caab.u1.v is              7
value of v in cb.u1.v is           22
value of v in def.u1.v is               7
```

18.2.3 '+' Wildcard

The single character + will match the preceding atom ONE or MORE times.

Listing 18.7: The + wildcard

```
        uvm_config_db #(uvm_bitstream_t)::set(null,"/a+b/", "s", 11);
```

This will yield the following matches,

```
value of s in a.u1.s is             0
value of s in aa.u1.s is             0
value of s in aaa.u1.s is             0
value of s in aaaaa.u1.s is              0
value of s in b.u1.s is             0
value of s in ab.u1.s is           11
value of s in aaaaab.u1.s is              11
value of s in abc.u1.s is           11
value of s in abbc.u1.s is            11
value of s in abbbc.u1.s is             11
value of s in aaaaabbbb.u1.s is               11
value of s in aaabbbccc.u1.s is              11
value of s in abd.u1.s is           11
value of s in abcdef.u1.s is             11
value of s in abcdefabc.u1.s is              11
value of s in cab.u1.s is           11
value of s in caab.u1.s is            11
value of s in cb.u1.s is            0
value of s in def.u1.s is             0
```

18.2.4 Anchors

The ^ character matches the start of a pattern when used as the first character of an expression, or the first character of a sub-expression.

The $ character matches the end of a pattern when used as the last character of an expression, or the last character of a sub-expression.

Consider the following example:

Listing 18.8: ../examples/config_db/beginning.log

```
        uvm_config_db #(uvm_bitstream_t)::set(null,"/^topenv\.a{1,2}\.u1/",
            "s", 8);
```

This example will match the properties in instances topenv.a and topenv.aa. It will not match the rest although it initially appears a match.

Listing 18.9: ../examples/config_db/beginning.log

```
value of s in a.u1.s is               8
value of s in aa.u1.s is              8
value of s in aaa.u1.s is              0
value of s in aaaaa.u1.s is             0
value of s in b.u1.s is             0
value of s in ab.u1.s is             0
value of s in aaaaab.u1.s is              0
value of s in abc.u1.s is             0
value of s in abbc.u1.s is            0
value of s in abbbc.u1.s is            0
value of s in aaaaabbbb.u1.s is               0
value of s in aaabbbccc.u1.s is               0
value of s in abd.u1.s is             0
value of s in abcdef.u1.s is              0
value of s in abcdefabc.u1.s is               0
```

18.2.5 Repeat Operators

The repeat operator is in curly braces and has a few different syntax options.

- a {2} Matches 'a' repeated exactly 2 times.

- a{2,} Matches 'a' repeated 2 or more times.

- a {2,3} Matches 'a' repeated either 2 or 3 times.

Here is an example.

```
uvm_config_db #(uvm_bitstream_t)::set(null,"/topenv\.t(omm)
    {2,}[1*].\.u1/", "s", 62);
uvm_config_db #(uvm_bitstream_t)::set(null,"/topenv\.tom(m)
    {2,}[1*].\.u1/", "v", 52);
```

The first configuration settings expect to set the property s in instance u1 for the pattern 'omm' repeated exactly three times to 62.

The second configuration settings expect to set the property s in instance u1 for the pattern 'm' repeated exactly three times to 52.

```
value of v in tomm10.u1.v is             7
value of v in tomm11.u1.v is             7
value of v in tommm12.u1.v is            52
value of v in tommm13.u1.v is            52
value of v in tommmm14.u1.v is             52
value of v in tomm15.u1.v is             7
value of v in tommommomm16.u1.v is               7
value of v in tommommommomm17.u1.v is              7
value of v in TOMMMM18.u1.v is             7
value of v in TOMMMM19.u1.v is            7
value of v in tom20.u1.v is           7
value of v in tom21.u1.v is           7
value of v in tom22.u1.v is           7
value of v in tom23.u1.v is           7
```

```
value of v in tom24.u1.v is                7
value of s in inst00.u1.s is              0
value of s in inst01.u1.s is              0
value of s in inst02.u1.s is              0
value of s in inst03.u1.s is              0
value of s in inst04.u1.s is              0
value of s in tom05.u1.s is             0
value of s in tom06.u1.s is             0
value of s in tom07.u1.s is             0
value of s in tom08.u1.s is             0
value of s in tom09.u1.s is             0
value of s in tomm10.u1.s is              0
value of s in tomm11.u1.s is              0
value of s in tommm12.u1.s is               0
value of s in tommm13.u1.s is               0
value of s in tommmm14.u1.s is                0
value of s in tomm15.u1.s is              0
value of s in tommommomm16.u1.s is                62
value of s in tommommommomm17.u1.s is                62
```

18.2.6 Marked Sub Expressions

A section beginning (and ending) acts as a marked sub-expression and treated like an atom.

```
        uvm_config_db #(uvm_bitstream_t)::set(null,"/topenv\.t(omm)
          {3}[1*].\.u1/", "s", 42);
```

In the above example, the pattern 'omm' is treated as a single unit. It is set to to repeat thrice for a match to happen. Note that it does *not* match the next instance.

```
value of s in tomm10.u1.s is              0
value of s in tomm11.u1.s is              0
value of s in tommm12.u1.s is               0
value of s in tommm13.u1.s is               0
value of s in tommmm14.u1.s is                0
value of s in tomm15.u1.s is              0
value of s in tommommomm16.u1.s is                42
value of s in tommommommomm17.u1.s is                0
```

18.2.7 Alternation

The | character allows you to select from one group of characters and another.

In the example below, we are looking for instance abc OR instance def to set the property s in instance u1 to 41.

```
        uvm_config_db #(uvm_bitstream_t)::set(null,"/abc|def/", "s", 41);
```

The result therefore shows as:

```
value of s in aaa.u1.s is              0
value of s in aaaaa.u1.s is               0
value of s in b.u1.s is            0
value of s in ab.u1.s is             0
value of s in aaaaab.u1.s is               0
value of s in abc.u1.s is            41
value of s in abbc.u1.s is              0
value of s in abbbc.u1.s is              0
value of s in aaaaabbbb.u1.s is               0
value of s in aaabbbccc.u1.s is               0
value of s in abd.u1.s is            0
value of s in abcdef.u1.s is             41
value of s in abcdefabc.u1.s is               41
value of s in cab.u1.s is            0
value of s in caab.u1.s is              0
value of s in cb.u1.s is           0
value of s in def.u1.s is            41
```

18.2.8 Precedence Among Operators

With all these operators, there is a precedence and ordering specified by the POSIX standard. The table below has the order of precedence between the various operators.

Escaped characters	\<special character>
Bracket expression	[]
Grouping	()
Single-character / duplication	* + ? {m,n}
Concatenation	
Anchoring	^ $
Alternation	|

Meta characters / regex in field names have been disabled due to performance and semantic issues in the later releases of UVM.

set_config_*, get_config_* now deprecated. Be careful when converting *_config_object when using clone().

Chapter 19

Advanced Core Utilities in IEEE 1800.2

Chapter 4 introduced operations on classes deriving from uvm_object using policies. Section 4.5 introduced many macros to simplify usage. These `uvm_object_utils macros and their field variants made it easy to control inclusion of class properties in many common operations.

The pre-IEEE versions of the library implemented these macros using undocumented methods and classes. This created many undesirable complications and restricted users from making any changes to the library; it was difficult for any user to modify the library or any of the macros to obtain changes their testbenches needed.

Nowadays, debugging a testbench or a failing test now takes a substantial portion of the verification activity, and many vendors now add debug hooks for their simulators to simplify matters. By instrumenting additional code into the library, some vendors also optimize some portions of the library to improve performance. This now introduces a new problem: if any user has their own version of the library, it becomes difficult for a simulator vendor to automatically detect and optimize the library implementation, given the significant complexity involved. While this may not be a significant issue in small verification environments, large environments put together with multiple sub-environments are a different matter altogether. One usually finds that the testbench now becomes a substantial portion of the time consumed in simulation.

This problem makes things challenging. The sections below describe how the core utilities were re-architected, keeping in mind the dual principles of extensibility and documentation in IEEE 1800.2. Users who need to implement specialized functionality can now do so without altering the library. Also, testbenches can be quickly updated as new versions of UVM are available. Two factors of this standardization effort led by multiple organizations in the committee:

- Provide extensibility for operations on the library
- Implement the library using documented methods and classes.

It is hoped that this actually makes it easier for users to implement specific changes that they would require in their environments without too much effort while enabling debug and other enhancements from simulator vendors.

This chapter covers advanced usage scenarios. You should be well versed with the contents of either Chapter 4 or Chapter A before you proceed with this topic. It covers changes that were made in the IEEE version, to support advanced and power users to accomplish their goals. Strict backward compatibility has been maintained, and hence, it is possible that the changes described below may not impact most users.

Recommendation 19.0.0: *Unless there is a bug fix for the library that is mandatory for your testbench, I strongly recommend leveraging the existing capabilities in the IEEE version of the library. Use the extension capabilities described below, which enables you to leverage the work done by others. It reduces the amount of code that you have to maintain. You can obtain bug fixes from the Accellera or other implementations without too much work on your part. You also benefit from the bug reports and fixes reported by the community.*

19.1 Infrastructure Additions

The UVM-1.2 and earlier library implementations had many undocumented macros, and it was effectively a closed system. Introducing a new class uvm_field_op, and a new method do_execute_op() addressed the following issues in the implementation:

- With the earlier versions of the UVM macros, additional hooks cannot be added into the do_* policy operations.

- You could not add your own operations (For example, A streaming pack if you were packing transactions for a C language-based scoreboard) that wasn't provided by the library.

- You could not intercept do_* policy in specific use cases, which resulted in significant hours of additional work and code complexity.

19.1.1 uvm_field_op

IEEE 1800.2 introduces a new class called uvm_field_op. This class extends from uvm_object and acts as a container for all the operations performed on a field. This class is used in the macros and provides extensibility to the user if needed. The class provides a user_hook bit that you can use to selectively disable the do_* callbacks in your user code.

This facility gives you some power (which can be abused, so please use it responsibly!). You could, in theory, add operations into your verification infrastructure. (like the above-mentioned streaming operation to do some work before the actual do_pack() occurred in particular cases similar to those in Section 19.1.6.). You can keep your code separate from the released based class library from the vendor, allowing you to quickly upgrade in case of bug fixes provided by a vendor. The functions in the class mentioned below are all virtual, allowing you to override them.

These functions are available to you from the uvm_field_op class:

```
virtual function void set( uvm_field_flag_t op_type, uvm_policy policy = null,
uvm_object rhs = null);
virtual function string get_op_name();
virtual function uvm_field_flag_t get_op_type();
virtual function uvm_policy get_policy();
virtual function uvm_object get_rhs();
function bit user_hook_enabled();
function void disable_user_hook();
virtual function void flush();
```

The above methods can be used to interact with a policy class. Almost all of these methods are used in the `uvm_field_* macros. Take a quick look at the implementation after you have read this chapter if you wish to gain a deep understanding of how they are used. Figure 19.1 provides an overview.

(i) Note that this uvm_field_op class itself is *factory replaceable*. Mull the infinite possibilities it provides. I haven't yet used this capability, but I choose to mention it here so that you know what it is capable of.

19.1.2 do_execute_op

This is a new method in the uvm_object base class. The uvm_object class now calls do_execute_op under the `uvm_field_utils macros. The uvm_object class has an empty method that is overridden with the contents in the macros. Figure 19.1 shows the order of calls and how they interact with one another.

```
function void uvm_object::do_execute_op ( uvm_field_op op);
```

19.1.3 How Does This All Work?

When you place the macros for the `uvm_field_utils_begin(<classname>), the macros instrument code to register the class with the factory, this is shown in Listing 5.2 of Chapter 5.

Figure 19.1 shows the flow diagram starting with the user-provided class along with the uvm_object_utils macros. In the Figure, policy_p could be any of the common policies like copy/compare/pack—unpack/print.

In addition to the factory registration, the macros add the do_execute_op() method call to the classes under the do_execute_op method. The do_execute_op method under the hood implements code to get all the relevant policy objects in effect.

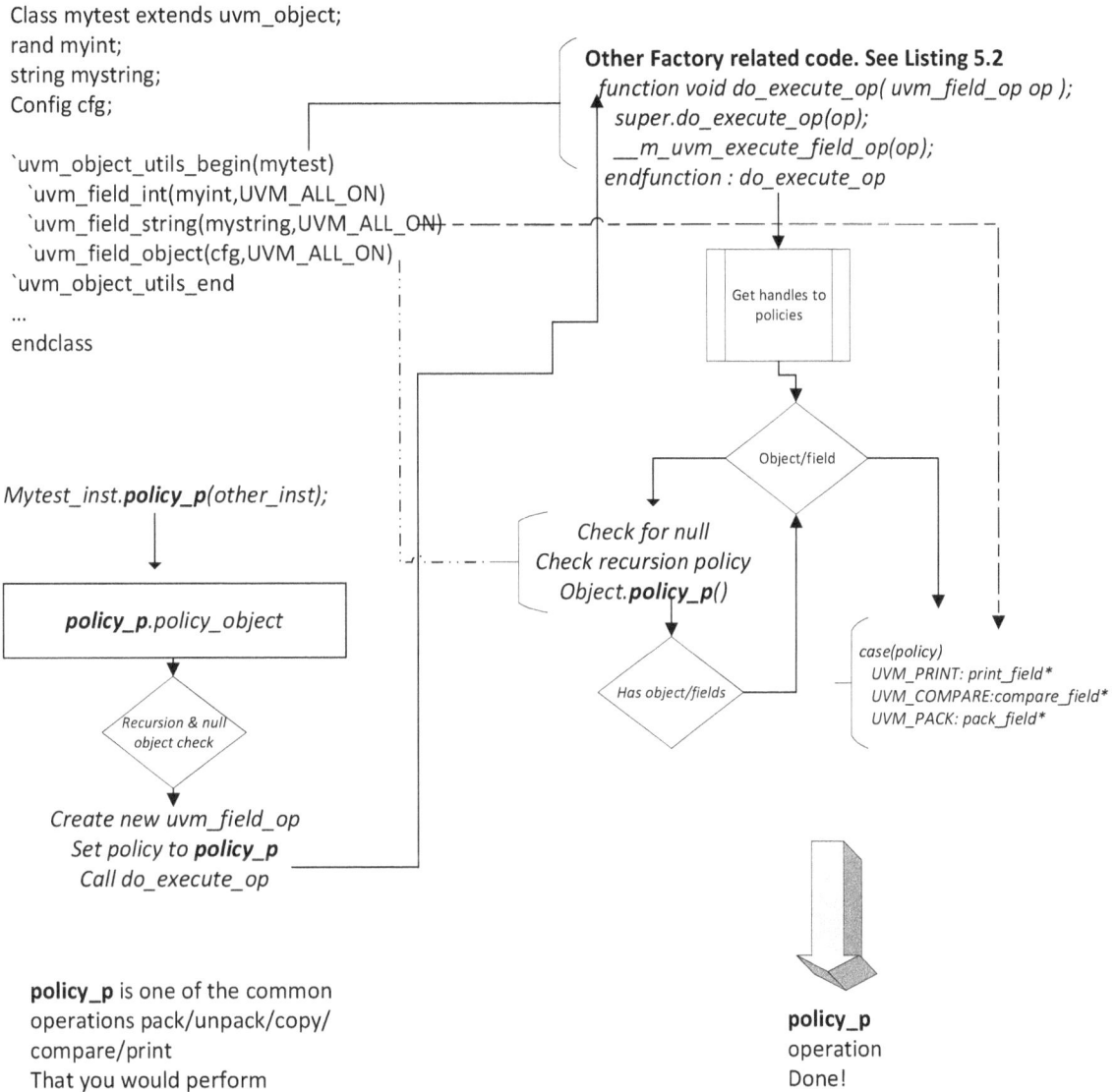

```
Class mytest extends uvm_object;
rand myint;
string mystring;
Config cfg;

`uvm_object_utils_begin(mytest)
  `uvm_field_int(myint,UVM_ALL_ON)
  `uvm_field_string(mystring,UVM_ALL_ON)
  `uvm_field_object(cfg,UVM_ALL_ON)
`uvm_object_utils_end
...
endclass
```

Other Factory related code. See Listing 5.2
function void do_execute_op(uvm_field_op op);
   super.do_execute_op(op);
   __m_uvm_execute_field_op(op);
endfunction : do_execute_op

Get handles to policies

Object/field

Check for null
Check recursion policy
Object.policy_p()

Has object/fields

case(policy)
   UVM_PRINT: print_field*
   UVM_COMPARE:compare_field*
   UVM_PACK: pack_field*

*Mytest_inst.**policy_p**(other_inst);*

policy_p.policy_object

Recursion & null object check

Create new uvm_field_op
*Set policy to **policy_p***
Call do_execute_op

policy_p is one of the common operations pack/unpack/copy/ compare/print That you would perform

policy_p operation Done!

Fig. 19.1: Policy Operation

Each of the `uvm_field_* macros now adds additional code that selects the policy for the relevant operation via a case statement (obviously only if enabled!) to the do_execute_op method. Code is implemented to check if the operation should be performed depending on the flags supplied by the user. Note that the code added is slightly different from one macro to another to accommodate the corresponding data types.

When you conduct an operation on the class (compare/pack/print/copy), the macros create a new uvm_field_op class and then call do_execute_op() after setting up the operation type. If you follow through Figure 19.1, you see that the code obtains the various policies and depending on the `uvm_field_* macros. It utilizes a CASE statement to pick the relevant actions for the policy in effect. The process repeats itself for each uvm_field_* operation. The policy operation is complete after cycling through all the code provided by the macros.

19.1.4 Additional Policy Callbacks

Assuming you had a testbench with either a buggy DUT or a testbench component when you were using the earlier release, you could not "intercept" the do_(copy—compare—print—pack/unpack) operations. The library now provides an additional callback after any of the policies (copy/compare/print/pack/unpack is called) before the do_* methods are called.

You could choose to disable some specific policy operations if you wanted to by setting a flag, as illustrated in Listing 19.1 on Line 106.

Note that this was not possible with earlier versions of UVM. Figure 19.2 shows where the do_execute_op() method is called.

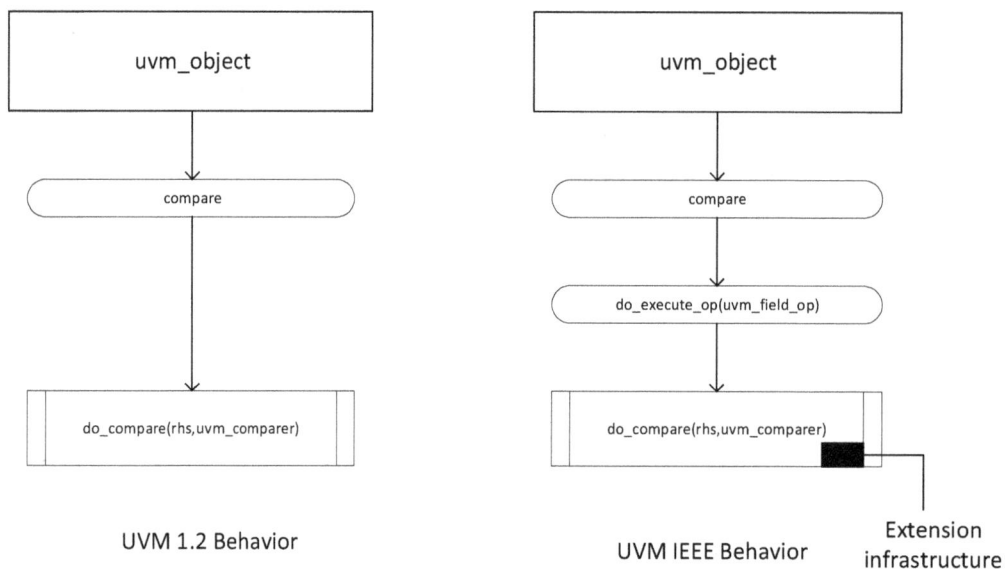

Fig. 19.2: Policy Callback hook shown for compare operation. Others are similar.

The do_execute_op infrastructure allows you to add an additional intercept point into the core operations. This capability is not restricted to built-in methods. You can also leverage this infrastructure if you choose to add your own policy classes, as will be seen in Section 19.3.

19.1.5 Creating Your Own Behaviour with do_execute_op - A Print Policy Example

The infrastructure provided by the do_execute_op is quite powerful. Recognize that the policy can be customized to do many things. You can detect the operation you are performing and also create your own print policy behavior. The listing below shows how the code would look if *you did not use* the macro expansion for the field utilities.

Listing 19.1: Do Execute Op for your own policy implementation Usage

```
38     class  class_P extends uvm_object;
39
40         // basic datatypes
41         rand int par_int;
42         rand byte par_address;
```

```
43            string par_string;
44
45            // Some objects to demonstrate the copy recursion policy
46
47            class_A cl1; // UVM_SHALLOW
48            class_A cl3; // UVM_DEEP
49            /*
50     `uvm_object_utils_begin(class_P)
51     `uvm_field_int(par_int,UVM_DEFAULT)
52     `uvm_field_int(par_address,UVM_DEFAULT | UVM_NOCOPY)
53     `uvm_field_string(par_string,UVM_NOCOPY)
54     `uvm_field_object(cl1,UVM_DEFAULT|UVM_NOCOPY)
55     `uvm_field_object(cl3,UVM_DEFAULT | UVM_NOCOPY)
56   `uvm_object_utils_end
57            */
58            `uvm_object_utils(class_P)
59
60            function new(string name="");
61                super.new(name);
62                cl1 = new(name);
63                cl3 = new(name )   ;
64                par_string  = name;
65            endfunction
66
67            function void do_copy(uvm_object rhs);
68                class_P rhs_;
69                super.do_copy(rhs);
70                $cast(rhs_,rhs);
71                par_int = rhs_.par_int;
72                par_address = rhs_.par_address;
73                par_string = rhs_.par_string;
74                cl1 = new rhs_.cl1;
75                cl3 = new rhs_.cl3;
76                cl1.copy(rhs_.cl1);
77                cl3.copy(rhs_.cl3);
78            endfunction
79
80
81            function void do_execute_op(uvm_field_op op);
82                class_P rhs_;
83                uvm_copier copier;
84                uvm_printer m_printer;
85                uvm_copy_filter_ext copy_filter_ext;
86
87                `uvm_info("POLICY",$sformatf("Operation Name %s",op.
                      get_op_name()),UVM_LOW)
88
89                if(op.get_op_name() == "copy") begin
90                    $cast(copier,  op.get_policy());
91                    if(copier.extension_exists(uvm_copy_filter_ext::get_type()
                        )) begin
92                        op.disable_user_hook(); // do_copy disabled
93                        // Our own implementation
94                        if ($cast(rhs_,op.get_rhs())) begin
```

```
95                          par_int = rhs_.par_int;
96                          par_address = rhs_.par_address;
97                          cl1 = new rhs_.cl1;
98                          cl3 = new rhs_.cl3;
99                          cl1.copy(rhs_.cl1);
100                         // dont copy cl3.
101                     end
102                 end
103             end
104             if(op.get_op_name() == "print") begin
105                 $cast(m_printer,  op.get_policy());
106                 op.disable_user_hook(); // do_copy disabled
107                 m_printer.print_field("par_int",par_int,32,UVM_NORADIX);
108                 m_printer.print_field("par_address",par_address,32,
                        UVM_NORADIX);
109                 //m_printer.print_object("cl1",cl1);
110                 //m_printer.print_object("cl3",cl3);
111             end
112
113         endfunction
```

- Line 38 declares Class_P.
- Lines 81 - 111 are the do_execute_op infrastructure that was developed **instead of macro expanded code that was commented out on Lines 49 - 57.**
- Line 58 registers this with the factory. **This is a key step you must take.**
- Line 89 checks if the operation is a copy() operation. If so, it copies the elements from source to destination after getting the copy policy on line 61.
- Line 104 checks if it is a print() operation. If so, it gets the printer policy on Line 105 and processes the print.
- Line 104 onwards processes the print. Note that the do_print hook is disabled on Line 106.

Note that the name of the operation is checked before proceeding with an operation on Lines 89 and 104. You can create your own operations by following the instructions in Section 19.3. For some specific classes, you can have your own definitions if you wish.

Note that the macros under the hood have implementations that are similar to what is shown in Listing 19.1 on lines 81-113

When you look at the log file, you will see the reporter messages from the `uvm_info macro on Line 87. This is shown in the abbreviated listing below:

Listing 19.2: Do Execute Op Log Usage

```
1
2       (Specify +UVM_NO_RELNOTES to turn off this notice)
3
4 UVM_INFO ../src/do_execute_op.sv(87) @ 0: reporter [POLICY] Operation Name
      print
5 ----------------------------------------
6 Name            Type       Size   Value
7 ----------------------------------------
8 first_inst      class_P    -      @116
9   par_int       integral   32     'hdc1c6b6b
10  par_address    integral   32     'hffffffa1
```

```
11 ----------------------------------------
12 UVM_INFO ../src/do_execute_op.sv(87) @ 0: reporter [POLICY] Operation Name
       print
13 ----------------------------------------
14 Name            Type        Size   Value
15 ----------------------------------------
16 second_inst     class_P     -      @126
17   par_int       integral    32     'h76760997
18   par_address   integral    32     'h7a
19 ----------------------------------------
20 UVM_INFO ../src/do_execute_op.sv(87) @ 0: reporter [POLICY] Operation Name
       copy
21 UVM_INFO ../src/do_execute_op.sv(87) @ 0: reporter [POLICY] Operation Name
       print
22 ----------------------------------------
23 Name            Type        Size   Value
24 ----------------------------------------
25 second_inst     class_P     -      @126
26   par_int       integral    32     'hdc1c6b6b
27   par_address   integral    32     'hffffffa1
28 ----------------------------------------
```

You will see the operation being identified and the output from the respective print policy in the output with a UVM_INFO message.

19.1.6 The Extensions Infrastructure

When you were using the UVM core utility macros from the earlier versions, you effectively had a "one size fits all" approach. If you wanted to change the behavior of any one of the do_* policy methods, you had to change it for all instances of that class. Otherwise, you had to extend the class and then deal with typecasting all over the environment where this class was used or accessed. This is certainly a bit inconvenient. Assuming that there was some extremely specific cases where you may want to shut off copy/compare or one of the policies. If you were using the macros, it was going to be difficult to accomplish your task.

Similar to the do_execute_op, and uvm_field_op infrastructure provided callbacks, an additional hook has been provided via an extensions infrastructure. These extensions are similar to the TLM2 generic payload extensions. You can create these in specific tests/environments and use them to influence how your testbench is going to operate. You can also exchange data with the object under a specific policy after checking for the presence of the extension. I hope you can see why this feature is so powerful! For specific tests, by merely writing a small check, you can have a huge change in behavior without impacting whatever was already working.

The use model for these extensions is as follows:
You create classes derived from uvm_object with any properties you need. You then check the presence of the extensions either in the do_* methods or in the do_execute_op method that is called. The example below is shown for the compare() operation. Note that this is similar for the other common operations like copy()/pack()/print() as well.

The methods available to check/set an extension are:

```
virtual function bit extension_exists( uvm_object_wrapper ext_type );
virtual function uvm_object set_extension( uvm_object extension );
virtual function uvm_object get_extension(uvm_object_wrapper ext_type );
```

The check for the extensions is type-based. Only one extension of a given type can exist.

An example of a simple extension is shown below. This extension has a couple of bits that dictate whether integers or strings will be compared.

Listing 19.3: A Simple Extension

```
61 class compare_extension_1 extends uvm_object;
62    `uvm_object_utils(compare_extension_1)
63    function new(string name = "compare_extension_1");
64       super.new(name);
65    endfunction
66
67    bit compare_integers;
68    bit compare_strings;
69 endclass
```

This extension is then created somewhere in your environment and assigned some values, as seen in the listing. You would also add the extension to your policy.

Listing 19.4: A Simple Extension assignment

```
189       compare_ext1 = new("compare_ext1");
190       compare_ext2 = new("compare_ext2");
191       comparer_B_policy_with_extensions = new("
             comparer_B_policy_with_extensions");
192       compare_ext1.compare_integers = 0;
193       compare_ext1.compare_strings = 1;
194       comparer_B_policy_with_extensions.set_extension(compare_ext1);
```

You connect the extension you created with the policy, as shown in the steps below.

Listing 19.5: A Simple Extension assignment

```
189       comparer_B_policy_with_extensions.set_extension(compare_ext1);
```

You check for the presence of the extension in your do_* methods, as shown below.

Listing 19.6: Check for existence of extension

```
108    virtual function bit do_compare(uvm_object rhs, uvm_comparer comparer);
109       class_P rhs_;
110       uvm_comparer my_comparer;
111       uvm_recursion_policy_enum  my_recur_policy;
112       compare_extension_1  compare_extension;
113       do_compare = super.do_compare(rhs,comparer);
114       $cast(my_comparer,comparer);
115       $cast(my_recur_policy,my_comparer.get_recursion_policy());
116       $cast(rhs_,rhs);
117       if(my_comparer != null) begin
118          if(my_comparer.get_active_object_depth() != 1 )
119             `uvm_fatal("compare policy depth","Expected value of 1")
120          if(my_comparer.extension_exists(compare_extension_1::get_type()))
                   begin
121             $cast(compare_extension, my_comparer.get_extension(
                   compare_extension_1::get_type()));
122             if(compare_extension.compare_integers == 1) begin
```

```
123                 do_compare &= comparer.compare_field_int("par_int",par_int,
                        rhs_.par_int,32,UVM_NORADIX);
124                 do_compare &= comparer.compare_field_int("par_address",
                        par_int,rhs_.par_int,32,UVM_NORADIX);
125             end
126             if(compare_extension.compare_strings == 1) begin
127                 do_compare &= comparer.compare_string("par_string",
                        par_string,rhs_.par_string);
128             end
129         end
130     else begin
131             do_compare &= comparer.compare_field_int("par_int",par_int,
                    rhs_.par_int,32,UVM_NORADIX);
132             do_compare &= comparer.compare_field_int("par_address",par_int
                    ,rhs_.par_int,32,UVM_NORADIX);
133             do_compare &= comparer.compare_string("par_string",par_string,
                    rhs_.par_string);
134     end
135         do_compare &= comparer.compare_object("cl1",cl1,rhs_.cl1);
136         do_compare &= comparer.compare_object("cl3",cl3,rhs_.cl3);
137       end
138     endfunction
139 endclass
```

- Line 120 checks to see if the extension exists.

- Line 121 then assigns that to a local handle. Notice that the get_extension method looks up extensions by *type*.

- Line 122 now checks a specific property compare_integers to determine if the integer properties need to be compared.

- Line 126-127 performs a similar operation with the string properties.

- Lines 131-134 would perform similar operations if the extension did not exist.

19.2 Introducing Callbacks in the Field Operations

The previous section described the use of the extensions infrastructure. This section now goes into how you can customize the effects of the policies using the do_execute_op() method. We will modify and reuse the same example as provided in Listing 19.6 and focus on the extensions infrastructure in this section.

Consider the following listing: Class_P extends uvm_object with a few properties as shown below:

Listing 19.7: Do Execute Op Usage

```
38    class  class_P extends uvm_object;
39
40        // basic datatypes
41        rand int par_int;
42        rand byte par_address;
43        string par_string;
44
45        // Some objects to demonstrate the copy recursion policy
46
47        class_A cl1; // UVM_SHALLOW
48        class_A cl3; // UVM_DEEP
49        /*
50    `uvm_object_utils_begin(class_P)
```

```
51        `uvm_field_int(par_int ,UVM_DEFAULT)
52        `uvm_field_int(par_address ,UVM_DEFAULT | UVM_NOCOPY)
53        `uvm_field_string(par_string ,UVM_NOCOPY)
54        `uvm_field_object(cl1 ,UVM_DEFAULT|UVM_NOCOPY)
55        `uvm_field_object(cl3 ,UVM_DEFAULT | UVM_NOCOPY)
56      `uvm_object_utils_end
57            */
58          `uvm_object_utils(class_P)
59
60        function new(string name="");
61            super.new(name);
62            cl1 = new(name);
63            cl3 = new(name )   ;
64            par_string  = name;
65        endfunction
66
67        function void do_copy(uvm_object rhs);
68            class_P rhs_;
69            super.do_copy(rhs);
70            $cast(rhs_,rhs);
71            par_int = rhs_.par_int;
72            par_address = rhs_.par_address;
73            par_string = rhs_.par_string;
74            cl1 = new rhs_.cl1;
75            cl3 = new rhs_.cl3;
76            cl1.copy(rhs_.cl1);
77            cl3.copy(rhs_.cl3);
78        endfunction
79
80
81        function void do_execute_op(uvm_field_op op);
82            class_P rhs_;
83            uvm_copier copier;
84            uvm_printer m_printer;
85            uvm_copy_filter_ext copy_filter_ext;
86
87            `uvm_info("POLICY",$sformatf("Operation Name %s",op.
                get_op_name()),UVM_LOW)
88
89            if(op.get_op_name() == "copy") begin
90                $cast(copier,  op.get_policy());
91                if(copier.extension_exists(uvm_copy_filter_ext::get_type()
                    )) begin
92                  op.disable_user_hook(); // do_copy disabled
93                  // Our own implementation
94                  if ($cast(rhs_,op.get_rhs())) begin
95                      par_int = rhs_.par_int;
96                      par_address = rhs_.par_address;
97                      cl1 = new rhs_.cl1;
98                      cl3 = new rhs_.cl3;
99                      cl1.copy(rhs_.cl1);
100                     // dont copy cl3.
101                  end
102              end
```

```
103                end
104                if(op.get_op_name() == "print") begin
105                    $cast(m_printer,  op.get_policy());
106                    op.disable_user_hook();  // do_copy disabled
107                    m_printer.print_field("par_int",par_int,32,UVM_NORADIX);
108                    m_printer.print_field("par_address",par_address,32,
                         UVM_NORADIX);
109                    //m_printer.print_object("cl1",cl1);
110                    //m_printer.print_object("cl3",cl3);
111                end
112
113        endfunction
114
115    endclass
```

- on Line 50, we called the uvm_object_utils macro without the begin/end variants, although we had fields. This allows us to get the factory registration completed on Line 58. Note that the do_execute_op method was not instrumented by the macros in this case.

- The do_execute_op method is listed from line 81 onwards.

- Lines 83-84 bring in the copier and printer policy handles.

- Line 89 checks the name of the operation being performed.

- Line 91 checks to see if there is an available extension

- Line 92 calls the disable_user_hook() method for that operation. What this does is set a flag internal to the library not to call the do_copy() method after this method is complete.

- Lines 93-100 implement the equivalent of the do_copy method for this class, copying across specific members.

- Lines 104-111 now perform the print operation for the print policy.

19.3 Adding New Policy Classes to UVM

(i) This is advanced usage and I would not expect a vast majority of users to need this. Information presented in this section allows you to glimpse at possibilities, embodying the reasoning for opening up the library. A complete example has not been provided here as it would consume a lot of space, and benefit only a few readers. I'm sure you can accomplish your goals by following the recipe below.

For the most part, most users will use the provided utilities and macros to implement their verification environments. In some specific cases, it may be needed to provide a new policy (for example, you need to implement a streaming operator based packing policy that goes across language boundaries). Earlier versions of UVM would have made this exceedingly difficult to accomplish without spending a lot of time. In the IEEE 1800.2 version, however, you can make a policy extension without too much trouble while minimizing the impact of the change.

The essential steps you would follow are:

1. Add a new parameter to the UVM library. You can find examples of this in the uvm_globals.svh in the source code.

2. Note that you should not use the first few bits which are reserved for existing parameters. Choose a parameter and its corresponding "off" switch. (The first 20 or so bits are reserved for internal UVM use. I would not replace those definitions because there are bit calculations in the macros that depend on them.)

3. Note that there is both an integer parameter and a string that are used. You will need to make sure to make both entries!

4. Create a policy class that controls what happens when recursion and other operations happen. I would suggest you make a copy of the uvm_comparer policy and look at using it as a starting point.

5. Create default instances of your policy with set/get methods and add them to the uvm_coreservice class.

6. Make a copy of the uvm_object_defines.svh macro and add your operation for the various data types (`uvm_field_int and similar).

7. Note that for array properties, you need to make more than one entry. One for the datatype and one for the array.

8. Override the uvm_field_op and alter the set() method to account for your operation. See Listing 19.1

You can then have a new type of operation used in all the macros after you follow these steps.

19.4 Summary

This chapter introduced advanced techniques to customize commonly performed operations in the library. The inner workings of the uvm object and field macros are explored in this chapter. The addition of extensions and newly provided intercept points grant you a high degree of flexibility in your verification environments using the IEEE 1800.2 version without having to modify the core library elements.

Part IV

Practical Verification using UVM - Applications

Chapter 20

UVM Registers with the VGA LCD Module

This chapter highlights essential features in UVM register modeling in context of a VGA module. We create a register model of the registers and memories in design at a higher abstraction level by using the UVM register package in a UVM verification environment. A complete verification environment is presented in this chapter so that you can explore UVM in greater depth. This chapter highlights the following key areas:

- Creation of the register model

- The register model and connecting it to the DUT

- Understanding the predictor model

- Front door and back door access to RAL

- Various built-in sequences available from the Register Layer from UVM

- Various tests pre-built into RAL

- Unlocking the model and reconfiguring registers

Figure 20.1 shows the block diagram of the VGA LCD module. There are three major interfaces to the core: the slave interface, the master interface, and the display interface. The slave interface is used to program the core. Upon completion of programming, the core is enabled, and it fetches data from the video memory using its built-in master interface. It then processes and sends the processed data through the display interface. The operation can be seen in Figure 20.2.

This core is programmed through the slave interface using a master agent. All registers are accessible through this interface. A slave agent is connected to the master interface. The core produces a display, which is captured and analyzed using a display agent that is configured to check the timings and image. Figure 20.2 shows the three agents connected to the core.

- The wishbone master agent

- The wishbone slave agent

- The display agent

The master agent from Chapter 8 is reused here. The VGA core acts as a master. The slave agent from Chapter 16 is used here for this environment as a responsive, reactive agent; it is a slave memory agent that responds to the VGA core which treats it as video memory and contains image data displayed on the output of the VGA core. The LCD agent has a monitor that keeps track of the various timings programmed into the core. It collects the data, and the monitor can potentially be connected with a scoreboard and be used to verify the proper operation of the module. The LCD agent and the slave agents are not used in the discussions below.

20.1 Integrating Register Models Into UVM Environments

The UVM Register Layer is a set of base classes that can be used to create a high-level, object-oriented abstraction model of the registers and memories in a design. The library of base classes can be used to abstract the read/write operations to

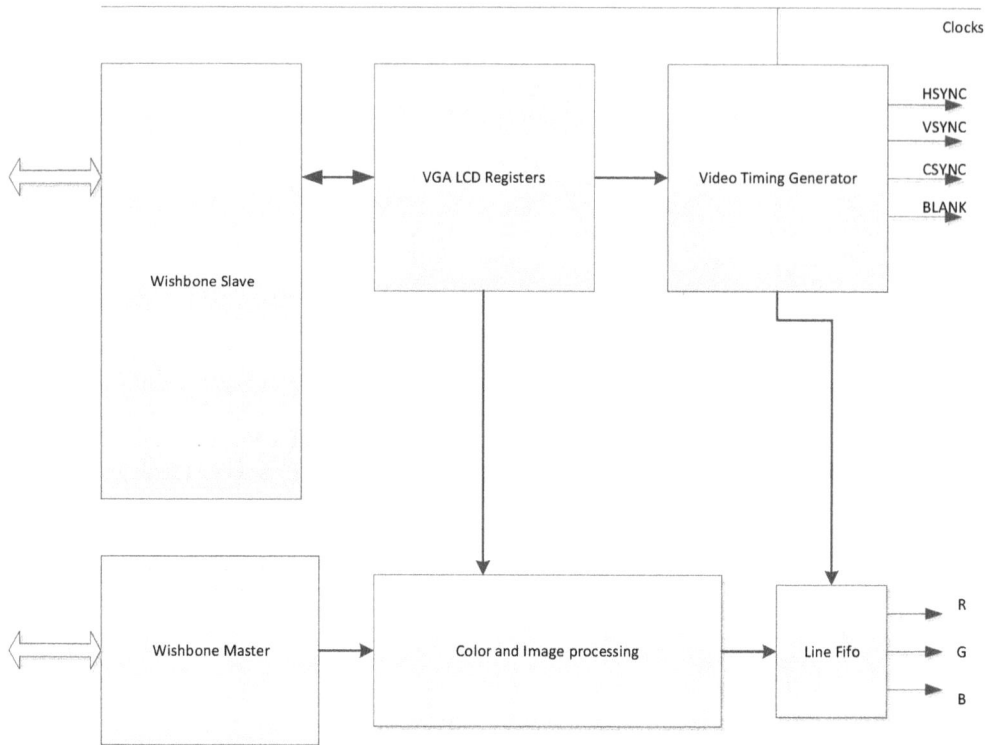

Fig. 20.1: VGA Core Block Diagram

the registers and memories in a DUT. It includes a sequence library that can be used to verify the correct implementation of the registers and memories in the design. The register model can be used to implement a functional coverage model to ensure that every bit of every register is exercised. You can also verify the different combinations of values being driven to the DUT registers. One essential aspect of the abstraction mechanism is to enable a smooth migration of verification environments and tests from block to system levels without needing any source code modification.

Table 20.1 shows registers in the DUT extracted from the documentation of the core. For the discussion on UVM registers below, the details of operations performed by each of these registers are not essential at this time. Our work initially focuses on integrating a register model into the environment[1].

The typical use model for this core involves programming the core with various timing parameters defining the size and resolution of the displayed image. If you take a close look at the register definitions, you find that the process of documentation, implementation, and verification can be carried out from a single starting point with the right set of tools, as described in Section 12.1.

---

[1] The Verilog testbench supplied with the core provides functional tests that exercise the functionality of the core in depth using macros for registers. Look at the exercises to migrate those Verilog tests to exercise the core using UVM.

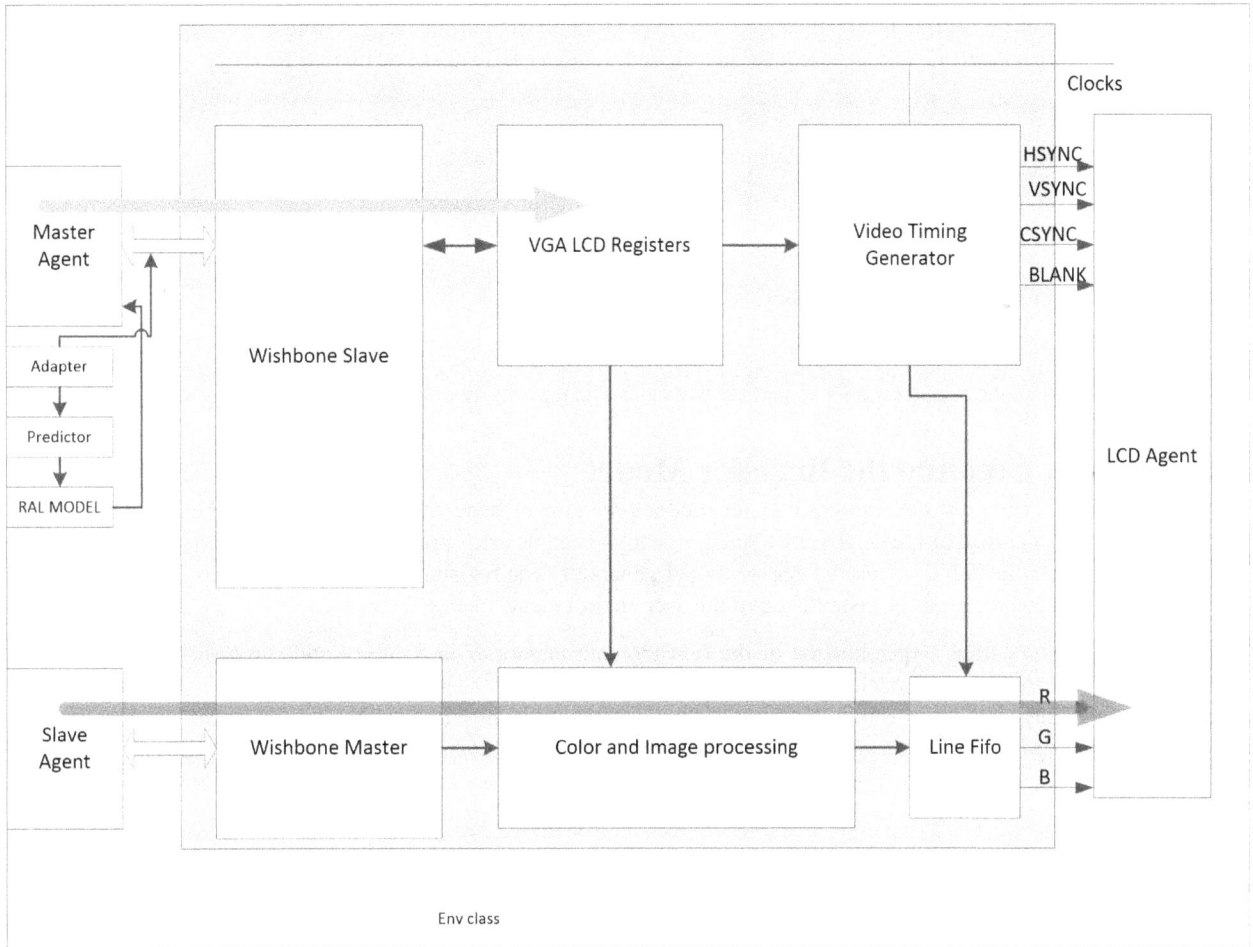

Fig. 20.2: VGA Core Data/Control Flow and Environment Block Diagram

Table 20.1: Listing Of The VGA LCD Registers

Name	Address	Description
CTRL	0x000	Control Register
STAT	0x004	Status Register
HTIM	0x008	Horizontal Timing Register
VTIM	0x00C	Vertical Timing Register
HVLEN	0x010	Horizontal and Vertical Length Register
VBARa	0x014	Video Memory Base Address Register A
VBARb	0x018	Video Memory Base Address Register B
	0x01C-0x02C	reserved
C0XY	0x030	Cursor0 X,Y Register
C0BAR	0x034	Cursor0 Base Address Register
	0x038-0x03C	reserved
C0CR	0x040-0x05C	Cursor0 Color Registers
	0x060-0x06C	reserved
C1XY	0x070	Cursor1 X,Y Register
C1BAR	0x074	Cursor1 Base Address Register
	0x078-0x07C	reserved
C1CR	0x080-0x09C	Cursor1 Color Registers
	0x0A0-0x7FC	reserved
PCLT	0x800-0xFFC	8bpp Pseudo Color Lookup Table

Integrating the register model into the verification environment involves multiple steps. While these steps are provided in the context of the wishbone VGA LCD core, they are the same for any DUT that you choose to verify.

1. Create the register model.

2. Create an adapter that can map between bus transactions and register items.

3. Choose between using an explicit predictor or an implicit predictor.

4. Instantiate the register model into the top-level environment.

5. Lock the model to disallow further changes.

6. Connect the model to the register adapter.

7. Provide a handle to the register model so that users can use the register model API to read and write from the registers.

20.1.1 Step 1. Creating the Register Model

The register model can be created using a register model generator or handwritten. While it may be possible to write this model by hand, because of the details involved, the results become error-prone. It is strongly recommended to write a script that abstracts the details or use a register model generator. The register model generator can quickly provide a correct-by-construction model to be instantiated in the user environment.

Model generators work from a specification of the registers and memories in a design and can provide an up-to-date, correct-by-construction register model. For verifying thousands of registers as well as maintaining them, model generators are a must-have in any verification setup. Without model generators, you must update the register model by hand to reflect any change in the input specifications. This can translate to a lot of updates, especially during the initial phases of a design verification environment bring up. The file format for the model generators is outside the scope of both UVM and this book.

This section introduces a commonly used specification, the Register Abstraction Layer Format (RALF). The UVM Users Guide [3] also describes the IPXACT specification for the register model. A typical model generator can take this input format and generate and update the UVM register model for the verification engineer. The RALF file is a specification of the host accessible registers and memories available in the design. It is captured by hand from the specification above, or it can be automatically generated from a suitably formatted specification document, such as an EXCEL spreadsheet.

The RALF structure mimics the UVM register model hierarchy, as seen in Table 20.1. The smallest unit that can be used to represent a design in a RALF description is the block. The name of the block should be relevant and unique. This allows the RALF description of the block to be included in a RALF description of the system that instantiates it. The bytes attribute defines the width of the physical data path when accessing registers and memories in the block. The register model assumes that the address granularity is equal to the width of the data path.

Listing 20.1 shows an abstract description of the model. Not all the registers are shown in this listing; for the complete model, please download the sources from GitHub. This abstract register model is fed into a tool that then generates a complete SystemVerilog file that can then be instantiated into the environment. Listing 20.1 shows the register model specification using syntax used by the Synopsys RALGEN©generator. This tool takes in a TCL formatted file and produces SystemVerilog output.

Note that only a partial listing is provided. See download for the complete file.

Listing 20.1: Abstract definition of VGA LCD model

```
1 register CTRL {
2    left_to_right;
3    field unused {bits 6;}
4      field HC1R {
5   bits 1; access rw  ;
6    coverpoint { bins x = {0,1}}
7        }
8      field HC1E {bits 1 ; access rw }
9      field unused {bits 2; }
10     field HC0R {bits 1; access rw }
11     field HC0E {bits 1 ; access rw }
12     field unused {bits 2; }
13     field BL {bits 1; access rw }
14     field CSL {bits 1 ; access rw}
15     field VSL {bits 1 ; access rw}
16     field HSL {bits 1 ; access rw}
17     field PC {bits 1 ; access rw}
18     field CD {bits 2 ; access rw}
19     field VBL {bits 2 ; access rw}
20     field CBSWE {bits 1 ; access rw}
21     field VBSWE {bits 1 ; access rw}
22     field CBSIE {bits 1 ; access rw}
23     field VBSIE {bits 1 ; access rw}
24     field HIE  {bits 1 ; access rw}
25     field VIE  {bits 1 ; access rw}
26     field VEN  {bits 1 ; access rw}
27 }
28
29 register STAT {
30    left_to_right;
31    field reserved {bits 7; }
32    field HC1A {bits 1; access ro }
```

The generated file after passing it through RALGEN is quite large, and only a small part is shown in this listing to illustrate the various concepts.

Listing 20.2: Generated code from The VGA LCD Abstract model

```
// You will NOT SEE THESE COMMENTS in the code!

// Class Declarations
class ral_reg_CTRL extends uvm_reg;
  rand uvm_reg_field BL;
    ...
  rand uvm_reg_field VSL;
  // Other entries
                  // COVERAGE
  covergroup cg_bits ();
    option.per_instance = 1;
    option.name = get_name();
    HC1R: coverpoint {m_data[23:23], m_is_read} iff(m_be) {
       wildcard bins bit_0_wr_as_0 = {2'b00};
```

```
....
        wildcard bins bit_0_rd_as_1 = {2'b11};
        option.weight = 4;
    }
    HC1E: coverpoint {m_data[22:22], m_is_read} iff(m_be) {
        wildcard bins bit_0_wr_as_0 = {2'b00};
...
        option.weight = 4;
    }
  endgroup
  ... similar groups here.
          // CONSTRUCTOR
  function new(string name = "CTRL");
    super.new(name, 32,build_coverage(UVM_CVR_REG_BITS));
    if (has_coverage(UVM_CVR_REG_BITS))
      cg_bits = new();
  endfunction: new
          // BUILD PHASE

  virtual function void build();
      this.HC1R = uvm_reg_field::type_id::create("HC1R",,get_full_name());

  ... Other fields here

  endfunction: build
        // UTILITIES
  `uvm_object_utils(ral_reg_CTRL)

        // COVERAGE SAMPLING
  virtual function void sample(uvm_reg_data_t data,
                              uvm_reg_data_t byte_en,
                              bit            is_read,
                              uvm_reg_map    map);
    if (get_coverage(UVM_CVR_REG_BITS)) begin
        m_data    = data;
        m_be      = byte_en;
        m_is_read = is_read;
        cg_bits.sample();
    end
  endfunction
endclass : ral_reg_CTRL

class ral_block_vga_lcd extends uvm_reg_block;
  rand ral_reg_CTRL CTRL;
// Other registers

  CTRL : coverpoint m_offset {
    bins accessed = { `UVM_REG_ADDR_WIDTH'h0 };
    option.weight = 1;
  }

// Other

  virtual function void build();
```

```
    this.CTRL.build();
        this.CTRL.add_hdl_path('{
            '{"wbs.ctrl[31:0]", -1, -1}
        });
        this.default_map.add_mem(this.CLUT1, `UVM_REG_ADDR_WIDTH'hC00, "RW",
            0);
  ...
 `endif
```

The explanation below assumes you have downloaded the examples from GitHub and are reviewing it with this book. You recognize the complexity of building the register model by hand for all but the most simple models. The generated model includes all the classes extending from uvm_reg and uvm_field, and uvm_reg_block. We haven't provided line numbers here, but you can open the download and look at the relevant lines.

Upon study of the listing, you notice three main categories of classes and entries in the code.

- The first category is the register classes. Each class is a separate specific entity that reflects the register from the DUT. It has field class instances as properties. These class properties are customized to have the exact number of bits that are in the specific field of the register in the DUT.

- The second category of entries are the various parts of the coverage model.

- The third category is the top-level block creation where all the registers and the register map are created as a part of the ral_block_vga_lcd entry from line 730 (In downloaded listing) onwards. (See Section 12.2 for a description of the register model hierarchy.)

You usually create an instance of the register block in your environment. You can place a handle to the register block in the config_db and make it available for any class in your environment or testcase.

20.1.2 Step 2. Creating an Adapter to Translate Bus Operations

The register model is a collection of classes with information about the values programmed in it, and a prediction of the value of the corresponding register in the DUT. It does not know any protocols. Depending on the type of access to the register model (read/write), the register model issues a register read or write operation. This operation is abstract. There is no information stored in the model regarding the transaction type or bus (Example: APB, AHB, AXI, wishbone, OCP) used in the RTL. Because of this, a conversion must be developed from an abstract transaction to a transaction that is specific to the bus where the transaction is driven. This translation must occur at the point when the register model is integrated with a bus agent.

To integrate the register model with a bus agent, one must convert the generic read/write operations that are available with the register model into the bus-specific operations available with the agent. It is noted here that the only requirement for the register model is that a translation function is made available to translate between the generic model and the required bus protocol descriptor. This translation is wrapped into a translation adapter class. A simple figure that illustrates this translation is shown in Figure 20.3.

The transaction adapter itself is implemented by extending the uvm_reg_adapter class and implementing the ***reg2bus()*** and ***bus2reg()*** functions. The class itself extends from uvm_object and it uses the standard UVM methods and macros to enable factory usage. The bus2reg() function translates the bus operation from the BUS protocol to the register operation.

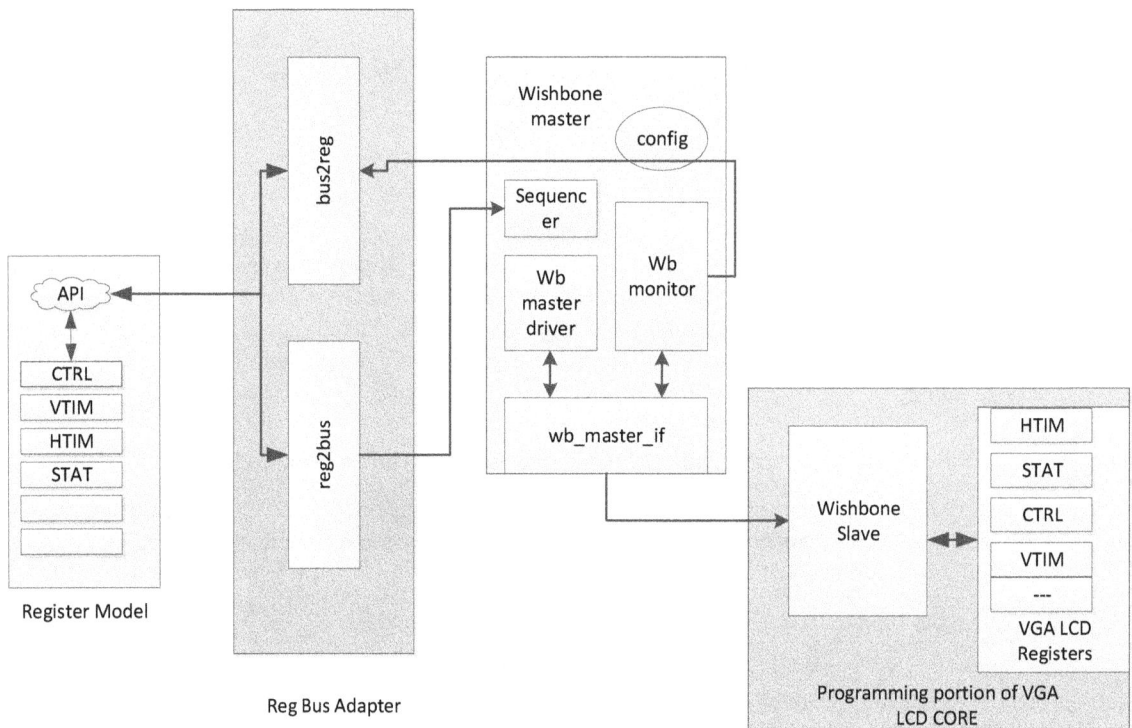

Fig. 20.3: Bus Adapters

Listing 20.3: Adapter for the register model

```
2 class vga_ral_adapter extends uvm_reg_adapter;
3
4    `uvm_object_utils(vga_ral_adapter)
5
6    function new (string name="");
7       super.new(name);
8    endfunction
9
10   virtual function uvm_sequence_item reg2bus(const ref uvm_reg_bus_op rw)
        ;
11      wb_transaction w_trans;
12      w_trans = wb_transaction::type_id::create("w_trans");
13      w_trans.address = rw.addr;
14      w_trans.sel = 4'hf;
15      w_trans.data = rw.data;
16      w_trans.kind = (rw.kind == UVM_READ)? wb_transaction::READ:
           wb_transaction::WRITE;
17      return w_trans;
18   endfunction
19
20   virtual function void bus2reg (uvm_sequence_item bus_item,
21                                  ref uvm_reg_bus_op rw);
```

```
22          wb_transaction trans;
23          if(!$cast(trans,bus_item))
24            `uvm_fatal("BUS2REF","Wrong type received");
25
26          rw.addr = trans.address;
27          rw.data = trans.data;
28          rw.kind = (trans.kind == wb_transaction::READ)?UVM_READ:UVM_WRITE;
29          rw.status = UVM_IS_OK;
30
31      endfunction
32
33 endclass: vga_ral_adapter
```

- Line 2 shows the declaration of the register adapter.

- Lines 6-8 show the constructor of the class.

- Lines 10-18 show the reg2bus method. This method takes a register operation and converts it to a wb_transaction, which is used by the driver. Various properties in the register operation are translated to the transaction, as shown in the listing.

- Lines 20-31 show the bus2reg method. This method takes a transaction and converts it to a register operation used to update the model. Various properties in the register operation are populated from the transaction, as shown in the listing.

> The register model is 2-state representation. The model has an abstraction of the register operation. It is essential to check for x/z in the adapter as a conversion occurs from a physical concept to an abstract concept in the adapter

20.1.3 Step 3. Choose a Predictor for the Register Models

Section 12.5.3.7 describes the built-in register mirror in the register model. As one drives stimulus into the design, it becomes necessary to ensure that the register model mirror is in sync with the values in the DUT. When an operation is carried out on the DUT using either the front door mechanism or the backdoor mechanism, the values in the register model need to be updated. This process by which the values are determined is termed as prediction. There are three structural bus agent integration approaches for keeping the register model's mirror values in sync with the DUT: implicit prediction, explicit prediction, and passive prediction.

20.1.3.1 Implicit Prediction

This integration is the simplest and quickest, but it does not observe bus operations that did not originate from the register model. In Figure 20.4 below, a register model is used to program the DUT. This approach is straightforward because the mirror is updated when the registers are read/written. No user code is needed. The drawback of this approach is that the mirror is only aware of all register operations that happen through the sequences. If a bus write happens *without using the agent*, then the mirror model is out of sync with the DUT.

Implicit prediction only needs the integration of the register model with one or more bus sequencers. Updates to the mirror are predicted automatically by the register model after the completion of each read, write, peek, or poke operation. No other user code is needed for this mode. The read and write method calls automatically update the mirror.

When a sequence reads or writes from a register in the DUT, the adapter linked into the model causes a prediction to predict the values of the mirror based on the values seen on the reg2bus and bus2reg adapters. While this mode is simple and easy to use, it suffers from many drawbacks. At the cost of simplicity, some issues are brought up. Changes to DUT model by other bus agent or sequences which access the register space in the DUT w/o using the register model methods effectively corrupt the mirror copy. Also, the timing of the mirror update may not be cycle accurate. Changes internal to DUT are not reflected in the mirror. It is not the right choice if the mirror value may be needed in user tests.

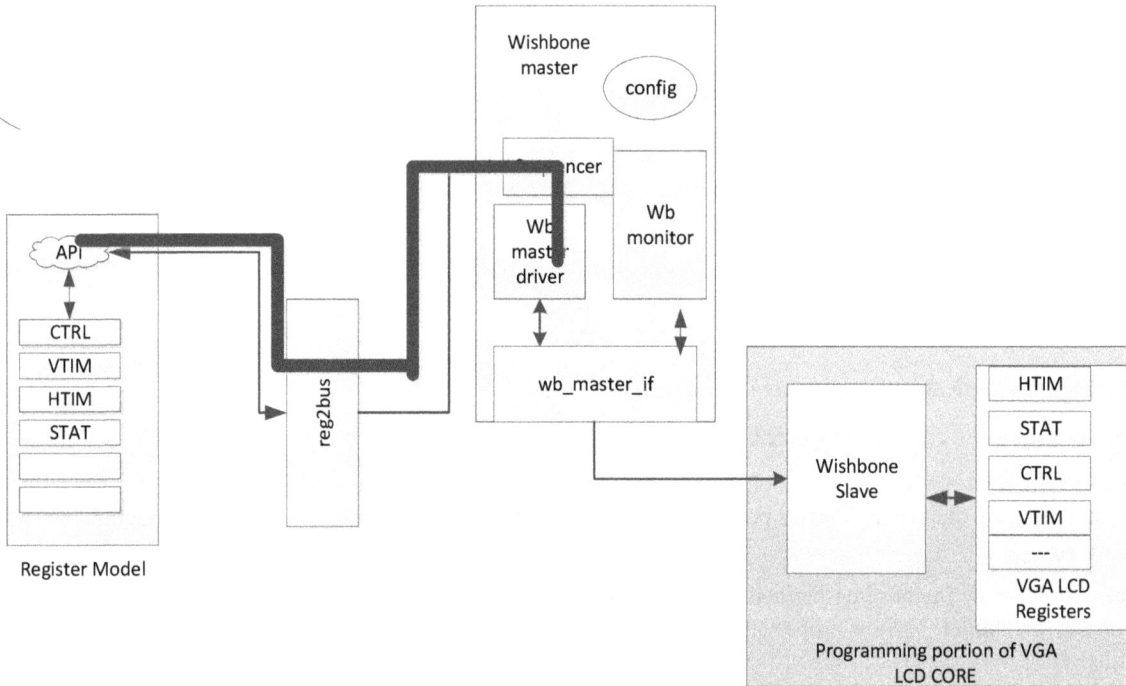

Fig. 20.4: Implicit Prediction

20.1.3.2 Explicit Prediction

Some of the problems in implicit prediction are solved using an explicit prediction mechanism. This mechanism uses both the bus sequencers and monitors. In this mode, the implicit prediction is turned off, and all updates to the mirror are predicted externally by a uvm_reg_predictor component, shown in Figure 20.5. There is a separate predictor component for each bus interface connected to a bus monitor.

The monitor component looks at the bus and creates transactions. The output of the monitor is written to an analysis port that is present on the predictor. The predictor receives the bus operations observed by a connected bus monitor. The predictor determines the register being accessed by performing a reverse-lookup using the observed address for the specific map and then calls the appropriate register's predict() method explicitly to update the mirror. This integration requires more work. However, the monitor observes all bus operations, whether originating from the register model or a third-party bus agent and appropriately updates the corresponding mirror values.

Table 20.2 shows how the two predictors compare.

Table 20.2: Comparison of Predictors

Internal Predictor	External Predictor
Easy to use. No additional work needed	Requires you to create additional components.
Cannot detect transactions to register addresses not initiated by a register sequence	Can detect and predict correctly values depending on the bus adapter and monitor code used.
Cannot add any Backdoor hooks	You can change the predicted value/register using a backdoor hook in the predictor
	Manually need to add additional instances of predictors and maps for each separate map.

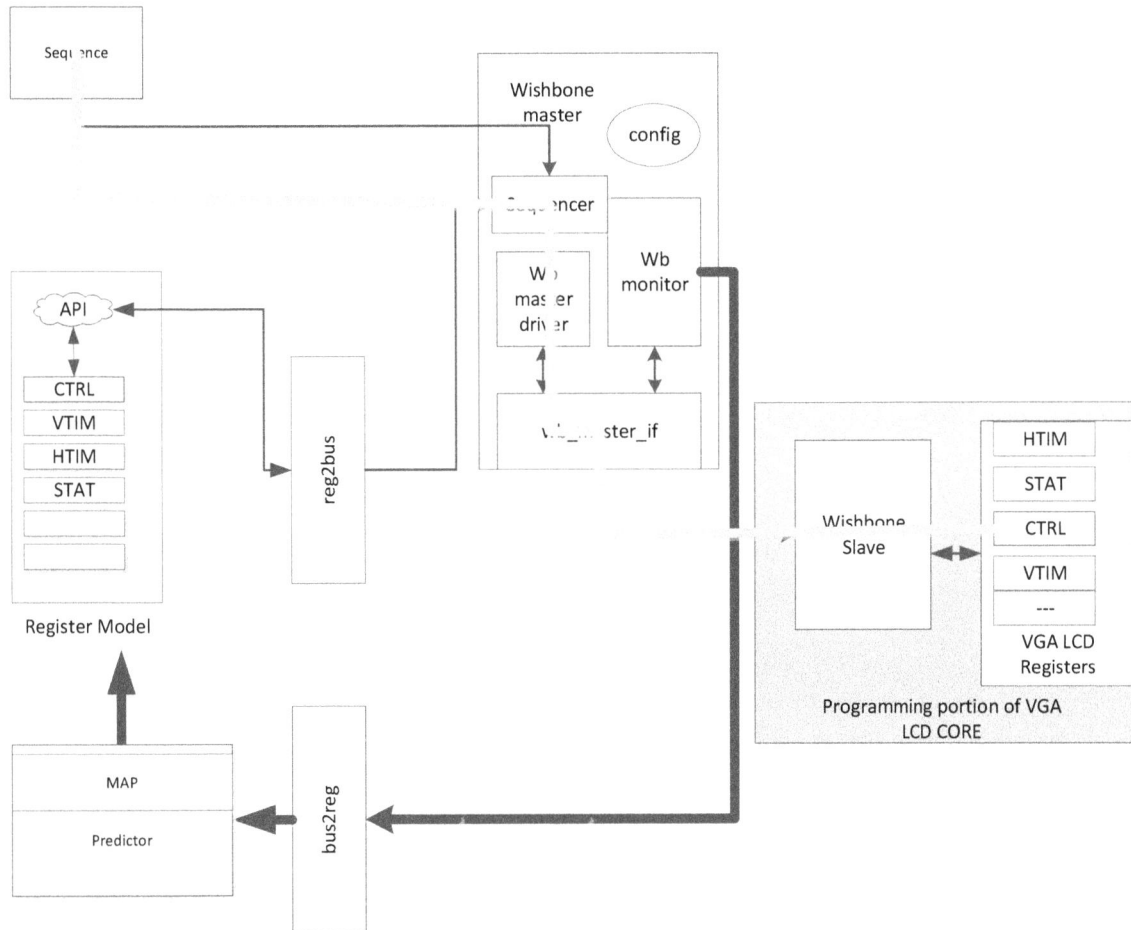

Fig. 20.5: Explicit Prediction

Recommendation 20.1.0: *Choose either the explicit or implicit depending on your application. However, leave some `ifdef hooks in your environment which enables switching between the external and internal predictors when you write the environment class code and test it early. This way, fewer modifications and review of modifications are needed.*

20.1.3.3 The Register Predictor

The uvm_reg_predictor component is derived from a uvm_subscriber and is parameterized with the type of the target bus analysis transaction. You configure the predictor with the register to target bus adapter and the register model map that is being used to interface to the bus agent sequencer. The predictor uses the register adapter to convert the analysis transaction from the monitor to a register transaction, and then it looks up the register by address in the register models bus specific map and changes the contents of the appropriate register.

The uvm_reg_predictor component is part of the UVM library and does not need to be extended. However, to integrate, the following steps must be taken:

1. Declare the predictor using the target bus sequence_item as a class specialization parameter.

2. Create the predictor in the env build() method.

3. In the connect_phase() method - set the predictor map to the target register model register map.

4. In the connect_phase() method - set the predictor adapter to the target agent adapter class.

Fig. 20.6: Predictor Component

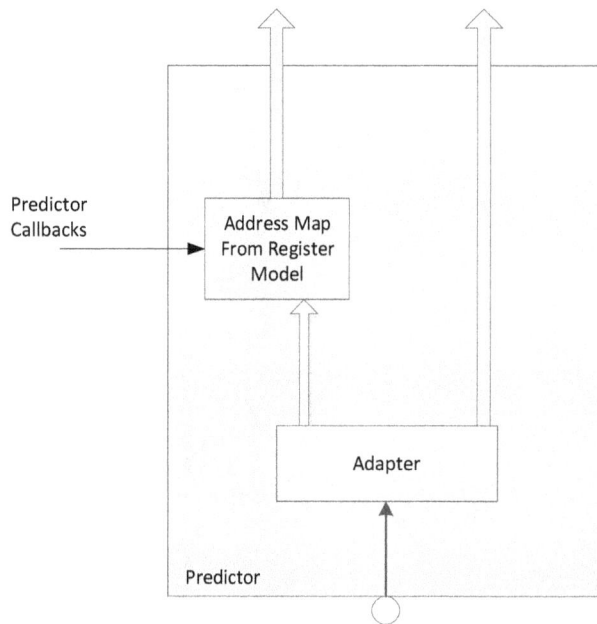

5. In the connect_phase() method - connect the predictor analysis export to the target agent analysis port.

The predictor accepts bus transactions from a connected bus monitor. It uses the preconfigured adapter to obtain the address and data from the bus operation. The map is used to look up the register object associated with that address. The register's predict() method is then called with the observed data to update the mirror value. If the register width is wider than the bus, the predictor collects multiple observed bus operations before calling predict() with the register's full value. As a final step, a generic uvm_reg_item descriptor representing the abstract register operation is broadcast to subscribers of its analysis port.

When UVM_NOT_OK status is obtained, the prediction in the UVM 1.2 implementation continues the prediction. This behavior is a bit counter-intuitive. You must make a note of this in UVM-1.2. Note that this has NOT been fixed in the IEEE 1800.2 as well.

20.1.3.4 Passive Prediction Without Active Components
The third approach of passive integration only needs the integration of the register model with the bus monitor as described above for the predictor. The register sequencers and the register adapters are not used in the environment. All the monitoring of the register operations is performed externally to (i.e., explicitly) the register model. All bus operations, whether they originated from the register model or a third-party bus agent, are observed and thus appropriately reflected in the corresponding mirror values. Because the register model is not integrated with a bus sequencer, it cannot be used to read and write register and memories in the DUT, only to track and verify their current value.

Refer to the GitHub repository to see how a passive predictor is used. This has significant value if you are assessing a non-UVM environment to assess the quality of your verification effort. There is a complete chapter on using this mode in non−UVM testbenches.

Recommendation 20.1.1:   *Look at trading off simplicity for flexibility by using an independent predictor*

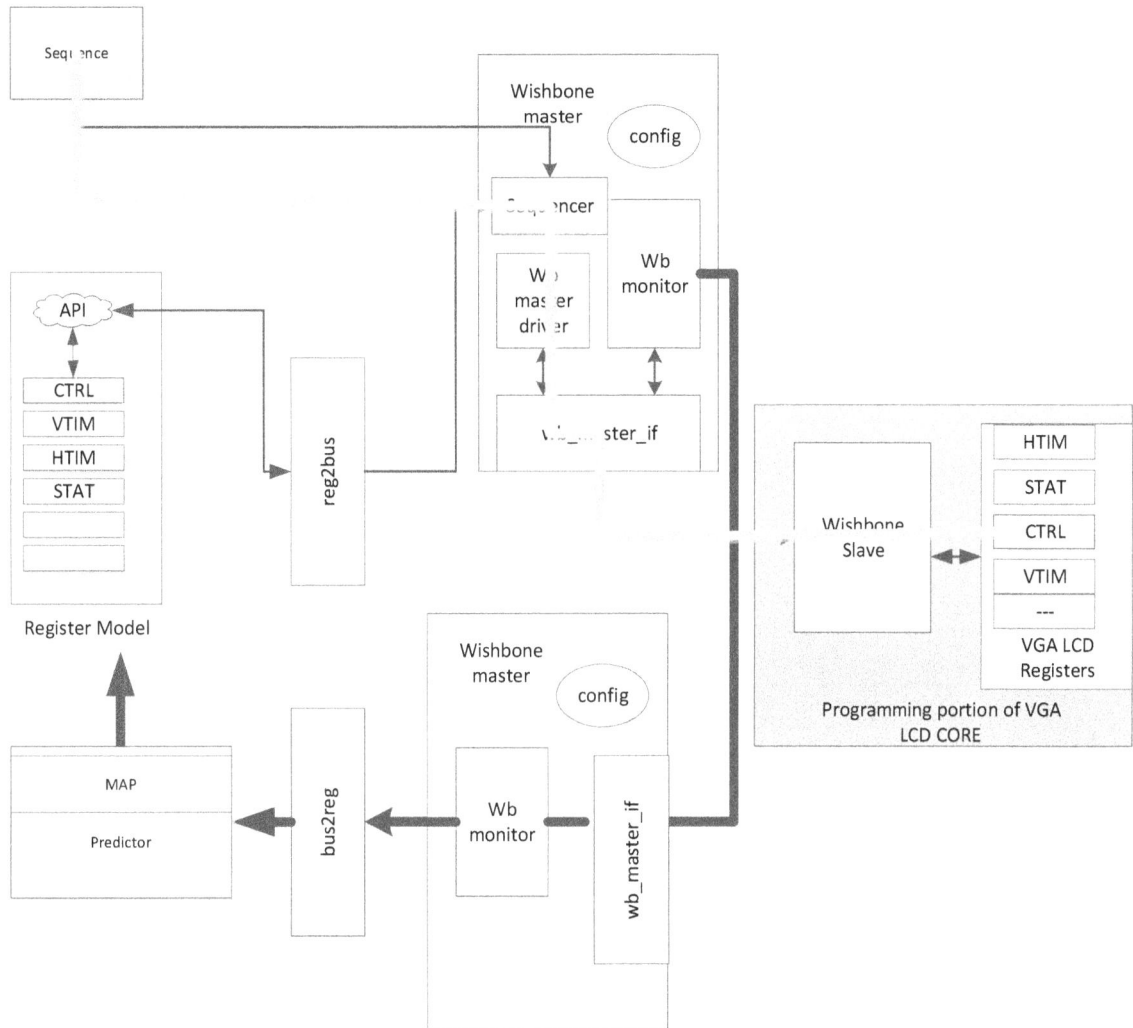

Fig. 20.7: Passive Prediction

The choice between an internal predictor and an external predictor is a matter of choice and capabilities. In general, the internal predictor works well if the register model is the source for the programming of the model, and there are no other sources that can program the DUT and the register model. If any agent connected to the DUT can program the DUT without the register model being updated, then the implicit model rapidly breaks down.

The external predictor needs a little more work in the environment. You can easily add a predictor model, which supplies a couple of additional callback routines that allow customizing the prediction. The external predictor can determine ALL the transactions that occur on the DUT interface regardless of whether they originated from the register model for the addresses that reside in the register model's memory map. The other advantage is that one can now use a 3rd party Verification IP to do the bus detection and allow the verification engineer to focus on the memory map and other operations.

20.1.4 Step 4. Instantiating the Register Model

The register model is instantiated in the top-level environment class, along with the other components of the environment. *Although the register model is derived from uvm_object and is a dynamic class as such (it is not derived from uvm_component), it is effectively a quasi-static component and is treated as such in the build() and connect() phases. Note that the register model does not have any phasing or other methods available to it.*

The register adaptor class instances are made a part of the environment as seen in the listing below.

Listing 20.4: Instantiation of VGA LCD register model

```
19   class vga_lcd_env extends uvm_env;
20     //vga_lcd_scbd sb;
21     ral_block_vga_lcd ral_regmodel;
22     wb_slave_agent slave_agent;
23     wb_master_agent master_agent;
24     vga_lcd_env_cov cov;
25     reset_agent rst_agent;
26
27     uvm_reg_predictor #(wb_transaction) wishbone_reg_predictor;
28
29     vga_ral_adapter reg2host;
30     vga_drv_mon_2cov_connect mon2cov;
31
32     `uvm_component_utils(vga_lcd_env)
33
34     extern function new(string name="vga_lcd_env", uvm_component parent=
           null);
35     extern virtual function void build_phase(uvm_phase phase);
36     extern virtual function void connect_phase(uvm_phase phase);
37
38   endclass: vga_lcd_env
39
40   function vga_lcd_env::new(string name= "vga_lcd_env",uvm_component
         parent=null);
41     super.new(name,parent);
42   endfunction:new
```

Listing 20.4 shows the vga_lcd_env class.

- Line 21 shows the instance of the register model.
- Lines 23 shows the master_agent that is used by the register model to program the DUT.
- Line 27 shows an instance of the uvm_reg_predictor class parameterized to the type wb_transaction.
- Line 29 shows the instance of the ral_adapter class. The various components are now described in the sections that follow.

20.1.5 Step 5. Creating the Register Model in the Environment

In the environment build phase, the register block instance needs to be created via the factory method. This is shown in the listing below.

Listing 20.5: Building The VGA LCD Register model

```
53    mon2cov.cov = cov;
54
55    this.ral_regmodel = ral_block_vga_lcd::type_id::create("ral_regmodel",
          this);
56    ral_regmodel.build();
57    reg2host = new("reg2host");
58    this.ral_regmodel.lock_model();
59
60    wishbone_reg_predictor = uvm_reg_predictor #(wb_transaction)::type_id
          ::create("wishbone_reg_predictor",this);
```

Listing 20.5 shows the creation of the register model in the environment.

- Line 55 shows model creation. This model instance is only created by the factory method. The rest of the register hierarchy is not created by the create() method.

- Line 56 builds the register model. If you study the source code for the model, you find that it builds each register and memory for each block in the model. Each of the register class instances calls the creation and build methods for each field in the register. When the build() method is completed, the entire register model hierarchy is in existence.

- Line 60 now builds the external predictor as a part of the build_phase.

20.1.6 Step 6. Locking the model

After the register model instantiated in the environment is built, the various class instances for registers and fields now come into existence. The register class hierarchy is completely created when the build() method is completed. The memory model map class instance is available. To prevent further changes to the register model once this process is complete, the *lock_model ()* method must be called.

There is quite a bit of infrastructure inside the model. When the locking is turned on, there are a few connections made inside the model in addition to some caching mechanisms kicking in. This method goes down through each register and sets the internal lock bit. This lock bit signifies that no further structural changes can be made to the model. The lock bit is checked by various utility functions in the register map and elsewhere. You get a UVM_ERROR if the model is not locked. *Once a model is locked, it is not possible to either make changes to the model or unlock it.* . The listing below shows you the steps in locking the register model for use by your tests and sequences.

See Line 58 in Listing 20.5 where we lock the model.

UVM
IEEE

The UVM 1.2 version does not allow for unlocking the model or making changes once locked. This can be a problem when verifying some devices that incorporate relocatable addresses like the Base Address Register in PCIe and all other registers affected by it. A regmodel unlock_model() method is available in the IEEE version to allow users to make changes to the model programmatically. See Section 20.1.10 for details

20.1.7 Step 7. Connecting the Register Model Adapter

The register model must now be connected to various components so that they all work in harmony. The register model in previous sections was built as a hierarchy. The predictor default maps are assigned to the register model in this example. The monitor analysis port on the agent is also connected to the predictor. The predictor adapter is also connected to the adapter. This is shown in the listing below.

Listing 20.6: Connecting the register model

```
65    ral_regmodel.default_map.set_sequencer(master_agent.mast_sqr,reg2host)
        ;
66    ral_regmodel.add_hdl_path("vga_lcd_env_top.vga_enh_top.u0","RTL");
67
68    wishbone_reg_predictor.map = ral_regmodel.default_map;
69    wishbone_reg_predictor.adapter = reg2host;
70
71    master_agent.mast_mon.mon_analysis_port.connect(wishbone_reg_predictor
        .bus_in);
```

- Line 68 shows the default map for the predictor is assigned to the register model

- Line 69 shows the predictor's adapter is assigned to the adapter we just created on Line 42 (previous step, and on Line 55)

- Line 71 shows the bus monitor analysis port is connected to the input port of the predictor.

20.1.8 Step 8. Set the Front-Door Sequencer

The model was connected to an adapter in step 7. You must set up the front door sequencer so that you can create a sequence using the register model to write values to either the model or the DUT. In the example below, we have only one front door sequencer to this model. The next chapter presents the same register model connecting to multiple sequencers.

In Listing 20.6:

- Line 65 shows the register model sequencer being set to the master agent master sequencer using the reg2host adapter that was created in the previous step.

20.1.9 Step 9. Accessing the Register Model

Now that a register model is has been created and instantiated in the environment (in the previous steps), it is now time to access the model and program the registers with it. A simple test that reads and writes to the model is shown in listing 20.7. The test writes a value to the HTIM register. Note that you could write any sequence of register reads and writes to the model in any order you choose.

20.1.9.1 Front Door Access

Normal register access is achieved by applying read and write commands through the driver class of our master wishbone agent using the normal wishbone protocol. This access takes simulation cycles to complete using their respective operations. For example, to write into our HTIM register without a register model, we need to specify the address of this register and the appropriate bit-fields, and then issue a write on the wishbone bus. A similar process holds when we want to read this register. We can easily verify that the value we write to a register is the value that is read. While this is a good test, it is not sufficient as there could be field inversions in both the read and write path that would never be caught. The example below shows you how to perform front-door access using the register model. I hope you see how much simpler it is!

Listing 20.7: Accessing register Model Front Door

```
18  class vga_lcd_reg_single_access_test_frontdoor extends
       vga_lcd_env_base_test;
19
20    `uvm_component_utils(vga_lcd_reg_single_access_test_frontdoor)
21
22    ral_block_vga_lcd ral_regmodel;
23    uvm_status_e status;
24
25    uvm_reg_data_t value_w;
```

```
26      uvm_reg_data_t value_r;
27      uvm_reg rg;
28
29      function new(string name, uvm_component parent);
30        super.new(name, parent);
31      endfunction
32
33      task main_phase(uvm_phase phase);
34        uvm_objection phase_done = phase.get_objection();
35        value_w = 32'h00001111;
36        env.ral_regmodel.set_coverage(UVM_CVR_ALL);
37        phase_done.raise_objection(this);
38        rg = env.ral_regmodel.HTIM;
39        `uvm_info(get_full_name(),"Starting Back door",UVM_LOW)
40        rg.write(status, value_w,.path(UVM_FRONTDOOR));
41        `uvm_info(get_full_name()," Done Back door",UVM_LOW)
42        `uvm_info(get_full_name(),"Starting Back door",UVM_LOW)
43        rg.read(status, value_r,.path(UVM_FRONTDOOR));
44        `uvm_info(get_full_name()," Done Back door",UVM_LOW)
45
46        phase_done.set_drain_time(this,200);
47        phase.drop_objection(this);
48      endtask : main_phase
```

- Line 33 shows the run_phase task in the test

- Line 35 has our desired value that is being programmed into this register.

- Line 36 turns on coverage in the register model. Note that it is not needed to do so. This was a way for us to show how coverage can be explicitly turned on in the register model.

- Line 38 shows handle rg being obtained to the register. Note that you can still access the model directly, as can be shown by lines 26,27.

- Line 40 performs the actual write. The value is written to the DUT and the register model.

- Line 43 performs the actual read. The value is read to the DUT, and the register model is updated.

20.1.9.2 Back Door Access

SOC validation often needs techniques to accelerate the register programming by the backdoor, by forcing the RTL signals. This is needed when the configuration sequences are already verified, and multiple tests go through the same long configuration cycles. In the absence of any standard methodology, all such force statements to various RTL hierarchies are error-prone. Also, given that these "force" statements are not a part of the register specification, they are not generated when the register model is created through a generator. If these are done separately after the simulation executable is created in some simulator flow, simulation can be slowed down; this would be a tedious manual process.

During the early integration phase, some of the frontdoor paths may not be fully functional. In this case, it is imperative to configure the register values through the backdoor paths. When the environment is created, there should be an option to choose accesses dynamically from frontdoor and backdoor paths in a simulation. A 'backdoor 'write followed by a 'frontdoor 'read helps verify the frontdoor path during the SOC integration phases as well as ensuring no other problems exist. The UVM register library supplies both frontdoor and backdoor accesses. It offers a set of predefined sequences to verify frontdoor functionality using backdoors as well.

Backdoor access provides an independent mechanism to both read and write into the registers. The normal register access is bypassed by using this mechanism. Backdoor access can uncover bugs that could be hidden by using the normal access path. Another advantage of backdoor access is that it's more efficient and does not consume simulation time. This access mechanism requires the user to specify the complete hierarchical reference to each of the registers. The mechanism to use the backdoor is like the front door; the only difference is in the .path argument to the write() function. The below example shows backdoor access to the register.

Listing 20.8: Accessing Register Model Using the Backdoor

```
4    class vga_lcd_reg_single_access_test_bkdoor extends
        vga_lcd_env_base_test;
5
6      `uvm_component_utils(vga_lcd_reg_single_access_test_bkdoor)
7
8      uvm_status_e status;
9
10     uvm_reg_data_t value_w;
11     uvm_reg_data_t value_r;
12     uvm_reg rg;
13
14     function new(string name, uvm_component parent);
15       super.new(name, parent);
16     endfunction
17
18     task main_phase(uvm_phase phase);
19       uvm_objection phase_done = phase.get_objection();
20       phase_done.raise_objection(this);
21       value_w = 32'h00001111;
22
23       rg = env.ral_regmodel.HTIM;
24       `uvm_info(get_full_name(),"Starting Backdoor write access to VTIM",
            UVM_LOW)
25       rg.write(status, value_w, .path(UVM_BACKDOOR));
26       `uvm_info(get_full_name(),"Ending Backdoor write access to VTIM",
            UVM_LOW)
27       `uvm_info(get_full_name(),"Starting Backdoor read access to VTIM",
            UVM_LOW)
28       rg.read(status, value_r, .path(UVM_BACKDOOR));
29       `uvm_info(get_full_name(),"Ending Backdoor read access to VTIM",
            UVM_LOW)
30       // Another way of doing this
31       env.ral_regmodel.HTIM.write(status, value_w, .path(UVM_BACKDOOR));
32       env.ral_regmodel.HTIM.read(status, value_r, .path(UVM_BACKDOOR));
33
34       phase_done.set_drain_time(this,200);
35       phase_done.drop_objection(this);
36     endtask : main_phase
```

- Line 18 shows the main_phase task in the test.

- Line 21 has our desired value that is being programmed into this register.

- Line 23 shows handle rg being obtained to the register HTIM. Note that you can still access the model directly, as can be shown by lines 31,32.

- Line 25 performs the actual write. The value is written to the DUT and the register model using the backdoor.

- Line 28 performs the actual read. The value is read to the DUT, and the register model is updated using the backdoor mechanism. This means the transaction never goes out on the bus.

- Lines 31,32 show another way of doing the same operation without the use of the handle rg.

If backdoor access is needed, and the backdoor is not defined, the library throws up a UVM_ERROR, which must be fixed.

Recommendation 20.1.2:   *Instead of hard-coding the access path, use a variable that can be overridden through the configuration database to have the same sequence work with different modes. That allows significant flexibility. The UVM register model supplies the APIs to set the HDL path roots dynamically, and you must take advantage of this feature in larger SOC integration environments.*

The table below provides a comparison of the front and back door accesses.

Backdoor Access	Frontdoor Access
Take zero simulation time	Use a bus transaction which will take at least one RTL clock cycle
Write direction accesses force the HW register bits to the specified value	Write direction accesses do a normal HW write
Read direction accesses return the current value of the HW register bits	Read direction accesses to a normal HW read, data is returned using the HW data path
In the UVM register model, backdoor accesses are always auto-predicted - the mirrored value reflects the HW value	Frontdoor accesses are predicted based on what the bus monitor observes
Only the register bits accessed are affected, side effects may occur when time advances depending on HW implementation	Side effects are modelled correctly
Bypasses normal HW	Simulates real timing and event sequences, catches errors due to unknown interactions

Table 20.3: Comparison Between Back Door and Front Door Accesses

Note that we added a few extra `uvm_info statements to the backdoor test in comparison with the frontdoor test. The idea behind this was to allow you to see that the time that was printed in the backdoor case in Listing 20.8 was quite different from that in the front door case in Listing 20.7.

20.1.10 New in IEEE: Unlocking the model

The UVM 1.2 version does not allow for unlocking the model or making changes once locked. This can be a problem when verifying some devices that incorporate relocatable addresses like the Base Address Register in PCIe and all other registers affected by it. This restriction came from the implementation artifact that the model performed some caching operations to speed things up and could not allow changes after that. Various other workarounds involved creating a new map and then using the new map to address the registers. To solve this problem, a new unlock capability is available.

The use model for this feature involves calling the unlock_model() after the model has been locked/used. You can then make some changes to the model.

To illustrate this feature, we have created an example by making some changes to the RALF description of the registers from Section 20.1.1. We have set the offset of the CTRL register to 0x0000_0010. The generated model through Step 6 in the earlier sections carried this value to the environment. The model is locked during the build_phase, and in earlier versions of UVM, you could not change it in the default map for the block.

However, if you look at the RTL documentation, the CTRL register is at offset 0x0000_0000. To access this register, post-reset, you will need to reconfigure the register model to be at 0x0000_0000. To do so, unlock the model and reconfigure the register to be at address 0x0000_0000. This is illustrated in the listing below.

Listing 20.9: Unlocking and Reconfiguring the Register model

```
34    task main_phase(uvm_phase phase);
35      uvm_objection phase_done = phase.get_objection();
36      value_w = 32'h00001111;
37      env.ral_regmodel.CTRL.get_offset();
38      `uvm_info("RAL_REGMODEL_OFFSET",$sformatf("Offset of CTRL register
          is %x", env.ral_regmodel.CTRL.get_offset()),UVM_LOW)
39      env.ral_regmodel.unlock_model();
40      env.ral_regmodel.CTRL.set_offset(env.ral_regmodel.default_map,0,0);
41      env.ral_regmodel.lock_model();
42      `uvm_info("RAL_REGMODEL_OFFSET",$sformatf("Offset of CTRL register
          is %x", env.ral_regmodel.CTRL.get_offset()),UVM_LOW)
```

- Line 39 unlocks the register model that was locked earlier in the environment's build_phase().

- Line 40 sets the offset of the CTRL register back to 0.

- Line 41 locks the model so that tests can use it.

(i) You can repeat this process any number of times any time you wish to lock and unlock the model. However, be aware that for every lock() and unlock() operation, the model walks through the register model and makes some changes to the register and field data structures.

Recommendation 20.1.3: *In case you have a large register model with tens/hundreds of thousands of registers, this can slow you down if you do it repeatedly. Plan out your lock/unlock test architecture before implementing it*

20.2 Burst Read and Write

At the current time, the UVM library does not support burst read or write operations. There are some challenges that arise when conducting a burst read/write, notably the approach to take when there are "holes" in the burst or if there are specialized registers (read only/write only) registers. To save memory, the register operation was defined as a struct instead of a class in UVM.

To work around this problem, several users have suggested using the extension mechanism available in the register model to carry information about the burst. Other approaches may involve adding additional API to the library and making some changes to the way register operations are calculated.

There is still some ongoing work to clarify the burst read and write operations from the library. When the standard is clarified, I will update the website.

20.3 Various Built-in Tests Available From UVM

The UVM library comes with some predefined sequences. After DUT integration, one can execute any of the predefined register test sequences to verify the proper operation of the registers and memories in the DUT. The simplest test (and one that finds the most bugs) is the hardware reset test. This allows you to debug the register model, the environment, the physical driver, and the DUT to a point if the environment is scalable, and the register model can be used in more elaborate tests. Some of the predefined test sequences require backdoor access depending on their definition per Tables 20.5 and 20.4. The tables presented were excerpted and used from the UVM Users guide [3] with my added comments and grouping.

Type of checks	Use for single instances of Reg/Memories	Sequence Name	Description	Attributes
Register	Single register Only	uvm_reg_single_bit_bash.seq	Sequentially writes 1's and 0's in each bit of the register, checking it is appropriately set or cleared, based on the field access policy specified for the field having the target bit.	Skip register if any of the following attributes is defined: NO_REG_BIT_BASH_TEST or NO_REG_TESTS
Register	Single register Only	uvm_reg_single_access.seq	Needs the backdoor be defined for the register. For each address map in which the register is accessible, writes the register then confirms the value was written using the backdoor. Subsequently writes a value via the backdoor and checks the corresponding value that can be read through the address map.	Skip register if any of the following attributes is defined: NO_REG_ACCESS_TEST or NO_REG_TESTS
Register	Single register Only	uvm_mem_single_walk.seq	Write a walking pattern into the memory then checks it can be read back with the expected value.	Skip memory if any of the following attributes is defined: NO_MEM_WALK_TEST or NO_MEM_TESTS or NO_REG_TESTS
Register	Single register Only	uvm_mem_single_access.seq	Needs the backdoor be defined the memory. For each address map in which the memory is accessible, writes the memory locations for each memory then confirms the value was written using the backdoor. Subsequently writes a value via the backdoor and checks that the corresponding value can be read through the address map.	Skip memory if any of the following attributes is defined: NO_MEM_ACCESS_TEST NO_MEM_TESTS or NO_REG_TESTS
Register	Uses Hierarchy API to check All registers	uvm_reg_hw_reset.seq	Reads all the register in a block and check their value is the specified reset value.	Skip block or register if any of the following attributes is defined: NO_REG_HW_RESET_TEST or NO_REG_TESTS
Register	Uses Hierarchy API to check All registers	uvm_reg_bit_bash.seq	Executes the uvm_reg_single_ bit_bash.seq sequence for all registers in a block and subblocks.	Skip block if any of the following attributes is defined: NO_REG_BIT_BASH_TEST or NO_REG_TESTS
Register	Uses Hierarchy API to check All registers	uvm_reg_access.seq	Executes the uvm_reg_single_ access.seq sequence for all registers in a block and sub-blocks.	Skip block if any of the following attributes is defined: NO_REG_ACCESS_TEST NO_REG_TESTS

Table 20.4: Built In Tests In UVM For Registers

These tests are available in source form in the UVM installation. Take a look into the sources once you become familiar with UVM.

Recommendation 20.3.0: *Note that some tests change a value from 1 to 0 and vice versa during the test (IE, each register test runs twice inside the sequence). This makes sure that both the values are covered.*

Type of checks	Use for single instances of Reg/Memories	Sequence Name	Description	Attributes
Memories	Uses Hierarchy API to check All memories	uvm_mem_walk_seq	Executes the uvm_mem_single_ walk_seq sequence for all memories in a block and sub-blocks.	Skip block if any of the following at- tributes is defined: NO_MEM_WALK_TEST NO_MEM_TESTS NO_REG_TESTS
Memories	Uses Hierarchy API to check All memories	uvm_mem_access_seq	Executes the uvm_mem_single_ access_seq sequence for all memories in a block and sub-blocks.	Skip block if any of the following at- tributes is defined: NO_MEM_ACCESS_TEST NO_MEM_TESTS NO_REG_TESTS
Registers in Maps		uvm_reg_shared_access_seq	Needs the register to be mapped in mul- tiple address maps. For each address map in which the register is accessible, writes the register via one map then confirms the value was written by reading it from all other address maps.	Skip register if any of the following attributes is defined: NO_SHARED_ACCESS_TEST NO_REG_TESTS
Memories in Maps	Uses Hierarchy API to check All registers	uvm_mem_shared_access_seq	Needs the memory to be mapped in mul- tiple address maps. For each address map in which the memory is accessible, writes each memory location via one map then confirms the value was written by reading it from all other address maps.	Skip memory if any of the following attributes is defined: NO_SHARED_ACCESS_TEST NO_MEM_TESTS NO_REG_TESTS
	Uses Hierarchy API to en- list all registers and memo- ries and walks through them	uvm_reg_mem_shared_seq_access_seq	Executes the uvm_reg_shared_ ac- cess_seq sequence for all registers in a block and subblocks. Executes the uvm_mem_shared_ access_seq sequence for all memories in a block and sub-blocks.	Skip block if any of the following attributes is defined: NO_SHARED_ACCESS_TEST NO_MEM_TESTS NO_REG_TESTS
	Runs all the above se- quences	uvm_reg_mem_built_in_seq	Execute all the selected predefined block level sequences. By default, all predefined block level sequences are selected.	Applies attributes governing each predefined se- quence, as defined above.
		uvm_reg_mem_hdl_paths_seq	Verify the HDL path(s) specified for regis- ters and memories are valid.	Skip register or memory if no HDL path(s) was specified.

Table 20.5: Built In Tests in UVM For Memories

These memory tests are also available in source form in the UVM installation. I would suggest that you look into the sources once you become familiar with UVM. If you design your own tests, it may be worthwhile to look at these as a template.

The nice thing about these sequences is that you can use them to automate most of the simple tasks in register verification quickly. They are all built for you! You can combine these sequences and use some of these sequences as subsequences in another sequence. Take a moment to look at the sequences in the $UVM_HOME/src/reg directory. Some these sequences use the register hierarchy API that was briefly covered in Section 12.5.2

20.4 Build and Run Instructions

In this environment, a complete Makefile is provided. The test can be compiled and run with the following simple command in the run directory:

```
% make
```

20.5 Exercises for Further Exploration

This chapter introduced the VGA core. After creating a simple environment, some steps were followed to create a register model and integrate it into the environment. Some tests and sequences using the register model were run on the environment. A study of both the implicit and explicit prediction mechanisms and a study of the front door and backdoor methods were undertaken in this chapter. The provided environment can be easily extended to test out other features in the core. Such an exercise is worth your time.

This environment, while mostly complete, doesn't exercise the DUT in a functional mode entirely. Complete the DVI monitor code (only a simple clocking block is provided in the example) and see if you can get traffic through the block. I have provided a rudimentary set of sequences, but the checking infrastructure and other files are supplied in a skeletal form. The code for the actual checks is placed in the Verilog directory of the example. It should not be difficult to do. You learn how to write checkers once you do this.

1. Modify the provided examples to see what happens during the access of various registers by turning off testing for different fields and registers. Turn on coverage and see the results of how the register programming affect the register coverage. Pay some attention to how the coverage is affected by the in-built tests.

2. Update the register model from the backdoor in a test and then do front door access to the register.

3. Force a value from the simulator. What kind of errors do you get when the register model is out of sync with the DUT? How do you reconcile them?

4. Change the environment so that you can pass some frames through the DUT and then shut itself down once the sequence is completed.

Chapter 21

Factories, Multiple Register Interfaces, Reporting, Callbacks and Command Line Control using the Wishbone Conmax Crossbar

Any SOC typically has a cross-connect component that interconnects blocks of IP that perform various functions. Creating a verification environment for this cross-connect is a good exercise since many master and slave components are present in the environment. Many UVM concepts can be learned through a single environment while testing this core. This chapter uses the central crossbar in a verification environment to discuss the following topics:

- Factory scheme

- Register model with multiple interfaces

- Virtual Sequences

- Scoreboard with multiple input ports and a simple comparison function

- Report suppression from some components

- Flat sequences

- Config DB usage

- Use of the command line processor in UVM

- Virtual Sequences

- Messaging and verbosity

- Callbacks

- Flat Sequences

It is assumed that you have had read Parts 1,2 and 3 as these Parts provide the background information that is related to this chapter. Most of the content presented builds upon the example discussed in those Parts[1].

21.1 Verification Environment

The Wishbone Conmax Crossbar is an RTL core that is constructed with 8 masters and 16 slaves. It uses a memory-mapped scheme to partition its address map amongst the slave devices. Any master can address any slave by issuing a transaction in the address range connected to the slave. A complete verification environment can be constructed to test out the crossbar using UVM. Input transactions are generated on the master interface, monitored on the appropriate slave interface to ensure that they were routed correctly and checked to ensure data integrity is met. The crossbar has many configuration registers, which are modeled using the approach presented in Chapter 20.

The wb_conmax module has 8 master interfaces and 16 slave interfaces, which are all connected to agents in the verification environment. To interface with each of the master ports, a master agent is needed. To interface with each of the slave ports, a slave agent is needed. This brings us to a total of 24 different master and slave components in the testbench.

---

[1] You should extend the provided environment to explore other aspects of UVM with this example. Look at provided documentation for further details of the crossbar if you choose to learn more about its capabilities.

Each of the components must be configured with many parameters. Since this design is essentially a "router" that moves transactions from one interface to another depending on the address range, a scoreboard is needed to ensure that the transactions are transferred correctly. This scoreboard needs to consider the fact that any of the 8 masters can interface with any of the 16 slaves. Addressing registers implies that a register model is required.

Figure 21.1 shows the overall block diagram of the environment. This environment consists of 8 masters and 16 slaves. Since there are 8 different interfaces by which the register model can program the DUT, each of them is connected to a map since each of them could have a separate address range for the interfaces going to the registers in the DUT.

The scoreboard is one of the more interesting components in this environment. The scoreboard must accept inputs from 8 masters and all 16 slaves and keep track of the master requests and the corresponding slave responses in the address mapping. It also must make sure that the transaction is transferred correctly.

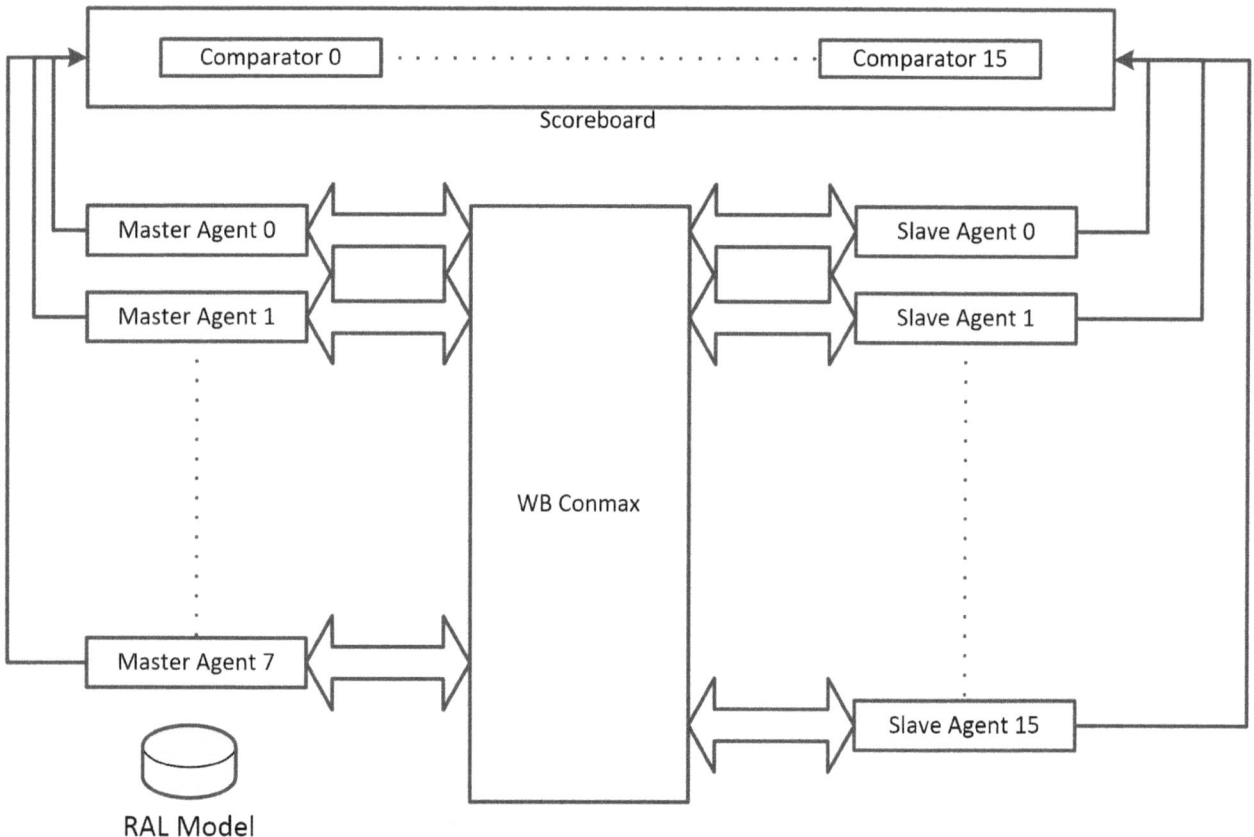

Fig. 21.1: Block Diagram of the Wb Conmax Testbench Environment

Each of the components that make up the environment is discussed in the following sections. You can draw parallels between the discussion in Chapters 2 and this chapter and see how the concepts from the simple example in that chapter map to the examples in this current chapter.

The master agent used in the environment is the master agent that was developed in Chapter 8. The slave agent used in the environment is the slave agent developed in Chapter 16. See those sections for the details of the agent implementation.

21.1.1 Register Programming Model

Each of the slaves in this WB Conmax block is allocated a region of memory configured in the RTL. A portion of the memory region for slave 15 is allocated for configuring the registers for the WB Conmax block. The register file consists of 16 registers of 16 bits each. The register file is selected when a master selects slave interface 15 and when the second nibble from the top address bits (MSB-4 through MSB-7) is equal to the parameter "rf_addr".

Table 21.1: Conmax Registers

Register	Address	Mode	Description
CFG0	0	RW	Configuration Register for Slave 0
CFG1	4	RW	Configuration Register for Slave 1
CFG2	8	RW	Configuration Register for Slave 2
CFG3	c	RW	Configuration Register for Slave 3
CFG4	10	RW	Configuration Register for Slave 4
CFG5	14	RW	Configuration Register for Slave 5
CFG6	18	RW	Configuration Register for Slave 6
CFG7	1c	RW	Configuration Register for Slave 7
CFG8	20	RW	Configuration Register for Slave 8
CFG9	24	RW	Configuration Register for Slave 9
CFG10	28	RW	Configuration Register for Slave 10
CFG11	2c	RW	Configuration Register for Slave 11
CFG12	30	RW	Configuration Register for Slave 12
CFG13	34	RW	Configuration Register for Slave 13
CFG14	38	RW	Configuration Register for Slave 14
CFG15	3c	RW	Configuration Register for Slave 15

Registers CFG0-15 are identical in structure. They provide priority settings for each of the slaves. The steps to create and integrate a register model for the wb_conmax module are identical to the steps shown in Chapter 20. These steps include the description of an abstract register description of the model and generating these with a register generation tool and integrating them into the environment, as shown in Section 20.1. All the nine steps described in Section 20.1 were executed here to create a register model for use with the wb_conmax environment. For more information, you are referred to Chapter 20. Table 21.1 shows a listing of the various registers that are in the register map for the RTL.

21.1.2 The Register Model for Multiple Interfaces

The wb_conmax module has eight master ports. Any of the eight masters could access the register file in the address space of slave 15 and program the registers. Each of the masters is attached to a different physical interface. It is possible that each of the masters can access the register model independently completely asynchronous from the other masters. This can lead to interesting conflicts depending on the sequencing of the register writes (and obviously the order/priority of the sequences that do so). To prevent corruption of values, the UVM register model has a built-in semaphore to prevent accidental overwrites.

In the wb_conmax example, there are eight different interfaces, and each has its map. (In this case, all the maps are identical as all the masters have access to the entire address space, but this may not be true in other devices.) Eight different maps are added to the register model. Each of the registers CFG0-CFG15 is associated with each of the maps as seen in the generated model.

Each of the maps needs a register adapter (described in Section 20.1.2). This example contains eight identical masters, and hence eight copies of the register adapter are created. Note that on a SOC bus, one input could be AHB, another could be OCP, and a third one could be an AXI 64-bit bus, and a fourth one could be a 32-bit AXI bus for instance. Hence, they could all be different. Each of the adapters is then associated with the respective maps, as shown in the code.

Figure 21.2 shows the various register adapters all connected to the same register model. Each of the maps is connected to a master agent. These connections are shown in Listing 21.1. Note that each of the maps is called a domain numbered 0-7 in the listing. Note that the listing is partial and shows a part of the build_phase() and part of the connect_phase().

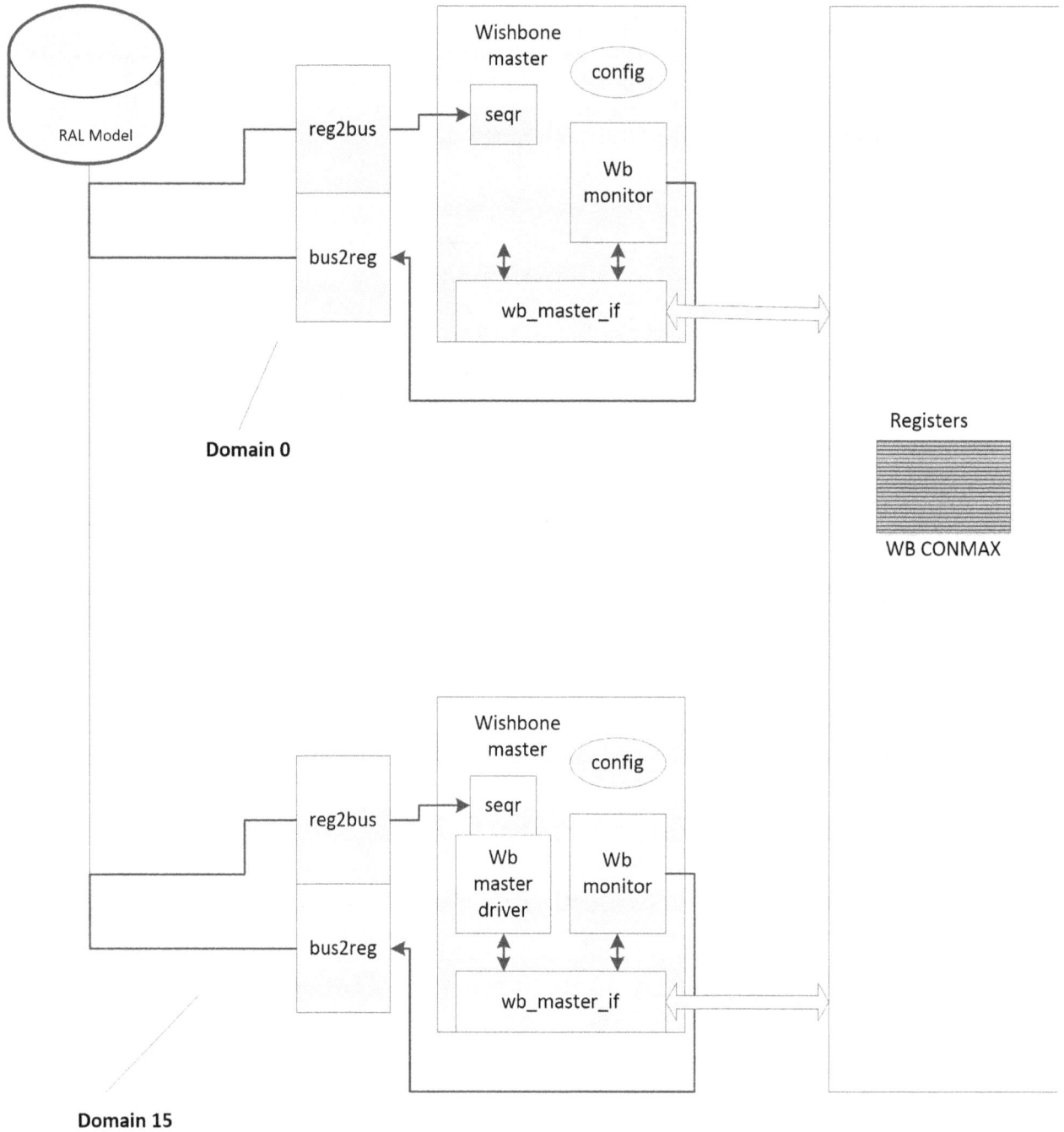

Fig. 21.2: Register Adapters Connected To Different Masters And Different Maps

Listing 21.1: Register Model Multiple Map Connections

```
73
74     for(integer i = 0; i < 8; i++) begin
75       ral_adapter[i] = new($sformatf("reg2agent_ral_adapter[%d]",i));
76     end
77   endfunction: build_phase
78
79   function void wb_conmax_env::connect_phase(uvm_phase phase);
80     super.connect_phase(phase);
81
82     // Set up the domain sequencers
83
84     ral_regmodel.wb_conmax_domain0.set_sequencer(master_agent[0].mast_sqr,
         ral_adapter[0]);
85     ral_regmodel.wb_conmax_domain1.set_sequencer(master_agent[1].mast_sqr,
         ral_adapter[1]);
86     ral_regmodel.wb_conmax_domain2.set_sequencer(master_agent[2].mast_sqr,
         ral_adapter[2]);
87     ral_regmodel.wb_conmax_domain3.set_sequencer(master_agent[3].mast_sqr,
         ral_adapter[3]);
88     ral_regmodel.wb_conmax_domain4.set_sequencer(master_agent[4].mast_sqr,
         ral_adapter[4]);
89     ral_regmodel.wb_conmax_domain5.set_sequencer(master_agent[5].mast_sqr,
         ral_adapter[5]);
90     ral_regmodel.wb_conmax_domain6.set_sequencer(master_agent[6].mast_sqr,
         ral_adapter[6]);
91     ral_regmodel.wb_conmax_domain7.set_sequencer(master_agent[7].mast_sqr,
         ral_adapter[7]);
```

Note that 21.1 intentionally has partial listings of two different methods.

- Lines 74-76 shows the creation of the register adapters. The adapters are built in a for loop, Each of the adapters has a unique name: "reg_2agent_ral_adapter[00]". These are executed during the build_phase.

- Line 84 shows the register model map 0 having its default sequencer set as that of master_agent[0] using ral_adapter[0].

- Any time the register model uses master_agent[0] and map0, the ral_adapter[0] is used to convert the abstract register transaction into a transaction that is understood by master_agent[0].

- Similar operations occur for maps 1-7 on lines 85-91.

Refer to the provided sequences in the download for examples on how to program the registers using different maps. Note that when the registers in the DUT become accessible via more than one physical bus interface, the same register sequence may instead be started as a virtual sequence as the sequencer used in each write/read call is not directly referenced. The register model routes the operation to the appropriate sequencer, based on the map that is in effect.

21.1.3 Using a Scoreboard with Multiple Input Ports and a Simple Comparator

The scoreboard is one of the most complex pieces of this environment. This scoreboard must take in the various master inputs and slave inputs and compare the transactions. In our case, our scoreboard has to get inputs from 8 masters and 16 slaves. Figure 21.3 shows the block diagram of our scoreboard. This contains 24 analysis ports to accept transactions from the master and slave monitors.

As soon as you begin to design a scoreboard, you can only declare a single write() function when you use an analysis port. This is a problem. Fortunately, UVM supplies us with macros to solve this problem. Listing 21.2 shows you how:

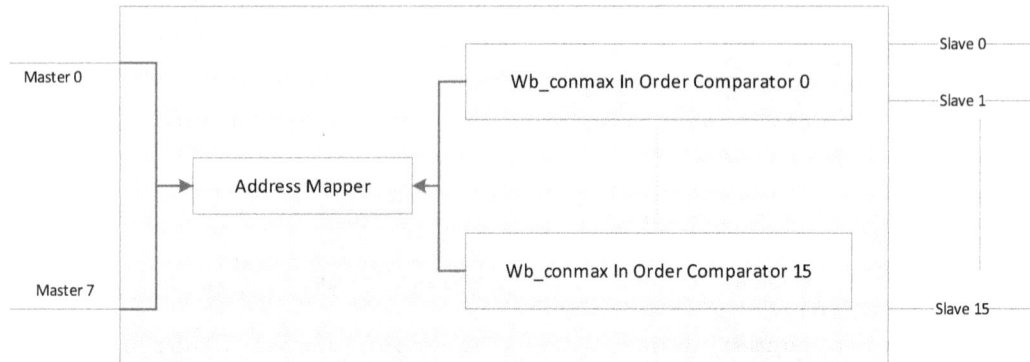

Fig. 21.3: Block Diagram Of The Scoreboard

Listing 21.2: Scoreboard Class

```
17    `uvm_analysis_imp_decl(_master)
18    `uvm_analysis_imp_decl(_slave)
19
20    typedef class wb_transaction;
21    class wb_conmax_scoreboard extends uvm_scoreboard;
22
23        `include "wb_conmax_env_defines.svh"
24        uvm_analysis_imp_master #(wb_transaction,wb_conmax_scoreboard)
             master_export[8];
25        uvm_analysis_imp_slave #(wb_transaction,wb_conmax_scoreboard)
             slave_export[16];
26
27        uvm_tlm_analysis_fifo #(wb_transaction) master_fifo[8];
28
29        wb_conmax_in_order_class_comparator #(wb_transaction) comparator
           [16];
30
31        `uvm_component_utils(wb_conmax_scoreboard);
32        extern function new(string name = "wb_conmax_scoreboard",
33            uvm_component parent = null);
34        extern virtual function void build_phase (uvm_phase phase);
35        extern virtual function void connect_phase (uvm_phase phase);
36        extern virtual function void end_of_elaboration_phase (uvm_phase
             phase);
37        extern virtual task run_phase(uvm_phase phase);
38        extern virtual function void report_phase(uvm_phase phase);
39        extern function void write_master(wb_transaction tr);
40        extern function void write_slave(wb_transaction tr);
41        extern function void report();
42        extern function int get_addr(ref wb_transaction tr);
```

```
43          extern function bit report_info_hook(input id, string message, int
                 verbosity, string filename, int line) ;
44
45     endclass: wb_conmax_scoreboard
```

- Lines 17-18 show the `uvm_analysis_imp_decl macros that allow you to declare *multiple* master and slave implementations. If you did not use these macros, you would be restricted to having only *one* write() method in the class. The macro allows you to declare *multiple* methods and associate them with the appropriate port write() implementations.

> The earlier edition of this book used a simple comparator. The comparators are not part of the IEEE Standard. They were primitive in terms of their capabilities and are present in UVM 1.2.
>
> In this edition of the book, I have added a new comparator wb_conmax_in_order_class_comparator. The details of this are not essential to the discussion below.

This is a simple cross connect, which is not as sophisticated as some of the more complex contemporary interconnects. A simple address decoding will be more than enough to see the transactions being routed to various slaves. In a more sophisticated scheme where a priority/arbitration scheme is in effect, such a simple system would be inadequate. However, this will suffice for the simple purpose of exploring UVM. The actual decoding, in this case, is simple as can be seen in the listing:

Listing 21.3: Scoreboard Multiple Analysis Port Implementation

```
89     function void wb_conmax_scoreboard::write_master(wb_transaction tr);
90         `uvm_info("SCOREBOARD_MASTER",tr.sprint(),UVM_HIGH)
91         comparator[get_addr(tr)].before_export.write(tr);
92     endfunction
93
94     function  void wb_conmax_scoreboard::write_slave(wb_transaction tr);
95         `uvm_info("SCOREBOARD_SLAVE",tr.sprint(),UVM_HIGH)
96         comparator[get_addr(tr)].after_export.write(tr);
97     endfunction
```

Listing 21.3 shows the effect of the two macros described in the earlier listing. As a result of the `uvm_analysis_imp_decl macro(_master) and the `uvm_analysis_imp_decl macro(_slave) on Lines 1-2 I can *create two write methods* to connect to the analysis ports which would not otherwise be possible in a single class. The write() methods are named write_master() and write_slave() (the second part after the write in the method name is whatever you pass to the macro. Do not introduce spaces in it!)

- Line 89 declares the write_master() method. This method is used instead of the write() method provided by the analysis port.

- Line 91 shows the corresponding comparison function indexed by the relevant slave being used.

- The write() method of the appropriate comparison function is invoked by the write_master method to write to the analysis port of the comparator.

- A similar process is carried out for the slaves on Lines 94-97.

- Note that the get_addr() method is not shown here, it returns an integer indexing the right slave.

> There are many other macros not shown here, which you can use for the other kinds of ports. Look in the src/macros/uvm_tlm_defines.svh file in your UVM sources for the specific flavor of the macro you would like to use.

21.1.4 Putting it All Together: The Top-level Environment

All the various components were defined in the earlier sections; it is time to integrate the various components into an environment so that it can be used in a testcase. To do so, the following components must be made a part of the environment:

- Eight instances of master agents, one per port of the master interface

- Sixteen instances of slave agents one per port of the master interface

- A scoreboard component that connects all the instances of masters and slaves for checking

- A virtual sequencer component to drive multithreaded stimulus to the DUT

- The register model containing the register model

- The adapters for the register model to allow the model to connect to the master agents

- A coverage component to cover the options given to the environment

This is shown in Listing 21.4.

Listing 21.4: Top Level Environment

```
17   class wb_conmax_env extends uvm_env;
18
19     wb_master_agent master_agent[8];
20     wb_slave_agent slave_agent[16];
21     wb_conmax_scoreboard conmax_scbd;
22     wb_conmax_virtual_sequencer wb_conmax_virt_seqr;
23
24     // reset Agent
25     reset_agent rst_agent;
26
27     // This is the RAL Model.
28     wb_conmax_env_ral_block ral_regmodel;
29     // This is the adapter
30     wb_conmax_ral_adapter    ral_adapter[8];
31
32     `uvm_component_utils(wb_conmax_env)
33
34     // Function declarations
35     extern function new(string name="wb_conmax_env", uvm_component parent=
           null);
36     extern virtual function void build_phase(uvm_phase phase);
37     extern virtual function void connect_phase(uvm_phase phase);
38
39   endclass: wb_conmax_env
```

Listing 21.4 shows part of the definition of the wb_conmax class.

- Line 17 shows the declaration of the environment.

- Line 19 shows the eight master agent instances.

- Line 20 shows the 16 slave agent instances.

- Line 21 shows the scoreboard.

- Line 25 shows the reset agent.

- Lines 28 and 30 show the register model and the adapters, respectively.

These various components are built during the build_phase(), which are then interconnected in the connect_phase() methods.

21.1.5 The Build Phase

The build_phase is where everything is created in the environment. Various class instances are created using the factory as can be seen in the listing below:

Listing 21.5: Top Level Environment Build Phase

```
45   function void wb_conmax_env::build_phase(uvm_phase phase);
46     super.build_phase(phase);
47     // Build Reset Agent
48     rst_agent = reset_agent::type_id::create("rst_agent",this);
49
50     // Build Masters
51     for(integer i = 0; i < 8; i++) begin
52       master_agent[i] = wb_master_agent::type_id::create($sformatf("
             master_agent[%02d]",i),this);
53       uvm_config_db #(uvm_object_wrapper)::set(this, {master_agent[i].
             get_name(), ".", "seqr.run_phase"}, "default_sequence",
             sequence_0::get_type());
54     end
55     // Build Slaves
56     for(integer i = 0; i < 16; i++) begin
57       slave_agent[i] = wb_slave_agent::type_id::create($sformatf("
             slave_agent[%02d]",i),this);
58       uvm_config_db #(uvm_object_wrapper)::set(this, {slave_agent[i].
             get_name(), ".", "seqr.run_phase"}, "default_sequence",sequence_0
             ::get_type());
59     end
60
61     // Scoreboard
62     conmax_scbd  = wb_conmax_scoreboard::type_id::create("Scoreboard",this
             );
63
64     // Build the RAL Model
65     if(ral_regmodel == null) begin
66       ral_regmodel = wb_conmax_env_ral_block::type_id::create("
             ral_regmodel",this);
67       ral_regmodel.build;
68       ral_regmodel.lock_model();
69     end
70
71     // Build the virtual Sequencer
72     wb_conmax_virt_seqr = wb_conmax_virtual_sequencer::type_id::create("
             wb_conmax_virt_seqr",this);
73
74     for(integer i = 0; i < 8; i++) begin
75       ral_adapter[i] = new($sformatf("reg2agent_ral_adapter[%d]",i));
76     end
77   endfunction: build_phase
```

• Line 48 shows the construction of the reset agent.

- Lines 51-54 show the construction of the master agent. The default sequence for each of the agents is set to the type sequence_0 in the environment.

- Lines 56-59 show the construction of the slave agents in a fashion similar to the master agent.

- Line 62 shows the factory creation of the scoreboard.

- Line 66 shows the creation of the register model.

- Line 67 shows the register model being built. Note that there are no factory methods used with the register model, although it is a structural component.

- Lines 68 shows the register model being locked. No further changes are allowed in the model.

- Line 72 shows the virtual sequencer being created.

- Lines 74-76 show the creation of 8 adapters. Note that in our case, all the adapters are identical, and hence I put them into an array. *In most of the other cases, you need to put individual adapters based on the protocol.*

21.1.6 Connect Phase

The build_phase illustrated the creation of various components of the environment. The connect_phase interconnects the environment sub-components so that everything works as intended.

Listing 21.6: Top Level Environment Connections

```
79   function void wb_conmax_env::connect_phase(uvm_phase phase);
80     super.connect_phase(phase);
81
82     // Set up the domain sequencers
83
84     ral_regmodel.wb_conmax_domain0.set_sequencer(master_agent[0].mast_sqr,
            ral_adapter[0]);
85     ral_regmodel.wb_conmax_domain1.set_sequencer(master_agent[1].mast_sqr,
            ral_adapter[1]);
86     ral_regmodel.wb_conmax_domain2.set_sequencer(master_agent[2].mast_sqr,
            ral_adapter[2]);
87     ral_regmodel.wb_conmax_domain3.set_sequencer(master_agent[3].mast_sqr,
            ral_adapter[3]);
88     ral_regmodel.wb_conmax_domain4.set_sequencer(master_agent[4].mast_sqr,
            ral_adapter[4]);
89     ral_regmodel.wb_conmax_domain5.set_sequencer(master_agent[5].mast_sqr,
            ral_adapter[5]);
90     ral_regmodel.wb_conmax_domain6.set_sequencer(master_agent[6].mast_sqr,
            ral_adapter[6]);
91     ral_regmodel.wb_conmax_domain7.set_sequencer(master_agent[7].mast_sqr,
            ral_adapter[7]);
92
93     for(integer i = 0; i < 8; i++) begin
94       master_agent[i].mast_mon.mon_analysis_port.connect(conmax_scbd.
            master_export[i]);
95
96     end
97     for(integer i = 0; i < 16; i++) begin
98       slave_agent[i].slv_mon.mon_analysis_port.connect(conmax_scbd.
            slave_export[i]);
99     end
100
```

```
101      wb_conmax_virt_seqr.seqr0 = master_agent[00].mast_sqr;
102      wb_conmax_virt_seqr.seqr1 = master_agent[01].mast_sqr;
103      wb_conmax_virt_seqr.seqr2 = master_agent[02].mast_sqr;
104      wb_conmax_virt_seqr.seqr3 = master_agent[03].mast_sqr;
105      wb_conmax_virt_seqr.seqr4 = master_agent[04].mast_sqr;
106      wb_conmax_virt_seqr.seqr5 = master_agent[05].mast_sqr;
107      wb_conmax_virt_seqr.seqr6 = master_agent[06].mast_sqr;
108      wb_conmax_virt_seqr.seqr7 = master_agent[07].mast_sqr;
109
110   endfunction: connect_phase
```

- Lines 84-91 show the register model maps being set with a sequencer. Each of the entries sets a sequencer to a different map for the same register model. For instance: Line 94 shows the master sequencer of master_agent[1] being set as the sequencer for map1.

- Lines 93-96 show the analysis port of the master agent monitor being connected to the scoreboard export ports.

- Lines 97-99 show the analysis port for the slave agent monitors being connected to the scoreboard.

- Lines 101-108 shows the virtual sequencer's subsequencer handles being assigned to the appropriate master sequencers. If the virtual sequencer runs a sequence on seqr0, it is running on the master_agent[0] master sequencer.

21.1.7 Top-Level Base Test

The top-level test instantiates the environment and brings together all the default settings to be able to run a test. As a reminder, the various master and slave agents were completely configurable. These configurations are features in the verification plan; they were placed in the test rather than in the environment.

Normally, many tests usually share many settings. Hence, it makes sense to keep all the settings in one common base class and then extend that base class to create tests that perform test-specific actions.

The top-level test needs to accomplish several things:

1. Create an instance of the environment class.

2. Create 16 configuration instances for the 16 masters in the environment.

3. Create 8 configuration instances for the 8 slaves in the environment.

4. Place the configuration instances in the config_db.

5. Build the environment.

Listing 21.7 illustrates these steps in code.

Listing 21.7: The Base test

```
20    class wb_conmax_base_test extends uvm_test;
21
22        wb_config master_configs[8];
23        wb_config slave_configs[16];
24
25        int slave_adr_max ;
26        int slave_adr_min;
27
28        `uvm_component_utils(wb_conmax_base_test)
29
30        wb_conmax_env env;
31
32        function new(string name, uvm_component parent);
```

```
33              super.new(name, parent);
34          endfunction
35
36          virtual function void build_phase(uvm_phase phase);
37              uvm_coreservice_t cs = uvm_coreservice_t::get();
38              uvm_root r = cs.get_root();
39              uvm_factory fact = cs.get_factory();
40              slave_adr_max = 32'h0fffffe;
41              super.build_phase(phase);
42
43              uvm_config_db #(uvm_object_wrapper)::set(this, "env.rst_agent.
                    mast_sqr.reset_phase", "default_sequence", reset_sequence::
                    get_type());
44
45              // create the configurations
46              // Master config
47              for(int i = 0; i < 8; i++) begin
48                  master_configs[i] = wb_config::type_id::create($sformatf("
                        master_configs[%02d]",i));
49                  master_configs[i].randomize with {min_addr == 0; max_addr
                        == slave_adr_max; max_n_wss == 5; };
50              end
51
52              // create the configurations
53              // Slave config
54              for(int i = 0; i < 16; i++) begin
55                  slave_adr_min = 0;
56                  slave_configs[i] = wb_config::type_id::create($sformatf("
                        slave_configs[%02d]",i));
57                  slave_configs[i].randomize with {min_addr == slave_adr_min
                        ; max_addr == slave_adr_max; max_n_wss == 2; };
58                  slave_adr_min =slave_adr_max + 1;
59                  slave_adr_max = slave_adr_max + 1 + 32'h00fffffe;
60              end
61
62              // Set the default sequencer in all the master agents
63              for(int i = 0; i < 8; i++) begin
64                  uvm_config_db #(uvm_object_wrapper)::set(this, $sformatf("
                        env.master_agent[%02d].mast_sqr.main_phase",i), "
                        default_sequence", null);
65                  uvm_config_db #(wb_config)::set(null,$sformatf("
                        uvm_test_top.env.master_agent[%02d]",i),"config",
                        master_configs[i] );
66              end
67
68              // Slave configuration
69              for(int i = 0; i < 16; i++) begin
70                  uvm_config_db #(wb_config)::set(null,$sformatf("
                        uvm_test_top.env.slave_agent[%02d]",i),"config",
                        slave_configs[i] );
71              end
72
73              env = wb_conmax_env::type_id::create("env", this);
74
```

```
75                    fact.print();
76             endfunction
77
78      endclass : wb_conmax_base_test
```

In Listing 21.7:

- Line 22-23 shows the various master and slave agent configurations being instantiated in the test.

- Lines 47-50 show the master agent configurations being built and randomized with constraints for the number of wait_states and min and max addresses.

- Lines 54-60 show a similar configuration for the slave agent.

- Lines 64 sets the default sequence in each of the master agents to null. Notice that this setting overrides the default configuration setting seen in the build_phase of the environment.

- Line 65 shows the master agent configurations being inserted into the config_db. These are retrieved by the respective master agents during their build_phase() execution. We discuss the need for this in Section 21.3.

- Lines 69-71 repeat this operation on the slave agents.

- After all the config_db settings are completed, the environment is created on line 73. It takes in all the configuration settings and recursively builds all the components in the environment as per the build_phase description in Section 21.1.5.

- Line 75 shows a debug print option to print the contents of the factory.

21.1.8 Creating a Specific Test

The base test contains all the settings that are used by multiple tests in the testbench. The wb_conmax_flat_sequence_test extends from the wb_conmax_base_test and sets a default sequence. It extends the base test and derives all the other settings from the base test. By inheriting the settings from the base test, the specifics of the test separate from the general settings that are needed in the environment can be organized.

Listing 21.8: Flat Sequence

```
20   class wb_conmax_flat_seq_test extends wb_conmax_base_test;
21
22      `uvm_component_utils(wb_conmax_flat_seq_test)
23
24      function new(string name, uvm_component parent);
25        super.new(name, parent);
26      endfunction
27
28      sequence_0 seq0;
29
30
31      virtual task main_phase(uvm_phase phase);
32        super.main_phase(phase);
33        phase.raise_objection(this,"Test Main Objection");
34        seq0 = sequence_0::type_id::create("sequence_1",this);
35        seq0.start(env.master_agent[00].mast_sqr,null);
36        seq0.wait_for_sequence_state(UVM_FINISHED);
37        phase.drop_objection(this,"Dropping Test Main Objection");
38      endtask
39
40   endclass :  wb_conmax_flat_seq_test
```

- Line 20: Class wb_conmax_flat_seq_test extends from the wb_conmax_base_test from the earlier section. It inherits all the various settings for the master/slave agents etc. from the base test.

- Lines 24-26 show the constructor for the test.

- The sequence_0 is the sequence that is executed in the test. It performs a set of reads and writes through the master agent[0].

- The connect_phase and other phases are used from the base test in this example.

21.1.9 Selecting a Specific Test to Run

In a typical verification environment, there are usually multiple tests that are compiled, and a specific test is made available for execution. The simulator's command-line plusarg +UVM_TESTNAME=testname specifies the name of the test to run (a name is associated with a test by registering the test class with the factory). If this plusarg is not used, then the test name argument of run_test may be used to specify the test name instead. If no test name is given, or it cannot find the test registered with it, no environment is created, and the simulation dies. See Section 11 for details on how to set the default test using the command line.

The uvm_top.run_test task() or the global run_test() task is called from an initial block in the top-level testbench module to instantiate a test using the factory and then run it (run_test is a wrapper that calls uvm_top, run_test.) The test's build_phase method creates the top-level environment. Configuration and/or factory overrides may be used within the test to customize a reusable test environment (or any of its components) without having to modify the environment code.

21.2 Factory Usage for Environment Creation

Chapter 5 provided a detailed discussion about the factory. Using the factory, one can create components and classes, and instruct the factory to provide alternate class types in lieu of the requested classes. This section focusses on using the factory to generate the various components in the wb_conmax environment. All the components are generated using factory methods. Subsequent sections show you how to override the components generated by the factory in some ways. The following listing shows how the various components are created by the factory.

See Section 21.1.5 and observe the create() command in the listing (Lines 52 and similar ones) where the factory creates the objects.

21.2.1 Using a Type Override

The build_phase of the environment showed how the factory method could create various components. Consider a situation where you had a different agent that was derived from the master_agent class, which had some additional functionality. (perhaps a different set of configurations, or a more updated driver?). If you had to replace all the instances of the master agent in the simulation, as shown by Figure 5.4, then you could use a type override. This is illustrated by the test below.

Listing 21.9: A Type Override Example

```
20 class wb_conmax_factory_type_override_test extends wb_conmax_base_test;
21
22    `uvm_component_utils(wb_conmax_factory_type_override_test)
23
24    sequence_1 seq1;
25
26    function new(string name, uvm_component parent);
27       super.new(name, parent);
28    endfunction
29
30    virtual function void build_phase(uvm_phase phase);
31       // Using the uvm_coreservice_t:
32       uvm_coreservice_t cs;
33       uvm_root r;
```

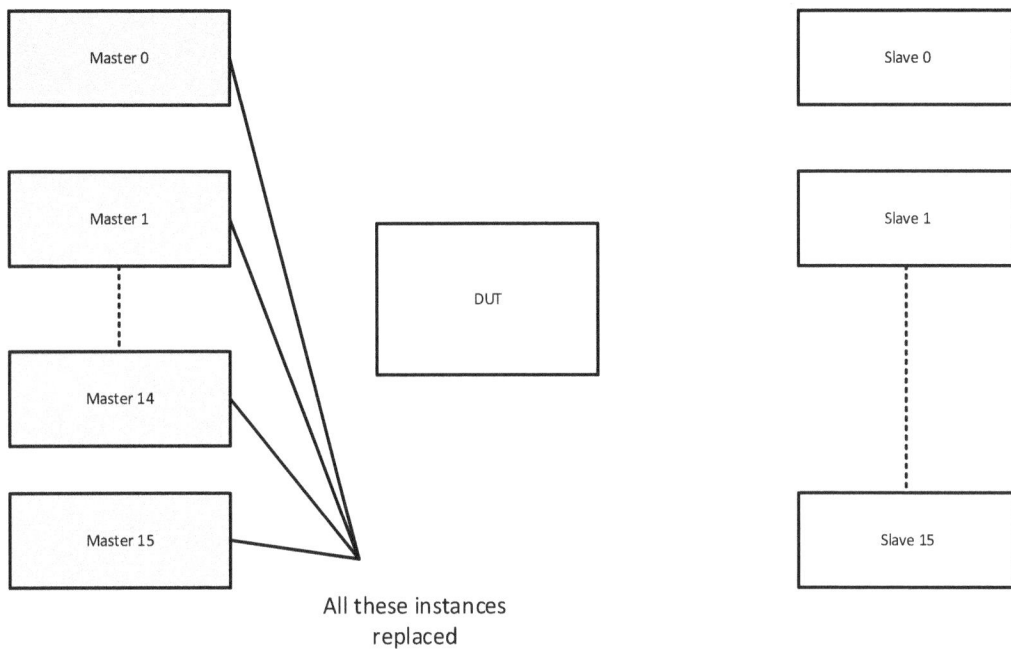

Fig. 21.4: Type Override

```
34        uvm_factory fact;
35        super.build_phase(phase);
36        // uvm_config_db #(wb_config)::set(null,$sformatf("uvm_test_top.env.
             master_agent[%02d]",i),"mstr_agent_cfg",master_configs[i] );
37
38        cs = uvm_coreservice_t::get();
39        r = cs.get_root();
40        fact = cs.get_factory();
41        fact.set_type_override_by_type(wb_master_agent::get_type(),
             wb_master_agent_n::get_type(),1);
42        // For you to to try out. Comment above line and uncomment one of
             the below.
43        // fact.set_inst_override_by_type(wb_master_agent::get_type(),
             wb_master_agent_n::get_type(),"env.master_agent[00]");
44        // set_inst_override_by_type(wb_master_agent::get_type(),
             wb_master_agent_n::get_type(),my_full_path);
45        // wb_master_agent::type_id::set_inst_override(wb_master_agent_n::
             get_type(),my_full_path);
46        // uvm_factory::set_inst_override_by_type(wb_master_agent::get_type
             (),wb_master_agent_n::get_type(),my_full_path);
47        fact.print();
48        // Set the default sequencer in all the master agents
```

In this example, consider that all instances of type master_agent were replaced by instances of type master_agent_n. To do so, the type override must have been registered with the factory, as was done using the 'uvm_component_utils() methods. Listing 21.9 shows a factory override test that replaces these agents.

- Lines 32-40 shows an example of how to get a handle to the factory using the uvm_coreservice class. This coreservice class is a singleton instance of uvm_coreservice_t, and this provides a common point for all central uvm services such as uvm_factory, uvm_report_server, and others. This coreservice class while acting as a container, provides many set() and get() accessor methods [2].

- Line 38 gets the coreservice handle so that one can access the singleton

- Line 41 gets a handle to the factory.

- Line 42 implements the actual type override instructing the factory to replace the wb_master_agent class with type wb_master_agent_n.

- Line 47 instructs the factory to print all its registered and override types.

Note that there was another way to accomplish it. You could use the set_type_override from the class itself.

21.2.2 Using Instance Overrides to Override Specific Instances

In Section 5.5.2 a discussion of the factory overrides on an instance specific basis was presented. The Factory API allows the function to be called in a test as can be seen in the section below.

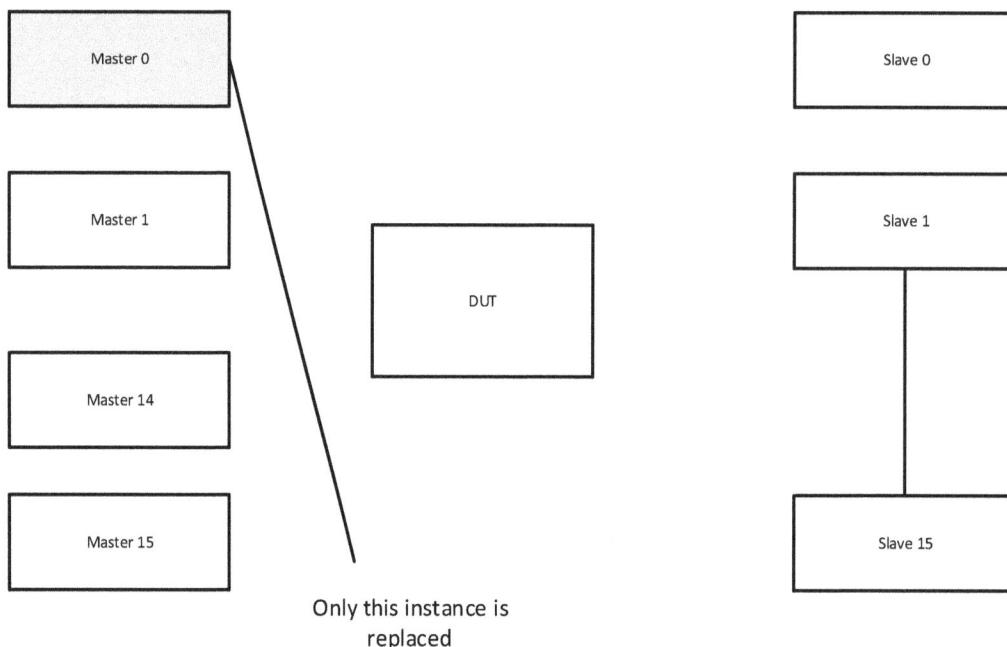

Fig. 21.5: Instance Override

There are two different ways to create instance overrides:

- Using the command line for instance overrides See Section 21.9.6 for an example.

- Using the test for instance overrides described below.

---

[2] The reason for providing this class in UVM is so that you can choose to replace even the factory, report server, etc. with an instance you create. This is advanced usage, not explored in this book. You must be incredibly careful if you try this.

In Section 5.5.2, the function set_inst_override_by_name() was described to set up the instance overrides. By observing our verification environment, we can replace the master_agent component in the environment for the first and third ports with following steps:

1. Define the class that is going to override the specific instance.

2. Create the override for the instance by calling the set_inst_override_by_name() method.

3. Build the environment after creating the override.

The actual override is done in the test class. The listing below provides an example.

Listing 21.10: Instance Override Example

```
21 class wb_conmax_factory_instance_override_test extends wb_conmax_base_test
      ;
22
23     `uvm_component_utils(wb_conmax_factory_instance_override_test)
24
25     function new(string name, uvm_component parent);
26         super.new(name, parent);
27     endfunction
28
29     virtual function void build_phase(uvm_phase phase);
30         string my_full_path;
31         string orig_type_name, override_type_name;
32         uvm_coreservice_t cs;
33         uvm_root r;
34         uvm_factory fact;
35
36         cs = uvm_coreservice_t::get();
37         r = cs.get_root();
38         fact = cs.get_factory();
39         my_full_path = "env.master_agent[00]";
40         orig_type_name = "wb_master_agent";
41         override_type_name = "wb_master_agent_n";
42
43         set_inst_override(my_full_path,orig_type_name,override_type_name);
44
45         fact.print();
46         super.build_phase(phase);
47         // Set the default sequencer in one of the master agents
48         uvm_config_db #(uvm_object_wrapper)::set(this, "env.master_agent
              [00].mast_sqr.main_phase", "default_sequence", sequence_1::
              get_type());
49         r.enable_print_topology=1;
50         r.print_topology();
51
52     endfunction
```

• Lines 42 shows a way to perform an instance override. The rest of the steps are similar to the previous example.

21.3 Use of Config DB to Apply Various Environment Settings

Chapter 7 provided a detailed description of the configuration database, and Section 7.7 provided guidelines to encapsulate several config settings into a class. This section provides a simple example of the concept. In Section 21.1 the master agent and slave agents had three configuration variables:

- Starting address

- End address

- Number of wait cycles

In this test environment, there are 8 masters and 16 slaves, which supports at least 72 ((8 + 16) * 3) config settings. By encapsulating these in a class, there are 8 master configuration classes and 16 slave configuration classes for a total of 24, which is a third of the original number. In other words, each class could contain hundreds of variables and yet, has only one entry in the config_db. This concept is illustrated in Listing 21.5.

The drastic reduction in the number of calls to the config_db helps you to eliminate multiple lookups amongst the tables in the config_db. This has a direct impact on performance. The order of calls is shown in Figure 21.6.

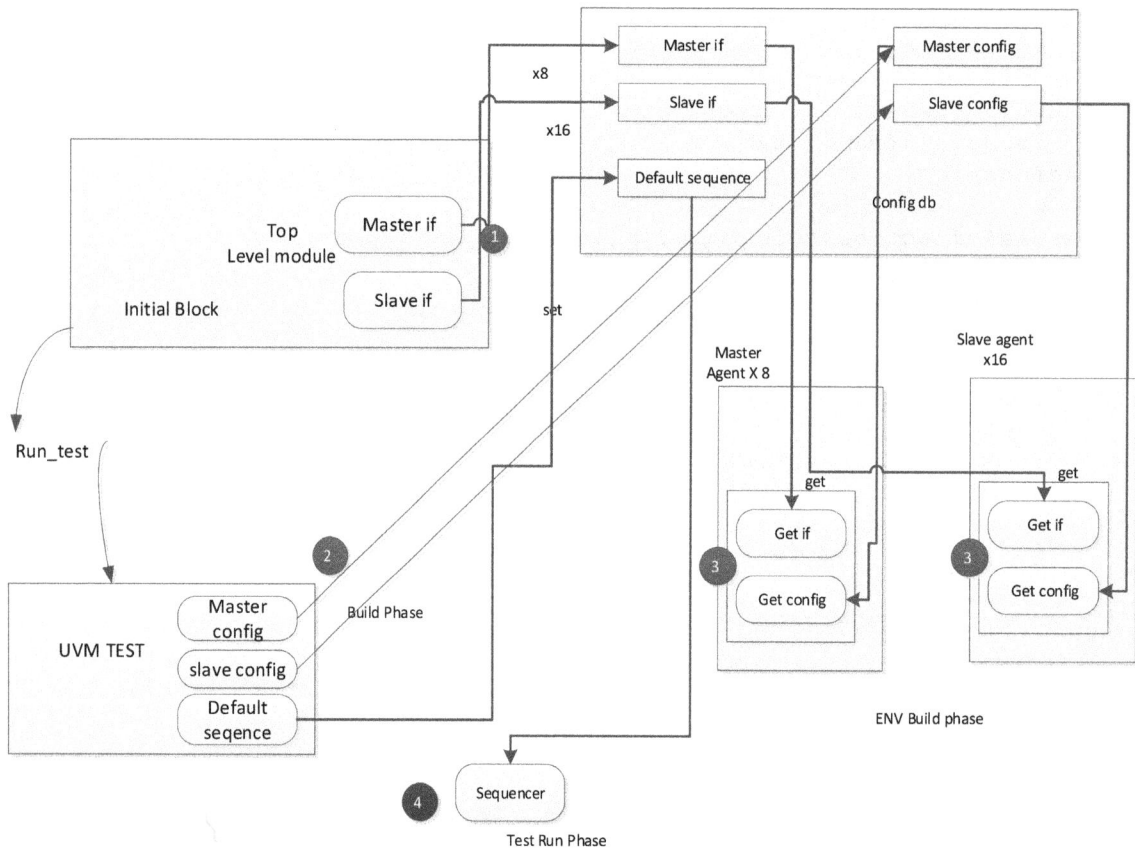

Fig. 21.6: Sequence Of Config_db Calls In The Verification Environment.

During the runtime in the environment, the simulation execution follows a certain pattern with the respect to the config_db calls. This sequence is described below for the wb_conmax verification environment.

Step 1: The figure shows the top-level test and the various configuration calls in the order that they happen in. In the top-level test, the 8 master and slave interfaces are placed in the config_db in step 1.

Step 2: The running test creates the 8 master configurations and 16 slave configurations and puts them in the config_db.

Step 3: During the build_phase of the environment, the environment creates the master and slave agents. These agents retrieve their configuration from the config_db. These agents retrieve the virtual interface handles from the config_db.

Step 4: The sequencer retrieves the default_sequence from the config_db and starts the appropriate sequence on the sequencer.

21.4 Use Of a Virtual Sequencer to Direct Traffic to Wishbone Crossbar

There are 8 masters and 16 slaves in this verification environment in addition to scoreboards, maps, and other classes. Our environment is completely set up to send traffic from one to 8 masters and to any of the slaves connected to the DUT. Since the stimulus can be applied in parallel, they could come from any sequence running on any sequencer. A virtual sequencer, therefore, fits ideally into this scenario. To use a virtual sequence on a virtual sequencer, one must create and instantiate a virtual sequencer in the environment. One must then create and run a sequence on the sequencer.

21.4.1 Creating a Virtual Sequencer

The wishbone environment has 8 masters. It is possible for any or all the masters to send traffic to the crossbar. There are 8 sequencers in this environment, and each of the individual masters can send traffic on its interface based on the sequence that is running on the sequencer in the agent. In one scenario, one of the masters may be running a register sequence, and another could be running a parallel sequence and so on. In this case, one would like to have a collection of sequences that are running on the various masters organized by sequences. This is where the virtual sequencer comes in. It acts as a" conductor" and allows orchestrating the stimuli from the various masters to the cross-connect. Since it has handles to all the sequencers in each of the master agents, it can run any sequence that is registered on any of the sequencers.

Listing 21.11: WB Conmax Virtual Sequencer

```
20 class wb_conmax_virtual_sequencer extends uvm_sequencer;
21    `uvm_component_utils(wb_conmax_virtual_sequencer);
22    int my_seq_lenght;
23
24    // The seven master agent sequencers are here
25    wb_master_seqr seqr0;
26    wb_master_seqr seqr1;
27    wb_master_seqr seqr2;
28    wb_master_seqr seqr3;
29    wb_master_seqr seqr4;
30    wb_master_seqr seqr5;
31    wb_master_seqr seqr6;
32    wb_master_seqr seqr7;
33
34    function new(string name = "wb_conmax_virtual_sequencer", uvm_component
          parent = null) ;
35       super.new(name,parent);
36    endfunction
37
38 endclass
```

Listing 21.4 shows a simple virtual sequencer for our wishbone cross-connect.

- Line 20 shows the wb_conmax_virtual_sequencer extending uvm_sequencer. Note that in this case, it is not specialized to any type of data item.

- Lines 25-32 show the handles from the virtual sequencer to each of the individual sequencers in the environment. Note that there is no connection that is made to any of the sequencers in the sequencer build phases. This is covered in the next section.

21.4.2 Connecting the Virtual Sequence to Subsequncers

After the virtual sequencer has completed the build_phase, connect the sequencers that were built in each of the master agents to the virtual sequencer. Doing so allows the virtual sequencer to start sequences on the appropriate sequencer. The code snippet from the wb_conmax_env.sv file shows how the connections are created in the connect_phase() method in the environment class that instantiates the virtual sequencer.

Listing 21.12: WB Conmax Virtual Sequencer Connections

```
101    wb_conmax_virt_seqr.seqr0 = master_agent[00].mast_sqr;
102    wb_conmax_virt_seqr.seqr1 = master_agent[01].mast_sqr;
103    wb_conmax_virt_seqr.seqr2 = master_agent[02].mast_sqr;
104    wb_conmax_virt_seqr.seqr3 = master_agent[03].mast_sqr;
105    wb_conmax_virt_seqr.seqr4 = master_agent[04].mast_sqr;
106    wb_conmax_virt_seqr.seqr5 = master_agent[05].mast_sqr;
107    wb_conmax_virt_seqr.seqr6 = master_agent[06].mast_sqr;
108    wb_conmax_virt_seqr.seqr7 = master_agent[07].mast_sqr;
```

In Listing 21.12

- Lines 101-108 show the virtual sequencer handles connected to each of the individual sequencers.

- The Virtual sequence running on the virtual sequencer can "see" all the sequencers and is aware of them. It can run a sequence on any of these sequencers.

21.4.3 Creating a Virtual Sequence and Controlling Other Sequencers

Section 14.4.5 provided a discussion on virtual sequences. This section provides an example of how to run a virtual sequence on the sequencer. The wb_conmax environment has a virtual sequencer. This is created in the build_phase() and connected up. It is time to run some simple sequences on the virtual sequencer. ***Note that the class is extending from uvm_sequence and is not parameterized to the type of the transaction in the various sequencers!*** . The listing below illustrates this.

Listing 21.13: WB Conmax Virtual Sequence on Sequencer

```
23 class wb_conmax_virtual_sequence extends uvm_sequence;
24
25    `uvm_object_utils(wb_conmax_virtual_sequence)
26
27    // get a handle to the sequencer
28    `uvm_declare_p_sequencer(wb_conmax_virtual_sequencer)
29
30    sequence_0 sequence0;
31    sequence_1 sequence1;
32
33    virtual task body();
34
35       `uvm_info("UVM_VIRTUAL_SEQUENCER","Starting a virtual sequence on
             the virtual sequencer",UVM_MEDIUM);
36
37       `uvm_info("VIRT_SEQQ","Starting Virtual Sequence: PART 0",UVM_MEDIUM
             )
38
39       `uvm_do(sequence0, p_sequencer.seqr0, -1, {});
40
41       `uvm_info("VIRT_SEQQ","Starting Virtual Sequence: PART 1",UVM_MEDIUM
             )
```

```
42
43         `uvm_do(sequence1, p_sequencer.seqr1, -1, {});
44         `uvm_info("VIRT_SEQQ","Starting Virtual Sequence: PART 2",UVM_MEDIUM
              )
45
46         `uvm_do(sequence0, p_sequencer.seqr2, -1, {});
47         `uvm_info("VIRT_SEQQ","Starting Virtual Sequence: PART 3",UVM_MEDIUM
              )
48
49         `uvm_do(sequence0, p_sequencer.seqr3, -1, {});
50         `uvm_info("VIRT_SEQQ","Starting Virtual Sequence: PART 4",UVM_MEDIUM
              )
51
52         `uvm_do(sequence0, p_sequencer.seqr4, -1, {});
53         `uvm_info("VIRT_SEQQ","Starting Virtual Sequence: PART 5",UVM_MEDIUM
              )
54
55         `uvm_do(sequence0, p_sequencer.seqr5, -1, {});
56         `uvm_info("VIRT_SEQQ","Starting Virtual Sequence: PART 6",UVM_MEDIUM
              )
57
58         `uvm_do(sequence0, p_sequencer.seqr6, -1, {});
59         `uvm_info("VIRT_SEQQ","Starting Virtual Sequence: PART 7",UVM_MEDIUM
              )
60
61         `uvm_do(sequence0, p_sequencer.seqr7, -1, {});
62
63     endtask
64
65     function new(string name="wb_conmax_virtual_sequencer");
66         super.new(name);
67         set_automatic_phase_objection(1);
68     endfunction
69
70 endclass
```

Listing 21.13 shows the listing for a simple virtual sequence. This listing shows a couple of child sequences in it.

- Lines 30-31 show two child sequence instances.

- Line 33-63 shows the body() task, which is the main sequence method. In this task:

- Line 39 shows the sequence_0 instance sequence0 being run on the master agent for master[00].

- Line 43 shows the sequence_0 instance sequence0 being run on the master agent for master[01].

Other instances are similar to the one above.

While we have only illustrated a simple sequence example, it is possible to combine many other sources. You are encouraged to create other virtual sequences that exercise other complex combinations, to enhance your knowledge of virtual sequences and virtual sequencers.

21.5 Altering Message Verbosity From Some Components

It is often desired to change the verbosity for some components in a simulation. This may be because a simulation is misbehaving, and it may be possible to analyze what is going on by looking at an enhanced verbosity from the simulation.

Depending on the situation, changing the verbosity for all components or for a specific component in a simulation may be useful.

Changing the verbosity for all components is possible either programmatically or by using a command line argument. Programmatically, this is accomplished by attaching the report catcher to a" null" instance instead of a specific one, as shown in the example below. The command line method is easy to use. However, in the case of changing the verbosity for a particular component, either programming or the command line could be used.

21.5.1 Using Methods

The approach of using methods allows more flexibility than the broad brush of using the command line arguments described in the next section. The main advantage here: in addition to changing the actual contents of a specific message, the message severity can be altered. One disadvantage of this method is that you are forced to recompile the design and testbench every time you make a change to this code. This can be challenging for a large design.

Listing 21.14: Altering verbosity specific Components Using Methods

```
1   class message_promoter  extends uvm_report_catcher;
2     function new(string name="message_promoter");
3       super.new(name);
4     endfunction
5
6     //This example demotes "MY_ID" errors to an info message
7     function action_e catch();
8       if(get_severity() == UVM_INFO && get_id() == "SLAVE_DRIVER")
9         set_severity(UVM_ERROR);
10      return THROW;
11    endfunction
12  endclass
13
14  class wb_conmax_alter_verbosity_specific_component_test extends
        wb_conmax_base_test;
15
16    `uvm_component_utils(wb_conmax_alter_verbosity_specific_component_test
        )
17
18    message_promoter promoter = new;
19
20    function new(string name, uvm_component parent);
21      super.new(name, parent);
22    endfunction
23
24    virtual function void build_phase(uvm_phase phase);
25      super.build_phase(phase);
26      // Set the default sequencer in all the master agents
27      uvm_config_db #(uvm_object_wrapper)::set(this, "env.
          wb_conmax_virt_seqr.main_phase", "default_sequence",
          wb_conmax_virtual_sequence::get_type());
28
29      uvm_report_cb::add(null,promoter);
30
31    endfunction
32
33    function void end_of_elaboration_phase(uvm_phase phase);
34      uvm_report_cb::add(this.env.slave_agent[0].slv_drv, promoter);
```

```
35       endfunction
36
37     endclass :   wb_conmax_alter_verbosity_specific_component_test
```

In the above listing,

- Lines 1-12 define a report catcher class. This class has a constructor.

- Lines 7-11 Function catch intercepts all the messages, and if the message is from the SLAVE_DRIVER, sets the message to have ERROR severity.

- Lines 14-37 define the simple test

- The report catcher class is declared on Line 18 and created.

- Line 29 adds the promoter class as a typewide report callback class.

- Line 34 shows another way to add the callback class to a specific instance. This line of code is provided as an illustration. It should have been overridden by Line 29.

21.5.2 Using the Command Line
For information, please refer to Section 21.9.7

21.6 Logging Messages From a Specific Component to a File
It is often imperative to log messages from a specific component into a file. A typical scenario for this would occur if one were attempting to debug the behavior of one component or have some specific messages going to a specific log file for being post-processed later. The reporting infrastructure in the library makes it possible to have many ways to achieve this goal. This is illustrated in Listing 21.15.

Listing 21.15: Altering verbosity specific Components and Logging into a file

```
20     class wb_conmax_report_file_test extends wb_conmax_base_test;
21
22       UVM_FILE file_master;
23
24       `uvm_component_utils(wb_conmax_report_file_test)
25
26       function new(string name, uvm_component parent);
27         super.new(name, parent);
28         file_master = $fopen("master_output","w");
29       endfunction
30
31       virtual function void build_phase(uvm_phase phase);
32         super.build_phase(phase);
33       endfunction
34
35       virtual function void end_of_elaboration_phase(uvm_phase phase);
36         super.end_of_elaboration_phase(phase);
37         //env.set_report_default_file_hier("SCOREBOARD_MASTER",UVM_LOG);
38         env.set_report_default_file_hier(file_master);
39         env.conmax_scbd.set_report_id_file_hier("SCOREBOARD_MASTER",
             file_master);
40         env.conmax_scbd.set_report_id_action("SCOREBOARD_MASTER",
             UVM_DISPLAY|UVM_LOG);
41
42       endfunction
```

- Line 22 shows the declaration of a filehandle of type UVM_FILE. It is an integer.

- Lines 26-29 shows the constructor for the test in which the file is opened for writing using the standard $fopen SystemVerilog tasks.

- Lines 38-39 show the scoreboard component messages being redirected to a file. All the messages from the scoreboard and its child components are redirected to the file.

When you observe the output after running the simulation, you see all the relevant messages in the file. Please examine the log file in the download.

21.7 An Illustration of Flat Sequences

Section 14.4.1 presented a discussion on flat sequences. These sequences are simple sequences that generate a stream of items with no other relationships. Below is an example of a flat sequence running on one of the master agents.

You should be able to recognize that this sequence is only generating a series of atomic transactions that run on any sequencer. The actual sequence itself is running in a test.

Listing 21.16: A Flat Sequence

```
1    class wb_conmax_flat_seq_test extends wb_conmax_base_test;
2
3      `uvm_component_utils(wb_conmax_flat_seq_test)
4
5      function new(string name, uvm_component parent);
6        super.new(name, parent);
7      endfunction
8
9      sequence_0 seq0;
10
11
12      virtual task main_phase(uvm_phase phase);
13        super.main_phase(phase);
14        phase.raise_objection(this,"Test Main Objection");
15        seq0 = sequence_0::type_id::create("sequence_1",this);
16        seq0.start(env.master_agent[00].mast_sqr,null);
17        seq0.wait_for_sequence_state(UVM_FINISHED);
18        phase.drop_objection(this,"Dropping Test Main Objection");
19      endtask
20
21    endclass :   wb_conmax_flat_seq_test
```

- Line 1 shows the declaration of the test

- Line 9 has an instance of the flat sequence sequence_1.

- Line 15 shows the creation of the sequence using the factory.

- Line 16 starts this on the sequencer of master_agent[00].

- Line 17 waits for the sequence to finish before allowing the objection on Line 17 to drop terminating the test.

21.8 Using Callbacks

Chapter 9 discusses callbacks in the UVM simulation. This section provides simple examples of how to use callbacks in context of our environment for the driver components. This environment has 8 masters, and 16 slaves; there are many components to which a callback can be attached. This leads us to two possibilities. One is to have a callback attached to every driver component in the environment (termed as a typewide callback). The other possibility is a specific driver in one specific instance (this is usually the case if injecting errors from a specific source). In the examples below, the callback class is extended from Section 9.1.4. The callback alters the driver output and response, as shown in the listing below.

Listing 21.17: Using the callback in the wb_conmax test

```
21      class wb_master_driver_new_cb extends wb_master_callbacks;
22
23          function new(string name="bus_driver_cb_inst");
24              super.new();
25          endfunction
26
27          // Called after a transaction has been executed
28          virtual task post_tx( wb_master xactor, wb_transaction tr);
29              tr.tgc = 4'h1;
30              `uvm_info("post_tx()",      tr.sprint(),UVM_LOW)
31          endtask: post_tx
32
33          virtual task pre_tx( wb_master xactor, wb_transaction tr);
34              tr.tga = 4'hf;
35              `uvm_info("pre_tx()",      tr.sprint(),UVM_LOW)
36          endtask : pre_tx
37
38      endclass
```

- Line 21 in the above listing declares a new callback class called wb_master_driver_new_cb that extends from the facade class wb_master_callbacks that was provided by the component developer of the wb_master class.

- Line 23-25 shows the constructor for this class.

- Line 28 shows the task post_tx which is called after the transaction is executed.

- The post_tx task alters the tgc property of the transaction. It prints the transaction.

- Line 33 shows the task pre_tx which is called after the transaction is executed.

- The pre_tx task alters the tga property of the transaction. It prints the transaction and prints the transaction.

See Section 9.1 for the description of the intercept points where the callback is called during the driver execution.

21.8.1 Instance Specific Callback Example
In Figure 21.7, Only one of the instances of the driver has a callback attached to it, which shown in Listing 21.18.

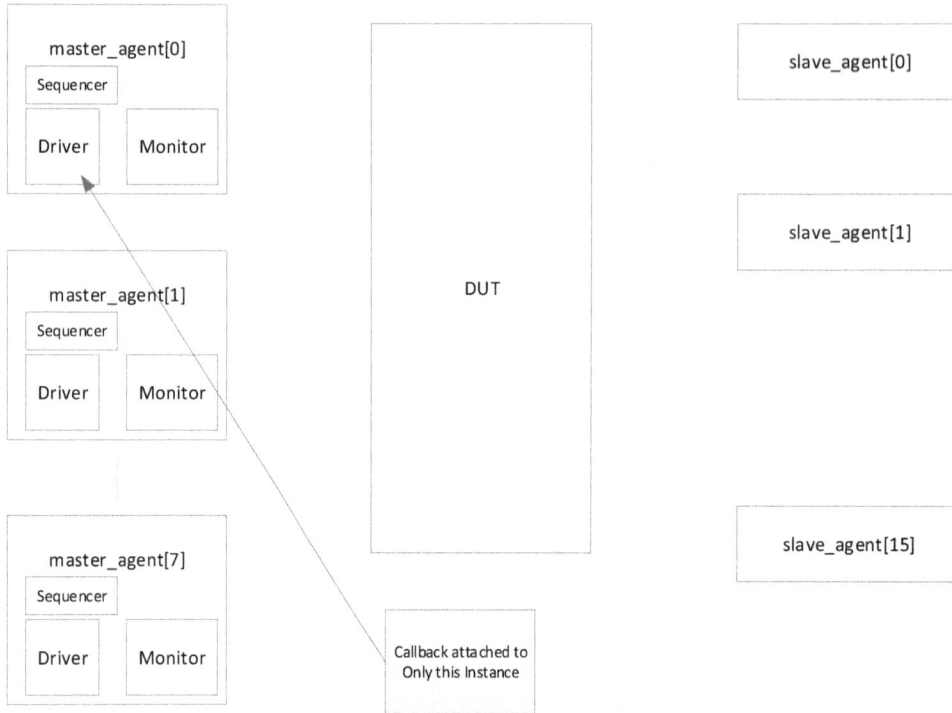

Fig. 21.7: Instance Specific Callbacks in WB_conmax environment.

Listing 21.18: Instance Specific Callback Example

```
40    class wb_conmax_instance_callback_test extends wb_conmax_base_test;
41
42        `uvm_component_utils(wb_conmax_instance_callback_test)
43
44        wb_master_driver_new_cb new_cb1 = new("New Callback #1");
45        wb_master_driver_new_cb new_cb2 = new("New Callback #2");
46
47
48
49        function new(string name, uvm_component parent);
50            super.new(name, parent);
51        endfunction
52
53        wb_conmax_virtual_sequence virt_seq1;
54        virtual task main_phase(uvm_phase phase);
55            uvm_callbacks #(wb_master,wb_master_driver_new_cb)::add(env.
                 master_agent[00].mast_drv,new_cb1);
56            phase.raise_objection(this,"Test Main Objection");
57            virt_seq1 = wb_conmax_virtual_sequence::type_id::create("
                 wb_conmax_virtual_sequence",this);
58            virt_seq1.start(env.wb_conmax_virt_seqr,null);
59            virt_seq1.wait_for_sequence_state(UVM_FINISHED);
```

```
60                phase.drop_objection(this,"Dropping Test Main Objection");
61          endtask
62
63      endclass :   wb_conmax_instance_callback_test
64
65 `endif //WB_CONMAX_CALLBACK_VERBOSITY_TEST
```

- Line 40 shows the top-level test.
- Line 44-45 show new instances of the callback being created in the test.
- Line 65 adds this callback to the master_agent[00] driver.
- The rest of the lines in the test help with test execution.

21.8.2 Type Wide Callback Example
You may want to attach a callback to all the instances. Figure 21.8 shows this application. All instances of the driver have a callback attached to them.

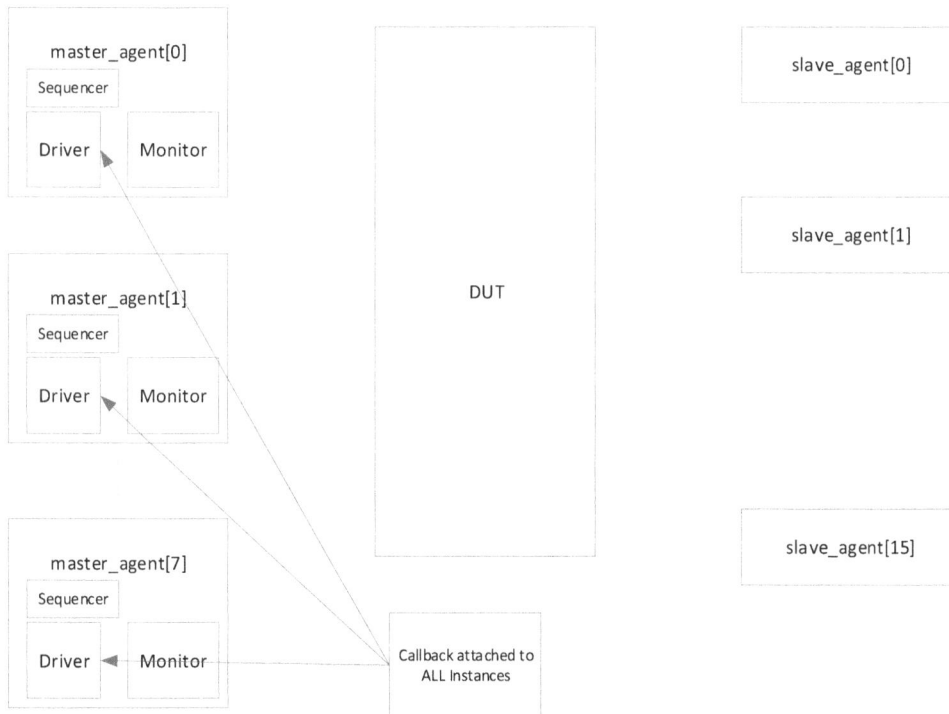

Fig. 21.8: Typewide Callbacks in WB_conmax environment.

Listing 21.19 shows the creation of a test. The creation of a typewide callback affects all the instances of the master driver. In this example, a callback function prints the transaction after it has completed. This is shown for all the 16 masters in the environment, depending on which ones were active based on the testcase.

Listing 21.19: Type Wide Callback Example

```
36   class wb_conmax_typewide_callback_test extends wb_conmax_base_test;
37
38     `uvm_component_utils(wb_conmax_typewide_callback_test)
39
40     wb_master_driver_new_cb new_cb1 = new("New Callback #1");
41     wb_master_driver_new_cb new_cb2 = new("New Callback #2");
42
43     function new(string name, uvm_component parent);
44       super.new(name, parent);
45     endfunction
46
47     virtual function void build_phase(uvm_phase phase);
48       super.build_phase(phase);
49
50       uvm_callbacks #(wb_master,wb_master_driver_new_cb)::add(null,new_cb1
             );
51       // Set the default sequencer in all the master agents
52
53     endfunction
54
55     wb_conmax_virtual_sequence virt_seq1;
56     virtual task main_phase(uvm_phase phase);
57       phase.raise_objection(this,"Test Main Objection");
58       virt_seq1 = wb_conmax_virtual_sequence::type_id::create("
             wb_conmax_virtual_sequence",this);
59       virt_seq1.start(env.wb_conmax_virt_seqr,null);
60       virt_seq1.wait_for_sequence_state(UVM_FINISHED);
61       phase.drop_objection(this,"Dropping Test Main Objection");
62     endtask
63
64   endclass :   wb_conmax_typewide_callback_test
```

- Line 36 shows the top-level test.
- Lines 40-41 show new instances of the callback being created in the test.
- Line 50 adds this callback to all the instances of the master_agent driver.
- The rest of the lines in the test help with test execution.

21.9 Use Of The Command Line Processor

The command line processor is a hidden gem within UVM. The capabilities of the processor are described in Chapter 11. This section focuses on the practical applications of the processor.

In modern designs, one must not only analyze and compile the design but must debug it as well. The debug cycle in contemporary verification environments takes a long time. With large designs, it takes a considerable amount of time for the design to be recompiled if you make a small change or debug something with a higher verbosity. With such turnaround times, you are looking at a few turnaround cycles in any given day. Using the command line processor with some planning ahead can save you much time in debugging. The following sections show you in a practical way how to use the command line processor to accomplish many actions:

- Control of sequences
- Override a class type with another type that has already been compiled in using the factory

- Replace an instance of a specific class with another using the factory

- Change the verbosity of all or specific components in the simulation

- Change the behavior of the reporting subsystem to either error out or increase verbosity for components in the simulation

- Pass parameters to your test

The sections that follow go over all these examples. Each example uses the base test described in Section 21.1.7 as a foundation. Some of the command lines indicated have been saved in the provided Makefiles as targets, and you can examine and modify the command lines to deepen your understanding. All of these use the base test shown in Section 21.1.7.

21.9.1 Command Line Options to Affect the Entire Simulation

In Section 11.6, the various command line options were explored. Now that we have a complete working environment, the command line processor can be put through its paces. To dump the command line, one can pass +UVM_DUMP_CMDLINE_ARGS to the simulation. This dumps out everything that the command line processor sees and can help identify if something that was passed in was not interpreted.

To recap from Section 11.5, the following arguments are useful during debug of any UVM simulation:

> +UVM_TESTNAME=name of test.
> +UVM_VERBOSITY=value This sets the verbosity of all the components in the simulation.
> +UVM_SEVERITY=(INFO|WARNING|ERROR|FATAL)
> +UVM_PHASE_TRACE
> +UVM_OBJECTION_TRACE
> +UVM_RESOURCE_DB_TRACE
> +UVM_CONFIG_DB_TRACE
> +UVM_MAX_QUIT_COUNT=<count>,<override> +UVM_TIMEOUT=<value>

Try these out in your simulation to see the effect of these command line options.

21.9.2 Getting a Command Line Argument Into the Simulation

When reusable tests are developed, provisions are often made to pass parameters into the test to control test behavior. These parameters can be sent to the test from the command line. In such circumstances, it is necessary to bring a command line argument passed into a simulation. The UVM command line processor comes to the rescue in these situations. An instance of the command line processor can be instantiated and then used to parse arguments. Consider a situation where it is desirable to constrain the masters to all send transactions to a specific area of the address range. For example, use the slave[0] and constrain its maximum address as seen by the master, and using a command line parameter to tell the master configuration what the maximum address is. This can be accomplished by using the command line processor as shown in the listing below:

Listing 21.20: Using the command Line processor to get a parameter into the simulation

```
22   class wb_conmax_simple_cmdline_proc extends wb_conmax_base_test;
23
24     wb_config master_configs[8];
25     wb_config slave_configs[16];
26
27     int slave_adr_max ;
28     int slave_adr_min;
29
30     `uvm_component_utils(wb_conmax_simple_cmdline_proc)
31
32     function new(string name, uvm_component parent);
33       super.new(name, parent);
```

```
34        endfunction
35
36        virtual function void build_phase(uvm_phase phase);
37
38          uvm_cmdline_processor clp;
39          string arg_values[$];
40          clp = uvm_cmdline_processor::get_inst();
41          void'(clp.get_arg_values("+slave_adr_max=", arg_values));
42          slave_adr_max = arg_values[0].atoi();
43          `uvm_info("CMDLINE_VALUE",$sformatf("SLAVE ADR = %h",slave_adr_max),
              UVM_LOW)
44
45          // slave_adr_max = 32'h0fffffe;
46          super.build_phase(phase);
47          // create the configurations
48          // Master config
49          for(int i = 0; i < 8; i++) begin
50            master_configs[i] = wb_config::type_id::create($sformatf("
                master_configs[%02d]",i));
51            master_configs[i].randomize with {min_addr == 0; max_addr ==
                slave_adr_max; max_n_wss == 5; };
52            master_configs[i].print();
53          end
54
55          // create the configurations
56          // Slave config
57          for(int i = 0; i < 16; i++) begin
58            slave_adr_min = 0;
59
60            slave_configs[i] = wb_config::type_id::create($sformatf("
                slave_configs[%02d]",i));
61            slave_configs[i].randomize with {min_addr == slave_adr_min;
                max_addr == slave_adr_max; max_n_wss == 2; };
62            slave_adr_min =slave_adr_max + 1;
63            slave_adr_max = slave_adr_max + 1 + 32'h00fffffe;
64            slave_configs[i].print();
```

In Listing 21.20:

- Line 40 shows a handle for the command line processor in the test.

- Line 42 assigns the global instance to the handle.

- Line 43 shows the value of slave_adr_max parameter being captured into the simulation from the command line using the command line processor.

- Line 42 slave_adr_max was declared as a string, and it's converted to an integer.

- Lines 59-65 use the value passed in from the command line to configure the slave agents.

You can pass a command line argument to the simulation by simply using the command line :

```
./simv +UVM_TESTNAME=wb_conmax_simple_cmdline_proc +UVM_DUMP_CMDLINE_ARGS
    +slave_adr_max=16777214 -l dump_cmdline.dat
```

Results can be viewed by looking at the output from the simulation.

21.9.3 Controlling Sequences Using the Built-In Command Line

UVM 1.2   Note that this is a new feature in the UVM 1.2 version

The command line processor can set default sequences in the sequencer. To do so, pass in the full hierarchical path name to the sequencer and default sequence. The following example shows you how to set the default sequence for a couple of sequencers in the simulation.

See my comments in Section 11.4.4. I do not like the feature for reasons cited there. While it's true that some may feel that the long compile times are worth it, the test writer can easily add additional tests with minimal overhead and then use the tests for tracking and mapping features to testcases. In any case, having understood the concerns I raise here, use it if you feel you can address them.

An example of a command line for the +uvm_set_default_sequence is provided in the command line below.

```
./simv -l uvm_set_default_sequence.dat +uvm_set_default_sequence=
    uvm_test_top.env.master_agent[00].mast_sqr,main_phase,sequence_1 +
    uvm_set_default_sequence=uvm_test_top.env.master_agent[00].mast_sqr,
    main_phase,sequence_0 +UVM_TESTNAME=wb_conmax_base_test
```

Results can be viewed at the output of the simulation.

21.9.4 Using the Command Line Processor to Configure Components

Chapter 5 showed the use of the factory to replace a given type with an override type. To accomplish this, send the factory the corresponding override requests. Both type and instance overrides are possible using this approach, as detailed below. I would recommend that you also use this for initial debugging for the same reasons as the uvm_set_default_sequence option.

21.9.5 Setting Type Override from the Command Line

Section 21.2.1 showed an example of how to create a type override in a test case. A similar effect can be accomplished in our base test by using the command line processor.

An example of a command line for the +uvm set type override is provided in the command line below:

```
./simv -l uvm_set_type_override.dat +uvm_set_type_override=wb_master_agent
    ,wb_master_agent_n +UVM_TESTNAME=
    wb_conmax_factory_instance_override_test_cmdline
```

Results can be viewed at the output of the simulation.

21.9.6 Setting an Instance Override from the Command Line

The previous section allowed you to replace all the components of a specific type. In some instances, that may not be what you want. You may want to replace the specific component with another using the factory, as shown in Section 21.2.2. The listing below shows you how to accomplish that using the command line:

An example of a command line for the +uvm_set_inst_override is provided in the command line below.

```
./simv -l s.d2 +uvm_set_inst_override=wb_master_agent,wb_master_agent_n,
    uvm_test_top.env.master_agent[00] +UVM_TESTNAME=
    wb_conmax_factory_instance_override_test_cmdline
```

If you look at the output of the simulation, you see the hierarchy printed into the log file. A grep of wb_master_agent from the log file yeilds the following results:

```
390:     master_agent[00]              wb_master_agent_n    -    @556
424:     master_agent[01]              wb_master_agent      -    @568
458:     master_agent[02]              wb_master_agent      -    @579
492:     master_agent[03]              wb_master_agent      -    @590
526:     master_agent[04]              wb_master_agent      -    @601
560:     master_agent[05]              wb_master_agent      -    @612
594:     master_agent[06]              wb_master_agent      -    @623
628:     master_agent[07]              wb_master_agent      -    @634
```

- Line 390 of the log file shows the master_agent[00] being of type wb_master_agent_n instead of being of type wb_master_agent.

- None of the other instances is affected by the command line as seen in the output. Note: only a portion of the output is shown.

21.9.7 Setting Verbosity for Specific Components on Command Line

As with other capabilities of the processor, you may want to increase the verbosity of a single component to debug what is happening with your simulation. This can be done without recompiling a simulation; instead, pass in arguments to the simulation.

An example of a command line for the +uvm_set_verbosity is provided in the command line below.

```
./simv -l uvm_set_inst_verbosity.dat +uvm_set_verbosity=uvm_test_top.env.
    master_agent[00].mast_drv,_ALL_,UVM_DEBUG,run +UVM_TESTNAME=
    wb_conmax_flat_seq_test
```

This command line increases the master_agent[00] verbosity to UVM_DEBUG, leaving all the other components at their configured verbosity (the default in this case). Only the output for the master_agent[00] is at the specified level. Notice that the _ALL_ parameter selects all the messages emitted by the agent.

```
4     Compiler version P-2019.06; Runtime version P-2019.06;  Jun 29
        13:54 2019
5      UVM_INFO /global/apps/vcs_2019.06/etc/uvm-ieee/base/uvm_root.svh
        (460) @ 0: reporter [UVM/RELNOTES]
6      **********          IMPORTANT RELEASE NOTES          **********
....
....
115    UVM_INFO @ 305000: uvm_test_top.env.Scoreboard.comparator
                0 [Comparator Match]
116    UVM_INFO ../../common/wb_master.sv(271) @ 315000: uvm_test_top.
    env.master_agent[00].mast_drv [WB_MASTER]

        ------------------------------------------------------------
117    Name                              Type          Size  Value
```

```
118      -------------------------------------------------------------
119      req                          wb_transaction   -        @6707
120        address                    integral         32       'h4
121        data                       integral         32       'hbeefdead
.....
.....
131        depth                      int              32       'd2
132        parent sequence (name)     string           10       sequence_1
133        parent sequence (full name)  string         53
      uvm_test_top.env.master_agent[00].mast_sqr.sequence_1
134        sequencer                  string           42
      uvm_test_top.env.master_agent[00].mast_sqr
135      --------------------------------------------------------------
136
137      UVM_INFO ../../common/wb_master.sv(191) @ 315000: uvm_test_top.
      env.master_agent[00].mast_drv [wb_env_DRIVER] Completed transaction
      ...
138      UVM_INFO ../../common/wb_master.sv(163) @ 315000: uvm_test_top.
      env.master_agent[00].mast_drv [wb_env_DRIVER] Starting transaction
      ...
139      UVM_INFO ../../common/wb_master.sv(241) @ 325000: uvm_test_top.
      env.master_agent[00].mast_drv [Wb master] Got a write transaction
140      UVM_INFO ../../common/wb_slave.sv(158) @ 346000: uvm_test_top.
      env.slave_agent[00].slv_drv [uvm_test_top.env.slave_agent[00].
      slv_drv] responding in this cycle
141      UVM_INFO ../../common/wb_slave_mon.sv(141) @ 346000:
      uvm_test_top.env.slave_agent[00].slv_mon [WB slave Monitor] got a
      write transaction  from Master
142      UVM_INFO ../../common/wb_slave.sv(198) @ 375000: uvm_test_top.
      env.slave_agent[00].slv_drv [SLAVE_DRIVER] Completed transaction...
143      UVM_INFO @ 375000: uvm_test_top.env.Scoreboard.comparator
              0 [Comparator Match]
144      UVM_INFO ../../common/wb_master.sv(271) @ 385000: uvm_test_top.
      env.master_agent[00].mast_drv [WB_MASTER]
         -------------------------------------------------------------------

145      Name                         Type             Size   Value
146      --------------------------------------------------------------
147      req                          wb_transaction   -        @6761
148        address                    integral         32       'h5
149        data                       integral         32       'h23456678
150        sel                        integral         4        'h3
......
......
161        parent sequence (full name)  string         53
      uvm_test_top.env.master_agent[00].mast_sqr.sequence_1
162        sequencer                  string           42
      uvm_test_top.env.master_agent[00].mast_sqr
163
         -------------------------------------------------------------------

164
```

```
165     UVM_INFO ../../common/wb_master.sv(191) @ 385000: uvm_test_top.
   env.master_agent[00].mast_drv [wb_env_DRIVER] Completed transaction
   ...
166     UVM_INFO ../../common/wb_master.sv(163) @ 385000: uvm_test_top.
   env.master_agent[00].mast_drv [wb_env_DRIVER] Starting transaction
   ...
167     UVM_INFO ../../common/wb_master.sv(201) @ 395000: uvm_test_top.
   env.master_agent[00].mast_drv [Wb master] Got a read transaction
168     UVM_INFO ../../common/wb_slave.sv(158) @ 416000: uvm_test_top.
   env.slave_agent[00].slv_drv [uvm_test_top.env.slave_agent[00].
   slv_drv] responding in this cycle
169     UVM_INFO ../../common/wb_slave_mon.sv(151) @ 416000:
   uvm_test_top.env.slave_agent[00].slv_mon [Wb_slave Monitor] got a
   read transaction
170     UVM_INFO ../../common/wb_slave.sv(198) @ 445000: uvm_test_top.
   env.slave_agent[00].slv_drv [SLAVE_DRIVER] Completed transaction...
171     UVM_INFO @ 445000: uvm_test_top.env.Scoreboard.comparator
             0 [Comparator Match]
172     UVM_INFO ../../common/wb_master.sv(191) @ 455000: uvm_test_top.
   env.master_agent[00].mast_drv [wb_env_DRIVER] Completed transaction
   ...
173     UVM_INFO ../../common/wb_master.sv(163) @ 455000: uvm_test_top.
   env.master_agent[00].mast_drv [wb_env_DRIVER] Starting transaction
   ...
174     UVM_INFO ../../common/wb_master.sv(201) @ 465000: uvm_test_top.
   env.master_agent[00].mast_drv [Wb master] Got a read transaction
175     UVM_INFO ../../common/wb_slave.sv(158) @ 486000: uvm_test_top.
   env.slave_agent[00].slv_drv [uvm_test_top.env.slave_agent[00].
   slv_drv] responding in this cycle
....
```

Sometimes, in a long simulation, you may find that the component produces much output, which can make it difficult to focus on the problem. Alternately you could choose to have verbosity for a specific time only using the time parameters.

An example of a command line for the +uvm_set_verbosity where the same example as earlier with a time range between 250 and 300ns is provided in the command line below.

```
./simv -l uvm_set_inst_verbosity_time.dat +uvm_set_verbosity=uvm_test_top.
   env.master_agent[00].mast_drv,_ALL_,UVM_DEBUG,time,250,330 +
   UVM_TESTNAME=wb_conmax_flat_seq_test
```

If you see the output, only the master agent is configured to be at UVM_DEBUG level only between Time 250 and 350 (a specific transaction in this example), which allows seeing the details of what is going on. This feature is handy. Rather than cluttering the log file, the information" zeroed in" to a specific time for a specific agent

21.9.8 Setting a Specific Report Action for a Specific Component on the Command Line

It may be desirable to change a specific message from a specific component, which may be an informational message into an ERROR or a fatal condition. This situation may occur under a variety of circumstances. This promoting/demoting activity is supported by the command-line-processor.

In the example below, the message from the "Wb_Master" is being changed from an UVM INFO message to an UVM_FATAL message. This can be accomplished from the command line. An example of a command line for the +uvm_set_severity is shown in this listing:

```
./simv -l uvm_set_inst_severity_no_action.dat2 +uvm_set_severity=
    uvm_test_top.env.master_agent[00].mast_drv,Wb master,UVM_INFO,UVM_FATAL
     +UVM_TESTNAME=wb_conmax_flat_seq_test
```

21.9.9 Setting a Specific Action for a Specific Error for a Component on the Command Line

After completing the debug, if the simulation is failing because of an error, and you wish to continue the simulation as if nothing had happened, set the report action to UVM_NO_ACTION from the command line. The command line below shows the same example from the previous section where the UVM_FATAL is overridden from the command line.

```
./simv -l uvm_set_inst_severity_no_action.dat +uvm_set_severity=
    uvm_test_top.env.master_agent[00].mast_drv,Wb master,UVM_INFO,UVM_FATAL
     +UVM_TESTNAME=wb_conmax_flat_seq_test +uvm_set_action=uvm_test_top.env
    .master_agent[00].mast_drv,Wb master,UVM_FATAL,UVM_NO_ACTION
```

21.10 Build And Run Instructions

Building and running the example can be done by using the provided Makefile. This Makefile contains all the compile and run commands.

If your favorite simulator is VCS, you can run the test using any of the command lines above, or use <path to simv>with the relevant options.

The build and run process is straightforward. A supplied Makefile in the run directory compiles all the files. Use the command line below to execute a particular UVM test you see in the tests directory:

make UVM_TEST=<Test Name> and you can run any of the provided tests/command lines. Inspect the provided Makefile for more information.

21.11 Exercises for Further Exploration

Several concepts in UVM were explored in this wb_conmax example. More concepts in UVM can be explored by extending the base test that was provided. Verify if the correct behavior is achieved.

1. Create many Sequences and add them to the wb_master_sequence_library class. These sequences must use the BLOCK READ/WRITE commands in the master. You may need to enhance the wb_transaction class and the master_driver classes a bit to make this work.

2. Use grab() and lock() as a part of a sequence that grabs any of the master sequencers. Note the order of transactions in the scoreboard may vary since other masters can write into the slave. Write some more logic into the scoreboard comparison so that the comparison happens correctly.

3. Change the logic in the master driver so that it can automatically detect a transaction regardless of the number of wait states. Right now, one needs to pass the same constants to both the master and the slave.

4. After studying the register model, attempt to write many tests for the registers in the wb_conmax design.

5. Attempt to change priorities in the wb_conmax arbiter and see how the verification environment behaves.

Chapter 22

Stimulus Generation with Ethernet

Chapter 3 described the various aspects of stimulus generation. This chapter provides some practical examples using an Ethernet Media Access Controller design using UVM. Key features of UVM highlighted as a part of the provided example are:

- Basic usage of a register model in a sequence

- Interrupt sequences

- Hierarchical sequences

- Virtual sequencer

The Ethernet IP core used in this chapter is a Media Access Controller (MAC) with a PHY interface and two wishbone interfaces. The core has been designed to offer much flexibility and allowing you to send data using the Ethernet protocol. The master wishbone interface interacts with the host CPU. The slave wishbone interface connects to the interconnect on the system and allows the core to fetch data from memory and encapsulate it using the ethernet protocol before sending it out on the PHY interface. For more details on the operation of the core, see the provided documentation in the Docs directory provided in the download.

Like the other designs in this book, the core is instantiated in a top-level testbench. The master interface connects to a memory, and the slave interface is used for programming. The other side of the MAC controller is connected to transmit and receive media agents. A register model is also created in the environment following the steps from Chapter 20 for this particular core. A simple block diagram is shown in Figure 22.1.

To transmit the frame through the controller, one must enable the TX part of the Ethernet Core by setting the TXEN bit to 1. The Ethernet IP Core continuously reads the first TxBD descriptor when enabled. When the descriptor is marked as ready, the core reads the pointer to the memory, storing the associated data and starts then reading data to the internal FIFO. When the FIFO is full, transmission begins. At the end of the transmission, the transmit status is written to the buffer descriptor, generating an interrupt.

In our code we must:

- Store the frame to the memory.

- Create a transaction and identify the properties of the buffer descriptor used to identify the transaction.

- Associate a Tx BD buffer descriptor in the Ethernet MAC core with the details of the packet written to the memory (length, pad, CRC, amongst others).

- Depending on the programming of the WR bit in the descriptor, the core either chooses the next descriptor or reuses the same buffer descriptor.

If the receive function is enabled, the Ethernet IP Core reads the Rx BD (Receive Buffer Descriptor) and starts receiving frames if the buffer is empty. The receive function receives an incoming frame nibble by nibble. After the frame has been received and stored in the memory, the receive status is written to the Rx BD. The successful reception generates an interrupt. The process is repeated after enabling the next buffer descriptor.

Follow these steps to receive a frame:

- Set the receive buffer descriptor (Rx BD) to be associated with the received packet and mark it as empty.

- Enable the Ethernet receive function by setting the RECEN bit to 1.

After studying the core and its capabilities, a complete verification environment for the MAC core may be developed. A master agent is connected to the slave interface. This master agent is used to program the DUT. The master agent is connected to a register adapter using the steps provided in Section 20.1. The master interface in this environment is connected to the slave interface of a memory agent. Two separate agents are connected to the MII side of the MAC core. An MII RX agent helps receive the packets from the MAC core, and the MII TX agent helps send packets to the MAC core. A complete verification environment is shown in Figure 22.1.

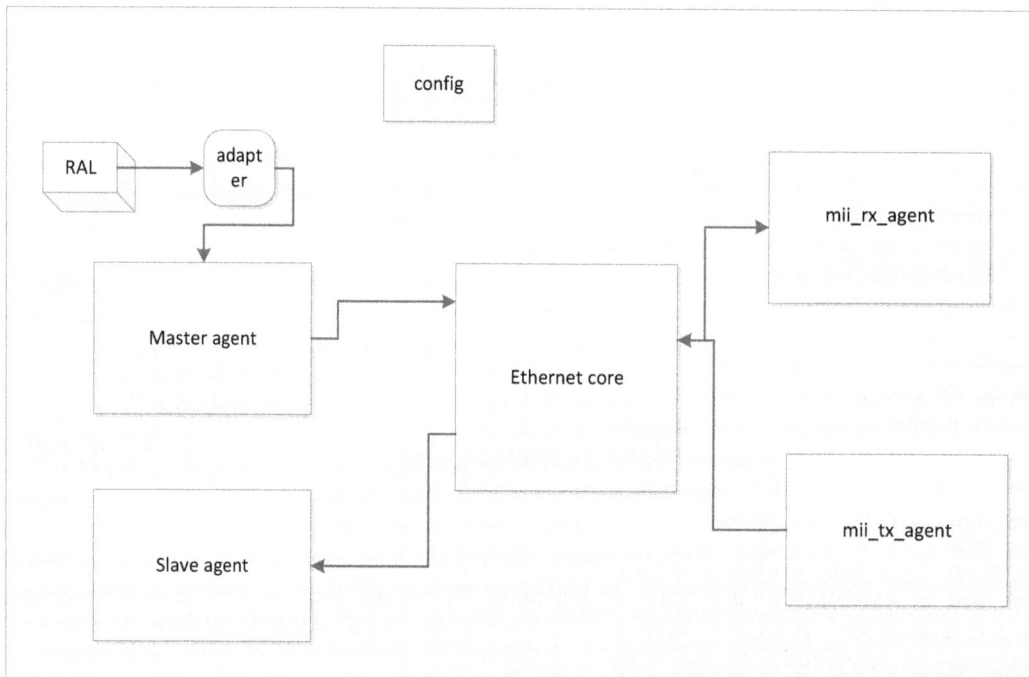

Fig. 22.1: Block diagram of Ethernet Environment

22.1 Data Modeling of Ethernet Packets

To provide stimulus to the DUT, we need an Ethernet packet to be transmitted by the DUT. This ethernet packet is primarily a packet descriptor for the Ethernet protocol. This packet descriptor, in our example, contains the following properties.

- Source address

- Destination address

- Payload

- Frame Check Sequence (CRC)

- Other properties.

The process of arriving at these properties is identical to the process of Section 3, and hence, this process is not repeated here[1].

22.2 Developing Interrupt Sequences in UVM

Some DUT implementations include an interrupt option. This interrupt is usually available as a signal from the DUT, indicating that additional steps need to be taken to service the DUT. Upon receipt of the signal, the servicing agent is expected to have a response servicing the interrupt. Once the interrupt is serviced and taken care of, normal processing can continue. To be able to handle an interrupt sequence, the sequence must be aware of the signal, and the following steps must occur:

1. Detect the interrupt event that is supposed to occur by waiting for it.

2. After the event has occurred, request the sequencer for exclusive access.

3. Run an interrupt handler sequence to take care of the interrupt.

4. Return control to the sequencer for normal operation of the agent.

In the case of the ethernet module, the MAC core provides an interrupt pin designed to be connected to a CPU subsystem. In this example, the pin is connected to a separate interrupt interface, as shown in the listing below. Note that this may not always be the case, and one could undoubtedly wrap it along with the rest of the signals and passed to the agent, as shown in Section 8.3.4.2. However, one view is that having a separate interface, which allows for greater flexibility in using it in mixed RTL/GATE environments, and also allows passing the interface handle to the config_db without requiring the other signals.

22.2.1 Step 1: Adding an Interface to the Environment

Listing 22.1 shows the interface that is connected to the ethernet interrupt pin in the top-level module. The interface has some tasks.

Listing 22.1: The Interrupt Interface

```
1 interface eth_rst_intr_if (input rst,intr);
2
3    task wait_for_reset_assert;
4       @(posedge rst);
5    endtask
6
7    task wait_for_reset_deassert;
8       @(negedge rst);
9    endtask
10
11   task wait_for_intr_pos;
12      @(posedge intr);
13   endtask
14   task wait_for_intr_neg;
15      @(negedge intr);
16   endtask
17
18 endinterface
```

---

[1] You can look at many examples available online to create the packet to verify the various aspects of the Ethernet protocol. A sample ethernet packet is supplied in the download, and you are encouraged to look and modify the provided code to verify the DUT after looking at the Verilog examples. You may also choose to modify the same packet so that a MAC side packet is also available to test the MAC receive functions. This is left as an exercise for practice.

- Line 11 shows the wait_for_intr_pos task waiting for the interrupt signal to become 1. This is a blocking task. The task waits for the interrupt signal to be asserted.

- Line 14 shows the wait_for_intr_pos task waiting for the interrupt signal to become 0. This is a blocking task. The task waits for the interrupt signal to be deasserted.

22.2.2 Step 2: Make the Interface Available Via config_db

This interface is put into the config_db in the top level test module as shown in the listing below.

Listing 22.2: The Interrupt Interface in the top testbench

```
22 module eth_blk_env_tb_mod;
23    import uvm_pkg::*;
24    import wb_eth_test::*;
25    typedef virtual mii_if mii_intf;
26    typedef virtual wb_master_if mast_if;
27    typedef virtual wb_slave_if slv_if;
28    typedef virtual interrupt_eth_if eth_rst_intr_if;
29    typedef virtual reset_if v_rst_if;
30    initial begin
31       uvm_config_db #(v_rst_if)::set(null,"uvm_test_top.env.rst_agent","
             rst_if",eth_env_top.rst_if);
32       uvm_config_db #(mast_if)::set(null,"uvm_test_top.env.wb_master_agt
             ","mst_if",eth_env_top.mast_if);
33       uvm_config_db #(slv_if)::set(null,"uvm_test_top.env.wb_slave_agt","
             slv_if",eth_env_top.slv_if);
34       uvm_config_db #(mii_intf)::set(null,"uvm_test_top.env.mii_rx_agt","
             mii_if",eth_env_top.mii_if_b);
35       uvm_config_db #(mii_intf)::set(null,"uvm_test_top.env.mii_tx_agt","
             mii_if",eth_env_top.mii_if_b);
36       uvm_config_db #(eth_rst_intr_if)::set(null,"uvm_test_top.env.
             wb_master_agt.mast_sqr","ethernet_int_if",eth_env_top.intr_if);
37
38       run_test();
39    end
40
41 endmodule
```

Listing 22.2 shows the top-level module of the testbench. This module contains all the UVM tests.

- Line 30-38 shows the main initial block.

- Line 36 shows the interrupt interface from the earlier step being placed in the config_db.

22.2.3 Step 3: Use the Interface From the config_db in Your Sequence

This example takes the interface handle from the config_db and makes it available through the sequencer. This enables other sequences to use this interface. An alternate approach is having it pulled into a base sequence so that other derived sequences could benefit from it. Both approaches are valid and are usually selected by preference.

If you chose the sequencer approach, we suggest creating this sequencer by extending the generic sequencer from example 8.3.3 and replacing it using a factory override.

Listing 22.3: The sequencer

```
19 class wb_master_seqr extends uvm_sequencer # (wb_transaction);
20
21    wb_config cfg;
22    int my_seq_lenght;
23    ral_block_ethernet_blk regmodel;
24    typedef virtual interrupt_eth_if int_if_t;
25    int_if_t int_if;
26
27    `uvm_component_utils_begin(wb_master_seqr)
28       `uvm_field_int(my_seq_lenght,UVM_DEFAULT);
29    `uvm_component_utils_end
30    function new (string name,
31                  uvm_component parent);
32       super.new(name,parent);
33    endfunction:new
34
35    function void build_phase(uvm_phase phase) ;
36       super.build_phase(phase);
37       if (!uvm_config_db#(int_if_t)::get(null, "uvm_test_top.env.
          wb_master_agt.mast_sqr", "ethernet_int_if", int_if)) begin
38          `uvm_fatal("SEQUENCER/NOVIF", "No virtual interface specified for
                this Sequencer instance %m. Cannot get the interrupt handle")
39       end
40    endfunction
41 endclass:wb_master_seqr
```

- Line 25 shows the virtual interface in the sequencer.

- Lines 35-40 show the build_phase() for this sequencer. The virtual interface is assigned in build_phase. You may note that we have not assigned the handles to the register model in this phase. This is accomplished in the base_test after all the components are built properly.

The tx_interupt_seq in the listing below illustrates an example of an interrupt sequence. This sequence could be run as a hierarchical sequence from a sequencer or forked off and run in parallel with the sequences running on the sequencer.

Listing 22.4: The Interrupt Sequence

```
2 class tx_interrupt_seq extends base_sequence;
3     `uvm_object_utils(tx_interrupt_seq)
4
5    function new(string name = "tx_interrupt_seq");
6        super.new(name);
7    endfunction:new
8
9    virtual task body();
10       uvm_reg_data_t reg_data;
11       uvm_status_e reg_status;
12
13       `uvm_info(get_full_name(),$sformatf("waiting for Interrupt %d",
             $time),UVM_MEDIUM)
14       p_sequencer.int_if.wait_for_intr_pos();
15       `uvm_info(get_full_name(),$sformatf("Got Interrupt %d",$time),
             UVM_MEDIUM)
```

```
16          grab();
17          p_sequencer.regmodel.INT_MASK.read(.status(reg_status),.path(
                UVM_FRONTDOOR), .parent(this),.value(reg_data));
18          p_sequencer.regmodel.INT_MASK.write(.status(reg_status),.path(
                UVM_FRONTDOOR), .parent(this),.value(32'h0000007f));
19          p_sequencer.regmodel.INT_SOURCE.read(.status(reg_status),.path(
                UVM_FRONTDOOR), .parent(this),.value(reg_data));
20          p_sequencer.regmodel.INT_SOURCE.write(.status(reg_status),.path(
                UVM_FRONTDOOR), .parent(this),.value(reg_data));
21          `uvm_info(get_full_name(),$sformatf("Completed interrupt sequence
                %d",$time),UVM_MEDIUM)
22          ungrab();
23      endtask
24 endclass
```

Regardless of the mode in which the tx_interupt_seq is started, the sequence waits for the interrupt to be provided by the DUT.

- Line 14 forces the sequence to be blocked until the interrupt is made available.

- Line 16 requests that the sequencer service it by using grab(). This method locks out the sequencer from running other sequences until the interrupt sequence is completed.

- Lines 17 – 20 show the sequence reading the INT_MASK register and clearing the interrupt.

- Line 22 releases the sequencer to examine other items.

This is a simple sequence that clears only the transmit interrupt, and serves to illustrate how to handle interrupt sequences. The processing of other interrupt sources, and using this sequence in a parallel sequence is also possible. A less disruptive approach to implementing interrupt handling using sequences is instead using sequence prioritization. Here, the interrupt monitoring thread starts the tx interrupt seq sequence with a priority higher than the main process. This has the benefit of holding off regular sequence operations while at the same time allowing still higher priority interrupts to inject themselves and win arbitration on the sequencer. A third alternate approach would be to implement another agent to handle these interrupts.

With the priority approach, however, multiple ISR sequences can be active on a sequencer regardless of the priority settings. Priority only affects the ability of an individual sequence to send a sequence_item to the driver. Therefore, whatever processing is happening in an interrupt sequence can continue even if a higher priority sequence interrupts it. Section 14.3.2, reveals that the only time that priority is considered is when multiple sequences have been called and are blocked in their start_item() tasks simultaneously.

22.3 Developing Layered Sequences in UVM

Layering can be implemented either as hierarchical sequences on the same sequencer or by using a layered sequencer. Hierarchical layering is described here while using layered sequences is described in [3].

22.3.1 Developing Hierarchical Sequences in UVM

Section 14.4.2 presented a detailed look at hierarchical sequences. In this section, the sequencer and a simple hierarchical sequence are examined. To transmit a packet through the ethernet module, several things need to occur in a sequence. These steps are detailed in the document for the core. The buffer descriptors need to be initialized, and the registers must be programmed with the correct values. In our example below, these are performed using a set of sequences. Details of the sequences are not described below as the complete source code, and relevant information is provided.

To transmit a packet, the following steps need to occur:

- Buffer descriptor registers need to be initialized in the ethernet core.

- Data to be transmitted must be placed in the memory.

- The registers in the core must be set to the buffer, and the core enabled.

- Wait for the interrupt to ensure the packet was transmitted.

To allow various sequences to program the core, the sequencer must contain a reference to the register model. It must also be able to determine when an interrupt has occurred.

Listing 22.3 describes the sequencer used for this activity. In the listing,

- Line 21 shows the configuration required by the sequences set in the environment.

- Line 23 shows the register model handle.

- Line 25 shows the virtual interface handle for the interrupt handling sequence from the earlier discussions in this chapter.

The hierarchical sequence now calls the various sequences one by one. It initializes the core by calling the following sequences in order one by one in the listing below. Without going into the details of the register programming required by the core, the listing below provides a good example of a hierarchical sequence.

Listing 22.5: The Hierarchical Sequence

```
1    class send_2_packets_event_sync_sequence extends base_sequence;
2
3      init_tx_seq tx_seq;
4      setup_txbd_sequence  txbd_sequence;
5      tx_interrupt_seq  tx_int_sequence;
6      initialize_txbd_rxbd_sequence  initialize_desc_seq;
7      write_master_single single_seq;
8      read_master_single single_seq_read;
9      uvm_event send_2_pkt_event;
10
11     `uvm_object_utils(send_2_packets_event_sync_sequence)
12     `uvm_declare_p_sequencer(wb_master_seqr)
13
14     function new(string name = "
   send_2_packets_event_sync_sequence");
15         super.new(name);
16     endfunction:new
17
18     virtual task body();
19         uvm_reg_data_t reg_data;
20         uvm_status_e reg_status;
21
22         uvm_config_db #(uvm_event)::get(null,"","transmit_b",
   send_2_pkt_event);
23
24         p_sequencer.regmodel.MODER.write(.status(reg_status), .
   value(0), .path(UVM_FRONTDOOR), .parent(this));
25         p_sequencer.regmodel.MAC_ADDR0.write(.status(reg_status),
   .value(32'h03040506), .path(UVM_FRONTDOOR),\part{title}.parent(this
   ));
26         p_sequencer.regmodel.MAC_ADDR1.write(.status(reg_status),
   .value(32'h00001020), .path(UVM_FRONTDOOR), .parent(this));
27         tx_seq = init_tx_seq::type_id::create("tx seq");
28         txbd_sequence = setup_txbd_sequence::type_id::create("TXBD
   data Sequence");
```

```
29                  initialize_desc_seq = initialize_txbd_rxbd_sequence::
      type_id::create("initialize_desc_sequence");
30                  tx_int_sequence = tx_interrupt_seq::type_id::create("
      tx_init_sequence");
31                  single_seq_read = read_master_single::type_id::create("
      single_seq");
32                  single_seq = write_master_single::type_id::create("simple
      seq read");
33                  // Clean up descriptors
34                  initialize_desc_seq.start(p_sequencer);
35                  p_sequencer.regmodel.INT_MASK.write(.status(reg_status),.
      path(UVM_FRONTDOOR), .parent(this),.value(32'h0000007f));
36                  p_sequencer.regmodel.MODER.write(.status(reg_status),.path
      (UVM_FRONTDOOR), .parent(this),.value(32'h00002403));
37

....
47                  txbd_sequence.mem_addr = 1000;
48                  txbd_sequence.start(p_sequencer);
49
50                  single_seq_read.read_address = 32'h00000400;
51                  single_seq_read.read_data = 32'h007c5800;
52
53                  repeat (5)   // Apparently this is a magic number that
      kicks off the machine
54                       single_seq_read.start(p_sequencer);
55                  send_2_pkt_event.trigger();
56              endtask
57          endclass
```

Above is an abbreviated listing. See

$DOWNLOAD/IEEE_version/Practical_Applications/soc/tb/uvm/ethernet/src/sequences/
wb_master_agent_send_2_packets_event_sync_sequence.sv

In Listing 22.5

- Lines 3-8 show the various instances of the subsequences. These subsequences program the registers, set up the core, and perform other functions needed for transmission.

- Lines 18-58 list the body() task. Essential lines are shown in this listing. The constructor for each of the sequences is called to create the sequence.

- Line 48 shows the txbd_sequence being started as a subsequence on the sequencer.

- Line 54 shows the read sequence, which kicks off the read in the core being started as a subsequence on the sequencer.

22.3.2 Developing Sequences as a Collection of Layers

To manage complexity, sequences can be written as a collection of subsequences. Using such an approach can help you to manage complexity on the one hand, while allowing the reuse of sequences on the other.

One crucial consideration when creating layered sequences is to be aware of a "waterfall" effect. The waterfall effect occurs when a set of constraints for the higher-level sequence are used to constrain the range of values that can be exercised by the lower-level sequence. As a result, the overall space is a more constrained than it should be. This effect occurs due to the capabilities of the constraint solver in modern simulators, which tend to look at the whole constraint space to arrive at a solution. When you create a layered sequence, you are fundamentally constraining the range of values into which the stimulus can be generated; the choice of a layered sequence should be taken with care exercised in the design of the sequences.

To completely describe layering in Ethernet is beyond the scope of this book. The layering example for Ethernet can be implemented in many ways.

1. Layering using a collection of agents. In this case, each of the layers would be implemented in a separate agent. A lower to upper agent and an upper to lower layer agent would be used in the implementation. The driver from the upper agent would produce sequences used by the lower layer sequence to be decomposed into a set of read/write operations using a hierarchical sequence, as described above. On the return path, various lower layer items would be combined to create a single upper-layer item.

2. Using an integrated protocol agent. In this approach, there are few agents present, and a single agent handles the complete translation from high-level sequences to low-level writes to the wb_master agent.

22.4 Exercises for Further Exploration

The above chapter provided a template for a complete verification environment to test a Wishbone based ethernet MAC controller. It would be instructive to try the following as an extension of the environment provided in this chapter.

1. Explore the provided documentation for the programming of the core.

2. Add a simple configuration class to the config_db to control how many packets are transmitted in the MAC direction

3. Add a few tests for the controller based the tests in the Verilog directory

4. Using the environment provided, add a few more agents and create the layering for this sequencer.

Appendix A

UVM Core Utilities in UVM 1.2

Chapter 2 provided an overview of the class library and some of the effects to consider when designing SystemVerilog environments. Class-based environments often create class instances and perform several operations using these instances. Upon further analysis of our simple SystemVerilog testbench in Section 1.3, you realize that creating, copying, and printing class instances for debug are common operations that occur in any class-based environment. These common operations are called core utilities, which are described in this chapter.

UVM supplies many commonly used utilities for any object that derives from the uvm_object class. The uvm_object class is a base class for all data and hierarchical classes. The primary function of this class is defining a set of methods for common operations like copy, compare, print, pack/unpack performed during verification. These operations are available to every uvm_object and its subclasses, which extend from uvm_object.

In the sections that follow, we will explore each of these operations in some level of detail. At the end of this chapter, you should be able to perform all of the common operations on classes derived from uvm_object.

(i) The code and examples in this chapter refer to the **UVM-1.2 version only**. Study Chapter 4 if you are trying to learn the UVM-1800.2 API.

If you are migrating code and need to compare the UVM-1.2 and UVM-1800.2 approaches, use the examples in Chapter 4 for an explanation of the API and behavior in the UVM IEEE version with the content of this chapter. The examples that are illustrated in this chapter are also available when using UVM-1800.2 API in the download. Use a simple text diff tool to quickly identify differences between the two versions.

The rest of this chapter uses examples in[1]:

$DOWNLOAD_DIR/**uvm-1.2**/UVM_Building_Blocks/Uvm_Core_Utils/src/

A.1 Simple Example Classes

To begin exploring UVM, we begin with a couple of simple SystemVerilog classes used in the examples in this chapter. The below listing presents a simple class with an integer property, string property, and an integer associative array as its members. This class extends from uvm_object class.

---

[1] See the Preface for download instructions

Listing A.1: A Simple Class

```
2 class class_A extends uvm_object;
3
4    int cl_int;
5    string cl_string;
6    int     cl_int_arr[];
7    int unsigned logic_data[int];
8
9    `uvm_object_utils_begin(class_A)
10       `uvm_field_int(cl_int,UVM_DEFAULT)
11       `uvm_field_string(cl_string,UVM_DEFAULT)
12       `uvm_field_array_int(cl_int_arr,UVM_DEFAULT)
13       `uvm_field_aa_int_int(logic_data,UVM_DEFAULT)
14    `uvm_object_utils_end
15
16    function void set_value(int value);
17       cl_int   = value;
18    endfunction
19
20    function new(string name="");
21       super.new(name);
22       cl_string = name;
23       set_value(10);
24       cl_int_arr = new[cl_int];
25       for(int i = 0; i < cl_int; i++) begin
26    cl_int_arr[i] = i + 1;
27       end
28    endfunction
29
30 endclass
```

Listing A.1 presents a simple class class_A. This class has the following properties:

1. An integer: cl_int

2. A dynamic array of integers: cl_int_arr

3. A string: cl_string

4. A associative array: logic_data

5. Lines 9-16 describe the constructor new() function which initializes various properties of the class at the time of creation of an instance of the classA_cl class.

6. Ignore all the macros on Lines 9-14. We will learn about them later in this chapter.

A second simple class that instances the first one shown above is provided in the next listing.

```
1  class class_P extends uvm_object;
2
3    // basic datatypes
4    rand int par_int;
5    rand byte par_address;
6    string par_string;
7
8    // Some objects to demonstrate the copy recursion policy
9
10   class_A cl1; // UVM_SHALLOW
11   class_A cl3; // UVM_DEEP
12
13   `uvm_object_utils_begin(class_P)
14      `uvm_field_int(par_int ,UVM_DEFAULT)
15      `uvm_field_int(par_address ,UVM_DEFAULT)
16      `uvm_field_string(par_string ,UVM_DEFAULT)
17      `uvm_field_object(cl1 ,UVM_DEFAULT)
18      `uvm_field_object(cl3 ,UVM_DEFAULT)
19   `uvm_object_utils_end
20
21   function new(string name="");
22      super.new(name);
23      cl1 = new(name);
24      cl3 = new(name )   ;
25      par_string  = name;
26   endfunction
27
28 endclass
```

The above class_P has the following properties as a part of the class.

- An integer called par_int
- A byte property called par_address
- A string property called par_string
- Two child objects of the class_A class called cl1 and cl3.
- Lines 21-26 describe the constructor for the class similar to the one whihc is provided in Listing A.1
- Ignore all the macros on Lines 13-19. We will learn about them later in this chapter.

The two examples for class_A and class_P classes above are not parameterized. Subtle differences between normal classes and parameterized classes exist and are discussed in Section 5.3. For now, recognize that it is possible to use parameterized classes in UVM.

Listing A.3 shows the listing for a parameterized object class. In this file, class packet is defined as a specialization of *param_packet_base*.

Listing A.3: Simple Parameterized Class

```
1  class param_packet_base extends uvm_object;
2     function new(string name="TypeT");
3        super.new(name);
4     endfunction
5  endclass
6
7  class packet #(type T=int) extends param_packet_base;
8     const static string type_name = $sformatf("packet#(%s)",$typename(T));
9
10    T my_var;
11    `uvm_object_param_utils(packet#(T))
12
13    function new(string name="TypeT");
14       super.new(name);
15    endfunction
16
17    virtual function string get_type_name();
18       return type_name;
19    endfunction
20
21 endclass
```

Ignore the macros in the listing on line 11. They are explained later in this chapter.

A.2 Object Creation

Common object creation activities with uvm_object classes are broadly divided into the following operations:

- Create via constructor or factory
- Object cloning

UVM makes use of some well-known paradigms such as design patterns, policies, and other concepts [9] from the software world. By leveraging these concepts, UVM offers more flexibility to the verification engineer to complete verification.

A.2.1 Create

UVM supplies the **create()** method to create a new object of a given type returning a handle to a new object. This method is implemented by every class that is derived either directly or indirectly from **uvm_object**. The factory method in Chapter 5 makes extensive use of this method to create the object. The create() method is extensively used throughout this book. The difference between using the new() method instead of the create() method is that when you call create(), the factory determines if it should substitute it with a different type. The factory calls the **new()** method after making this determination under the hood. *I recommend that you always call create().* If you call new() directly, the factory cannot substitute the object even if you want it to do so. The create() method signature is defined as:

```
virtual function uvm_object create ( string name = "" )
```

For usage examples of the create() method, see Listing 2.7 Line 26.

Recommendation A.2.0:   *Match the object's handle name with the string name passed into the create() call; this simplifies debugging.*

UVM 1.2 requires you to declare a constructor in the class. Earlier versions of UVM did not. If you want the older behavior in UVM-1.2 because you have somebody else's code that you cannot change, you have to define UVM_OBJECT_DO_NOT_NEED_CONSTRUCTOR at compile time to override this behavior.

A.2.2 Clone

UVM supplies the clone() method to help you make an exact copy of the object. The clone() method calls a constructor under the hood and creates a new object of the specific type followed by a copy().

(i) *Note that clone() returns a handle of type uvm_object and hence **you will need** to typecast it before you use it. Else your code will not compile!*

Listing A.4: Simple Cloning operation

```
1 module top;
2    import uvm_pkg::*;
3 `include "class.sv"
4
5    // Class definition
6
7    class_A     class_A_inst1;
8    class_A     class_A_inst2;
9    initial begin
10      // free children
11      class_A_inst1 = new("child_inst1");
12
13      class_A_inst1.randomize();
14      class_A_inst1.print();
15      $cast(class_A_inst2,class_A_inst1.clone());
16      class_A_inst1.print();
17
18    end
19 endmodule
```

- Lines 7 -8 show the instantiations of the class_A class.

- Line 11-13 create a class and randomize and print it.

- Line 15 shows the use of the clone() utility. As mentioned, the $cast operation is essential.

A.3 Common Operations on Objects

UVM supplies automation for common operations like copy,compare,print and pack/unpack using policy classes. These policy classes perform a specific task for each of these operations and are implemented separately from the uvm_object class. The intention behind this implementation is to allow the user to plug in different policies based on the desired object *without modifying the uvm_object subclasses*. By simply applying a different policy, the behavior of the operation can be changed. These classes come with user-configurable parameters that have defaults thereby making it easy for the user to use defaults wherever applicable. You can subtype the policy classes and replace the defaults in your environment by using the factory mechanisms described in Chapter 5 if you need to. You can also write your own customized version of the operation using a callback hook that is provided by UVM as shown in Figure A.1.

A.3.1 Copy

To copy one object to another, UVM supplies built-in functions. The following two methods support the copy operation for classes derived from the uvm_object class. The copy() function copies the contents of the *rhs* to itself. To override this default mechanism, you must use the do_copy() method.

```
function void copy (uvm_object rhs, uvm_copier = null );
virtual function void do_copy (uvm_object rhs );
```

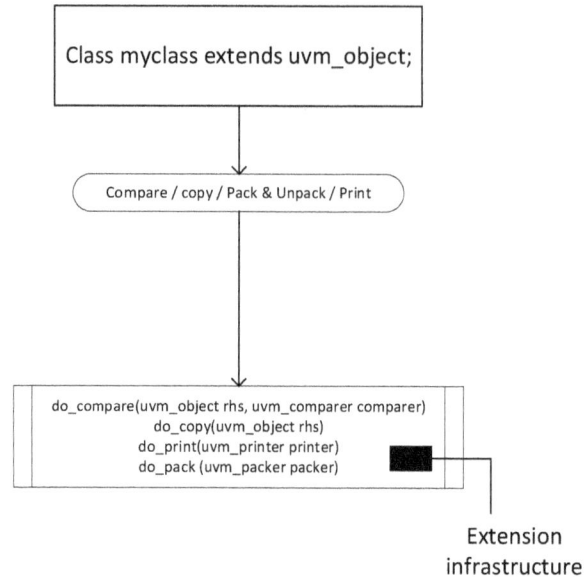

Fig. A.1: Additional Policy Callback hooks

Using the classes from the earlier portions of this chapter, the listing below shows an example of how the copy function in UVM. In this listing, class class_P is instanced in a module, and illustrates the copy method.

Listing A.5: A Simple Copy example

```
1 module top;
2    import uvm_pkg::*;
3    typedef class class_A;
4
5 `include "class.sv"
6
7    class_P  class_P_inst1;
8    class_P  class_P_inst2;
9    initial begin
10      // Create and print instances
11      class_P_inst1 = new("first_inst");
12      class_P_inst1.randomize();
13      class_P_inst1.print();
14
15      class_P_inst2 = new("second_inst");
16      class_P_inst2.randomize();
17      class_P_inst2.print();
18
19      class_P_inst2.copy(class_P_inst1);
20      class_P_inst2.print();
21
22    end
23 endmodule
```

In Listing A.5:

- Lines 10-13 create the class_P_inst1 instance and randomize and print it.

- Lines 15-17 create the class_P_inst2 instance and randomize and print it.

- Line 19 shows the class_P_inst2 instance copying into itself the contents of class_P_inst1. Note that the contents of the children are copied as well.

Rule A.3.0:   *Note that the supplied copy() method is not virtual by design* **and should not be overloaded in derived classes**

The underlying implementation of the copy() method from the previous example calls the do_copy methods in class_P. This method can be used to have your implementation of the copy() method. The do_copy method for class_P is shown below.

Listing A.6: A simple do_copy() example

```
41    function void do_copy(uvm_object rhs);
42        class_P rhs_;
43        super.do_copy(rhs);
44        $cast(rhs_,rhs);
45        par_int = rhs_.par_int;
46        par_address = rhs_.par_address;
47        par_string = rhs_.par_string;
48        cl1 = new rhs_.cl1;
49        cl3 = new rhs_.cl3;
50        cl1.copy(rhs_.cl1);
51        cl3.copy(rhs_.cl3);
52    endfunction
```

In the above listing for the do_copy method for class_P:

- Lines 45-47 copy par_int, par_address, par_string over to the target.

- Lines 48 and 49 create new child objects.

- Lines 50-51 copy the children cl1 and cl3 to the target.

Rule A.3.1:   *You must never call the do_copy() method directly. Implement the method and allow the copy() method implementation to call it under the hood.* UVM supplies macros that provide a default copy() implementation. You can override the default implementation by calling the do_copy() method. To enable overriding the copy() method, you must set some flags in the macros to enable the do_copy() method call.

A.3.2 Compare

Quite often, in a scoreboard or other application, you may need to compare two objects. UVM supports the comparison operation between two different uvm_objects using the following two methods. These methods utilize a comparer policy. A default comparer policy object is provided in UVM. To override the default, you use the do_comparer() method.

```
function bit compare (uvm_object rhs, uvm_comparer comparer=null);
function bit do_compare (uvm_object rhs, uvm_comparer comparer);
```

The compare() function is used to compare all the automated fields of a class configured to be in the compare operation. You can also create an instance of the comparer policy and customize it as shown in Listing A.7 below to control the output of the comparer. Table A.1 shows the various policy settings available with the uvm_comparer class.

Listing A.7: Simple Comparison

```
1 /* This example illustrates a custom comparer
2  * and the copy operation
3  */
4
5 module top;
6 `include "uvm_macros.svh"
7    import uvm_pkg::*;
8 `include "class.sv"
9    // Class definition
10    class_P    class_P_inst1;
11    class_P    class_P_inst2;
12
13
14
15    initial begin
16       uvm_comparer c_comp = new();
17       c_comp.show_max = 1;
18       c_comp.sev = uvm_pkg::UVM_WARNING;
19
20       class_P_inst1 = new("class_P_inst1");
21       class_P_inst1.cl1.set_value(32);
22       class_P_inst2 = new("class_P_inst2");
23       class_P_inst2.cl1.set_value(16);
24
25       class_P_inst1.randomize();
26       class_P_inst2.randomize();
27       // Make a copy into class_P_inst2.
28       class_P_inst2.copy(class_P_inst1);
29       // Change the values in class_P_inst1.
30       class_P_inst1.cl1.logic_data[16 ] = 2;
31       class_P_inst1.cl1.logic_data[32 ] = 2;
32       class_P_inst1.cl1.logic_data[64] = 2;
33       class_P_inst1.cl1.logic_data[128] = 1;
34       // We should see miscompares.
35       class_P_inst1.compare(class_P_inst2, c_comp);
36       // We can get all the miscompares into a string and print them
37       `uvm_info("COMPARES",c_comp.miscompares,UVM_LOW)
38
39    end
40 endmodule
```

In this listing, class c_comp is an instance of uvm_comparer. For illustration purposes, we redefine settings that are available in class uvm_comparer and their default settings.

- Lines 17 and 18 shows how the setting for these properties can be assigned using based on Table A.1

- Note that you could also do this before the policy object is passed to the compare operation line 35

- The show_max of the compare policy object is set to 1 so that only the first compare result is printed. The rest of the miscompares are suppressed because show_max was set to 1.

- The miscompares string on line 37 returns a string of all the miscompares (4 in this case)

Rule A.3.2:   *Note that the supplied compare() method is not virtual by design* **and should not be overloaded in derived classes**

The UVM 1.2 versions for the compare functions had many member properties that are outlined below. In Section A.3.2, the examples illustrates the use of set/get methods to set the values of these properties. The older style was to directly set the property values in the comparer as shown below.

Table A.1: UVM Comparer Policy knobs

Property	Description
policy	Determines whether comparison is UVM_DEEP, UVM_REFERENCE, or UVM_SHALLOW.[2]
show_max	Sets the maximum number of messages to send to the messager for miscompares of an object.
verbosity	Sets the verbosity for printed messages.
sev	Sets the severity for printed messages.
miscompares	This string is reset to an empty string when a comparison is started.
physical	This bit provides a filtering mechanism for fields.
abstract	This bit provides a filtering mechanism for fields.
check_type	This bit determines whether the type, given by uvm_object::get_type_name, is used to verify that the types of two objects are the same.
result	This bit stores the number of miscompares for a given compare operation.
compare_field	Compares two integral values.
compare_field_int	This method is the same as compare_field except that the arguments are small integers, less than or equal to 64 bits.
compare_field_real	This method is the same as compare_field except that the arguments are real numbers.
compare_object	Compares two class objects using the policy knob to determine whether the comparison should be deep, shallow, or reference.
compare_string	Compares two string variables.
print_msg	Causes the error count to be incremented and the message, msg, to be appended to the miscompares string (a newline is used to separate messages).

The do_compare() method is the override of the compare() method and is called by the class library under the hood. It allows comparing of fields that need special handling or cannot be configured by the field automation macros. The listing below shows an example of this method.

Listing A.8: A simple do_compare() example

```
28    virtual function bit do_compare(uvm_object rhs, uvm_comparer comparer);
29       class_P rhs_;
30       do_compare = super.do_compare(rhs,comparer);
31       $cast(rhs_,rhs);
32       do_compare &= comparer.compare_field_int("par_int",par_int,rhs_.
              par_int,32,UVM_NORADIX);
33       do_compare &= comparer.compare_field_int("par_address",par_int,rhs_.
              par_int,32,UVM_NORADIX);
34       do_compare &= comparer.compare_string("par_string",par_string,rhs_.
              par_string);
35       do_compare &= comparer.compare_object("cl1",cl1,rhs_.cl1);
36       do_compare &= comparer.compare_object("cl3",cl3,rhs_.cl3);
37    endfunction
```

You will recognize that the operations are similar to the one for the do_copy() method.

Rule A.3.3:   *You must never call the do_compare() method directly. Define the method and allow the compare() method implementation to call it under the hood.*

UVM supplies macros that provide a default compare() implementation. You can override the default implementation by calling the do_compare() method. To enable overriding the compare() method, you must set some flags in the macros to enable the do_compare() method call.

UVM
1.2
We have found that the support for UVM_DEEP and UVM_SHALLOW are not complete as a part of the implementation under some circumstances, although they have been documented in the library. Hence, I recommend that the user performs the required operations by using the do_* methods.

A.3.3 Print

One of the more common operations of printing from UVM is accomplished using the following predefined methods to support the print operation for classes derived from uvm_object:

```
function void print(uvm_printer printer=null);
function string sprint(uvm_printer printer=null);
virtual function void do_print (uvm_printer printer);
```

Rule A.3.4:   *Note that the supplied print() method is not virtual by design* **and should not be overloaded in derived classes**

The print() function prints out all the fields configured using the macros to be a part of the print operation.

Function sprint() is similar to print() except that it returns a string instead of printing the result to the screen. The do_print() provides a callback mechanism for handling fields of the calling object that require special handling or are not configured by field automation macros to be included in the print operation. The print() and do_print() functions use a similar use model to that of the copy() policy described earlier.

The print operation makes use of print policy object uvm_printer. This policy object contains settings for controlling the print operation, as well as many methods that customize the way object data is printed. It is possible to define a new print policy object that redefines the settings of the default printer and hence achieves a modified print behavior. The following global print policy objects are automatically created by loading the UVM class library: Listing A.9 shows you how to use

uvm_printer_policy	Action
uvm_default_printer	Prints the object in a tablular formatted way
uvm_default_line_printer	Prints the object on a single line
uvm_default_tree_printer	Prints the object in a tree like format
uvm_default_table_printer	Prints the object in a tabular way (same as the default printer)

Table A.2: Printer Policies

different printers that come with UVM.

If no printer policy object is passed to print functions (i.e., print() and sprint()), then the global printer uvm_default_printer is used by default. Each printer policy object contains field knobs that can be used for customizing the printer output. Table A.3 shows a summary of knob properties that can be configured.

When an object's print function is called without the optional printer argument specified, **then the uvm_default_printer is used**. The uvm_default_printer variable may be assigned to any printer derived from uvm_printer. Often, it is desirable to redirect the output of a printer to a file so that it may be studied later. On other occasions, a slightly different output may be desired. UVM supports these customizations quite well.

Listing A.9: A Simple Print Example using various printers

```
1 module top;
2    import uvm_pkg::*;
3 `include "class.sv"
4
5    uvm_line_printer local_line_printer = new;
6    uvm_tree_printer local_tree_printer = new;
7    uvm_table_printer local_table_printer = new;
8    UVM_FILE myfile;
9
10   class_A cl1 = new("Child Class");
11   initial begin
12      myfile = $fopen("Data","w");
13      //uvm_default_printer = uvm_default_table_printer; //default, so not
             needed.
14      cl1.print();
15      uvm_default_printer = uvm_default_line_printer;
16      cl1.print();
17      uvm_default_printer = uvm_default_tree_printer;
18      cl1.print();
19      local_table_printer.knobs.type_width = 20;
20      local_table_printer.knobs.header = 1;
21      local_table_printer.knobs.value_width = 20;
22      local_table_printer.knobs.mcd = myfile;
23      cl1.print(local_table_printer);
24   end
```

The implementation of the print policy allows the output of print functions to either follow the global setting of the printer policy object or to be customized depending on the local requirements. Local customizations are done by instantiating a local copy of a printer policy object and then modifying its properties before passing it explicitly to the print function. The printer policy object that is passed to callback function do_print() is the same printer policy object provided as an argument to the print() functions.

You could customize the output of the printer using settings in the policy class. In UVM-1.2, these settings were placed in a class called uvm_printer_knobs. The members of this class were public and you could assign them directly.

Table A.3 provides a listing of the various printer knobs to alter the way your output looks[3].

Here is an example of how to use the print policy settings to control your output:

Listing A.10: Customizing Print

```
1 module top;
2    import uvm_pkg::*;
3    typedef class class_C;
4
5    // Class definition
6 class class_C extends uvm_object;
7
8    int cl_int;
9    string cl_string;
10   int    cl_int_arr[];
11   int    cl_int_sarr[40];
```

---
[3] This was adapted from [13]

Table A.3: Printer Knobs

Type	Property	Default value	Description
int	begin_elements	5	Number of elements at the head of a list that should be printed
string	bin_radix	"'b"	String prepended to any integral type when UVM_BIN used for a radix
int	column	0	Current column that the printer is pointing to
string	dec_radix	"'d"	String prepended to any integral type when UVM_DEC used for a radix
radix_enum	default_enum	UVM_HEX	Default radix to use for integral values when UVM_NORADIX is specified
int	depth	-1	Indicates how deep to recurse when printing objects, where depth of -1 prints everything
int	end_elements	5	Number of elements at the end of a list that should be printed
bit	footer	1	Specifies if the footer should be printed
bit	full_name	1	Specifies if leaf name or full name is printed
int	global_indent	0	Number of columns of indentation printed when newline is printed
bit	header	1	Specifies if the header should be printed
string	hex_radix	"'h "	String prepended to any integral type when UVM_HEX used for a radix
bit	identifier	1	Specifies if an identifier should be printed
int	max_width	999	Maximum column width to print
integer	mcd	UVM_STDOUT	File descriptor or multi-channel descriptor where print output is directed
string	oct_radix	"'o"	String prepended to any integral type when UVM_OCT used for a radix
bit	reference	1	Specifies if a unique reference ID for an UVM_object should be printed
bit	show_radix	1	Specifies if the radix should be printed for integral types
bit	size	1	Specifies if the size of the field should be printed
bit	sprint	0	If set to 1, prints to a string instead of mcd
string	truncation	"+"	Specifies truncation character to print when a field is too large to print
bit	type_name	1	Specifies if the type name of a field should be printed
string	unsigned_radix	"'d "	Default radix to use for integral values when UVM_UNSIGNED is specified

```
12
13     `uvm_object_utils_begin(class_C)
14        `uvm_field_int(cl_int,UVM_DEFAULT);
15        `uvm_field_string(cl_string,UVM_DEFAULT);
16        `uvm_field_array_int(cl_int_arr,UVM_DEFAULT);
17        `uvm_field_sarray_int(cl_int_sarr,UVM_DEFAULT);
18     `uvm_object_utils_end
19
20     function new(string name="");
21        super.new(name);
22        cl_string = name;
23        cl_int = 8;
24        //cl_int_arr = new[cl_int];
25        for(int i = 0; i < cl_int; i++) begin
26     cl_int_arr[i] = i + 1;
27        end
28        for(int i = 0; i < 40; i++) begin
29     cl_int_sarr[i] = i * 2;
30        end
31     endfunction
32
33 endclass
34
35
36     class_C class_C_inst;
37     uvm_printer my_printer;
```

```
38    initial begin
39       // free children
40       my_printer = uvm_default_table_printer;
41       my_printer.knobs.type_name = 0;
42       my_printer.knobs.begin_elements = 7;
43       my_printer.knobs.end_elements=2;
44       class_C_inst = new("class_C_inst");
45       class_C_inst.randomize();
46       class_C_inst.print(my_printer);
47
48    end
49 endmodule
```

- Lines 6-33 declare class_C. For now, dont worry about the macros on Lines 13-18. Their operation is described later on in this chapter.

- Line 36 creates an handle for class_C as class_C_inst.

- Line 37 creates a handle for a printer.

- Line 40 assigns the printer to the default table printer

- Line 41 sets the printer to *not display the type names*

- Line 42 -43 set the number of elements in the beginning and end of arrays to be printed

- Line 44-45 creates and randomizes the class_C_inst.

- Line 46 prints the class using the table printer.

Here is the output (partially shown) :

```
1    11  --------------------------------------------------------------
2        12 UVM-1.2.Synopsys
3        13 (C) 2007-2014 Mentor Graphics Corporation
4        14 (C) 2007-2014 Cadence Design Systems, Inc.
5        15 (C) 2006-2014 Synopsys, Inc.
6        16 (C) 2011-2013 Cypress Semiconductor Corp.
7        17 (C) 2013-2014 NVIDIA Corporation
8        18 --------------------------------------------------------------
9        19
10       20  **********          IMPORTANT RELEASE NOTES          **********
11       21
12       22  You are using a version of the UVM library that has been
            compiled
13       23  with `UVM_NO_DEPRECATED undefined.
14       24  See http://www.eda.org/svdb/view.php?id=3313 for more details.
15       25
16       26  You are using a version of the UVM library that has been
            compiled
17       27  with `UVM_OBJECT_DO_NOT_NEED_CONSTRUCTOR undefined.
18       28  See http://www.eda.org/svdb/view.php?id=3770 for more details.
19       29
20       30       (Specify +UVM_NO_RELNOTES to turn off this notice)
21       31
22       32 ------------------------------
23       33 Name            Size   Value
```

```
24    34  -------------------------------
25    35  class_C_inst    -       @335
26    36    cl_int        32      'h8
27    37    cl_string     12      class_C_inst
28    38    cl_int_arr    0       -
29    39    cl_int_sarr   40      -
30    40      [0]         32      'h0
31    41      [1]         32      'h2
32    42      [2]         32      'h4
33    43      [3]         32      'h6
34    44      [4]         32      'h8
35    45      [5]         32      'ha
36    46      [6]         32      'hc
37    47      ...         ...     ...
38    48      [38]        32      'h4c
39    49      [39]        32      'h4e
40    50  -------------------------------
```

Looking at the output above, observe the settings on line 39-46 and 48of Listing 5 control the number of array elements in the output. Notice that the type name is also not printed in the output.

UVM supplies macros that provide a default print() implementation. You can override the default implementation by calling the do_print() method. To enable overriding the print() method, you must set some flags in the macros to enable the do_print() method call.

The do_print() method is the override of the print() method and is called by the class library under the hood. It allows printing of fields that need special handling or cannot be configured by the field automation macros. The listing below shows an example of this method.

Listing A.11: A simple do_print() example

```
34        function void do_print(uvm_printer printer);
35            printer.knobs.type_name = 1;
36            printer.print_field_int("Class Integer",cl_int,32,UVM_NORADIX
                ,".","");
37            printer.print_string("Class String",cl_string,"");
38            printer.print_array_header("cl_int_arr",3,"cl_int_sarr(int)");
39            foreach(cl_int_sarr[i])
40                printer.print_field($sformatf("[%0d]", i), cl_int_sarr[i],
                    32);
41            printer.print_array_footer();
42        endfunction
```

Rule A.3.5: *You must never call the do_print() method directly. Implement the method and allow the print() method implementation to call it under the hood.*

A.3.4 Packing And Unpacking

UVM supplies utility methods to pack class objects into a bitstream, as well as unpack objects from a bitstream and populate the class contents. To accomplish this goal, UVM supplies a uvm_packer class which provides a policy object for packing and unpacking uvm_objects. This policy object determines how the packing and unpacking routines should behave. When packing an object, the object is placed into an array of bits. Such an array may then be sent across a language boundary or used inside a networking frame or other applications. The unpack operation in the application can then disassemble the bitstream array and obtain the values of the class properties. Please see Figure 10.8 for an illustration of how packing and unpacking can be used across language boundaries.

The pack operation makes use of a pack policy object called uvm_packer. This policy object contains settings for controlling and customize the way the object data is packed. It is possible to define a new pack policy object that redefines the settings of the default packer and hence achieves a modified pack behavior. If you do not choose to create a new policy object and yet wish to override the default behavior, use the do_pack() callbacks.

The essential functions for packing and unpacking are:

```
function int pack ( ref bit bitstream[], input uvm_packer packer = null);
virtual function void do_pack (uvm_packer packer);
function int unpack (ref bit bitstream[],input uvm_packer packer = null);
virtual function void do_unpack (uvm_packer packer);
```

UVM supplies macros that provide a default pack() implementation. You can override the default implementation by calling the do_pack() method. To enable overriding the pack() method, you must set some flags in the macros to enable the do_pack() method call. Listing A.12 shows you an example of a pack/unpack on a pair of classes.

Listing A.12: A Simple Pack/Unpack Example

```
1    import uvm_pkg::*;
2 `include "class.sv"
3
4    bit      pack_bytes[];
5    class_P  class_P_inst1;
6    class_P  class_P_inst2;
7    initial begin
8       // Create and print children
9
10       class_P_inst1 = new("first_inst");
11       class_P_inst1.randomize();
12       class_P_inst1.print();
13       // Pack object
14       class_P_inst1.pack(pack_bytes);
15
16       class_P_inst2 = new("second_inst");
17       //     class_P_inst2.randomize();
18       class_P_inst2.print();
19
20       // Unpack object
21       class_P_inst2.unpack(pack_bytes);
22       class_P_inst2.print();
23
24    end
25 endmodule
```

- The pack operation on line 14 packs class class_P_inst1 into the bit stream pack_bytes declared in Line 5.

- The unpack operation on Line 21 unpacks the bitstream into class class_P_inst2.

if you wish to use the do_pack() and do_unpack() methods, There are many helper methods available that help simplify the packing and unpacking operations.

```
virtual function void pack_field (uvm_bitstream_t value, int size);
virtual function void pack_field_int (logic[63:0] value, int size);
virtual function void pack_string (string value);
virtual function void pack_time (time value);
virtual function void pack_real (real value);
virtual function void pack_object (uvm_object value);
virtual function bit is_null ();
```

The pack_field function allows you to pack an arbitrary field of up to 4096 bits into the bitstream. The size variable can be computed for any variable by using the $bits system function. The pack_field_int, pack_string, pack_time, pack_real functions pack their corresponding variable types into the bitstream.

To unpack an object from a bitstream, you have corresponding methods as shown below: These unpacking functions take the input bitstream and unpack back the values from the bitstream into the class object.

```
virtual function logic[63:0] unpack_field_int (int size);
virtual function uvm_bitstream_t unpack_field (int size);
virtual function string unpack_string (int num_chars=-1);
virtual function time unpack_time ();
virtual function void unpack_object (uvm_object value);
virtual function int get_packed_size();
```

These functions can be used to pack any arbitrary data variable into the packed array. The use_metadata flag indicates whether to encode metadata when packing dynamic data or to decode metadata when unpacking. The do_pack and do_unpack routines which are user developed should use the following interpretation when using the metadata flags. For strings, pack an additional null byte after packing the string if the flag is set.

For objects, pack 4 bits before packing the object itself. The notation of 4'b0000 is used to indicate the object being packed is null. Otherwise, one must pack 4'b0001. Do not use any of the other bits.

if you are not using the automation macros or the metadata flag, For queues, dynamic arrays, and associative arrays, pack 32 bits to indicate the size of the array before packing individual elements. When you unpack, the first thing you do is read the array and get the size. After obtaining the size, unpack the relevant number of array elements in the do_unpack routines.

Rule A.3.6: *You must never call the do_pack() method directly. Implement the method and allow the pack() method implementation to call it under the hood.*

Here is an example of the do_pack and do_unpack methods.

Listing A.13: A simple do_pack() example

```
54    function void do_pack (uvm_packer packer);
55        super.do_pack(packer);
56        packer.pack_field_int(par_int,32);
57        packer.pack_field_int(par_address,8);
58        packer.pack_string(par_string);
59        packer.pack_object(cl1);
60        packer.pack_object(cl3);
61    endfunction
62
63
64    function void do_unpack (uvm_packer packer);
65        super.do_unpack(packer);
66        par_int = packer.unpack_field_int(32);
67        par_address = packer.unpack_field_int(8);
68        par_string = packer.unpack_string();
69        packer.unpack_object(cl1);
70        packer.unpack_object(cl3);
71    endfunction
```

You will recognize that the operations are similar to the one for the do_copy() method.

A.3.5 What Does The use_metadata Flag Do?

Figure A.2 illustrates how the library adds a few extra bytes. In Listing A.13 on Line 59, This flag does a couple of things. It packs a NULL 4 byte in case of a null object being packed and a NULL terminating character when using the string data type.

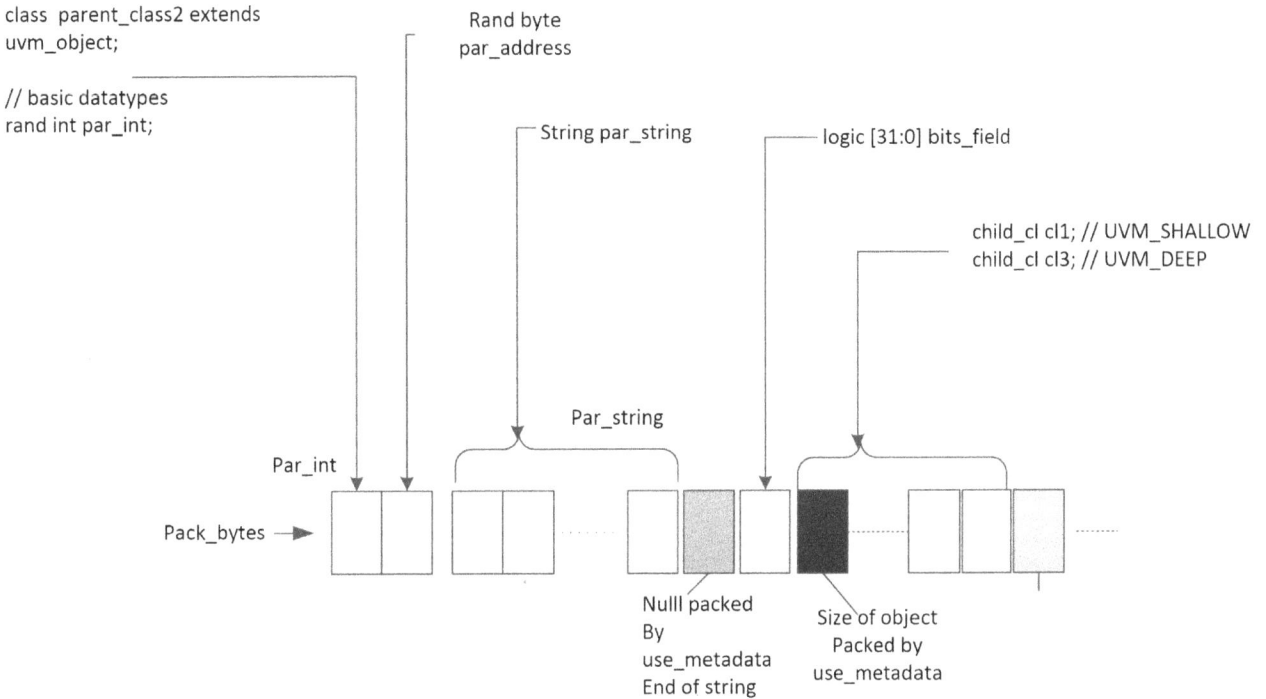

Fig. A.2: Pack/Unpack and use_metadata

A.4 Core Operations Summary

Please study Sections 4.4 onwards to learn more about UVM core utilities.

References

1. Accellera. A specification for a register description language. *Prepared by the Register Description Working Group of the Spirit Consortium*, 2009.
2. Accellera. *UVM 1.2 Class reference Manual*. Accellera, 2014.
3. Accellera. *UVM Users Guide V 1.2*. Accellera, 2014.
4. Janick Bergeron. *Verification Methodology Manual for System Verilog*. Springer Science & Business Media, 2006.
5. Janick Bergeron and Mark Glasser. Tlm 2.0 in systemverilog.
6. Janick bergeron and Adiel Khan. Tlm2 in systemverilog and vmm.
7. V Cooper and Paul Marriott. Demystifying the uvm configuration database. *DVCon 2014*, 2014.
8. Srinivasan Venkataraman Doug Perry and Srivatsa Vasudevan. Uvm tips and tricks.
9. Ralph Johnson Eric Gamma, Richard Helm and John Vissides. *Design Patterns: Elements of Reusable Object-Oriented Software*. Wiley.
10. Mark Glasser. Advanced testbench configuration with resources. *DV-Con 2011*, 2011.
11. Mentor Graphics. *OVM Users Guide*. 2011.
12. Brian Hunter. *Advanced UVM*. Createspace, 2015.
13. Sasan Iman. *Step-by-step Functional Verification with SystemVerilog and OVM*. Hansen Brown Publishing, 2008.
14. Doulos Inc. Easier uvm coding guidelines.
15. Doulos Inc. Run time phasing in uvm.
16. Synopsys Inc. The uvm ral generator.
17. Mark Litterick and Marcus Harnisch. Advanced uvm register modeling. 2014.
18. OpenCores. *Wishbone Protocol Guide*. OpenCores.org, 2002.
19. Mark Peryer. There's something wrong between sally sequencer and dirk driver –why uvm sequencers and drivers need some relationship counselling.
20. Justin Refice. Run-time phasing in the uvm: The long lost user's guide.
21. Srivatsa Vasudevan. *Effective functional verification principles and processes*. Springer, 2006.
22. Wikipedia. Directed graph.

Index